Egypt, Canaan, and Israel in Ancient Times

Egypt, Canaan, and Israel in Ancient Times

Donald B. Redford

PRINCETON UNIVERSITY PRESS

PRINCETON, NEW JERSEY

Copyright © 1992 by Princeton University Press
Published by Princeton University Press, 41 William Street,
Princeton, New Jersey 08540
In the United Kingdom: Princeton University Press, Oxford

Library of Congress Cataloging-in-Publication Data
Redford, Donald B.
Egypt, Canaan, and Israel in Ancient Times / Donald B. Redford.
p. cm.
Includes bibiliographical references and index.
1. Egypt—Relations—Palestine. 2. Palestine—Relations—Egypt.
3. Egypt—History—To 332 B.C. 4. Palestine—History—To 70 A.D.
I. Title.
DT82.5.P19R43 1992 303.48'26205694—dc20 91-19245 CIP

ISBN 0-691-03606-3

This book has been composed in Linotron Sabon

Printed in the United States of America

In Memoriam Patris,
Cyril Fitzjames Redford

Contents

List of Illustrations and Tables

FIGURES

TABLES

List of Abbreviations

JOURNALS

ADAJ	*Annual of the Department of Antiquities of Jordan*
AfO	*Archiv für Orientforschung*
AIPHOS	*Annuaire de l'institut de philologie et d'histoire orientale*
AION	*Annali istituto orientale di Napoli*
AJA	*American Journal of Archaeology*
Ann Natur Hist Museum, Vienna	*Annalen des Naturhistorischen Museums in Wien*
Anz Österr Akad Wissenshaften	*Österreichische Akademie der Wissenschaften, Anzeiger*
ArOr	*Archiv Orientalni*
ASAE	*Annales du service des antiquites de l'Egypte*
ASTI	*Annual of the Swedish Theological Institute*
BA	*Biblical Archaeologist*
BAR	*Biblical Archaeology Review*
BASOR	*Bulletin of the American Schools of Oriental Research*
BES	*Bulletin of the Egyptological Seminar* (New York)
BibOr	*Bibliotheque Orientale*
BIE	*Bulletin de l'institut d'Egypte*
BIFAO	*Bulletin de l'institut français d'archeologie orientale*
BJRL	*Bulletin of the John Rylands Library*
BMQ	*British Museum Quarterly*
BN	*Biblische Notizen*
BSFE	*Bulletin de la société française d'Égyptologie*
Bull Soc Geog Égypt	*Bulletin de la société de géographie d'Égypte*
BZ	*Biblische Zeitschrift*
BZAW	*Beihefte, Zeitschrift für die alttestamentalische Wissenschaft*
CBQ	*Catholic Biblical Quarterly*

CdE	Chronique d'Egypte
CJT	Canadian Journal of Theology
CRAIBL	Comptes rendus de l'academie des inscriptions et belles lettres
CRIPEL	Cahiers de recherches de l'institut de Papyrologie et d'Egyptologie de Lille
FIFAO	Fouilles de l'institut français
GM	Göttinger Miszellen
HTR	Harvard Theological Review
HUCA	Hebrew Union College Annual
IEJ	Israel Exploration Journal
JANES	Journal of the Ancient Near Eastern Society
JAOS	Journal of the American Oriental Society
JARCE	Journal of the American Research Center in Egypt
JBL	Journal of Biblical Literature
JCS	Journal of Cuneiform Studies
JdS	Journal des Savants
JEA	Journal of Egyptian Archaeology
JEOL	Jahrberichte "Ex Oriente Lux"
JESHO	Journal of the Economic and Social History of the Orient
JHS	Journal of Hellenic Studies
JJS	Journal of Jewish Studies
JMEOS	Journal of the Middle East and Oriental Society
JNES	Journal of Near Eastern Studies
JOAI	Journal of the Oriental and African Institute
JPOS	Journal of the Palestine Oriental Society
JQR	Jewish Quarterly Review
JRAI	Journal of the Royal Asiatic Institute
JSOT	Journal of the Society of Old Testament
JSS	Journal of Semitic Studies
JSSEA	Journal of the Society for the Study of Egyptian Antiquities
JTS	Journal of Theological Studies
JWH	Journal of World History
LdÄ	Lexikon der Ägyptologie
MDAIK	Mitteilungen, des deutschen archäologischen Institut, Kairo
MDOG	Mitteilungen des deutschen Orientgesellschaft
MIOF	Mitteilungen des Institut für Orientforschung

MVAG	Mitteilungen der vorderasiatisch-aegyptischen Gesellschaft
NGWG	Nachrichten der Akademie der Wissenschaften in Göttingen
OLP	Orientalia Lovaniensia Periodica
OLZ	Orientalistische Literaturzeitung
OTS	Old Testament Studies
PEFQS	Palestine Exploration Fund Quarterly Statement
PEQ	Palestine Exploration Quarterly
RA	Revue assyriologique
RB	Revue biblique
RdA	Revue d'Assyriologie
RdE	Revue d'Egyptologie
RHA	Revue Hittite et Asiatique
RHJE	Revue de l'histoire juive en Egypte
RHR	Revue de l'histoire des religions
RIDA	Revue International des Droits de l'Antiquité
RSO	Rivisti di studi orientali
RT	Receuil de travaux
SAK	Studien zur altägyptische Kultur
SBAW	Sitzungsberichte der bayerischen Akademie der Wissenschaften
SMEA	Studi Micenei ed Egeo-Anatolici
Stud Class Oriental	Studi Classici e Orientali
ThWAT	Theologisches Wörterbuch zum Alten Testament
ThZ	Theologische Zeitschrift
TLZ	Theologische Literaturzeitung
UF	Ugarit Forschungen
VT	Vetus Testamentum
VTS	Vetus Testamentum Supplements
WO	Welt des Orient
WZKM	Wiener Zeitschrift für die Kunde des Morgenlandes
ZA	Zeitschrift für Assyriologie
ZÄS	Zeitschrift für ägyptische Sprache und Altertumskunde
ZAW	Zeitschrift für die alttestamentliche Wissenschaften
ZDMG	Zeitschrift der deutschen morgenländischen Gesellschaft

ZDPV   *Zeitschrift des deutschen Palästina-Vereins*
ZThK   *Zeitschrift für Theologie und Kirche*

MAJOR WORKS

ANET²   *Ancient Near Eastern Texts Relating to the Old Testament*, ed. James B. Pritchard (Princeton, N.J., 1969)

CAH³   *Cambridge Ancient History* I–III (Cambridge, 1971–1982)

IDB   *International Dictionary of the Bible*, ed. G. A. Buttrick (New York, 1962)

OCD   *Oxford Classical Dictionary*, ed. N.G.L. Hammond and H. H. Scullard (Oxford, 1970)

RE   *Real-Encyclopädie der klassischen Altertumswissenschaft* ed. A. Pauly, G. Wissowa, and W. Kroll

Wb   *Wörterbuch des ägyptischen Sprache*, 5 vols., ed. A. Erman and H. Grapow (Berlin and Leipzig, 1971)

ANCIENT WRITINGS

ARM   *Archives royales de Mari*, ed. A. Parrot and G. Dossin (Paris, 1950–)

BM   British Museum

CAD   *The Assyrian Dictionary*, ed. I. J. Gelb, T. Jacobsen, B. Landsberger, and A. L. Oppenheim (Chicago, 1956–)

CGC   *Catalogue général du musée de Caire* (Cairo, 1904–)

CT   Coffin Texts

EA   The El-Amarna Letters

FGrHist   *Fragmente der griechischen Historiker*, ed. F. Jacoby (1923–1958)

KBo   *Keilschrifttexte aus Boghazköi* (Berlin and Leipzig, 1916–1921)

Koehler-Baumgartner   *Hebräisches und aramäisches Lexikon zum Alten Testament*, ed. L. Koehler and W. Baumgartner (Leiden, 1967–1974)

KRI   *Ramesside Inscriptions*, 7 vols., ed. K. A. Kitchen (London, 1969–)

KUB   *Keilschrifturkunden aus Boghazköi* (Berlin, 1921–1944)

NBC   Niesse Babylonian Collection

P-M/P-M² B. Porter and R. Moss, *Topographical Bibliography of Ancient Egyptian Hieroglyphic Texts, Reliefs and Paintings*, 7 vols. (London, 1927–)

PT Pyramid Texts

RS Ras Shamra

Urk Urkunden des ägyptischen Altertums, ed. G. Steindorff (Leipzig and Berlin, 1906–1958)

MISCELLANEOUS

L.P.H./l.p.h. Life, prosperity, health

Preface

THE PRESENT work represents, broadly speaking, an overview of the relations between Egypt and Western Asia from the earliest times down to the destruction of Jerusalem in 586 B.C. As in similar cases of inscripturation, publication freezes a viewpoint in time, and already new returns have come in on topics on which the author satisfied himself in the fall of 1989 that his view was generally accurate. An effort has been made to incorporate most significant additions to ongoing discussions, but inevitably some will have been missed.

A number of people must receive hearty thanks for the assistance they have offered the writer: my wife Susan for graphics and maps; G. Mumford, S. Shubert, and P. Sodtke for typing the manuscript and for sundry bibliographical research; numerous colleagues for their shrewd counseling, including J. S. Holladay, Jr., E. Oren, S. Ahituv, W. Murnane, A. R. Schulman, G. W. Ahlström, J. van Seters. All of these would quail, I am sure, if this acknowledgment were taken to mean that they were responsible for any particular view herein espoused; and I hasten to emphasize that this is not the case. Finally to members of seminars and classes, too numerous to mention individually, whom I have taught over the past decade goes my warm appreciation; for outside the heated debate of the classroom scholarship does not flourish.

Introduction

THE 13,000-SQUARE-KILOMETER tract of the north Sinai, separating modern Israel and Jordan from the Delta of the Nile, always conjures up, for the author, three distinct memories that are permanently fixed in his consciousness. The first is dated to early June 1967 when, in receipt of permission to study inscriptions in the ancient Egyptian mines in the Sinai, he was deterred at the last moment from boarding a plane to Cairo by the alarming news of the day. The second is a memorable trip of the same year, through Gaza and Khan Yunis, along the Mediterranean coast toward Egypt from the east. Finally, from a hot July night eight years later, comes the recollection of a dawn vigil on the roof of the house of the commander of United Nations forces in Ismailia, to watch the heliacal rising of Sirius on the eastern horizon of the Sinai.

Surprisingly at first recall, it is not the terrain of the north Sinai that has left an indelible impression. The prospect of low undulating sand dunes and a horizon obscured in the haze does not linger long in the mind's eye, for in contrast to the majestic mountains of the southern sector of the Sinai or the Egyptian Red Sea coast, the 150 kilometers between Port Said and Gaza are nondescript and uninviting. The traveler between Egypt and Palestine, faced with the slow going of this inimical littoral, might well be forgiven if he opted for a sea route. Only nomads, one might imagine, would be best equipped to negotiate the sands of Sinai.

The nature of the north Sinai, however, belies its importance in antiquity and its use as a transit corridor. For here we are not only on the route between two local regions, Egypt and the Levant, but more especially on the land bridge between the two largest continents, Asia and Africa. From remote prehistory, migrants, caravans, armies, pilgrims, and fugitives have crossed this threshold in both directions, bearing goods, religion, and culture. Funneled into its narrow passage, things and ideas from as far afield as black Africa, the steppes of Russia, and the Far East have flowed to and fro, leaving unmistakable traces not only on the routes of transit, but also on the peoples inhabiting the threshold itself.

Nonetheless, these peoples enjoy an impressive pedigree in their own right. In the Nile Valley shortly before 3000 B.C. appeared the first nation-state in the world, adorned with all the sophisticated trappings of civilization. Within the first four centuries of its existence, a native culture had taken root, expressing itself in belles lettres, metaphysics, and an accomplished and refined architecture that remains the wonder of the world.

Permanence and changelessness were the hallmarks of the ancient Egyptian way of life: language, script, religion, and iconography of this Nilotic civilization during the time of Christ had changed rather less than might have been expected from the period of its inception three thousand years earlier. "The Kingdom of the Two Lands" seemed immutable. Not so the society on the other side of the threshold. Here, even the unity of country, geographically or politically, was a hope rarely realized. Called by the Egyptians "Retenu" or "Kharu," by the Syrians of the second millennium B.C. "Canaan," by the Hebrews "Israel," and the Greeks, Romans, and Saracens "Palestina," the Holy Land has remained over the centuries a land that displays no inherent unity or cultural autochthony. A true threshold, it has witnessed an ethnic osmosis over five thousand years of recorded history, with communities drifting in and out from the four corners of the compass and finding lodgment for a brief period. All have brought new cultural traits and ideas for promulgation; few as integral cultures have been content to remain in the land.

The communities on both sides of this continental threshold have been *and* are too fundamentally disparate in culture for any substantial borrowings to take place, not to mention syncretism. As the Egyptians might have put it, in anticipation of Kipling's "East is East, and West is West," a papyrus stalk cannot grow on the desert, nor a cactus on the banks of the Nile. On a wider scale, the Sinai frontier proved difficult of passage for goods and ideas coming from much farther afield. Babylon and Byblos might be crossroads for the transit of caravans from the Mediterranean to the Punjab; the "Wilderness of Sin" could never be so described. For most of the four millennia covered by this book, Egypt successfully kept a sort of "Wacht am Suez."

Yet on both sides of the Sinai divide men knew of their hither neighbors, and the latter's presence cannot help but have produced a reaction even if borrowings were eschewed. Egypt and Asia may well have viewed each other with an apprehension that consciously sought to block interaction; but subtle influences could not be prevented.

The aim of the present work is first to chronicle as empirically as possible the nature and extent of the relationship between Egypt and hither Asia in the more than three thousand years covered herein, and second to try to ferret out the causes that might be elicited on the basis of the extant evidence. Comparison with past efforts in this field shows that the endeavor is fraught with grave risk: there is a scylla and charybdis to steer through. On no account can a prejudice in favor of a sort of "Pan-Egyptianism" or an "Israel-first" syndrome be allowed to compel the evidence to dance to its own tune. If it happens to be the case, for example, that Egyptian wisdom strongly influenced Hebrew belles lettres, or that Israel's earliest "constitution" was "democratic," this will emerge as the facts are paraded or the model set up. One must not become an apologist for the ancient people whose culture and history constitute one's discipline.

Chronology is a subject that cannot be discussed at length in this book, but a few words of explanation cannot be avoided. For the period down to the beginning of the 18th Dynasty there is no essential disagreement among scholars—a variety of means (carbon-14 tests included) has provided parameters which are ever closing; however, for the New Kingdom on a narrower front controversy reigns. This book follows the so-called high chronology (accession of Thutmose III in 1504 B.C.), although we are now assured that scholarly consensus would opt for the middle or low chronology (accession of the same king in 1490 or 1479 B.C., respectively).[1] Be that as it may, and the notion of "chronology by consensus" conjures up amusing examples from the past, the present choice of the high dates provides a traditional though provisional framework for New Kingdom chronology, which may well be adjusted by future discovery.

[1] P. Ahström, "High, Middle or Low?" in Acts of an International Colloquium on Absolute Chronology Held at the University of Gothenberg (Gothenburg, 1987).

Egypt and the Levant from Prehistoric Times to the Hyksos

CHAPTER 1

Villages, Camps, and the Rise of a Colossus

ONE OF THE great anomalies in the long story of civilization on the face of the globe is the stark contrast between Egypt of the 4000s and 3000s before Christ and its immediate progeny of the early pyramid age. Only generations separate the two, and yet in terms of relative societal and political development a vast gulf interposes itself. Unlike the Tigris-Euphrates Valley, where human society over millennia of prehistory displays a linear evolution at a constant rate and where the temples at Uruk presage the glories of Sumer centuries in advance, Egypt bounced overnight, as it were, out of the Stone Age and into urban culture. High-rises suddenly replaced mud huts; a civil service superseded the village elders. A new sophisticated focus for human organization filled the void where only chiefdoms had occasionally appeared: a king sat over Egypt.

How do we explain this quantum leap? The question has often been posed, but no satisfying answer has been given. Of course, our problem may be lack of evidence. Egyptian prehistory, although the object of intense research since World War II, continues to yield spotty evidence in some areas, to withhold evidence over large "gaps," and broadly speaking to prevent us from generalizing. And yet by and large we are not mistaken: around 3300 to 3200 B.C. a catalyst or combination of factors catapulted the Neolithic village into history.[1]

THE STONE AGE IN EGYPT AND PALESTINE

There can be no doubt that man has occupied northeast Africa for hundreds of thousands of years. Although very few skeletal specimens have been recovered from remote Paleolithic times, countless stations and lithic assemblages have been recovered both in the deserts and along the

[1] For general works on Egyptian prehistory, see J. Mellaart, *The Earliest Civilizations of the Near East* (London, 1965); idem, *The Neolithic of the Near East* (London, 1975); W. C. Hayes, *Most Ancient Egypt* (Chicago, 1965); M. Hoffman, *Egypt before the Pharaohs* (New York, 1979); J. L. de Cenival, *L'Égypte avant les pyramides* (Paris, 1973); V. Gordon Childe, *New Light on the Most Ancient Near East*[4] (London, 1953); F. Debono, in J. Ki-Zerbo, ed., *General History of Africa* (London, 1981), 634–55; D.A.E. Garrod and J.G.D. Clark, *CAH*[3] I (1971), 70–89. Those wishing a complete listing of sources should consult K. R. Weeks (A) *Bibliography of Egyptian Prehistory* (New York, 1985).

edge of the Nile. Close examination of these remains along with the faunal and climatic record of these times has enabled scholars to sketch in outline the general nature of the Old Stone Age society and ecology and, in the process, to put right the flawed views of earlier scholars, which, until recently, continued to dominate laymen's views of prehistoric Africa.[2]

The modern Nile is the descendant of a prehistoric river of Pleistocene origin whose bed had been hewn through the rocky plateau of northeast Africa already in the Pliocene, five million years before.[3] During the four great advances of the ice sheet over the northern hemisphere during the last million years, the concomitant fluctuations in rainfall in the area were responsible for a series of alternating increases and retardations in the flow of the river. These are marked today by eight distinct edges to the valley of the Nile, which are marked by an equivalent number of "terraces" in the rocky cliffs that give onto the eastern and western deserts. It is on the three lowermost of these terraces, each representing an ancient bank of the river at floodtime, that the earliest artifacts of man in the valley are encountered. The sixth terrace from the top, about 24 to 27 meters above the present floodplain, yields assemblages of crude handaxes of a pear-shaped type, known as Acheullian, that are found over Europe and much of northern Africa and Asia, and are usually dated to the second Interglacial period.[4] Although Egypt helps little in this regard, finds elsewhere in Africa suggest the humanoid species *Homo erectus* as responsible for this industry. The lowest terraces (9 meters and 3 to 4 meters) display Mousterian artifacts in which worked flakes constitute the staple and are used for various purposes, including projectile points.[5] Again, to judge from finds outside the bounds of Egypt, the Mousterian culture was produced by that subspecies of *Homo sapiens* known universally as Neanderthals; and the span of their floruit is usually assigned to the close of the third interglacial and the fourth (and last) glacial, about 100,000 to 50,000 years B.P.

The final retreat of the ice around 20,000 B.P. witnessed an acceleration in the cultural evolution of human society. Neanderthal man in Europe perished—under what conditions no one seems sure—and true *Homo sapiens* ultimately was left with the field. The "tool kit" of primitive man becomes larger and more varied. New techniques of implement manufac-

[2] P.E.L. Smith, *Scientific American* 235 (1976), 30–38.

[3] C.B.M. McBurney, *The Stone Age of North Africa* (Harmondsworth, 1960), 122; W. C. Hayes, *JNES* 23 (1964), 78; R. Said and F. Yousri, *BIE* 45 (1986), 1–30.

[4] F. Bordes, *The Old Stone Age* (London, 1968), 64–76; D. Gilead, *World Archaeology* 2 (1970), 1–11; P. M. Vermeersch et al., *Paleorient* 4 (1978), 245–52.

[5] K. S. Sandford, *Palaeolithic Man and the Nile Valley in Upper and Middle Egypt* (Chicago, 1934); J. Vandier, *Manuel d'archéologie égyptienne* (Paris, 1952), 41.

ture, including blade making and polishing, begin to replace the more primitive methods of the past. The decorative arts take on a new importance as a form of the community's cultural expression.

It is not altogether clear to what extent Egypt shared in the innovations of Epipaleolithic Europe. Increasingly in the past decades, excavation in the Nile Valley has revealed campsites of the period 16,000 to about 9000 B.C. of a community subsisting on intensive hunting and fishing. This culture (known as Sebilian)[6] shows a marked decrease in the size of all tools, which are largely manufactured from flakes secondarily worked for hafting into composite tools ("microliths"). Although semisedentary and, toward the end of the period, knowledgeable about animal domestication, the Sebilians remain squarely within the tradition of the hunter-gatherers of the Old Stone Age.

One of the outstanding questions plaguing prehistorians of Egypt is when did that fundamental change in human economy from food gathering to food production take place in northeast Africa? Was it an indigenous development, or were the primitive Nile dwellers beneficiaries of the importation of agriculture from outside? Leaving aside the reason why primitive man of this period was compelled to devise a new means of subsistence (diminishing wild game reserves, an increase in population, reduced living space?), we must confess that hard data have not been bequeathed to us for that crucial period from around 9000 to 6000 B.C. in the Nile Valley. We enter this "Dark Age" with the Epipaleolithic Sebilians firmly ensconced in the valley; we emerge from it to find agricultural, "Neolithic" communities everywhere dotting the landscape. The economy of these little villages is a curious composite of relatively advanced methods of farming superimposed on a base livelihood of hunting and fishing. It almost looks as though agriculture was introduced from outside to hunter-gatherers who proved only lukewarm to its arrival.[7]

The optimum habitat for the domestication of wheat and barley, sheep and cattle is the "Mediterranean type woodlands of the Fertile Crescent";[8] and archaeology has now borne this out. The earliest known hu-

---

[6] R. W. Fairbridge, *Kush* 11 (1963), 98ff.; K. W. Butzer and C. L. Hansen, *Desert and River in Nubia* (Madison, Wis., 1968); K. W. Butzer, *Environment and Archaeology* (Chicago, 1971), 553; J. Mellaart, *The Neolithic of the Near East* (London, 1981), 264; F. Hassan, in L. G. Freeman, ed., *Views of the Past* (The Hague, 1978), 153–76.

[7] It should be borne in mind that the contention that in prehistoric times swampy conditions prevailed in the Nile Valley and that it was man's task to drain these swamps and claim land for agriculture (McBurney, *Stone Age*, 142) is now known to be in error. Cf. K. W. Butzer, *Bull Soc Geog Égypte* 32 (1959), 47: "The extent of perennial swamps and lakes in the valley was small, almost unimportant, even in early settlement times. The greater part of the plain consisted of seasonally flooded basins as today." Idem, *Environment and Archaeology*, 601.

[8] Butzer, *Environment and Archaeology*, 547.

man society that we see in process of developing an economy based first on the systematic gathering of wild cereals and then on their artificial production was to be found in Palestine, Transjordan, and Lebanon between about 10,000 and 8000 B.C.[9] Dubbed by prehistorians "Natufian" after the type site just north of Jerusalem, this culture was the product of a human type of slight build with long heads (dolichocephalic) that can confidently be classified as *Homo sapiens*. Natufians, like the modern Bantus, practiced evulsion of the incisors and apparently wore skins and at times headgear made of shells. Although obliged to adopt a partly migratory existence because of their hunting and fishing, the Natufians did possess more or less permanent settlements, which centered upon caves or were located on hilltops close to springs. Their houses often consisted of circular huts from 3 to 8 meters in circumference, built of fieldstone and roofed presumably with boughs. Stone was widely used for tools in the same microlith tradition as the Sebilians, blades and lunate projectile points being common. Bone was employed for pins, awls, and fishhooks, and shells (some imported from the Red Sea) were strung together for jewelry. While hunting and fishing continued as the main means of livelihood, mortars, pestles, storage bins, and sickles suggest the harvesting of grain was known and practiced by the Natufians. This evidence does not prove, of course, that horticulture and animal domestication had been discovered and were developing; but by the beginning of the eighth millennium with the establishment of the first permanent town sites, these techniques had undoubtedly been invented. We can, then, speak of a *food-producing*, farming economy in the final stages of the Natufian in Palestine.

THE EGYPTIAN AND HIS VILLAGE

If one feels compelled to explain the spread of such major changes in human society as the introduction of agriculture by a theory of diffusion, it will be easy to postulate the gradual osmosis of this new kind of economy outward from its place of origin in the southern Levant during the eighth millennium. Whether this area provided a model for the inception of the Neolithic in Syria, Anatolia, and the Zagros may be a moot point; but in Egypt we encounter difficulties. For not only are we faced with a gap of nearly three millennia in the archaeological record, but when neolithic sites do appear after 6000 B.C., the source from which they derived their knowledge of agriculture, it is claimed, must be sought in the south

[9] On the Natufians, see D. Garrod, *The Natufian Culture* (London, 1957); K. M. Kenyon, *Advancement of Science* 26 (1969–1970), 1–17; Mellaart, *The Earliest Civilizations of the Near East*, 22–32; idem, *The Neolithic of the Near East*, 28–38.

and west rather then the northeast.[10] Indeed, the general demographic
flow that seems to be charted in the distribution and sequence over time
of Neolithic sites in the Nile Valley would seem to be south to north.
Consonant with this pattern is the apparent African connection of so
many of the early traits of Neolithic culture in Egypt—for example, the
dolichocephalic crania, the familiarity with ivory working, the fashion-
ability of steatopygy, and the morphology and decoration of the pottery.[11] Still, it is almost inconceivable that Palestine, separated from the
Nile by scarcely 160 kilometers, should not have played some role in the
arrival of a knowledge of farming in Egypt.[12]

By the fifth millennium B.C. we can speak of a Neolithic in the Nile
Valley. Small farming communities on outcrops of rocks or levees in the
valley seem to push their way northward over time (unless unmethodical
survey and excavation have skewed the evidence).[13] Each comprises a
small number of reed huts plaited with mud, and surrounded by some
kind of protective circumvallation. Although mud brick was introduced
around the middle of the fourth millennium in the Amratian period,[14] it
was not extensively used until after 3500 B.C. with the remarkable advances of the Gerzean. Similarly, throughout most of the period covered
by the Neolithic there is some evidence of increased population and
slowly expanding settlements,[15] but the general level of culture remained
that of a fairly primitive farming community, still wedded to the hunting
economy of the past. For man resists change, innovation, and the advent
of new ideas until forced to accept them by dire necessity; and in the Nile
Valley the climate was so salubrious and fish and game so plentiful that
the prehistoric residents felt little compunction to transform their economy to a rigorous agricultural one.[16]

The study of the "predynastic" period of Egypt's past—that is, that
encompassing the Neolithic during the fifth and fourth millennia B.C.—
has become in large measure the purvue of anthropologically trained pre-

[10] For the western route, see K. W. Butzer, *Early Hydraulic Civilization in Egypt* (Chicago, 1976), 11; for the Khartoum Mesolithic, see B. Trigger, in *Ancient Egypt, A Social
History* (Cambridge, 1983), 16; Cf. also Clark, *CAH³* I (1971), 34ff.; R. Derricourt, *JNES*
30 (1971), 1–9.

[11] On the south-north flow, see McBurney, *Stone Age*, 128, 161; R. Solecki, *Kush* 11
(1963), 70; E. Strouhal, *Journal of African History* 12 (1971), 1–9.

[12] J. M. Renfrew, in P. Ucko and G. W. Dimbleby, *Domestication and Exploitation of
Plants and Animals* (London, 1969), 149ff.; Trigger, *Ancient Egypt*, 17ff.

[13] Trigger, *Ancient Egypt*, 10.

[14] M. Hoffman, *JNES* 39 (1980), 119–37.

[15] Butzer, *Bull Soc Geog Égypte* 32 (1959); idem, *Environment and Archaeology*, 602.

[16] On this resistance to change, resulting in a mixed hunting, fishing, and farming economy for the Egyptian Neolithic, see W. C. Hayes, *JNES* 23 (1964), 226; K. A. Wittfogel,
Oriental Despotism (New Haven, Conn., 1957), 19; Trigger, *Ancient Egypt*, 20.

historians who have the commitments to a much broader area. This is as it should be, and the subject of this chapter gains much by the involvement. Egyptologists, however, have a function here too. After the material culture of Egypt's Neolithic has been examined through excavation and survey, and after models of the rise of complex societies have been called forth and compared, there remains a number of significant questions a philologist might possibly contribute to answering. What can we tell about the government and social organization of the communities wherein these Neolithic artifacts were made? Was it effective organization and were the members of the community satisfied? How did one community get along with its neighbor? Do we know anything of the religious beliefs of the time? These questions cannot be answered merely by an examination of archaeological remains: written records are necessary to give satisfactory answers. And in the absence of contemporary records, one will have to extrapolate from later documents that seem to be describing basic institutions of antiquity. For Neolithic Egypt had reached a plateau that was to provide a foundation for Egyptian society for all time, in the form of the farming village, the home, and native habitat of the Egyptian peasant from 5000 B.C. to the present.[17]

When, after 3000 B.C., the invention of the hieroglyphic script reveals the language of Egypt, several words were current designating human settlements, each with its own nuance. *Neywet*, usually translated "city," in fact meant a collection of reed huts surrounded by some kind of protective circumvallation; *demy^e*, "town" from a root meaning "to touch," referred to the spot on the riverbank where ships put in. *Ehy^e* referred to a bower for domesticated animals; *yat* designated a "mound" on which stood a settlement in the floodplain and its important buildings; *wahyet*, "clan, family," was applied to those small hamlets or encampments of kin groups. Thus the principal raisons-d'être for coming together in collectives in the Nile Valley may be elicited from the lexical material as follows: protection of farmers and animals, transportation and transshipment of produce, protection from the inundation, and base camps for (hunting?) groups.

Another early word for a type of settlement was "seat" or "abode," specifically that of a god; and archaeology as well as early epigraphic records, has underscored the importance of the shrine in predynastic settlements.[18] One should imagine—and now the excavations at Hierakonpolis provide a concrete image—a simple shrine of light material (reeds, boughs, and wood), with a curved roof and horns protruding from the

---

[17] On urbanism in ancient Egypt, see B. J. Kemp, *Antiquity* 51 (1977), 185ff.; M. Bietak, in K. Weeks, ed., *Egyptology and the Social Sciences* (Cairo, 1979), 98–105; on urbanization in general, Y. V. Andreev, *Oxford Journal of Archaeology* 8 (1989), 167–78.

[18] Hoffman, *Egypt before the Pharaohs*, 307.

facade. This served not only as a place wherein the service of the god was performed, but also as the center of the administration and as a focus for local markets and festivals. The divine inmate, possibly in origin a tribal ancestor,[19] was "the town god,"[20] the protector and liege of all those dwelling in the settlement or its immediate bailiwick. His sphere of activity encompassed the entire range of the community's interest, and thus he was at once creator of the world, founder of the town, sustainer (of fertility), mortuary god, and leader in war. Outside the shrine on a pole floated a strip of cloth later to become the hieroglyphic for "god," as well as the god's "emblem," an object or animal enjoying a loose connection with the deity, also elevated for all to see.[21] These emblems, which often seem to identify a predynastic community, as well as its god, begin to proliferate in the decorative arts of the last Neolithic phase, the Gerzean, about 3300 to 3050 B.C.

By what mechanism these early communities were governed is difficult to say. Only toward the close of the Gerzean, and in fact on the very threshold of history, do some graves become sufficiently large to postulate the existence of a chiefdom. Early historic texts speak of "great ones" or "chiefs" at the provincial level, possibly a throwback to independent tribal rulers of prehistoric times;[22] and there is some evidence for the existence of a council or corporation (presumably of elders) who would approve the selection of a new chief.[23] Some have suggested that the early title that came to mean "king of Upper Egypt" was of local predynastic origin. This title, pronounced *ensi*, meant literally "he-of-the-*swt*-plant" and, according to some, designated a ruler who owned the land and had right of disposal of its produce;[24] yet there is evidence that in predynastic

[19] H. Goedicke, *JSSEA* 16 (1986), 57–62.

[20] K. Sethe, *Urgeschichte und älteste Religion der Ägypter* (Leipzig, 1930), 3ff.; on the nature of the local god in Ancient Egypt, see E. Hornung, *Conceptions of God in Ancient Egypt* (Ithaca, 1982), 70–74.

[21] The nature of the association varies from place to place from complete identification to a tenuous connection between two divine things of independent status. See H. Frankfort, *Ancient Egyptian Religion* (New York, 1948), 3–29; Sethe, *Urgeschichte*, 6–7; S. Schott, *Hieroglyphen* (Mainz, 1950), 15ff.; J. Assmann, *BN* (1980), 46ff. Emblems represented include animals (cow, lion, bull, crocodile), birds (falcon, ibis, vulture), insects (beetle, centipede), plants (sycamore, oleander), inanimate objects (pillar, fossil bundle of stakes). It is a moot point whether the prevalence of such "emblems" militates in favor of an early "totemic" stage in the evolution of Egyptian religion.

[22] W. Helck, *Untersuchungen zu den Beamtentiteln des ägyptischen Alten Reiches* (Glückstadt, 1954), 51. In historic times the title was reserved for foreign rulers.

[23] Cf. the "corporation" and the "council" of Heliopolis, and its role in the Old Kingdom: R. Anthes, *JNES* 18 (1959), 192–94.

[24] See E. Otto, *WO* 1 (1947–1952), 445; H. Goedicke, *Die Stellung des Königs im alten Reich* (Wiesbaden, 1960), 17–37; E. J. Baumgartel, *The Cultures of Predynastic Egypt* (Oxford, 1960), 2:142–43; idem, *JEA* 61 (1975), 28–32.

times some land at least was communally owned and apportioned.[25] In any event, a firm connection between the ruler of a community and fertility of the soil through the agency of the river seems to be endemic to ancient Egypt, a bequest of the African substratum of its civilization.[26]

Very few predynastic settlements have survived at a level or in a condition to be excavated with ease—much of the Delta has aggraded and those sites in the floodplain are similarly out of reach; consequently, it is to the better preserved cemeteries that one turns for evidence of material culture and religious beliefs. In particular three separate but overlapping sets of mortuary beliefs and practices may be elicited. In one the heavens capture the imagination of the primitives, who translate the stars into glorified beings, human-headed bird-souls of the departed. Orientation of the corpse toward the sunrise also attests a preoccupation with a celestial hereafter, awakened by the prospect of resurrection with the sun.[27]

In the valley of the Nile, the vast western desert, always visible and identifiable as the place where the sun "died" every evening, naturally attracted popular attention. Here was the realm of the dead, in the *West*, and the "westerner" became a euphemism for the dead. Cemeteries were separated from the living and placed usually, but by no means always, on the western desert edge; consequently death involved a journey from the home of the living to the house of the dead in the desert. The Realm of the Dead was in fact projected over the trackless desert wastes, and out here only the instincts of a canine—jackel, dog, or wolf—would avail. Such a quadruped can always be seen prowling among the tombs or over the desert, seeming to find his way where no path exists. And thus it is no surprise that, in Middle Egypt especially, where the low sandy desert emerges at a gentle gradient from the valley floor, the canine quadruped should have become the essential town deity, protecting the dead and leading them to the West. The names are transparent: Khentiamentiu, "the First of the Westerners"; Wepwawet, "the Opener of the Ways" (i.e., the Trailblazer); Anubis, "he who is upon his hill, lord of the High Ground (i.e., the necropolis)."[28] When the pharaonic monarchy came into being, it borrowed heavily on the symbolism of the first two named.[29]

In the Delta, where the landscape is one of marsh, islands, and low-

[25] J. G. Griffiths, *The Conflict of Horus and Seth* (Liverpool, 1959), 147–48.

[26] Baumgartel, *Predynastic Egypt*, 2:152–53; Trigger, in Weeks, *Egyptology and the Social Sciences*, 51–52.

[27] J. Černý, *Ancient Egyptian Religion* (London, 1952), 16; Otto, *WO* 1 (1947–1952), 434; I.E.S. Edwards, *The Pyramids of Ancient Egypt* (Harmondsworth, 1962), 34; the circumpolar stars, "they that know not destruction," particularly fascinated the ancients.

[28] S. Schott, *Bemerkungen zum ägyptischen Pyramidenkult* (Cargo, 1950), 142; H. Kees, *Ancient Egypt: A Cultural Topography* (London, 1961), 25.

[29] W. Helck, *ArOr* 20 (1952), 83; J. G. Griffiths, *The Origins of Osiris and His Cult* (Leiden, 1980), 166.

lying land, two other components informed the ideas about death. One involved burial within the town on its mound—the desert edge is usually too remote—under the protection of the local town god. Here the family context was all important. As head of the house, the father must remain with the family, and thus burial beneath the floor and preservation of the corpse were in order. The eldest son must minister to his father, and summon him to the daily offering meal, a role also to become later a symbolic rationalization of the kingship.[30] A second belief had it that the dead were translated to one of the inaccessible "islands," of which the Delta in antiquity boasted many amid the marshes, a sort of Avalon called "the Field of Rushes."

THE MOVE TO A COMPLEX SOCIETY IN EGYPT AND PALESTINE

It is not altogether clear to what extent the town whose structures, economy, and religion we have sketched in the Nile Valley exerted any influence as a model on neighboring countries. But for Palestine, at least, throughout most of the Neolithic the influence would have been slight.

For the period about 8000 to 6000 B.C., the so-called Prepottery Neolithic, the culture of Palestine and Syria shows a progressive development of farming techniques, including the domestication of animals, and sedentarization in permanent towns. This demographic shift, which may have been occasioned in part by the onset of dessication in the Levant, is one of the most important changes in human life-style during the period. While in Egypt the needs of the farmer and hunter and the service of the gods provide the basic reason for coming together in human communities, in the Levant defense seems to have been uppermost in the thinking of the population. Jericho, a settlement of about two thousand and one of the earliest to be excavated, was surrounded by a stone wall 3 meters wide and about 4 meters high, interspersed with towers. (Plate 1).[31] The lexical evidence bears out this preoccupation. Although the languages of the Levant long remembered a seminomadic stage in societal development—the most common word for "city," *âlu* in Akkadian, goes back to the plural of the word "tent"[32]—other terms for settlement derive from roots meaning basically to fortify.

When after 3000 B.C. Egyptian written sources are obliged to describe

[30] Schott, *Pyramidenkult*, 142, 162–64; A. Scharff, *Das Grab als Wohnhaus in der ägyptischen Frühzeit* (Munich, 1947); see H. Kees, in S.A.B. Mercer, *The Egyptian Pyramid Texts* (New York, 1952), 124–27; J. Settgast, *Untersuchungen zu altägyptischen Bestattungsdarstellungen* (Glückstadt, 1963), 114.

[31] K. Kenyon, *PEQ* (1960), 1–21; idem, *Digging Up Jericho* (New York, 1957), 65–76.

[32] G. Buccelati, *Cities and Nations of Ancient Syria* (Rome, 1967), 40–41.

Plate 1. Circular tower in the fortifications of Prepottery Neolithic Jericho, c. 8000–6000 B.C.

cities in Palestine, they call them *wnwt*, meaning fortified enclosures.[33] While fortifications may serve to protect men from animal predators, the size of the Jericho walls can scarcely be construed as anything other than a defense against the threat of other communities.

On a cultural level Egypt and Palestine share little during the earlier part of the Neolithic. A sort of ancestor worship seems to be attested for the seventh millennium B.C., manifest in the curious cult of skulls.[34] Otherwise burials are poor and nondescript, and the orientation and position of the dead unrevealing. Some trade with the Negeb is in evidence, but this did not apparently extend to the Delta. In fact by 6000 B.C. the progressive aridity that had invaded the south had forced the abandonment of many Palestinian settlements, and in the subsequent millennium Palestine becomes merely a culture province of Syria.[35]

In Egypt, with the first traces of the Neolithic in the Fayum, about 4500 B.C.,[36] a sequence may be established that leads us without interruption through the so-called Chalcolithic age ("copper-stone") and into history.

[33] See chapter 2.
[34] Mellaart, *The Neolithic of the Near East*, 61–62.
[35] Ibid., 67–69.
[36] A. J. Arkell and P. J. Ucko, *Current Anthropology* 6 (1965), 145–65. For Fayum A, see F. Wendorf, *Science* 169 (1970), 161ff.; Trigger, *Ancient Egypt*, 21–22.

The sequence is still not quite so well known, or so well attested as comparable sequences in western Asia, but the course is fairly convincingly charted. If one examines the ongoing record of these fifteen centuries with an eye to a progression from simpler to more complex forms, one will be struck by the initial stagnation of civilization in Egypt for the first twelve of those centuries, followed by a dramatic acceleration in societal evolution, which plummets us into the most sophisticated of contemporary states. Two questions we must ask are fundamental to the present study: what caused this extraordinary speedup in social and political evolution, and why did it take place in Egypt rather than the Levant?

In fact, for Egypt, a number of models for the rise of the pharaonic complex have been advanced, but none is particularly satisfying. The problem is that in almost every case the evidence, or at least some portion of it, does not square with the model. Those who place all the emphasis on advancement in irrigation techniques[37] as the catalyst will now have to admit that widespread irrigation *followed* the establishment of the monarchy, and improved techniques were at most its concomitant.[38] Those who argue that the pharaonic monarchy arose as a result of the invasion of Egypt in the late predynastic period by a superior "dynastic race" which imposed itself on the autochthonous population[39] will have to think again; for the ethnic bifurcation in Egypt is much older than the Gerzean.[40] The economic historians who see the energy generated by the clash between two economies as the spark that caused the pharaonic "explosion" will have to face up to our present awareness of the complexity of this matter, as the hunting, pastoral, and farming economies had long existed and melded in the Nilotic landscape.[41]

One feature of the Egyptian landscape, often observed but poorly assessed as to our present purpose, provides at once a marked contrast to the Levant and a valuable clue toward solving the conundrum already enunciated. I refer to the river itself. The Nile not only offers itself as a transit corridor and accelerates travel—three weeks to a month to cover the one thousand kilometers between the First Cataract and the apex of the Delta—it virtually forces a broader, more grandiose view of the world

[37] On irrigation, see W. Schenkel, *Die Bewasserungsrevolution in alten Ägypten* (Mainz, 1978); Butzer, *Early Hydraulic Civilization*; idem, in D. Schmandt-Besserat, ed., *Immortal Egypt* (Malibu, Calif., 1978), 13–18.

[38] On the so-called urban revolution, see V. Gordon Childe, *Man Makes Himself* (London, 1936), 157–201; idem, *New Light*, 98ff.; J. Wilson, *The Burden of Egypt* (Chicago 1951), 29ff.; cf. the remarks of Butzer in *Environment and Archaeology*, 603–4.

[39] R. Engelbach, *ASAE* 42 (1943), 193–221; D. E. Derry, *JEA* 42 (1956), 80–85; W. B. Emery, *Archaic Egypt* (Harmondsworth, 1962), 38–40.

[40] See A. C. Berry, R. J. Berry, and P. J. Ucko, *Man*, n.s. 2 (1967), 551–68; Trigger, *Ancient Egypt*, 12–13.

[41] Kees, *Ancient Egypt: A Cultural Topography*, chap. 1.

on the inhabitants on its banks. The possibility of goods transiting far longer routes under the aegis of one authority had long since stretched the Egyptian imagination. In historic times it became the norm that grain should "hasten" from one township to another in time of drought through the agency of a single headman; and the latter, though possibly from an impoverished part of the country, gained immense prestige and influence through his entrepreneurial skill. A township ruler will boast of controlling and effecting the passage of minerals, foodstuffs, and luxury items into his bailiwick; and even people from distant stretches of the valley will drift into his jurisdiction through the attraction of his personality and good administration. The relative success or importance of one headman vis-à-vis another will not necessarily depend on a simple one-to-one correspondence with the availability of food stocks in his region. The Nile Valley in Middle Egypt, from Abydos to Cairo, boasts the broadest width of floodplain and the greatest acreage under cultivation; yet it was the relatively poor stretch of valley from Aswan to Abydos that provided Egypt with the chiefdom that translated itself into the royal family of the 1st Dynasty.[42] It is in this remote south that during the fourth millennium we find certain centers beginning to outstrip other settlements in size and political importance; and each is situated in an area where control of a manageable floodplain at time of inundation is possible, and where the proximity of a wady makes control of a transit corridor relatively easy.[43] Abydos, in what was later to become the eighth township of Upper Egypt, lay at the mouth of a wady and route leading to the oasis of Dakhleh in the western desert. Naqada, about thirty kilometers to the north of modern Luxor, on the west bank of the river, was situated directly opposite the western end of the wady Hammamat, which provided easy access to the Red Sea through the eastern desert.[44] Hierakonpolis midway between Luxor and Aswan, had grown up also at a wady's mouth, linking it with the oasis routes of the Sahara desert.[45] Of these three it was the last, Hierakonpolis, that won the day; but the compromising spirit of the entrepreneur is in evidence in the victory: Abydos became a favored residence and burying ground for the Hierakonpolitan kings,[46] and the wild-pig god 'Ash (or Seth) of Naqada was co-opted as tutelary deity of Upper Egypt.

[42] Trigger notes (*Ancient Egypt*, 14) that the flood plain from Abydos south has smaller natural basins, making irrigation easier than further north.

[43] K. Bard, *JARCE* 24 (1987), 81–94.

[44] W.M.F. Petrie and J. E. Quibell, *Naqada and Ballas* (London, 1896); J. J. Castillos, *JSSEA* 11 (1981), 97–106.

[45] W. Kaiser, *MDAIK* 16 (1958), 183–92; B. Adams, *Ancient Hierakonpolis* (Warminster, 1974); idem, *LdÄ* 2 (1977), 1182–86; on the new excavations, see M. Hoffman, *Expedition* 18 (1976), 32–41; idem, *Anthropology* 4 (1980), 51–70.

[46] Cf. B. J. Kemp, *JEA* 52 (1966), 21; but there may also have been early royal burials at Hierakonpolis: idem, *JEA* 59 (1973), 36ff.

The breadth of vision and all that was entailed thereby that blessed the leadership in Upper Egypt is absent from its counterpart in the Delta. Here the landscape is low lying and flat, the river branches and watercourses many, the desert nowhere to be seen. Orientation is difficult, and one clings to a "home base." Fishing, fowling, cattle raising, and goat herding are the principal means of livelihood, but the prevalence of bees makes honey production viable. Lotus, papyrus, and aromatic herbs abound; while on the western side of the Delta and along the coast viticulture is practiced. The proximity of swamps forced communities to high ground and towns were built on "islands" or on the "sand backs" that abound on the east side. Everywhere, except at the apex of the Delta, marsh and watercourse tended to isolate communities from one another and to reinforce independence, self-sufficiency, and parochialism. Under such conditions, uniting Lower Egypt politically was so difficult that the goal did not readily suggest itself to the imagination.

Nevertheless, as in the valley, three communities had signalized themselves in the late fourth millennium, at the dawn of Egyptian history. Two lay on the west side of the Delta. Buto was situated on the westernmost, Rosetta, branch of the Nile, 24 kilometers from the Mediterranean coast;[47] Sais was 20 kilometers south of Buto on the same branch.[48] Until the nineteenth century both were "marsh-locked," and the evidence of a swampy locale increases the farther back in time one consults the sources. Mendes, on the other hand lies on a "sand back" on the west side of the Delta, about 110 kilometers north-northeast of Cairo, and about 55 kilometers south of the Mediterranean.[49] None of the three had vaulted to a position of dominance over the others by the end of the millennium, although Buto enjoys a primacy of place. The site of Buto and Mendes have been subjected to modern excavation; Mendes awaits further investigation in the immediate future, but Sais's predynastic levels are far beneath the present water table.

In contrast to Upper Egypt, and even the Delta, in Palestine the genesis and growth of communities with a manifest destiny to control vast tracts of land were impossible. The mountains divide the land into circumscribed regions—valley, upland, steppe, coast—and prevent the development of anything beyond a canton. Automatically population growth was limited, and complexity of government and society never achieved anything beyond a rudimentary level. Moreover transit corridors in western Asia are more difficult to negotiate than the Nile, and control of lengthy stretches of them virtually impossible. The result was that, although human society in Palestine shared with Egypt the foundation of the agricul-

---

[47] In general on Buto, see H. Altenmüller, LdÄ 1 (1975), 887–89; D. B. Redford, BES 5 (1983), 67–101; in prehistoric times the coast may have been much closer to the site.

[48] J. Baines and J. Malek, Atlas of Ancient Egypt (London, 1980), 170.

[49] See E. S. Hall and B. V. Bothmer, eds., Mendes, 2 vols. (Warminster, 1976–1980).

tural village, it could not partake in the permanent evolution of a larger whole, and thus never conceived of the "nation-state."

But it is not sufficient to put the rise of complex societies down to geographic determinism. In Egypt additional factors seem to be operating, and for these we must look briefly at the latest predynastic culture, the Gerzean.[50]

The Gerzean period covers the three centuries from about 3400 to 3050 B.C., on the basis of carbon-14 tests,[51] and shows a far more sophisticated society and economy than what went before. The culture is thought to have affinities with Lower Egypt where it perhaps originated, although excavation in the Delta is still in its infancy and nothing certain can be said as yet on the subject. It rapidly moved south and Gerzean settlements are found in the valley from the Fayum to Hierakonpolis, although further south in Nubia it failed to dislodge the older more primitive Amratian culture.[52] For the first time in Egypt's history there is evidence of a marked increase in population: settlements are large, some reaching five thousand inhabitants,[53] are sometimes fortified; and are made up of rectangular houses of mud brick and wood. In the economy hunting now definitely occupies a less important position, as farming based on limited irrigation provides most of the communities' food. The cultural assemblage of the Gerzean shows an advanced lithics industry in which bifacial knives recede in popularity in the face of beautiful, thin, "ripple-flaked" knives, mace heads, axheads, and chisel-shaped arrowheads. Copper, known from the end of the fifth millennium, is now worked with some skill and cast into adzes, chisels, daggers, hoes, harpoons, and axheads inspired by the stone forms; while silver, gold, lapis, and faience are used in small quantities for toilet articles. Most charming is the Gerzean pottery made of desert marl and adorned in dark red paint. The decoration is much more varied than in the earlier Amratian period, and for the first time the motifs are scenes taken from life. We see the multifarious fauna of the prehistoric landscape: rows of ostriches, cows, bulls, flights of birds, crocodiles, ships with cabins and standards, marching men, dancing women. Pottery shapes sometimes copy stone prototypes: cylindrical jars with tubular handles, double jars, theriomorphic jars depicting hippopotamuses, elephants, birds, and fishes.

[50] C. Aldred, *Egypt to the End of the Old Kingdom* (London, 1965), 36–42; E. J. Baumgartel, *CAH³* I (1971), chap. 9; J. Eiwanger, in J. Assmann, ed., *Problems and Priorities in Egyptian Archaeology* (London, 1987), 81–104.

[51] Butzer, *Early Hydraulic Civilization*, 7; idem, *JNES* 44 (1985), 306. The beginning of the 1st Dynasty would appear to fall close to 3050 B.C.: F. A. Hassan and S. W. Robinson, *Antiquity* 61 (1987), 125.

[52] B. Trigger, *History and Settlement of Lower Nubia* (New Haven, Conn., 1959), 68–72.

[53] Butzer, *Environment and Archaeology*, 602.

THE ASIATIC CONNECTION

Clearly major changes were taking place in Egypt during the Gerzean period, and we would not be wrong in construing them as the dynamics associated with the rise of the monarchy. We have already reviewed the geographic factor at work in the process but there were others. A decline of rainfall from the Neolithic subpluvial has been invoked to explain the increased concentration of population during the Gerzean,[54] and it may be that the population increase had something to do with necessitating the development of new irrigation techniques.[55]

Be that as it may, there can be no questioning the fact that the Gerzean displays numerous cultural features that are not the products of autochthonous development, but which have all the earmarks of having been introduced from outside suddenly.[56] Cylinder seals of wood or stone make their appearance[57] and, as we have seen, the craft of the coppersmith advances dramatically in technique. Mud brick is used in much more elaborate types of building, which can truly be called monumental, and towers, battlements, and elaborate recessed paneling in the form of vertical niches are all within the capacity of the architect.[58] New pottery forms, with no antecedents in the Nile Valley, dominate the Gerzean repertoire.[59] The art of the stonecutter now extends to the manufacture of vessels of the hardest stones,[60] and pear-shaped mace-heads also emerge from his atelier. An array of new and strange art motifs appears in the repertoire of the graphic artist. These include long rows of animals, predators tearing their prey, fantastic animals with long necks intertwined, a heroic figure separating two felines, and captives being clubbed to death.

Thanks to the German excavations at Warka in Iraq and the French excavations in Iran, convincing parallels to most of these new features can be found in that region of western Asia dominated by the late Uruk culture of Mesopotamia (c. 3300–3100 B.C.).[61] Moreover, in the Tigris-

[54] Hoffman, *Egypt Before the Pharaohs*, 309–10.

[55] Wilson, *Burden*, 29ff.; Wittfogel, *Oriental Despotism*, 16ff.; E. Boserup, *The Conditions of Agricultural Growth* (Chicago, 1965), 11.

[56] Of the voluminous literature on this subject, one might consult as convenient compendiums H. Frankfort, *The Birth of Civilization in the Near East* (Bloomington, Ind., 1951); Baumgartel, *CAH*[3] I (1971), chap. 9; W. S. Smith and W. K. Simpson, *The Art and Architecture of Ancient Egypt* (Harmondsworth, 1981); Trigger, *Ancient Egypt*; Aldred, *Egypt*, 31ff.

[57] A. L. Kelley, *JSSEA* 4 (1973), 5–8.

[58] For such architecture at Hierakonpolis, see K. R. Weeks, *JARCE* 9 (1971–1972), 29–33; W. A. Fairservis, Jr., *The Hierakonpolis Project*, vol. 3 (Poughkeepsie, N.Y., 1986).

[59] H. Kantor, in R. Ehrich, ed., *Relative Chronologies in Old World Archaeology* (Chicago, 1965), fig. 2.

[60] A. Lucas, *JEA* 16 (1920), 200–212.

[61] On the contemporaneity of the late Uruk with the Gerzean, and the Jemdet-Nasr with the 1st Dynasty, see F. Hassan and S. W. Robinson, *Antiquity* 61 (1987), 125.

Euphrates Valley and southwest Iran[62] the cultural evolution that produced these forms and motifs can be traced back over centuries of indigenous development, whereas in Egypt there are no antecedents. Few would dispute, therefore, the obvious conclusion that we are dealing with the comparatively sudden importation into Egypt of ideas and products native to Mesopotamia.[63]

But three questions arise immediately. How—that is, by whom or what agency—were those ideas and products brought to the Nile Valley? What route did they take? What relationship existed, if any, between the arrival of Mesopotamian influence and the rise of the pharaonic monarchy? Final answers to these puzzling queries will probably not be given for many years, but some tantalizing possibilities are suggested by recent discoveries.

We can narrow the possible range of answers by drawing some obvious inferences. First, as has often been pointed out, the Egyptians, no matter how the Asian prototypes became known to them, did not slavishly reproduce them, but adapted them to their own environment. Seals, although as in Mesopotamia sometimes providing identifying "signatures," were pressed into service also as objects with funerary scenes. Such motifs as the hero dominating two carnivores were modified by substituting Egyptian elements (in this case, crocodiles).[64] The first attempts at writing in the Tigris-Euphrates Valley, while possibly providing the Nile with a concept, had no influence at all on the developing hieroglyphic script.[65] In the second place it seems clear that we can discount any hypothesis that introduces an intermediary through whom only ideas were transmitted. Several cylinder seals of Mesopotamia manufacture have in fact been found in Egypt, apart from those numerous specimens made in Egypt and bearing witness to Mesopotamia inspiration,[66] proving at least the presence in the Nile Valley of objects of Mesopotamian make.

[62] LeBretton, *Iraq* 19 (1957), 79–124.

[63] See the works cited in n. 57; to which one might add, A. L. Kelley, *JSSEA* 4 (1974), 2–11; A. J. Arkell, *The Prehistory of the Nile Valley* (Leiden, 1975), 48–50; Hoffman, *Egypt Before the Pharaohs*; Trigger, *Ancient Egypt*, 36–40; D. O'Connor, *Cambridge Encyclopedia of Archaeology* (Cambridge, 1980), 129–31. I also had access to a useful paper written for me by my student, Mrs. Helke Ferrie, in 1984.

[64] P. Amiet, *La glyptique mésopotamienne archaïque* (Paris, 1961), sealing R (I am indebted to Mrs. Ferrie for drawing my attention to this example).

[65] M. V. Pope, *Antiquity* 40 (1966), 17ff.; E. S. Meltzer, in P. A. Kolers et al., eds., *Processing of Visible Language* (New York, 1980), 2:43–66; W. Schenkel, *GM 52* (1981), 83–95; W. Helck, in P. Posener-Kriéger, ed., *Mélanges Gammal eddin Mukhtar* (Cairo, 1985), 1:395–408; idem, *Untersuchungen zur Thinitenzeit* (Wiesbaden, 1987), 138–43. It should be noted that the principle of syllabic writing that informs the cuneiform script has no place in the evolution of the Egyptian hieroglyphs.

[66] H. Kantor, in Ehrich, *Chronologies*, 10; A. Kelley, *JSSEA* 4 (1973), 5–8.

But the problem remains: did Mesopotamians themselves set up contact with the Nile Valley and arrive there in person, or did third parties act as "middlemen"? Although it is an argument from silence, it is difficult to find such a "third party." Admittedly we may have to look to one of the provincial extensions of Uruk-Jemdet-Nasr culture in North Syria for the "jumping off" point for the Egyptian leg of the route, but this is not exactly a third party. Another point ought to be stressed. Although art motifs, especially for the minor decorative arts, invite mimesis at long range for which no direct contact is required, it is difficult to see how such a specialized craft as the brick architecture of the Gerzean period could be introduced by anyone who had not *seen* the style in its Tigris-Euphrates home. A like argument could be advanced with respect to the costume and coiffure—kilt, fillet, beard—of the Jemdet-Nasr "hero" who appears in Egypt on the Gebel el-Araq knife handle, and the ships with raised prows of Mesopotamian origin.

If individuals from the Tigris-Euphrates Valley or regions contiguous that enjoyed the same culture[67] did establish direct contact with Egypt, one wonders what drew them and by what route did they come. The gold deposits of the eastern desert have been suggested by some as the source of attraction, and it is true that in historic times Naqada at the Nile opening of the Wadi Hammamat was called "gold town";[68] but it seems doubtful that gold mining was already extensive in Gerzean times. Since the change from small towns to large, urban centers in ancient Mesopotamia is linked to the switch in dependence from fishing to cereal production,[69] one wonders whether the grain trade sparked the increase in contact. Yet surely Mesopotamia was self-sufficient in this realm. Again: we have seen that the gradual movement of people, goods, and ideas in the Nile Valley before the Gerzean was from south to north, and thus the river constituted a corridor through which African products could move quickly and easily to the Mediterranean and the northeast. Were the Uruk people tempted to tap this flourishing transit of goods closer to its source?

A similar uncertainty has always surrounded the determination of which route (or routes) were used in the establishment of contact with Egypt. Long ago Petrie opined that the Gerzean had originated in the eastern desert.[70] While this notion is now disproved, the presence of indicators of a "Mesopotamian" presence at Naqada and Hierakonpolis

---

[67] In fact some of the best parallels come from Iran: LeBretton, *Iraq* 19 (1957), 79–124; E. Heinrich, *Die Tempel und Heiligtümer in alten Mesopotamien* (Berlin, 1982), 1:38.

[68] H. Heinrich, *Kleinfunde aus den archäischen Temtelschichen in Uruk* (Berlin, 1936), 11; Trigger, *Ancient Egypt*, 39.

[69] J. Makkay, *Iraq* 45 (1983), 1–6.

[70] Petrie, *JRAI* 31 (1911), 250; see W. Davis, in P. R. Robertson, *History of African Archaeology* (London, 1990), 277–78.

has been taken by some to suggest a sea route ending at Quseir on the Red Sea coast, and giving access to the Wady Hammamat, Koptos, and Naqada. These indicators include the "Mesopotamian" motifs on the Gebel el-Araq knife handle (reportedly found in the area), the late Gerzean tomb scene from Hierakonpolis,[71] the numerous ivories and palettes from the latter site, and especially the alien ships. These do indeed bear a striking resemblance to vessel shapes known from Uruk and Jemdet-Nasr sealings; and it is quite true that the Wady Hammamat route that seaman of such ships would have used is known to have been well traveled in the late predynastic and archaic periods (Plate 2).[72]

There are, however, a number of indications that we ought to look north rather than east for the debouchment of the route that brought the Tigris-Euphrates culture into northeast Africa.[73] The increased skill in working copper may argue a greater familiarity with the sources of copper ore in the north and in Sinai;[74] and silver would certainly have to have been imported from Anatolia, as there are no deposits in Egypt.[75] Certain signs in the hieroglyphic script, which is first encountered at the close of the Gerzean, show a curious rooting within the linguistic horizon of a speaker of West Semitic (at home in the Levant);[76] also the Egyptian word for "west" is cognate with West Semitic for "right hand," thus implying an orientation from the north, facing south.

The problem until recently has been that, as no Delta site has been excavated, no evidence was forthcoming from that part of Egypt that would have felt the brunt of Mesopotamian "incursions," if the northern route should turn out to be the corridor we are seeking; and Palestinian archaeology provides equivocal evidence at best. Throughout the Neolithic significant contact between Egypt and Palestine seems not to have occurred. In the later Neolithic and the earlier Chalcolithic, Palestine supported a rather backward culture, enjoying little contact with the north, and having little to offer Egypt.[77] Even in the main phase of the Palestin-

[71] W. Kaiser, *MDAIK* 16 (1957), 189ff.; H. Case and J. C. Payne, *JEA* 48 (1962), 11; J. C. Payne, *JEA* 59 (1973), 31–35.

[72] Cf. A. Scharff, *SBAW* (1942), 3, 23; E. J. Baumgartel, *Ar Or* 20 (1952), 281; S. Yeivin, *Polotsky Festschrift* (Jerusalem, 1964), 27.

[73] W. F. Albright, *The Archaeology of Palestine* (Harmondsworth, 1949), 72; E. Anati, *Palestine before the Hebrews* (New York, 1963), 354; Trigger, *Ancient Egypt*, 39; W. M. Davies, *JSSEA* 11 (1981), 21–27.

[74] Baumgartel, *Cultures*, 1:42.

[75] Ibid., 2:14–18; A. Lucas, *JEA* 14 (1928), 313ff.

[76] Hieroglyphic signs for "eye," "ear," and "hand" have phonetic values identical with West Semitic roots, but the Egyptian words for these members are wholly different: K. Sethe, *ZÄS* 50 (1907), 91ff.; E. Otto, *WO* 1, no. 3 (1948), 144; see D. B. Redford, in B. Bryan, ed., *Festschrift for Hans Goedicke* (Baltimore, 1991), forthcoming.

[77] K. A. Kenyon, *Archaeology in the Holy Land* (London, 1979), 49–50.

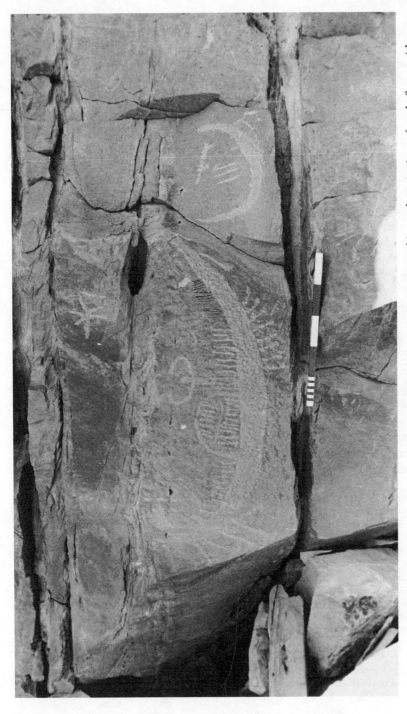

Plate 2. Petroglyphs in the Wady Hammamat. The ship on the left has steering oars, a cabin, and a prominent female figure with arms above her head thought on the basis of other examples to be a goddess. Gerzean period, c. 3400–3050 B.C.

ian Chalcolithic, the Ghassulian (mid-fourth millennium B.C.), contact with the Nile remains slight,[78] and it is only with the last half of the period and the Early Bronze I (contemporary with the 1st Dynasty) that advances in metalworking and similarities in pottery suggest an increase in Palestinian exports to Egypt.[79] At the same time cylinders and sealings with Jemdet-Nasr affinities show an opening up of commercial contact with the north.[80] But by the mid-1st Dynasty, when Palestine contacts are on the increase with Egypt, evidence of Mesopotamian imports dies out.[81]

If this evidence casts doubt on an inland corridor via Palestine, a *sea* route has more to be said for it. During the historic period, beginning at least as early as the twenty-seventh century B.C. but undoubtedly of much higher antiquity, the Pharaohs enjoyed a formal trade relationship with Byblos on the Phoenician coast (see chapter 2). Already in the Gerzean the similarity of artifacts with the Byblian assemblage militates in favor of trade contact, clearly by sea, between the Delta and Byblos.[82] The recent excavations by the Germans at Buto under the direction of Van der Way virtually seals the argument. Here in the northwest Delta, twenty-four kilometers from the Mediterranean, the excavations have revealed predynastic levels ceramically in touch with the ʿAmuq in North Syria. In addition to this, colored clay cones have been brought to light of the sort that, at Uruk in Mesopotamia, are used to adorn the facades of temples, in a sort of mosaic. That a Delta site as remote as Buto should have been in contact with Syria and the Upper Euphrates militates strongly in favor not only of a northern route, but also a sea route (Figure 1).[83]

Although it is perhaps premature to arrive at conclusions, the evidence for contact with Mesopotamia is more extensive and specific than can be accommodated by a theory of intermittent and casual trade. It would seem that besides trade items, a *human* component of alien origin is to be sought in the Gerzean demography of Egypt. This is *not* to resuscitate the

[78] Ibid., 63; cf. H. Kantor, *JNES* 1 (1942), 177; J. Kaplan, *IEJ* 9 (1959), 134–36.

[79] Kantor, in Ehrich, *Chronologies*, 6–9; B. Hennessey, *The Foreign Relations of Palestine during the Early Bronze Age* (London, 1967), 26–35; R. Amiran, *Ancient Pottery of the Holy Land* (New York, 1970), 22–35; O. Bar Yussef, *IEJ* 27 (1977), 65ff.; W. S. Smith and W. K. Simpson, *Art and Architecture of Ancient Egypt*[2] (Harmondsworth, 1983), 433, n. 27.

[80] Albright, *Palestine*, 71; Kenyon, *Holy Land*, 80.

[81] G. E. Wright, *The Bible and the Ancient Near East* (New York, 1965), 100, and 130, n. 46; Kantor, in Ehrich, *Chronologies*, 11–14.

[82] O'Connor, *Cambridge Encyclopedia of Archaeology*, 131; M. Saghieh, *Byblos in the 3rd Millennium B.C.* (Warminster, 1983), 129.

[83] See J. Leclant, *Orientalia* 55 (1986), 242–43; 56 (1987), 301–2: T. von der Way, *MDAIK* 43 (1986), 241–57; for the spread of Sumerian culture into North Syria in the fourth millennium B.C., see J. Oates, *Babylon* (London, 1986), 29 and n. 1; on the demography of the northern Delta, see Redford, in Bryan, *Goedicke Festschrift*.

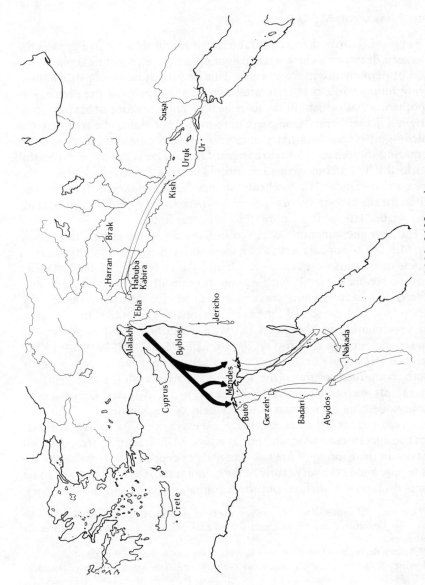

Figure 1. Egypt and the Near East in the Late Gerzean (c. 3300–3100 B.C.).

moribund "dynastic race" theory, but we should be careful not to misread the evidence or ignore its real weight.

THE PHARAONIC MONARCHY

The political turmoil and cultural ferment we dimly sense in Egypt as the Gerzean draws to a close were to spin off and exalt a political phenomenon of permanence and longevity. This had its embodiment in a human being filling a role that translated him into the realm of the divine. His apotheosis was evident in the titles he bore and the scope of his power. In origin a "chief" and "One-pertaining-to-the *swt* plant," he was now the falcon-god Horus incarnate; once ruler of a circumscribed community requiring diplomacy and entrepreneurial skill, he was now a successful warlord who had bludgeoned or intimidated the entire Nile Valley to the apex of the Delta. His forebears' names (or remembered designations) stood for the bloody victory: (Horus)-is-here-to-stay, (Horus) fights, (Horus) seizes, (Horus) is a Cobra, (Horus) decapitates.[84]

The new phenomenon was, of course, the divine monarchy, the rule by a god.[85] As it appears first to view—and its rise and crystallization in visible memorials were rapid—it is founded on a broad and unmistakably African *soubassement*,[86] with equally prominent borrowings from elsewhere. The Egyptian king was closely tied from the outset to the fertility of the Nile and the soil of Egypt. He personally guaranteed this fertility; his very coming to "his lakes . . . with green fields and meadows . . . causes the herbage to grow on the banks" (PT 508–9). In death he triumphed over decay and chaos and, as Osiris, the personification of the tomb, continued to imbue the soil and the river with his energizing effluxes; his son and successor, the new Horus, defeated chaos (Seth), championed his father, and with the help of his mother the "Throne" (Isis) restored his father to an otherworld existence.[87] As elsewhere in Africa the ancestors en bloc, and not as a specific, finite family tree, counted heavily in the rooting of the new-fangled concept of monarchy in the remote past and in the very fabric of the community. The king was not some jumped-up power wielder, but the legitimate successor to the ancestors,

[84] On the royal names of the 1st Dynasty, see most recently Helck, *Thinitenzeit*, 115–18 for earlier literature. (One can and probably will take exception to a number of Helck's renderings.)

[85] Among the many works on ancient Egyptian kingship, one might profitably consult the following: W. Barta, *Untersuchungen zur Göttlichkeit des regierenden Königs* (Munich, 1975); H. Brunner, *Universitas* 11 (1956), 797–806; H. W. Fairman, in S. H. Hooke, ed., *Myth, Ritual, and Kingship* (Oxford, 1958), 74–104; H. Frankfort, *Kingship and the Gods* (Chicago, 1951); H. Goedicke, *Die Stellung des Königs im alten Reich* (Wiesbaden, 1960); J.-P. Lauer, *BIFAO* 55 (1956), 153ff.; G. Posener, *De la divinité du pharaon* (Paris, 1960).

[86] Cf. E.L.R. Meyerowitz, *Divine Kingship in Ghana and Ancient Egypt* (London, 1960).

[87] See Griggiths, *Origins of Osiris*.

and the "eldest of the eldest" and the beloved of the gods. All the community, high and low, the ancestral "souls" and the town gods and local numina, all convened to lend their approbation to the incarnate god-king, and reassembled in conclave at sundry times during the ongoing reign to reaffirm their acceptance.[88]

But if his "African" persona impresses us most, there are certain of the king's accoutrements and symbolism that take us further afield. At the very close of the Gerzean, when the erstwhile chieftain of remote Hierakonpolis had all but completed the aggrandizement of his kingdom as far as the apex of the Delta, he self-consciously took to wearing specific headdresses as an outward symbol of his status. A green (later red) openwork crown had long been known in the valley, and was shortly to be (artificially) identified as the crown emblematic of rule of the Delta; but the king's native headdress was a tall, white bulbous crown, which has a parallel from the archaic levels at Susa.[89] To underscore and broadcast the ruthlessness and bellicosity of a regime that would brook no rivals, the monarch had recourse to a number of specific motifs and symbols. The execution of prisoners strongly recalls Mesopotamian examples,[90] and the one triumph motif, the head-bashing scene, made famous by the Narmer Palette, springs suddenly into the repertoire in the 1st Dynasty: but it has an exact antecedent in Susa level C.[91] Motifs involving lion and bull mauling or crushing an adversary, whether on standards as designations of new territorial divisions (townships or nomes) or as heraldic devices, all are to be read as allomorphs of the king (Plate 3): they too have long-standing parallels all over the Near East but appear relatively suddenly in Egypt with the creation of the monarchy.

Despite traces of its disparate roots, the monarchy was a new concept and its promoters thought in new forms. From a "standing start" in which climatic exigencies had produced an increasing concentration of population and forced on the tribal headman not only the need to improvise, but also the golden prospect of controlling movement over greater distances, the incipient institution of kingship had conceived the goal and had been impressed by the "manifest destiny" of ever-expanding control of resources. Nubia and the Delta were next;[92] and beyond them why not Libya, Sinai, and the Levant (Plate 3)?

[88] On the "ancestors," see D. B. Redford in *Pharaonic King-lists, Annals and Day-books* (Toronto, 1986), 137–40 and passim.

[89] Amiet, *La glyptique mesopotamienne*, no. 282; Heinrich, *Tempel und Heiligtümer*, 1:38; note the hooped palanquin carried in procession. The type is well known in the *sed* festival in Egypt.

[90] Quibell, *Hierakonpolis*, 1: pls. XI; XII, no. 4–6; XV.

[91] LeBretton, *Iraq* 19 (1957), fig. 18, no. 4.

[92] The forced annexation and absorption of Lower Egypt, the Delta, into the New Kingdom was a long, drawn-out affair, and it is wrong to see it memorialized only in the Narmer palette: W. Kaiser, *ZÄS* 91 (1964), 86ff.

Plate 3. The "City" palette showing, on left, a series of rectangular fortified settlements under attack by numina associated with the monarchy. The town names, although uncertain, may indicate the region of Buto in the northwest Delta. On the right, cattle, donkeys, sheep, and bushes recall a coastal setting, as the hieroglyph T̠hnw, "Libya," indicates.

The demographic changes in Egypt at the outset of the 1st Dynasty present us with a dramatic contrast with Palestine. The manifest destiny of the protégé of Horus had transformed the community into the nation: the country was the agricultural town enlarged to accommodate the new political form.[93] To win the day those involved in the triumph and organization had to grow in numbers as the community grew. The day-to-day control of a "town," the extremities of which could not be reached in one day, necessitated couriers, residents, transporters; the application of sanctions necessitated a body of retainers, a host; to feed and house these new dependents, the headman required producers and purveyors of food, service personnel. In the Levant and Mesopotamia, the city or "metropolis" of any state had come into being slowly by spontaneous growth, the product of market and social forces at work over the centuries; in Egypt the "metropolis," called "White Fort" (later Memphis)[94] came into being suddenly, the conscious behest of one man, and as the result of *political* necessity. Its keynote was the concentration of manpower: vast enclosures surrounded with crenellated mud-brick walls provided shelter for the aggregations of labor needed by the new regime (Figure 2).[95] The "residence" (of the king) provided a focus for an always growing number of

[93] Otto, *WO* 1 (1947–1952), 445–46.

[94] K. Zibelius, *Ägyptische Siedlungen nach Texten der alten Reiches* (Weisbaden, 1978), 39–42.

[95] *Ḥwt*, "enclosure," later "domain," often (later) of a mortuary nature. On the word, see H. Jacquet-Gordon, *Les noms des domaines funéraires* (Cairo, 1962), 4ff.; M. Atzler, *CdE* 47 (1972), 17ff.; A. Badawy, *LdÄ* 2 (1978), 194–203.

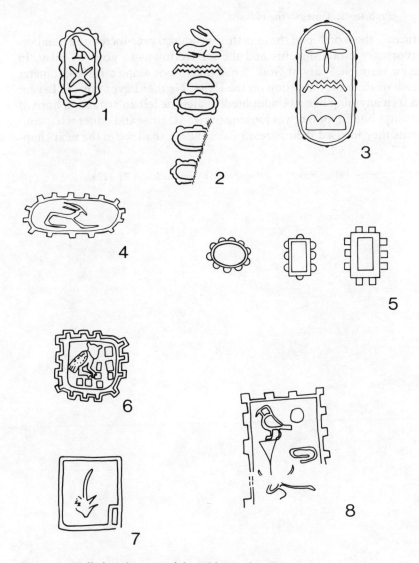

Figure 2. Walled enclosures of the Old Kingdom:

1. Jar sealing of the late 1 and 2 Dynasties
2. Inscription from the tomb of Weni, Abydos, in the reign of Merenre
3. From a statue dated to the 12th Dynasty of a regulator of phyles in the Teti Pyramid temple
4. Wooden tablet of the 1 Dynasty from Abydos
5. From the Pyramid Texts 1837 a–b (Pepy II only)
6. Fragment of a stone palette
7. Wooden label of Udimu from Abydos
8. Wooden label of Hor-aha from Abydos

"offices"; the worship of the ancestors produced ever-increasing numbers of mortuary establishments and the service towns to go with them. In short a veritable "City of God"[96] had taken root along a forty-kilometer stretch of the valley abutting on the Delta. Neither Egypt nor the Levant had seen anything like it. Undoubtedly Palestine felt an attraction born of curiosity; but Egypt too was looking outward. How and under what conditions they focused their gaze on Palestine we shall see in the next chapter.

[96] Cf. "(Divine) Falcon-town" as a designation of the residence: PT 417a.

CHAPTER 2

Upper and Lower Egypt and the Walled Towns of Asia

LATE predynastic and 1st Dynasty art abounds in figures who, in the somewhat stereotyped motifs fashionable at the time, fulfill the role of the "vanquished." The subconscious urge to depict such enemies as thoroughly discredited and disreputable led to a consistent representation of an unkempt individual, often naked, no matter what the identity of his homeland.[1] Thus it is often difficult to break through the stylization and determine what foreign people is being recorded as defeated.[2] Only when the artist sees fit to include the insignia or accoutrements,[3] or to gloss his picture with a *name*, do we suddenly become aware that we are in the presence of such-and-such a foreigner.

Thanks to such glosses and consistency of representation throughout the Old Kingdom, we may describe the typical Asiatic man of the early third millennium B.C. as bearded and with long braided hair confined by a fillet and falling behind the ears. The basic costume is a kilt reaching from waist to knee.[4] Possibly a heavier cloak, or sheepskin, was worn in winter.[5]

PALESTINE DURING THE OLD KINGDOM

Although these scattered and unflattering representations of Asiatics might suggest a Palestine undeveloped and of meager importance, the archaeological picture rectifies this false impression. Early Bronze Age levels in most Palestinian tells lie so deep beneath the superimposed strata of later periods that they often cannot be excavated and studied as extensively as we would wish. Thanks, however to the concerted effort by such

[1] Cf. B. G. Trigger, *in* M. Görg, ed., *Festschrift Elmar Edel* (Bamberg, 1979), 409ff.

[2] Cf. the repetitive slaughter of prisoners: J. E. Quibell, *Hierakonpolis* (London, 1900), 1: pl. XV, nos. 1, 2, 4.

[3] Cf. the "phallic sheath" and feather, both indicative apparently of Libyans: J. Capart, *Primitive Art in Egypt* (London, 1905), 100, fig. 70; W. B. Emery, *Great Tombs of the First Dynasty* (Cairo, 1949), 1:60, n. 565.

[4] Cf. W.M.F. Petrie, *The Royal Tombs of the First Dynasty* (London, 1900), 1: pl. 17 (30); L. Borchardt, *Das Grabdenkmal des Königs Sa³hu-re'* (Berlin, 1913), 2: pl. 13.

[5] M. Saghieh, *Byblos in the Third Millennium* (Warminster, 1983), fig. 7B, pl. 33; P. Matthiae, in *Studies in the History and Archaeology of Jordan* (Amman, 1982), 1:79ff.

contemporary scholars as R. Amiran and R. Gophna in Israel, the late Dame Kathleen Kenyon of Great Britain, W. Dever, R. T. Schaub, W. Rast, and S. Helms in America, and B. Hennesey in Australia, we are now in a much better position to appreciate the nature of these settlements in Palestine and to speculate on population and economic factors (Figure 3).[6]

It should be noted that, although with an estimated population of 150,000 and some nine hundred identified settlements Early Bronze Age Palestine clearly enjoyed a prosperity equaling that of its later halcyon days during the Roman Empire, the society and economy of the time can scarcely be characterized as "urban." Even the largest sites do not exceed sixteen hectares, contrasting dramatically with Uruk's four hundred hectares in Mesopotamia, or the five square kilometers of Egypt's Memphis. In fact these communities are not "cities" at all, but rather walled towns into which a rural population might retreat when danger threatened.

Despite this caveat, Palestine shows marked signs of a wealthy and energetic population, enjoying municipal life and a healthy international trade. Population was relatively evenly distributed throughout the lowland and the upland, with the greatest density in the upper Jordan valley, the valley of Jezreel, and the northern coastal plain. The inhabitants are concentrated in about twenty large towns, accounting for about half of the total population of the country and providing the nuclei for a much larger number of very small hamlets. The latter seemed grouped no farther than about a day's journey from the major, "parent(?)" settlement, a fact that might militate in favor of postulating a political structure based on a series of (semi?) independent cantons. Each major town was very well fortified with walls of brick and stone (depending on local building materials), some exceeding ten meters in thickness and provided with glacis for defense. Gates were fortified and walls strengthened with square, rectangular, or semicircular towers. Within, houses and public buildings of the rectangular, "broad-room" type were usually laid out in a regular pattern, which bespeaks a consciousness of town planning.

While the material culture of Early Bronze Age Palestine is attested widely and is now well known, little if anything can be said about the politics, society, and religion of the country. No native texts have as yet come to light, and it is a moot point what script, if any, was employed in the region at this time. The quest for information, then, must of necessity

---

[6] See in particular R. Amiran, *in* J. A. Sandars, ed., *Near Eastern Archaeology in the Twentieth Century* (New York, 1970), 83ff.; idem, in *Biblical Archaeology Today* (Jerusalem, 1985), 108ff.; M. Broshi and R. Gophna, *BASOR* 253 (1984), 41ff.; P. W. Lapp, in Sandars, *Near Eastern Archaeology*, 101ff.; W. Rast, *Scripta Mediterranea* (1980), 1:5ff.; R. T. Schaub, in *Studies in the History and Archaeology of Jordan*, 1:67ff.; R. de Vaux, *CAH*[3] I (1971), 232ff.

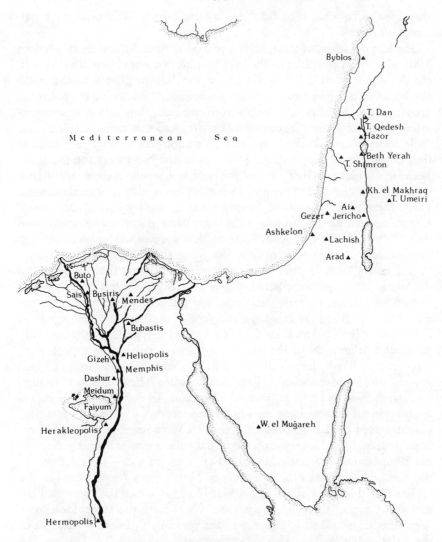

Figure 3. Egypt and the Levant in the third millennium B.C.

direct itself toward the writings of major, adjacent cultures; and for Palestine, this means the rather meager literature of Old Kingdom Egypt.

THE ETHNIC IDENTITY OF EARLY BRONZE AGE PALESTINIANS

Who were these unshaven rustics "beyond the pale," as it were, who occupied these walled towns of the southern Levant?[7] What language did

[7] See D. B. Redford, *JARCE* 23 (1986), 125–32, for detailed discussion.

they speak? To what race did they claim to belong? What did the Egyptians call them?

The last question, at least, finds a partial answer. When, shortly before 3000 B.C. the appearance of the hieroglyphic writing system lifts the veil, the designations used by the Egyptians for their neighbors to the north can be seen to derive from personal observation, pejorative propaganda, geographic knowledge, and linguistic awareness. They called these northerners after the leather (?) costume that they had seen them wearing, thus "kilt wearers" or "kilties," or "shoulder knot people" after the fashion they employed in supporting a jerkin by a tied band over the shoulder. Because of their proclivity to use the bow and arrow in their subsistence economy, "archers" or "people of the bow" were also appropriate terms. From their hostility toward Egyptian expeditionary forces, occasional brigandage along the frontier, the Egyptians occasionally designated them "the wild men of Asia," a term that approaches in meaning and association our current term *terrorist*. Since they came from the north, "northerners" was an obvious appellative; but because they lived beyond the Sinai, "those-who-are-across-the-sand" also suggested itself.

A more interesting term, and one that incidentally helps answer the questions regarding the language and race of the Early Bronze Age folk, is the word *ʿ3mw*, which modern students of Egyptology provisionally pronounce *a'amu*. Now the *ayin*-sound designated by the supralinearʿ, represents a harsh, laryngeal sound in the West Semitic family of languages, wholly absent in most European tongues. The same sound though less harsh, was present in ancient Egyptian. The *alif, 3*, a pharyngeal sound present in most languages that open words with a vowel, was consistently used by the Egyptians to render a West Semitic "dark," or perhaps uvular, *1* used intervocalically. That such a uvular *1* was present in the West Semitic dialects of the third millennium B.C. is now proved by the newly discovered Eblaite dialect of North Syria (represented in the tablets found by the Italians at Tel Mardikh),[8] in which the common verb *alakum*, "to go," turns up as *ayakum*. We should, therefore, look for a West Semitic word, which the Egyptians presumably heard on the lips of the Asiatics themselves, with the consonantal sequence ʿ + *1* + *m*. The search is not difficult. Most West Semitic languages—Phoenician, Ugaritic, Amorite, Hebrew—all share a root *ʿalamu* that means "young man" or, more generally, the generic "man(kind)." It is now clear that the Early Bronze Age Palestinians used the word to identify members of their own community. They were "men," "people" in the same ethnocentric, parochial sense in which many primitive peoples (cf. the Amerindians) reserved the generic term for themselves alone.

---

[8] See G. Pettinato, *The Archives of Ebla* (New York, 1981).

EGYPTIAN CONTACTS WITH ASIA IN THE ARCHAIC PERIOD

Evidence of Egyptian involvement in the affairs of Palestine and Syria during the 1st and 2nd Dynasties is unmistakable.[9] In the surviving fragments of annals from the reigns of the immediate successors of Menes, one often encounters an entry such as "smiting the Asiatics," or "first occasion of smiting the east," as an identifying event by which to designate a year.[10] Artistic motifs sometimes incorporate a shaggy-haired, kilted foreigner, with arms manacled, who is glossed by the simple hieroglyphs for "Asia." And the archaeological record confirms the textual evidence. First Dynasty cenotaphs from Abydos throw up clear examples of Early Bronze (EB) II pottery, and attest to the use of Lebanese timber in their construction.[11]

On the Asiatic side the picture is no less clear. Egyptian pottery is found widely throughout the Negeb and southern Palestine in EB II levels. Not infrequently vessels from royal workshops come to light, with the "Horus" name of Pharaoh incised; and Egyptian seal impressions on clay stoppers with which jars were plugged are also attested. It has even been suggested that the Egyptian-inspired construction techniques show up, both in brick and stone, in some localities.[12]

But despite the apparent uniformity of the evidence, numerous questions remain unanswered. Egyptian remains seem to delineate a sphere of influence confined to the coastal route between the western Delta and the region of greater Gaza, the southern Shephelah, and the Negeb around Arad and westward. What geopolitical facts conspired to define such a tract? Was the Egyptian presence there the result of an armed incursion, or peaceful contact inspired by the prospect of trade? Any expedition, peaceful or military, across the 160-kilometer Sinai desert must have cost a pretty penny. Who paid? Are we dealing with royally funded enterprises or private entrepreneurial commerce? And what attracted the Egyptians? The territory just demarcated is not today particularly rich in resources: was the situation different in antiquity, or was it then a transshipment area for lands further afield? And how did the locals accept Egyptian overtures? Did they resist Egyptian intimidation (which might explain the

[9] M. Wright, *BA* 48 (December 1985), 240ff.; also see Redford, *JARCE* 23 (1986), 125–32.

[10] On the Egyptian annals, see D. B. Redford, *Pharaonic King-lists, Annals and Daybooks* (Toronto, 1986), 86ff.

[11] W. S. Smith and W. K. Simpson, *The Art and Architecture of Ancient Egypt*[2] (Harmondsworth, 1983), 35ff.

[12] W. F. Albright, *The Archaeology of Palestine* (Harmondsworth, 1949), 76; J. B. Hennessey, *The Foreign Relations of Palestine during the Bronze Age* (London, 1967), 73; R. Gophna and D. Gazit, *Tel Aviv* 12 (1985), 9ff.

battle and prisoner motifs), or did they welcome the periodic arrival of the prototype of the "Wells-Fargo" wagons?

It is far easier to pose these questions than to answer them. The mere presence of foreign pottery and foreign construction techniques at a particular site does not necessarily imply that foreigners had been there; commodities could easily be brought back and skills learned by natives who had spent time away from home in contact with foreigners. On the other hand, seal impressions that point to supplies officially packaged and dispatched from Egypt, can scarcely suggest anything other than an Egyptian-inspired initiative.

That Egypt was attracted to the region of southern Palestine and Sinai is beyond question. Most prominent in the surviving record looms the turquoise- and copper-rich terrain of western Sinai where for nearly two thousand years from the close of the first quarter of the third millennium the Egyptians were to expend immense energies in the mining and transportation of these minerals.[13] They attached such importance to their free access to the mining district in the Wady Mughara ("Valley of Caves") that they were willing to neutralize the autochthonous inhabitants or the neighboring communities in southern Canaan by any means in their power—by co-opting them in times of peace, or by expelling them by military force when they proved recalcitrant. Imposing, rock-cut tableaux lined the walls of the Wady, giving notice of the fact that "the Perfect God" Sneferu or Sahure or Izezy had "put down all foreign lands" and "struck down the wild men of Asia." The giant figure of the god-king, striding forward to beat the groveling foreigner, served notice on the latter's congeners that Egypt would not tolerate any interference with its mining operations.[14]

Further north the evidence ceases to be epigraphic, and greater reliance must be placed on archaeology. The survey of the north Sinai coast by professor Eliezer Oren of the Ben Gurion University of the Negeb[15] has demonstrated the presence during the Egyptian 1st Dynasty of a well-traveled route between the eastern Delta and the region of Raphia and greater Gaza. From here a chain of sites with evidence of Egyptian artifacts, stretches to the east toward Beer Sheba, an inhospitable and poorly endowed tract of land. Surely such sites as Ein Beer, although from the evidence of the aforementioned clay sealings in close contact with Egypt,[16] could not have been the ultimate destination of caravans from

---

[13] The standard work on the Sinai mines is that of A. H. Gardiner and J. Černý, *The Inscriptions of Sinai* (London, 1952–1955); cf. also R. Giveon, *The Impact of Egypt on Canaan* (Göttingen, 1978), 51ff.

[14] On the head-smiting scene in Egyptian art, see H. Schafer, *WZKM* 54 (1957), 168ff.

[15] E. Oren, *IEJ* 23 (1973), 198ff.

[16] R. Gophna, *Atiqot* 11 (1976), 5.

the Nile, nor the place of origin of expeditions Delta-bound. They could only have been way stations along a route which from the beginning had been designed to link Egypt with the only major political power in the Negeb, namely the great city of Arad.

Arad is situated on a saddle-shaped hill in the gently rolling terrain of the eastern Negeb, about thirty kilometers east of Beer-sheba (Plate 4).[17] Although there is no spring in the vicinity, the town planners with the aid of resevoirs skillfully sited the settlement so as to capture the natural run-off. The EB II town, excavated in the 1960s by R. Amiran, occupied about nine hectares and was surrounded by a stone wall 2.4 meters in thickness and 1,170 meters in circumference. At intervals of 20 to 25 meters semicircular towers projected from the outer face of the wall. The town had been planned in a regular fashion by people aware of the importance of defensive considerations and the need for organized town life. Houses were grouped into insulae around the outer perimeter, while public buildings were grouped in the center. Within a day's march of Arad were situated at least twenty satellite villages, suggesting a fairly extensive

Plate 4. Part of the EB II fortifications of Arad in the Negeb of Israel (twenty-ninth to twenty-eighth centuries B.C.). The semicircular towers belong to a type often depicted by the Egyptians in their renderings of Asiatic towns.

[17] R. Amiran, *IEJ* 23 (1973), 241–42; idem, *IEJ* 24 (1974), 257–58; idem, in M. Avi-Yonah ed., *Encyclopaedia of Archaeological Sites in the Holy Land* (Jerusalem, 1975) 1:74ff.; idem, in *Biblical Archaeology Today*, 108ff.

political organization; and the town's effective control extended far to the south into the eastern Sinai. That in fact trade, or an exchange of goods in some form, had taken place between Egypt and Arad prior to the latter's destruction at the hands of an unknown enemy is proved by the presence of Egyptian ceramics and artifacts throughout all levels of occupation.

With the close of the EB II period, roughly coincident with the fall of Arad,[18] a change overtakes the relations between Egypt and Asia. The coastal route and the chain of sites in southern Palestine and the Negeb no longer command the prior interest of Pharaoh, and the new focuses of cultural interest and commercial exploitation begin, gradually it must be admitted, to come to the fore.[19]

This period of transition corresponds, broadly speaking, with the 2nd Dynasty in the traditional framework of Egyptian history.[20] While it remains a moot point whether insurrection occurred on the death of Qaʿa, last king of the 1st Dynasty, his immediate successors were clearly able to rectify any imbalance in the kingdom brought on by the time of stasis and, to judge by the size and putative appointments of their mortuary structures, to maintain a high degree of prosperity. But after the reign of one *Weneg*, if that truly was his name—by an all too frequent copying error in the king list he was later transmuted into *Wadj-nes* in the New Kingdom and *Tlas* in Greek times[21]—there appears an occupant of the throne well attested in the contemporary inscriptions but absent from the king list. This is the "Seth: Peribsen" who, by placing the "Seth"-animal[22] above the *serekh*, where normally the Horus-falcon would appear, seems to signal some fundamental change in the theological underpinning of the monarchy. In view of the mythological antithesis of Seth and Horus,[23] one is tempted to interpret the symbolic change in terms of

[18] F. A. Hassan and S. W. Robinson, *Antiquity* 61 (1987), 127; on the fall of Arad, see R. Amiran, *IEJ* 36 (1986), 74–77.

[19] W. Rast, *Scripta Mediterranea* 1 (1985), 5; Hennessey, *Foreign Relations*, 73–74.

[20] The 2nd Dynasty, thanks partly to the paucity of the archaeological and textual evidence, is given a short shrift in the literature; cf. E. Drioton and J. Vandier, *L'Égypte*[4] (Paris, 1962), 142–43; W. B. Emery, *Archaic Egypt* (Harmondsworth, 1962), 91ff.; I.E.S. Edwards, *CAH*[3] I (1971), chap. 11; W. Kaiser, *ZÄS* 86 (1961), 46ff.; A. H. Gardiner, *Egypt of the Pharaohs* (Oxford, 1961), 415ff.

[21] W. Helck, *Untersuchungen zu Manetho und den ägyptischen Königslisten* (Berlin, 1956), 13.

[22] On the cult animal of Seth, usually identified as an extinct species of pig, see P. E. Newberry, *Klio* 12 (1912), 397ff.; idem, *JEA* 14 (1928), 211ff.; S. Donadoni, *MDAIK* 37 (1981), 115ff.; on the god himself, see J. G. Griffiths, *The Origins of Osiris and his Cult* (Leiden, 1980); H. Te Velde, *Seth, God of Confusion* (Leiden, 1967).

[23] See the work by Griffiths in the preceding note. The theory on a "Seth-rebellion," as worked out in detail by P. E. Newberry (*Ancient Egypt* [1922], 40ff.), has been effectually answered by J. G. Griffiths (*Glimpses of Ancient Egypt* [Warminster, 1979], 174ff.). On

some violent rupture in the sociopolitical fabric of Egypt. Be that as it may, one has to admit that there is no concrete evidence from Peribsen's reign of an upheaval. In fact his jar sealings and jar inscriptions show that produce continued to be received from foreign lands, perhaps Canaan among them; and that such receipts were in such quantity that a special "administrator of foreign lands" had to be appointed.[24] The aftermath, however, might support the initial suspicion. One of Peribsen's successors, and possibly the one that followed him immediately, Kha'sekhem, coupled the Seth-animal and Horus-falcon atop his *serekh*, as though indicating reconciliation; and shortly modified his name to Kha'sekhemwy Nebwy-hotpimef, which means "The Two Powerful Ones have arisen, the Two Lords (i.e., Horus and Seth) are at peace in him."[25]

How the problems of Egypt's internal politics affected its relations with Palestine at this time is unclear. But it may not be without significance that certainly by the close of the 2nd Dynasty, the lines of foreign contact and trade had shifted noticeably. The Sinai mine land was now more than ever the jealous preserve of the Egyptian state, while the land route through Sinai and the Negeb had been abandoned. More significant, perhaps, for Egypt's long-range commercial relations is a brief entry in the royal annals, by chance surviving from the close of Kha'sekhemwy's reign one particular year, that is identified by the laconic notice "ship-building," an unmistakable reference to a sea-going fleet.[26] Is it only fortuitous that Kha'sekhemwy's is the earliest Egyptian royal name to be found at the site of Byblos on the Phoenician coast?[27]

EGYPT AND BYBLOS

Byblos is situated on a slight sandy promontory jutting out into the Mediterranean about forty-two kilometers north of Beirut.[28] Immediately north of the site a shallow indentation of the coast provided a harbor in

---

Peribsen, see further Edwards, *CAH*[3] I (1971), chap. 11; J. S.-F. Garnot, *BIE* 37 (1956), 317ff.; J.-P. Lauer, *BIFAO* 55 (1956), 162–63.

[24] P. Lacau and J.-P. Lauer, *La pyramide à degrés* (Cairo, 1959), 4:77, no. 205 (cf. also pl. 18, nos. 87, 93; 5: no. 274; T. E. Peet, *The Cemeteries of Abydos* (London, 1914), 1: pl. 10.

[25] On Kha'sekhemwy, see Edwards, *CAH*[3] I (1971), chap. 11.

[26] Palermo Stone, recto V, 6; on the expression, see J. C. Darnell, *GM* 83 (1984), 17ff.

[27] P. Montet, *Byblos et l'Égypte* (Paris, 1928), 271.

[28] Cf. ibid., passim; P. Montet, *Kêmi* 1 (1928), 19ff.; H. Goedicke, *MDAIK* 19 (1963), 1ff.; S. H. Horn, *Andrews University Seminary Studies* 1 (1963), 52ff.; P. E. Newberry, *JEA* 24 (1938), 182ff.; M. S. Drower, *CAH*[3] I (1971), chap. 17; S. Herrmann, *ZÄS* 82 (1957), 48ff.; K. Sethe, *ZÄS* 45 (1908), 7ff.; M. Saghieh, *Byblos in the Third Millennium* (Warminster, 1983); W. A. Ward, *JESHO* 6 (1963), 1ff.; Griffiths, *Origins of Osiris*, 28ff.; O. Tufnell and W. A. Ward, *Syria* 43 (1966), 165ff.

antiquity, but this was subsequently covered with debris. The city itself, as revealed by the clearance operations of the French under P. Montet and (later) M. Dunand, occupied only about five hectares, and from the EB III period was surrounded by a stout wall. Within this circumvallation the settlement distribution centered upon the temple of the "Mistress of Byblos" (Ba'alat Gebel), the epithet of the local Astarte, and a sacred pool. Whereas the magnates of the community enjoyed large domiciles in prime locations overlooking the sea to the west, the rest of the inhabitants were housed in small dwellings squeezed together along narrow, winding streets.

As is usual at this point on the Levantine coast, the towering massif of the Lebanon range rising to its height less than forty kilometers to the east, narrows the coastal plain and virtually forces the inhabitants to look seaward. But it also placed them within easy reach of the vast stands of cedar that clothed the mountain slopes (Plates 5, 6). Although almost totally gone today because of the unrestricted logging that continued into the twentieth century, the cedar forests of the Lebanon provided excellent wood for shipbuilding and construction, and had long since attracted the attention of neighboring states. (The semilegendary Gilgamesh of Mesopotamia, whose historical inspiration dates to the late fourth millennium B.C., is reputed to have undertaken an expedition to the cedar forest.)[29] Byblos in the third millennium dominated that part of the coast from which access to the forest was easiest, and thus it comes as no surprise that the Byblians should have become both excellent seafarers and shrewd timber merchants.

Precisely when contact was established between Egypt and Byblos is not known, but the date must have been very early indeed. Byblian tradition took pride in the belief that it was the oldest city in the world, founded by El, high god of the Canaanite pantheon; and the French operations at the site have revealed a Neolithic stratum.[30] The appearance of a pharaonic state on the Nile, eager to memorialize its presence and accomplishments in monumental architecture, made the Egyptian rulers avid of good building materials; and there was simply no other source for good cedar than Byblos. The 1st Dynasty tombs certainly employed Byblian timber, and by-products such as cedar oil and resin are mentioned as well.[31] So regular did this commerce become, and so well traveled the sea route between the Nile Delta and Byblos, that one of the oldest Egyptian words for an ocean-going boat was "Byblos ship"— that is, a vessel of a sort that can make the crossing to the Lebanese coast (cf. our "East

[29] *ANET*², 82ff.; G. Roux, *Ancient Iraq* (Harmondsworth, 1966), 115–16.

[30] Drower, *CAH*³ I (1971), chap. 17.

[31] Ibid.; S. Tawfik, *GM* 30 (1978), 79; J. Strange, *Caphtor/Keftiu: A New Investigation* (Leiden, 1980), 71ff.

Plate 5. Stand of cedars in the mountains east of Byblos. Unrelieved logging in ancient and medieval times by the people of the eastern Mediterranean in quest of ship timber has almost completely denuded the region.

Plate 6. The Lebanon Mountains northeast of Beirut.

Indiaman").[32] Competent shipwrights as the Egyptians were, they could still learn from the Byblians new techniques in shipbuilding, and they acknowledged their debt: Hathor, "mistress of Byblos," is credited with skill in manufacturing oars.[33]

But Byblos gained far more from Old Kingdom Egypt in the realm of engineering technology and manufacturing, so rapid and all-encompassing was Egypt's technological revolution during the pyramid age, and much later traditions unmistakably reflect this fact. Fifteen hundred years later, in the eleventh century, B.C., a Byblian prince is reported to have acknowledged to an Egyptian emissary: "All lands did Amun (the New Kingdom king of the gods) found, and he founded them only after he founded the land of Egypt whence you have come; but technical skill spread from there as far as (this) place where I am."[34] The pantheon of the Phoenicians gives prominence of place to a god "Taut" who is none other than the Egyptian god of writing Thoth; and the Canaanite craftsman god Kothar is said to have his seat in HKPT—that is, Ḥwt-k³-Ptḥ, "Memphis."[35]

Just how early Egyptian technological influence was exerted over Byblos is now plain through the excavations. Masonry techniques derived from Egypt appear in the temple architecture of the third millennium B.C., and motifs such as the frieze of rearing uraei were adapted to local requirements (Plate 7).

It is important to note that Egypt's close relations with Byblos did not result from armed conquest, but were based on enlightened self-interest and mutual respect; and not always could that be said of pharaonic foreign policy. Pharaoh's dealings with Byblos, and to a certain extent with other cities in Palestine and Syria during the Old Kingdom, exemplified the age-old practice of gift giving to both temple (god) and palace (chieftain) with an eye to securing influence and favor between equals. Recent socioeconomic studies of so-called primitive economies have shown such gift exchanges at head-of-state level to be part and parcel of a shrewd policy of creating spheres of influence by setting up lines of mutual obligation.[36] Egyptian sources articulated such policy by referring to the king's unfailing generosity in rewarding "those that are upon his wa-

---

[32] Ch. Boreux, *Études de nautique égyptienne* (Cairo, 1925), 462; T. Säve-Söderbergh, *The Navy of the 18th Egyptian Dyansty* (Uppsala, 1946), 12, 48–49; P. Montet, *Kêmi* 13 (1954), 63ff.; 16 (1962), 86–87; A. B. Lloyd, *JEA* 58 (1972), 272ff.

[33] CT I, 262b; A. Altenmüller, *Synkretismus in den Sargtexten* (Wiesbaden, 1975), 133.

[34] From the Report of Wenamun: 2:19–22.

[35] H. W. Attridge and R. A. Oden, Jr., *Philo of Byblos. The Phoenician History* (Washington, D.C., 1981), 72, n. 6; II Aqhat v, 20ff.; T. H. Gaster, *Thespis* (New York, 1961), 161, 164–65.

[36] C. Zaccagnini, *Lo scambio dei doni nel Vicino Oriente durante i secoli XV–XIII*, (Rome, 1973); M. Liverani, *Three Amarna Essays* (Malibu, Calif., 1979), 21ff.

Plate 7. The so-called obelisk temple (Middle Bronze Age) at Byblos. Although the cultic(?) function of this form remains in doubt, Egyptian inspiration for it is easy to postulate.

ter"—those loyal to Egypt.[37] They also make plain how desirable it is, from a moral and pious point of view, for a monarch to bestow votive offerings on "a god in a land far away whom the people love."[38]

Just such a posture toward the Levantine coast and its hinterland informed Egypt's acts of state in this theater. Hardly an Old Kingdom monarch, beginning with Kha'sekhemwy, failed to send some object, inscribed with his name, as a present to the shrine of the "Mistress of Byblos," the patron goddess of the town.[39] Menkaure of the 4th, Unas of the 5th, and Pepy I of the 6th Dynasties are very well represented by votives, and the latter, with his predecessor Khafre, is now also known on alabaster vessels found at Ebla.[40] As for Palestine, one can cite the Egyp-

[37] W. Westendorf, *GM* 11 (1974), 47ff.

[38] Shipwrecked Sailor, 147–49; D. B. Redford, *JEA* 67 (1981), 174–75.

[39] See Montet, *Byblos et l'Égypte*; on Hathor, "mistress of Byblos," see ibid., pl. 28:11, p. 35; M. Chehab, *Bulletin de la Musée de Beyrouth* 22 (1969), 1ff.; R. Stadelmann, *Syrisch-Palästinensische Gottheiten in Ägypten* (Leiden, 1967), 97; J. G. Griffiths, *Plutarch's De Iside et Osiride* (Cambridge, 1970), 326; C. J. Bleeker, *Hathor and Thoth* (Leiden, 1973), 72–73.

[40] P. Matthiae, *CRAIBL* (1978), 229, 230–31, fig. 20; idem, in *Studies in the History and*

tian alabastra found at Et-tell, sixteen kilometers north of Jerusalem (Plate 8). Here, on a magnificent rocky eminence, some unknown Early Bronze Age chieftain founded a capital centered upon a citadel with stone-built, plastered walls and columned courts. Great casemate walls of Cyclopean masonry surround the whole, transforming the site into an impregnable fortress. The familiarity in the use of stone that the builders evince is perfectly in keeping with Et-Tell's relative proximity to Egypt, but the presence of Egyptian vessels suggests much more. Could it be that the local chieftain of the city controlled much of the south central highlands, and could be counted as one of those "on the water of Pharaoh"?[41]

We do not know whether the Egyptians of the Old Kingdom maintained a permanent residence at Byblos. Certainly private names occasionally turn up among the inscribed objects: Nefer-seshemre, scribe of royal carpenters left an offering table at Byblos, and one of Khufu's ship's crews lost an axhead nearby at the mouth of the Adonis River. But these need not have been residents.

Plate 8. Early Bronze Age structure of semidressed fieldstones at Et-tell (Biblical Ai), north of Jerusalem. Masonry techniques and the presence of alabastra suggest contact with Egypt.

Archaeology of Jordan, 1:89, fig. 22; G. S. Matthiae, *Studia eblaiti* (Rome, 1979), 1:33ff.; (Rome, 1981), 4:104, fig. 14.

[41] On Et-Tel (Biblical "Ai"), see J. A. Callaway, *The Early Bronze Age Sanctuary at Ai (et-Tel)* (London, 1972); Avi-Yonah, *Encyclopaedia of Archaeological Excavations in the Holy Land.* 1:36ff.

Even without a permanent colony of Egyptians living in the town, by the closing centuries of the third millennium Egypt knew Byblos very well indeed. To them it was *Kpny*,[42] principal city of the land of *Negaw* whence came timber. It was for the Egyptians the gateway to a vast tract of mountainous land trailing off into desert, a tract that the Egyptians heard the natives refer to as *Qedem* ("the East"), a word they subsequently adopted as their own toponym. The city was surrounded by a mighty rampart, that they knew, and pursuant thereto Egyptians spoke of "Fortress Byblos."[43] Native princes indeed, in contrast to other Levantine potentates, were so enamored of the Egypt that courted them that they were to strive later to pass themselves off as Egyptian "mayors" and took pride in their ability to carve inscriptions in the hieroglyphic script.[44]

In matters of religion and cult, Egypt and Byblos enjoyed a singular, though not prominent, community of interest and interpretation. But to explore this more fully we shall have to delve into the exciting, though treacherous, field of mythology.

A COMMUNITY OF MYTH

While an occasional Asiatic deity may turn up in the Egyptian pantheon, consciously "borrowed" and partly "Egyptianized" like Hathor of Byblos, for the most part the cults, pantheons, and mythologies of Egypt and western Asia remained distinct in outward expression.[45] The West Semitic "hero-god" Baʿal, the "Lord" par excellence, seems to spring spontaneously out of the rain-drenched mountains of the Levantine littoral; and equally, Khopry, the "Beetle," appears, as indeed the Egyptian creation myths maintain, from the mud flats arising out of the Nile's inundation. The mythology seems tailored to specific landscapes and climates, and the cults arise from markedly different societies.

If this suggests that the Near Eastern religions of historic times never enjoyed anything in common, one might be advised to beware. Long ago, for example, some scholars noted the striking similarities between Osiris and his cult and the "dying-and-rising" god of Canaanite mythology. Were not both "fertility" gods, associated with such cultic appurtenances

---

[42] The ancient transcription into hieroglyphics of the Canaanite *Gubla*, "mountain," which was the name of the town: W. F. Albright, *The Vocalisation of Egyptian Syllabic Orthography* (New Haven, Conn., 1934), 60; Z. S. Harris, *A Grammar of the Phoenician Language* (New Haven, Conn., 1936), 93; Koehler-Baumgartner, 1:166. Only certain dialects of ancient Egyptian possessed an *l*, and early transcriptions press an *n* into service when a foreign *l* is to be rendered.

[43] *Wntt Kbn*: J. Leclant, *Orientalia* 23 (1954), 73; P. Montet, *Kêmi* 16 (1962), 80.

[44] See chapter 4.

[45] See in particular D. B. Redford, "The Sea and the Goddess," in S. Groll, ed., *Studies in Egyptology Presented to Miriam Lichtheim* (Jerusalem, 1990), 824–35.

as flowering shrubs or trees, mounds or "high places," cultic pillars, and pastoral animals? Had not both been murdered and subsequently championed by a faithful goddess-consort? Was not even the name *Osiris* related to a Semitic root whence came *Asir* and even *Ashur*? The resultant theory to which these observations were to give rise was so faciley stated and simplistic that debunkers easily pointed up a host of differences, some of them major, between the two gods and their cults. Few students of comparative religion today would dare even to broach the subject, preferring to dwell on the native character and roles of the individual deities.[46] Nevertheless, one cannot help but be uneasy at the suspicion that we may have "thrown out the baby with the bath water": in mythology similarities do exist, if only in broad plot structure and plot roles. In cultures occupying adjacent stretches of the eastern Mediterranean coast, do such similarities have any meaning?

Central to the mythology of the maritime cities of the Levant in antiquity was the phenomenon of the cosmic struggle between land and sea, fair weather and storm. In keeping with man's tendency to humanize his environment and to bow to its inspiration by the creation of coherent narrative, this most striking of the environmental phenomena in the eastern Mediterranean was translated into a plot motif. A raging monster, dark and foul, invades the land but meets resistance in the form of a hero, larger than life, with all the force of elemental morality behind him. Many changes can be rung on this simple pattern, depending on the outcome of the struggle, the identity of ancillary characters, or the context in which the story is used. The venue can even be transferred to the land, where the monster becomes "Death." But the point must be stressed that the basic plot was in origin a "neutral" device, and not necessarily an etiological means of explaining creation or some phenomenon of nature.[47]

The story turns up in classic form in the mythology of North Syria, known best from the important archives of Ugarit.[48] Here, in texts of the Late Bronze Age, but certainly derived from material millennia earlier, is the story of *Yam*, "Prince Sea," the avaricious monster who lords it over the gods and lusts after the beautiful goddess Astarte, until defeated by Baʿal. In a parallel motif Baʿal is lured to a remote water hole during the

---

[46] On the Osiris cult and its alleged derivation from western Asia, see A. Scharff, *Die Ausbreitung des Osiriskultes in der Frühzeit und während des Alten Reiches* (Munich, 1948), 8; S.A.B. Mercer, *The Religion of Ancient Egypt* (London, 1949), 97ff.; Griffiths, *Origins of Osiris*.

[47] See O. Kaiser, *Die mythische Bedeutung des Meeres in Ägypten, Ugarit und Israel* (Berlin, 1959); A. Y. Collins, *The Conflict Myth in the Book of Revelation* (Missoula, Mont., 1976), 57ff.; cf. T. H. Gaster, *Thespis*[2] (New York, 1961), 153ff.; Attridge and Oden, *Philo of Byblos. The Phoenician History*, 76–77, n. 29.

[48] *ANET*[2], 129ff.; see also the preceding note.

hunt, and set upon and killed by the monster *Mot*, "Death," and his minions. "Death" in turn is now harried by Baʿal's consort, the maiden "ʿAnat," who administers a good thrashing to *Mot*, and then (apparently) proceeds to revive her unfortunate husband.

The plot roles thus demand three protagonists: monster, hero, and female consort; but, while at Ugarit both ʿAnat and Astarte are associated with the monster Yam, theirs is not a pivotal function. Further south, however, in the major coastal towns south of the Eleutheros River, the goddess is paramount in the worship of the populace to the point where her male partner often recedes into passivity. At Byblos whence comes the most ancient evidence, the "Baʿalat," mistress of the city, is manifestly the dominant member of the local pantheon. Her common epithet, of course, conceals Astarte, transmogrified by Egyptian usage into Hathor. Her male consort, however, the local Baʿal, is more difficult to identify. The Egyptians identified him with their own crocodile god, Arsaphes, a deity who, two thousand years later, was to be recognized by the Greeks as Herakles. But his native *name*, certainly in the pyramid age, was pronounced something like *Hay-ʿatul*, which means "the Living One is Exalted." Divine names often, by reason of their inviolability, are replaced in speech by epithets and circumlocutions (as is indeed the explanation of the prevalence of "Baʿal"); and in the case of the hero-god of Byblos, his "lordship" tended, as the centuries passed, to find expression in the local vernacular word for "lord," namely *Adon*, whence the classical "Adonis."[49]

The hero–monster struggle holds a prominent place in the Byblian cult; but here the myth displays significant differences from the one that was popular further north at Ugarit. Adonis does indeed engage the Sea in battle but is killed in the act and has to be revived by his female partner. The more widespread version of the tale, which translates the whole to a setting on land, has the god killed by a boar while hunting; and in consequence the local river (Nahr Ibrahim) runs with blood seasonally. The influence of the Byblian cult and mythology extended to the cities and regions along the coast to the immediate south. Sidon had its Eshmun and Astronome, Tyre its Melqart and Astronoe, and the coast of Palestine Baʿal (masquerading as Perseus in classical times), and Ketes the monster.

In the mythologies of the cities south of Byblos another motif, arising from the hero–monster combat, is stressed in our sources. This is the story of the lecherous Sea who directs his lust toward the goddess herself, Baʿal's consort, and pursues her relentlessly, sometimes forcing her to

---

[49] On Hathor of Byblos, see Griffiths, *Original of Osiris*, 33; C.J. Bleeker, *Hathor and Thoth* (Leiden, 1973), 72–73; on *Ḥʿy-tʒw*, see PT 518, Goedicke, *MDAIK* 19 (1963), 1ff.; on Adonis, see B. Soyez, *Byblos et les fêtes des Adoneis* (Leiden, 1977); N. Robertson, *HTR* 75 (1982), 313ff.

commit suicide. Such an episode underlies the form of the myth current at Aphek in the mountains above Byblos where Aphrodite (Astarte) leaped into the sacred pool and became a fish to escape the clutches of the monster.[50] At Tyre the classical sources that tell of Europa and the Bull conceal a more ancient tale of the goddess raped away by the Sea; and at Joppa the Andromeda–Ketes–Perseus melodrama again points to an older, native story of the same basic pattern.[51] The goddess of Ashkelon, Atargatis or Derceto, together with her son, leaps into a lake and is either eaten by, or becomes, a fish; and there is some evidence that a similar version, featuring an offspring, was to be found in the mythology of Gaza.

Thus far we have uncovered two related, though divergent, plot motifs: the battle between hero and monster issuing in a victory for the former; and the pursuit of the goddess by the monster resulting often in a cultic miracle. Both require three plot roles, the first hero, monster, and goddess-consort; the second monster, goddess, and goddess's son.

The battle between hero and monster in its "classical" localization (in Ugaritic mythology) at the mouth of the Orontes in North Syria, finds parallels, if not derived versions, in the mythologies of several adjacent cultures. In Mesopotamia the plot pattern turns up as the etiological explanation of creation in the struggle between Marduk, god of Babylon, and Ti'amat, the monster of chaos.[52] Classical mythology knows the North Syrian myth well: it is at the mouth of the Orontes and on the coast of neighboring Cilicia that the Greeks localized *their* version of the story, translating Ba'al into Zeus and sea into the monstrous Typhon.[53]

Most significant for our present investigation, the hero–monster motif is found in Egypt also, concealed in the substratum, as it were, of mythological thought, behind more popular myths. As elsewhere, the story is used in an account of creation or inauguration. In the twenty-first century B.C. King Merikare is advised by his father to "look after mankind, the flock of the gods; (for) he (i.e., the creator-god) made heaven and earth according to their desire, and subdued the water monster. He made the breath of life so that they might breathe; they are his image(s) who came forth from his body."[54] Often the hero role is filled by the sun-god or one of his minions and the allusion, which is only fleeting, refers to

---

[50] Soyez, *Byblos*, 30ff.; M. Astour, *Hellenosemitica* (Leiten, 1965), 116, n. 1.

[51] On Europa, see W. Buhler, *Europa. Ein Überblick über die Zeugnisse der Mythos* (Munich, 1968); Astour, *Hellenosemitica*, 128ff.; R. B. Edwards, *Kadmos the Phoenician* (Amsterdam, 1979), 79, n. 73; on Andromeda, see H. J. Rose, in *OCD²*, 63–64.

[52] J. Jacobsen, *JAOS* 88 (1968), 107–8.

[53] Hesiod, *Theogony*, 12.820ff.; Apollodorus, 1.41–44.

[54] W. Helck, *Die Lehre für Merikare* (Wiesbaden, 1977), 83–84; M. Lichtheim, *Ancient Egyptian Literature* (Berkeley, Calif., 1976), 1:106–7.

archetypal myths of a vaguely inaugurative kind. Thus one passage makes passing reference to "the adze of Atum which is in the vertebra of the Neheb-kau serpent which brings an end to the strife in Heliopolis"; another qualifies Atum as "he who quelled the raging in heaven, the strife in Heliopolis (at) the great battle."[55] The latter is further described as having taken place "on the northwest of the House of the serpent Es-ʿos, when Re had transformed himself into an ichneumon of 46 cubits (long) to fell Apophis in his rage."[56] Creation accounts in Egypt, however, did not commonly make use of the hero–monster motif. A much more popular employment of the latter was in the rationalization of the solar eclipse: Apophis, always lurking in the celestial Nile in wait for the solar boat, was confronted by the spear-brandishing hero Seth standing on the prow of the bark.[57]

One Egyptian myth, however, can be directly compared with the role triangle found in the southern Levant, namely monster–goddess–son, and that is the cycle of narrative dealing with the flight of Isis to the marshes of the Delta.[58] Upon the death of her husband Osiris at the hands of Seth, Isis is forced to flee to the marshes of the Delta for her own safety and that of her child Horus. At Buto especially, in the northwest Delta, and secondarily at Yamet in the east, the myth took on the ambience of a bucolic setting. The child Horus, the baby falcon, lies concealed in the nest while his mother Isis, "the Kite," keeps watch for the rampaging monster Seth, the wild pig. Approvingly and offering what protection they can, the denizens of the fens assist the frantic mother in her watch: Edjo, "the Green One" (the cobra), Djebat the heron, Sekhet-Hor the cow. Unlike the myth at Joppa, Ashkelon, and Gaza, however, where its purpose was to provide an etiological rationale for the cult, the essential humanity of the "Butic" cycle lent a much more positive tone to the whole. Despite numerous trials, Isis is not captured by the monster; her son Horus is not destroyed. The hero–monster motif is appended to the whole and issues in a triumph of the right: Horus issues from Buto on his maturity, and defeats Seth.[59]

Thus the "Butic" cycle, at home originally on the northern fringe of the Delta not far from the Mediterranean coast, shares with the urban centers

---

[55] PT 229; G. Daressy, *ASAE* 11 (1911), 188; 18 (1918), 116; Gasten, *Thespis*², 141, 152; A. W. Shorter, *JEA* 21 (1935), 43; K. Mysliewic, *Studien zum Gott Atum* (Hildesheim, 1978), 1:92ff., 124.

[56] Ibid.

[57] E. Hornung, *Conceptions of God in Ancient Egypt* (Ithaca, N.Y., 1982), 158–59.

[58] A. Klassens, *A Magical Statue Base (Socle Behague) in the Museum of Antiquities at Leiden* (Leiden, 1952); R. T. Rundle-Clark, *Myth and Symbol in Ancient Egypt* (London, 1957), 186ff.; A. Massart, *MDAIK* 48 (1957), 172ff.

[59] See D. B. Redford, *BES* 5 (1983), 67ff.

of the southern Levantine littoral a community of mythological pattern-
ing. Although a strictly maritime setting does not inform the Egyptian
stories, the motif is clearly the same. We must remember, however, the
very simple nature of the plot of these tales as well as the mutual awareness and interconnection through trade and travel enjoyed by communities around the Levantine and African coasts from time immemorial. We
are, in fact, plummeted back to a prehistoric age if we seek to identify in
time and place the point of origin of the story. It would be a bootless
search. Even if one gifted narrator is responsible for turning the storm-
lashing-the-coast into the hero—monster struggle, so many cult-centers in
the interim have adopted, changed, embellished, and pruned this common heritage, often unconscious of their debt to a more remote author,
that our quest would rapidly bog down into a form-critical evaluation of
varying versions. Suffice to say that Egypt and the Levant, in a way they
scarcely realized, were joint heirs five millennia ago to a powerful and
elemental creation in narrative, which, in one form or another, is still with
us today.

"THE FOREIGN LANDS BELONG TO THE KING"

The outgoing 2nd Dynasty had witnessed one of the great turning points
in Egyptian history: the final suppression of dissident elements in the Nile
Delta and the composite union of the land under pharaonic monarchy.
Within a generation of Kha'sekhem's tersely recorded victory march over
48,000 slain northerners,[60] there arises the first examplar of that monumental symbol that forever afterward was to mark the absolute monarchy of united Egypt, the royal pyramid (Plate 9).[61] It was as though the
new unity had released all the pent-up energies of the young nation. Beginning with the experimental structure in six steps that was built for
King Djoser of the 3rd Dynasty by the architect *cum* physician Imhotpe,
the form passed rapidly through several stages of evolution until within
75 years of Djoser's death it had achieved the smooth-faced, pyramidal
form we associate with the term today. In fact from Djoser to Khafre (4th
Dynasty), a period of about 150 years, the pyramid experienced a rapid
and incremental development in mass, height, and appointments. From a

[60] F. W. Green and J. E. Quibell, *Hierakonpolis* (London, 1900), 1: pl. 39–41.

[61] Literature on this subject is legion and shockingly uneven in scholarly excellence.
Among the best works are the following: D. Arnold, *LdÄ* 5 (1984), 1ff.; I.E.S. Edwards, *The
Pyramids of Egypt*² (Harmondsworth, 1971); A. Fakhry, *The Pyramids*² (Chicago, 1969);
L. V. Grinsel, *Egyptian Pyramids* (Bristol, 1947); J.-P. Lauer, *Les Pyramides de Sakkarah*
(Cairo, 1977); V. Maragioglio and C. Rinaldi, *L'architettura delle piramide Menfite* (Turin,
1962). Up-to-date bibliography on individual pyramids may be found in Smith and Simp-
son, *Art and Architecture of Ancient Egypt*².

Plate 9. The 4th Dynasty pyramids at Giza, viewed from the south. Though now stripped of the outer casing stones, the group fittingly symbolizes the apogee of Old Kingdom power in the twenty-sixth century B.C.

height of 62 meters under Djoser the form rose to a towering 157 meters under Khufu; from Djoser's relatively modest 126 by 110 meters the base measurements increased to 232 meters square under Khufu. Both site and setting were supposed to convey to men and gods the permanence and centrality of the king in this world and the next. Djoser's step pyramid silhouetted itself against the sky on the desert edge immediately above Memphis, the central royal city and residence, where no citizen could fail to see it or appreciate its significance; Khufu's massive monument arose on the desert edge at the exact point where the Nile debouches into the Delta, a fitting symbol of Pharaoh's absolute dominance of the two divisions of his kingdom. The complex of buildings around Djoser's pyramid symbolized in iconography and layout the union of the land, and memorialized the jubilee, a festival of kingship and rejuvenation.[62] The formal pyramid temple, which from the reign of Khafre displayed a standard design, pointed to the deceased king, the "Osiris," who as "Great God" continued to rule his subjects in the beyond.[63]

But to us the pyramid signalizes something more than the elaboration of new symbols and iconography, and the rapid development of new construction techniques. It is the visible sign of a revolution in the knowledge

[62] S. Schott, *Bemerkungen zum altägyptischen Pyramidenkult* (Cairo, 1950), 133ff.; K. Martin, *LdÄ* 5 (1983), 782–90.

[63] H. Junker, *Pyramidenzeit* (Zurich, 1949), 118ff.; R. Anthes, *JNES* 18 (1959), 169ff.; Griffiths, *Origins of Osiris*, 44ff., 173ff.

of how to handle human society and organize manpower; it is the indicator of a burgeoning bureaucracy that the centralization of the state in the person of the king has imposed on his growing residence-city.

By far the majority of textual sources from the Old Kingdom comprises lists of titles and functions found in the biographical inscriptions in private tombs.[64] From these it is possible to reconstruct a vast civil service that is startling in its sophistication. Immediately under the king and deputizing for him stands a sort of "grand vizier" or prime minister, who is responsible for all the departments of government, or "the offices of the (king's) residence" as contemporary jargon puts it. There were what we would call departments of agriculture and livestock, a department of the treasury comprising *inter alia* "the double house of gold and silver," "the repository of royal luxury goods," and the granary; a defense department ("the house of armor"); the secretariat along with the archives ("the house of books or rescripts"); and a number of other offices and organizations of which we only dimly perceive the function.

Understandably, those departments concerned with the recruitment, training and organization of manpower loom large during the "pyramid age."[65] Recruitment was based on the notion that all Egyptians owed service to the state, and the related assumption that all prisoners of war and foreign captives had lost any right they might have had to choose freely. Egyptians could thus be recruited by "the king's house" or by "any office of the residence"[66] for construction work, corvée labor, fieldwork, or hard labor; and foreigners could be pressed into service at the will of the state. Their work was organized under the aegis of the Department of Works, and they were divided into gangs of varying sizes (often in groups of ten), supervised by overseers of the residence. As with the service of priests or of palace personnel, the masses of unskilled labor on construction projects served in four divisions, each operating for three months of the year, thus permitting a large proportion of the peasants to return to the fields for planting, tilling, and harvesting.[67] While employed by the government, this work force, which was drawn from all over Egypt, was housed, fed, and clothed at the expense of the state, and there is some

[64] W. Helck, *Untersuchungen zu den Beamtentiteln des ägyptischen Alten Reiches* (Glückstadt, 1954); K. Baer, *Rank and Title in the Old Kingdom* (Chicago, 1960); N. Kanawati, *Government Reforms in Old Kingdom Egypt* (Warminster, 1980); for Old Kingdom administration, see idem, *The Egyptian Administration in the Old Kingdom* (Warminster, 1977); N. Strudwick, *The Administration of Egypt in the Old Kingdom* (London, 1985).

[65] Cf. Arnold, in *LdÄ* 5 (1984), 1–4.

[66] H. Goedicke, *Königliche Dokumente aus den Alten Reich* (Wiesbaden, 1967), fig. 5.

[67] H. Kees, *Ancient Egypt, A Cultural Topography* (London, 1961), 55.

evidence to suggest medical services were also provided.[68] The criteria of success on construction projects were speed and efficiency. One official claims to have quarried an alabaster offering table and transported it from quarry to work site, a distance of 290 kilometers, in seventeen days; another boasts of having floated the granite columns for the king's mortuary temple a journey of 950 kilometers in seven days![69] A letter of complaint from a superintendent of a gang of quarrymen protests the practice of monthly refitting of his crew: "Yours Truly (he says, referring politely to himself) has been in the habit of spending 6 days at the Residence with this gang before they are issued clothing. This is detrimental to the work which is in the charge of Yours Truly; for only a single day is deducted (from the quota) for this gang when it is issued clothing."[70]

Into this beehive of construction work our evidence now chronicles the influx of increasing numbers of foreigners from the end of the 3rd Dynasty.[71] This cheap manpower rapidly became what Egypt expected to receive from the adjacent lands, along with booty, enforced benevolences, gifts, and raw materials, as part of their obligations to Egypt ordained by the gods. Egypt sought to ensure a regular supply, not through the establishment of an imperial infrastructure permanently subjugating foreign lands, but through intimidation and the creation of a "sphere of influence." For foreign lands, "belonged to" the king, as did Egypt itself: the king tramples on alien peoples called collectively the "Nine Bows," and on Egyptians too. Egyptians and foreigners alike bow down before the god-king (Figure 4).[72]

The acquisition of the goods and personnel Egypt wanted beyond its frontiers could be ensured by a variety of means.[73] The Egyptians could trade with the natives or, at the summit of political power, engage in gift exchange. They could also make plain that they expected "benevolences" to be proffered "spontaneously" by the locals, on pain of incurring the displeasure of Egypt. If all else failed, a military expedition might be sent abroad. In fact the distinctions are blurred. Expeditions that went abroad comprised a "host" that, because it sometimes had to fight, we have fallen into the habit of calling an "army." But the "host" might not have to fight if the operation were a mining or a trading venture, and could then be used to transport bodily whatever commodity had been acquired. "Seal bearers of the god," a term often attached to expedition commanders,

[68] See n. 70; P. Ghalioungui, *Magic and Medical Science in Ancient Egypt* (London, 1963), 65.

[69] *Urk* I, 107–8; H. G. Fischer, *JEA* 61 (1975), 33ff.

[70] B. Gunn, *ASAE* 25 (1925), 242ff.; A. H. Gardiner, *JEA* 13 (1927), 75ff.

[71] D. B. Redford, *Scripta Mediterranea* 2 (1981), 8–9; idem, *JARCE* 23 (1986), 136ff.

[72] Redford, *JARCE* 23 (1986) nn. 80–83.

[73] See A. Ben-Tor, *JESHO* 29 (1986), 1–27.

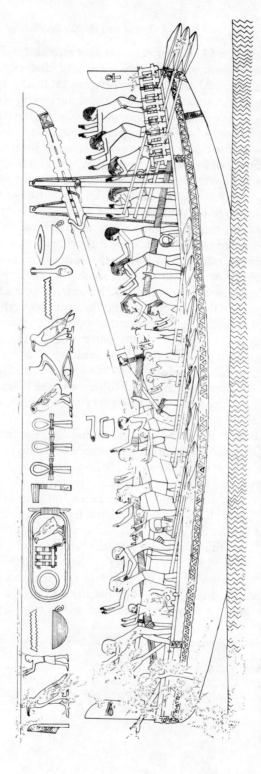

Figure 4. Scene from the pyramid temple of Sahure (twenty-fifth century B.C.), showing a boat full of Asiatics arriving in Egypt. (The king was probably pictured on the left.) The text reads "Hail to thee, O Sahure, god of the living! May we behold thy beauty!"

took "troops" with them on foreign expeditions, but usually these were present merely to show the flag and "to pacify" (as contemporary jargon had it) the local population.[74] Egyptians referred, somewhat archly one feels, to "putting the fear of Horus (i.e., the Pharaoh) among the foreign lands."[75] It was far less expensive, of course, to rely on the natives of Palestine voluntarily to bring their natural resources, produce, and servants to the king as "gifts." The Egyptians designated specific days of the year when such benevolences were deemed appropriate, and the foreigners must soon have learned when such "free-will" offerings were expected. Still, an Egyptian "host" and Egyptian ships may well have come out to accompany the gift bringers.

There is less information available for the Old Kingdom than for later periods on how Egypt acquired a foreign labor force. Captives from foreign expeditions account for a large proportion of the aliens in Egypt during the pyramid age (as noted previously), but surely not for the total number. Unfortunately the surviving annals do not always accompany the entry for foreigners returning with an expedition with an explanation as to how they were acquired. It is quite probable, however, that, as in later better-documented times, the inhabitants of Palestine and Syria needed little coercion to be persuaded to transfer their place of residence to the banks of the Nile and offer their services to Pharaoh. Egypt at all periods acted like a magnet on its neighbors. To people like those in the Levant whose prime concerns centered on the uncertainty of the harvest and the ever-present prospect of starvation, the constancy and superabundance of Egypt's grain production and the richness of its stock of fish, fowl, and wild game could scarcely be resisted. Better to live a well-fed factor in Egypt than die a starving "free man" on the steppes of Asia. Whether emigrating voluntarily, or sold by their village headman, or yet again captured in battle, it is doubtful whether any of the Asiatics we see conveyed in Egyptian vessels regretted their fate.

The evidence of trade and diplomatic gifts does not conceal the fact that the Egyptians could, and frequently did, resort to naked force in gaining their ends in Palestine. We are also in a position to say what precisely was considered a *casus belli*: when Egyptian commissioners were interfered with or killed, when Asiatic principalities "rebelled," sometimes egged on by external subversive elements, or when the expected benevolences were refused—then Egypt took punitive action. The few surviving texts from the Old Kingdom that deal with the subject do not equivocate. The most common verb used is "to smite," referring to mortal

[74] For this sense of the verb *sḥtp* the argument of G. E. Kadish is still the best: *JEA* 52 (1966), 29ff.

[75] Redford, *Scripta Mediterranea* 2 (1981), 6–7.

combat. The enemy are "slaughtered," "put to flight," or "cowed," and the survivors brought off to Egypt as prisoners. As punishment and an example, the rebellious city was demolished after capture, the mud-brick walls being systematically hacked down with hoes. Firing a town was occasionally referred to. The whole action took place within a legal context, betokened by such verbs as "to put down," and "to inflict punishment." Statue fragments of kneeling captives, which occasionally are unearthed in pyramid temples of the later Old Kingdom, reflect the motif of the execution of prisoners; and there is textual evidence of the ceremonial cursing of foreign peoples.[76]

The most detailed account of a military expedition into Palestine is that contained in the biographical statement of one Weny, who served during the reigns of Tety, Pepy I, and Merenre of the 6th Dynasty (twenty-fourth century B.C.).[77] Weny, although only a courtier and superintendent of royal market-gardeners, was chosen to lead the army because (as he tells us) he was "more capable in His Majesty's opinion than any of his magistrates, dignitaries or servants." Beyond the vague allusion to rebellion, no reason is given for the expeditions, but as the text was only for home consumption, none was required. The Egyptian reader would take for granted that the Asiatics had acted evilly.

> When His Majesty would punish the Asiatics who are across the sand, (he) made an army of many tens of thousands recruited from all Upper Egypt . . . and the Delta. . . . His Majesty sent me in command of this army. . . . It was I that took charge of them, although my office was only that of Superintendent of Palace market-gardeners, because of the exactitude with which I discharged my function. And the result was that no one quarreled with his fellow, no one stole a loaf or a pair of sandals from a traveler, no one seized a garment from any town, and no one seized a goat from any person. I led them by way of the "Northern Fort" (?), through the "Gate of Imhotpe," in the district of "Horus-Lord-of-Truth . . ."
>
> This army returned in peace, having hacked up the land of them that are across the sand!
>
> This army returned in peace, having pulverized the land of them that are across the sand!
>
> This army returned in peace, having razed its fortified towns!
>
> This army returned in peace, having cut down its fruit trees and vines!

[76] On statues of bound prisoners from Old Kingdom mortuary temples, see now M. Verner, *RdE* 36 (1985), 145ff.; on Execration Texts, see G. Posener, *Cinq figurines d'envoûtement* (Cairo, 1987), where a complete bibliography will be found.

[77] A. K. Grayson and D. B. Redford, *Papyrus and Tablet* (Engelwood Cliffs, N.J., 1973), 45–48; cf. also Lichtheim, *Literature*, 1:18ff.; Wilson, in *ANET²*, 227–28; H. Goedicke, *RSO* 38 (1963), 187ff.; B. Couroyer, *RB* 78 (1971), 558–59; J. Osing, *Orientalia* 46 (1977), 165ff.

This army returned in peace, having set all its dwellings(?) on fire!

This army returned in peace, having slain the enemy troops that were in it by the many tens of thousands!

This army returned in peace, having brought off very much of the enemy troops that were in it as prisoners!

And His Majesty praised me for it beyond anything. His Majesty sent me to lead this army on five occasions, to smite the land of them that are across the sand every time they rebelled, with these troops. I did it so well that His Majesty praised me for it beyond anything.

Then it was reported that there were troublemakers among these foreigners in the land of "Gazelle-nose(?),"[78] and so I crossed the sea in transport ships with these troops, and put to shore behind the height of the ridge on the north of the land of them that are across the sand. With a full half(?) of these troops afar off, I returned, having captured them all; and the troublemakers among them were slain.

The ebullience, the naiveté, and the boastfulness are all typical of private biographical statements with which ancient Egyptian tombs of all periods are inscribed; and the historian has automatically to "scale down" the degree of intensity and success the speaker claims characterized his actions. Nevertheless, in Weny's case two important points cannot be distorted by the rhetoric and they are, first, that an enormous expeditionary force was required and, second, that the Asiatics were successful enough in their rebellion to repeat it five times. In view of the momentous events that were shortly to bring the Early Bronze Age to a dramatic close, we may allow ourselves to pose some fundamental questions. Do Weny's expeditions reflect the beginning of the end in Palestine? And who were the "troublemakers" who had infiltrated among "these foreigners"? Answers will probably never be forthcoming, but the queries are of vital importance nonetheless. Within a century of Weny's escapades, both Egypt and Palestine were to experience a complete economic and political collapse.

[78] Unknown place on the Levantine coast, sometimes identified with the Carmel range.

CHAPTER 3

"Lo, the Vile Asiatic!"

AMONG THE shifting sands of south Saqqara, the vast necropolis of the Egyptian capital city Memphis, stands the pyramid complex of Pepy II, last of the great Pharaohs of the Old Kingdom (c. twenty-third century B.C.), and longest-lived monarch in history with a reign of 94 years. Although badly preserved, the complex was subjected in the 1930s to the careful excavations of G. Jequier, and these revealed a layout and functional design thoroughly in keeping with the Old Kingdom tradition that had been evolving over five centuries.[1] A "valley temple" on a canal communicating with the Nile gave access to the customary causeway, which led up to the desert plateau, whereon stood the pyramid and its temple. Here on the day of interment the mummy of the aged Pharaoh was conveyed, its physical faculties having been restored in the magical ceremony of "Opening the Mouth." The priests and acolytes deposited the sarcophagus in the burial chamber, placed various foods and funerary goods in the storage chambers, and offered the first sacrifices to the spirit of their departed king in the temple abutting the eastern face of the pyramid. Thus was set in motion the elaborate apparatus designed to serve the dead king throughout eternity.

As the procedures adhered to tradition, so the plan, architecture, and design of "Pepy-is-firm-and-living" (the official name of the pyramid complex of Pepy II) followed time-honored models. The architects might have dispensed with basalt in favor of the more easily acquired limestone, and have replaced the delicate papyriform or palm columns with simple piers, but nonetheless the pyramid temple displayed the requisite grandeur for a god-king departed to rule over a new realm. The pyramid itself indeed comprised an easily constructed core of rubble faced with fine limestone to provide the pyramid shape; but its size (seventy-eight meters square) and external appearance compared favorably with the dozen or so pyramids that had preceded it in the 5th and 6th Dynasties: all rubble-filled and "veneered." And as had become customary since the time of king Unas of the 5th Dynasty, the burial chamber was carved with the myriad of spells, hymns, and liturgies that collectively constitute the "Pyr-

[1] On the pyramid complex of Pepy II, see G. Jequier, *Le monument funéraire de Pepy II* (Cairo, 1936–1941).

amid Texts," a corpus of religious texts used primarily in the ritual of the temple cult to assist the king in the beyond.[2]

THE COLLAPSE OF THE OLD KINGDOM

When the pyramid and temple of Pepy II first arose on the western plateau, not a cloud was perceived on any horizon. Pharaoh's host still freely traveled to any mine or quarry the sovereign chose; caravan conductors brought ass trains from the south laden with all the exotic products of Africa. Votive offerings in the name of the king were still presented in far-off places.[3] The necropolis of Saqqara and Giza continued to boast large, private tombs of rectangular shape (called "mastabas" by the modern Arabic-speaking population, after the resemblance to benches outside the doors of village houses), each replete with painted or relief scenes depicting the life, accomplishments, and pious hopes of the owner.[4] Provincial centers had long since spawned cemeteries of rock-cut tombs in the wadys leading off into the desert, wherein the local "lords of the manor," the municipal officials of the royal administration, were laid to rest amid a parochial pomp that could only ape the sophistication of the capital.[5] Most of these burying grounds were thriving when Pepy II came to the throne, and continued throughout the first half of his reign to throw up the proud biographies we are accustomed to associate with the Old Kingdom. The quality of the arts of sculptor and smith, always a bellwether of the stability of the community, causes no alarm at the outset of the reign: the examples of relief from the king's mortuary temple are as aesthetically pleasing and technically excellent as anything executed during the 5th or 6th Dynasty.

By the last quarter of Pepy's reign the picture has changed dramatically. Expeditions to mines and quarries have been suspended. When caravans venture abroad, the might of Egypt ceases to overawe the natives: one expedition leader is slain in Nubia by rebellious tribesmen and his son has to ransom his corpse; another is murdered by Asiatics on the shores of the Red Sea.[6] The royal administration lapses into inactivity. The last

---

[2] On the Pyramid Texts, see, among others, J. H. Breasted, *The Development of Religion and Thought in Ancient Egypt* (New York, 1912); R. O. Faulkner, *The Ancient Egyptian Pyramid Texts* (Oxford, 1969): H. Altenmüller, *Die Texte zum Begrabnisritual in den Pyramiden des Alten Reiches* (Wiesbaden, 1972); W. Barta, *Die Bedeutung der Pyramiden Texte für die verstorbenen König* (Munich, 1981).

[3] Cf. P. Montet, *Byblos et l'Égypte* (Paris, 1929), nos. 56, 58.

[4] On Saqqara, see J. Baines and J. Malek, *Atlas of Ancient Egypt* (London, 1980), 142ff.

[5] E. Drioton and J. Vandier, *L'Égypte*[4] (Paris, 1962), 226; N. Kanawati, *The Egyptian Administration in the Old Kingdom* (Warminster, 1977).

[6] *Urk* I, 134, 136ff.

dated text of the reign is dated to year 67.[7] Later folklore depicts Pepy as a voluptuary and (possibly) a homosexual, unflattering labels from an ancient Egyptian point of view.[8] In fact, during his lifetime already he may have been held in contempt: in the last half of his reign, in contrast to the beginning, there is a tendency on the part of the nobility to drop titles connected with his pyramid temple.[9] Contemporary archaeological evidence reveals an impoverished Memphis where people can afford only a small mud-brick mastaba, decoration requiring artists being beyond their means;[10] and where such a high-ranking officer as the vizier can only have himself buried in a usurped tomb.[11] The elaborate "pecking order" or ranking system that supporting framework of Old Kingdom society was ostensibly breaking down. Titles that from the dawn of time had been reserved for the queen are now found brazenly added to the titularies of common women. Everyone is a "king's favorite" and men and women[12] both usurp the lofty rank of "vizier."[13]

The aftermath struck the ancients as no less horrendous. Although contemporary evidence fails, the king-list tradition of later times conveys what must be a reasonably accurate picture, at least in its general impression. The Turin Canon (c. 1250–1200 B.C.), our one true king list from ancient Egypt,[14] follows the entry for Pepy II with seven names: [Merenre II(?)], Nitokerty, Neferka (the) child, Nefer, Aba, and two lost names, in total reigning for something in excess of a decade. But the copiest had a gap of six years in his sources, and faithfully notes it.[15] This gap is filled by the so-called Abydos king list, a list of royal names placed in historical sequence, and used in the rite of offering to the royal ancestors.[16] Here, following Pepy II, occur eighteen names of wholly ephemeral kings who in sum can account for scarcely twenty years. According to Herodotus Pepy II was followed by a Menthsouphis who reigned for little more than a year and was murdered in a palace conspiracy. His sister Nitocris (Nitokerty?) took revenge on the conspirators by convening them in a large

---

[7] *Urk* I, 174.

[8] G. Posener, *RdE* 11 (1957), 119ff.

[9] Kanawati, *JEA* 63 (1977), 60, n. 5.

[10] Drioton and Vandier, *L'Égypte*[4], 221–22.

[11] W. Helck, *Untersuchungen zu den Beamtentiteln des ägyptischen Alten Reiches* (Glückstadt, 1954), 142.

[12] J. Malek, *JSSEA* 10 (1980), fig. 2.

[13] On *Špst-nsw*, see D. Meeks, *Année lexicographique* (Paris, 1980), 1:368; cf. also Jequier, *Monument funeraire*, 2: pl. 90; H. G. Fischer, *JAOS* 76 (1956), 99–100.

[14] A papyrus now in the Turin Museum found by the consul Drovetti in 1822 in a tomb in western Thebes. Editions: G. Farina, *Il papiro dei Re* (Rome, 1938); A. H. Gardiner, *The Royal Canon of Turin* (Oxford, 1959).

[15] D. B. Redford, *Pharaonic King-lists, Annals and Day-books* (Toronto, 1986), 12ff.

[16] Ibid., 18ff.

hall, ostensibly for a banquet, then by means of a dam diverting the waters of the Nile so that it drowned them all.[17] Manetho, two centuries later in the third century B.C., elaborates on the king-list tradition from folkloristic sources. Thereafter, says Manetho, a 7th Dynasty took power, consisting of seventy kings for seventy days, followed by an 8th Dynasty of twenty-seven kings.[18]

Conflicting as these accounts may appear, they convey an impression of the same historic fact: the morrow of the passing of Pepy II witnessed a lapse into political anarchy. Contemporary records are silent, but the aftermath is clear. Within a generation the Memphite family of kings, which had held power for nearly a thousand years, had thoroughly discredited itself and disappeared ignominiously. The initial turmoil at that point was temporarily quelled by the assumption of power on the part of "the House of Akhtoy" at Herakleopolis. Akhtoy and his seventeen successors, noblemen in origin, provided Egypt with a century-long regime, called traditionally the 9th and 10th Dynasties. Their hold over a united Egypt, however, was soon broken when, shortly after 2140 B.C. the southernmost townships of Egypt broke away under the leadership of the upstart city of Thebes, and formed their own rebel state in the south.

In the light of the absence of contemporary evidence of the sort that an economic historian might use, and the gap of four thousand years that separate us from the event, it would appear the height of sophomoric hubris to imagine that we could even come close to assigning causes to the collapse of the Old Kingdom. But certain facts do, indeed, stand out unmistakably. First, it is quite clear that at the close of Pepy II's reign the court at Memphis did not dispose of the revenues it had once received to excess. The impoverishment of the courtiers and the decline in the arts (brought on by inability to continue financing the ateliers of the artisans?) derive directly from these reduced circumstances in which Pharaoh found himself. Second, it is also clear that the person of *this* Pharaoh did not, at least in the later years of his life, command the respect he might have argued was his due. Third, in general, in contrast to the hiatus suffered in the occupancy of the Memphite necropolis, the provincial cemeteries continue to show succeeding generations in the landed, manorial families throughout the period of stasis.

The collapse of the economy of the pharaonic regime is the most difficult to explain. It is sometimes claimed that the cost of erecting such gigantic, "noneconomic" structures as the Giza pyramids crippled the state.[19] But twelve generations separate Menkaure from Pepy II, and the

[17] Herodotus, 2.100.
[18] W. G. Waddell, *Manetho* (London, 1940), 54–55.
[19] J. Wilson, *The Burden of Egypt* (Chicago, 1951), 98.

intervening period shows no obvious diminution of prosperity. Pepy II's pyramid was not more or less costly to build than that of Userkaf, three centuries before. Moreover, pyramids were not white elephants. They were the focal point of a temple and a priestly community that constituted a land-owning, economic unit producing real wealth in the form of food, livestock, and manufactured goods. In a regime where redistribution along hierarchial lines governs the economy, rather than the marketplace, the proliferation of such estates seems beneficial, not deleterious. Again, we are told that the constant provision of landed endowments for pyramid temples, private courtiers, and provincial cults constituted an obvious drain on the royal treasury. If so, and if the process was allowed to go on unchecked, one can only conclude that the rulers and their advisors were all fools. For it requires no heightened intelligence to realize that, if one continues to lop off parcels of land from one's domain, eventually nothing will be left. But there is evidence the regime would allow such an endowment to be appropriated by the descendants of the person for whom it had originally been set up, thus obviating the need to hand out even more land.[20] To a certain extent, however, and especially in the region of Memphis and the Delta, it may be true that the proliferation of cultic services for the ancestors and the state gods may have committed substantial tracts of land over which the king had once held wholly the right of disposal to institutions enjoying increasing autonomy.

This latter possibility raises the prospect of the progressive attenuation of the regime's discretionary rights over "property" of all kinds, which, at the beginning of the 4th Dynasty, we may imagine it enjoying to the full. How did this come about—through the relentless working of inevitable economic factors, or through short-sightedness and bad planning?

The question becomes acute when we address the problem of the charters of immunity.[21] While the term "charter," "legal document"[22] is ubiquitous in texts of the Old Kingdom with reference to all sorts of legal instruments, the particular form under discussion here is a royal edict, transcribed and sealed in the king's presence, and issued in favor of a temple or community with exemptive force. The fortunate recipient is thereby rendered exempt from taxation and forced labor. Two examples will illustrate tenor and intent. Neferirkare I (c. 2520–2500 B.C.) issues an edict to Hemwer, the local bishop, in favor of the temple at Abydos:

I do not empower anyone to take any priests who are in the township where you are for any agricultural or construction work of the township, exclusive of

[20] H. Kees, *Ancient Egypt, A Cultural Topography* (London, 1961), 63.

[21] H. Goedicke, *Königliche Dokumente aus dem Alten Reich* (Wiesbaden, 1967).

[22] H. Goedicke, *JNES* 15 (1956), 30; P. Posener-Krieger, *Les archives du temple funéraire de Nefereirkare-Kakai* (Cairo, 1976), 2:479.

the performance of ritual for his god in the temple where he is, and the repair of the temples in which they are. They are exempted throughout eternity by command of the King of Upper and Lower Egypt, Neferirkare. There is no charter contradictory thereto in any temple service.[23]

Nearly two centuries later Pepy I decrees in favor of the pyramid towns belonging to the mortuary estate of his remote ancestor Sneferu of the 4th Dynasty: "My Majesty has commanded that these two pyramid towns be exempt for him throughout the course of eternity from doing any work of the palace, from doing any forced labor for any part of the royal residence throughout the course of eternity, or from doing any forced labor at the word of anybody in the course of eternity."[24]

The question is, Were these acts of unmerited favor, or was the monarch trying to right wrongs? Was he, as has been suggested, attempting to purchase the support of a priestly class that had lately become increasingly influential? Whatever the motive, the edicts become more numerous as the Old Kingdom draws to an end. Of thirty-one known edicts, nine come from the reign of Pepy II and thirteen from the ephemeral kings of the 8th Dynasty. It may well be that here we have a major, though partly concealed, clue as to the reason for the economic collapse, were we but able correctly to interpret it. Certainly if such exemptions were granted on a large scale under Pepy II, the net result would have been the inevitable shrinking of the taxation base.

And such a shrinkage can be the only explanation of the impoverishment of the court. A contributing factor may well be found in the growing independence of royal officials now living permanently in the provinces, whose provincial cemeteries we have already had occasion to mention. Although they give prominent place in their titularies to the titles betokening connection with the royal family, as was the time-honored custom, their biographical statements betray an independence of spirit unheralded in the inscriptions of their forebears. With less than absolute control over the future of a provincial tax man (who in the 4th and early 5th Dynasties had been a mere court factor, whose domicile, family, and eventual burial remained in Memphis), the royal court of the 6th Dynasty was not in a position to reckon on the revenues of a Khufu or a Khafre.[25]

The intriguing suggestion has been made that the poverty of Egypt at the close of the Old Kingdom owes more to ecology than to economics and administration. The incidence of famine increases in the late 6th Dy-

---

[23] Goedicke, *Königliche Dokumente*, 23, fig. 2.
[24] Wilson, *Burden*, 99.
[25] H. Fischer, *JAOS* 74 (1954), 26; idem, *Dendera in the Third Millennium B.C.* (Locust Valley, N.Y., 1968), 12; N. Kanawati, *Governmental Reforms in the Old Kingdom* (Warminster, 1980).

nasty and early First Intermediate Period, and a reduction in rainfall and the annual flooding of the Nile seems to have afflicted northeast Africa with progressive dessication as the third millennium draws to a close.[26]

Other postulated factors in the collapse of the Old Kingdom command less attention. Did Old Kingdom Egypt so depend on "foreign trade" that disturbances beyond its northern and southern frontiers and the increasing hostility of its neighbors result in a drastic curtailment of needed commodities?[27] Perhaps a demographic problem faced the Pharaohs of the 6th Dynasty. What in fact are the "new cities" that turn up in titles of the 5th and 6th Dynasties, and do they have anything to do with shifts of population?[28] Toward the close of the Old Kingdom we hear of the flight of population from township to township,[29] of corruption and arrests.[30] Was this characteristic of the times?

It would be interesting to learn whether the Egyptians of the outgoing Old Kingdom sensed the impact of any of these factors we have passed in review. The likelihood is that they did not. Literature of the First Intermediate Period is not reticent in assigning causes to national ills, but in the main it tends to externalize the problem. It smacks of timeless psychological defense—it's not *our* failings but the result of outside forces—when someone tries to lay the blame on the king or god himself;[31] and of equal frequency are allusions to the depredations of foreigners from the outside.

Now Egypt of the Old Kingdom had long since secured its northeastern frontier. Fortresses and the commandants thereof are known from the inscriptions.[32] Such titles as "he who is privy to classified information from the foreign entry point"[33] betray concern about who or what can come across the frontier. In the celestial realm even the gods themselves fight on Egypt's behalf to protect the eastern border.[34]

But, after a pattern to be repeated in the long course of Egyptian his-

---

[26] B. Bell, *AJA* 75 (1971), 1ff.; K Butzer, *Early Hydraulic Civilization in Egypt* (Chicago, 1976), 28–29.

[27] Wilson, *Burden*, 100, 108.

[28] *LdÄ*, 2 (1987), 153.

[29] Cf. N. de G. Davies, *The Rock Tombs of Deir el-Gabrawi* (London, 1902), 2: pl. 25: "I resettled underpopulated(?) towns with citizens of other townships; those who had been destined for serfdom therein I made their offices into townships."

[30] Cf. *Urk* I, 233; P. Berlin 8896 (P. C. Smither, *JEA* 28 [1942], 16ff.).

[31] As does Ipuwer: cf. M. Lichtheim, *Ancient Egyptian Literature* (Berkeley, Calif., 1976), 1:149ff.; G. Fecht, *Der Vorwurf an Gott in den "Mahnworten des Ipu-wer"* (Heidelberg, 1972).

[32] D. B. Redford, *JARCE* 23 (1986), 133 and n. 84.

[33] H. Kees, *Nachrichten Göttingen* (1933), 590; on ḥry sšt³, see D. B. Redford, *JSSEA* 15 (1985), 42.

[34] Redford, *JARCE* 23 (1986), 133 and n. 86.

tory, the breakdown of central authority inevitably leads to unguarded frontiers and unrestricted access to the country by foreigners. From the close of the Old Kingdom the resultant pressure of Asiatics is reflected in the texts. The later corpora of the Pyramid Texts speak of "the Ram gate which repulses the Fenekhu," possibly a reference to the potential for foreign incursions into the eastern Delta.[35] Frustration and bluster are characteristic of the times: "fear of me extends to heaven," boasts the deceased, "my slaughter impresses the Fenekhu."[36] The Admonitions of Ipuwer and the Instruction for Merikare make it quite clear that, in the aftermath of the collapse, groups of Asiatics encountered no resistance to their penetration of the Delta. But at most, it could be argued, their ingress was a concomitant, not a cause, of Egypt's troubles.

THE END OF EARLY BRONZE AGE PALESTINE

The archaeological record provides a clear picture of the close of EB III. Sites in Cis-Jordan for the most part do not survive as settlements into the subsequent transitional phase from the Early to the Middle Bronze Age (EB IV–MB I period), and a movement is detectable from large fortified tells to smaller centers. Some destruction is in evidence, but in many cases (it is alleged) the historian is justified in using no more than the term abandonment. In EB IV only Transjordan, parts of the Jordan Valley, and later Negeb exhibit limited settlement; and while there is a clear cultural continuum between EB III and IV, there has come about a marked change in the economy of society. In place of the semi-industrialized society of EB III, which could indulge in international trade, nought is left but rustic pastoralism in which stockbreeding looms large at the expense of agriculture.[37]

That the causes of this breakdown were as complex as those we have elicited for the Egyptian disaster is truistic in the extreme. The older hypothesis of an external agent in the form of an invading community of alien ethnic background, the "Amorite theory,"[38] has foundered on the demonstration that EB III and what came after it constitute a cultural continuum and that the putative newcomers are nowhere to be found, archaeologically or textually. An external agent from the south in the

[35] Faulkner, *The Ancient Egyptian Pyramid Texts. Supplement*, 63; CT I, 302c; E. Edel, *ZÄS* 102 (1975), 36; J. Leclant, *SAK* 2 (1984), 458.

[36] CT III, 394f–g.

[37] S. Richard, *BASOR* 237 (1980), 12; W. Dever, ibid., 38; R. Cohen and W. Dever, *BASOR* 243 (1981), 57ff.; Dever, in *Biblical Archaeology Today* (Jerusalem, 1985), 113ff.; W. Rast, ibid., 155–56; P. Gerstenblith, *The Levant at the Beginning of the Middle Bronze Age* (Philadelphia, 1983), 117.

[38] See, e.g., P. W. Lapp, in J. A. Sandars, ed., *Near Eastern Archaeology in the Twentieth Century* (New York, 1970), 116ff.

form of punitive raids by Egypt likewise appeals no longer to Palestinian archaeologists, convinced as they are that we are dealing with the abandonment, not the destruction, of EB III cities.

The causes currently being considered relate rather to ecology, sociology, and demography.[39] As in northeast Africa, a climatic change may have brought progressive dessication to Palestine and resulted in famine and perhaps disease, With all this, exhaustion of natural resources and political corruption are suggested.

This new approach to the problem far outstrips in perception the old naive theory of an "Amorite invasion"; but there remains a tendency to view the evidence in isolation. First of all, several of the postulates are at present beyond the realm of verification, and probably will remain there permanently. No one has any proof that the Palestinian towns suffered from political corruption, or that they were beset by famine and disease to an inordinate degree. As for the overworking of natural resources, there now appears to be convincing evidence for it; but whether this was cause, concomitant, or result is impossible to say. With respect to climatic change, it may have had some impact on the Levantine littoral; but its precise effect remains to be determined.

It seems to me that one body of evidence deserves closer scrutiny. The discontinuity in the urban tradition at the close of EB III is known primarily from central Palestine, Syria, and at first even Transjordan remaining unaffected.[40] The zone thus delimited belonged precisely within Egypt's sphere of influence; and it is here that we must locate the numerous acts of unbridled bellicosity we have found attested toward the close of the Old Kingdom. The Weny text reflects a determined policy on the part of Pepy I to lay waste extensive tracts of prosperous countryside; and by the time of Pepy II "destroying the fortresses of Asia" had become a cliché.[41] These acts of destruction, moreover, involve demolition after assault, not accidental or intended firings. It would be blind to deny that the increase of a nonurban, transhumant economy in post–EB III Palestine could be put down in large measure to the depredations of the Egyptian armed forces.

EGYPT AND PALESTINE IN THE FIRST INTERMEDIATE PERIOD

Dividing history into periods sounds artificial, and interest in nomenclature the preserve of schoolmen. But to the time under discussion the as-

---

[39] Richard, *Basor* 237 (1980), 25; W. Dever, *BASOR* 210 (1973), 37ff.; idem, in *Biblical Archaeology Today*, 123.

[40] Dever, *BASOR* 237 (1980), 52; idem, in *Biblical Archaeology Today*, 129; Rast, ibid., 155–56; P. Matthiae, *Studies in the History and Archaeology of Jordan* (Amman, 1982), 1:90.

[41] Redford, *JARCE* 23 (1986), 139.

signment of an apt term and a point of division is of more than passing significance. The term Intermediate Period may not satisfy many (including the present author); yet it does embody a widely held value judgment, and corresponds to a period definable by verifiable limits in human experience.

The present divisions in the archaeological history of Palestine, however, strike one as purely arbitrary. For one thing, the use of the qualifiers "Chalcolithic," "Bronze," and "Iron," though once in the early history of the discipline deemed applicable, are now known to be wide off the mark, bronze having come into wide use only in the "Late Bronze Age" and iron only in "Iron II". But these discrepancies can be tolerated, if only because the terminology is of such long-standing that all serious scholars have agreed to maintain it.

With the internal divisions of the "Bronze Age," however, scholars have voiced widespread dissatisfaction.[42] The archaeological explorations between World Wars I and II demonstrated conclusively that from the end of the predynastic period in Egypt until roughly the closing decades of the Old Kingdom Palestine had witnessed the flowering of an indigenous culture developing *in continuum* with limited external influence. This was termed, largely at the instigation of W. F. Albright, "Early Bronze I, II, III." Similarly, from a point roughly contemporary with the mid-13th Dynasty in Egypt until the conquests of the 18th Dynasty, a sedentary culture had held sway in Palestine, identified by artifacts (largely ceramic) and architecture as being of single inspiration and autochthonous evolution. This span of four centuries Albright called "Middle Bronze II A, B, C." But the intervening period posed a problem, and no scholarly consensus has yet emerged. Pursuant to his investigations at Bab edh-dhra east of the Dead Sea, and at Tell Beit-Mirsim, southwest of Jerusalem, Albright identified an "EB IV," a period of urban decline and seminomadism at the end of the third millennium B.C.; and an "MB I" (contemporary with Egypt's 12th Dynasty), a period of complete nomadic culture to the exclusion of city living. Latterly however, scholars have pointed out that it is misleading to refer to the latter as "MB I"; for it is an intrusive culture and not an early stage of MB II. Likewise, EB IV, while morphologically descended from EB III, represents a lapse into nomadism (by survivors?) and shares something in common with the succeeding "MB I" period. Of late the solution to this state of confusion has involved a tendency to lump EB IV and MB I together under a variety of heads: "Intermediate EB–MB I" (Kenyon), "MB I" (Mazar), "Intermediate Bronze" (Lapp, Kochavi), "EB IV, a, b, c" (Dever).

If such lumping has been generally agreed upon, the absolute chronology that delimits the period under discussion has not. Palestinian, Cypri-

[42] Gerstenblith, *The Levant*, 2–3.

ote, and Aegean archaeologists rely, for want in their own baliwicks of king lists, chronicles, and written observations of datable phenomena, on the comparatively firmly dated history of Egypt. In the present case, debate centers on when, in terms of Egyptian chronology, did nomadic society in Palestine give place to the sedentarization of MB II: during the 12th Dynasty (c. 1991–1786 B.C.) or the 13th (c. 1786–1665 B.C.)?[43]

This is not the place to deal *in extenso* with the archaeological evidence from Palestine on the refounding of towns and the evolution of Middle Bronze Age fortifications. The debate now fills the organs of the discipline. What will be done at this point is to pass in review the inscriptional evidence from Egypt from the 9th through 12th Dynasties that has a bearing on not only military and economic interests in western Asia but also the picture of society in the region.

For the two centuries following the end of the Old Kingdom, we possess three major sources that reflect the fact, and the Egyptian perception of, Asiatics on the Eastern frontier and within the Delta. These are the Admonitions of Ipuwer, the Instruction for Merikare, and the Prophecy of Neferty.[44] Of these three the last mentioned was written with the reign of Amenemhat I (c. 1991–1961 B.C.) in mind and must, therefore, belong to the early 12th Dynasty; but it purports to describe conditions prior to the inception of the new regime.

Ipuwer belongs to Egyptian "lament" literature, which became very popular in the Middle Kingdom, and later achieved a sort of classical status.[45] The genre belongs very definitely within the realm of oral composition and tradition, although the dominance of a scribal tradition in ancient Egypt has caused such compositions to attain canonicity in written form.[46] The extant copies of Ipuwer all date to the New Kingdom, but a passage was excerpted as early as the 12th Dynasty for inclusion in the Instruction of Amenemhet; and the historical milieu of the piece clearly points to the period between Pepy II and the rise to power of the 11th Dynasty for its formulation.[47] The composition consists of a long monologue by the wiseman Ipuwer in poetic form (full of mnemonic devices)

[43] Cf. J. M. Weinstein, *BASOR* 217 (1975), 10–11; Gerstenblith, *The Levant*, 101–8.

[44] For the pertinent bibliography, see Wilson in *ANET*², 414, 441, 444; Lichtheim, *Literature*, 1:98, 139, 150; W. Helck, *Die Lehre für König Merikare* (Wiesbaden, 1977), 1; idem, *Die Prophezeiung des Nfr.ty* (Wiesbaden, 1970), 1–2; H. Goedicke, *The Protocol of Neferyt* (Baltimore, 1977), 1ff.; R. J. Williams, *JAOS* 101 (1981), 1ff. The particular designations are those of modern scholarship, the ancient titles having been lost.

[45] Egyptian *nhwt*: H. Grapow, *Sprachliche und Schriftliche Formung ägyptischer Texten* (Glückstadt, 1936), 60, n. 29; contrast H. Goedicke, *The Report about the Dispute of a Man with His Ba* (Baltimore, 1970), 183.

[46] See my forthcoming *Oral Tradition and the Scribe in Ancient Egyptian Historiography.*

[47] I have argued this date elsewhere: cf. *King-lists*, 144, n. 69. Van Seter's date in the Second Intermediate Period (*JEA* 50 [1964], 13–23) has long since been rejected.

describing the lamentable state of the land in the throes of anarchy and revolution. Toward the close the poet turns his rage against the "Eternal Lord" (the sun-god), to whom he appears to have been speaking, and ends in a diatribe on the Almighty's negligence.

Ipuwer does not dwell on the Asiatic threat to Egypt at length, but he does in fact mention their presence within the land as a consequence of the weakness of the government. "Lo, the face grows pale (for) the bowman is ensconced, wrong doing is everywhere, and there is no man of yesterday" (2, 2). "Lo, the desert pervades the land, townships are laid waste, and a foreign bow-people are come to Egypt!" (3, 1). "Lo, the entire Delta is no longer hidden . . . foreign peoples are conversant with the livelihood of the delta" (4, 5–8). "People flee . . . and it is tents that they make like bedu" (10, 1–2). "The bedu are apprised of the state of the land, which indeed formerly all foreign people showed respect for" (15, 1–2).

Akhtoy III (?), father of king Merikare of the 10th Dynasty, purports to be the author of a book of instruction, which to the ancients would have been classified with the category of *seboye*, "teaching, wisdom."[48] While most exemplars of this genre take the form of the fatherly chat to a son about how to make his own way in the world, and preach the same pragmatic wisdom to be found alike in the Book of Proverbs and Dale Carnegie's *How to Win Friends and Influence People*, Merikare is unique in that both father and son are royalty; and Akhtoy's words therefore frequently approximate a Macchiavellian discourse on statecraft. The father often draws on his own experience, a bent that rejoices the heart of the historian in a period short on historical texts. In the course of ruminating on various threats to the security of the kingdom, Akhtoy has occasion to dwell at length on the Asiatics of his day:

The East has a wealth of bow-people . . . (but) look! [the land] which they destroyed is (now) made into townships and very many townspeople [are there] (pp. 83–86). . . . Speak now of the bowman! Lo, the vile Asiatic! It goes ill with the place where he is, lacking in water and covered in brushwood, the paths thereof tortuous because of the mountains. He never dwells in one place but has been forced to stray through want, traversing the lands on foot. He has been fighting since the time of Horus, never conquering nor yet being conquered. He never announces a day for fighting, like an outlaw thief of a (criminal) gang. But as I live! As long as I was around those bowmen were walled off, and the fortress that lay open I closed up on them(?). And so I made the

---

[48] On "Wisdom," see M. V. Fox, *ZÄS* 107 (1980), 120ff.; E. Hornung and O. Keel, *Studien zu altägyptische Lebenslehren* (Göttingen, 1979); R. J. Williams, in J. R. Harris, ed., *The Legacy of Egypt*² (London, 1971), 257ff.; idem, *JAOS* 92 (1972), 215ff.; idem, *JAOS* 101 (1981), 1–19.

Delta smite them, and I plundered their chattels and siezed their cattle. . . . Don't give them a thought! The Asiatic is a crocodile on the riverbank: he snatches on the lonely road, (but) he will never seize at the harbor of a populous city (pp. 91–98).

There is no better description in Egyptian literature of the transhumant pastoralist of western Asia. Although he possesses chattels and cattle, he is always on the move and perpetually in want. Given to fighting and incapable of being subdued because of his furtive and unorthodox methods of fighting, the Asiatic is nonetheless naught but a marauder on a small scale, easily intimidated by manned forts and populous urban centers.

Committed to writing in the reign of Senwosret I as a piece of transparent propaganda, the prophecy of Neferty comprises a prediction of the "Time of Troubles" at the close of the First Intermediate Period and the restoration of the kingdom by the 12th Dynasty.[49] The whole is placed in the mouth of the wiseman Neferty (who may or may not be historical) and backdated to the reign of Sneferu of the 4th Dynasty. As such the piece preserves a vivid picture of the state of affairs in Egypt and adjacent parts of Asia during the last decades of the third millennium B.C.

He (i.e., Neferty) meditated on what would happen in the land and called to mind the state of the east, how the Asiatics would come in their might, bringing terror to the hearts of those who are at harvest, and seizing the teams as they ploughed (Pet. 17–19). . . . A foreign bird shall lay her young in the marshes of the Delta, when she has made her nest close to the townsfolk. People shall welcome her in through want (Pet. 29–30). . . . All good things are gone and the land is prostrate through misery because of those well-provisioned Asiatics throughout the land. Enemies have put in an appearance in the East, and Asiatics will descend upon Egypt. The keep is invested (even when) help is near, and its garrison will pay no heed: the siege ladder will be run up in the night, the fortress entered and the ramparts crossed while people slumber. I go to rest saying "I (must) stay awake!" The wildlife of the desert will drink at the river of Egypt, and through lack of someone to drive them away will refresh themselves on their (sic) banks (Pet. 31–37). . . . The Asiatics shall not be allowed to come down to Egypt, that they might ask for water beggar-fashion to water their flocks (Pet. 67–68).

In some respects that Asiatic in Neferty resembles the description vouchsafed by the Instruction for Merikare, about one hundred years earlier. He is still characterized by his dependence on cattle for his livelihood, and is avid of the water resources of the Delta to water his flocks. His

[49] For the propaganda output of Senwosret I, see G. Posener, *Literatur et politique dans l'Égypte de la XIIe dynastie* (Paris, 1956).

obsequiousness is remarked upon as a well-known trait. But in contrast to his ancestors he now descends upon Egypt in strength, raids farms, steals cattle, settles down, and enjoys the fraternization of the natives. If the third pericope translated is understood correctly, he has even mastered the art of siege warfare. Neferty's evidence will be of some significance later in our discussion of the civil war that preceded the 12th Dynasty.

THE AGRESSIVE POLICY OF THE 11TH DYNASTY

For all his pride in having restored the inviolability of his eastern frontier, Merikare's father never claims to have carried war into Asia; and contemporary tomb scenes do not show or imply the presence of Asiatics in Egypt. We are probably correct, therefore, in concluding that the Herakleopolitan regime was obliged, *faute de mieux*, to confine its interests to its own restricted bailiwick.

This all changed, however, with the collapse of Herakleopolis. About 2050 B.C. the rebel Theban kingdom in the south, under the leadership of its king Montuhotpe I,[50] defeated the forces of the 10th Dynasty, destroyed Herakleopolis, and reunited Egypt under the Theban 11th Dynasty. The pent-up energies of the belligerent though backward southland now found an outlet in the resumption of punitive razzias into Asia along the lines practised by the Old Kingdom monarchs.

The evidence for the pursuance of this policy under Montuhotpe seems to increase yearly. Not only do we possess the rather stereotyped scenes of headsmiting showing the king "wielding the throw-stick (against) the eastern foreign lands," equivocal attestations[51] at best, but also specific references, both royal and private, to military activity in Asia. A fragmentary stela from Deir el-Ballas, just north of Thebes, mentions the "*Qedem*-lands"—that is, the territory of Coele-Syria—in a military context.[52] The king's steward Henenu states in his biographical inscription: "[My lord l.p.h. despatched me] to create an army [. . . in order to subdue (?) them-who-are-across]-the sand," and later alludes to "[cedar] of the cedar slopes."[53] The king's general, Antef, includes in his tomb a fascinating

---

[50] With the praenomen Neb-hepet-re. On the variety of the name-forms adopted by this king, see D. Arnold, *MDAIK* 24 (1969), 38ff.; H. Goedicke, *JSSEA* 12 (1982), 157–58. For the date of the fall of Herakleopolis, see F. Gomàa, *Ägypten während der Ersten Zwischenzeit* (Wiesbaden, 1980), 157.

[51] For the reliefs and texts from Gebelein, Thebes, and Dendara, see W. Schenkel, *Memphis, Herakleopolis, Theben* (Wiesbaden, 1964), 209–10, 216ff.; J. J. Clère and J. Vandier, *Textes de la première period intermédiaire* (Brussels, 1949), 36ff.

[52] H. G. Fischer, *Inscriptions from the Coptite Nome* (Rome, 1964), pl. 37; Schenkel, *Memphis*, 214ff.

[53] W. C. Hayes, *JEA* 35 (1949), pl. 4; Schenkel, *Memphis*, 242–43.

depiction of a river fight and the siege of a fortress.[54] Although no text glosses the scene, it is clear that the attackers are Egyptian, while Asiatic soldiers defend from the parapets. In light of the unanimous testimony of the archaeological and textual record that EB IV Palestine knew only a nomadic, transhumant society, one might be inclined to discount the weight of Antef's pictorial claim: was he not a military man, and was not the genre of siege scenes popular at the time? On the other hand Syria and parts of the coast and Transjordan continued to support some urban centers; and the scene in Antef's tomb displays a sufficient number of peculiar details to cast doubt on the allegation that it is merely a stereotype.

Most revealing, perhaps, is the scrawled graffito of one Tjehemau, a Nubian mercenary, who left an account of his career on the rocks at Abisko, south of Aswan.[55] The text reads: "Stela that Tjehemau made (in?) the year of smiting the foreign land. 'The year when I began to go to war was in the time of Nebhepetre (i.e., Montuhotpe I) in the army, when he came to Buhen.[56] My son embarked with me to (meet) the king. He fared through the entire land, having purposed to slay the Asiatics of D^3ty, and he (the king?) sailed southward with the wind.' " Overlooking the amusing boast of having won the day single-handed, Tjehemau's account one must conclude is a relatively sober description of a historical campaign in Asia under Montuhotpe I. Where D^3ty is to be located poses problems; but the transcription suggests an original $Z/Ṣ-R-T1(\ )$. Interestingly a Zarethan is known from the Jordan Valley.[57]

[54] J. Leclant, *Orientalia* 34 (1965), 185–86, figs. 8–11; O. Keel, *VT* 25 (1975), 419, fig. 1.

[55] Redford, *JARCE* 23 (1986), 129, n. 41.

[56] The chief Egyptian administrative center at the Second Cataract.

[57] Josh. 3:16; cf. Jud. 7:22.

CHAPTER 4

"Trampling the Foreign Lands": Egypt and Asia during the Middle Kingdom

THE PERIOD OF roughly four centuries that intervenes between the triumph of Montuhotpe I and the advent of the Hyksos remains one of the most enigmatic periods in the sphere of foreign relations this book attempts to address. In contrast to the empire period that follows, the Middle Kingdom and the Second Intermediate Period have bequeathed us precious little evidence. Even the historical events are poorly known, and policy and motivation are often the subject of sheer speculation. So preliminary is the state of our historical researches in the period that the publication of a new stela often changes the picture completely, or appears to do so. This being the case, one must proceed with caution and with one's critical wits well honed in order to produce a passable analysis of Egypt's relations with Palestine during this period.

THE CIVIL WAR

The 11th Dynasty, to which Montuhotpe I belonged, suffered an abrupt termination within fifteen years of the death of that great monarch. No connected account of the disaster has survived, but the scattered pieces of circumstantial evidence agree sufficiently to support the postulate of a disastrous civil war.

It was apparently upon the second successor of Montuhotpe I that the blow fell, one Neb-towi-re Montuhotpe (III), whose name significantly does not appear either in the king list or the ancestral offering lists.[1] He is known primarily in inscriptions from quarries, especially those in Wadi Hammamat. These are remarkable for their number, size, and excellence of execution.

The purpose of the mission was the routine quarrying of stone for a sarcophagus, and nothing out of the ordinary; but, we are told, Min the god of the highland, so loved "his son" the king that he performed two miracles for him. The first[2] involved "the coming of a pregnant gazelle

---

[1] D. B. Redford, *Pharaonic King-lists, Annals and Day-books* (Toronto, 1986), 15; termed Montuhotpe IV by Von Beckerath: *LdÄ* 4 (1982), 69–70.

[2] J. Couyat and P. Montet, *Les inscriptions hiéroglyphiques et hiératiques de Ouadi Hammamat* (Cairo, 1912), no. 110.

moving straight toward the people in front of her . . . without turning back, until she reached (this part of) the noble mountain and this (very) block while it was still in position. . . . Then she gave birth upon it, while this army of the king was looking on." Not content with this, Min performed again:

> The power of this god was seen and his might manifested to the plebs: the upland was turned into a lake, and water arose over the hard stone. (For) a well was found in the midst of the valley, 10 cubits square (c. five meters square), filled with water to its brim, kept pure and clean from the gazelles and hidden from the mountain tribesmen. It had been bypassed by the former expeditions of kings who were aforetime; but no eye had seen it, nor human gaze fallen upon it. Only to His Majesty alone was it revealed.[3]

These were wonders indeed, sufficient to excite the admiration of the populace, but they would never have been recorded had Amenemhet, the leader of the expedition, not wished it. And oddly enough he figures in one inscription much more prominently and with much more effusive self-praise than any other expedition leader before or since in the valley inscriptions.[4]

With such a paragon of administrative skill and moral rectitude as prime minister, one wonders why King Montuhotpe did not simply retire and transfer the reins of power to his right-hand man. That Amenemhet did indeed shortly find the reigns of power in his hands makes the preceding sentence less facetious than it appears. Already in the Wady Hammamat inscriptions one senses a situation not fully explained by the wordy texts. Why the insistence on miracles? Why is Amenemhet so prominent? Did the purpose of the expedition necessitate such an extensive mustering of manpower from all over Egypt? The figure of ten thousand men is certainly substantial, and far in excess of what would be required for the quarrying and transport of the paltry number of blocks Amenemhet was after.

But Amenemhet was not alone in executing assignments abroad on behalf of King Neb-towi-re. At an unknown date in the same reign "the general responsible for the highlands and steward over Egypt . . . Se'onkh" went to Hammamat with an "army" of 130 (including children as well as adults) recruited from Middle Egypt.[5] In Neb-towy-re's first year a "commander of alien (troops) and steward" Shed-ptah son of Antef was despatched to Wady el-Hudy in the south."[6]

---

[3] Ibid., no. 191.

[4] Ibid., 79–81 (no. 113).

[5] Ibid., no. 1.

[6] A. Fakhry, *The Inscriptions of the Amethyst Quarries at Wady el-Hudi* (Cairo, 1952), 19ff. (figs. 14–17).

Again from a quarry, this time the alabaster quarry at Hatnub, comes an even more suggestive group of texts chronicling the exploits of Count Nehry and his two sons Kay and Thutnakht.[7] The inscriptions bear dates in regnal years 5 through 8 and, although these are assigned to the "reign" of Nehry himself, there can be no doubt that the events they speak of occurred during the transition from the 11th to the 12th Dynasty.[8] Nehry, who was the nomarch of the fifteenth township of Upper Egypt with its capital at Hermopolis, describes himself with the braggadocio common to the biographical statements of the time:[9] "Count, controller of the Two Thrones, superintendent of prophets, baron of the Hare Nome (i.e., the fifteenth township), acquaintance of the king, foremost of the southland . . . a brave commoner . . . whose arrival is awaited everywhere, possessed of a strong arm, greatly loved, whom the king said to summon on the day of council—this entire land subsists through every policy he enunciates!" The inscriptions of all three men boast of the participation of each in the internecine strife of a period of stasis in the kingdom. Nehry records the curious fact that the king had challenged him.[10] " 'Draw you up the battle line! See, I too am in battle line!' (But I was) a fortress for fighting in *Shedyet-sha* to which all the people rallied . . . skipper of all the people, who rescued [his city on the day of terror] instigated by the king's house." Kay is even more specific. Charged with mustering the militia of Hermopolis, he claims[11] "I recruited (the city's) draftees of young men in order that its levies be numerous; for the draftees had retired into the (ranks of the) commons, dwelling in their houses, and never marched forth during the period of terror of the king's house"; and again[12] "I trained my draftees of young men and went to fight along with my city. I acted as its fortress in *Shedyet-sha*. When there was no one with me except my retainers; the Medjay, Wawat, southerners, Asiatics, the Southland and the Delta being united against me. I emerged, the affair being a success, my entire city being with me without loss."

Through the hyperbole one can visualize a civil war in which, *inter alia*, a small township found itself pitted against government forces ("the king's house"), but happily had allied itself with the side that won out.

[7] R. Anthes, *Die Felseninschriften von Hatnub* (Leipzig, 1929), nos. 16–26.

[8] Debate has warmed in the past over the precise date of Nehry and Kay, but in fact there can be little doubt that their floruits must be placed just prior to the assumption of power by Amenemhet I: see the principal discussions by R. Anthes, *ZÄS* 59 (1924), 100–108; R. O. Faulkner, *JEA* 30 (1944), 61–63; E. Blumenthal, *Altorientalische Forschungen* 4 (1976), 35–62; W. K. Simpson, *LdÄ* 2 (1977), 1043–45; and especially H. O. Willems, *JEOL* 28 (1985), 80–102.

[9] Anthes, *Felseninschriften*, no. 20.

[10] Ibid., no. 25:6–12.

[11] Ibid., no. 24:2ff.

[12] Ibid., no. 16:4–8.

Kay's exaggeration may amuse us, but it is interesting that he includes Asiatics among his opponents and, by implication, allies of the king's house.

Texts from Amenemhet, after he took the throne as founder of the 12th Dynasty, and his coterie are quite vague, and help very little in delineating the cause of the strife. In the posthumous testament of Amenemhet I for his son Senwosret I,[13] from the grave as it were, he describes his seizure of power in the following words:[14] "I tramped to Elephantine, I went in the opposite direction as far as the Delta swamps; I stood on the limits of the land and surveyed its interior. I curbed lions and caught crocodiles, I supressed those of Wawat and caught the Medjay; I made the Asiatics do the 'dogwalk' ."[15] In other words, he physically touched the limits of the land, thus taking possession of it, and taking stock of it; as an elemental colossus of nature and human society alike, he quelled both wild beasts and wild foreigners, both north and south. This is nothing more than the fulfillment of the expected role of the good Pharaoh: we can scarcely squeeze these statements to provide any factual history.[16]

The autobiographical statement of one Khnumhotpe who participated in the civil war is only slightly more helpful.[17] Khnumhotpe, later appointed count of a small subdivision of the sixteenth township of Upper Egypt, says:

> [The Majesty of my lord] l.p.h. the king of Upper and Lower Egypt Sehtepibre, son of Re, Amenemhet (I), living for ever and ever!—appointed me retainer(?) . . . I embarked with him to ⌜Upper Egypt⌝ (?) in a flotilla of 20 cedar ships. Then he came (back) having calmed the land and subdued it along both banks. The southerners ⌜restrained⌝ (their) evil, the Asiatic nomads fell back; he gave regulations to the land, foreign parts being treated (?) as the "Two Banks." . . . the commons were established in their stations, and the kingship came to rest [with the Uraeus] upon the brow of her master.

Apart from the references to Khnumhotpe'a appointment and participation, and to the fleet of twenty boats, the text comprises the expected platitudes: the land put to rest, foreigners quelled, the common people put in their place, and the kingship reestablished. In a word, *ma'at* (order, truth, justice) has been reintroduced into nature and human society. We

[13] See W. Helck, *Der Text der "Lehre Amenemhets I für seiner Sohn"* (Wiesbaden, 1969); Lichtheim, *Ancient Egyptian Literature* (Berkeley, Calif., 1976), 1:135–39.

[14] Helck, *Text*, 68–78.

[15] For the last expression, see the literature in ibid., 79, n. *a*.

[16] W. A. Ward, *Egypt and the East Mediterranean World 2200-1900 B.C.* (Beirut, 1971), 67.

[17] P. E. Newberry, *Beni Hasan* (London, 1893), 1: pl. 44; *Urk* VII, 12; J. H. Breasted, *Ancient Records of Egypt* (Chicago, 1906), 1: sec. 465.

are vouchsafed no clues whatsoever from this text as to who was Amenemhet's principal adversary, or in which part of the land the battle took
place; and it is nothing but wishful thinking to postulate a locale in the
northeast Delta and a prior interest in the route to Byblos.[18]

Briefly to sum up the investigation to this point: the evidence we have
adduced is woefully short on detail and has suppressed fact in favor of
comforting stereotype. Through the verbiage we can discern: an unusual
mustering of manpower by influential officials early in the reign of Neb-
towy-re Montuhotpe; a period of "terror" perpetrated by the king's
house; civil strife in which opportunists like Nehry and Khnumhotpe
took sides with Amenemhet and were later rewarded with baronies; a
great battle in a place (?) called *Shedyet-sha*, involving foreign mercenaries as well as Egyptians; and punitive campaigns north and south, undertaken by Amenemhet after the victory was won.

The Asiatic role in all this does not loom large, at least not on the evidence presented. But additional texts are now available that put the matter in a slightly different light.

Twenty years into the floruit of the new regime, Amenemhet for
reasons unclear associated his son, the future Senwosret I, with him as
joint ruler upon the throne of Egypt. During the ten years this coregency
was to run, the young heir presumptive had already decided upon a program of temple building.[19] In the third year of the coregency Semwosret
proclaimed that he would refurbish the temple of Atum and build his
palace in Heliopolis. By the ninth year he had turned his attention to
the south. In that year, according to an inscription recopied in the 18th
Dynasty by Thutmose III, Senwosret convened his court and, although
the remainder of the text is lost, he probably announced his intention to
build a temple of Amun at Thebes. Around the same time must fall visits
by the king to points further south, and the setting up of inscriptions at
Tod[20] and Elephantine.[21] The shrines at both sites were abandoned and
in ruins.

There can be no question from the content of the inscriptions that the
king pins the blame on the agency of foreigners. References to the "terraces" (i.e., the slopes of the Lebanons) and "Asiatics" leave no doubt as
to whom the king had in mind; and the severity of the punishment yields
a clue to the seriousness with which Senwosret viewed the whole affair.

---

[18] W. A. Ward, *Index of Egyptian Administrative and Religious Titles of the Middle Kingdom* (Beirut, 1982), 66. His reading *I[met]* (*JEA* 55 [1969], 215–16) is wrong; the text has
Šm³w, "Southland."

[19] See W. K. Simpson, *LdÄ* 5 (1984), 890–99.

[20] W. K. Simpson, *LdÄ* 5 (1984, 898, n. 15; W. Helck, in *Ägypten, Dauer und Wandel*
(Mainz, 1985), 45–52; D. B. Redford, *JSSEA* 17(1987), 36–55.

[21] W. Schenkel, *MDAIK* 31 (1975), pl. 33(a); W. Helck, *MDAIK* 34 (1978), 69ff.

But when did all this happen? What situation would have permitted Asiatics to run amok inside Egypt? Since Senwosret is clearly describing a general condition of ruination he witnessed early in his coregency, the event must have transpired sometime prior to his appointment. Indeed, to account for overgrown ruins, silted-up wells, blocked-up canals, and the like, we must postulate the passage of years, not months, and cannot help but be tempted to see in the king's vivid word pictures the aftermath of the civil war. Neferty, as we have seen, hints at the trespassing of the frontiers and the investment and destruction of forts and towns; now the Tod text suggests that the affects were sufficiently grievous to engage the resources of the state many years in the process of rebuilding. That Senwosret I was still thus engaged and considerably exercised as well over the depredations of the Asiatics makes us painfully aware of the importance of a page of history we seem to have almost wholly lost.

"Retenu Belongs to Thee Like Thy Dogs!"[22]

Over fifty years ago the gifted Biblical scholar and archaeologist W. F. Albright opined that "the Pharaohs of the 12th Dynasty claimed, and often held, the suzerainty over Palestine and Phoenicia extending their influence as far as Ugarit and Qatna."[23] Twenty-four years later he remained committed to "the conquest of Phoenicia by the Thebaid kings of the 12th Dynasty,"[24] and seems never to have changed his mind.[25]

It might be contended that Albright had a tendency to adopt a position on an ad hoc basis before all the evidence had been garnered. And in the present case it was easy to point to the paucity, or total absence, of Egyptian objects from Palestinian contexts in that period contemporary with the 12th Dynasty.[26] Statues of Egyptian noblemen of Middle Kingdom date excavated in Palestine could easily and persuasively be proved to have been deposited in their archaeological find spots decades or centuries after their manufacture, and therefore are not evidence of Egyptian occupation.[27] Moreover, a perusal of Egyptian historical texts of the 12th Dynasty revealed but one dubious record of a military campaign into western Asia, namely that of Senwosret III (c. 1878–1842 B.C.) to the land of *Skmm* (usually identified with Shechem) mentioned by one of his

[22] Sinuhe B 223.
[23] *JPOS* 15 (1935), 221. Of course Albright was careful to "stress the fact that the imperial organization of the Middle Empire must have been very loose in comparison with the practice of the new . . ."
[24] *BASOR* 155 (1959), 33.
[25] Cf. his views on MB I Megiddo as an Egyptian fortress: *BASOR* 168 (1962), 39.
[26] J. M. Weinstein, *BASOR* 217 (1975), 1–16.
[27] W. Helck, *UF* 8 (1976), 101–14.

soldiers Sebekkhu.[28] And when to this evidence is added what appears to be the unequivocal testimony of Sinuhe regarding the foreign policy of Senwosret I—"he will seize the southern lands, he will not be concerned about the northern countries"[29]—it seemed certain that the 12th Dynasty had purposely turned its back on western Asia.

Yet a growing body of evidence sounds a discordant note in what we have been given to understand is a harmonious strain. Both kings and commoners glory in epithets constructed around claimed victories over Asiatics. Senwosret I is "he for whom all lands are bound,"[30] "throat slitter of them that are in Asia."[31] Montuhotpe, vizier and treasurer of Senwosret I, calls himself "one that put his (the king's) terror among the foreigners, who put to silence them that are across the sand";[32] Montemhet, the general is "he whom the king recommends before his nobles to put down the enemies of Asia, the rebels of the northern lands."[33] The "very great general of the entire land," Nessumontu,[34] describes how, late in the reign of Amenemhet I, he "destroyed the wild bow-people, namely them that are across the sand. I demolished fortresses and prowled like a jackal (?) on the desert edge, roving freely through the streets."[35] In the reign of Amenemhet III, Amenemhet's commander of shock troops boasts of having "smitten the Nubians and opened the land of the Asiatics";[36] some forty-three years later the treasurer Ptah-wer claims to have "˥bound˺ Asia for Him-that-is-in-the-Palace."[37]

If the sincerity of these speakers may be called in question by the obvious bombast of their declamations, certain other passages of a casual, non-self-serving nature tend to underscore their witness. From a tomb of the reign of Amenemhet II or Senwosret II (nineteenth century B.C.) comes a painting of cattle with the identifying caption "cattle of the Asiatics brought as [. . .]."[38] A Middle Kingdom literary piece, belonging to the genre of "oratory," [39] commences: "Beginning of the discourse which the priest of Sakhmet Rensoneb said [when] he [came back(?)] from Syria in

[28] See now J. Baines, in M. Görg, ed, *Form und Mass* (Wiesbaden, 1987), 43–61.

[29] Sinhue B 71–72.

[30] A. H. Gardiner and J. Černý, *The Inscriptions of Sinai* (Oxford, 1952), no. 64 (pl. 19).

[31] E. Blumenthal, *Untersuchungen zum ägyptischen Königtum des mittleren Reiches* (Berlin, 1970), 1:229.

[32] Cairo 20593 verses 10–11.

[33] J. J. Janssen, *Ar Or* 20 (1952), 442–45; D. Dunham, *Second Cataract Forts*, vol. 1: *Semna-Kummeh* (Boston, 1960), 59, pl. 90, fig. 4(2).

[34] D. Wildung, *MDAIK* 37 (1981), 506, fig. 2.

[35] K. Sethe, *Ägyptische Lesestücke* (Leipzig, 1928), 82, lines 12–15.

[36] Couyat and Montet, *Inscriptions*, 48, no. 43, pl. 13.

[37] Gardiner and Černý, *Sinai*, p. 18, no. 54.

[38] A. M. Blackman, *The Rock-Tombs of Meir* (London, 1915) pl. 4.

[39] *Mdt*, literally "word, discourse"; on the genre, see G. Posener, *RdE* 6 (1951), 46–47.

the suite of the superintendent of treasurers Senebtify."[40] In addition to this, administrative documents from the eighteenth and seventeenth centuries B.C. make occasional mention of Asiatics, both men and women, employed in sundry services associated with temples and private estates as domestics, doorkeepers, or dancers.[41] Once a chieftain is attested.[42] Most bear assumed Egyptian names, often compounded with "Ptah," as though Memphis were a sort of clearinghouse for Asian immigrants. One roster of domestics on a private estate comprising seventy-seven legible names (of an original ninety-five) shows at least forty-eight to have been Amorite, and mainly female.[43]

This evidence cannot be shoved aside. On the one hand, the epithets unequivocally claim the king's right to punish and exploit Asia, and record the fact that he and his lackeys did so. On the other, passing references in business documents reveal the presence in Egypt of the sort of booty and personnel to be expected from such expeditions.

The publication in 1980[44] of an important new inscription from Saqqara fully confirms the direction the discussion is taking at this point, and casts a flood of light on what the Egyptians really wanted in Asia, and how they went about getting it. As presently preserved the inscription has lost its beginning and ending, and in consequence the intent of the sculpting scribe in copying it out is lost to us. But there can be little doubt that we are dealing with an original and extended excerpt from the daybook of the king's house,[45] secondarily committed to stone, perhaps the events of an *annus mirabilis* deemed so important that publication on a monument was considered appropriate.

The text as preserved begins with a record of festival offerings and pious donations (undoubtedly of royal authorization) to the deceased Senwosret I, including a processional statue of Amenemhet II, offering tables, and containers and their contents for the cult of Senwosret I in the mortuary temple of Tety (x 1–7). Then (x + 7) comes the laconic statement "dispatch of the army to Khenty-she (i.e., the Lebanese coast)." The next

[40] G. Posener, *MDAIK* 25 (1969), 101ff.

[41] L. Borchardt, *ZÄS* 37 (1900), 98.

[42] W. Wreszinski, *Aegyptische Inschiften aus dem Königliche Hofmuseum in Wein* (Leipzig, 1906), 27, no. 32.

[43] W. C. Hayes, *A Papyrus of the Late Middle Kingdom in the Brooklyn Museum* (Brooklyn, 1955), 87–109; W. F. Albright, *JAOS* 74 (1954), 222–32.

[44] S. Farag, *RdE* 32 (1980), 75ff.

[45] On daybooks, see D. B. Redford, *LdÄ* 6 (1986), 151–53; idem, *King-lists*. The interest of the present inscription is precisely that of a daybook: dispatch to the palace of Amenemhet II; disbursements of commodities, booty, and cult objects to the ancestral cults; distribution of rewards; perambulations of the court, etc.

column records "the dispatch of the army together with the commander of elite troops and (the commander of) the army to hack up *Iw³s* (in) Asia [. . .]." There follows the record of benefactions to the god Montu and a goddess, and then the arrival of Nubians and Asiatics with tribute (x + 11–13). Next comes the entry "arrival of the army sent to the turquoise terraces. What they brought: . . ." (a list of commodities, some in large quantity). Following a list of cultic benefactions, including a number of architectural pieces for a temple of Senwosret I,[46] comes the entry: "coming . . . of the suppliants of the *Tmp³w*. With them they brought: lead, 238 ingots [. . . (x + 16) Arrival (?)] of the shock troops sent to destroy (the towns of) *Iw³y* and *I³sy*.[47] Tally of prisoners of war brought back from these two foreign lands: 1,554 Asiatics; copper-cum-wood:[48] (battle)-axes, 10; scimitars,[49] 33; daggers, 12; knives (?), 11 . . ." The list goes on to include ingots of copper, peeling knives, javelins, gold, staves, lapis, gems, and Asiatic pottery. "⟨Return of⟩ the army dispatched to Khenty-she in 10 ships. What they brought: silver, 1665 units [. . . (x + 19) . . .] gold (?) 4882 units, copper 15,961 units . . ." There follows an extensive tally of items, all listed in substantial quantity, including edibles, precious stones, oil, trees, copper weapons (inlaid with gold, silver, and ivory), vessels, wine, and precious wood. The remaining columns of text record the recreation of the king and court on an outing to the Fayum, the rewarding of the military officers charged with the expeditions, and the beginning (apparently) of the entry for a new regnal year of Amenemhet II.

It would be difficult to exaggerate the importance of this document. Suddenly, as it were, the veil is lifted on the 12th Dynasty, and we see a court and government immensely rich, powerful, and efficient, able to work its will not only inside the country but beyond the borders as well. Moreover, one senses the resolve to be ruthless. In a single year paramilitary expeditions of some size are dispatched to tap the resources of Sinai and the Lebanons, two punitive campaigns are mounted against three Asiatic places, and tribute-bearing suppliants arrive from Kush and perhaps Asia. The amount of produce, minerals, and manufactures brought back are enormous, and even the number of prisoners is substantial, al-

[46] Kheperkare.

[47] For indentifications of the place-names in the text, see W. Helck, *GM* 109 (1989), 27–30. *Iw³s* is New Kingdom Alse (E. Edel, *Orientalia* 48 [1979], 82–85); *I³sy* seems to be Alashiya (Cyprus); for *Tmp³w* cf. *Ibr* at Ugarit (C. Gordon, *Ugaritic Handbook* [Rome, 1956], no. 2643).

[48] I.e., the general entry for the weaponry which follows. Manufactured items of metal hafted on to wooden handles is what is meant.

[49] Literally, "reaping implements" as the determinative shows.

though the numbers of weapons (which *may* indicate the number of enemy dead in conflict) appear modest. No longer can scholars contend that the Middle Kingdom had no interest in Asia: it is now abundantly clear that, in imitation of their Old Kingdom forebears, the Pharaohs of the 12th and 13th Dynasties viewed hither Asia and the Levant as theirs to exploit to the full.

On the other hand, it is equally clear that we cannot speak of "empire" in the formal sense. Titles denoting colonization, occupation, and military surveillance are certainly known from the Middle Kingdom, but they turn up mainly in the Nubian theater. In the north a prior decision had been taken already in the days of the 10th Dynasty to "hold the line." At that time cities along the eastern frontier of the Delta had been peopled and fortified in an effort to provide protection against the depredations of the Asiatics.[50] With the coming to power of Amenemhet I a new fortress had been erected, probably in the Wady Tumilat, and dubbed "The Wall of the Ruler."[51] Further north, at the beginning of the "Ways of Horus," that tract of barren desert northeast of the eastern tip of the Delta,[52] there was ensconced a "commander . . . in charge of the (border) patrol," a platoon of police responsible for the oversight of the neighboring wastes.[53] But among the communities beyond the Sinai no attempt was made to exert any sort of permanent control.

This statement can be made with confidence, since the argument from silence on this occasion is cogent. Numerous private inscriptions, in addition to the annalistic text already reviewed conspire to leave us in no doubt as to the presence and purpose of Egyptians beyond the Delta frontier. There were "prospectors," "who course through the lands,"[54] looking for mineral-bearing regions and produce that might be of use to Pharaoh. In their wake came the paramilitary to "open up the foreign lands, trampling through every land,"[55] treading through the foreign lands for

---

[50] For Tel ed-Dabʿa in the First Intermediate Period, see M. Bietak, *Avaris and Pi-Ramesse* (London, 1981), 290; for the "Mansion-of-the-Roads-of-Akhtoy," see H. Kees, *MDAIK* 18 (1962), 9; for construction and occupation of the fortified frontier town at Ezbet Rushdi under Amenemhet I, see S. Adam, *ASAE* 56 (1959), 213–14. Tell er-Retabeh in the Wady Tumilat was apparently already fortified in the 10th Dynasty: for a jaspar weight of Neb-kau-akhtoy, see W.M.F. Petrie, *Hyksos and Israelite Cities* (London, 1928), 32, pl. 32A.

[51] Mentioned in Neferty (W. Helck, *Die Prophezeihung des Nfr.tj* [Wiesbaden, 1970], 56) and Sinuhe B 16, possibly to be identified with Tell er-Retabeh (F. Gomàa, *Die Besiedlung Ägyptens ïwarhend des Mittleren Reiches* [Wiesbaden, 1987], 2:129–30.

[52] On the "Ways of Horus," see Gomàa, *Besiedlung*, 224–25.

[53] Sinhue B 242.

[54] *Smntyw*: see H. G. Fischer, *GM* 84 (1975), 25ff.; K. J. Seyfried, *GM* 20 (1976), 45ff.; the epithet is taken from the Tod texts of Senwosret I.

[55] Couyat and Montet, *Inscriptions*, 48, pl. 5, no. 17; pl. 13, no. 43; Gardiner and Černý, *Sinai*, pl. 18, no. 54; pl. 22, no. 88.

the Lord of the two Lands (on) missions of Horus of the Palace, quelling the foreign lands."[56] Then came the "treasurers and god's chancellors"[57] with armies of technicians, "commanding multitudes in an alien land . . . attaining the limits of foreign lands on foot, treading difficult valleys,"[58] in order to fetch precious gems for His Majesty,"[59] or simply "to bring what his lord desires."[60] Sometimes, especially from archaeological contexts contemporary with the 13th Dynasty, come scarabs left behind by members of such expeditions:[61] "seal-bearers of the King of Lower Egypt," a title for expedition commanders; "the eldest of the hall," a curious designation of a sort of commercial agent for temples; "palace manager"; "scribe of the army (or expedition)";[62] "steward"; "chief of the tens of Upper Egypt" (i.e., a labor foreman); "member of the ruler's staff (or table)" (i.e., royal ships' captains). These are the grades of officers found on mining, trading, or quarrying expeditions in Nubia, the deserts or the Sinai; but none represents any function connected with permanent occupation of an imperial kind.

Where exploitation and intimidation failed, Pharaoh practiced the cultivation of friends. This entailed the sort of mutual gift-giving at a high level encountered principally among oriental potentates, and signalized by such epithets of royal officials as "he who accompanies the sovereign's monuments to far-off lands."[63] The gifts in question have, in fact, turned up in excavations in the Levant, chiefly in the important cities of Syria: Ebla, Ugarit, Qatanum, Ba'albek, Byblos, and Beirut.[64] While some of these may owe their provenience to the pillage of the Hyksos rulers,[65] the unequivocal statement of Sinuhe shows that the practice was common from the beginning of the 12th Dynasty.[66] In fact there is ample evidence

[56] Cairo 20278 (*šmsw*, a "retainer"); Gardiner and Černý, *Sinai*, pl. 36, no. 118 (a treasurer).

[57] Ibid., pl. 51, no. 140.

[58] Ibid., pl. 18, no. 54.

[59] Ibid., pl. 85, no. 405.

[60] Ibid., pl. 18, no. 51; cf. pl. 22, no. 101A.

[61] R. Giveon, *Tel Aviv* 7 (1980), 179ff.

[62] R. Dunand, *Les fouilles de Byblos* (Paris, 1939), 1: no. 3594 (pl. 129, p. 246).

[63] Cairo 20086.

[64] For Elba, see G. S. Matthiae, *Studi eblaiti* 1 (1979), 119ff.; G. Matthiae, *Antike Welt* 13 (1982), 14ff. (Hetep-ib-ra); for Ugarit see W. A. Ward, *Orientalia* 30 (1961), 130 (Senusert-onkh); P-M VII, 395 (Amenemhet III); for Qatanum, see P-M VII, 392 (Amenemhet II's daughter); for Ba'albek, see J. Von Beckerath, *Untersuchungen zur politischen Geschichte der zweiten Zwischenzeit in Ägypten* (Glückstadt, 1965), 250 (Sobekhotpe VI); for Byblos, P. Montet, *Byblos et l'Égypte* (Paris, 1929), nos. 610, 611, 614 (Amenemhet III and IV); for Beirut, see *BMQ* 2 (1937), 87 pl 58a (Amenemhet IV).

[65] W. Helck, *UF* 8 (1976), 101ff.

[66] B 175–76: "Then His Majesty sent to me with presents from the king, that he might gladden the heart of yours truly, like the ruler of any foreign land."

to picture the crisscrossing of the Levant by Egyptian messengers. When Sinuhe the exile had achieved the status of a great sheikh among the bedu of Palestine, he could boast "the courier who went north or south from or to the (Egyptian) Residence, used to stop off at my place."[67] Senwosret I's "runners wax numerous in all lands,"[68] and the profession of emissary was so well known that its hazards could be satirized: "The emissary who goes abroad to a foreign land, his chattels willed to his children, in terror of lions and Asiatics."[69]

FROM NOMAD TO TOWNSMAN: PALESTINE UNDER THE 12TH AND 13TH DYNASTIES

But what was the land like, this "Retenu" toward which Pharaonic interests were actively directed from 2000 to 1700 B.C.? As we have seen, Antef the general and Nessumontu had both claimed to have destroyed fortified settlements in that part of Asia to which they led expeditions; and the Amenemhet text from Saqqara writes foreign toponyms in crenelated ovals, denoting walled settlements with protective towers. A plausible interpretation of a passage in Neferty might suggest that the inhabitants of hither Asia in the early 12th Dynasty had mastered siege techniques. All this might militate in favor of the view that the twentieth and nineteenth centuries B.C. had once more witnessed the appearance of a sedentary, urban population in Palestine. But is the evidence consistent throughout?

The archaeological picture that we have examined earlier[70] shows a Palestinian community during the last two centuries of the third millennium transformed by a transhumant, nonsedentary population. The place of origin of this culture seems to be the steppes of Transjordan, whence a cultural and demographic thrust westward and southward resulted in a shift of population to southern Palestine and the Negeb.[71] While the Negeb thereafter supports a rather larger community than formerly, it nonetheless remains "nonnucleated" and nomadic, and sedentarization does not result.[72] Just what a Negeb settlement looked like in

---

[67] Sinuhe B 94–95.

[68] Blumenthal, *Untersuchungen*, 199.

[69] W. Helck, *Die Lehre des Dw³-Htjj* (Wiesbaden, 1970), 2:xvia.

[70] In general for the older discussions, see among others K. Kenyon, *CAH³* I (1971), chap. 21; J. Van Seters, *The Hyksos, A New Investigation* (New Haven, Conn., 1966), 9ff.; also the notes which follow.

[71] W. Dever, *BASOR* 210 (1973), 58ff.; S. Richard, *BASOR* 237 (1980), 22; W. Dever, *BASOR* 237 (1980), 36, 38–39; idem. in *Biblical Archaeology Today* (Jerusalem, 1985), 123, 127.

[72] B. Mazar, *IEJ* 18 (1968), 68, n. 7; Dever, *BASOR* 237 (1980), 48–49; T. L. Thompson, *The Settlement of Sinai and the Negeb in the Bronze Age* (Tübingen, 1975), 20.

the days of EB IV is revealed by the excavations of William Dever at Bir Resisim. Here approximately eighty curvilinear huts provided sleeping accommodation, apparently on a seasonal basis, for a small clan of about seventy-five persons who lived by dry farming, pastoralism, and a little trade.[73] Most of Palestine and southern Syria must have been home to such seminomadic pastoralists, wandering around the ruin-mounds of Early Bronze Age cities, but never settling. If, in fact, they did return periodically to the cities of the past, it was only in summer to bury their dead in the traditional burying grounds hallowed by time, in deep shaft tombs leading to the rock-cut chambers. Here dismembered corpses were deposited, or heroes laid out with a dagger to protect them in the afterlife.[74] Their pottery was crude, handmade with incised decoration, often bearing caliciform rims and envelope ledge-handles.[75] In contrast, however, their knowledge of metallurgy was surprisingly advanced. To judge by the famous Beni-Hassan tomb painting it would appear that small clans traveled about with bellows and anvil, perhaps earning here and there from tinkering, and one is put in mind of the later Biblical Kenites.[76] Caches of copper ingots and weapons for recasting that have turned up in archaeological contexts of EB IV–MB I date fully substantiate the epigraphic evidence.[77]

The story of Sinuhe the exile, to which we have already referred, corroborates the archaeological picture to perfection.[78] Sinuhe, a middle-ranking official in the employ of the queen, fled at the time of the assassination of Amenemhet I, believing himself to be proscribed in the civil war he felt was bound to ensue. His flight took him eastward toward the Delta frontier and, after passing the border fortress at night, he struck out into the Sinai. "I continued my journey at time of evening and, when day dawned, I had reached Peten and come to rest on an island in the 'Great Black.'[79] Thirst overwhelmed me: I was dry, my throat parched. I said 'This is the taste of death!' Then I composed myself and collected my limbs, (for) I had heard the lowing of cattle and I espied some Asiatics.

---

[73] Dever, in *Biblical Archaeology Today*, 1117ff.; see also *BASOR* 237 (1980), 57–58; L. K. Horwitz, *BASOR* 275 (1989), 15–25.

[74] K. M. Kenyon, *Archaeology in the Holy Land* (New York, 1979), 121–36; S. Gittin, *Eretz Israel* 12 (1975), 46ff.; W. Dever, *Eretz Israel* 15 (1981), 22ff.

[75] R. Amiran, *Ancient Pottery of the Holy Land* (New York, 1970), 80–89.

[76] For the Beni Hasan painting, see Newberry, *Beni Hasan*, 1: pls. 28, 30–31; D. Kessler, *SAK* 14 (1987), 147–66.

[77] W. Dever and H. Tadmor, *IEJ* 26 (1976), 163ff.; Dever, in *Biblical Archaeology Today*, 117.

[78] Translated *ANET²*, 18–22; Lichtheim, *Literature*, 1:222–35; see in particular A. F. Rainey, *The World of Sinuhe*, Israel Oriental Studies 2 (Jerusalem, 1973), 368ff.; R. Parent, *L'affaire Sinouhe* (Paris, 1982).

[79] Apparently the region of the Bitter Lakes.

Their chief[80] who had previously been in Egypt recognized me." Saved by this stroke of luck, Sinuhe passed through community after community, heading north. "Land gave me to land. I set out for Byblos, I turned back to Kedem and spent one and a half years there. ῾Ammu's son Neshi, who was the chief of Upper Retenu, brought me and he said to me 'You shall be happy with me, you shall hear the language of Egypt!' He said this for he knew my character, and had heard that I was skilled: the people of Egypt who were with him had given testimony of me." The years of civil strife in Egypt had apparently propelled many Egyptians into exile in the Levant, where they formed a close-knit fraternity.

Nenshi married Sinuhe to his eldest daughter and settled him in a territory belonging to the tribe. So Sinuhe lived the life of a beduin skeikh, becoming prosperous and renowned and acquiring much wealth. He does not reveal how long he spent abroad, but as he claims to have seen his sons mature and become heads of clans, it must have been several decades.

But his very success excited the envy of the natives.

There came a mighty man of ⟨Re⟩tenu who challenged me in my (own) tent. He was a hero without equal, and had beaten all comers. He said he was going to fight with me, thinking he would beat me and intending, on the advise of his tribe, to take my cattle as plunder. (Nenshi) took council with me. I said "I do not know him. I do not know him. I am not, indeed, a confederate of his that I should swagger about in his encampment. Is it a fact that I have ever opened his door, or crossed his stockade? It is animosity (only), because he sees me performing your messages. . . ." At night I strung my bow, I practiced shooting my arrows, I brandished my dagger and polished up my weapons. When dawn broke ⟨Re⟩tenu was come having stirred up its tribes, and (fully) half of it was now gathered together. All interest was on this fight. He (i.e., the champion) approached me as I was standing waiting, and I put myself within his range. Every heart burned for me, men and women groaned, every heart was ill for me. Said they, "Is there another mighty man who can fight against him?" Then he took up his shield, ax and armful of javelins. Now after I had dodged his missiles and let his arrows pass by me harmlessly, one after the other, then he charged me. But I shot him and my arrow lodged in his neck. With a cry he fell on his nose. Then I felled him with his own ax, and emitted my battle cry on his back while every Asiatic roared. I gave praise to Montu while his friends mourned for him.

In spite of the obvious relief with which our swash-buckling hero recounts his adventures, he cannot conceal his longing to return to Egypt. Plainly he was homesick. Discreet inquiries were made, feelers put out,

[80] *Mtn*, perhaps "path-finder."

and letters sent. At last the king himself, Senwosret I, replied in person. Of course Sinuhe could come home. He had done nothing wrong, there was nothing to forgive. His place was in Egypt in the queen's suite, not among the fuzzy-wuzzies in some godforsaken outback.

So Sinuhe made preparations to return. He was met at the Egyptian frontier by a deputation that conveyed him up river to the Residence at Itj-towy (modern Lisht), where Amenemhet I had founded his capital. Still doubts about the king's sincerity assailed him. Could it be a ruse to entice him back to Egypt, then throw him in prison or execute him? The account of the audience with Pharaoh is a masterpiece of sensitive, psychological description.

> When day dawned I was summoned while ten men were coming and going to introduce me into the palace. I bowed to the ground between the sphinxes while the royal children waited in an alcove above me. The courtiers introduced me into the broad hall and directed me to the private apartments. I found His Majesty upon the Great seat in an alcove of electrum, and at once I was stretched flat on my belly. I did not know myself in his presence. This god addressed me kindly, but I was like a man seized at night time: my soul was gone, my limbs trembled, my heart it was not in my body! Thereupon His Majesty said to one of the courtiers "Pick him up. Make him speak to me." Then said His Majesty "Behold! You are come after journey in flight through the foreign lands. Old age has attacked you, feebleness has caught up with you. The burial of your corpse is no small affair: you should not be buried by bedu! No, no indeed! . . . You do not speak when your name is pronounced; are you afraid of punishment?" I made answer like the answer of one who is afraid: "What is it that my lord says to me? . . . it was simply the hand of god. . . . Behold, I am before you. Life belongs to you. May Your Majesty do as he wishes." Thereupon His Majesty had the royal children ushered in, and His Majesty said to the queen: "Look! Here is Sinuhe, come as an Asiatic, a creation of the bedu!" She uttered a very great cry, and all the royal children squealed together. They said to His Majesty "It is not really he, O sovereign my lord?" Said His Majesty, "It is really he."

Sinuhe, whether fictional or not,[81] provided the 12th Dynasty with a marvelous piece of propaganda literature. In spite of the turmoil and factionalism created by the civil war, Egypt was still home for *all* Egyptians:

---

[81] The text has some of the earmarks of an "expanded" stela inscription, or biographical statement. Among the more recent treatments of Sinuhe, see J. Assmann, in M. Görg, ed., *Fontes atque Pontes* (Wiesbaden, 1983), 18ff.; J. Baines, *JEA* 68 (1982), 27ff.; P. Derchain, *RdE* 22 (1970), 79ff.; idem, *GM* 87 (1985), 7ff.; G. Fecht, in F. Junge, ed., *Studien zu Sprache und Religion Ägyptens* (Göttingen, 1984), 465 ff.; J. Foster, *JSSEA* 12 (1982), 881ff.; H. Goedicke, *JARCE* 21 (1984), 197ff.; idem, *RdE* 35 (1984), 95ff.; A. Herrmann, *OLZ* 48 (1953), 101ff.

come home, O exile! All is forgiven! Loyalty and service to the god-king will bring happiness and prosperity. The king is patient, understanding, forgiving, and knows how to care for his own. He is not vindictive. Let us all bury the past and work in concert for a greater, happier homeland. For our present purpose this obvious moral pales in comparison to the candid and detailed picture the storyteller unwittingly paints of Palestine in the second half of the twentieth century B.C. Sinuhe mentions no city except Byblos in his extensive travels. Wherever he went in Palestine and Coele-Syria he encountered groups of transhumants living in tents or within stockades,[82] pasturing their flocks and herds and raiding each other. Domesticated animals include sheep, cattle, goats, and donkeys, with cattle being far the most important;[83] and in consequence pasturage and wells assume a paramountcy in the life of the clan that only nomads comprehend.[84] The communal diet comprises beef, poultry, wild game, milk, and wine,[85] and the latter together with the mention of fruit trees[86] proves that some horticulture was practiced. In spite of this evidence for working the land, and the limited dry farming attested for EB IV communities, hunting remained a principal means of livelihood.[87] Dead were buried in sheepskins, and interred in a shallow grave surrounded by a low wall, a practice anathema to the Egyptians.[88]

Political organization was rudimentary and followed tribal lines. Tribes were divided into clans and clans into families;[89] and the verb used of the chieftain's role vis-à-vis his people—dr, "to put down, quell, suppress"—vividly expresses the unsophisticated nature of his function.[90]

Archaeology has demonstrated these people's expertise in manufacturing a high quality of weapon, and the presence of weapons in graves suggests warlike traits. Sinuhe's famous fight with the champion of Retenu underscores the fact that tribal custom provided a channel for such bellicosity. Significantly, the weapons Sinuhe dwells on are those that excavation and epigraphy have also brought to light: the bow (pdt), the dagger (b^3gsw), the javelin ($nywy$), and the ax ($minb$).[91]

Despite the welcome Sinuhe and other exiles received among these seminomads, the essential antipathy remained between the settled Egyptian peasant and the wandering Palestinian of EB IV. Sinuhe epitomizes

[82] For stockades, see Sinuhe B 115, 146, 201; for tents, see B 110, 145.
[83] Sinuhe B 103, 144, 147, 240.
[84] Cf. Sinuhe B 102.
[85] Sinuhe B 87–92.
[86] Sinuhe B 241; Thompson, Settlement, 64.
[87] Sinuhe B 89–91.
[88] Sinuhe B 198.
[89] Sinuhe B 92–94, 200.
[90] Sinuhe B 93–94.
[91] Sinuhe B 127–28, 135, 140.

the relationship succinctly: "There is no bowman that fraternizes with a Delta dweller. Who can plant a papyrus stalk upon a mountain?"[92]

There seems little doubt, in the light of this weighty evidence, that the society reflected in what has come to be known as EB IV–MB I remained firmly ensconced in Palestine until the close of the twentieth century B.C. Can we muster any evidence from an Egyptian source as to when it passed out of existence and sedentarization set in?

The data for the nineteenth century B.C.,—that is, the reigns of Amenemhet II, Senwosret II and III, and Amenemhet III—are less tractable and permit several interpretations. Despite the rich content of the annals of Amenemhet II, it remains unclear what sort of economy dominated among the Asiatics of the time, save that two or three fortified places attracted the attention of the Egyptian expeditionary force. But *two* walled towns do not make a wholly urban society. The thirty-seven-member family of chief Absha, who visited the sixteenth township of Upper Egypt in the reign of Senwosret II (c. 1897–1877 B.C.),[93] has often been considered representative of typical bedu of the Middle Bronze Age; but we are hardly justified in declaring them representative of the dominant way of life in Palestine at that time. They might as easily hail from the periphery of a more urban community.[94]

The most precious source bearing on Egypt's relations with Asia in the late Middle Kingdom, the so-called Execration Texts, must be dated from about 1850 to 1750 B.C. These reflect an act of magical annihilation of persons and things inimical to Pharaoh and Egypt. The rite involved either figuring the individual in a terra-cotta, stone, or wooden representation, inscribed or uninscribed, or writing the names on pottery vessels. The curse formula was undoubtedly then pronounced and the object broken.[95] During the Old Kingdom nearly every major pyramid temple yields fragments of statues of bound foreigners (Nubians or Asiatics), but thus far only one lot on inscriptions has been published (Nubian).[96] For the

---

[92] Sinuhe B 121–22.

[93] See n. 76.

[94] They do in fact hail from *Shutu*, which has been equated with Biblical *Sheth* of Num. 24:17; S. Ahituv, *Canaanite Toponyms in Ancient Egyptian Documents* (Leiden, 1984), 184.

[95] S. Schott and K. Sethe, *ZÄS* 63 (1928), 101–3; L. Borchardt, *ZÄS* 64 (1929), 12–13; apart from the works mentioned in the immediately following notes, see on the Execration Texts W. F. Albright, *BASOR* 184 (1966), 26–35; A. Alt, *Kleine Schriften zur Geschichte des Volkes Israel* (Munich, 1959), 3:49–71; A. Goetze, *BASOR* 151 (1958), 28–33; H. B. Huffmon, *Amorite Personal Names in the Mari Texts* (Baltimore, 1965); W. L. Moran, *Orientalia* 26 (1957), 339–45; G. Posener, *LdÄ* 1 (1972), 67–69; idem, in *Studien zu Sprache und Religion Ägyptens*, 1:613–18; J. Vercoutter, *CRAIBL* (1963), 97–102; S. Yeivin, *Atiqot* 2 (1959), 155ff.

[96] J. Leclant, *RdE* 21 (1969), 55–62; M. Verner, RdE 36 (1985), 145–52; A.-M. Abubakr and J. Osing, *MDAIK* 29 (1973), 97–113.

12th and early 13th Dynasties four lots of texts have relevance: figurines from Helwan (?), early 12th Dynasty (no Asiatics names preserved);[97] figurines and pottery from the Nubian fortress of Mirgissa, 1900 to 1850 B.C.;[98] pottery purchased on the market and now in Berlin, dating from the reign of Senwosret III or (early) Amenemhet III;[99] and clay figurines excavated at Saqqara and now in Brussels, dating one or two generations after the Berlin bowls, thus sometime during the first half of the eighteenth century B.C.[100]

The basic format of the texts may be appreciated best through a perusal of the Berlin group. Here, for both Nubia and Asia (and for Libya as well, although the section is brief), we have the following "paragraphs": (A) a listing of named chieftains each preceded by the denomination "chief of (toponym) N, and all the henchmen who are with him"; (B) a generalizing statement encompassing "all the Nubians/Asiatics of (Toponym)" followed by a list of places[101]; (c) a second generalizing statement listing various functions: "their mighty men, their runners, their confederates, their associates . . ."; qualifying clauses ". . . who may rebel, who may conspire, who may fight, who intend to rebel in this entire land." While the generalizing and qualifying sections tend to remain constant over time,[102] perhaps reflecting an early Middle Kingdom prototype, the list of section A displays considerable fluidity. The Mirgissa texts have six entries for section A with three toponyms mentioned ('Anaqi four times), and five for B with five toponyms mentioned (three reproduced from A); the Berlin texts show thirty-one entries for section A with fifteen toponyms mentioned, while B has twenty-one entries with nineteen toponyms, all three of which occur in A. The Brussels group yields sixty-five entries for A, of

---

[97] G. Posener, *Cinq figurines d'envoûtement* (Cairo, 1987), 16; for a convenient list of such texts known to the author, see pp. 2–6.

[98] J. Vercoutter, *CRAIBL* (1963), 97–102; G. Posener, *Syria* 43 (1966), 277–87; as the fort of Mirgissa was built no earlier than the reign of Amenemhet II, the texts can scarcely predate the second quarter of the nineteenth century, and could be as late as the early years of Senwosret III: K. Zibelius, *LdÄ* 4 (1982), 144–45.

[99] K. Sethe, *Die Achtung feindlicher Fürsten, Volker und Dinge auf altägyptischen Tongefasscherben* (Berlin, 1926); for a good résumé of the ongoing discussion on date and interpretation, see T. L. Thompson, *The Historicity of the Patriarchal Narratives* (Berlin, 1974), 98–113.

[100] G. Posener, *Princes et pays d'Asie et de Nubie* (Brussells, 1940).

[101] By and large intended to cover the same places as section A.

[102] Since they reproduce a more or less standard *Vorlage* and are therefore not "current," but rather "catchall" clauses, it is of no avail to any argument to use the content of the "generalizing" sections to suggest imprecision and incompleteness in the specific list of A (Thompson, *Historicity*, 116). Brussels e.64 lists "all the chiefs of 'Anaqi" simply because the pattern of this section demanded it—it is already there in Mirgissa E.6—and this should not be taken to mean that the Egyptians at the time *knew* of more chiefs of the place, even though in E.36 they had listed but one.

which the first sixty give the expected format and prosopographical information, with fifty-five toponyms mentioned. The last five entries really belong in the B section, which would then total eleven entries with seven toponyms of which three occur in section A.

Before proceeding it is well to bear in mind the following. The purpose of the exercise is to prevent by *magical* means plot, conspiracies, and acts of rebellion and warfare that might be perpetrated by anyone on earth, even Egyptians. Since the act is one of magic, it will be used primarily in cases in which direct action (police, punitive, military) is impossible—that is, when the potential rebel is physically beyond Pharaoh's jurisdiction.[103] The rite will be used against any the state is not sure of—any who are not a *foederatus* ("on the water of" the king)—which meant virtually all of Asia, apart from Byblos. The interest of those carrying out the rite is clearly directed toward *persons*, not *places*: the toponymic content of the texts serves only to identify and locate the individual(s); there is, therefore, a prima facie probability that the list of potential malefactors will be comprehensive rather than selective.[104] Finally, since individuals are the prime focuses of attention, section A will resist any tendency toward degenerating into a stereotype to be reproduced over several generations; archaizing and obsolescent forms are not, therefore, to be expected in section A,[105] although conservatism shows through plainly in the generalizing, "catchall" sections.

Although it is now certain that the Berlin bowls and the Mirgissa group are only about one or two generations earlier than the Brussels figurines, marked differences characterize the number and arrangement of places in the two groups as well as the relationship of named individuals to these places. For one thing there is a stunning increase in the number of places mentioned from only five in Mirgissa to over sixty in Berlin. For another, in Mirgissa and Berlin several chiefs are associated with a single toponym,

[103] This may mean that the Egyptians named among the possible rebels are not *in* Egypt, but abroad. Sinuhe of course and other Middle Kingdom texts bear eloquent witness to the widespread phenomenon of exile. The texts from the mastaba of Senwosret-ankh at Lisht, to be published by the late G. Posener, in C. Hoelzl, *The South Cemetary at Lisht. The Mastaba of Senwosret-ankh* (forthcoming), seem to curse Egyptians in the main; but titles are rare and nothing indicated the victims' whereabouts. Could they be fugitives?

[104] Hence the inclusion of "all evil words, all evil speech, every evil conjuration, every evil concept, every evil plot, every evil strife, all evil uproar, every evil plan, every evil thing, all evil dreams, all evil sleep." Thompson's claim (*Historicity*, 114) that "the texts reflect . . . Egyptian concerns about Palestine rather than an objective and complete description of Palestine itself" is only half true: the "concerns" are of such a nature that the list in the aggregate approaches completeness. Gaps in fact are in most cases explainable: foreign chiefs, for example, may be above reproach, but their tribal enclaves may not be (e.g., Byblos).

[105] Contra Thompson, *Historicity*, 107. Note how orthography keeps pace with the times, e.g. in the spelling of *Kush*: Posener, *Cing figurines*, 23; idem, *Princes*, 48.

in six cases no less than three. In the Brussels texts, however, each place is linked to one chief.[106] Also, in the Berlin bowls there seems to be no geographical order to the sequence of places: Rehob in Galilee is followed by Ashnah in western Judah;[107] Arqata north of Byblos precedes Ashkelon. But the Brussels texts group their toponyms by *region*, if not in the sequence of itineraries.

It has long been suspected that the differences between the groups of texts, separated as they are over time, conceal important historical or societal facts.[108] Discussion has centered upon the question, Why has the number of places tripled in the time that has elapsed between the Berlin group and the Brussels group? It cannot simply reflect the growing progressive awareness of the Egyptians with the political geography of Palestine and southern Syria: the evidence we have reviewed unanimously speaks for a familiarity in detail (through repeated military forays) with the hither parts of western Asia.

One salient fact must be the starting point for the investigation: when the Berlin texts were written identification of a particular chief by *place of residence* counted for less than it did one or two generations later. Under Senwosret III the Egyptians knew of various chiefdoms *through* a limited number of places, identifying individuals as the "chief of" that place (although that may have been an oversimplification on Egypt's part). At the time the Mirgissa texts were written, four of the toponyms refer to locations on the sea (Byblos, Ullaza, and probably ⟨'⟩naqi and Mugar),[109] and one in Trasjordan (Shutu). Central Palestine is not mentioned. This complements the picture that can be elicited from the first half of the 12th Dynasty as attested in the historical texts we have reviewed, namely Egyptian interest and activity extended to the coast, contact with nomads in Transjordan, and avoidance of the underpopulated central portion of the country. Of the roster of toponyms in the Berlin texts, four are certainly

---

[106] Among the explanations tendered, that of Alt (*ZDPV* 64 [1941], 37), which sees territorial divisions in Brussels which went unnoted in the Berlin texts, is not as attractive as might first appear. It is true that Brussels differentiates sometimes (though not as often as the hypothesis requires) between "upper" and "lower," or "north" and "south," but these are artificial terms—note that there are no "east" and "west" qualifiers—introduced to explain multiple listings.

[107] Josh. 15:43; on the identification see S. Yeivin, *Eretez Israel* 4 (1953), 37; note that this place-name is also found on a seal of the Second Intermediate Period: G. Martin, *Egyptian Administrative and Private Name Seals* (Oxford, 1971), pl. 27:25 (306).

[108] For a résumé of the problem, see Thompson, *Historicity*.

[109] 'Anaqi has rightly been compared with the ͨAnaqim of the Bible: Koehler-Baumgartner, 3:813 (references); it is to be located along the south coast from Gaza to Ashdod (Alt, *Kleine Schriften*, 3:52). The occasional omission of the *ayin* reflects more on the weakness of the sound in Egyptian than on the state of this laryngeal in Canaanite. *Mgr* can plausibly be equated with the West Semitic word for "cave."

coastal areas (Arqata, Ashkelon, Ullaza, and Byblos), and three probably
maritime ('Anaqi, Mugar, and S'apa).[110] Of those of the remainder that
are identifiable, one appears to be a general designation of Transjordan
(Shutu), one a town in western Galilee (Rehob), another a district in western Judah (Ashnah), another in the south-central highland (Jerusalem),
and a fourth probably east of Batrun in Phoenicia (Mutara).[111] Since the
rest cannot be identified with certainty, it is difficult to claim that large
gaps exist in the distribution of place-names; but none of the names can
be placed north of the sources of the Orontes or north of the Eleutheros
Valley. That is to say: we are dealing with the same general sphere of
interest on Egypt's part that appears in the New Kingdom, and was
fought over and legalized by treaty over a long period of two centuries.

A number of indications may point to the toponyms being used as designations of *regions* rather than towns. Several names are preceded by a
triple reed-leaf sign that can, at times, be used to render a West Semitic
preformative -*y*-. In the names in question, however, they do not represent a precative form of the verb, but seem to indicate a separate mor-
pheme אִיֵּי־ *iyē*-,[112] "the coasts (or locality) of, "a usage familiar in
Biblical Hebrew. Thus we would have "coast/region of S'apa" (Sethe,
e.31), "coast/region of height" (Sethe, f.9, 13). Another toponym suggests
a dispersal of the chiefdoms' names around a central meeting point,
"(place of) assemblies" (Sethe, e.8).[113] Elsewhere, although the toponyms
in question are indubitably towns, the interest is explicitly stated to lie in
the rural population of the environs: "the tribes of Byblos" (Sethe, f.2),
"all the Asiatics of Ullaza" (Sethe, f.3), ". . . of the coast/region of the
Height" (Sethe, f.9, 13).

One can scarcely escape the conclusion that the Palestine that the Mirgissa–Berlin group describes is a region of rural enclaves in which towns
were few or of limited importance. "Townsfolk" are known, but they are
relegated to penultimate position (Sethe, f.16). In contrast, Egypt is fa-

[110] S'apa has been equated with a toponym attested a millennium later south of Gaza, viz.
Asapa: Alt, *Kleine Schriften*, 3:52, n. 3 Certainly neither this place-name, nor the New Kingdom *Ysp-ᵓr* has anything to do with the Biblical "Joseph": R. Weill, *Journal Asiatique*
(1937), 37–38, 54–55; O. S. Wintermute, 2:981.

[111] Ahituv, *Canaanite Toponyms*, 146.

[112] The use of the triple reed-leaf is already know in the transcription of the diphthong
-*aye*- in Old Egyptian: A. Abubakr and J. Osing, *MDAIK* 29 (1971), 107, 109; for the
Canaanite "islands, coasts," see Koehler-Baumgartner, 1:37; Z. Harris *A Grammar of
Phoenician* (New Haven, Conn., 1936), 76; R. S. Tomback, *A Comparative Semitic Lexicon of the Phoenician and Punic Languages* (Missoula, Mont., 1978), 12–13; it has been
claimed to occur in Eblaite place-names (e.g., *i-ya-puᵏˡ*, "the coasts of Joppa": M. Dahood,
in G. Pettinato, *The Archives of Elba* [New York, 1981], 295), but this remains dubious.

[113] Cf. Num. 33:22.

miliar with the country by regions, not logically ordered, but in the haphazard order in which their representatives may have appeared in audience before the king; for one well-attested way in which the Egyptian government came into face-to-face contact with Asiatic chiefs was through the obligatory attendance of the latter at the Egyptian court.[114]

When the Brussels texts were penned, on the other hand, one could not mention a foreign chief without identifying him with a place-name, and this meant usually (but not always)[115] a *town* name. Brussels knows of the presence of "clans" presumably of nomadic transhumants, but they are confined to Midian (Kushu)[116] or the Phoenician coast.[117] For the rest the ordering makes sense from the standpoint of a list of itineraries: the south coastal plain and Shephelah (e.1–5); the lateral route from the coast via Shechem to Pella in the Jordan Valley (e.6–8); the plain around Haifa and east of Carmel (e.9–14); the route through the north Jordan Valley to the Bek'a (e.15–20); a Transjordanian route (e.25–29); the upper Orontes and Damascus (e.30–34); and the Phoenician coast (e.35–38). From this point, difficult readings and unknown toponyms render interpretation hazardous; but among the more or less certain entries are Jerusalem (e.45), 'Acco (e.49), Shamkhuna (e.55), Lakish (e.59), Beth-Shemesh (e.60). The territory covered by the Brussels figurines is essentially the same as that of the Berlin texts, but the population is segmented and identified by single chiefdoms, and appears to be on the increase. It is, moreover, distributed in settlements that have appeared along *routes* connecting Egypt with the north and east, a pattern quite different from what can be detected in the earlier texts. The Brussels material reflects an increase in land travel along a north-south axis and, as a consequence, the siting of permanent settlements along transit corridors.

The Execration Texts contain some evidence on the economy and society of the chiefdoms they list. When the generalizing section C was composed, the administration and social functions that could be listed revealed a small, rudimentary community in which closeness to the chief and his trust counted toward status.[118] Use of the term *nḫt*, "mighty man, champion," takes us into the tribal, transhumant society of Sinuhe, as does the term "confederate";[119] and even "runners" conjures up the most

---

[114] Sinuhe B 25–26, cf. 73–75; Redford, *King-lists*, 108.

[115] At least fourteen of the names in the Brussels texts can plausibly be construed as regions or topographic features.

[116] E. 50–51: W. Albright, *BASOR* 83 (1941), 34, n. 8.

[117] E. 61–4, F.2; or the mountainous hinterland, reached only from the coast.

[118] This is the inference to be drawn from the use of the word *mhnk*, "henchman": D. Meeks, *Année lexicographique* (Paris, 1980), 1:169; (Paris, 1982), 3:129.

[119] Sinhue B 109–14.

basic and primitive means of communication.[120] In the Brussels texts, however, these terms are suppressed, and two others put roughly where the others formerly would have occurred, namely "townsfolk" and "harvesters."[121] The Brussels texts, therefore, not only witness an increase in settlements along transit corridors, but also attest to a sedentary, agriculturally based economy.

It is hard to avoid the obvious conclusion. The Mirgissa and Berlin texts form a group different in essence from the Brussels texts. They reflect essentially the same MB I world as does the story of Sinuhe. The Brussels texts, on the other hand, witness the development of commerce along north-south transit corridors and to the concomitant sedenterization of the population identified archaeologically as MB IIA.[122]

THE GREAT KINGDOMS OF THE LEVANT

The great empire of Ur in southern Babylonia (c. 2050–1950 B.C.), which had included most of western Asia as its sphere of influence, collapsed in the middle of the twentieth century B.C. and on its ruins arose a group of warlike successor states. The ruling classes and most of the population of these states spoke a West Semitic language generally dubbed "Amorite," but while they could look back on an early stage in their development when they had lived a rustic, nomadic life on the Syrian steppes, they had by now for several generations been exposed to the influences of Akkadian culture.[123] In Mesopotamia the historic focus is on the states of Isin, Larsa, Eshnunna, and (later) Babylon in the south, Mari and Khana on the

[120] In foreign parts even Pharaoh had recourse to "runners" see p. 82 above.

[121] *Hz sm*, literally "cutters of herbage"; cf. Akk. *ḫuṣṣuṣu*, "to break, cut," and *sammu* "herbage": CAD, 4:131; the root descends also into Egyptian; cf. *ḥz* "to put to death (by knife)," *ḥz³w* (type of plant), etc., *Wb* III; D. Meeks, *Année lexicographique* (Paris, 1982), 3: 224.

[122] MB IIA has, over the past decade and a half, undergone an elevation in date which can be termed nothing short of astounding, and a beginning around 2000 B.C. is now accepted virtually as an article of faith: W. G. Dever, in J. A. Sandars, ed., *Near Eastern Archaeology in the Twentieth Century* (New York, 1970), 132–63; idem in F. M. Cross, ed., *Magnalia Dei: The Mighty Acts of God* (New York, 1976), 3–38; P. Gerstenblith, *The Levant at the Beginning of the Middle Bronze Age* (Winona Lake, Ind., 1983), 101ff.; the entire argument, however, is based on the "middle" chronology, which necessitates a jacking up of dates by over half a century, and is unacceptable on the basis of Egyptian evidence. From an examination of the latter it ought to be quite clear that the nonsedentary culture of MB I (using the old terminology) is in evidence throughout the twentieth century and well into the nineteenth. But this is not the place to continue the debate.

[123] On the problems in terminology and identification that arise from the application of MAR.TU (*Amurru*) to Northwest Semitic, see I. J. Gelb, *JCS* 15 (1961), 29; Thompson, *Historicity*, 68ff.; Gerstenblith, *Levant*, 123ff.; whether "Akkadianized" or not, the Amorite dynasts of the time certainly experience a "rise to power." On Larsa's roots, for example, as an erstwhile Amorite tribe and chiefdom, see M. B. Rowton, *JNES* 32 (1973), 214.

middle Euphrates, and Assyria on the upper Tigris; and the historic process at work is the gradual subversion of all these states through intestine feuding to the rule of Babylon by 1700 B.C.

In Palestine and Syria too by the mid-nineteenth century Amorite communities were in the ascendancy. Yamkhad, centered upon Aleppo in North Syria, was for its contemporaries the most powerful of all the Amorite kingdoms, deferred to by both Zimri-lim of Mari and the famous Hammurabi of Babylon. One of its kings, Yarim-lim, possessed a fleet of five hundred merchant vessels, which plied the Euphrates and intervened effectively in Mesopotamian politics. Located athwart the major trade routes, Yamkhad could tap commerce coming from as far west as Cyprus and the Aegean and as far east as Iran.[124] Qatanum, enjoying an optimum location on the upper Orontes in central Syria with access to the Mediterranean through the Eleutheros Valley, was the major power on Yamkhad's southern flank. Geography made it a close partner with Mari on the middle Euphrates: joint military operations were undertaken from time to time, trade flourished, and Mari citizens even had rights to sheep pasturing in Qatanum.[125] Hazor dominated southern Syria and northern Palestine from its optimum position in the upper Jordan Valley. Messengers passed to Mari, Babylon, and Ugarit, and its trade extended in the west to the Aegean. Something of its importance may be gauged by the relative size of shipments of tin from Mari: 10 minas to Muzunnim near Damascus, 8.33 minas to Laish, and 70 minas to Hazor. It may well be that the statement in Joshua 11:10 that "Hazor formerly was head of all those kingdoms" stems from a dim memory of the Middle Bronze Age importance of the place.[126]

The picture painted by the textual sources from Mari, Alalakh, Babylon, and other similar archive-bearing sites is born out by the archaeological record, which is extensive and impressive. Following the impoverished MB I, with its sparse population of elusive transhumants, there comes the birth of a new cultural phase, which is not descended from MB I. MB IIA represents the introduction into the Levant of a culture with contacts with the north.[127] Most distinctive is the ceramic assemblage,

[124] In general on Yamkhad, see H. Klengel, *Geschichte Syriens* (Berlin, 1965), 1:102ff.; (Berlin, 1970), 3:142ff.; for the famous letter from Ibalpiel to Zimri-lim, see G. Dossin, *Syria* 19 (1938), 117; for Yarim-lim's fleet, see G. Dossin, *Syria* 33 (1956), 63ff.; on its trade, see J.-R. Kupper, *CAH³* II, pt. 1 (1973), 18–19.

[125] Klengel, *Geschichte Syriens*, 2:98ff.

[126] On Hazor, see A. Malamat, *JBL* 79 (1960), 12–19; idem, in Sandars, *Near Eastern Archaeology*, 164–77; idem, *IEJ* 21 (1971), 31–38; idem, in M. Libeau and P. Talon, ed., *Reflets des deux fleuves* (Louvain, 1989), 117–18; H. Limet, *Archives royales de Mari* (Paris, 1986), 25: no. 43.

[127] Cf. B. Mazar, *IEJ* 18 (1968), 69ff.; R. Amiran, *Anadolu* 12 (1968), 559–62; there is no reason, however, to postulate an invasion from the north (Van Seters, *The Hyksos*, 32,

which shows evidence of the fast wheel, sophisticated burnishing techniques, and ornamentation. Loop handles, pointed bases, and fine clay all suggest a complete break with the past; and the carinated profiles point to metallic prototypes.[128] The presence of an advanced weaponry provides corroboration of the postulated skill in metallurgy: bronze duckbill axes, socketed spearheads, ribbed daggers, and scimitar-shaped swords are all in evidence.[129]

The warlike tendencies of the Amorite successor states are clearly reflected in the town architecture of MB IIA and B (Plate 10). To accommodate an increase in population—the population of Palestine in MB IIA has been estimated at 100,000, that of MB IIB at 140,000—cities were enlarged and (in MB IIB) fortifications introduced.[130] The latter exhibit two basic types. On existing tells the summit was built outward by means of artificial fills in layers; the sloping surface was then plastered or cobbled, and a stone revetment with fosse built at the bottom. In new settle-

Plate 10. South gate of the Canaanite city of Shechem in the Middle Bronze Age.

38ff.), or even "considerable population movements" (W. Ward, *UF* 8 [1976], 353). The role played by trade and transit corridors is itself considerable: Gerstenblith, *The Levant*, 109ff.

[128] Amiran, *Pottery*, pls. 25, 27, 33, 35; Kenyon, *Archaeology*, 163f., figs. 36, 37; Gerstenblith, *The Levant*, chaps. 4–5.

[129] Gerstenblith, *The Levant*, 89–100.

[130] On the population estimate, see M. Broshi and R. Gophna, *BASOR* 261 (1986), 73–90.

ments vast rectangular enclosures were walled in by earthen ramps and surrounded by moats. Towered gates with multiple apertures on a single axis make their appearance at many sites. These new provisions for defense can only mean that new tactics had been devised in the art of warfare somewhere in the Middle East; and the increased use of transit corridors in the Levant and the concomitant unsettled politics necessitated their introduction in Palestine's MB IIB. It has from time to time been suggested that the introduction of the horse and chariot from the north and northeast, and the revolution this effected in mobile warfare, lie behind the evolution of this type of military architecture.[131] But at Mari in the late eighteenth century B.C. the horse is still a novelty and its use of doubtful propriety; and while Mari texts indicate Amurru in Syria to have been a horse-rearing area,[132] actual horse burials are rare before the 18th Dynasty.[133] A much more likely catalyst in the development of new techniques of defense is the siege engine developed in central Mesopotamia and perfected by the Hurrians. Both the battering ram (yašibu in Akkadian) and the siege tower (dimtu) are attested, against both of which the sloping ramp or glacis would have proved the obvious defense.[134]

While one gains the distinct impression that by the end of MB IIA Palestine and southern Syria had been irrevocably drawn into the ambit of the warring Amorite states of the north and east, and hence obliged to adopt a more hostile stance toward Egypt, one city in the Levant distinguishes itself as the exception to this generalization. That is Byblos, which, as we have seen, had entertained amicable relations with Egypt for a millennium and a half. While the North Syrian coast had fallen to Yamkhad,[135] and although Byblos itself around 2000 B.C. is found within the pale of the great 3rd Dynasty of Ur,[136] its chief is conspicuous by his absence from the Execration Texts. A gap in our sources prevents us from commenting on the city throughout most of the 12th Dynasty, but by the

[131] On the introduction of the horse and chariot into the Near East, see M. Littauer and J. H. Crouwel, *Wheeled Vehicles and Ridden Animals in the Ancient Near East* (Leiden, 1979); R. Drews, *The Coming of the Greeks* (Princeton, N.J., 1988), 74–93; on the horse in Egypt, see J. Leclant, *Syria* 37 (1960), 17–18; L. Storock, *LdÄ* 4 (1982), 1009–13.

[132] B. Landsberger, *JCS* 8 (1954), 56; Gelb, *JCS* 15 (1961), 41ff.

[133] The horse burial from Buhen (J. Leclant, *Orientalia* 31 [1962], 127) defies dating because of the methods of excavation employed at the site (Drews, *The Greeks*, 102–3); that there exists indirect evidence for the presence of the chariot at the beginning of the Hyksos regime in Egypt (so. W. Helck, *JNES* 37 [1978], 337–40) remains moot.

[134] Y. Yadin, *BASOR* 137 (1955), 23ff.; P. Parr, *ZDPV* 84 (1968), 18ff.; G.R.H. Wright, *ZDPV* 84 (1968), 1ff.; for the appearance of these engines in Mesopotamia, see Kupper, *CAH³* II, pt. 1 (1973), 5; A. Goetze, *Iraq* 25 (1963), 128.

[135] Ugarit as subservient to Yamkhad: F. M. Tocci, *La siria nell' eta di Mari* (Rome, 1960), 69ff.

[136] E. Sollberger, *AFO* 19 (1960), 120ff.; A. Malamat, in *Assyriological Studies in Honor of Benno Landsberger* (Chicago, 1965), 373, n. 43.

reign of Amenemhet III it is back within the Egyptian fold. A series of nine rock-cut tombs, still yielding grave goods despite plundering, apprises us of the same number of city rulers, apparently of the same family. Surprisingly almost all have chosen at one time or another to commemorate themselves in writing by using the hieroglyphic script. Egyptian gods and epithets appear in these short inscriptions, a type of Egyptian hymn is attested, and even Egyptian-style reliefs are attempted by local craftsmen.[137] Most intriguing are the titles the chiefs choose to designate their political status: *iry-pᶜt* and *ḥ³ty-ᶜ*, which are usually translated "hereditary prince" and "count." While the first is a polite though banal indicator of general association with a hereditary elite, the second is a functional title applied to a nonhereditary function of king's frontman in the governing of a settlement. By the time the rulers of Byblos are blessed with the title, it is well on its way to becoming little more than "mayor of the town." Had the Byblian chiefs been obliged, each upon his accession, to repair to Pharaoh's court to undergo the formal bestowal of the rank? Or had they simply arrogated the term as the closest equivalent to a native title?

With the Byblian ruler Antin, a new stage in the history of Byblos is reached. The title "ruler of rulers" that he assumes (in hieroglyphic) betokens an exalted status, which is amply born out by the Mari archives where he is also mentioned;[138] tombs 6 through 9 in the royal necropolis, which follow Antin's floruit, are among the largest and best appointed of the group.[139] Assuming they cover an equal number of generations reckoned between twenty and twenty-five years, and commencing in the last half of the nineteenth century B.C., we are taken down to the middle of the seventeenth century for the termination of the line. Perhaps significantly from one of the later tombs comes a jar text (in hieroglyphs) that reads "foreign ruler" (*ḥk³ ḫ³swt*).[140] With this epithet we shall shortly become familiar.

[137] On the royal tombs at Byblos, see P. Montet, *Monuments Piot* 27 (1924), 1–29; idem, *Byblos et l'Égypte*, 146ff.; on the Byblian dynasty of the period, see K. A. Kitchen, *Orientalia* 36 (1967), 39–54; W. Helck, *Die Benziehungen Ägyptens zur Vorderasien²* (Wiesbaden, 1972), 63–67; on the epithets, see Montet, *Kêmi* 16 (1962), 95–96; 17 (1964), 62ff.

[138] Montet, *Kêmi* 16 (1962), 96, fig. 6; W. F. Albright, *BASOR* 99 (1945), 10–18.

[139] Montet, *Byblos et l' Égypte*, 205ff.

[140] Ibid., 208, no. 826.

CHAPTER 5

The Hyksos in Egypt

Tutimaeus. In his reign, for what cause I know not, a blast of
God smote us; and unexpectedly, from the regions of the East,
invaders of obscure race marched in confidence of victory
against our land. By main force they easily overpowered the rulers of the land, they then burned our cities ruthlessly, razed to
the ground the temples of the gods, and treated all the natives
with a cruel hostility, massacring some and leading into slavery
the wives and children of others. Finally, they appointed as king
one of their number whose name was Salitis. He had his seat at
Memphis, levying tribute from Upper and Lower Egypt, and always leaving garrisons behind in the most advantageous positions. Above all, he fortified the district to the east, foreseeing
that the Assyrians, as they grew stronger, would one day covet
and attack his kingdom.

In the Saite [Sethroite] nome he found a city very favorably
situated on the east of the Bubastite branch of the Nile, and
called Auaris after an ancient religious tradition. This place he
rebuilt and fortified with massive walls, planting there a garrison of as many as 240,000 heavy-armed men to guard his frontier. Here he would come in summertime, partly to serve out rations and pay his troops, partly to train them carefully in
maneuvers and so strike terror into foreign tribes.

—Manetho, *Aegyptiaca*, frag. 42, 1.75–79.2

THUS SPEAKS the Egyptian historian Manetho of the third century B.C., in
a fortunately surviving excerpt quoted *in extenso* by Flavius Josephus in
the late first century A.D. Josephus had an ax to grind in his rebuttal of
the anti-Jewish Egyptian writer Apion, but he nonetheless appears to
have faithfully reproduced the Manethonian text. A certain mystery has,
perhaps because of the use of the English word "obscure" to render the
Greek ἀσήμοι, attached itself to the foreign element whose invasion is
here described; and because Manetho uses the term "Hyksos" almost as
though it were a gentilic, the search was on for a mysterious "race" that
had burst suddenly on the Egyptian horizon and a century later had disappeared.

"Men of Ignoble Race"

Already in classical times identifications had begun to proliferate. Josephus records that "some call them Arabs," a statement not so inexplicable as once thought. This derives solely from the constant use of "Arabia"—that is, the "East"—in classical writers to designate the regions of Asia closest to the Suez frontier, regions that in pharaonic times would have been known collectively as "the northern countries," namely Palestine and Syria.[1] Josephus himself, speaking as a Jew, refers to the Hyksos as "our ancestors," a curious half-truth which we shall analyze later.[2]

With modern discovery and contemporary research, identifications began to reflect the trends in scholarship. The uncovery of the Hittite capital at Boghaz Keui in Asia Minor and the consequent reconstruction of the history of an otherwise unknown people led quickly to the suggestion that they in fact had been the Hyksos.[3] But the Egyptians were quite familiar with the Hittites and had faithfully and consistently transcribed their name by Ht^3; moreover there was, and is, no evidence whatsoever that in the seventeenth century B.C. the Hittites played any role outside the confines of the limited bailiwick bounded by the Halys River. Nevertheless attempts to find a candidate beyond the Taurus persisted. Albright found in a Hittite text a chief of the "Umman Manda," a vague term often employed for seminomadic hordes in northern Mesopotamia, one named Ča-lu-ti which he at once compared with Salitis, the first Hyksos king in the Manethonian list.[4] Others displayed a fixation with the alleged use of the horse and chariot by the Hyksos, and promoted an identification with the Indo-European elements, which by the sixteenth century B.C. had imposed themselves as a ruling elite on the native stock of Mesopotamia.[5] In recent years a proposed identification with the Hurrians, that aforementioned native stock, has gained some respectability.[6] But no one has been able to demonstrate the presence in the seventeenth century B.C. of large numbers of Hurrians in the territory intervening between Mesopotamia and Egypt; and their arrival in Syria and Palestine seems now definitely to have taken place *after* the Hyksos conquest.[7]

This frantic search has been not only premature but wrongheaded from

[1] D. B. Redford, *Pharonic King-lists, Annals and Day-books* (Toronto, 1986), 278, n. 77.

[2] *Contra Apionem*, 1.74, 91.

[3] Cf. J. G. Duncan, *Digging up Biblical History* (London, 1931), 69–72.

[4] W. F. Albright, *BASOR* 146 (1957), 30–31; idem, *Yahweh and the Gods of Canaan* (New York, 1969), 57, n. 12; cf. B. Mazar, *IEJ* 18 (1968), 88, n. 61.

[5] R. M. Engberg, *The Hyksos Reconsidered* (Chicago, 1939); Z. Mayani, *Les Hyksos et le monde de la Bible* (Paris, 1956); cf. Mazar, *IEJ* 18 (1968), 91–92.

[6] W. Helck, *Die Beziehungen Ägyptens zur Vorderasien²* (Wiesbaden, 1972), 104.

[7] See subsequent discussion in this chapter.

the start. The Greek ἀσήμοι means simply "vile, ignoble," which is surely only a rendering of the common Egyptian *ḥsy*, "vile," which in Egyptian texts of all periods characterizes foreign peoples. As such it is not a confession of ignorance but a pejorative. Moreover, "Hyksos" is not a gentilic at all, but, as numerous examples from the third and second millennium will attest, merely the Greek garbling of the common way of designating a "foreign ruler" (*ḥk³ḫ³swt*, literally "ruler of foreign lands"); therefore, it applies to the regime and not the people.[8]

The true identity of the Hyksos can now easily be ascertained through the examination of two bodies of evidence: archaeological and linguistic. We shall have occasion below to look more closely at the archaeological record; but suffice it to say for the present that recent excavations at such Hyksos sites in the eastern Delta as Tel-ed-Dab'a and Tel el-Maskhuta have revealed an intrusive culture whose ceramic and artifactual content differs not at all from the culture of contemporary MB IIb Palestine and Phoenicia. The linguistic picture is wholly consistent. Contemporary Egyptian texts from the time of the wars of liberation and the early 18th Dynasty call the invaders ʿ³*mw*—that is, speakers of a West Semitic tongue. Although the Hyksos have left behind no inscriptions in their native language, a number of their personal names have turned up on seals and dedicatory texts, and these can be analyzed syntactically and lexically. It is abundantly clear from such an analysis that we are dealing with personal names from a West Semitic dialect—all but two names sustain a West Semitic derivation, and none permit a Hurrian.

It remains difficult to ascertain more specifically where the dynasty Manetho called "fifteenth" originated. The apparent predilection for the "mountain (deity)" might favor the highlands of Palestine or the Lebanon against the Negeb, Shephelah, or inland Syria; but this is of minimal weight. Recently attention has been drawn to the similarity in the lowest Hyksos levels excavated at Tell-ed-Dab'a between the local "Tel el-Jehudiya ware" and that of Byblos;[9] and one recalls in this connection the notice of the Christian chronographer Africanus (second century A.D.), in reproducing the Epitome of Manetho, that the Hyksos hailed from Phoenicia.[10] But the latter in Egyptian demotic of the period of Manetho is always a rendering of *Ḥ³rw*, a term with wider reference than the narrow littoral of the eastern Mediterranean north of Haifa, and roughly equivalent to our Palestine and southern Syria. We may for the time being be obliged to satisfy ourselves with nought but these broad limits: no further

[8] D. B. Redford, *Orientalia* 39 (1970), 1–51; idem, *King-lists*, 240–42.

[9] M. Bietak, in A. F. Rainey, *Egypt, Israel, Sinai* (Jerusalem, 1987), 41–56.

[10] W. G. Waddell, *Manetho* (London, 1940), 90.

north than the Lebanon ranges, no further south than the Judaean highlands.

THE HYKSOS CONQUEST OF EGYPT

When we address the question as to *how* the Hyksos extended their control over Egypt, we involve ourselves in a warm and ongoing debate. Manetho has long since set the tone by insisting on an invasion; but one can
easily argue that events closer in time to his life-span than the Hyksos
period have influenced him. The successive invasions, extremely destructive all, of the Assyrians (671, 666, 663 B.C.), the Babylonians (600, 567
B.C.), and the Persians (525, 343 B.C.) had created a perception and awakened an expectation that the destroyer always appeared suddenly out of
the north and in the form of a conquering army.[11] Possibly Manetho's
source, which probably dates to the fourth century B.C., saw in the Hyksos a prototype of these later hordes and credited them (falsely) with the
same intent to wreak havoc in Egypt. Manetho's reliability as a source
having thus been called in question, we are free to recast our views in
rather different form. The Brooklyn Museum Papyrus, and other brief
notices passed in review in the last chapter, demonstrate clearly the presence in Egypt during the 12th and 13th Dynasties of a sizable Asiatic
population of servile status, presumably brought back as the result of foreign wars. Although there is nothing to suggest that this population was
any larger in the eastern Delta than elsewhere, it is not unreasonable to
suppose that with the gradual weakening of royal authority, the Delta
defenses were allowed to lapse, and groups of transhumants found it easy
to cross the frontier and settle in Lower Egypt. Although the next step in
the argument is largely inferential, one can be led to believe that in time
the Asiatic population of the eastern Delta grew to exceed in number the
native Egyptian stock. Having persuaded oneself of this, the postulate of
an invasion becomes unnecessary: the Hyksos assumption of power reveals itself as a peaceful takeover from within by a racial element already
in the majority.[12]

Now this argument, as adumbrated largely a priori, although its exponents have sought desperately to shore it up with stray evidence, contains a number of serious flaws. First, the allegation that the advent of the
Hyksos was attended by grievous destruction is not new with Manetho,
but dates back to the early New Kingdom. Kamose, who helped inaugu-

[11] See subsequent discussion.
[12] See T. Säve-Söderbergh, *JEA* 37 (1951), 53–71; J. Van Seters, *The Hyksos, A New
Investigation* (New Haven, Conn., 1966); A. H. Gardiner, *Egypt of the Pharaohs* (Oxford,
1961), 156–57; W. C. Hayes, *CAH* II³, pt. 1 (1973), 54 ff.; cf. M. Bietak, *LdÄ* 3 (1980),
94–103; idem, in Rainey, *Egypt, Israel, Sinai*, 52.

rate the wars of liberation, speaks of "Egypt which the Asiatics have destroyed";[13] and Hatshepsut, scarcely half a century later, recalls the "nomad groups" among the Hyksos who had "destroyed what had been made."[14] The wholesale rape of monuments throughout the Memphite region and their dispersal to Avaris (and later Tanis) and to points farther north in the Levant most probably must be put down to the depredations of the Hyksos.[15] This is not, arguably, the expected practice of a race acculturated to Egypt by long settlement within Egypt's borders. While other foreign groups, long resident in Egypt, like the Libyans, were thoroughly Egyptianized and treated politically as though they were native Pharaohs, the Hyksos remained throughout their century of power in Egypt "Asiatics," and their kings "foreign rulers" or "princes of Retenu." This also is not what we should expect of a group with a long prior residence within Egypt's borders.

Second, the mere presence of Asiatics in Egypt prior to the Hyksos accession to power has no bearing whatsoever on the nature of the political coup that produced the 15th, or Hyksos, Dynasty. There were Greeks in Egypt before the Ptolemies, Arabs before 641 A.D., and British before Tel el-Kebir; but the coming to power of these three groups constituted nonetheless military invasions along more or less formal lines. One other point needs to be stressed, and that pertains to the economy of the newcomers. Egypt had long known the infiltration of transhumant pastoralists when border forts were abandoned, but these had appeared in *small numbers*, a nuisance perhaps, but no threat to towns.[16] These certainly could not have constituted the mainstay of a coup, nor, a fortiori, could a prisoner-of-war population such as our 12th and 13th Dynasty texts attest to the presence of. But if one removes the argument based on the mere presence in Egypt of foreign elements before the Hyksos period, the prima facie case disappears. What remains to be explained are the major sites such as Tel ed-Dab'a, Tel el-Yehudiyeh, and Maskhuta, where an urban but thoroughly Middle Bronze Canaanite population had insinuated itself.[17] And this population surely did not take shape through sporadic infiltration but through the migration en bloc of communities already urban in nature.

It would be gratifying to be able to report extensive destruction levels about this time, in evidence in archaeological excavations; but such is not the case. Many Delta sites had been picked over before archaeology be-

[13] Kamose I, 4–5: W. Helck, *Historisch-biographische Inschriften der 2. Zwischenzeit* (Wiesbaden, 1975), 84.

[14] A. H. Gardiner, *JEA* 32 (1946), 43–56.

[15] J. M. Weinstein, *BASOR* 217 (1975), 1–16; W. Helck, *UF* 8 (1976), 101–14.

[16] See the observations of Merikare's father and of Neferty, reviewed in chapter 3.

[17] For discussion and bibliography on these sites, see now M. Bietak, H. Goedicke, and A.-P. Zivie, *LdÄ* 6 (1986), 321–51.

came the scientific endeavor it is today, while others have either permanently concealed their Middle Kingdom strata below a high water table, or show a hiatus in occupation. Avaris itself, undoubtedly the modern Tel ed-Dab'a, is never claimed in Manetho to have been sacked, and the excavations reveal only a change in settlement planning and the occupation of the site by "complete newcomers."[18] Places like Tel el-Maskhuta were, presumably, new settlements.[19] While the excavations at Karnak have revealed a thin layer of wind-blown ash over the 13th Dynasty building phase,[20] one would be rather rash at this stage in our research to ascribe it to the Hyskos.

The counterargument just presented sounds negative and perhaps borders on a counsel of despair, so that we may well ask ourselves at this point: What do we really know about the Hyksos conquest?

Between the close of the 12th Dynasty and the first Hyksos ruler, the Turin Canon of kings, a papyrus of Ramesside date reflecting a king list begun in the Middle Kingdom, lists between 120 and 130 names, which it groups under a single rubric "[k]ings [who follo]wed (?) [the House of] king [Seh]etepibre L.P.H." (i.e., the 12th Dynasty). In Manetho at this point a 13th and 14th Dynasty are inserted with a total of 136 kings, a close approximation of the total that must once have been computable from the Turin Canon. Although Diodorus in the first century B.C. has misleadingly reduplicated the last kings of the 12th Dynasty and confused them with the early kings of the 18th, he nonetheless preserves a generally accurate assessment of the period:[21]

Seoosis I (1.53)

Seoosis II (1.59)

"After this king a long line of successors on the throne accomplished no deed worth recording." (1.60)

Amasis (1.60)

Aktisanes the Ethiopian (1.60)

Mendes (Marrus), builder of the laybrinth (1.61)

Interregum: "no kings for five generations" (1.62)

Cetes Proteus (1.61)

"Seoosis II" and "Mendes" are to be identified with Amenemhet III, builder of the Hawara pyramid complex (i.e., the Labyrinth).[22] The "long

[18] M. Bietak, *Proceedings of the British Academy* 65 (1979), 244 (stratum F).

[19] J. S. Holladay, Jr., *Cities of the Delta*, vol. 3: *Tel el-Maskhuta* (Malibu, Calif., 1982).

[20] D. B. Redford, *JSSEA* 11 (1981), 253; idem, *Akhenaten, the Heretic King* (Princeton, N.J., 1984), 98.

[21] Diodorus, 1.59–61; A. Burton, *Diodorus Siculus, Book I. A Commentary* (Leiden, 1972), 179–82.

[22] See A. B. Lloyd, *JEA* 56 (1970), 81ff.; K. Michalowski, *JEA* 54 (1968), 219ff.; D. Arnold, *MDAIK* 35 (1979), 1ff.

line of successors" and the interregnum clearly reflect the 13th Dynasty, and five generations (c. 125 years) is in fact nearly correct.[23] The adverse comment on their regime stems equally from the facts that individual kings followed each other in rapid succession, and that relatively few of them left buildings or inscriptions.

Now at viii, 27, and ix, 9 of the Turin Canon, occurs a name, partly damaged, that probably is to be read *Dd-[ms]{r}*. Scholars have long considered most probable an identification of this king with *Dd-ḥtp-rʿ* (var. *Dd-nfr-rʿ*) *Ddw-ms*, a king who is mentioned in several contemporary texts from the Thebaid,[24] and have construed both forms as the historical basis of the Tutimaios of Manetho, under whom the Hyksos invasion is supposed to have taken place. Unfortunately the contemporary inscriptions say nothing about the invasion, although one might infer from them that Ded-mose's activities were confined to Upper Egypt and that the north was outside his jurisdiction. But inscriptions, all from the south, from about this time do convey a somewhat bellicose air, which would be consonant with the sudden eruption of warlike activities within Egypt. Common epithets include "a mighty king beloved of his army . . . overthrowing the ⟨refractory⟩ who had rebelled against him, who directs slaughter against them that had attacked [him]; . . . who repels all foreign lands and rescues his city . . . who overthrows them that had trespassed . . . who acts with his mighty arm," and so forth.[25] Two of the stelae mentioning Ded-mose come from military men, fortress commandants who worked for him.[26]

That these oblique references to strife are, in fact, to be understood as indicating hostilities that broke out pursuant to an *incursion* of "foreign lands," and that the latter were the Hyksos is virtually proved by Ka-

[23] Roughly 1786 to 1660 B.C. The chronology of the period continues to be bedeviled by uncertainty as to the exact dates of the 18th and 19th Dynasty kings (see among others E. F. Wente and C. C. van Siclen III, in J. H. Johnson, ed., *Studies in Honor of George R. Hughes* [Chicago, 1976], 217–62; E. Hornung, in M. Görg, ed., *Festschrift Elmar Edel* [Bamberg, 1979], 247ff.; R. Krauss, *GM* 70 [1984], 37–44; idem, *Sothis- und Monddaten* [Hildesheim, 1985]). In the present work we are following the "high" chronology used in the *CAH*, computing the accession of Thutmose III at 1504 B.C. (the "middle" chronology would lower this date by fourteen years, and the "low" by twenty-five), and the expulsion of the Hyksos between 1555 and 1550 B.C. For recent discussions on the chronology of the Hyksos, see M. Bietak, *AJA* 88 (1984), 471–85; W. G. Dever, in *Palestine in the Bronze and Iron Ages* (London, 1985), 67–87.

[24] Helck, *Historisch-biographische Inschriften*, 41–44.

[25] For these epithets, see the stelae of Neferhotpe Ikhernofret (ibid., 45; P. Vernus, *ASAE* 68 [1982], 129–35) and Montuhotpi (J. Von Beckerath, *Untersuchungen zur politischen Geschichte der zweiten Zwischenzeit in Ägypten* [Glückstadt, 1965], 288; P. Vernus, *RdE* 40 [1989], 145–61), both found at Karnak.

[26] Helck, *Historisch-biographische Inschriften*, 41–44.

mose's ubiquitous allusions to them a century later. They are "Asiatics"[27] who have "destroyed the land"; they hail from "the land of the Asiatic,"[28] their leader is a "Syrian chief";[29] they have "overrrun Egypt."[30]

The international climate prevailing in the Near East in the second quarter of the seventeenth century B.C. commends itself for examination, for measured against the backdrop of the contesting states of the Fertile Crescent of MB IIB–C, the sudden and outright conquest of Egypt by the 15th Dynasty becomes much more likely. It was a period of internecine warfare in which great power centers vied with one another for the feudal allegiance of lesser kings, and when adventurers roved far abroad fighting for and winning kingdoms.[31] Armies were large and moved swiftly: "For four days, ten thousand soldiers of Babylon have passed by, coming from Sippar, and three thousand men have set out from Shubat-enlil for Eshnuna. Maybe he has taken them via Ashnakum, maybe via Sususum. Who knows?"[32] Marches were long and the stakes high: Yahdunlim cf Mari, on the mid-Euphrates, destroys a coalition and raises his frontiers on the Mediterranean;[33] Yarim-lim of Yamkhad (Aleppo in North Syria) swears to march to Der (south of the Zagros Mountains) to avenge a slight.[34] Always jockeying for position, the potentates of the day make and break alliances as their immediate interests dictate: "The king of Eshnuna will support me. Now send me troops so that I may reach my goal and then I will, together with your troops, send you strong forces in order that you may reach your goal";[35] "if the enemy comes against you again, my troops will come to your aid; but if the enemy comes against me, may your troops come to my aid!"[36] Failure to be vigilant meant sudden attack from a neighbor: "The king of Eshnuna has decided to build the city. . . . While he is building the city shall I do nothing but watch him? (No!) I shall attack his land!"[37] "It is an opportune time for your coming . . . these three cities are not well fortified: we can take them in a single day!

[27] ꜣmw (Kamose I, 4–5, 13; II, 11–12, 15–16, etc.); Sttyw (Kamose I, 4, 11).

[28] Kamose I, 7.

[29] Kamose II, 4.

[30] Kamose I, 13. The verb used is btn, which means "to set oneself in opposition to" (WB I, 485:17–486:2; E. Blumenthal, Untersuchungen zum ägyptischen Königtum des mittleren Reiches [Berlin, 1970], 1:212). This usually takes the "face" determinative, but when "walking-legs" are used, there seems to be a semantic overlap with bt, "to run (through)": cf. PT 140, 253, 769.

[31] Redford, Orientalia 39 (1970), 16.

[32] C. F. Jean, RA 39 (1942), 78, 81.

[33] G. Dossin, Syria 32 (1965), 1–28; J. D. Safren, JESHO 32 (1989), 28–29.

[34] G. Dossin, Syria 33 (1956), 63–69.

[35] ARM II, 33.

[36] ARM II, 72.

[37] ARM I, 123.

Come quickly now and take these cities in order that your troops may get booty!"[38] Pillaging and brutality were commonplace: "The troops of Eshnuna will take to pillaging and will set their face toward the Euphrates;"[39] "Thirty Sutu who have slaughtered all their sheep are preparing to make a raid;"[40] "The Banu-yamina have taken to raiding. Once they made a raid and took sheep, and I sent auxiliary troops who caught them";[41] "I sent N to the land of Ahuzim with an army. . . . he has wiped out the sortie of troops of the lands of the Turukeans who had assembled around him! Not one man escaped! On that same day the whole land of Ahazim was taken!"[42]

These references provide a paradigm of the kind of raid that the Hyksos conquest seems initially to have been. The motivation and the situation are alike optimal for postulating such an event: a strong Amorite state in the Levant, a weakened Egypt, the prospect of easy conquest and much booty. It remains to ascertain who were these foreign kings.

THE FIFTEENTH DYNASTY

Between the entry for *Dd-[msi]* in the Turin Canon ix, 9, and the section devoted to the Hyksos in Turin Canon x, 15, approximately thirty-two names intervene that have defied interpretation for many years. In fact it now appears that these are west Asiatic names, garbled in many cases beyond recognition in the course of transmission.[43] The appearance of six or seven entries tantalizingly resembling names known from Shamshi-adad's genealogy in the Assyrian king list[44] yields a clue to the true nature of this puzzling section. One well-attested trait in the culture of the west Asian Amorite kingdoms of the Middle Bronze Age is the worship of the royal ancestors in the form of a pedigree, which lent legitimacy to the regime;[45] and several examples of such pedigrees survive in written form. The thirty-two names in the Turin Canon immediately preceding the Hyksos constitute the family tree of the 15th Dynasty, preserved in the ancestor-cult at Avaris and transmitted in the area down to the 19th Dynasty. Their "foreign" (*ḫȝst*) association being misconstrued as an origin

---

[38] *ARM* V, 16.

[39] *Syria* 19 (1938), 121–22.

[40] *ARM* VI, 58.

[41] G. Dossin, in *Mélanges syriens offerts à M. R. Dussaud* (Paris, 1939), 981.

[42] *ARM* I, 69.

[43] Redford, *Orientalia* 39 (1970), 20 and n. 4; idem, *King-lists*, 199–200 and n. 245.

[44] Redford, *King-lists*, 201, n. 252.

[45] On the strength of the ancestral cult among the tribal Amorites, see D. Charpin and J.-M. Durand, *RdA* 80 (1986), 141–83.

in Xois (H^3sww), they turn up in the first millennium labeled a 14th Dynasty from Xois.[46]

If in their family tradition the Hyksos again demonstrate their unmistakable origins in a Middle Bronze "Amorite" kingship, once they had established themselves in Egypt they duly entered the Egyptian king-list tradition. Manetho lists six names for the 15th Dynasty, and the number is also six in the Turin Canon a millennium earlier; so that we may with considerable justification consider the number historical. At this point, however, the congruence of the two sources ceases. Whereas Turin Canon contains but one entry for Hyksos rulers, the epitome of Manetho (Africanus's version) records "Shepherd Kings again" for the 16th and 17th. Committed to a single, linear list of kings, Manetho can do nothing to indicate the contemporaniety of *two* regimes other than to list the same group as many times as there were coeval regimes. Failure to recognize this mechanism in the past has resulted in some comic reconstructions of the Hyksos era.[47] In the three versions of the epitome of Manetho's *Aegyptiaca* widely differing time spans are given for Hyksos rule: 250 years (Eusebius), 284 years (Africanus), and 511 years (Josephus).[48] The most plausible restoration of the figure in the Turin Canon, on the other hand, records 108 years, or a credible 18 years per reign on average.[49] The relative chronology of Egyptian history, combined with the evidence of carbon-14 tests, the ceramic chronology of western Asia, and the tightly meshed political history of Mesopotamia will permit only about a century for Hyksos rule. Manetho's (or his epitomizer's) organization and figures may therefore by safely ignored.

But what of Manetho's names? These too vary somewhat from version to version, but not to the same extent as the totals already listed.

Josephus	Africanus[50]	Eusebius
Salitis, 19 yrs.	Saites, 19 yrs.	Saites, 19 yrs.
Bnon, 44 yrs.	Bnon, 44 yrs.	Bnon, 40 yrs.
Apachnan, 36 yrs, 7 mos.	Pachnan, 61 yrs.	——
Apophis, 61 yrs.	Staan, 50 yrs.	——
Iannas, 50 yrs., 1 mo.	Archles, 49 yrs.	Archles, 30 yrs.
Assis, 49 yrs., 2 mos.	Apopis, 61 yrs.	Apopis, 14 yrs.

[46] Failure to recognize the 14th Dynasty as chimerical continues to result in strange reconstructions of the period immediately preceding the 15th Dynasty: see M. Bietak, *SAK* 11 (1984), 59–76; J. Yoyotte, *BSFE* 114 (1989), 17–63.

[47] Involving in the main theories of a "Greater" and a "Lesser" Hyksos dynasty: D. B. Redford, *History and Chronology of the Egyptian Eighteenth Dynasty. Seven Studies* (Toronto, 1967), 43–46.

[48] Waddel, *Manetho*, 86, 90, 92.

[49] A. H. Gardiner, *The Royal Canon of Turin* (Oxford, 1959), 17 (note).

[50] Listed under the 17th Dynasty.

Common to all three lists are the names Salitis (Saites), Bnon, and Apophis. Of the remaining names, Staan can plausibly be derived from Iannas through an orthographic error, while Archles through position and assigned length of reign can be identified with Assis. The total is thus reduced to six in agreement with the historical tradition. The only glaring discrepancy that remains, the position of Apophis, can now be resolved in favor of Africanus, thanks to an inscription from Tel el-Dab'a strongly implying that one 'lansas was the eldest son of Khayan.[51]

When we attempt to work back before Manetho, we encounter major difficulties in that the names do not match. An unfortunate lacuna in the papyrus of the Turin Canon has deprived us of the first five entries, and the sixth and sole surviving name is *Ḥ³mwdi*, which suits neither Assis nor Apophis. A genealogy of Memphite priests, drawn up in the eighth century B.C. mentions a certain king *Sharek* during what to us would be the Second Intermediate Period, preceded one generation earlier by a king *'A-ken*,[52] and followed by Apophis. Are these garbled forms of *Salitis* and *'-ḳn-r'* (one of the praenomens of Apophis), the latter treated derisively by construing it as "Brave Ass"?[53] To be sure, Apophis does appear in a piece of folklore of Ramesside date, about three hundred years after he must have lived, as one of the protagonists at the outbreak of the wars of liberation; but, beyond a vague recollection of the period, the story is devoid of historical reliability.[54]

Texts contemporary with the Hyksos occupation (mainly scarabs and seals, rarely stone inscriptions or papyrus documents) have yielded an impressive number of attestations of Hyksos royal names.[55]

1. The Good God *M³'-ib-r'*, the son of Re, Sheshy (attested on numerous scarabs from Egypt, Nubia, and Palestine).[56]

2. The Good God *Mr-wsr-r'*, the son of Re, Ya'kob-har (attested on numerous scarabs from Egypt, Nubia, and Palestine).[57]

---

[51] M. Bietak, *MDAIK* 37 (1981), pl. 6.

[52] L. Borchardt, *Die Mittel zur zeitlichen Festlegung von Punkten der ägyptischen Geschichte* (Cairo, 1935), 92ff. (fifth generation from Senwosret III).

[53] From *'³-ḳnn-r'*, "Great-of-Courage-is-Re."

[54] Redford, *Orientalia* 39 (1970), 35–38; efforts to read historical or cultic overtones into this "Shaggy Dog" story are quite wrongheaded in my view: L. Störk, *GM* 43 (1981), 67–68; H. Goedicke, *The Quarrel of Apophis and Seqenenre'* (San Antonio, 1986).

[55] See in general Von Beckerath, *Untersuchungen*, 269–80; Helck, *Beziehungen*², 89–106; idem, *Historisch-biographische Inschriften*, 54–58; W. A. Ward, *UF* 8 (1976), 353–65; A. Kempinski, in S. Groll, ed., *Pharaonic Egypt, the Bible and Christianity* (Jerusalem, 1985), 129–38.

[56] Von Beckerath, *Untersuchungen*, 278.

[57] A good deal has been written on this name (cf. *inter alia*, S. Yelvin, *JEA* 45 [1959], 16ff.; R. Giveon, *Tel Aviv* 3 [1976], 133). While it is clear that we have a West Semitic precative form, presumably from *'ḳb*, "to protect" (Ward, *UF* 8 [1976], 359) plus the divine

3. The Good God, the son of Re, Ya'am (var. 'am) (attested on a small number of scarabs lacking provenience).[58]
4. Horus: "He-who-Encompasses-the-Lands," the Good God, *Swsr.n-rʿ*, the son of Re Khayan (attested on monuments from the Delta and Upper Egypt, small objects from Mesopotamia, central Anatolia, and Crete, and on numerous scarabs from Egypt, one from Palestine, but none from Nubia).[59]
5. The eldest king's son, Yansas-X (attested on a door-jamb from Tel ed-Dab'a).[60]
6. The Good God, Lord of the Two Lands, *Nb-ḫpš-rʿ*, the son of Re, Apophis (attested on two small objects and a scarab).[61]
7. Horus: Who-Pacifies-the-Two-Lands, the Good God, *ʿ3-ḳnn-rʿ*, the son of Re, Apophis, Beloved of Seth (attested from half a dozen monuments and small objects mainly from Memphis or the Delta).[62]
8. The Good God / king of Upper and Lower Egypt, *ʿ3-wsr-rʿ*, the son of Re, Apophis (attested on monuments from Tel ed-Dab'a, Bubastis, Memphis, Thebes, Gebelein, and Spain, on the Rhind Mathmatical Payprus, on a scribe's kit, and on scarabs from Egypt and Palestine).[63]

Certain conclusions may be drawn at once and with confidence. First, the position of numbers 1 and 2 at the head of the list (although not their relative order) is put beyond doubt by the style and lack of sophistication

name, the identity of the latter is not at all clear, thanks to the vagaries of the orthography. Most examples give *-ḥr*, presumably "mountain deity," but some sixteen contain variant writings, *Yʿḳb-ʿ(r)*, *Yʿḳb-ʿr*, or *Yʿḳb-ʿm*. The latter (see Von Beckerath, *Untersuchungen*, 278; Giveon, *Tel Aviv* 3 [1976], 133 [8]) may be at once dismissed as an erroneous form: an original *ʿr* in hieratic has been misinterpreted as *mw* through the similarity of ligatures. But the question remains whether in the forms with *-ʿr* we have a different divine name. Two suggestions have been tendered: first that the *-ʿr* indicated the presence of *ʿali*, "the exalted one," or second that we are dealing with *bʿl*, i.e. "Ba'al," the two *b*s being written only once, as is the rule (see W. C. Hayes, *CAH³* II, pt. 1 (1973), 59; Albright, *Yahweh and the Gods*, 57, n. 10). On the other hand, since it is reasonably clear that all attested forms refer to the same individual, it may well be that the rarer *-ʿr* is an orthographic mistake for the common *-ḥr*.

[58] Von Beckerath, *Untersuchungen*, 278.
[59] Ibid., 271–72; Hayes, *CAH³* II, pt. 1 (1973), 60ff.; H. Stock, *MDOG* 94 (1963), 73–80; R. Giveon, *JEA* 51 (1985), 202–4; W. Helck, *Die Beziehungen Ägyptens und Vorderasiens zur Ägäis* (Darmstadt, 1979), 48–50.
[60] M. Bietak and M. Görg, *MDAIK* 37 (1981), 63–73; Kempinski, in *Pharaonic Egypt, the Bible and Christianity*, 131.
[61] Von Beckerath, *Untersuchungen*, 275; H. Gauthier, *Le livre des rois d'Égypte* (Cairo, 1912), 2:144, n. 7; Helck, *Historisch-biographische Inschriften*, 55 (no. 75).
[62] *Untersuchungen*, 274–75; Gauthier, *Livre des rois*, 2:141–43, no. 6; Helck, *Historisch-biographische Inschriften*, 55–56 (nos. 76–78).
[63] Von Beckerath, *Untersuchungen*, 272–74; Gauthier, *Livre des rois*, 2:139–43, nos. 5–6; Helck, *Historisch-biographische Inschriften*, 56–58 (nos. 79–85); I. Gamer-Wallert, *Ägyptische und ägyptisierende Funde auf der Iberischen Halbinsel* (Wiesbaden, 1978), 39–40; R. Giveon, in M. Görg, ed., *Fontes atque Pontes* (Wiesbaden, 1983), 155–61.

of their scarabs, the uncertain orthography, and the absence of any monumental inscriptions. Second, the sequence of numbers 4 and 5 is assured from the doorjamb referred to previously. Third, that number 8 is close to the end of the list finds support in the fact that *'3-wsr-r'* is now known to have been the opponent of Kamose within a decade of the expulsion of the Hyksos.[64] Finally, it is likely that numbers 6 and 7, both rarely attested, should be construed as earlier forms of number 8, and that we are dealing with but a single Apophis.[65] We may thus reconstruct the sequence of kings of the 15th Dynasty as follows:

The Historical Fifteenth Dynasty[66]	Manetho
1. *M3'-ib-r'* Sheshy	Salitis
2. *Mr-wsr-r'* Ya'kob-har	Bnon / Pachnan
3. *Swsr.n-r'* Khayan	Iannas
4. [————] Yansas-X	Assis
5. Three names, Apophis	Apophis
6. [————] *H3mwdi*	————

This list does not, however, exhaust the number of names to which aptly the term "Hyksos" may be applied. A handful of scarabs, mostly lacking provenience, provides evidence for five or possibly six names preceded by the title *hk3 h3s(w)t*:

1. Yat (?)[67]
2. 'Aper-'Anat[68]
3. 'Anat-har[69]
4. User-'Anat[70]
5. Khyan[71]
6. Samkuna[72]

Now in spite of the small number of attestations, the glyptic style of these scarabs proves them to date early in the Hyksos occupation of

[64] L. Habachi, *The Second Stela of Kamose and His Struggle against the Hyksos Ruler and His Capital* (Glückstadt, 1972).

[65] Redford, *History and Chronology*, 44, n. 90.

[66] Ordered somewhat differently, on the basis of glyptic styles, by W. A. Ward, in O. Tufnell, ed., *Studies on Scarab Seals* (Warminster, 1984), vol. 2, no. 1, 162ff., esp. 172. In a period of slightly over a century, where two of the six kings account for well over half the span (and probably over two-thirds of it), it is difficult to accept stylistic variations as a chronological indicator. See D. Franke, *Orientalia* 57 (1988), 260ff.

[67] R. Giveon, *Tel Aviv* 7 (1980), 90–91: "the (foreign) chief Yat(?), repeating life."

[68] G. T. Martin, *Egyptian Administrative and Private-Name Seals* (Oxford, 1971), no. 318.

[69] Ibid., nos. 349–50; Von Beckerath, *Untersuchungen*, 279.

[70] W. M. F. Petrie, *Scarabs and Cylinders with Names* (London, 1917), xxi, D 15.1.

[71] *Untersuchungen*, 272.

[72] Martin, *Seals*, no. 1453.

Egypt.[73] The fact that none displays any *Egyptian royal* epithets, but only an expression long used for *foreign* rulers, places them within a known political category: they are not kings of Egypt, but rulers of and from alien lands who have, however, come sufficiently within the penumbra of Egyptian culture and government for someone to deem it appropriate to write their names in Egyptian. Their names, in fact, *must* be used in day-to-day affairs. It would appear to me that the persons named here carry us back to the very generation of the conquest, and quite likely reflect the federated chiefs attending Sheshy/Salitis on the morrow of his victory.

HYKSOS RULE IN EGYPT

The evidence has led us to the reasonable conclusion that the advent of the Hyksos took the form of a real military conquest along the lines that we see reflected in the great archives of the eighteenth and seventeenth centuries in western Asia.[74] Along with Sheshy (Salitis) came a number of lesser "kings," following their suzerain, just as was the practice in west Asia. If, as the Turin Canon indicates, Sheshy's reign proved relatively short, the second and third generations of Hyksos kings may have even participated in the conquest, which would lend credence to the assumption that in the "*ḥk³ ḫ³swt* Khayan" we should recognize the future king. The conquest may well have involved the kind of destruction that Manetho describes, and Memphis and Itj-towy were probably taken quickly and pillaged.[75] Dedu-mose, we may well imagine, beat a hasty retreat and took up quarters in Thebes far to the south.

About the same time, or perhaps slightly earlier, another blow fell: the Middle Kingdom holdings in Lower Nubia, long neglected by the 13th Dynasty, broke away. Native tribesmen sacked some Egyptian fortresses, took over and refurbished others, and may even have smelted copper.[76] Shortly there developed on the upper Nile, centered upon Kerma at the Third Cataract in the Dongola reach, an amorphous Nubian "kingdom"

[73] H. Stock, *Studien zur Geschichte und Archäologie der XIII. bis XVII. Dynastien Ägyptens* (Hamburg, 1942), 473, n. 2; 492; 534, n. 3; 729–30.

[74] Cf. G. Dossin, *Syria* 19 (1938), 117; J. Munn-Rankin, *Iraq* 18 (1956), 68ff.

[75] F. Gomàa, *Die Besiedlung Ägyptens während des mittieren Reiches* (Wiesbaden, 1987), 39. The pillaging, which resulted in the scattering far and wide over the Delta of Middle Kingdom memorials (cf. A. Dodson, *ZÄS* 114 [1987], 44), has misled many into false reconstructions of 13th Dynasty history: see n. 89. Both Ahmose and Hatshepsut refer to the refurbishing of temples (Helck, *Historisch-biographische Inschriften*, 109–10; A. H. Gardiner, *JEA* 32 [1946], pl. 6:36ff.), but it may well have been only in Thutmose III's time that a full-scale program of rebuilding in the Delta was set on foot: *Urk* IV, 1443.

[76] B. G. Trigger, *History and Settlement of Lower Nubia* (New Haven, Conn., 1959), 104; A. W. Lawrence, *JEA* 51 (1965), 72; W. B. Emory, *Egypt in Nubia* (London, 1965), 166–68; H. S. Smith, *The Fortress of Buhen. The Inscriptions* (London, 1976), 80ff.

shaped along the lines of the pharaonic monarchy, and looking to Egypt for its cultural expression. Egyptian settlements in Nubia, and perhaps even some in southern Upper Egypt, were pillaged to provide statuary and other items of adornment for the "residency" at Kerma.[77]

The weakened 13th Dynasty, driven back to the original homestead whence the ancestral house had come, now faced hostility on two fronts. It is very likely that the belligerent tone of two stelae from Karnak finds a context in this period of the threat of even deeper incursions into the narrowed Thebaid. On one,[78] King Sekhem-re 'Onkh-towy Neferhotpe Ikhernofret describes himself as

> he who entered his city with sustenance preceding him, one united with holiday, a mighty king beloved of his army, good Horus who brings offerings, who causes his city to live when it had fallen into want, leader of victorious Thebes, the Good God, beloved of Re, son of Amun king of the gods, who protects his city when it had "gone under" when it was submerged, together with the foreigners, [who pacifies] on its behalf the rebellious foreign lands through the power of his father Amun, who overthrew [for her the enem]ies that had rebelled against him.

On the second,[79] a king Montuhotpi is eulogized:

> One ought with jubilation to praise [. . .] before him, at the departure from his house, like a sun disk beloved of his army; he has overpowered [. . .] one lives by his plans [————] of victorious Thebes! I am a king of the interior [homeland] of Wese, this city of mine, master (sic) of the entire land, the victorious town [mistress of] every town! The great god, the likeness of Re, with none to emulate him, forever! Over me does every one exult, the [. . .] of the gods, who drove back all foreign lands and rescued his city in his might; there is no plundering of people in ⟨his presence (?)⟩ ⟨traces⟩ like Sekhmet in the year of her vengeance (i' ⟨ḥr⟩.s), one feared for his flaming breath, who overthrows his attackers [who had come to (?)] the drinking hole (?)[80] of his fortress, like cattle (around ?) his battlements; from whose fortress (like) crocodiles of the inundation, the army came forth as comes forth terror from [. . .] There was none that could stand up to them . . . (fragment C) who gives timely . . . and it comes to pass through his utterance, who acts with his overpowering arm, sharp-witted one who comes forth from [. . . five groups] who is over the Two Lands, . . .

---

[77] F. Hintze, ZÄS 91 (1964), 84; W. Helck, UF (1976), 8, 102ff.; B. J. Kemp, in *Ancient Egypt, a Social History* (Cambridge, 1983), 162–68. For the Kerma kingdom, see W. Y. Adams, in E. Endesfelder, ed., *Ägypten und Kusch* (Berlin, 1977), 41ff.; C. Bonnet, in J. Vercoutter, ed., *Hommage à Serge Sauneron* (Cairo, 1979), 3ff.; D. O'Connor, *JARCE* 21 (1984), 65ff.

[78] See n. 25.

[79] See n. 25. The present translation is from the author's hand copy.

[80] Cf. CT VI, 231m.

Bombastic though the phraseology appears to us moderns, specific events prompted the inscribing of both texts. We see in one a city in want, relieved by the timely arrival of the king with food, and the repulse of the enemy, "the foreign lands"; and in the other, the defeat and rout of "attackers," undoubtedly the "foreign lands" again, who are likened to animals slinking around a fortress to drink at the watering hole. It is tempting to see in both texts the poetic commemoration of a desperate defense of Thebes itself against Nubian or Asiatic invaders, or perhaps against both. It is equally attractive to interpret the destruction level over the ruins of the last Middle Kingdom city at Thebes as the result of one such attack, perhaps the one that brought a final end to the hopelessly weakened Thirteenth Dynasty.[81] But whether the agent was Nubian or Hyksos remains a moot point. At any rate, at one stage in their occupation, the Hyksos could claim sufficient domination over the Thebaid to erect a monumental construction at Gebelein, just south of Thebes.[82]

Certainly the Hyksos had lost no time in making contact with the Nubians, probably employing the oasis route through Bahriya, Dakhleh, and Dush to gain access to the Nubian Nile at Toshka.[83] Numerous scarabs and sealings of Sheshy are attested from the former Egyptian fortress of Uronarti,[84] and from Kerma;[85] and Ya'kob-har appears also at the latter site.[86] A lively "trade" (exchange of goods) took place in oil[87] and luxury items such as furniture and weaponry.[88] As we shall see, this trade also involved a political relationship of dependence, couched in terms familiar *mutatis mutandis* from western Asia.

The Hyksos's choice of a residence, according to Manetho, fell upon Memphis; but the route of their entry made them keenly aware of the strategic value of the eastern Delta. Here, on the easternmost branch of the Nile, thirty-seven kilometers northeast of Bubastis, had long stood an administrative and defensive settlement called "The Mansion of the Two Roads of Akhtoy," to judge from its name, a foundation of the kings of the 9th and 10th Dynasties of Herakleopolis. (The name itself indicates

---

[81] But see the caveat on p. 103 and n. 20.

[82] G. Daressy, *RT* 16 (1894), 42.

[83] Redford, *JSSEA* 7, no. 3 (1977), 2–3f.

[84] O. Tufnell, *JEA* 61 (1975), 69.

[85] G. A. Reisner, *Excavations at Kerma* (Cambridge, 1923), 2:75, fig. 168, nos. 57–58, 61–62.

[86] Ibid., 2:75, fig. 168, no. 56.

[87] If this is what the Tel el-Yehudiya juglets contained; on this ware, see M. Kaplan, *The Origin and Distribution of Tell el-Yahudiyeh Ware* (Göteborg, 1980); J. M. Weinstein, *AJA* 86 (1982), 450; Bietak, in Rainey, *Egypt, Israel, Sinai*, 46–49. Certainly the shape of this juglet places it within the *ḥnm*-type, which was mainly an oil container (Compte du Mesnil de Buisson, *Les noms et signes égyptiens désignant des vases* [Paris, 1935], 45ff.). These are found only at Buhen and Aniba: Kemp, in *Ancient Egypt*, 167.

[88] Kemp, in *Ancient Egypt*, 160–73.

the optimum location of the site, at the divide between the route north-west to Mendes and the central Delta, and the route northeast to the Sinai and Gaza.) The town, originally a planned, walled settlement, was expanded in the 12th Dynasty by Amenemhat I and by Senwosret III through the addition on the north side of a *ku*-temple dedicated to the founder of the house, surrounded by large mud-brick houses of the priests and administrators. Possibly because of its location, it became known (colloquially?) as the "Mansion of the Desert Tract," in Egyptian, *Ḥwt-w'rt*, rendered into Greek Ἀυάϱις, or Avaris; and the local district, again because of the proximity of the desert, was dubbed "The Opening of the Farmland." All through the 13th Dynasty the town and its environs retained their importance as an administrative center and were patron-ized especially by king Nehesy (first quarter of the seventeenth century B.C.)[89]

The excavations from 1966 of the Institute of Egyptology of the University of Vienna, under the direction of Manfred Bietak, at the site of Tel ed-Dab'a, immediately south of Ezbet Rushdi, have cast a flood of light on the Hyksos occupation. Here were uncovered no less than six discern-ible strata of MB IIB–C, along Canaanite lines. The domestic and cultic character of the quadrants excavated owed nothing to Egyptian culture, being wholly of northern, Levantine inspiration. Family tombs sur-rounded the temples. Burials with weapons and the sacrifice of sheep were common, and often teams of donkeys had been interred before the door of the tomb. A few tombs yielded rich appointments, including diadems. The size of the site, which continued to grow throughout the period, as well as the monumentality of its architecture and the wealth of its occu-pants, marks it as a major settlement of invaders, and possibly also the residence and place of burial of their rulers.[90]

The extent of Asiatic occupation in the Delta in the seventeenth and sixteenth centuries B.C., as revealed by recent archaeological work, is con-fined to the eastern, Bubastite, branch of the Nile and the Wady Tumilat,

---

[89] On the "Mansion of the Two Roads of Akhtoy," see S. Adam, *ASAE* 56 (1959), 207–26; Gomàa, *Besiedlung*, 232–33; M. Bietak, *Marhaba* 3 (1983), 41; idem, *Avaris and Pi-Ramesse* (London, 1981), 290. On Nehesy's patronage of this region, see M. Bietak, *SAK* 11 (1984), 59ff.; the provenience of Nehesy's monuments in the eastern Delta have, how-ever, nothing to do with the territorial extent of his domain. So little remains from this king (and others of the same period), and so widely scattered in later times were 13th Dynasty memorials, that it is building a house of cards to endow Nehesy and his reign with such specifics as Bietak does (in Rainey, *Egypt, Israel, Sinai*, 50). Archaeological evidence in gen-eral, no matter how aesthetically pleasing it may appear to those whose calling limits them to excavation, cannot sustain such weight.

[90] M. Bietak, *Tell el-Dab'a* (Vienna, 1975); idem, *Avaris and Pi-Ramesse*; for the palace, see M. Bietak, *AnzÖsterrAkadWissenschaften* 121 (1984), 312–49; D. Eigner, *JOAI* 56 (1985), 19–25; J. Leclant, *Orientalia* 56 (1987), 303–4.

thus the eastern fringe of the Delta.[91] Here, as at Tell ed-Deb'a-Avaris, we have to reckon with a large immigrant population of Palestinian or Syrian origin, which lived unto itself apart from, and with little or no intercourse with, any native Egyptian population that may have been in the area (Plate 11).

Elsewhere, in the central and western Delta, and in the Nile Valley proper, we may safely assume the Egyptian population to have survived intact, albeit subverted now to Hyksos authority. During the later war of liberation, Kamose the Theban patriot inveighs against his fellow countrymen "who allowed themselves to hearken to the call of the Asiatics, having forsaken Egypt, their mistress" (Kamose II, 18), so that collaboration was at least perceived to have occurred. Manetho states that Salitis posted garrisons throughout the territory reduced by him,[92] and contemporary texts prove this to have been the case. Kamose refers to "the places of the Asiatics" in Middle Egypt (Kamose I, 11), uses the locution "a nest of Asiatics" of the town of Nefrusy (ibid., 13), and speaks of an Asiatic garrison and border patrol in Pr-š³ḳ (ibid., 16). Manetho's claim that Salitis taxed the country is also corroborated by Kamose's exasperated comment: "No one can be at ease when they are milched by the taxes of the Asiatics!" (ibid., 4).

Of native forms of Hyksos administration, we know next to nothing. In the light of the destruction of the Hyksos monuments by the vengeful Egyptians once the foreigners were at last expelled, it is no wonder that we know so little; and it is left to the reader to assign appropriate weight

Plate 11. Rampart of packed sand and stones, Tell el-Yehudiyeh, a Hyksos settlement about sixteen kilometers north-northeast of Heliopolis.

[91] Bietak, SAK 11 (1984), 69, fig. 5.
[92] Waddell, Manetho, 80.

to the following spotty evidence. No texts have come to light to suggest the office of vizier was maintained. On the other hand, an apparent plethora of scarab seals belonging to treasurers militates, in the opinion of some scholars, in favor of the assumption that this office ranked high in the Hyksos bureaucracy.[93] A number of inscriptions mentioning "king's-(eldest)-sons" similarly test our interpretive powers. As already noted, the title "king's son" had undergone a weakening resulting in an extended sphere of reference. Are these Hyksos "king's sons" in reality courtesy offspring, or are they genuine princes? The title "he who follows his lord," or in our parlance "retainer," occurs but once,[94] but it seems in keeping with a rationale derived from Egyptian practice of the First Intermediate Period and 12th Dynasty. Similarly, the choice of praenomen by the Hyksos kings follows a pattern in vogue under the kings of the 13th Dynasty, their predecessors. One might, with some reason, conclude that the Hyksos thus adopted forms they found ready to hand in Egypt, and suffered native mentors to counsel them.

One can only wish that some evidence on the "feudal" traditions of the Hyksos had come to light in an Egyptian context. The "Amorite" tradition in the Levant and the Tigris-Euphrates Valley had taken the form of a number of "great kings" constituting the focuses around which "lesser" kings had gravitated. The lesser, dependent, kings were viewed by the Great King as his "sons," and he, from their vantage point, as their "father."[95] One, and perhaps the prime, piece of evidence from an Egyptian source is the letter of Apophis to the ruler of Kush, preserved in the second Kamose stela, in which Apophis calls his correspondent "my son."[96] The Theban administrator, the earliest contemporary of Apophis, appears with the praenomen *Sknn-rˤ*, which has suggested to some a vassal's mimicry of his suzerain who early adopted the praenomen *ˤ3-knn-rˤ*.

HYKSOS RELIGION

The Asiatic kings who founded the 15th Dynasty showed their alien origin to no greater degree than in the gods they worshiped. While they suffered Egyptian lector-priests to fashion for them throne-names with the infixed name of the Egyptian sun-god Re, the Hyksos kings remained de-

[93] W. Helck, *Zur Verwaltung der mittleren und neuen Reiches* (Leiden, 1958), 79–80; for the individual treasurers Hur, ʿAper, Saˀdy, Per-em-wehat and Redi-haˀ, see P. Labib, *Das Herrschaft der Hyksos in Ägypten und ihr Sturz* (Berlin, 1936), pl. 6; T. Säve-Söderbergh, *JEA* 37, 65; W. A. Ward, *Orientalia Lovaniensia Periodica* 6–7 (1976), 589ff.; Martin, *Seals*, nos. 479–508, 904–12 and passim; Helck, *Historisch-biographische Inschriften*, 57:83.

[94] G. Daressy, *ASAE* 7 (1906), 115ff.

[95] Munn-Rankin, *Iraq* 18 (1956), 68–110.

[96] R. Stadelmann, *MDAIK* 20 (1965), 62–69.

voted to the native cults they had brought with them from Asia. Since 90 percent of our textual evidence on Canaanite religion comes from the Late Bronze Age, the accuracy of our identifications and the propriety of our use of this evidence for the Middle Bronze Age may be questioned. Nonetheless, it is usually assumed that there is a continuum in the tradition between the seventeenth century B.C. and the fourteenth.

Weight is added to this sanguine argument by the divine infixes in some of the "Hyksos" names examined previously. Prominent here are two deities, male and female. The latter is referred to as 'Anat, well known from the Ugaritic archives as the bloodthirsty consort of the "Lord" Ba'al;[97] and presumably it is she that appears as a quasi "Hathor" in certain Hyksos scarabs as "Mistress of the Two Trees."[98] The male (partner?) is referred to by the epithet hr, "the mountain (deity)," and in this connection one can only compare the strong connection of Ba'al in the Late Bronze Age with mountains, especially Mount Sapon.[99]

In fact, there is more evidence for this identification. The story of Apophis and Sequenenre, circulating in Egypt in Ramesside times, describes how Apophis "made Seth his personal lord, and served no other god in this entire land except Seth. He built a temple of fine and eternal work beside the 'House of Apophis' l.p.h., and [there] he appeared [every] day to make daily sacrifice to Seth, while the courtiers [of the Palace] l.p.h. carried garlands, exactly as it is done in the temple of Re-harakhty."[100] The god Seth enjoyed an equivocal role in the Egyptian pantheon. Opponent of Osiris and adversary of Horus, a wild and ruddy god associated with the desert, sterility, and confusion, he nonetheless fulfilled a positive function as champion of the sun-god, and author of thunder.[101] In the New Kingdom, he was to be identified, thanks to an *Interpretatio Aegyptiaca*, with the Canaanite Ba'al, and the chances that this was already the case under the Hyksos are heightened by the "Four Hundred Year Stele." This monument, set up by Ramesses II at Avaris, some time after his thirty-fourth year (i.e., 1270 or 1257), commemorates the four hundreth year of the "reign" of the god Seth, who is pictured in the vignette quoted

[97] Van Seters, *The Hyksos,* 175–78. R. Stadelmann, *Syrisch-Palästinensische Gottheiten in Ägypten* (Leiden, 1967), 88–95.

[98] I. Beste, *Corpus Antiquitatum Aegypticarum: Scarabaen,* Kestner Museum (Hanover, 1979), no. 2844.

[99] A. S. Kapelrud, *Ba'al in the Ras Shamra Texts* (Copenhagen, 1952), 57–58; C. H. Gordon, *Ugaritic Handbook* (Rome, 1965), no. 2185; S. M. Olyan, *Asherah and the Cult of Yahweh in Israel* (Atlanta, 1988), 62–63; for Ba'al Saphon at Tell ed-Dab'a, see Bietak, in Rainey, *Egypt, Israel, Sinai,* 43.

[100] A. H. Gardiner, *Late Egyptian Stories* (Brussels, 1931), 85–86; Goedicke, *The Quarrel,* 10.

[101] H. Te Velde, *Seth God of Confusion* (Leiden, 1967).

previously in the guise of Baʿal.[102] It would seem most likely that this "reign" is the period since the inception of Hyksos rule in Avaris, still commemorated four centuries later, and ascribed to the Seth-Baʿal deity whose association with the Hyksos lived on in memory.[103]

Seth had enjoyed a cult in the northeastern Delta prior to the coming of the Hyksos, and Nehesy had made dedications to him.[104] In hieroglyphic texts the Hyksos too maintain the use of "Seth" when, in their native parlance, Baʿal would undoubtedly have appeared.[105]

The Reign of Apophis and the Hyksos "Empire"

The reign of Apophis (c. 1615–1575 B.C.) marks the pinnacle of Hyksos power in Egypt and abroad. The words put in Apophis's mouth by Kamose (Kamose II, 16–17) probably accurately reflect the "legal" extent of Hyksos suzerainty once the formative stage of their incursions had passed: "I am lord without equal from Hermopolis to Pi-Hathor ⟨as well as⟩ Avaris and on both rivers." The territory thus delimited takes us from the southernmost populous town under the Hyksos's control, namely Hermopolis in the fifteenth Upper Egyptian nome—Kamose I, 5, proves the actual southern frontier to have been at Cusae,[106] in the fourteenth Upper Egyptian nome—to the site of Pi-Hathor northeast of Avaris and close enough to the eastern frontier that it could be considered an "Ultima Thule."[107] The allusion to Avaris and the "Two Rivers" encompasses the entire Delta, the reference to Pi-Hathor and Avaris having accounted for the eastern branch of the Nile, and the Two Rivers being the central and western branches.[108] Later tradition was to credit Apophis (Epafos) with

[102] Redford, *Orientalia* 39 (1970), 23–31; Van Seters, *The Hyksos*, 97ff.

[103] Stadelmann's unfortunate persistence in construing the four hundred years as a temple jubilee, computed from the founding of a cult and shrine of the god in Avaris (see most recently *LdÄ* 6 [1986], 1042), would have the effect of rupturing the connection between the "reign" of the god and the regime of those who worshiped him. But clearly the "reign" of Seth, like the "reigns" of other gods, is modeled on the terrestrial phenomenon; and no earthly king dates the inception of his reign from the building of his palace.

[104] W.M.F. Petrie, *Tanis* (London, 1885), 1: pl. 2.

[105] Helck, *Historisch-biographische Inschriften*, 55, no. 76.

[106] Von Beckerath, *Untersuchungen*, 147, n. 4.

[107] H. Gauthier, *Dictionnaire des noms géographiques contenus dans les textes hiéroglyphiques* (Cairo, 1926), 2:117; cf. the Nitocris adoption stela where it is placed between Tanis and Bubastis (line 25: R. A. Caminos, *JEA* 50 [1964], 93). In P. Anast. III, 3:3, it is noted for its rushes, suggesting a location close to the marches of *Ṯwfy*. In New Kingdom papyri an "Upper Mansion" and a "Lower Mansion" are located immediately before the "Ways of Horus" (i.e., the start of the Sinai route into Asia), and two places after Avaris: R. A. Caminos, *Literary Fragments in the Hieratic Script* (Oxford, 1956), pl. 6, 3:14. These are possibly a playful or garbled rendering of *Pr-Ḥwt-Ḥr*: Gomàa, *Besiedlung*, 2:235.

[108] On the eastern, Bubastite, branch as the "Water of Avaris," see A. H. Gardiner, *Ancient Egyptian Onomastica* (Oxford, 1947), 2:155*.

having "founded Memphis," but this may refer, if genuine, to nothing more than construction work (a palace?) in that city.[109]

The Thebaid, under the expiring 16th Dynasty, probably constituted an embarrassing and indigestible part of Egypt, more trouble than it was worth to subjugate completely. Kamose's taunt to Apophis (Kamose II, 1–2), "Your authority is restricted inasmuch as you, in your capacity as suzerain, have made me a chief," suggests that Apophis maintained the fiction that the Thebaid was administered by the Theban kings as vassals on Apophis's behalf. Nonetheless, the presence of some kind of Hyksos fort at Gebelein south of Thebes[110] shows that Hyksos control was something more than a legal fiction.

The degree of Hyksos control over the land whence they had emerged remains problematical. Design scarabs dubbed "Hyksos" simply because they are ubiquitous in Egypt and Palestine during the period of the 15th Dynasty may or may not be proof of political rule: at most they attest to the presence of a sort of cultural penumbra. Since they combine Asiatic with Egyptian motifs, executed with traces of an alien treatment, their assignment to the Hyksos period is strengthened. Hyksos royal sealings and scarabs, on the other hand, are much rarer in Palestine.[111] Sheshy and Yaq'obhar are attested, the latter as far north as Galilee;[112] a sealing of Khiyan comes from the Shephelah,[113] and two of $'3$-wsr-(r'), probably Apophis, from Palestine, with unknown provenience.[114] Other scarabs with heraldic designs and the liberal use of royal terms and epithets may signal the presence of royal plenipotentiaries of one sort or another. One wonders whether such phrases, couched within cartouches as "The Good Sun," "He whom Re has caused to appear," "the Sun of Every Land," are not direct references to the reigning monarch.

We are not, however, left to flounder in a sea of scarabs, notoriously difficult, as they are, to interpret for the benefit of the chronologist and historian alike; for we have more specific textual references. The assumed names of Khayan and Apophis, namely "He-who-encompasses-the-lands," and "Re-is-master-of-the-Sword,"[115] must excite some suspicions. The text on an offering table, dedicated to Seth by Apophis, originally

---

[109] Eusebius, *Hieronymus Chronikon* (ed. Helm), 32, 44 (for year 92 of Hyksos rule, i.e. late in Apophis's reign). There remains the possibility that this tradition arises solely out of the confusion of Apophis with "Apis," here misconstrued as a founding father of the city.

[110] See p. 113; cf. also the ax blade in the British Museum calling Apophis "beloved of Sobek, lord of Su-menu": T.G.H. James, *BMQ* 24 (1961), 40.

[111] See R. Giveon, *CdE* 49 (1974), 222ff.

[112] R. Giveon, *GM* 44 (1981), 17–20.

[113] R. Giveon, *JEA* 51 (1965), 202–4.

[114] A. Rowe, *Catalogue of Scarabs in the Palestine Archaeological Museum* (Cairo, 1936), nos. 210–11.

[115] See p. 109.

from Avaris, reads as follows: "Horus-He-Who-Pacifies-the-Two-Lands, the Good One, '3-knn-r', living ⟨forever⟩! He made it as his monument for his father [Seth], Lord of Avaris, when he placed all lands beneath his feet."[116] To be compared at this juncture are the epithets Apophis assigns himself on that most candid of personal revelations, the scribal palette of Atju: "Stout-hearted on the day of battle, with a greater reputation (literally, name) than any other king, who protects strange lands that have never seen him . . . there is not his peer in any land!"[117] Here is a fighting king who has made a name for himself, and who perceives himself a universal monarch with far-flung obligations. Kamose's description of the harbor at Avaris during the reign of Apophis now takes on a new light. The Theban rebel refers to the "hundreds of ships of fresh cedar which were filled with gold, lapis, silver, turquoise, bronze axes without number, not to mention the moringa-oil, fat, honey, willow, box-wood, sticks, and all their fine woods—all the fine products of Syria!" (Kamose II, 13–15).

Though meager, this evidence cannot be misinterpreted. Military conquest, clearly in the north, the status of a great king, vast amounts of tribute—all this accrued to the great Apophis, and perhaps to his forebear Khiyan as well. The latter's name is known from a number of small objects[118]—a weight from Baghdad, an unguent vessel from Boghaz Keui (the later Hyksos capital), and the lid of an alabaster vessel from Knossos—which at one time was enough to conjure up to some scholars the vision of a world empire.[119] There was nothing of the sort, of course, during Hyksos times; but these scattered objects do tell us something. When combined with the vessel inscribed for T^3w^3, the princess and sister of Apophis from Spain, and the plate of Ḥrit, a daughter of Apophis from Amenhotep I's tomb at Thebes, can we catch a glimpse of an active court at Avaris, with international interests, sending diplomatic presents and perhaps arranging marriages with the city states of Palestine and Syria and the Aegean?[120] As evidence for the same kind of diplomatic contact

---

[116] Helck, *Historisch-biographische Inschriften*, 55, no. 76.

[117] Ibid., 58.

[118] Von Beckerath, *Untersuchungen*, 271–72, for references.

[119] W. Fr. von Bissing, *AfO* 11 (1936–37), 325–35.

[120] While the weight purchased in Baghdad has no reliable provenience, the checkered histories of the other pieces are more certain. The piece from Boghaz Keui undoubtedly ended up there in the fourteenth century B.C. as booty or tribute from one of the Hittite dependencies in Syria (Stock, *MDOG* 94 [1963], 73–80). The Spanish find was probably carried to the Iberian peninsula at a much later date from one of the coastal towns when in the first millennium Phoenician trade was dispersing many objects of Egyptian manufacture all over the western Mediterranean (Gamer-Wallert, *Ägyptische Funde*; J. Padro i Parcerisa, *Egyptian-Type Documents from the Mediterranean Littoral of the Iberian Peninsula* [Leiden, 1983]). The jar from Knossos was uncovered in a contemporary locus (R. W. Hutch-

we must construe the numerous statuary of Middle Kingdom date found all over western Asia from Gaza to the Euphrates. These objects must have formed part of the "booty" seized during the initial expansion of Hyksos power throughout Egypt, and later put to use in the gift exchange with Levantine states.[121]

Whether anything more than a sphere of interest should be postulated beyond the Sinai for the Hyksos dynasty is difficult to say at present. The ease with which the survivors of the war of liberation could hold out aginst Ahmose at Sharuhen near Gaza has suggested to some the existence of a Hyksos dependency centered in that city, and controlling most of the Philistine plain north to about Joppa.[122] It should be remembered that during the age of Shamsi-adad and Hammurabi (late eighteenth and early seventeenth centuries B.C.) Hazor in the north Jordan Valley had been a major power center, presumably exercising control over much of northern Palestine and the Golan.[123] The MB IIB–C strata revealed in Yadin's excavation of the site show a continuing prosperity throughout the seventeenth and into the sixteenth centuries B.C., only terminating in a great destruction at the outset of Late Bronze I;[124] so that presumably the Hazor regime would have maintained its powerful position through most, if not all, the Hyksos period. Unless Apophis himself is the author of the destruction of MB IIC Hazor, we can only assume Hazor's continued hegemony would have blocked Hyksos attempts to expand their control northward.

Hyksos relations with transmarine neighbors pose many problems, in spite of the undeniable evidence of the Khiyan text from Knossos. There is remarkably little other evidence supporting any contact between Egypt and the Aegean at this time. There are no Middle Minoan III objects from Egypt, and very few Egyptian objects from contemporary Crete or the Greek mainland.[125] Aegean trade was directed mainly eastward toward North Syria, and via Syrian ports to Meospotamia. The palace frescoes at

---

inson, *Prehistoric Crete* [Harmondsworth, 1962], 197; Helck, *Beziehungen* Ägäis, 48), and was probably sent directly to Crete.

[121] J. M. Weinstein, *BASOR* 213 (1974), 56; 217 (1975), 9–10; Helck, *UF* 8 (1976), 101ff.; idem, *Beziehungen Ägäis*, 45–48.

[122] A. Alt, *Kleine Schriften zur Geschichte des Volkes Israel* (Munich, 1959), 3:107; Helck, *Beziehungen*², 121; on Sharuhen, see A. Kempinski, *IEJ* 24 (1974), 145ff.; R. Giveon, *LdÄ* 6 (1984), 532; there is no reason to make of Tel el-Ajjul more than it really is, viz. the hastily chosen, last stronghold of a fleeing regime: the wealth excavated at the site may simply indicate that Khamudi, the last king, holed up there: C. Vandersleyan, *Les guerres d'Amosis* (Brussels, 1971), 127, n. 1.

[123] See p. 94.

[124] Y. Yadin, *Hazor* (London, 1970), 31, 124–25.

[125] J. Vercoutter, *Essai sur les relations entre Égyptiens et pre-Héllènes* (Paris, 1954), 82; J.D.S. Pendelbury, *Aegyptiaca* (Cambridge, 1930), nos. 33, 34, 57, 297–98.

Ugarit, Mari, and Alalakh have rightly been compared with similar frescoes in the palace at Knossos;[126] and the Mari archives actually refer to products imported from Kaptara (Crete).[127] Was it indirectly, via Syria, that the Hyksos enjoyed contact with the Aegean?[128]

Through the retrieval and examination of widely scattered pieces of evidence, the reign of Apophis is appearing through the mists of history as a time of some cultural prosperity. The century that had elapsed since the conquest had sufficed to lend a veneer of Nilotic sophistication to the royal family at least. Apophis even had pretensions to literacy and expertise in the hieroglyphic script. On the aforementioned scribal palette he calls himself "a scribe of Re, taught by Thoth himself . . . multitalented (literally, with numerous [successful] deeds) on the day when he reads faithfully all the difficult (passages) of the writings, as flows the Nile." We may well believe his claim to be interested in literature, for it was in his reign (year 33) that the Rhind Mathmatical Papyrus was copied; and other literary pieces such as the Westcar Papyrus may well date from the same reign. Kamose paints, unwittingly we may be sure, a charming picture of the capital Avaris under Apophis, well fortified and rich during this last period of its supremacy. Its walls are high and crowned with harems with windows through which the women peer out, like animals in their holes. A crowded harbor stands to the north, and the land around it is flat. While desert lies to the east, there are vineyards in the vicinity; and these produce wine for the court.[129] Oblivious of what was in store, the Hyksos rulers were not to imbibe this wine for long.

[126] Helck, *Beziehungen Ägäis*, 107.

[127] G. Dossin, *RA* 64 (1970), 97ff.; A. Malamat, *IEJ* 21 (1971), 31ff.; F. Matz, *CAH*[3] II, pt. 1 (1973), 162–63; J. Strange, *Caphtor/Keftiu. A New Investigation* (Leiden, 1980), 90–93.

[128] On this trade, see Matz, *CAH*[3] II, pt. 1 (1973), 162–63. It has been suggested, largely on the basis of the fabulous treasure of the shaft graves at Mycenae that the relations between Egypt and Greece in the MM III period extended also to the military. One theory ascribes the wealth to mercenaries who aided the Egyptians in their battle with the Hyksos (A. W. Persson, *New Tombs at Dendra near Medea* [Lund, 1942], 178–96; F. Schachermeyer, *ArOr* 17 [1947], 331ff.; idem, *Anthropos* 46 [1951], 705ff.); another conjures up fugitive Hyksos as an ingressing element to account for the "new" ruling class the tombs represent (cf. F. H. Stubbings, *CAH*[3] II, pt. 1 [1973], 633–37). No evidence from Egypt supports either contention. One feels that a too literal interpretation of the Io-Danaus cycle of legends has prompted a somewhat prejudiced view of the period: see R. B. Edwards, *Kadmos the Phoenician* (Amsterdam, 1979), 59–61, 169–72, 189, n. 208; R. Drews, *The Coming of the Greeks* (Princeton, N.J., 1988), 172–75. As will be shown (p. 413) the legend of Io is originally a Canaanite interpretation of the Hyksos occupation of Egypt, only secondarily expanded to accommodate Greece.

[129] For the excavation of one, see M. Bietak, *AnzÖsterrAkadWissenschaften* 122 (1985), 267–78.

PART TWO

The Egyptian Empire in Asia

"Extending the Frontiers of Egypt": The Imperialist Wars of the 18th and 19th Dynasties

AT THE HEIGHT of its power around 1580 B.C. and beginning to ape the ways of the natives, the Hyksos regime had nonetheless doomed itself by its very nature and its reliance on force to be a pariah, on no surer footing than a Mari or an Isin. Within the territory ruled from Avaris the Egyptians undoubtedly made the best of the situation and worked with the foreigners. What else could they do? But in the south feeling ran high and it was here, at Thebes, that the rebellion began.

THE EXPULSION OF THE HYKSOS

Some time in the first decade of the sixteenth century B.C., a new family came to power in Thebes, replacing the ephemeral and discredited 16th Dynasty. The likelihood is that Ta'o, the founder of the house, was recognized by or perhaps even appointed by Apophis as vassal in the south, since his praenomen, *Sqn-n-r'*, is modeled on that of Apophis *'3-qnn-r'*. But from the outset no love was lost between the two.[1]

The opening of hostilities is not reflected in any extant text. The tale of Apophis and Seqenenre, which circulated in the 19th Dynasty and laid the blame on Apophis's gratuitous harrassment of his vassal, is nothing more than a "shaggy dog" story, devoid of historical value.[2] The initiative for the rebellion must have come from the Thebans, but at first they suffered frustration. Our earliest item of solid evidence regarding the war is not an inscription—would that a stela one day be unearthed—but the mummy of Seqenenre Ta'o himself preserved in the Deir el-Bahri cache of royal mummies. The wounds on the corpse witness eloquently to how he died: he must have been surrounded and cut down by spear, ax, and dagger. The long-held suspicion that he fell in some unrecorded battle with

[1] On the family of the 17th Dynasty, see R. Tanner, *ZÄS* 102 (1975), 50ff.; C. Blankenberg-van Delden, *GM* 54 (1982), 31ff.; C. Vandersleyan, *GM* 63 (1983), 67ff. E. F. Wente, in K. Weeks and J. Harris, eds., *An X-Ray Atlas of the Royal Mummies* (Chicago, 1980), 122ff.

[2] D. B. Redford, *Orientalia* 39 (1970), 35–39; attempts to treat the tale more soberly than it deserves are naive, it seems to me: for the latest treatment and literature, see H. Goedicke, *The Quarrel of Apophis and Seqenenre* (San Antonio, Tex., 1986).

the Hyksos has now been brilliantly confirmed by a careful examination of the wounds, which has proved that they were made by weapon types well known among Asiatics at the time (Plate 12).[3]

Ta'o's defeat and death did not, however, unseat his family. With the accession of Kamose, relations with Avaris seem to have returned to the status quo ante, a reflection either of the resilience of Thebes or the weakening of the Hyksos.[4]

We are fortunate to possess a long inscription of Kamose giving details of his pursuance of the war. The text was inscribed on two stelae (an anomaly indicating lack of forethought in drafting the text), set up before the temple of Amun at Thebes. The first was later smashed, and only fragments were recovered and published in 1939; but fortunately an aspiring scribe in the New Kingdom made a copy of part of it on a drawing board, which was found by Lord Carnarvon's expedition at the turn of the century. The second stela had been reused in the foundations of a statue late in the 19th Dynasty, and was only recovered in the early 1950s.[5] The account begins with the king in council chafing under his inability to act, and restrained by the caution of his advisors, a motif often

Plate 12. Head of the mummy of Seqenenre showing the fatal wounds he apparently sustained in battle with the Hyksos.

[3] M. Bietak and E. Strouhal, *AnnNaturHistMuseum, Vienna* 78 (1974), 29–52.

[4] On the problems relating to the genealogy of Kamose, see Wente, in *X-Ray Atlas.*

[5] An extensive literature has built up around these two stelae: see in particular A. H. Gardiner and B. Gunn, *JEA* 5 (1918), 36–56; L. Habachi, *ASAE* 53 (1956), 195–202; idem., *The Second Stela of Kamose and His Struggle against the Hyksos Ruler and His Capital* (Glückstadt, 1972); P. Montet, *CRAIBL* (1956), 112–20; P. Lacau, *ASAE* 39 (1939), 245–71; H. S. Smith and A. Smith, *ZÄS* 103 (1976), 48ff.; J. A. Wilson, in *ANET²*, 232–34.

used in royal texts to highlight the heroism and daring of the monarch. A treaty had been drawn up after the demise of Ta'o giving both Thebes and Hyksos access to each other's territory for goods and services; and the Hyksos had so far shown no signs of bad faith. Nonetheless, Kamose decides to attack and crosses the frontier without warning. Perhaps because of the element of surprise or the elan of his troops, he has little difficulty with towns in Middle Egypt, where he wreaks havoc with the settlements of collaborating Egyptians and finds himself (to his own surprise, one senses from the text) beneath the walls of Avaris. A raid on the harbor, however, and his own furious taunts hurled at the enemy are not nearly enough to carry the day. Apophis attempted to elicit the aid of the Nubians and to persuade the Nubian king to attack Thebes from the south; and although Kamose's troops intercepted the messenger whose passage in their rear had been somehow facilitated and sent him back to Apophis, the Thebans were forced to retire. There were still, it seems, Egyptians in Middle Egypt who could be persuaded to help Apophis. Desultory raiding in and around Cynopolis in the seventeenth township of Upper Egypt, and attempts to secure the oasis route preceded a retirement to Thebes.

It is difficult at first glance to assess the exact historical weight of this most precious document. The highest year date of Kamose is year 3, cut over the beginning of the first stela, and thus added as an afterthought; and he must have disappeared from the scene shortly thereafter, leaving no son and his grand design unfulfilled. One can only wonder whether he died of wounds. Nevertheless, his exploits in the north had accomplished a great deal. The Hyksos had, on any reading of the text, suffered a reverse that had severely weakened them. More important perhaps, any aura of invincibility that may have surrounded them was now dashed: Kamose had proved that Hyksos territory could be penetrated with impunity. It now became evident that Hyksos power resided solely within the walls of Avaris and relied on those ramparts alone.

Kamose's sudden death elevated his younger brother (?) Ahmose to the throne.[6] Unfortunately, no text such as the Kamose stelae has yet come to light from their reign, and so the denouement of the war of liberation must be pieced together from sundry asides in contemporary biographies, daybook entries, and later tradition. All are brief, factual, and dispassionate and, because of the very natures of the genres in question, lack the verve of Kamose's personal style.

The town of El Kab, south of Thebes, where Nekhbit the tutelary goddess of Upper Egypt was worshiped, had maintained itself as a thriving

---

[6] On the family relationship, see Wente, X-Ray Atlas; the reign of Ahmose is comprehensively analyzed in C. Vandersleyan, Les guerres d'Amosis (Brussels, 1971).

center throughout the impoverished years of the Second Intermediate Period. From the ranks of its inhabitants came several who fought in the Theban army of liberation: Baba, a professional soldier under Seqenenre; his son, the marine Ahmose-si-Abina (later to become admiral); his relative, the treasurer Ahmose-pa-Nekhbit; the commando(?) Apu-sonb and his like-titled son Amenmose.[7] The biography of the second named is the fullest. It is of peripheral value as a *vita* showing what must have been the course of advancement in the military at the time; and what to us constitutes its prime importance, namely, incidents in the war, are passed off as "pegs" on which to hang Ahmose's exploits. He served as a young man on three ships in succession, one of which was named "Ahmose (i.e., the king) appears in Memphis," and thus signals the capture of that town. Three engagements with the Hyksos are recorded just south of Avaris, and the final fate of the town is conveyed in the laconic statement: "Then Avaris was sacked."

Of perhaps more importance to the historian are the scribblings of some scribe whose name is lost to history on the reverse of the Rhind Mathematical Papyrus.[8] Within two decades of the writing of the mathematical text on the recto, dated to year 33 of Apophis, someone used the verso to record what he felt to be the momentous event of his time:

> Regnal year 11, second month of *shomu*—Heliopolis was entered. First month of *akhet*, day 23—this southern prince broke into Tjaru. Day 25—it was heard tell that Tjaru had been entered. Regnal year 11, first month of *akhet*, the birthday of Seth—a roar was emitted by the Majesty of this god. The birthday of Isis—the sky poured rain.[9]

Here without doubt is the view through *northern* eyes[10] of the Theban advance from the south. The "southern prince" (i.e., Ahmose) moves relatively quickly, entering Heliopolis in early July, and then bypassing Avaris to capture Sile, the frontier fort on the edge of the Sinai, in mid-October. Dimly we glimpse a superior strategy designed to cut off support from Asia and then to blockade the capital. The archaeological record

---

[7] On El Kab in general, see P. Derchain, *Elkab* (Brussels, 1971); on Baba, see H. Brugsch, *Thesaurus Inscriptionum Aegyptiacarum* (Leipzig, 1883–1891), 1527–28; the texts of the two Ahmoses are given in *Urk* IV, 1–11, 32–39; see further, C. Vandersleyan, *CdE* 45 (1970), 68–69; H. Goedicke, *JARCE* 11 (1974), 31ff.

[8] Vandersleyan, *Les guerres*, 34–35; W. Helck, *Historische-biographische Texte der 2. Zwischenzeit* (Weisbaden, 1975), 78; idem, *GM* 19 (1976), 33–34f.

[9] The "birthdays" of five gods—Osiris, Horus, Isis, Seth, and Nephthys—constitute the five epagomenal days at the end of the Egyptian calendar.

[10] No one should be deluded by the Theban provenience of the Rhind Papyrus. The dating system used by the scribe, viz. clearly the reign of the Hyksos king (Helck, *Historische-biographische Texte*, s.v. the names in n. 9) and the reference to Ahmose as "this southern prince" both conspire to prove a northern, rather than a southern, vantage point.

confirms that Ahmose pursued the same policy as his brother in committing enemy enclaves to a fiery destruction; and when Avaris finally capitulated, it too was burned and abandoned.[11] The remnants of the Hyksos regime—what happened to Khamudy and the royal family is uncertain—fled across the Sinai and holed up in Sharuhen on the seacoast south of Gaza. Presumably the majority of the Asiatic community in the eastern Delta retired eastward also, if they had not already done so. Some Asiatics will have been captured in engagements or taken as part of the booty and dispersed as domestics among the Egyptian troops; but these were relatively few, and the absence in Egypt during the next fifty years of a servile community of aliens speaks against the postulate of a seizure of a large segment of the Hyksos population by the liberators.[12]

Whether the surviving Hyksos in Sharuhen nursed any hopes of a counterattack we do not know; but Ahmose was not about to allow them to make one. On three successive campaigning seasons he marched across Sinai and assaulted them in their new redoubt, eventually capturing the fort and committing it to destruction. The Hyksos realm of the 15th Dynasty had ceased to exist.[13]

THE "NEO-HYKSOS" IN ASIA: THE COMING OF THE HITTITES and HURRIANS

Egypt on the morrow of the Hyksos withdrawal and annihilation in their "Festung-Sharuhen," had attained for good or ill a new perception of what was required for its own security and defense. The Egyptians at first did not realize the import of their own victory, and contemporary events did nothing to lessen their continuing apprehension. The destruction of Sharuhen was followed by razzias and then a full-scale invasion of Nu-

[11] See M. Bietak, *Avaris and Pi-Ramesses* (London, 1979), 268. Other sites, such as Tell el-Yehudiyeh and Tell el-Maskhuta, were presumably also abandoned about this time: J. S. Holladay, Jr., *Cities of the Delta, vol. 3: Tell el-Maskhuta* (Malibu, Calif., 1982) 44–47.

[12] Cf. the domestics Ahmose si-Abina acquired: *Urk* IV, 10. Of nineteen persons named, only seven or eight *may* be Asiatic. But as Ahmose served later in life on the Asiatic campaigns of Thutmose I, these may reflect later rewards.

[13] The precise connexion of Sharuhen with the Hyksos royal house remains unknown. The site itself (Tel el-Ajjul, seven kilometers south of Gaza on the coast) is ideally located at the mouth of the Wady Ghazzeh where it can intercept trade and communications along the *Via Maris* and through the Negeb; not surprisingly, during the Hyksos period, it was one of the richest towns in Palestine (see W.M.F. Petrie, *Ancient Gaza* 1–4 [London, 1931–1952]; A. Kempinski, *IEJ* 24 [1974], 145–52; O. Tufnell, in M. Avi-Yonah, ed., *Encyclopedia of Archaeological Excavations in the Holy Land* [Jerusalem, 1975], 1:52–61; J. Weinstein, *BASOR* 217 [1975], 4; D. Collon, in J. N. Tubb, ed., *Palestine in the Bronze and Iron Ages* [London, 1985], 57–68). It clearly controlled the western Negeb and the southern coastal plain, but whether as an appendage of the 15th Dynasty is at present unknown. See D. B. Redford *JAOS* 99 (1979), 283, n. 69.

bians against the south, as though the old strategy of Apophis to involve Thebes in a two-front war by calling up his southern ally was belatedly being put into effect. It was evident that the old complacent trust in their own innate superiority over peoples "beyond the pale" would serve the Egyptians ill in the cold atmosphere of this brave new world (Figure 5).

The fifty years following the expulsion of the Hyksos—roughly the second half of the sixteenth century B.C.—comprise a major period of transition in the history of western Asia. As the exhausted Ahmose, on the morrow of his victory at Avaris, gazed northward over the sands of the Sinai, he contemplated pretty much the same political map of Palestine and Syria as his predecessor Dudumose had pored over 110 years before. The "Amorite" kingdoms of the high Middle Bronze Age continued to maintain themselves: Babylon in the Tigris-Euphrates basin, Assyria on the upper Tigris, Yamkhad ruled from Aleppo in North Syria, Qatanum on the middle Orontes, and Hazor dominating Galilee and the upper Jordan. True, some new states had come into being, like Khana on the middle Euphrates, but these were modeled on Middle Bronze Age political patterns, and could be classed culturally as "Amorite."

But Ahmose could not help but have sensed that winds were beginning to blow from new quarters. From the west a lively trade had sprung up with Cyprus, which brought opium, copper, and a distinctive painted pottery to the cities of the Levant.[14] (In Egypt the revival of commerce with Cyprus seems to date to the close of the Hyksos age.)[15] On the east Babylon was finding itself unable to meet the demands of an empire, at least in the Mesopotamian plain, and was forced to retire within the confines of its own immediate territory. Its withdrawal created a power vacuum in this area, and the history of western Asia in the next two centuries may be largely explained as the filling of this vacuum. The Kassites, a race from the Zagros mountains of western Iran, were beginning to exert an influence on the Euphrates Valley. Following the death of Hammurabi these barbarians had invaded Babylonia, establishing a presence at Khana, south of Mari,[16] and another (?) at Terqa on the Euphrates sixty-five kilometers north of Babylon.[17] Initially the Kassite hold was insecure. Their attempts to enter Babylon proper met with but qualified success; twice they were thrown back, once they apparently sacked the city and held it for a short time.[18] A generation after the passing of Ahmose in

[14] See R. S. Merrilees, *Antiquity* 36 (1962), 289–94; idem, *Trade and Transcendence in the Bronze Age Levant* (Göteborg, 1974); L. M. Artzy, *The Origin of Palestinian Bichrome Ware* (Ann Arbor, 1972).

[15] R. S. Merrilees, *Levant* 3 (1971), 56ff.; E. Vermeule, *AJA* 80 (1976), 178.

[16] I. J. Gelb, *JCS* 15 (1961), 36–37.

[17] H. Lewy, in *Isidore Levy Festschrift*, 246ff.

[18] G. Roux, *Ancient Iraq* (Harmondsworth, 1986), 218–19.

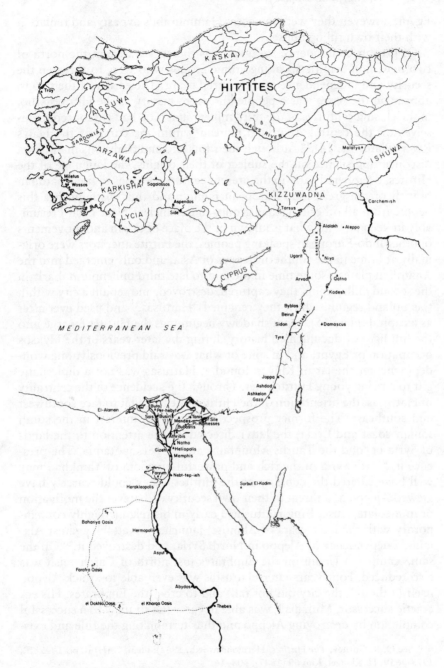

Figure 5. The eastern Mediterranean in the Late Bronze Age.

Egypt, however, they were to unseat Hammurabi's dynasty and replace it with their own ruling house.

Of greater consequence to Egypt was the appearance in the north of two new, non-Semitic speaking ethnic groups who were to threaten the security and independence of the entire Levant. The earlier of the two to appear on the scene was a people known to history as the Hittites who, in the closing centuries of the third millennium B.C., had ensconced themselves on the central Anatolian plateau within the curve of the Halys River (Plates 13, 14).[19] Although their folklore and traditions maintain a disconcerting silence on the subject of their origins, the language of the Hittites, deciphered early in the present century, belongs to the Anatolian branch of the great Indo-European family; and thus distinguishes this people from all other language groups in the ancient Near East. Presumably in keeping with what is known of the place of origin and movements of other Indo-European speaking peoples, the Hittite ancestors were originally at home in the southern steppes of Asia, and only emerged into the Anatolian plateau some time in the mid-to late third millennium. Early in the second millennium, they captured, destroyed, and rebuilt a city within this upland region, which they renamed "Hattusas," and used ever after as a capital (Plate 15). From shadowy beginnings the Hittites emerge into the full light of documented history during the later years of the Hyksos occupation of Egypt; and in spite of what was said previously, one wonders whether the jar of Khiyan found at Hattusas was not a diplomatic gift to a rising young Hittite ruler. Through the accidence of the centrality of Hattusas, the orientation of the Hittite state forced it to face southwest and southeast. The former prospect cultivated an interest in the south Ionian coast and Lycia; the latter directed Hittite attention to the lands of Syria beyond the Taurus Mountains and to Mesopotamia. The presence in North Syria of the rich and powerful kingdom of Yamkhad may well have excited the cupidity of the Hittites—they could scarcely have viewed Aleppo as a threat to their own security. Whatever the motivation or immediate cause, King Hattusilis I early in his reign (roughly contemporary with the later years of Ahmose) launched an attack against Alalakh, a dependency of Aleppo in North Syria, and destroyed it.[20] On the same campaign Urshu on the Euphrates just north of Carchemish was also reduced. Four years later Hattusilis was even able to attack Aleppo itself (although the city did not fall) and to cross the Euphrates. His energetic successor, Mursilis I, was able to carry the strategy to a successful completion by destroying Aleppo and thus terminating the rule and exis-

[19] See O. R. Gurney, *The Hittites* (Harmondsworth, 1962); idem, *CAH*³ II, pt. 1 (228ff., 1973), 659; H. Klengel, *Klio* 69 (1987), 308–16.

[20] Gurney, *Hittites*, 241–43; M.-H. Carre Gates, *Alalakh Levels VI and V: A Chronological Reassessment* (Malibu, Calif., 1981).

Plates 13 and 14. Hittites and their North Syrian allies. Note the figure-of-eight shield and the tonsure that leaves the front of the scalp bare. Abydos temple of Ramesses II, thirteenth century B.C.

Plate 15. The "warrior" gate at the Hittite capital of Hattusas (modern Boghaz Keui) in central Asia Minor. (Photo: Courtesy, D. Graf)

tence of Yamkhad once and for all. As a much later treaty between the Hittites and Aleppo recalls: "Formerly the kings of Aleppo had acquired a great kingship; but Hattusilis, the great king, the king of the land of Khatte, terminated their kingship. After Hattusilis the king of the land of Khatte, Mursilis the great king, the grandson of Hattusilis, the great king, destroyed the kingship of Aleppo and Aleppo (itself)."[21]

A second and more celebrated feat of arms by Mursilis I, was to wreak havoc with the political configuration of Mesopotamia and change the demography of the region. Both Hittite and Babylonian sources record a lightning military campaign that carried Hittite arms clean down the Euphrates and resulted in the capture and annihilation of the city of Babylon (shortly before 1530 B.C.). A razzia only, bent on booty after the manner of the Middle Bronze Age Amorite "freebooters," Mursilis's campaign destroyed the 1st Dynasty of Babylon, swept away the state of Khana, and allowed the rising power of the Kassites to move in and occupy Babylonia.[22]

It also gave a much freer hand to a second ethnic group looming large on the horizon of the eastern Mediterranean, namely the Hurrians. Al-

[21] See H. Klengel, *Geschichte Syriens im 2. Jahrtausend v.u.Z.* (Berlin, 1965), 1:177–78, 183ff.; idem, *MIOF* 10 (1964), 213ff.; N. Na'aman, *JCS* 32 (1980), 34ff.

[22] Gurney, *CAH³* II, pt. 1 (1973), 249–51.

though they were to exert a major influence in the Near East, and must long have formed the autochthonous element in central Mesopotamia, the Hurrians remain an enigma among the peoples of the ancient world. Their literature made a profound impact on the Hittites (and later the Greeks), yet their language (non-Semitic and non-Indo-European) remains little known.[23] Their beautiful painted pottery is common in Mesopotamia and eastern Syria—even the Egyptians of the New Kingdom prized "Hurrian-ware"—yet their material culture has not yet been intensively investigated.[24] Like the Kassites, the Hurrians had come from the northern Zagros and perhaps from Armenia,[25] and already in the late third millennium Hurrian names occur sporadically in northern Mesopotamia and the area of Kirkuk.[26] By the time of Hammurabi of Babylon, a trickle of Hurrians is attested entering the region of Chagar Bazar, and in the half century following his death (c. 1670–1620 B.C.) they are found also in North Syria where, at Alalakh for example, they constitute 30 percent of the population.[27] By 1600 a Hurrian name appears in the onomasticon of the rulers of Khana, and we hear of a "Dagon of the Hurrians" in the pantheon of the district.[28]

What transformed the Hurrian nation from a group of "perioikoi," peripheral to the great focuses of civilization, into a sophisticated political force of its own was the arrival of an Indo-European element from the north; its amalgamation, between about 1600 and 1550 B.C., with the Hurrians resulted in a symbiosis of "rulers" and "subjects."[29] The Indo-Aryans in question were clearly an offshoot geographically and culturally of the great Aryan migrations southward from the Russian steppes during the sixteenth and fifteenth centuries B.C., which brought a sizable body of Indo-European speaking peoples to northern India; and, as in the Punjab so in Mesopotamia, the Aryans provided the dominant aristocracy in the society that resulted. The phenomenon was in fact remembered in the Puranas: "Pracetas had 100 sons, all kings. They were overlords of bar-

[23] In general see E. A. Speiser, *JWH* 1 (1953), 311–27; H. G. Güterbock, *JWH* 2 (1954), 383ff.; also *RHA* 36 (1978); G. Wilhelm, *The Hurrians* (Warminster, 1990).

[24] B. Hrouda, *Archeologia Geographica* 7 (1958), 14–19; P. Zamonsky, *Context* (Boston University Center for Archaeological Studies), 6, nos. 1–2 (Fall 1987), 4–8; H. Otten, *Fischer Weltgeschichte* 3 (1966), 135–36.

[25] M. Astour, *RHA* 36 (1978), 8 and nn. 74–75.

[26] E. A. Speiser, *JAOS* 72 (1952), 99–100; Roux, *Ancient Iraq*, 211; P. Michalowski, *ZA* 76 (1986), 4–12.

[27] I. J. Gelb, *Hurrians and Subarians* (Chicago, 1944); J. R. Kupper, *Les nomades en Mesopotamie au temps des rois de Mari* (Paris, 1957), 230ff.; E. A. Speiser, *JAOS* 74 (1954), 19; I. J. Gelb, *JCS* 15 (1961), 39, and 40, n. 43.

[28] Gelb, *Hurrians and Subarians*, 63.

[29] M. Mayrhofer, *Die Indo-Aryer im alten Vorderasien* (Wiesbaden, 1966); A. Kammenhuber, *Die Arier im Vorderen Orient* (Heidelberg, 1968); idem, *RHA* 36 (1978), 84–90.

barian kingdoms, having moved to the northern quarter."[30] Although these Aryan invaders soon lost their language and adopted the Hurrian vernacular, the onomasticon retained Aryan names replete with the infixes of the principal Vedic gods Mithra, Indra, and Varuna.[31] Aryan customs lingered on as well, including the use of the horse and chariot, cremation in place of interment, and the designation of the feudal aristocracy by the term *maryannu* (Sanskrit *maurya*, "young man").[32]

The new Aryo-Hurrian society displayed an *élan vital* that propelled its members far and wide to south and west.[33] By the third quarter of the sixteenth century a number of strong enclaves of Hurrians were in the process of coalescing into states in northern Mesopotamia, the most powerful of which was called by the loose geographical term *Khanigalbat*. Although its center of gravity lay on the upper Tigris to the north of Assyria where its capital Ta'ida was located,[34] Khanigalbat by geographical outlook and necessity oriented itself westward and looked toward the Euphrates and beyond.

Thus, Hittites and Hurrians, perceiving their manifest destiny to expand in opposite directions, each to dominate the territory claimed by the other, were fated to come to blows; and North Syria and the upper Euphrates would be the battleground. Already during the reign of Hattusilis I Hurrian expansion westward had brought Hittites and Hurrians into conflict,[35] and Mursilis's ability to raid into North Syria and down the Euphrates should in no way be taken to mean the Hurrians had suffered a reverse. To the contrary, the disappearance of Yamkhad and Khana facilitated their westward movement and occupation.[36] Traces of Hurrian dominance are found at Alalakh immediately following its destruction by Hattusilis (c. 1560–1550 B.C.);[37] and there is such a preponderance of Hurrian names in the toponymy and onomasticon of Alalakh IV (fifteenth century B.C.) that a massive invasion must have taken place in the

[30] R. M. Smith, *Dates and Dynasties in Earliest India* (Delhi, 1973), 38.243.

[31] Mayrhofer, *Die Indo-Aryer*, 28.

[32] Ibid., 26; on cremation see now M. van Loon, *Persica* 10 (1982), 47–64.

[33] See good résumés by Astour in *RHA* 36 (1978), 1–22; idem, in G. D. Young, ed., *Ugarit in Retrospect* (Winona Lake, Ind., 1981), 8–10; G. Wilhelm, *SMEA* 24 (1984), 286–87.

[34] E. F. Weidner, *AfO* 5 (1928–1929), 95, n. 1; A. Goetze, *JCS* 7 (1953), 59, n. 47; A. Harrak, *Assyria and Hanigalbat* (Hildesheim, 1987), 103–4; Ta'ida was not the capital of Mitanni, the latter being formally distinct from Khanigalbat (*pace* W. Mayer, *UF* 18 [1986], 231–36).

[35] H. Otten, *MDOG* 91 (1958), verse 11; 79, n. 16; Gurney, *CAH³* II, pt. 1 (1973), 242ff.; E. von Schuler, in M. Liverani, ed., *La Siria nel tardo bronzo* (Rome, 1969), 102–3; H. Klengel, *RHA* 36 (1987), 101.

[36] Astour, *RHA* 36 (1978), 9.

[37] Gates, *Alalakh*, 11, n. 51; 27.

sixteenth century.[38] The momentum was even yet by no means spent. In the last quarter of the sixteenth century a Hurrian contribution is attested in the ethnic and cultural makeup of the incipient state of Kizzuwadna in the Cilician plain, northwest of Alalakh;[39] and even before this principality came to birth, an Aryo-Hurrian push southward toward Egypt must have taken place.

In connection with the last-name thrust contemporary sources might be expected to yield evidence but are unfortunately wanting. We know, thanks to the personal names in the Amarna letters, that by the close of the fifteenth century a surprisingly large number of the ruling families in the towns of Palestine and central Syria display Indo-Aryan names despite the fact that their bearers spoke "Canaanite."[40] Two generations earlier lists of personal names from Tanaach suggest that the combined Hurrian and Indo-Aryan population of Palestine, about 1450 B.C., amounted to as much as 37.5 percent.[41] The invasion must have taken place earlier still, since the term "Kharu" ($\underline{H}^3rw$), derived from Hurru-(land), is applied by Amenophis II to Palestine, and undoubtedly had enjoyed currency under Thutmose III. The latter indeed uses the plural gentilic "Kharians" in contexts where it is clearly simply a synonym for Asiatics in general and specifically those encountered in Palestine and Coele-Syria.[42] In Thutmose III's twenty-first year an old prisoner of war, now employed as a doorkeeper, described himself as a *Kharu*.[43]

The evidence thus conspires to suggest that the influx from the north that brought the Indo-Aryan-Hurrian amalgam into Canaan, and lent an indelible tinge to that land's demography and physical culture, had already transpired *before* the end of the sixteenth century B.C. Can we be more precise about time and circumstances?

Unfortunately no cache of texts has been unearthed to date that could shed light on the political history and demographic shifts of the second half of the sixteenth century, and one has the sinking feeling in approaching this period that a most significant page is missing in the record. The Alalakh archives terminate with the destruction of the city by Hattusilis and do not resume until the fifteenth century; similarly, the archives of Ugarit begin only in the later fifteenth century. For the Hittite "Old King-

---

[38] Astour, *RHA* 36 (1978), 11 and nn. 91–92; M. Liverani, *RHA* 36 (1987), 148–56.

[39] G. R. Meyer, *MIOF* 1 (1953), 108–9; B. Landsberger, *JCS* 8 (1954), 50; Mayrhofer, *Die Indo-Aryer*, 29; W. Helck, *LdÄ* 3 (1980), 443–44.

[40] See list in Mayrhofer, *Die Indo-Aryer*, 29–30; for Hurrian influence on the pantheon at Qatna, see J. Bottero, *RA* 43 (1949), 34–35.

[41] A. Glock, *BASOR* 204 (1971), 30.

[42] Cf. *Urk* IV, 743:8 (total of Asiatics given to Amun by Thutmose III); P. Berlin 10621 rs. 9 (workers on a tomb at Thebes); Helck, *LdÄ* 3 (1980), 87.

[43] *Urk* IV, 1069:7; see now A. J. Spalinger, in F. Junge, ed., *Studien zu Sprache und Religion Ägyptens* (Göttingen, 1984), 638–39.

dom" sources are rare and fragmentary, and the period of our interest is reflected elsewhere only in random allusions in later texts. No state archives have as yet come to light from any of the major centers of the Hurrians in Mesopotamia; and of the Middle Bronze Age giants of the Levant, Aleppo remains unexcavated, Hazor's archives have eluded the excavator, and Qatanum has bequeathed nought but inventories and a few business documents.[44] For their part, the Egyptians have left only sparse allusions to Asia prior to the campaigns of Thutmose III.

This gap in our written sources is doubly maddening in view of the upheaval attested in the archaeological record. Nearly every major town in Palestine and southern Syria is found, upon excavation, to have undergone a violent destruction sometime after the close of MB IIC—that is, the cultural phase roughly contemporary with the last stage in the Hyksos occupation of Egypt.[45] The assumption that MB IIC was coterminus with the end of Hyksos rule has contributed to the widely held view, amounting almost to an unquestioned tenet of faith, that it was the Eygptian armies of Ahmose that effected this devastation in their pursuit of their fleeing enemy.[46] Yet a moment's reflection will demonstrate the improbability of this view. The Egyptians of Ahmose's time were notoriously

---

[44] From which a skeletal king list might be reconstructed: cf. Bottero *RA* 43 (1949), 1–40, 137–215; C. Epstein, *JNES* 22 (1963), 242–46.

[45] For Tell Beit Mirsim, Megiddo, Tell el-Ajjul, Tell Farah (south), and Beth Shean, see G. E. Wright, *The Bible and the Ancient Near East* (New York, 1965), 112; Jericho: K. A. Kenyon, *Digging Up Jericho* (New York, 1957), 229; Hazor: Y. Yadin, *Hazor* (London, 1970), 31–32 and passim; Tell Kadesh (Galilee): M. Avi-Yonah, in *Encyclopedia of Archaeological Excavations in the Holy Land* (Jerusalem, 1976), 2:406; Gezer: W. G. Dever, *Gezer* (Jerusalem, 1974), 2:36 (and cf. J. A. Sauer, *BASOR* 233 [1979], 71); Tell Dor (abandoned?): E. Stern, *IEJ* 37 (1987), 205; Tell Kabri (abandoned?): A. Kempinski, *IEJ* 37 (1987), 177; Timnah: G. L. Kelm and A. Mazar, *IEJ* 36 (1986), 108; Shechem: W. G. Dever, *BASOR* 216 (1974), 37, 41, 48; Achzib: M. W. Prausnitz, *IEJ* 25 (1975), 207; Tanaach: P. W. Lapp, *BASOR* 173 (1964), 8–20; Tell Dan: Avi-Yonah, in *Encyclopedia*, 1:316. Transjordan was sparsely populated in MB IIB–C, but even those few sites for the most part terminate at the close of IIC: see S. Mittmann, *Beiträge zur Siedlungs und Territorialgeschichte der nördlichen Ostjordanlandes* (Wiesbaden, 1970), 256ff. It is uncertain how far north into Syria the levels of destruction extend at the close of MB IIC, because of the lack of archaeological excavations there and the generally inferior methods of digging employed by those few expeditions that have worked there (Dever, in J. W. Hayes and J. M. Miller, eds., *Israelite and Judaean History* [Philadelphia, 1977], 90). But surveys suggest the limit of MB IIC destruction may have lain south of the Beka'a since the number of settlements detected by survey had, in that region, shown a steady decline of 40 percent between EB III and LB I; this decline was not affected by and was independent of the devastation wrought further south: Marfoe, *BASOR* 234 (1979), 12.

[46] Cf. the list of some proponents in *BibOr* 30 (1973), 224; sadly this cant is still being parroted: cf. L. E. Toombs, *ADAJ* 17 (1972), 105; Gates, *Alalakh*, 19–21; Dever, *BASOR* 216 (1974), 48; J. D. Seger, *Eretz Israel* 12 (1975), 45*; idem, in Hayes and Miller, *Israelite and Judaean History*, 89; Sauer, *BASOR* 233 (1979), 71.

inept when it came to laying siege to, or assaulting, a fortified city: Avaris defied their attempts for more than one generation, and Sharuhen for three years. Even sixty years later under Thutmose III the medium-sized fortress of Megiddo held out for seven months.[47] Moreover, there is virtually a total absence of that type of significant evidence that would point to large-scale operations and an extended presence of Egyptians in Palestine under Ahmose: there are no names of resident governors, no Egyptian artifacts found in excavations, no extensive deportation of Asiatics who later turn up in Egypt. When we are apprised by texts that the empire is in existence (after Thutmose III), such evidence appears in abundance.[48]

But if the Egyptians did not do it, who in fact is responsible? First, it ought to be noted that the facile assumption that the end of MB IIC coincides with the expulsion of the Hyksos should not be allowed to affect the argument at all. One might, with equal justification, argue for a date before Ahmose ascended the throne, or for one well beyond the point of his death. From the stratigraphic evidence alone we simply are not in a position to judge, and then the door is left open for the possibility that many of the destruction levels are to be ascribed to the aftermath of Thutmose III's conquest.[49]

But if one were to object that putting the end of MB IIC after 1500 B.C., as would naturally follow, is too late, another candidate is waiting in the wings. The relentless pressure westward of the Hurrians and their Indo-Aryan leaders during the third-quarter of the sixteenth century gave birth to a new nation-state called "Mitanni" between the Euphrates and the Balikh by 1530 B.C.[50] Mitanni rapidly became the chief Hurrian state and leading exponent of Hurrian culture; and very soon it had subverted the states of central Mesopotamia and the upper Tigris (including Assyria). Its southern expansion is unrecorded. But one wonders whether the same *élan* that created Mitanni on the ruins of Khana and Mari, pro-

---

[47] See below, p. 157.

[48] The present case has been made several times by the author: see *BiblOr* 30 (1973), 224; *JAOS* 99 (1979), 273; *Studies in the History and Archaeology of Jordan* (Amman, 1982), 1:117; see also the incisive observations of W. H. Shea, *IEJ* 29 (1979), 1–5.

[49] The lively debate between J. K. Hoffmeier and W. G. Dever over the MB IIC destruction levels, initiated by the former's article in *Levant* 21 (1989), has had the salutary effect of reopening the question of date and rendering it increasingly likely that the reign of Thutmose III is the time span involved. It must be maintained, however, that the destructions could never have been effected in the heat of battle but must have been in the nature of intentional demolition demanded of the conquered by the king himself.

[50] See H. Klengel, *RHA* 36 (1978), 91–115; D. B. Redford *LdÄ* 3 (1980), 149–51; van Loon, *Persica* 10 (1982), 47–64; G. Wilhelm, *SMEA* 24 (1984), 286–87. The Egyptians also employ the vague geographical term *Naharin*, "River-land," for Mitanni (M. Astour, *JNES* 31 [1972], 103), while the Syrians and Hittites preferred the term *Khanigalbat*: H. Klengel, *MIOF* 10 (1964), 216; H. Otten, *Fischer Weltgeschichte* 3 (1966), 129.

pelled a body of Hurrians southward toward Palestine where they devastated Hazor and its dependencies in a bid to set up yet another state on the frontier of Egypt? Such a state, of course, did not come into being, for on the eve of Thutmose III's conquests early in the fifteenth century Kadesh on the Orontes seems to have dominated Palestine. But the rulers of Kadesh for the LB I period show consistently Mitannian names. Could Kadesh, then, be the "agent" we are seeking?[51]

Sources for the History of the Empire

For the period of the creation and the existence of the Egyptian empire in Asia—that is, from about 1550 B.C. under Ahmose until its final demise some time in the middle of the 20th Dynasty (around 1120 B.C.)—we possess a comparative wealth of primary source material. For the first time both Egyptian and cuneiform texts provide not only a contemporary record but also opposing vantage points for the same periods, and sometimes for the same events.

Egypt

ANNALS

Although for the Old Kingdom our roster of surviving text-genres includes yearly records of major events and data necessary for future generations, we are unsure as to how long this type survived. True, the term "annals" is a common noun in the lexicon to the end of Egyptian history, but it may refer after the end of the Old Kingdom to an obsolete form, or a drastically modified one.[52] In any case, no example survives from the New Kingdom.

JOURNALS

From the Middle Kingdom comes the genre called "the Daybook of" such-and-such an institution, a compilation of salient events, memoranda, and expenditures, organized calendrically by day, month, and year.[53] Temples, or departments of government and the king's house, all kept such journals, and these became the primary source for secondary

---

[51] Astour speaks of the "brief conquest of a large part" of Palestine by Mitanni about 1500 B.C. (*RHA* 36 [1978], 1), but gives no supporting evidence. Later (ibid., 12) he alludes to the "immense prestige" the creation of Mitanni gave to the Hurrian language, religion, and onomasticon. For rulers of Kadesh with Mitannian names, see Epstein, *JNES* 22 (1963), 245–46; Mayrhofer, *Die Indo-Aryer*, 30.

[52] See in general D. B. Redford, in Junge, *Studien zu Sprache und Religion Ägyptens*, 327–41; idem, *Pharaonic King-lists, Annals and Day-books* (Toronto, 1986), 65–96.

[53] Redford, *King-lists*, 97–126.

types of literature, including songs, encomia, and triumph texts. Most important for our purposes is the "daybook of the king's house," the palace diary that recorded not only the king's doings day by day, but also the receipts and disbursements of the royal household. When the king went on campaign, the daybook became virtually a war diary. No daybook of the king's house has survived from the New Kingdom, but under Thutmose III and (to a lesser extent) some of his successors extended excerpts were used in the composition of stelae.

CORRESPONDENCE

During the Late Bronze Age (c. 1550–1200 B.C.) international correspondence of a diplomatic variety was carried on between the major states of the ancient world using Akkadian as the *lingua franca*, written in cuneiform on clay tablets.[54] Pharaoh kept a "stable" of Akkadian-speaking letter-scribes at court who translated his letters, drawn up initially in Egyptian, into Akkadian, and rendered the replies back into Egyptian. For the reigns of Amenophis III, Akhenaten, and Tutankhamun, we have part of the cuneiform correspondence with Egypt preserved in the Amarna Letters, recovered from the ruins of the chancery at Amarna by peasants in 1887. Some of the correspondence of Ramesses II and his family and court has turned up in the excavations of Hattusas, the Hittite capital.[55]

TREATIES

Although references exist to international agreements entered into by Egypt and its neighbors, this form was not native to Egypt and only one, the peace treaty between Ramesses II and the Hittites, has come down to us, translated from the Hittite.

These four categories constitute an essentially private corpus in which writers seek to communicate with and influence one another, or a small group of individuals. The purposes are practical: to convey or put on record information, to persuade one person for immediate advantage. They are not intended for public consumption, and since they generally reflect what the writers perceive to be facts, the element of deception is

[54] See in general E. Edel, *LdÄ* 3 (1980), 482–85.
[55] For the Amarna Letters, see now W. L. Moran, *Les lettres d'El-Amarna* (Paris, 1987). No connected or complete edition of the Hattusas letters has yet been produced, but Edel has, over the past forty years, published the more important ones piecemeal: for references, see ibid., and add E. Edel, *NGWG* (1978), no. 4; *SAK* 7 (1979), 23–39; *Sitzungsberichte, Österreichische Akademie der Wissenschaften* 375 (Vienna, 1980); H. Otten, in M. Görg, ed., *Festschrift Elmar Edel* (Bamberg, 1979), 314–18.

not prominent. But such is not the case with the following "published" genres.

TRIUMPH STELAE

The Egyptian "victory inscription" (*wḏ n nḫtw*)[56] applies to a type of text that, although it may derive from an event signalized in a daybook, has been highly embellished in a narrative or oratorical manner for popular consumption. Often the theme is a victory in battle couched in a more or less artificial setting of which two are noteworthy. First, a crisis looms, but the king's councilors advise caution; the king ignores their advice and his daring wins out. Second, a messenger arrives with news of an uprising or the like; the king flies into a rage and again adopts a daring course of action, which proves successful.[57] Such stelae were set up at the approaches to temples where scribal "readings" could be heard by the populace.

ENCOMIA

The Egyptian "compilation of deeds," later simply "song,"[58] betokens a highly rhetorical poetic composition commemorating the mighty acts of the king (often in battle), usually sung to the accompaniment of the harp.

WAR RELIEFS

The New Kingdom developed an elaborate series of vignettes, blown up into larger-than-life depictions of various stages of a battle, inscribed on the exterior faces of temple walls and pylons for all to see.[59] The sequence includes the god commissioning the king, the king mounting his chariot, the march, the battle or assault, the homeward march, and the presentation of the captives to the god. Apart from the names of the enemies, which vary, the texts that gloss the scenes tend to be stereotyped and uninformative. Although the genre is already attested under the

---

[56] Redford, *King-lists*, 128, n. 3.

[57] Out of these artificial situations the term "Königsnovelle" (royal tale, "king's story") has been coined: see A. Herrmann, *Die ägyptische Königsnovelle* (Leipzig, 1938); S. Herrmann, *Wissenschaftliche Zeitschrift der Karl-Marx Universität, Leipzig* 3, no. 1 (1953–1954), 51–62; J. van Seters, *In Search of History* (New Haven, Conn., 1983), 160–64. But the term ought to be construed correctly as nothing more than a "topos," not a formal genre.

[58] The genre that might be dubbed "the mighty deeds of the king," well known from such 18th Dynasty examples as the Ermant stela, and the "Sphinx" stelae of Amenophis II (cf. *ANET*², 243–45), probably arises from extemporized recitations of royal encomia. By the 19th Dynasty the form is more rigid, clearly in meter, and intended to be sung: Redford, *King-lists*, 128, n. 3.

[59] See G. A. Gaballa, *Narrative in Egyptian Art* (Mainz am Rhein, 1976).

Thutmosids,[60] the best preserved exemplars come from the reigns of Sety I and Ramesses II.

HEADSMITING SCENES AND TOPONYM LISTS

The head-smiting motif is as old as pharaonic art, but was combined in the New Kingdom with groupings of foreign toponyms in ovals surmounted by the torsos of foreign captives to symbolize the far-flung conquests of the king. Such scenes were de rigueur on the external face of temple pylons where they would have the maximum propaganda effect. Apart from the extensive toponym lists of Thutmose III, which derive from itineraries, the lists of later kings decrease in value as reflections of historic events.[61]

PRIVATE BIOGRAPHICAL STATEMENTS

Addressed to the living from beyond the grave, such statements had long formed part of the decoration of the tomb chapel open to vistors.[62] In the 18th Dynasty soldiers who had been on campaign or officials whose task was to receive booty or tribute would often include their exploits in their statements. By Ramesside times interest in recounting specific events over a lifetime began to wane in favor of a more somber concern with ways and means to ensure a happy afterlife.

The Levant

From what has been passed in review, it will have become evident that the vast majority of our Egyptian sources belong in the monumental category, based on original texts to be sure, but inscribed for all to see. The state archives for the most part have suffered destruction, or at least have not yet come to light in quantity. Such is not the case in western Asia where monumental records are lacking—this mode of propaganda may

[60] Cf. B. Bruyère, *FIFAO* 4 (1926), pls. ii–iv; J. K. Hofmeier, in *The Akhenaten Temple Project* (Toronto, 1988), 2:40; A. H. Zayed, in P. Posener-Krieger, ed., *Mélanges Gamal Eddin Mokhtar* (Cairo, 1985), 1: pls. I–II.

[61] On the toponym lists, see J. Simons, *Handbook for the Study of Egyptian Topographical Lists Relating to Western Asia* (Leiden, 1937); E. Edel, *Die Ortsnamenlisten aus dem Totentempel Amenophis III* (Bonn, 1966); M. Noth, *ZDPV* 61 (1938), 26ff.; D. B. Redford, *JSSEA* 12 (1982), 55–74; the degree of historical worth in these texts remains problematical, and scholars must be on their guard against wishful thinking. To take but one example, the list of Sety I from Qurnah (Simons, *Handbook*, XV) contains a section of twelve names (nos. 13–24), which could plausibly be linked to the Beth-Shean campaign of year 1, only to include in the same list such impossible sites as Cyprus, Assyria, Paba(n)hi (in north Mesopotamia—twice!), Takhsy (twice!), and Qatna (ibid., XIV, no. 31) no longer in existence.

[62] Redford, *King-lists*, 154–58.

not have developed as it did in Egypt—and state archives have through excavation been recovered in quantity. Two corpora loom large in the history of the Late Bronze Age.

ALALAKH

The Alalakh Tablets[63] (in cuneiform in Akkadian) from level IV of that site number about 250 texts dating to the fifteenth century B.C. They were found in the excavations at the site by Sir Leonard Woolley, scattered through the rooms leading from the palace offices, as though dropped in flight as the building was being fired. The contents show clearly that these were part of the state archives for they include administrative texts (census and tax lists, lists of goods and slaves, ration-lists), legal decisions and royal edicts, and a few letters and copies of treaties.

UGARIT

The texts from Ugarit likewise emanate from a palace archive, but the total number far exceeds the number of the Alalakh tablets.[64] Unlike the latter they span the period between about 1425 and 1190 B.C., and are written on clay tablets mainly in two languages: Akkadian and Ugaritic (in a special alphabetic cuneiform), a West Semitic language related to Canaanite and Hebrew. Apart from a substantial body of religious texts (in Ugaritic), which has revolutionized our knowledge of Canaanite religion, the remainder of the archive sheds welcome light on the administration of this state and the history of North Syria in general. The tablets were found in a number of distinct locations in the building, reflecting the careful separation of the branches of government. The "central" archives are really a record office containing vast numbers of juridical texts, copies, deeds, wills, and contracts and bills for sale. The "west" archives come from the treasury and show administrative texts similar to those from Alalakh, whereas the east archive reflects the municipal administration of the city proper. Finally, the "south" archives reveal themselves as the records of the "foreign office" containing letters from foreign kings and officials, tribute lists, juridical texts, and treaties.

LESSER CACHES OF TEXTS

Nothing remotely comparable to the Ugaritic archives for size and illumination has come to light elsewhere in Palestine or Syria, but some finds of scattered tablets from excavations are worth noting. Some business documents from Emar on the Euphrates have been used for chrono-

---

[63] See D. J. Wiseman, *The Alalakh Tablets* (London, 1954).

[64] See C.F.A. Schaeffer, *Ugaritica*, 6 vols. (Paris, 1939–); C.F.A. Schaeffer and C. Virolleaud, *Le palais royal d'Ugarit*, 5 vols. (Paris, 1956–).

logical purposes;[65] and a series of inventory tablets recording bequests to a cult center at Qatna has been useful in establishing a king list.[66] A handful of texts, mainly letters, has come to light from Palestinian excavations at Tanaach,[67] Aphek,[68] and Kumide;[69] these have made a welcome, though limited, contribution to our understanding of the workings of the Egyptian empire in Asia.

Khatte

The excavations of the Hittite capital at Khattusas (modern Boghaz Keui) by the Deutsche Orientgesellschaft (from 1906–1914, 1931–1939, and 1952 to the present) have yielded a rich harvest of thousands of cuneiform tablets from the state archives.[70] Of the numerous genres (invaluable for the re-creating of the life of one of the "lost" peoples of the ancient world), the treaties, annals, letters, and "apologia" are the most important for our purposes. If composed by the Hittites themselves, these were drawn up first in Hittite, then translated into Akkadian; both Hittite drafts and Akkadian versions have often survived.[71]

ANNALS

A year-by-year account of the (military) activity of a king is a form that, although attested for the sixteenth century B.C. among the Hittites,[72] is best represented by the fragmentary royal annals from the fourteenth and thirteenth centuries B.C. These fall into the category that the Hittites call "manly deeds," and are designed to prove divine approbation of the king in battle.[73]

TREATIES

The Hittites had developed this instrument of international diplomacy to a high degree, although it was not new with them.[74] The form is essen-

[65] D. Arnaud, *Syria* 52 (1975), 87–92; J. Margueron, *Syria* 52 (1975), 53ff.

[66] Bottero, *RA* 43 (1949), 1–40, 137–215; and Epstein, *JNES* 22 (1963), 242–46.

[67] W. F. Albright, *BASOR* 94 (1944), 12–27; A. Glock, *BASOR* 204 (1971), 17–30.

[68] D. I. Owen, *Tel Aviv* 8 (1981), 1–17; I. Singer, *Tel Aviv* 10 (1983), 3–25.

[69] D. O. Edzard, *Kamid el-Loz-Kumidi* (Bonn, 1970).

[70] Cf. E. F. Weidner, *Politische Dokumente aus Kleinasien* (Berlin, 1923); A. Goetze, in *ANET*², 318–20; Gurney, *The Hittites*, 224–25 (8); H. Hoffner, *Orientalia* 49 (1980), 283–332; A. Kammenhuber, *Saeculum* 9 (1958), 136–55; H. Klengel, *Klio* 69 (1987), 314–16.

[71] For the languages represented in the archive, see Gurney, *The Hittites*, 117–31.

[72] H. Otten, *MDOG* 91 (1958), 78ff.; F. Cornelius, *Orientalia* 28 (1959), 292ff.; Kammenhuber, *Saeculum* 9 (1958), 143, n. 37; Hoffner, *Orientalia* 49 (1980), 293ff.

[73] Van Seters, *In Search of History*, 105–13.

[74] See Hoffner, *Orientalia* 49 (1980), 311; V. Korosec, *Hethitisches Staatsverträge* (Leipzig, 1931).

tially tripartite: a preamble, in which the historical relations between the two contracting parties is set forth; the particular provisions of the treaty; and the witnesses (the gods and goddesses of both parties). Important treaties for Syrian historians include those with Aleppo, Kizzuwadna, Tunip, Amurru, Ugarit, Mitanni, and Egypt.

LETTERS

Most of the extant correspondence dates from the thirteenth century B.C. (Hattusilis III and his successors). Fragments of about twenty-six letters from the court of Ramesses II have survived,[75] and a number of letters (or drafts thereof) to the kings of Assyria and Babylonia, and Khanigalbat.[76]

APOLOGIA

This catchall term covers a number of disparate pieces, each with the common intent of presenting the writer's personal position in a plea or explanation. We will mention three of historical import: the Edict of Telepinus (c. 1470 B.C.), which seeks to regulate the government and monarchy and, in passing, makes brief reference to earlier Hittite history;[77] the "Plague-prayer" of Mursilis II (c. 1335 B.C.), in which he tries to ascertain from the storm-god why the land is suffering pestilence, and has occasion to recount history;[78] and the "Apology" of Hattusilis III, in which the king seeks to justify the actions of a lifetime.[79] All display, like the annals and treaties, a well-developed sense of political morality, and the need to justify one's deeds before gods and men.

THE POLITICAL CONFIGURATION OF THE LEVANT ABOUT 1525 B.C.

These sources, so briefly described, begin to provide a coherent picture in the last quarter of the sixteenth century B.C., perhaps within a decade of the destruction of Aleppo by Mursilis I and the latter's untimely assassination.[80] It was a time when "the Hurri warriors" between the Euphrates and the Balikh rivers were organizing themselves into a state, and their rulers voluntarily ceding primacy to one of their number, Shutarna I son of Kirta, "King of the land of Mitanni."[81] At the same time the Hittites,

---

[75] E. Edel, LdÄ 3 (1980), 482–83.

[76] Harrak, Assyria and Hanigalbat.

[77] Gurney, The Hittites, 24–25.

[78] ANET², 394–96.

[79] H. Otten, Die Apologie Hattusilis III (Wiesbaden, 1981).

[80] See inter alia W. Helck, AfO 22 (1968–1969), 27ff.; N. Na'aman, UF 6 (1974), 265–74; Redford, JAOS 99 (1979), 270–87.

[81] Wiseman, Alalakh Tablets, nos. 13, 14 (seal).

suffering from the political weakness produced by the assassination and concomitant feuding, seemed to retire and leave the field to the newcomers. Hantilis I could, around 1520 B.C., attempt attacks on Ashtata and Carchemish, but they proved to be only ineffectual raids.[82] The Hurrians founded the state of Kizzuwadna in the Cilician plain, and Zidantas I, Hantilis's successor, after an attempt to withstand the newcomers by force of arms, was obliged to sign a treaty with Pa'illiya, king of Kizzuwadna, in which there was a mutual exchange of captured cities and a regulation of the frontier.[83] Thereafter through seven generations the Hittites centered their policy in the southeast upon maintaining Kizzuwadna as a buffer against encroachments of Mitanni and its minions.

Mitannian pressure westward was relentness. A new house had struggled to establish itself in Aleppo after Mursilis's raid, under one Abba-'el son of Sharra-'el;[84] but civil strife (fomented by Mitanni?)[85] swept his successor Ilim-ilimma off the throne and put to flight the scions of the royal family. Mitanni would henceforth not tolerate a revival of the "Great Kingship" of Aleppo, and its former dependencies became independent principalities: Alalakh and Mukishe to the west, the amorphous Nukhashshe lands east of the Orontes,[86] and Niya to the south at Apamea.[87]

Further south it was undoubtedly the Hurrian thrust that dealt the deathblow to the hegemony Qatna had enjoyed during the Middle Bronze Age. The independent "land of Zinzar" is attested for the early fifteenth century (Qal'at Sejar, about twenty-five kilometers northwest of Hamath on the Orontes), and undoubtedly already existed half a century earlier.[88] More important, the politics of the new age had liberated Tunip, a hitherto small commercial center contiguous to Zinzar on the south. Although not convincingly identified with any existing tell, Tunip must have lain a little northwest of Qatna and west of the Orontes, where it could dominate the Eleutheros Valley.[89] Some forty-four kilometers southwest

---

[82] A. Goetze, *JCS* 11 (1957), 55 and n. 30.

[83] H. Otten, *JCS* 5 (1951), 129–30f.; idem, *Fischer Weltgeschichte* 3 (1966), 127.

[84] Klengel, *Geschichte*, 1:175.

[85] Ibid., 228; S. Smith, *The Statue of Idrimi* (London, 1949), 59–60.

[86] A. H. Gardiner, *Ancient Egyptian Onomastica* (Oxford, 1947), 1:168*ff.; W. Helck, *Die Beziehungen Ägyptens zur Vorderasien*[2] (Wiesbaden, 1972), 152.

[87] Klengel, *Geschichte*, 1:45, n. 12; Helck, *Beziehungen*[2], 307. In the treaty between Suppiluliumas and Niqmaddu II (RS 17.340, 17.132: *Palais royal d'Ugarit*, 4:48ff.) Niya is clearly identified as belonging to the Nukhashshe lands.

[88] *Urk* IV, 891:17; Helck, *Beziehungen*[2], 299–300.

[89] Noth identified it with Tell Hana, sixteen kilometers northwest of Qatna (*ZDPV* 64 [1953], 71; see also Helck, *Beziehungen*[2], 139–40); H. Klengel, *Geschichte Syriens im 2. Jahrtausend v.u.Z.* (Berlin, 1965), 47, n. 39; Helck, *UF* 5 (1973), 286–87; M. Astour, *Ori-*

of Qatna, again on the Orontes, the city of Kadesh (Tell Nebi-mend) had also broken away and formed an independent principality. Between them, Tunip and Kadesh were to exercise a brief though significant hegemony over neighboring territories: Tunip over the middle Phoenician coast (as a cat's paw for Mitanni) and Kadesh over the upper Orontes and Galilee.[90]

We are poorly informed on the political status of the coastal cities but can presumably extrapolate from the situation a generation or so later. South of the mouth of the Orontes, Ugarit and the smaller Syannu on its southern border enjoyed a tenuous independence, as did presumably Arvad in its island fastness. While Irqata was falling under Tunip's influence, Byblos maintained favorable relations with Egypt, as did (we may be sure) Beirut, Sidon, and Tyre.

THE CREATION OF THE EGYPTIAN EMPIRE

Egypt involved itself in this welter of jockeying states gradually perhaps unconscious of the broader implications of its actions, but initially, we may be sure, apprehensive of the new Hurrian menace. While Egypt had long been aware (and avid) of the products, resources, and manpower of the adjacent tracts of western Asia, it had relied heretofore on the creation of a sphere of influence and periodic intimidation (razzias, punitive strikes) to gain access to them. But now, on the morrow of the Hyksos occupation, Egypt began to regard hither Asia in a new light and to value this region for its strategic location vis-à-vis points further north. For Pharaoh could not be sure that those "foreign rulers," the ḥḳ³w-ḫ³swt, were not about to attack Egypt again and restore the scions of the 15th Dynasty; and well into the 18th Dynasty the perception of himself as launching a preemptive strike against "the foreign rulers who had attacked him" or "who were intending to destroy Egypt" and "were on the march against him" dominated the 18th Dynasty monarch's thinking.[91] And so it was appropriate and necessary to "extend the frontiers of Egypt" and turn the territory thus engulfed into a buffer zone. Those within it would be transformed into Egypt's "serfs" and "Asia (would) become His Majesty's tenant," swearing fealty in Pharaoh's name.[92]

These quaint rationalizations of the embryonic phenomenon of empire derive from what was familiar to the Egyptians, namely their own social

---

entalia 46 (1977), 51ff.; A. Altman, *Bar-Ilan Studies in History* (Ramat Gan, 1978), 5, n. 12.

[90] M. S. Drower, *CAH³* II, pt. 1 (1973), 430–31; W. T. Pitard, *Ancient Damascus* (Winona Lake, Ind., 1987), 50–51.

[91] D. B. Redford, *Akhenaten the Heretic King* (Princeton, N.J., 1984), 15–16.

[92] *Urk* IV, 102:15, 138:9, 86:1.

and political relationships of the Middle Kingdom; and the initial moves into western Asia were likewise throwbacks to a well-known mechanism, in this case the razzia that had been the favorite tool of intimidation for over one thousand years. Ahmose, so our scant sources indicate, conducted operations of some kind inland from Byblos; and Amenophis I (if our ascription of the text is correct) ranged even farther north down the Orontes as far as Tunip (Plate 16).[93] Thutmose I's advance to the Euphrates may have looked like a raid, and therefore a continuation of the old-fashioned policy of desultory attacks, although in my view Thutmose perceived it as something different, as will be discussed. Again, in imitation of royal practice during the Middle Kingdom, when the age-old hunt of the king had enjoyed regular performance by the court,[94] the kings of the early 18th Dynasty transplanted the royal hunt to Asia where it became a regular feature of the campaign in the postvictory celebration.[95] Of course, the first three kings of the 18th Dynasty were more concerned with establishing their hegemony in Nubia, and this required much more effort than raids into Asia, since the dynasty had purposed to destroy the erstwhile Kushite kingdom, and to garrison and colonize the region. None of these measures were as yet considered appropriate for Asia. Nonetheless, in the broad lines of the concept, the reduction of Nubia was again within the limits of Egypt's traditional stance vis-à-vis the outside world.

If the first four reigns of the dynasty appear conventional in their formulation of foreign policy, and if the reign of Thutmose II inaugurates a new approach to relations with Asia, it is the twenty years of Hatshepsut's floruit that craves precise assessment (Plate 17).[96] Whereas in art the queen's reign is coming to be appreciated as the *end* of an era, her military and economic policies seem more a bridge between two distinct periods. True, the old idea that Hatshepsut intended to be a throwback to a much earlier type of king and turned out to be a pacifist requires considerable modification: it is abundantly clear that the queen did not eschew military activity, and at least once took the field herself.[97] Nonetheless, her campaigns are very few in number and were undertaken on a limited scale. Obviously use of the military did not constitute a major element in her program.

[93] Vandersleyan, *Les guerres d'Amosis*, 90ff.; Redford *JAOS* 99 (1979), 270–87.

[94] Cf. the literary motif of the "hunting/fowling king," which became surprisingly popular": R. A. Caminos, *Literary Fragments in the Hieratic Script* (Oxford, 1959).

[95] H. Altenmüller, *LdÄ* 3 (1980), 221–24 and n. 17.

[96] On Hatshepsut, see S. Ratié, *La reine-pharaon* (Paris, 1972); idem, *La reine Hatshepsout: Sources et problems* (Leiden, 1979).

[97] D. B. Redford, *The History and Chronology of the Egyptian 18th Dynasty. Seven Studies* (Toronto, 1967), 57–62.

Plate 16. Limestone doorjamb from Karnak (early 18th Dynasty) depicting personified places in Asia bringing offerings, and recording a campaign into Syria. The figure is that of Qedem, "the East."

Plate 17. Block from Karnak showing Hatshepsut (center), in one of her rare early depictions as queen, being offered life and dominion by Seth.

Hatshepsut herself has bequeathed us a number of personal statements, and these may be expected to yield clues as to her thinking. In fact, they do. Dominating every inscription is the queen's preoccupation with a vast project to rebuild Egypt,[98] and for this project, peace was required. Hatshepsut states explicitly "I ordained tranquility throughout the townships, all the cities were at peace,"[99] and was later to characterize her reign as "years of peace."[100] Her relations with foreign parts, then, may be expected to have been markedly affected by this prior interest in parochial matters.

The following is a selection of statements bearing on her attitude to the outside world. (Gods to Hatshepsut:) Mayest thou refound it (the land) and right its wrongs; mayest thou make thy monuments in thy temples and stock the altars of him that begot thee (Amun). ⟨Thou⟩ shalt course through the lands and ensnare many foreign countries, thou shalt triumph over the Libyans, and flex thine arm in smiting the bow-people. Thou shalt decapitate hosts and seize the chiefs of Syria through slaughter, them that remained over from thy father; thy tribute shall be millions of men of thy sword's captivity, and [in] thy train thousands of men for the temples.[101]

[Hatshepsut is] possessed of tribute from all lands . . . malcontents coming in obeissance [. . . and all that] the Sun disk [encircles] bearing its things; she that sends edicts to an unknown land and they do all she commanded . . . the chiefs of foreign lands come to her requesting peace [from Her Majesty, the . . .] are in her grasp, for she has seized every land with her [strong arm], and [ter]ror of her [has circulated] through all lands.[102]

[Hatshepsut speaks: [I am a] good [heir], . . . one to whom the kingship of the Black Land and the Red Land was given, all foreign lands being beneath my feet. My southern frontier is on the shores of Pwenet and [God's land is in my grasp]. My eastern frontier is on the marshes of Asia, and the Montiu of Asia are in my grip. My western frontier is at Manu-mountain and I rule [Libya. My northern frontier is at . . .] and my power overwhelms them that are across the sand all together. As grain is shipped, so is myrrh of Pwenet brought to me [. . .] and all the marvels of this foreign land—they are directed to my palace as a single item. The Asiatics provide [. . .] of turquoise from the land of Roshayt,[103] they bring me the choicest products of Negaw, namely cedar, juniper (?) and mrw-wood [. . .] all the fine woods of God's land. And I have brought the pro-

[98] Ibid., 80.

[99] P. Lacau and H. Chevrier, Une chapelle d'Hatshepsout à Karnak (Cairo, 1977), 144.

[100] E. Naville, The Temple of Deir el-Bahri (London, 1898), 3: pl. 62, lines 33–34.

[101] Urk IV, 247:14–248:9.

[102] Urk IV, 370:3–371:3.

[103] F. Gomàa, Die Besiedlung Ägyptens während des mittleren Reiches (Wiesbaden, 1986), 2:279 (Sinai or Arabah).

duce of Libya, namely 700 tusks of ivory that were there, numerous panther [hides], six cubits along the back and four in circumference, that is of the southern panther, apart from a variety of products from this foreign land.[104]

(Hatshepsut speaks:) Re authorized (it) in his plan: the banks are united under my authority, and the Black Land and the Red Land are in terror of me. My power causes foreign countries to kneel, while the uraeus that is upon my brow brings fear to all lands. Ro-shayt comes, unable to hide from My Majesty, Pwenet journeys to me from the fields of trees, bearing fresh myrrh. The roads that were formerly blocked up, are now (well) trod; and my army, which was formerly unequipped, now has riches since I appeared as king.[105]

(The uraeus speaks:) I shall set the awe [of her throughout] all lands, terror of her throughout every foreign country.[106]

(Hatshepsut speaks:) All lands are bound up in my grasp, the Nine Bows with none of them missing! My power reaches the limits of the Two Lands, I have attained the strength of 'Him-with-the-Mighty-Voice' (Seth), my might pervades the valleys. . . . I have gathered up those who knew not Egypt, whom a royal messenger had never visited. . . . My might terrifies the southland, the northland has (felt) my footsteps. . . . The northerners [. . .] their gods are fashioned as my amulets, with their arms extending life and dominion.[107]

Much of this verbiage is simply plucked from the traditional jargon, fashioned centuries before, and given an archaic cast by using stilted constructions and obsolescent vocabulary (cf. "Montiu," "bow-people," "them that are across the sand"). When one tries to read between the lines, one can isolate but a few, and rather innocuous, excursions into foreign lands, which provide the occasion for the hyperbole. These are the trading venture to Pwenet, which returned in year 9[108] with five shiploads of tropical products; a mining expedition to Sinai or the Arabah;[109] a trading(?) expedition to Byblos in quest of cedar; and a similar expedition to Libya, or possibly one of the oases.[110] Allusions to issuing edicts to a far-off land and the arrival of chiefs in quest of peace reflect the Pwenet expedition only. The reference to the remnant of the chiefs of

---

[104] *Urk* IV, 372:2–373:11.

[105] Speos Artemidos, lines 11–15.

[106] Lacau and Chevrier, *Chapelle*, 115.

[107] Ibid., 144, 147–48.

[108] A.-A. Saleh, *JEA* 58 (1972), 141, n. 1.

[109] There are inscriptions of Hatshepsut (and Thutmose III) at Serabit el-Khadim dated to years 5, 11, and 13 (J. Černý and A. H. Gardiner, *The Inscriptions of Sinai* [London, 1952], pls. 56–57, 61, 68; the expedition of year 20 [ibid., pl. 58] and perhaps year 16 [P-M VII, 343] are too late to have been the inspiration for what is quoted in the text).

[110] The products listed are tropical and not native to Libya; they may have come from the Sudan via the oasis route.

Syria and the donation of captives to the temples probably reflects her father's (or Thutmose II's) accomplishments. Hatshepsut's approach to foreign affairs is clearly traditional: an interest in the peaceful acquisition of goods and services, and recourse to force only when all else failed or rebellion loomed.

There is, then, no evidence for any active involvement, military or otherwise, in western Asia during the twenty years of Hatshepsut's regime; and this hiatus might be expanded to include the preceding reign of Thutmose II, who sent merely a punitive expedition against the Shasu in the Negeb.[111] Was anything happening in the north that would have permitted Egypt temporarily to withdraw from the scene? The answer is: all things have conspired to involve Pharaoh even more deeply in the affairs of western Asia; and if in fact Egypt did withdraw, the reason lies in its own internal condition.

For the new chapter in Egypt's approach to its northern neighbors really began with the reign of Thutmose I, the father of Hatshepsut.[112] This remarkable man, more than any other, was responsible for the final destruction of the Kushite kingdom of the Second Intermediate Period and the raising of the frontier at its remotest southern point, as well as the establishment of a pattern of conquest in the north. The king was methodical in his planning: two years devoted to southern wars; the establishing of residences in the region of Memphis (the better to oversee northern operations); the appointment of a "house steward" at the "Ways of Horus";[113] and the launching of the northern campaign (year 5 or 6). The official record of the campaign itself has not survived (or yet been found), but the event is alluded to in a number of biographical texts of those who participated in it. The old admiral Ahmose-si-Abina accompanied the expedition and recounts: "His Majesty reached Naharin and found that the fallen one[114] had mustered his troops. Then His Majesty made a great slaughter among them, there was no end to the living captives His Majesty took in his victory."[115] His relative Ahmose-pa-Nekhbit records more briefly his captures for Thutmose I "in the land of Naharin."[116] Also one Amenemhet, a scribe who had become king's horologist under Amenophis I, apparently accompanied the expedition, for he records in his fragmentary biographical statement (now lost) "[arrival at(?)] the foreign land of Mitanni—so people call it—and the enemy

[111] R. Giveon, *Les bédouins Shôsou des documents égyptiens* (Leiden, 1971), 9–10.
[112] For what follows, see Helck, *Beziehungen*², 115–16.
[113] *Urk* IV, 547:4.
[114] A pejorative reference to the king of Mitanni.
[115] *Urk* IV, 9.
[116] *Urk* IV, 36.

[. . .] Thebes(?). The ascent of [His] Majesty from this foreign land, after he had laid it waste [. . .]."[117]

For the first time in New Kingdom history, those ancilliary scenes and references to the concomitants and effects of foreign victories can be noted. We hear of a boundary stela the king set up on the banks of the Euphrates, a sure indicator that he was thinking in terms of permanent conquest.[118] A fragmentary text from Deir el-Bahari records an elephant hunt in Niya, clearly on the return from the Euphrates campaign.[119] The king's charioteer was rewarded with 150 *stat* of land, probably for service on the operation.[120] The scene of the return of foreign captives, to become so popular during the succeeding two centuries, makes its first appearance at this time;[121] and it is probably to the same, or the following reign, that we must date the earliest known scene depicting chariots in battle.[122]

There is thus good evidence to conclude that, in contemporary perception and in fact, Thutmose's was the first serious incursion of the New Kingdom into western Asia, mounted on a grand scale, and intended to effect permanent results; but did it have any effect on the states of North Syria?

Here we must confess a profound ignorance. Archaeological traces of the Egyptian invasion are conspicuous by their absence. A pot from Alalakh and a few vessels of Egyptian type in the Qatna inventories certainly do not constitute evidence of Thutmose's passage through the region.[123] And it would be a rash excavator indeed who links a destruction level in a Syrian site with this campaign. If indeed there is a southward orientation detectable in the ceramic repertoire of LB IA,[124] this need indicate nothing more than a revival of trade in which 18th Dynasty Egypt was once again exerting its influence.

The fact is that Thutmose's attack caused scarcely more than a minor

---

[117] L. Borchardt, *Altägyptische Zeitmessung* (Leipzig, 1920), pl. 18; H. Brunner, *MIOF* 4 (1956), 323–24; it is assumed, probably correctly, that the text alludes to Thutmose I, although his name does not appear in this pericope, and in the very next column Amenemhet begins an extended record of his service under Ahmose and Amenophis I: see W. Helck, *Oriens Antiquus* 8 (1969), 301–2; L. Bradbury, *Serapis* 8 (1985), 19.

[118] *Urk* IV, 697:5; A. J. Spalinger, *JNES* 37 (1978), 35ff.

[119] Naville, *Deir el-Bahri*, 3: pl. 80; on the ascription of the text to Thutmose I, see Gardiner, *Onomastica*, 1:158*.

[120] Berlin 14994: *Aegyptische Inschriften aus den staatlichen Museen zu Berlin* (Leipzig, 1924), 2:115.

[121] Ineni's tomb: N. de G. Davies, *Private Tombs at Thebes* (London, 1963), 4: pl. 22.

[122] B. Bruyere, *FIFAO* 3 (1926), pls. ii–iv; these were found in the mortuary temple of Thutmose II, and estimates of the date have ranged widely (see P-M²II, 456; Hoffmeier, in *Akhenaten Temple Project*, 2:40). In the light of Thutmose II's absence from the Asiatic theater, it is reasonable to construe them as a commemoration of his father's activity.

[123] Bottero, *RA* 43 (1949), 33.

[124] R. Dornemann, *BASOR* 241 (1981), 46.

"shudder" in North Syria because it was not repeated. Administering an oath to Syrian princes in Pharaoh's name was no substitute for the threat of another campaign and the planting of garrisons; and although Thutmose may have left a garrison somewhere in Asia, it was not nearly enough to deter Mitanni.

In the forty years that followed Thutmose's isolated attack—the period of Egypt's withdrawal from Asia—Mitanni was free to continue its aggressive subversion of Syria and Mesopotamia. One of the survivors of the civil war in Aleppo, Idrimi, was ensconced in the kingdom of Alalakh north of the lower Orontes (including Mukishe and Niya as well), and bound by a treaty imposed by "Barratarna, the mighty king, king of the warriors of the Hurri-land," apparently the successor of Shutarna I.[125] Although in fact a tribute-paying vassal of Mitanni,[126] Idrimi was allowed a free hand as a Hurrian cat's paw: he was allowed to sign independent treaties with Pa'illiya of the contiguous Kizzuwadna and with the king of Ugarit on the south,[127] and could raid Hittite towns with impunity.[128] To the east Aleppo had sunk to the status of a principality ruled directly from Mitanni,[129] and Niya through its subservience to Alalakh was indirectly under Mitannian control.

In central Syria, Tunip and Kadesh took advantage of the relative calm to expand; and more than any other single factor it was this that brought about the change in Egypt's policy and led to the most intense period of empire building Egypt had ever known. Whether Tunip and Kadesh acted as protégés of Mitanni is unclear, although under Niqmepa, Idrimi's son, Ir-teshup the king of Tunip gladly acknowledged the Mitannian ruler as suzerain, and as a vassal signed a treaty with Alalakh.[130] In any case, because its natural horizon lay to the west, Tunip began to exert its influence among the towns of the coast north of Byblos. Kadesh for its part looked south[131] and on the eve of Hatshepsut's death had made itself the de facto master of Coele-Syria and north Palestine. The king of Kadesh owned property in cities in Galilee and the north Jordan Valley[132] and the Palestinian towns were characterized as "those that are loyal to him." The fact that he was able to muster the headmen and the militias of the towns of

---

[125] On the Idrimi inscription, see Smith, *Idrimi*, 59–60; Klengel, *Geschichte*, 1:182 and n. 33; 228–29; M. Dietrich and O. Lorenz, *UF* 13 (1981), 201–69; Van Seters, *In Search of History*, 188–91.

[126] Wiseman, *Alalakh Tablets*, no. 395; Klengel, *Geschichte*, 1:219, 229.

[127] Cf. Wiseman, *Alalakh Tablets*, no. 4; Klengel, *Geschichte*, 1:229–30; 2:334–35.

[128] Wiseman, *Alalakh Tablets*, no. 3; Klengel, *Geschichte*, 1:219 and n. 3; Smith, *Idrimi*, 18–20.

[129] Cf. Wiseman, *Alalakh Tablets*, no. 101.

[130] Ibid., no. 2, lines 73–75; Klengel, *Geschichte*, 1:219 and n. 3; Smith, *Idrimi*, 18–20.

[131] See p. 156f.

[132] Cf. *Urk* IV, 664:1–665:2; cf. 744:3–8.

his sprawling bailiwick at Megiddo demonstrates not only his firm control over his vassals but also his intent to move south and annex territory. No matter when we date the catastrophe at the beginning of the Late Bronze Age, Egypt could scarcely cede control of Palestine to such an expansionist power. The expressed concern of Thutmose III over this threat must be accepted as a sincere statement, not deceptive propaganda: the massing of such a large force so close to the Egyptian frontier was a *casus belli* and a preemptive strike was clearly called for.

While it is now certain that the animosity of the young Thutmose III toward his aunt-consort Hatshepsut did not issue in the destruction of her monuments until long after her death,[133] nonetheless her continued presence as the dominant partner exerted a restraint on her nephew. Bellicose statements in inscriptions from year 20 may indicate that Thutmose III, perhaps chafing under his inability to act alone, was being given freer rein.[134] It is very likely that Hatshepsut was ailing toward the end of her life, and that her decline was widely bruited. When she at last passed away on the tenth day of the sixth month in the twenty-second year of the joint reign[135] (early February 1482 B.C.), the king of Kadesh must already have put his plan into effect and begun to muster his forces at Megiddo, perhaps intending to take advantage of the queen's imminent death.[136] Thutmose's resolve to meet this threat, and his crossing the frontier in May of the same year, set the stage for the first and most decisive of the great conqueror's campaigns.[137]

The battle of Megiddo, to judge from the booty list, involved the largest

---

[133] See C. F. Nims, *ZAS* 63 (1966), 97–100; P. F. Dorman, *Fourth International Congress of Egyptology. Abstracts of Papers* (Munich, 1985), 55–57.

[134] Gardiner and Černý, *The Inscriptions of Sinai*, pl. 57:181; T. Säve-Söderbergh, *Aegypten und Nubien* (Lund, 1941), fig. 16 (209).

[135] This is the unqualified opening date on the Armant stela (*Urk* IV, 1244), now universally accepted in the wake of M. S. Drower (in R. Mond and O. Myers, *The Temples of Armant* [London, 1940], 182–83) as the date of the queen's death: Ratié, *La reine Hatshepsout*, 295–96.

[136] The decision by the king of Kadesh to call up the vassal armies at Megiddo, preparatory to the move on Egypt (cf. the explicit wording of Barkal, lines 7–8; *Urk* IV, 1254:9, 758:7), must have been arrived at months before the date on the Armant stela. Since only ten weeks and five days elapsed between that date and the start of the campaign, Thutmose III must have begun his own mustering of the Egyptian forces shortly after Hatshepsut's death; and since what prompted him to act was news of the massing of Canaanite levies at Megiddo (which would have taken the best part of a month to reach him, under the most favorable conditions), the gathering of the forces at Megiddo must have taken place weeks before the queen's demise.

[137] For the campaigns one may consult with profit J. H. Breasted, *Ancient Records of Egypt* (Chicago, 1906), 2: sec. 391–540; J. Wilson, in *ANET²*, 234–41; H. Grapow, *Studien zu den Annalen Thutmosis des Dritten* (Berlin, 1949); S. Yeivin, *BiblOr* 23 (1966), 18–27; Helck, *Beziehungen²*, 119–56; A. J. Spalinger, *JARCE* 14 (1977), 41–54; Redford, *LdÄ* 6 (1984), 185–93. In a more popular vein, see A. Tulhoff, *Thutmosis III* (Munich, 1984).

forces (on both sides) that ever took part in Thutmose's forays into Syria, and showed the king's brilliance as a tactician to best advantage.[138] By a daring strike through the pass at Megiddo, Thutmose caught the Canaanite army off guard, effected a rout, and invested Megiddo for seven months (Figure 6). When the city fell in December 1482 B.C., all the Canaanite headmen, with the exception of the king of Kadesh who had fled,

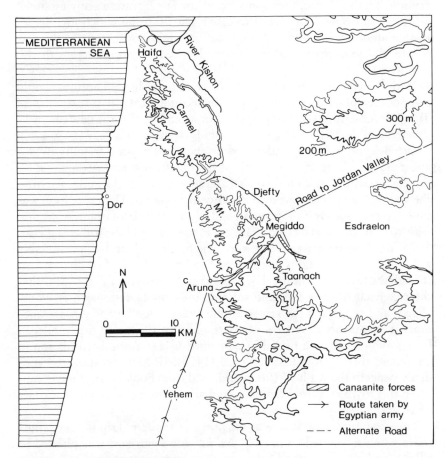

Figure 6. The battle of Megiddo.

[138] The Karnak annals date from nearly two decades after the event and represent the full-blown account, based on the daybook, but given a literary and rhetorical cast (see, among others, Grapow, *Annalen*; I. Shirun-Grumach, in A. Rofe and Y. Zakovitch, eds., *Israel Leo Seligman* [Jerusalem, 1983], 1:79–94; A. J. Spalinger, *MDAIK* 30 [1974], 221–22; idem., *GM* 33 [1979], 47–48; I am preparing a new edition of the annals in conjunction with a forthcoming monograph on Thutmose III). By judicious comparison of the varying accounts it is not difficult to arrive at a close approximation of what actually happened.

fell at one stroke into Egyptian hands and were made to take the oath: "The lands of Retenu shall not again rebel on another occasion," and "we shall not again act evilly against (Thutmose III) in our lifetime."[139] Humiliated by being deprived of their horses, the headmen were sent back to their towns now as Egyptian vassals; but if they thought with the passage of time Thutmose III would lose interest and tacitly concur in their renouncing the pledge, they were mistaken. The Egyptian army mounted a tour of inspection for three successive years (during which it collected tribute among other things)[140] and reaffirmed the royal claim to the new territory. The frontiers had thus been advanced to approximately the Litani River.

With the coalition destroyed and Kadesh discredited, Thutmose could now contemplate a move against the second northern threat, that of Tunip. It took three years to prepare, but when it broke, the new offensive was irresistible. In the early summer of his twenty-ninth year (1476 B.C.), Thutmose and his troops advanced up the coast beyond friendly Byblos and reduced Ullaza (at the mouth of the Eleutheros) and Ardata (six kilometers south of modern Tripoli), and took prisoner the entire garrison the king of Tunip had placed on the Phoenician coast. The expedition was timed to coincide with the harvest, and vast quantities of grain, wine, and fruit were dispatched by ship to Egypt. In the spring of the following year, 1475, the Egyptians were back, this time by ship,[141] landing presumably at Byblos. The mountains were crossed and Kadesh attacked directly. Although the terse entry of the daybook reads "destroying it," it is clear that the city itself did not fall, and suffered only the laying waste of its orchards and crops. On the return Sumur (near Tripoli?) and Ardata once more were assaulted. After a year's respite (for the king's first jubilee?), during which the king of Tunip refortified Ullaza and placed his son in command there, Thutmose returned (1473). In May he appeared suddenly beneath the walls of Ullaza and, as the daybook entry states, "captured this town in a brief moment, and all its property became a 'Come-and-Get-it.' "[142]

The coast was now secure as far north as modern Tripoli, and Thutmose was determined to hold it. An Egyptian garrison was planted in Ullaza, and all the chiefs of Lebanon placed under taxation. The harbors were turned into depots stocked with food and military supplies for future expeditions, and Lebanese timber was yearly shipped thence to

[139] Barkal stela, lines 21, 24.
[140] And in year 25 made a collection of exotic plants from Palestine! Cf. W. Wreszinzki, *Atlas zur altägyptischen Kulturgeschichte* (Leipzig 1935), 2: pl. 26.
[141] Cf. the determinative in *Urk* IV, 689:5.
[142] *Urk* IV, 691:10–11.

Egypt. All this shows farsighted planning; but Thutmose was also preparing his next move.

The direct attack on Mitanni, which must long have been seen as one of Thutmose's manifest goals, followed in his thirty-third year (1472 B.C.). Certainly the judgment of Thutmose III himself and his contemporaries was that it marked the apogee of his military career; and the modern historian would have to concur.[143] Besides its treatment in the annals, the eighth campaign became a favorite theme in Thutmose's speeches in which he reminisced before the court;[144] and officers who accompanied the expedition are as proud to record the fact as any participant at Agincourt or Crecy.[145]

Thutmose transported the army by ship to Byblos and there had prefabricated assault craft prepared of Lebanese timber. The whole expeditionary force then crossed the mountains to the Orontes Valley, the disassembled vessels being transported in carts in the rear, and proceeded northward. Kadesh and Tunip offered no resistance, perhaps taken aback by the surprise and speed of the operation, and the Egyptians passed through their territories unopposed. As soon, however, as the army entered the region of Aleppo, the Mitannians offered resistance. Three sharp engagements issued in Thutmose's favor and brought the Egyptians to the bank of the Euphrates at Carchemish. The king of Mitanni and his forces had withdrawn to the east bank, and had presumably destroyed or taken possession of all other river craft in the vicinity. Now Thutmose brought forward his assault craft, embarked his troops, and pursued the bewildered Mitannian ruler and his routed forces downstream and eastward toward the Balikh, while the nobility of the country took refuge in caves.[146] Wholesale destruction followed as Thutmose committed the towns along the Euphrates to the flames. "There was no one to save them throughout that land of Naharin," boasted the king in a speech fifteen years later, "which had been abandoned by its lord through fear. I destroyed his cities and his villages and set them on fire, and My Majesty turned them into ruin mounds, never to be resettled."[147] The erection of a stela on the riverbank beside that of his father marked the farthest point

[143] Some treatments: R. O. Faulkner, *JEA* 32 (1946), 39–40; Helck, *Beziehungen*², 138–39; P-M² II, 89 (240–44); Redford, *LdÄ* 6 (1984), 185–93.

[144] Barkal stela, lines 9–17; Armant stela, lines 7–8; seventh pylon inscription (*Urk* IV, 188–89); possibly *Urk* IV, 676–77; cf. also the "poetical" stela, lines 7–8, and the Constantinople obelisk (cf. L. Habachi, *The Obelisks of Egypt* [New York, 1977], 147).

[145] Yamu-nedjeh (*Urk* IV, 1370); Minmose (*Urk* IV, 1441); Montu-iwy (*Urk* IV, 1467); Amenemheb (*Urk* IV, 890–92).

[146] N. de G. Davies and A. H. Gardiner, *The Tombs of Menkheperrasonb. Amenmose and Another* (London, 1933), pls. 5 and 7.

[147] Barkal stela, line 9.

an Egyptian king was to attain in the north.[148] The leisurely homeward march and the obligatory hunt (this time for elephants at Niya) brought the campaign to a formal conclusion.

Thutmose's policy of following up his successes was pursued in this case also. The next year the king returned and plundered the region of Nukhashshe, and the next year after that he took on an even larger Mitannian force in North Syria and routed them. The Egyptian empire in Asia had reached its maximum extent.

THE UNEASY HEGEMONY AND THE TREATY WITH MITANNI (c. 1460–1440)

The immediate effect of Thutmose III's crowning achievement in defeating Mitanni was to bring Egypt to the attention of the entire ancient world as a potent factor in the politics of the eastern Mediterranean. These were halcyon days for Egypt, when "at the mere sight of an Egyptian the kings of Canaan would flee."[149] Those states that stood in strategic opposition to Mitanni, namely Babylon, Assyria, and Khatte, immediately sent diplomatic gifts to Pharaoh,[150] and very soon thereafter Cyprus followed suite.[151] Five years after the initial Egyptian invasion of North Syria, Alalakh too (perhaps under its young king Niqmepa, son of Idrimi) felt it expedient to send presents, undoubtedly to placate Thutmose and ward off future incursions.

Clearly Thutmose intended to annex the country he had traversed. Following local practice, he anointed local magnates and appointed them to the kingship at local principalities as his own vassals.[152] A garrison was assigned to Uga⟨ri⟩t,[153] and Thutmose reappeared personally year by year

[148] A. Spalinger, *JNES* 37 (1978), 35–42; W. Helck, *CdE* 56 (1981), 241ff.

[149] EA 109:44.

[150] *Urk* IV, 700–701, 727. The Egyptian sources do not mention the kings' names, but if our chronology is correct, the Assyrian must have been Ashur-nirari I (A. K. Grayson, *Assyrian Royal Inscriptions* [Wiesbaden, 1972], 33–34), and the Babylonian perhaps Burnaburiash I (Drower, *CAH³* II, pt. 1 [1973], 442). The Hittite is more difficult to identify, since no Hittite king list has as yet been found; but it may well have been Telepinus.

[151] *Urk* IV, 707–8, 724.

[152] Cf. EA 51:4–5: "Manahbi ⟨ri⟩ya, the king of Egypt, the father of your father, appointed Taku, the father of my father, in Nukhashshe, and poured oil on his head." If taken literally, "father of your father" would indicate Thutmose IV since this letter was sent to Akhenaten. But the locution can indicate simply "dynastic ancestor"; and in fact Thutmose III was later known as "father of the fathers" (Redford, *King-lists*, 52). A more serious objection is the vocalization of the name in Akkadian, which approximates more closely the form Thutmose III's praenomen would have taken: for discussion and references, see B. Bryan, "The Reign of Thutmose IV" (Ph.D. diss., Yale University, 1980), 431–34.

[153] Early in Amenophis II's reign an Egyptian garrison is mentioned as occupying a place called *I-k³-ti* (*Urk* IV, 1312). If this *is* Ugarit, we have an anomalous spelling, since the name

to collect taxes. Niya, formerly a dependency of Alalakh, now appears as a separate state with its own prince,[154] and the region briefly becomes the hunting estate of Pharaoh.

But the strength and resilience of the empire of Mitanni, that "land of the Hurri-warriors," showed itself almost before the dust had settled on the Euphrates campaign. Thutmose III does not tell us the identity of "that fallen one of vile Naharin" whom he defeated on the eighth campaign, but he gives the distinct impression that he fled eastward never to be seen again. Yet only two years later another "vile fallen one of Naharin" musters an even larger army to oppose the Egyptians. It is very tempting to see in the flight of the unnamed Mitannian ruler the end of the career of Barratarna, the contemporary of Idrimi and successor of Shutarna I.[155] In that case the Mitannian leader who confronted the Egyptians two years later may well be Barratarna's successor, who seems, from all the evidence known today, to have been Saussatar, son of Parsatatar, and "king of Mitanni."[156] If this is the case, the removal of one powerful

---

usually appears in Egyptian transcription as *I-k³-ri-ti*. Since, however, the Amenophis II passage is the earliest reference, it may well be that the scribe was proceeding under the influence of an archaic, Middle Egyptian standardization of the toponym. Astour has ingeniously tried to discredit the identification on geographical, not linguistic grounds (see *Ugarit in Retrospect* [Winona Lake, Ind., 1981], 14). The Karnak stela allows only ten days for the excursion from Niya to *I-k³-ti*, and back to *T³-r-ḫ*, "on the road from Niya to Qidsi," a round trip of 260 kilometers, if Ugarit is the town in question. But *T³-r-ḫ* is *not* on the road to Kadesh, but rather is to be identified with Zalkhi, a district close to Ugarit (cf. Edel, *Ortsnamenlisten*, 82; EA 126:5). The march from Niya to Ugarit and then on to Zalkhi, about 150 kilometers by the *longest* route, is easily negotiable in ten days. For further discussion, see Gardiner, *Onomastica*, 1:165*; E. Edel, *ZPDV* 69 (1953), 149ff.; Helck, *Beziehungen²*, 157; Klengel, *Geschichte*, 2:2, 336–39. Just when Ugarit was subverted to Egypt is not known, but two periods suggest themselves: a voluntary submission during Thutmose's Phoenician campaigns, or a conquest during the eleventh or twelfth campaigns (1469–1468). Certainly EA 46 and 47, with their references to the ancestral kings of Ugarit having been servants of Egypt, would push the subjection of the town well back in time.

[154] Klengel, *Geschichte*, 2:1, 68.

[155] His death is mentioned in a Nuzi text, which could be dated about this time: *Harvard Semitic Series* XIII, 165:3; W. F. Albright, *BASOR* 118 (1950), 17, n. 27; but see the following note.

[156] The lack of any Mitannian archives in which diplomatic correspondence or a succession of rulers might be found continues to bedevil all attempts to establish a king list. All we can say with certainty is that Barratarna was a contemporary of Idrimi and began to rule in the generation before Thutmose III (Smith, *Idrimi*, 16), that he is to be placed approximately one generation before Saussatar (on the basis of Nuzi evidence of witnesses in legal documents: H. Lewy, *AIPHOS* 13 [1953], 284, n. 4, and 286ff.; Klengel, *RHA* 36 [1978] 94–95), and that the latter was a later contemporary of Thutmose III, dying after the first decade of Amenophis II's reign (Klengel, *Geschichte*, 1:39; W. Helck, *Geschichte der alten Ägypten* [Leiden, 1968], 163). There is little reason to think that Parsatatar, Saussatar's father (R. Lachman, *BASOR* 78 [1941], 22), was ever king, and he probably represents a branch of the family distinct from that to which Barratarna belonged (*pace* F. Imperati, *I*

opponent did little to alleviate the intensity of the opposition to Egypt's incursion.

Saussatar set about vigorously to resist Egypt and to continue to extend Mitanni's authority. In 1463, scarcely a decade after the Euphrates campaign, we find an auxiliary force "of vile Naharin" dispatched to the king of Kadesh, and Tunip fomenting rebellion on the Lebanese coast. Thutmose was forced to march by land to deal with the insurrection in Arqata north of Byblos, then to march over the mountains against Tunip and Kadesh. Territory was devastated, orchards and crops destroyed, and possibly for the first time Kadesh assaulted and captured.[157] Although Thutmose set up headquarters for a time in Tunip, now captured, a residency long remembered by the Tunipians,[158] the revolts continued; and soon the land of Takhsi on the upper Orontes between Kadesh and Damascus[159] was in open rebellion. Despite the destruction of thirty towns and the deportation of headmen, chattels, and livestock,[160] the revolt continued into the coregency and early sole rule of Amenophis II, who, as one of his first acts, was forced to deport seven chiefs to Egypt and execute them.[161]

Elsewhere Saussatar had no difficulty in reasserting Mitannian authority. To the east he subdued Assyria, stripping Ashur of some of its treasures and extending his control to the Zagros.[162] In the west, Aleppo remained subservient to Mitanni and Niqmepa of Alalakh, despite his gifts to Pharaoh, reaffirmed his loyalty to Saussatar.[163] Ugarit, though not within Mitanni's pale, was planning to expel its Egyptian garrison. Southward up the Orontes Valley, Niya, Zalkhe, and towns as far south as Kadesh were beginning to fall once again under Mitannian influence.

Amenophis II's "raid" in his seventh year did nothing to win back ter-

---

Hurriti [Florence, 1964], 58ff.), although it is conceivable that he occupied the throne for a short time following Barratarna's death. See also G. Wilhelm, *Acta Antiqua* 24 (1976), 149–61. D. L. Stein has recently argued (*ZA* 79 [1989], 36–60) for the existence of a Barattarna II and for the redating of Saussatar to the end of the fifteenth century. I have difficulty, however, even on the "low" chronology of the 18th Dynasty, of accommodating a date so late.

[157] *Urk* IV, 729–30; presumably it is here, or on some unrecorded campaign shortly after—the Karnak annals end at this point—that Amenemheb distinguished himself by breaching the wall of Kadesh: *Urk* IV, 894:5–895:3.

[158] Cf. EA 59:6–10. On the identity, see p. 175.

[159] R. Hachmann, in D. O. Edzard et al., eds., *Kamid el-Loz-Kumidi* (Bonn, 1970), 85; S. Ahituv, *Canaanite Toponyms in Ancient Egyptian Documents* (Leiden, 1984), 187.

[160] *Urk* IV, 893:6–13; 1442:16–18. All references to the Takhsi revolt postdate year 42 and the conclusion of the annals.

[161] C. Kuentz, *Deux stèles d'Amenophis II* (Cairo, 1925), 47–56.

[162] Weidner, *Politische Dokumente*, 39; E. A. Speiser, *JAOS* 49 (1929), 269–70; Harrak, *Assyria and Hanigalbat*, 42–43.

[163] Cf. Klengel, *Geschichte*, 1:183; Wiseman, *Alalakh Tablets*, nos. 13, 14, and passim.

ritory.[164] This characterization is not unncessarily harsh: Amenophis II was a brave warrior and his army may have been substantial, but he met no large enemy force in a set-piece battle. The repulse of a small hostile contingent from Qatna at the crossing of the Orontes and the quelling of an incipient rebellion in Ugarit hardly constituted great victories; and although Niya and other towns on the Orontes opened their gates to him, Pharaoh would have been naive to believe this betokened a renunciation of allegiance to Saussatar. His uprooting and deportation of 15,070 Nukhashsheans seems in the event to be a move of desperation.[165]

The Hittites for their part had never underestimated their enemies beyond the Euphrates. Telepinus had signed a treaty with Ishputakhshu, the "great king of Kizzuwadna," effectually renewing that state's function as a buffer (c. 1450 B.C.);[166] and an unknown successor had concluded a similar agreement with Shunashshura I, Ishputakhshu's successor.[167] This last text is of some interest in our present concern, in that it envisages an imminent war between the Hittites and Mitanni, and one in which Mitanni might take the initiative. If that occurs, Shunashshura is to deny the Mitannians access to Khatte via the land of Shuwanta, although it will be within his discretion to participate on the Hittite side or remain neutral. The implied tension between Khatte and Mitanni may also be reflected in the border dispute between Niqmepa of Alalakh and the same Shunashshura over the border town of Alawari.[168]

The coming of peace between Egypt and Mitanni is, in its immediate background and details, a missing page in the documentation of the time. Amenophis II boasts that, some time after his ninth year (i.e., after c. 1443 B.C.), the impression his conquests and deportations had made forced the great kings of the earth to come to terms:[169] "When the chief of Naharin, the chief of the Hittites and the chief of Babylon heard about the victory I had achieved, each one vied with his fellow in presenting all sorts of gifts from every foreign source; and they intended in their hearts . . . to seek peace from My Majesty and to seek that there be given to them the breath of life (to wit): 'our labor is earmarked for thy palace, O (Amenophis II)!' " Later still in the reign (exact date unknown), a eulogist of the king has occasion to record on the columns of one of the halls at

---

[164] On the numbering of campaigns and year dates, see Edel, *ZDPV* 69 (1953), 158; A. Alt, *ZDPV* 70 (1954), 41, n. 29.

[165] See now the complete discussion and bibliography in P. der Manuelian, *Studies in the Reign of Amenophis II* (Hildesheim, 1987), 56–83.

[166] G. R. Meyer, *MIOF* 1 (1953), 110; H. Otten, *Saeculum* 15 (1964), 122.

[167] Meyer, *MIOF* 1 (1953), 122–23.

[168] Wiseman, *Alalakh Tablets*, no. 14; Klengel, *Geschichte*, 1:229.

[169] *Urk* IV, 1309:13–20.

Karnak[170] that "the Chiefs of Mitanni came to him, their tribute upon their backs, to seek the peace of His Majesty, desirous of his sweet breath of life. A notable event! (The like of this occurrence) had not been heard of since the time of the demigods (literally, god's people): this land which knew not Egypt was supplicating the Good God!"

One should be cautious in assessing these two passages. In view of Amenophis's bombast and braggart nature, there may lie behind the first no more than the receipt of diplomatic gifts of the same sort as Thutmose III had recorded more soberly on the morrow of his Euphrates campaign; and whatever else Amenophis II says about motivation may be nothing more than his eisegesis. The second passage, however, must be taken more seriously. The amplification of the stock phrases that open the pericope, together with the insistence that this was a unique event, suggests that a certain kernel of truth is concealed beneath the hyperbole. The excuse for the exaggerated claims probably lies in the arrival (after year 10, we may be sure) of a Mitannian embassy sent by Saussatar[171] with proposals of "brotherhood" (i.e., a fraternal alliance and renunciation of hostilities).[172]

The treaty arises, it seems to me, out of Mitanni's observation of two hard facts: the ferocity of the new Egyptian ruler and the revival of Khatte. Amenophis II may have been unable to maintain effectively Egypt's control over the middle and lower Orontes basin, but his mass deportations, both in Syria and especially in Palestine in year 9, served notice of what he might be prepared to do in the event of continued hostilities. They were, in a word, the tactics of terror. The Hittites may have appeared less brutal, but their threat was immediate. A new house had seized the reins of power in Khattusas and was intent on capturing the initiative from the Mitannians.[173] An early member of the family, Tudkhaliya (usually termed II), made overtures to Aleppo, which he construed as accepted, and in a Macchiavellian manner viewed Aleppo's con-

[170] *Urk* IV, 1326.

[171] The name of the Mitannian king is not known, but I prefer to see in the negotiator under Amenophis II a king earlier than Artatama, the son and successor of Saussatar (KBo I, 3, obv. 8), the contemporary of Thutmose IV. Only by postulating a change of reign can we explain a situation in which the new Pharaoh, Thutmose IV, can feel free to attack Mitannian holdings with impunity: he had never concluded a treaty with his counterpart in Khatte (see subsequent discussion).

[172] Klengel, *Geschichte*, 1:39; Helck, *Beziehungen*[2], 161; Bryan, "The Reign of Thutmosis IV," 423–24 (although I believe the Kurushtama treaty is better placed early in Akhenaten's reign: see subsequent discussion).

[173] On the thorny problem of the order and identity of the predecessors of Suppiluliumas, see in particular A. Kammenhuber, *Orientalia* 39 (1970), 278–301; H. G. Güterbock, *JNES* 29 (1970), 73–77; W. Helck, in M. Görg, ed., *Elmar Edel Festschrift* (Bamberg, 1979), 238–39; S. Kosak, *Tel Aviv* 7 (1980), 163–69.

tinued ties to Mitanni as evidence of duplicity. Therefore, says a later Hittite text,[174] he "destroyed the king of Mitanni[175] and the king of Aleppo together with their lands, and devastated the city of Aleppo." In spite of the fact that the Talmisharruma treaty, from which this excerpt was taken, dates over a century after the event and contains inaccuracies—Aleppo at the time was ruled by a Mitannian governor, not a king[176]—the text certainly reflects a historical attack upon Aleppo, Khatte's long-standing "whipping boy," and a reverse for Mitanni.

Under these circumstances there was little the Mitannians could do, save persevere alone in a "two-front war" or seek an alliance that would do away with one of the "fronts." Mitanni wisely chose the latter. The closer and more hostile Khatte could not be mollified, but the distant and volatile Amenophis II seemed susceptible to negotiations. Courageous but vain, athletic and convivial, and possibly easily won over by flattery—did the Mitannians know their man?—Amenophis II was apparently charmed and disarmed by the embassy from "Naharin," and perhaps even signed a treaty.[177] There is no doubt that Egypt's own interest would have been served by such a treaty, although the pharaonic state of the 18th Dynasty could, more easily than Mitanni, sustain the expense of periodic military incursions eight hundred kilometers into Asia.

The alliance was cemented in place by the marriage of Amenophis II's son, Thutmose IV, about 1415 B.C. to the daughter of Saussatar's son and successor, Artatama I of Mitanni.[178] His father's *concordat* with Saussatar (whatever form it in fact took) had not, however, prevented Thutmose IV from mounting an offensive in Asia early in his reign,[179] which took him up the coastal road to Phoenicia and then, following the route of his father and grandfather, across the mountains to the Orontes.[180] His intent was to continue the deportation of Palestinian inhabitants initiated by his father (he depopulated Gezer);[181] to "show the flag" in Phoenicia;[182] and to punish certain "rebels" in the Orontes Valley. But the whole operation seems to have been conceived on a modest scale, and motivated not by

[174] Talmisharuma treaty: for bibliography, see Klengel, *Geschichte*, 1:177–78; also N. Na'aman, *JCS* 32 (1980), 34ff.

[175] So according to another version: H. Klengel, *MIOF* 10 (1964), 216.

[176] Klengel, *Geschichte*, 1:189, n. 38.

[177] For the evidence for the character of this unusual Pharaoh, see p. 230.

[178] EA 29:16–18; A. R. Schulman, *JNES* 39 (1979), 189, n. 54; Bryan, "The Reign of Thutmosis IV," 158–61.

[179] C. Kühne, *Die Chronologie der internationalen Correspondenz von El-Amarna* (Neukirchen-Vluyn, 1973), 20, n. 85.

[180] A very judicious treatment of this campaign is offered in Bryan, "The Reign of Thutmosis IV," 422–25, where earlier literature is cited.

[181] *Urk* IV, 1556:10–11.

[182] On his stop in Sidon, see EA 85:71; Helck, *Beziehungen²*, 174.

political or military necessity but rather in imitation of what the imperial Pharaoh was increasingly being expected to do at the outset of his reign. In any event, this campaign (which need not, in any case, have been construed as "anti-Mitannian") terminated Egypt's military adventures in western Asia for sixty-five years. The marriage and the renewal of the treaty brought a peace to Egypt and Mitanni from which both states benefited and which, as it turned out, was never abrogated or broken.

THREE GENERATIONS OF PEACE: THE EMPIRE, 1440–1375

Although we lack the text of the treaty, we may be sure that the negotiators for the Egyptian and Mitannian sides would have been most concerned over the border between the two empires. The frontiers sanctioned by the pact can be elicited from contemporary and slightly later records, and represented the lines as they fell at the close of Amenophis II's reign. Through two hundred years, and with only slight modification, they were to become hallowed as traditional, and were to leave their mark subtly but indelibly on the history and culture of the entire Levant.

Essentially the line followed known geographical or cultural divisions and in the north coincided with the course of the Orontes River. Mukishe, with its capital Alalakh and the principality of Aleppo, continued to be dependents of Mitanni. Between Aleppo and Qatna, east of the Orontes, lay the Nukhashshe lands, which likewise, according to the evidence of the Talmisharruma treaty, remained within the Mitannian sphere.[183] Niya, although its "chief" had opened his gates to Amenophis II (as previously noted), continued to be closely tied to Mukishe and Alalakh;[184] and while the neighboring Zinzar[185] is missing from the records, it too presumably fell within the penumbra of Mitanni and its northern vassals.

Tunip too remained a vassal of Mitanni. Perhaps to weaken its position or to place the border region under the control of a stronger power, certain of its districts were separated off and given to Ilim-ilimma, son of Niqmepa of Alalakh, a later contemporary of Amenophis II and Thutmose IV. Whatever Egyptian control Thutmose III had enjoyed over Tunip

---

[183] Cf. Klengel, *Geschichte*, 2:1, 24; Na'aman, *JCS* 32 (1980), 38–39; on the location of the Nukhashshe, see Gardiner, *Onomastica*, 1:168*ff.; Klengel, *Geschichte*, 2:18; Helck, *Beziehungen*[2], 152. The Amarna Letters likewise prove that Nukhashshe was beyond the Egyptian pale: although the Nukhashshe kings love Pharaoh (EA 53:41–44), they have never paid tax to Egypt (EA 53:50–51), and Nukhashshe does not (yet) belong to Pharaoh (EA 55:21–22).

[184] Cf. Wiseman, *Alalakh Tablets*, no. 215:4 (list of landowners whose property is located in the vicinity of Niya); nos. 397:4, 398, 400:7 (copper and bronze distributed to Niya); nos. 364:5, 426:3 (passage of officials and presents).

[185] Qal'at Sedjar on the left bank of the Orontes, northwest of Hama: Klengel, *Geschichte*, 2:31, n. 8.

had been brief. When in the Amarna age the inhabitants of the city turned to Egypt and tried to persuade Pharaoh to help them, they could only cite Thutmose III's short residence in the town by way of argument that Tunip had traditionally been an Egyptian possession; and they knew that it was only the "old men" of Pharaoh's entourage that could corroborate this. In the recent past, it is clear, Tunip had not belonged to the kings of Egypt.[186]

The inland frontier between the Mitannian and Egyptian spheres left the Orontes between Tunip and Qatna and ran eastward to encompass the latter city. We know little of Qatna between its feeble attempt to block Amenophis II's advance and the letters of Akizzi to Akhenaten. The Qatna inventories provide the evidence for the reconstruction of a king list but say nothing of political history. Akizzi, however, indicates unequivocally that not only is he an Egyptian vassal but also so have his fathers been from of old, and that Qatna belongs to Pharaoh.[187] South of Qatna, Kadesh, the land of Upe, and Damascus all fell within the Nilotic empire.[188] The upper Orontes basin constituted the fertile farmlands of the Amki, while Damascus lay in the center of grazing country.[189] Egypt prized the area highly and would take stringent measures to retain its hold on it.

The territory west of the Orontes, as far as the Mediterranean coast, belonged to Egypt.[190] This is understandable in the light of Egypt's maritime power, since it could maintain contact by ship with the coastal cities of Phoenicia more easily than with the remote hinterland. These coastal lands south of the mouth of the Orontes, together with Cis-Jordan south of the sources of the Orontes, made up a single geographical area, which from of old had been called "Canaan."[191] The origin of the name is obscure, but clearly Alalakh, Aleppo, the Nukhashshe lands, and Qatna lay outside the region so designated in the Late Bronze Age; and one is almost

---

[186] Cf. *KUB* III, 16, 20 (Weidner, *Politische Dokumente*, 136–47, no. 10); EA 59. There is no evidence at all that Egypt controlled Tunip after the withdrawal of Amenophis II in his ninth year: *pace* A. Alt, *Kleine Schriften zur Geschichte des Volkes Israel* (Munich, 1959), 3:210; Helck, *Beziehungen*[2], 295; Pitard, *Ancient Damascus*, 57.

[187] EA 55:4–9; cf. 52:6, 53:64–65 (differently Klengel, *RHA* 36 [1978], 110).

[188] Pitard, *Ancient Damascus*, 64. There is a discrepancy where Kadesh is concerned, Etakkama stating in EA 189 that he is an Egyptian vassal, Suppiluliumas declaring in the "Seventh" tablet (H. Güterbock, *JCS* 10 [1956], 91) that he was a Mitannian protégé. The likelihood is that by the close of the fourteenth century, when the "manly deeds" were composed, the prior status of Kadesh had been blurred. It was now assumed to have been a Mitannian dependency.

[189] H. Klengel, in M. Liverani, ed., *La Siria nel tardo bronzo* (Rome, 1969), 18, n. 9.

[190] Ibid., 21.

[191] Gelb, *JCS* 15 (1961), 42; Klengel, *Geschichte*, 1:187, n. 8; W. F. Albright, *Yahweh and the Gods of Canaan* (New York, 1968), 116, n. 15; R. de Vaux, *JAOS* 88 (1968), 23–30; W. Helck, *LdÄ* 3 (1980), 309–10.

led to think that it referred to those parts of the Levant, still largely West Semitic speaking, not under the direct control of Hurrian Mitanni.[192] Ugarit (and presumably its southern dependency Siyannu) was Egypt's northernmost subject state within Canaan. Under Amenophis III its ruler Amishtamru I was a "servant" of Pharaoh,[193] as was his son Niqmaddu II under Akhenaten.[194] Niqmaddu's seal shows decidedly Egyptian influence in its design,[195] and its owner received presents from his suzerain;[196] prayers were offered on behalf of Pharaoh,[197] and Niqmaddu even married an inmate of the Egyptian harem and allowed his name to be written in hieroglyphs.[198] The status of Ugarit within the Egyptian administration approximated the "favored city" treatment afforded to the rest of the major cities of the Phoenician coast.[199] Although we know little of Arvad at this time, Byblos, Beirut, Sidon, and Tyre fall into this category of privileged state. The first named was the oldest ally of Egypt, and at this time was responsible for the towns further north as far as Sumur.[200]

Palestine and the route through Transjordan (the later "King's Highway") were wholly Egyptian possessions. It was here that the policy of deporting to Egypt huge numbers of the autochthonous population, whether hostile or not, was chiefly put into effect, and reached its apogee under Amenophis II, who carried off over 85,000 men, women, and children of all social strata.[201] In consequence the hill country was virtually

---

[192] The old idea that Kn'n derived from the West Semitic root KN', "to bend down, to bow the knee," and therefore meant something like "lowlands," and in the gentilic "lowlanders," has long since been given up: M. Astour, JNES 24 (1965), 347. So, in fact, have a number of others: that it derives from a Hurrian word for "purple dye" (W. F. Albright, in Studies in the History of Culture [Menasha, Wis., 1942], 25, n. 50; that Kn'ni meant "merchant," and "Canaan" the "country of merchants" (B. Maisler, BASOR 102 [1946], 7–12; M. Gibson, JNES 20 [1961], 218–19); that it meant originally "land of sunset," i.e., the West (Astour, JNES 24 [1965], 348; cf. S. Moscati, Studia Biblica et Orientalia (Rome, 1959), 3:268. When "Canaanites" first appear (in a Mari letter of the late eighteenth century B.C.), the usage is slightly pejorative (cf. G. Dossin, Syria 50 [1973], 277–78; A. F. Rainey, Tel Aviv 6 [1979], 158–59); and one reflects that commonly in Hebrew the root means "to be abased, put down, subdued," etc.

[193] Cf. EA 45–47.

[194] EA 49: W. F. Albright, BASOR 95 (1944), 30ff.; cf. C. Virolleaud, CRAIBL (1954), 257.

[195] C.F.A. Schaeffer, Ugaritica (Paris, 1956), 3:78; cf. 82, n. 3, and 85, fig. 106.

[196] Ugaritica, 3: fig. 120.

[197] C. Virolleaud, CRAIBL (1953), 209; (1955), 74; cf. Palais royal d'Ugarit, 2:18.

[198] C. Desroches-Noblecourt, in Ugaritica, 3:179–80; Schulman, JNES 38 (1978), 185.

[199] Astour, Ugarit in Retrospect, 16–17.

[200] See chapter 7.

[201] See further p. 208. This figure admittedly includes a small percentage of captives from the north (Nukhashsheans). Interestingly when, about ten years later, Amenophis II convened representatives "of Djahy (Palestine)" at his capital, only eleven cities are represented, from the coast (Achasph, Misha'el, Sharon, Ashkelon, possibly Tanuna and Hatom), from

depopulated and the country severely weakened.[202] Never again could the Asiatics use Palestine as a base from which to attack Egypt or, in the more familiar parlance of moderns in the same region: the territory was held as "insurance" against the hostility of Egypt's neighbors.

The long reign of Amenophis III reaped the fruits of the labor expended in subduing Asia during the three preceding generations.[203] A Pax Aegyptiaca had been forcibly imposed on Canaan, and Amenophis III had no need to go on campaign. Taxes and benevolences poured in at Pharaoh's behest, caravans from and to Egypt passed peacefully along the routes through Palestine, and merchant shipping around the eastern Mediterranean increased greatly. The ties with Mitanni grew tighter, and frontier problems largely ceased. Amenophis III, through his marriage to Gilukhepa, daughter of Shutarna II, grew especially close to his brother-in-law Tushratta, son of Shutarna; and later was to wed Tushratta's daughter as well. Substantial amounts of luxury goods passed between the two empires in the satisfaction of bride-prices and dowries and personal presents between the two monarchs. Babylon and Cyprus also courted Pharaoh, dispatching gifts and concluding diplomatic marriages. In a word, the habitable world was at Egypt's feet.[204]

THE END OF MITANNI

Peace had been made lasting between Egypt and Mitanni only through the agreement on the mutual border, and by closely defining the vassalage of existing principalities in Syria. If a new factor entered the equation in the form of a state not accounted for in the provisions of the agreement, trouble was bound to ensue. And it was just such a factor that was to create a problem for Egypt in central Syria and, left unresolved, to precipitate a long, drawn-out war.

As we have seen, the Eleutheros Valley (Nahr el-Kebir) on the north of the Lebanon range provided an access from the Mediterranean coast to the Orontes that entailed political consequences. It had enabled Egyptian armies to move from coast to interior with comparative ease and to exercise firmer control over the Qatna-Kadesh reach than points further north; but it had also permitted Tunip to realize political expansion west-

the Kishon valley and Carmel (Sam'una, Megiddo, Tanaach), and from the north Jordan Valley (Kinneroth, Hasor): C. Epstein, *JEA* 49 (1963), 53ff. Elsewhere the envoy of Lachish is mentioned: P. Leningrad 1116A, pl. 15:2.

[202] Cf. T. L. Thompson, *The Settlement of Palestine in the Late Bronze Age* (Wiesbaden, 1979), 59 and passim.

[203] For the organization and economy of the empire, see chapters 7 and 8.

[204] See G. Steindorff and K. C. Seele, *When Egypt Ruled the East* (Chicago, 1957); Helck, *Beziehungen*²; W. C. Hayes, *CAH*³ II, pt. 1 (1973), 338–401; E. Hornung, *LdÄ* 1 (1973), 206–10; Redford, *Akhenaten*, 34–54.

ward toward Sumur and Tripoli. Tunip had now suffered the attentua-
tion of its territory and, moreover, was on the wrong side of the frontier
to exploit its former advantage. The result was that the tract of land extending roughly from the Orontes Valley at the Lake of Homs westward
to the Phoenician coast became a sort of border zone, nominally in Egyptian hands but administered by no local vassal. From the last quarter of
the fifteenth century B.C., the local population of the coast and central
Syria began to call this tract *Amurru,* the "West," after an old term used
in the Middle Bronze Age by the Akkadians for the entire Levantine littoral.[205] Beginning in the reign of Amenophis III, Amurru became a favorite haunt for those "cossacklike" bands of outlaws known as ʿApiru,
as well as for seminomadic West Semitic speaking clans.[206] Under the
leadership of a family of Canaanite-speaking individuals headed by their
sheikh Abdi-ashirta, Amurru grew into a warlike canton that posed a political threat to its neighbors. It was Amurru's struggle for recognition and
its perceived "manifest destiny" to expand to the Phoenician coast and
the Orontes that posed the major problem in the northern empire for
Egypt.[207]

But how was Amurru to be controlled? It was not recognized as a "legitimate" state in the Egypto-Mitannian treaty; indeed, it may not even
have been in existence under Amenophis II. Nominally the region belonged to Egypt. Abdi-ashirta characterizes himself in a letter to Amenophis III as "a servant of the king and a dog of his house," and the protector on Egypt's behalf of "the entire land of Amurru";[208] and it is true that
he had undergone some sort of formal appointment.[209] But the high-
handed and violent tactics of Abdi-ashirta used to create a legitimacy for
himself, and impose his will on his neighbors, at the very least caused
Pharaoh embarrassment. Abdi-ashirta might argue that he was not responsible for the seizure and partial destruction of the Egyptian garrison
post of Sumur; but his attempt to extend his authority southward at Byb-

[205] Gelb, *JCS* 15 (1961), 29–34; J. R. Kupper, *Les nomades en Mesopotami au temps des
rois de Mari* (Paris, 1957), 149–50; H. Klengel, *MIOF* 10 (1964), 60, 68; idem, *Geschichte,*
2:178–79; idem, in Liverani, *La Siria nel tardo bronzo,* 17–18; Altman, *Bar-Ilan Studies in
History,* 4, n. 5; R. Giveon, *LdÄ* 1 (1973), 251–52. Was the term first applied from the
vantage point of the Orontes Valley? Or had Amurru by this time assumed a wholly linguistic connotation? For the "City of Amurru" (Sumur?), see R. R. Stieglitz, *JNES* 50
(1991), 45ff.

[206] On the ʿApiru, see p. 195.

[207] On Abdi-ashirta, see A. Altman, "The House of Abdiasirta" (Ph.D. diss., Bar Ilan
University, 1964); Klengel, *Geschichte,* 2:245–63; M. Liverani, *RSO* 40 (1965), 276–77;
G. Kestemont, *Orientalia Lovaniensia Periodica* 9 (1978), 27–28; W. J. Murnane, *The
Road to Kadesh* (Chicago, 1985), 183–96.

[208] EA 60:6–9.

[209] EA 101:29–31.

los's expense belies his words. Amenophis III's belated dispatch of a small punitive force to the Phoenician coast to keep the peace was perceived as too little too late.

One wonders whether it was with Egypt's tacit or explicit approval that Tushratta stepped into the picture and attempted to neutralize Amurru. (His correspondence with Amenophis III, his brother-in-law, indicates complete agreement over matters of empire.) The Amarna Letters indicate he was concerned over the growth of Amurru; and on one occasion even attempted an expedition against it.[210] Subsequently, Abdi-ashirta was obliged to present himself in Mitanni, and we hear of excessive taxation imposed on Amurru.[211]

But the recognition of the two superpowers and their sporadic attempts at coercion did not deter the House of Abdi-ashirta. When the latter was killed under mysterious circumstances at the end of Amenophis III's reign, his sons resumed his work. One of these, Aziru, soon took the lead[212] and invested Sumur (which had been forcibly removed by the Egyptians from his father's authority). When Sumur fell, Aziru moved south along the coast, taking town after town, until he eventually even succeeded in gaining access to Byblos. The mayor, Rib-addi, who had been responsible for a torrent of frantic letters to Pharaoh requesting help, was finally handed over to Aziru and put to death. A similar expansion was directed eastward toward Tunip, which subsequently became a possession of Amurru, and southeast toward the upper Orontes where the fertile Amki beckoned. In the north even Ugarit was threatened.[213]

The tactics of both Abdi-ashirta and Aziru were irregular for the times and confused their contemporaries, as they continue to confuse some modern investigators. Both were Egyptian vassals, duly instated and regularly taxed (although only Aziru used a formal seal, like a king, and was later considered the founder of the dynasty);[214] both corresponded with the court and followed diplomatic protocol. But Amurru was an ʿApiru community, but lately graduated from that type of stateless, lawless brigandage for which ʿApiru bands throughout the Levant were notorious. And it was the tactics of a brigand that Aziru used in all his diplomatic dealings with his equals. If a town could be taken and pillaged or a territory ransacked, Aziru did so without a second thought. If resistance was encountered, or was likely to be encountered, a more circuitous route was adopted: a conspiracy against the local mayor might be hatched, or a

---

[210] Cf. EA 95:27–31; 85:51–55.

[211] EA 90:19–23; 86:8–12.

[212] On Aziru, see H. Freydank, *MIOF* 7 (1960), 356–57; Klengel, *MIOF* 10 (1964), 57–83; idem, *Geschichte*, 2:264–65; Kühne, *Chronologie Road to Kadesh*, Murnane, 188–96.

[213] Klengel, *Geschichte*, 2:342.

[214] Ibid., 204.

rebellion fomented among the peasantry. *Mutatis mutandis*, such tactics are not unusual in the Middle East: at any period a rich golden-tongued outlaw can often persuade the peasantry to join him. But such peasant revolts arose endemically in the present instance where a quintessential ʿApiru state met and impinged upon settled, agricultural communities. The problem Amurru posed for its neighbors was unique to the region of *Syria Secunda* and middle Phoenicia: it should *not* be construed as a type of malaise widespread in the Canaanite social fabric of the time, and a *deus ex machina* to explain the origins of Israel.[215]

Were it not for its unexpected consequences, one might label the expansion of Amurru a storm in a teapot; for all contemporary eyes were certainly focused not on central Lebanon but on Anatolia. Here the scions of the Tudkhaliyas dynasty were continuing to press Mitanni and to keep alive their claims to freedom of action in North Syria. Once again under a Hattusilis (II) at the close of the fifteenth century, the overriding interest of the Hittites in Aleppo proved pivotal to their involvement in a contretemps with Mitanni. The states of Ashtata and Nukhashshe (south and east of Aleppo) sought, now that Aleppo had long since lost its independence, to expand at Aleppo's expense, and the subsequent adjustment of boundaries effected by the king of Mitanni, was viewed as a *casus belli* by Khatte.[216] Subsequent events reflect the ebb and flow of the assailants' advantage: Suppiluliumas, the crown prince, was sent to undertake operations near Mount Casius in the former territory of Aleppo;[217] but Mitanni was able to ween the strategic Kizzuwadna away from its treaty obligations to the Hittites.[218] The latter move was soon checked: Suppiluliumas forced treaties on Talzush, king of Kizzuwadna, and soon after on his successor Shunashshura II; and was even able to appoint his own son to the priesthood there. But this was only a quid pro quo: Ishuwa (the region of Malataya on the upper Euphrates) had earlier seceded from Khatte and gone over to Mitanni.[219]

The preliminary exchange of pawns in this elaborate chess game reached the stage of attacking pieces of higher value soon after Suppiluliumas mounted the throne.[220] A dispute between Tushratta and his erst-

---

[215] See further chapter 10.

[216] Klengel, *Geschichte*, 2:184–85; W. Helck, in Görg, *Festschrift Elmar Edel*, 238ff.; Naʾaman, *JCS* 32 (1980), 34–35.

[217] Güterbock, *JCS* 10 (1956), 61–63; Astour, in *Ugarit in Retrospect*, 18.

[218] *KBo* I, 5:6–7.

[219] *KBo* I, 5; *KUB* XIX, 25. A. Goetze, *Kizzuwatna and the Problem of Hittite Geography* (New Haven, Conn., 1940), 61ff.; Gurney, *The Hittites*, 78–79; Otten, *Fischer Weltgeschichte* 3 (1966), 142–43; on Ishuwa's secession, see *KBo* I, 1 verses 10–13 (Weidner, *Politische Dokumente*, 4–5); cf. also H. Klengel, *Oriens Antiquus* 7 (1968), 63ff.; 15 (1976), 85–89; idem, *RHA* 36 (1978), 102.

[220] For the events of Suppiluliuma's reign and the chronological problems involved, see

while vassal, Sarrupsi of Nukhashshe, gave Suppiluliumas the chance to intervene. While Ammishtamru of Ugarit was terrified at the sight of the Hittite army poised for action, and sent a desperate call for help to Amenophis III,[221] Hittite intentions lay elsewhere and were more narrowly focused. Troops were sent across the Taurus into Nukhashshe, ostensibly at Sarrupsi's request, and a set battle ensued engaging Hittite and Mitannian forces. Both sides claimed a victory, but the outcome was probably a standoff: Suppiluliumas was able to impose vassalage on Sarrupsi—a "first" for any Hittite king south of the Taurus—but Tushratta was able to gloat over his repulse of the enemy and to dispatch some of the booty to Egypt.[222]

The situation may well have appeared to Suppiluliumas to have degenerated into a stalemate. Now it was time to take a bold new tack, and this Suppiluliumas did by courting Egypt. Khatte and Egypt had never in the past engaged in hostile activity, and the exchange of gifts in the time of Thutmose III could be appealed to as evidence of amity. At the very least Suppiluliumas's overtures might neutralize Pharaoh and weaken his willingness to assist Mitanni; at most, he could drive a wedge between the two "brother" kings and destroy the alliance.

Suppiluliumas claims that Amenophis III had requested the normalization of relations between Egypt and Khatte;[223] but whether that be so or not, it was certainly he that first approached Akhenaten. In a fortunately surviving letter from the Amarna corpus, he calls the Egyptian "brother," congratulates him on his accession, and expresses the wish for the kind of gift exchange common between kings in an alliance of brotherhood.[224] Suppiluliumas's overtures succeeded rather well. For reasons unknown to us, Akhenaten was not, from the moment of his coming to the throne, on amicable terms with Tushratta, and relations cooled rapidly during the next five years, much to Tushratta's dismay.[225] Hittite envoys were present at Akhenaten's jubilee in year 3,[226] and shortly thereafter we hear that an alliance between Egypt and Khatte was in the offing.[227] The stage was now set for Suppiluliumas to mount a grand offensive.

K. A. Kitchen, *Suppiluliumas and the Amarna Pharaohs* (Liverpool, 1961); Kühne, *Chronologie*; Redford, *History and Chronology*, 216–25; idem, *Akhenaten*, 193–221; Murnane, *Road to Kadesh*, 177–242.

[221] Cf. EA 45:22–31.

[222] Weidner, *Politische Dokumente*, 58–59; EA 17:31–38.

[223] EA 41:8–9.

[224] EA 41; cf. EA 44 with similar requests (full bibliography in J.-G. Heintz, *Index documentaire d'El Amarna* [Wiesbaden, 1982], 119).

[225] Cf. the tenor of the four letters EA 26–29: see Redford, *Akhenaten*, 195.

[226] D. B. Redford, in *Akhenaten Temple Project*, 2:14, pl. 7:3.

[227] EA 35:49 (from the king of Cyprus); line 36 speaks of messengers detained three years.

The occasion was a dispute over the status of the territory of Ishuwa; but this soon appeared to be nought but an excuse for a major campaign (c. 1377 B.C.).[228] Suppiluliumas defeated Ishuwa, then suddenly turned south and made for Wassukani, the Mitannian capital. Unable to muster his forces in time, Tushratta and his family took to flight, much as Thutmose III's adversary had done nearly a century earlier; but, unlike the act of Barratarna, Tushratta's flight cost the empire. Suppiluliumas turned west and crossed the Euphrates into Syria unopposed. In Mukishe he received the submission of the North Syrian principalities with the exception of Niya, which resisted and had to be defeated in battle. Proceeding to Nukhashshe similarly to receive expressions of loyalty, Suppiluliumas was unexpectedly attacked by Shutatara of Kadesh and Ariwanahi of Abina.[229] Both were defeated, and all the rebels and their families were carted off to Khattusas. At one stroke the Hittites had annexed Mukishe, Aleppo, and Nukhashshe and fixed their frontier in the Lebanon mountains.

It is interesting to speculate on how Egypt might have viewed the legality of the Hittite takeover. Suppiluliumas makes quite plain in his account that his campaign was directed solely toward Tushratta's dependencies. This was intentional. As yet he had no quarrel with Egypt. He did not attack Ugarit, the Phoenician cities,[230] Amurru or Amki, and maintained the Orontes frontier inviolate. Of course, because of the relationship of "brotherhood," Akhenaten should have risen to Tushratta's defense; but he had no affection for Mitanni and did nothing. Undoubtedly, it was not he that authorized Shutatara, his vassal in Kadesh, to resist the Hittite advance; Shutatara acted spontaneously as a "march lord" eager to protect the frontier for his suzerain. In fact, Suppiluliumas showed a certain degree of sensitivity toward the special relationship Niya and Kadesh enjoyed with Egypt: after a short detention in Khattusas two of the rebels, Addu-nirari of Nukhashshe and Etakama, son of Shutatara of Kadesh, were allowed to return to their patrimonies. The former remained hopeful of Egypt's continued goodwill; the latter had seen the handwriting on the wall.

It must have been immediately following the Hittite annexation of Mitanni's Syrian possessions, when for the first time Egypt and Khatte shared a border, that the treaty was drawn up between Suppiluliumas and

---

Since the preceding letter (EA 34:52–53) had spoken of Akhenaten's accession, EA 35 probably dates around Akhenaten's fourth year.

[228] *KBo* I, 1 (Weidner, *Politische Dokumente*, 2ff.); cf. also A. Goetze, in *ANET²*, 318.

[229] Location unknown, but not to be identified with Upe: Pitard, *Ancient Damascus*, 66ff.

[230] Rid-addi of Byblos reflects Suppiluliumas's advance in EA 126:51 and 59, where he laments to Akhenaten that the Hittites are burning the lands with fire, and are on their way to take Byblos. Like so many of Rib-addi's statements, this is to be taken *cum grano salis*.

Akhenaten regularizing relations between the two states and, in particular, establishing the common frontier. The tablet of the treaty was seen by Mursilis II, Suppiluliumas's son, who avers that he had not abrogated it in any way. The decision on the boundary line soon attained a legal force that was long respected (if sometimes in the breach).[231]

While the reason need not detain us here,[232] Akhenaten never made clear his intentions toward his Asiatic empire. On one occasion he might admit a policy of leniency,[233] on another he might uproot a whole community and deport it to Nubia.[234] He might ignore correspondence and keep messengers waiting at court for years; yet on short notice he could summon the local mayors from all over his empire to the jubilee.[235] The great potential of Egypt was never lost on the Canaanite headmen, and that they mistook Akhenaten's resolve means only that they were not endowed with prescience.

Some time within the decade following Suppululiumas's campaign the Syrian states were seriously considering renouncing their oath to him.[236] Addu-nirari of Nukhashshe wrote Akhenaten directly, and Akizzi of Qatna interceded on behalf of other Nukhashshe kings, requesting to be taken back into the pharaonic fold, while Tunip besought the king for a ruler of its own.[237] Finally, the conspirators took action: Ituraddu of Mukishe, Addu-nirari of Nukhashshe, and Aki-teshup of Niya formed an ad hoc league, renounced their vassalage to Khatte, and attempted to force Niqmaddu II of Ugarit to join them, on pain of invasion. But now came the unexpected. Niqmaddu, a faithful Egyptian protégé, who had married an Egyptian and had cultivated close relations with Egypt, made a volte-face and appealed, not to Pharaoh, but to the Hittite king to extricate him from this dilemma. Suppiluliumas was not slow to seize the opportunity. Letters of reassurance came at once from Khattusas and troops were dispatched to drive out the rebel army from Ugaritian territory. Suppiluli-

---

[231] H. Güterbock, *RHA* 66 (1960), 57–63. Whether this is the same as the famous Kurushtama treaty (literature and discussion in Murnane, *Road to Kadesh*, 40–42) is a moot point. The wording of the reference in the Plague Prayer (Goetze, *ANET²*, 395) sounds as though the treaty that brought people of Kurushtama to Egypt was no sooner made than broken; but Suppiluliumas's purported words in his son's account (Güterbock, *JCS* 10 [1956], 95) suggest the treaty was an old one and not familiar to him. The problem is: at what time prior to Suppiluliumas's takeover of Mitannian territory in Syria did Egypt and Khatte have any significant relations at all?

[232] For speculation on the psychological makeup of the king, see Redford, *Akhenaten.*

[233] Cf. EA 162:40–41.

[234] D. O. Edzard, *Kamid el-Loz-Kumidi* (Bonn, 1970), 56–57.

[235] Redford, in *Akhenaten Temple Project*, 2:14–15.

[236] Confusion of the "Great Syrian" campaign (of the Shattiwaza Treaty) with the Nukhashshe revolt (of the Ugaritic sources) has seriously distorted the sequence of events in some recent histories.

[237] EA 51–55; 59.

umas came himself to Alalakh, and Niqmaddu dutifully crossed the Orontes and prostrated himself before the great king. Ugarit had voluntarily seceded from Egypt.[238]

But Suppiluliumas was not finished. Once again he crossed into Nukhashshe and took up residence, probably in Niya. Here the kings of the local districts and territory further south were expected to hasten to renew their oaths. Akizzi of Qatna and Biryawaza of Upe refused to go, since they were Egyptian regents.[239] For this affront, Qatna was assaulted by Hittite troops and the last we hear is the pitiable cry from Akizza that Hittites were seizing the men and chattels of the city. Shortly the town was given over to destruction and never reinhabited.[240] Biryawaza could only be got at with greater effort in Upe, and so was not attacked by the Hittites; but Etakama, determined to rehabilitate his image with Suppiluliumas, led a small detachment of Hittite troops to ravage the district.[241]

None of the implication of these events was lost on Aziru. Two city-states, but lately part of the Egyptian empire in Asia, had been taken over by the Hittites, and one of them destroyed. Suppiluliumas was obviously no longer observing the niceties of avoiding all but Mitanni's former holdings, no matter how he rationalized the situation. Akhenaten, however, had remained inactive through it all, as his northern border became destabilized; and rumor now had it that he *would not* act.[242] Even before the Hittites arrived in Syria, Aziru had decided to take advantage of the situation by allying himself to Etakama in an effort to get as much as he could as the frontier disintegrated. Aziru sent his own troops to assist Etakama against Amki and Upe, and he himself occupied Tunip.[243] When the Hittites advanced against Nukhashshe, he entertained messengers from Suppiluliumas, although he did not go north to greet the king.[244] This, however, proved too much even for the inactive Akhenaten, and Aziru was summoned to the Egyptian court. Thither, after several delays (suggesting a stubborn self-assertion), he repaired along with the Egyptian captain sent to fetch him.[245]

Aziru's detention at the court of Akhenaten lasted several years, and during its course he may have suffered blinding; but neither his spirit nor his resolve were broken, and when he was finally released Akhenaten may

[238] On the defection of Ugarit, see the texts in *Palais royal d'Ugarit*, 4:35–55 (of which RS 17.340 is the most detailed); also Astour, *Ugarit in Retrospect*, 19–20.

[239] EA 53:11–15; 197:25–26.

[240] Comte du Mesnil du Buisson, *Le site archéologique de Mishrife-Qatna* (Paris, 1935), 33–34.

[241] Cf. EA 174–76; on Biryawaza, see now Pitard, *Ancient Damascus*, 66–70.

[242] Cf. EA 53:46.

[243] Cf. EA 59:25–28 (Aziru threatening); EA 161:11–12 (Aziru residing in city).

[244] EA 161:48–50.

[245] EA 162, 164–67.

have sensed he had lost his man.[246] For no sooner "had he come out of the door of Egypt" and returned to Amurru than "he fell at the feet of the Sun, the Great King" of Khatte, and offered himself as vassal. Amurru had thus broken away from the Egyptian empire, whose border now shrank back to south of the Eleutheros Valley.[247]

THE EGYPTO-HITTITE WAR

The sequel shows that, while the Hittites considered their new southern frontier a legally recognized boundary, Egypt never accepted the new line. By a curious sort of "revisionism" the Hittites could, in later generations, consider all the states north of the new line, even Kadesh and Amurru, as once having belonged to Mitanni, and therefore fair game;[248] but Egypt was reluctant to accept this new political "fact." Its estimation that Khatte was in blatant violation of the treaty provoked a desultory war over the frontier, which lasted a century. Kadesh became from the outset the focus of Egyptian attacks and political pressure, and Pharaoh had occasional success in turning the city against the Hittites.[249] On one occasion a coastal campaign is attested, from Byblos as far as Carchemish, a route that would have taken the Egyptian expeditionary forces through Amurru; but the venture achieved no lasting success.[250] Hittite retaliation usually was directed against the Amki, but the Hittites equally were un-

[246] Cf. EA 169 in which a son of Aziru (DU-Teshup?) implies that Aziru's stay in Egypt is already of disturbing length: see E. F. Campbell, *The Chronology of the Amarna Letters* (Baltimore, 1964), 88–89; Klengel, *Geschichte*, 2:25, 293. Cf. also *KBo* XVI, 32: P. Cornil and R. Lebrun, *Orientalia Lovaniensia Periodica* 6–7 (1975–1976), 89–91. This last intriguing text contains fragmentary references to the Euphrates, Mount Siryanu (Mount Hermon: H. Gonnet, *RHA* 83 [1968], 135), and the distant sea. Verse iv, 4–5, mentions someone going to Egypt, "your father," a garrison of soldiers, and someone being blinded.

[247] H. Freydank, *MIOF* 7 (1960), 360, 380; cf. *KUB* XIX, 9.i.11ff.: "He (Suppiluliumas) made the land of Kadesh and the Land of Amurru his border."

[248] See n. 189.

[249] *KUB* XIX, 7 (Güterbock *JCS* 10 [1956], 85), an attack resulting in the burning of the city, possibly late in Akhenaten's reign. For the possibility that Akhenaten bestirred himself at the eleventh hour to dispatch an expedition, see EA 191, 195, etc. *KBo* V, 6.A.ii, 21–22. (Güterbock, *JCS* 10 [1956], 93), an attack on Kadesh by Tutankhamun: Redford, *Akhenaten*, 213–14; *Akhenaten Temple Project*, 2:19–20 (now expanded, thanks to the recent work of Ray Johnson, into a large, formal assault scene). On the rebellions of Kadesh against Khatte late in Suppiluliumas's reign and in the first decade of Mursilis's reign, see Klengel, *Geschichte*, 2:148–49. On the entire period, see A. J. Spalinger, *BES* 1 (1979), 55–89.

[250] D. B. Redford, *BASOR* 211 (1973), 36–49. The campaign is mentioned in a fragmentary passage in the annals of Mursilis II (year 7). The present inscription is carved on the rim of a granite bowl and, because of the faulty writing of the personal name Horemheb, has been declared to be a forgery. But the text itself shows such an extraordinary authenticity that it must have been exerpted by a modern forger to enhance the value of the bowl.

able to effect a permanent shift in the line of the frontier. The desperate plea of Tutankhamun's widow for a Hittite prince for a husband, and the subsequent assassination of one of Suppiluliumas's sons, did little to resolve the issue, save momentarily to excite passions.[251]

There were at least two reasons for the stalemate. On the one hand geography rendered it exceedingly difficult for either great power, based as the crow flies thirteen hundred kilometers apart, to control effectively any territory beyond the line of the Eleutheros Valley. North of this line a city-state lay within three days' march of Hittite garrisons in North Syria; south of it, the Egyptian strongpoints in Phoenicia and Upe could easily monitor recalcitrants on the upper Orontes. Failing a total breakdown in the will to preserve the empire, continued attacks along the frontier could only meet with limited, tactical success, and thus produce frustration and lower morale.

But a subtler factor is to be discerned in the formal ties Khatte forged to link the dependent principalities to itself. The mechanics of the Egyptian empire had been fashioned ad hoc, and its demands on members of the empire were irregular and quixotic. Year by year tax demands might change and were communicated either by letter or tax assessor. The vassal was not required to come to Egypt on a regular basis but might have to appear on a moment's notice should Pharaoh demand it. The legal bond to the Egyptian crown was solely the oath not to rebel, taken orally, and we have no indication that it was transcribed in writing. The Hittite king, on the other hand, wrote out for each vassal a formal treaty, which (apart from the historical preamble) stipulated in detail the Hittite king's demands. The vassal must appear yearly in Khattusas and had to pay the specified amounts in tax. He is to have no independent foreign policy but is to be friends with Khatte's friends and an enemy of Khatte's enemies.[252] Should the Hittite king be at war, he must assist him by sending auxiliary troops; and fugitives from Khatte must be extradited immediately.[253] Foreign powers who, at the time of writing, are enemies of Khatte are specified, and those on the southern "front" (like Aziru and Duppi-teshup) are forbidden to have any dealings with Egypt.[254] Such unilateral treaties between Khatte and its vassals did not prevent the latter from exercising a certain degree of freedom in jockeying for position among themselves.

[251] Güterbock, *JCS* 10 (1956), 94–95; Otten, *Fischer Weltgeschichte* 3 (1966), 146–47; Redford, *Akhenaten*, 217–21; Murnane, *Road to Kadesh*, 225–26.

[252] Weidner, *Politische Dokumente*, 60 (treaty with Tette); 70 (treaty with Aziru), cf. p. 78; *Palais royal d'Ugarit*, 4:51 (RS 17.340: Niqmaddu treaty); 89 (RS 17.353: Niqmepa treaty); Murnane, *Road to Kadesh*, 87, n. 23.

[253] Cf. Freydank, *MIOF* 7 (1960), 364; *Palais royal d'Ugarit*, 4:98.

[254] Freydank, 366; *ANET²*, 204; Cornil and Lebrun, *Orientalia Lovaniensia Periodica* 6–7 (1975–1976), 96–98.

They could contest at law,[255] contract marriages,[256] and even alter internal "allegiances."[257] Although this may have mirrored in a general way conditions under Egyptian hegemony, the formalization of relations through written agreement made sanctions easier to impose.

By the middle of the fourteenth century B.C., the 18th Dynasty had completely lost the confidence and respect of its subjects. Tutankhamun left no scion of the house to sit upon his throne, and power was at once seized by the military. The pitiable—and treasonous—appeal to Suppiluliumas for assistance and a husband by Tutankhamun's widow is the last squeak we hear from the once-great royal family. Under the energtic if somewhat pedestrian guidance of three generals who sat on the throne in succession—Ay (1356–1353 B.C.), Horemheb (1353–c. 1323 B.C.), and Ramesses I (1323–1321 B.C.)—Egypt underwent internal reorganization and the strengthening of the lines of communication with western Asia.[258]

Although it is quite clear that, apart from the loss of Amurru and Kadesh, Egypt did *not* give up any part of its empire during the Amarna period,[259] it is nonetheless apparent that during the third-quarter of the fourteenth century its holdings in the north were being subjected to new stresses. The success enjoyed by the ʿApiru enclaves in the north Lebanon in carving out a kingdom for themselves is not paralleled elsewhere by the bands of ʿApiru operating in Amki, Bashan, and the Palestinian highlands at the close of the period covered by the Amarna Letters. Akhenaten had deported some from Amki and set a military governor in Jerusalem to keep those in the hill country under surveillance; but ever since the great deportations of Thutmose III and Amenophis II, the northern empire and Palestine especially had suffered a weakening brought on by underpopulation. Not only did the ʿApiru banditry now take advantage of the vacuum in the highlands, but nomads from Transjordan also began to move north into Galilee and Syria and west across the Negeb to Gaza, Ashkelon, and the highway linking Egypt with Palestine. It was probably pressure from these marauders that led, at the end of the Amarna age, to the fortification of this route with a regular series of blockhouses.[260]

The coming to power of the general Paramesses as Ramesses I signaled

---

[255] *Palais royal d'Ugarit*, 4:284 (RS 19.68, line 5). This document dates to the very end of Aziru's reign, when both he and Niqmaddu were Hittite vassals.

[256] Ibid., 120–21.

[257] Ibid., 76–77 (RS 17.368 recto 1–3).

[258] For the history of this period, see R. Hari, *Horemheb et la reine Moutnodjmet* (Geneva, 1961); R. Krauss, *Das Ende der Amarna-zeit* (Hildesheim, 1976); J.-M. Kruchten, *Le decret de Horemheb* (Brussels, 1981); Redford, *Akhenaten*, 212–21; Murnane, *Road to Kadesh*, 39–51.

[259] M. Several, *PEQ* 104 (1972), 123–33; J. M. Weinstein, *BASOR* 241 (1981), 15–17.

[260] On this military route, see now E. Oren, in A. F. Rainey, ed., *Egypt, Israel, Sinai* (Jerusalem, 1987), 69–70; T. Dothan, in ibid., 121–22.

the rise of a new dynasty. Fifty years of succession to the throne by appointment came to an end, as Ramesses, possibly an old man at the time and already ailing, selected his own son, Sety, as his successor. As the father faded, the son became energetically involved in the government.[261] Drawing on jargon used for six hundred years, Sety proclaimed a new era characterized by the expressions "Repetition of Births" and "Beginning of Eternity."[262]

Translated into military action, the renewal entailed the resumption of an aggressive foreign policy reminiscent of that of Thutmose III. Sety was to be "the one who sets his boundary wherever he pleases . . . protector of Egypt who crushes foreigners and subdues other countries on their home territory."[263] Numerous "victory stelae" proclaimed his success in this endeavor, often backdated to year 1 for effect; but we lack any sober, connected account such as Thutmose III has vouchsafed. The main source for Sety's wars is the set of stunningly beautiful battle reliefs, carved on the exterior face of the north wall of the hypostyle hall of the temple of Amun at Karnak; but of these the upper registers have been removed and the preserved texts are banal and largely devoid of historical interest.[264] The latest attempt to interpret the order of the scenes and registers has placed us all in W. J. Murnane's debt,[265] and in general his results are followed here.

Some time shortly after his father's death Sety received a messenger's report on the state of Palestine: "Their chiefs are gathered together in one place, taking their stand on the hills of Palestine. They have begun to go wild, everyone of them slaying his fellow. They do not give a thought to the laws of the palace."[266] Too much weight should not be attached to this description. It is part of a shopworn topos in which a state of anarchy is tendered as sufficient grounds for a military strike: law and order must be restored. More specific was the report that Beth Shean was under attack from a Canaanite king and could not get help.[267] Sety successfully

---

[261] Murnane, *Road to Kadesh*, 70–72; idem, *Ancient Egyptian Coregencies* (Chicago, 1977), 183–85.

[262] The former expression is sometimes appended to the names of gods, or has reference to the restoration of their cult statues or temples. In the sense of "'(period or initiator of) Renewal/Renaissance," it is used by Amenemhet I, Hatshepsut, Tutankhamun, and Horemheb: see E. Blumenthal, *Untersuchungen zum ägyptischen Königtum des mittleren Reiches* (Berlin, 1970), 1:78.

[263] R. A. Caminos, *The Shrines and Rock Inscriptions of Ibrim* (London, 1968), pls. 39–40.

[264] *Reliefs and Inscriptions at Karnak*, vol. 4: *The Battle Reliefs of King Sety I* (Chicago, 1985).

[265] Murnane, *Road to Kadesh*, 53–54.

[266] KRI I, 9.

[267] Ibid., 12.

beat back the nomads who had severed the highway to Gaza and had little difficulty in relieving Beth Shean. Even when the ʿApiru in the central highlands in his rear made trouble, a small detachment of Egyptian troops was sufficient to quell the disorder.[268] Sety then proceeded north and captured Yeno'am near the sources of the Jordan, and there received the homage of "the great chiefs of the Lebanon" who were compelled in an act of deliberate humiliation to cut timber themselves for Amun's bark. Stelae were erected in Bashan and Tyre before the army turned homeward.[269]

This campaign was only the prelude. Sety was, consciously or unconsciously, following the overall strategy of Thutmose III. At an unknown date, but subsequent to year 2, Sety advanced up the coast and struck at Amurru and then, passing through the mountains, assaulted Kadesh.[270] Kadesh fell to the Egyptians and a commemorative stela was set up within the walls; and on a subsequent campaign we find the king fighting further north against the Hittites themselves. Sety's activities had obviously provoked a reaction on the part of the aged Hittite king Mursilis II.[271]

Reliant as we are on the generalizing propaganda of the war relief to reconstruct the Egypto-Hittite war in Sety's reign, we feel acutely the lack of that wealth of detail which comes from such state archives as the Amarna Letters or the Boghaz Keui texts. No archives survive from the last years of Mursilis II or for the entirety of the short reigns of Muwatallis and Urhi-teshup; and documents referring to this period in later reigns sometimes display tendentious argumentation.

In particular one wishes to know whether Sety, in carrying war to Amurru, Kadesh, and points north, was in defiance of a treaty he was obliged to uphold. Apart from the enigmatic Kurushtama treaty, we know of only two formal agreements that existed prior to the great Egypto-Hittite pact of Ramesses II's year 21. Both are alluded to briefly in the preamble to the latter as having been in force, one under Suppiluliumas, the other Mursilis II.[272] The evidence as we have it can accommodate a treaty during the time of Suppiluliumas, as we have seen;[273] but the pact with Mursilis poses problems of historical context. For from the later years of Suppiluliumas down to the period contemporary with Sety's campaigns no treaty is attested. In a broken passage in the annals for

[268] Ibid., 16.
[269] P-M² VII, 383; J. Leclant, *Orientalia* 30 (1961), 394; M. Chehab, *Bulletin du Musée Beyrouth* 22 (1969), pl. 8 (3); on the location of Yeno'am, see Ahituv, *Canaanite Toponyms in Ancient Egyptian Documents*, 198–200.
[270] KRI I, 24; Murnane, *Road to Kadesh*, 80–81.
[271] Murnane, *Road to Kadesh*, 91ff.
[272] Called by the dyanstic name Muwatallis in the passage in question: *ANET²*, 200.
[273] See p. 173.

Mursilis's seventh year there is mention of a "treaty," and "the king of Egypt"; but the former may refer to a treaty between Khatte and Nukhashshe.[274] Elsewhere, with specific reference to an old treaty tablet delineating the border between the two empires, Mursilis stresses the fact that he has simply maintained the agreement bequeathed to him by his father and made no changes in the balance of power vis-à-vis Egypt.[275] This avowal falls about the middle of his reign, and we are left to wonder what happened after that. Could it be that the ferocity and success of Sety's onslaught forced the old Mursilis to come to terms in the closing years of his life?

Exactly where the line of the border ran on the eve of Sety's death is difficult to say. At some time the Egyptians had had to give up Kadesh for it sided with Khatte in the battle of Ramesses II's year 5, and one wonders whether our putative treaty late in Mursilis's reign stipulated a return to the status quo ante. The status of Amurru is an even greater puzzle. There is nothing in the laconic statement in Sety's war reliefs to suggest that both Kadesh and Amurru were taken, and only Kadesh is pictured under attack.[276] A rereading of the sources suggests that Amurru defected to Egypt not too long before the battle of Kadesh and in fact precipitated that confrontation.

In the last decade of the fourteenth century B.C. the two old protagonists Sety and Mursilis died, the former unexpectedly one gathers, the latter under conditions we know nothing of; and two young men took their places who were remarkably similar to each other. Ramesses II, Sety's son and successor, had been groomed for the job, and had been given managerial tasks as early as year 9 of his father.[277] His training, in keeping with the family tradition, involved the military from an early age, and in his capacity of "chief of the shock troops and chariotry" he had presented his father with regular reports.[278] He already cut a dashing figure when he ascended the throne, and the adulation of his court is extreme even for Egypt: "Thou art Re, thy body is his body! There has been no ruler like thee, thou art unique. . . . Isis [has loved] no king since Re except thee and her son . . . every city should know that thou art the god of all the people!"[279]

[274] A. Goetze, MVAG 38 (1933), 83.

[275] Güterbock, RHA 66 (1960), 59–60.

[276] Wreszinski, *Atlas zur altaegyptische Kulturgeschichte*, 2:53; KRI I, 24. The text inside the mock-up of the fort is unequivocal: "The ascent which His Majesty made to destroy the land of Kadesh (of/belonging to) the land of *the* Amorite (*sic*)."

[277] L. Habachi, BIFAO 73 (1973), pl. XI:10; on the coregency, see Murnane, *Coregencies*, 57–87.

[278] Dedicatory inscription, Abydos: 44–45.

[279] Ibid., 55–69.

We know less of Muwatallis's upbringing, although he too was clearly imbued with a military spirit. The second of four children of Mursilis II, Muwatallis came into the heir apparency on the death of the eldest son. Devoid apparently of sibling jealousy, Muwatallis elevated his sickly, younger brother Hattusilis to the priesthood of Ishtar and gave him a high military command in central Anatolia.[280] This left him free to move his headquarters to the south where he could oversee operations in the Levant.

The uneasy peace that Sety and Mursilis had bequeathed was broken once again by the actions of Amurru. Because the reign of Ramesses II (especially his early years) is well documented,[281] the moment of Amurru's defection from Khatte ought to be capable of being deduced, if it is not specifically mentioned. Certainly there can be no doubt that Ramesses was mightily concerned with the northern empire; yet during his first two years we find him engaged in building operations and a tour of Nubia, wholly oblivious, it seems, of Asia. Late in his third year, however, he is in Memphis, and probably in May of that year leads his forces across the frontier in his first "campaign of victory." What caused this sudden dash northward must have been news that the people of Amurru under their king Benteshina had seceded from Muwatallis's authority and had offered themselves to Egypt. Allowing time for the passage of messengers and the mustering of the host, Amurru must have made its move in the winter of 1302–1301 B.C..[282]

Ramesses's first expedition into Asia took him up the coast, perhaps even as far as Amurru itself, to accept the homage of his new vassal, but it did not bring him into contact with any Hittite force. On his return march, in October, he was able to carve a stela (now badly worn) at the mouth of the Dog River in Phoenicia before returning to Egypt.[283] But the presence of an Egyptian army at the frontier was a goad to Muwatallis; and the following winter was spent mustering an enormous host. The treaty had been broken; a showdown was clearly coming.

The battle that followed, the "Battle of Kadesh," is better documented

[280] Otten, *Apologie*, secs, 3–5. Hattusilis had been born no later than his father's ninth year: Goetze, *MVAG* 38 (1933), 11–12.

[281] D. B. Redford, *JEA* 57 (1971), 110–19.

[282] Cf. the Shaushkamuwa treaty (C. Kühne and H. Otten, *Der Sausgamuwa-Vertrag* [Wiesbaden, 1971], obv. I, 13–39), the wording of which strongly suggests that the battle of Kadesh followed directly from Amurru's changing of sides; cf. K. A. Kitchen, *Pharaoh Triumphant* (Warminster, 1982), 24–25. Allowing about eight months between the end of Ramesses II's first campaign and the battle would give sufficient time for the mustering of the Hittite forces, some contingents of which (Lukka and Karkisha) came from western Asia Minor.

[283] P-M VII, 385; KRI II, 1; P. Montet, *Kêmi* 16 (1962), 78; H. Goedicke, *JEA* 52 (1966), 73–74.

than any other military engagement prior to Marathon in 490 B.C. Our sources include six versions of the set of colossal relief scenes inscribed on temple walls and pylons, five exemplars of the so-called poem on the battle, three copies of the hieroglyphic record, and a cuneiform letter from Ramesses II to Hattusilis III. For whatever reason, Ramesses obviously wished to make capital out of the event.[284] The Hittite account has not yet been discovered, and we have only passing references in unrelated documents; but Ramesses's candor in the cuneiform letter casts the Egyptian records in a favorable light.

In the early spring Ramesses, at the head of his forces, crossed the frontier and made his way rapidly up the coastal road. His exact route is still the subject of debate, but his final approach to Kadesh (which he intended to seize) was from the south down the Orontes. By the end of May, about a month after he had left Egypt, he and the army were encamped at the ford on the east bank of the river, barely fourteen kilometers south of the city. While the king was deliberating with his staff, the sentries brought in two bedu who had been found lurking suspiciously close to the camp. When questioned they claimed to be deserters from the Hittites and stated further that the Hittite forces were still at Aleppo, reluctant to march south through fear of Ramesses. Ramesses decided to march on to Kadesh as quickly as possible and to invest the town before Muwatallis could arrive.

Of course, it had been a ruse. Muwatallis had "planted" the bedu "deserters" with their false information, and he and his army were at the moment encamped on the east side of the Orontes behind the city. As Ramesses crossed the river and hastened northward to pitch his tent on the northwest side of Kadesh, his army, which he had outdistanced and which was following in four divisions strung out along the line of the march, was suddenly ambushed by the entire corps of Hittite chariotry. One division was decimated, and its remnants fled headlong toward the spot where the king and his household troops were setting up camp. Having learned from a messenger of the ambush and from captured spies of the true disposition of the Hittites, Ramesses scarcely had time to call a council of war before his camp was surrounded by the chariots of the pursuing enemy. If Ramesses had heretofore been guilty of slackness and overconfidence, he now showed what metal he personally was made of.

---

[284] From the voluminous literature on the battle one might profitably consult R. O. Faulkner, *MDAIK* 16 (1958), 93–94; G. Fecht, *SAK* 11 (1984), 281–82; A. H. Gardiner, *The Kadesh Inscriptions of Ramesses II* (Oxford, 1960); Goedicke, *JEA* 52 (1966), 71–72; idem, ed., *Perspectives on the Battle of Kadesh* (Baltimore, 1985); W. Helck, *AfO* 22 (1969), 23–24; A. Kadry, *BIFAO* 81 (1981), 47–48; Kitchen, *Pharaoh Triumphant*; C. Kuentz, *La bataille de Qadesh* (Cairo, 1928–1934); M. Noth, *WO* 1, no. 3 (1948), 223–24; B. G. Ockinga, *CdE* 62 (1987), 38–48; A. F. Rainey, *UF* 5 (1973), 280–81.

Gathering whatever chariots he had on the spot, he charged repeatedly into the mass of the enemy, sending some hurtling over the bank and into the Orontes, until one of his divisions still on the march could come up and relieve him.

It was at this point that Muwatallis let a sure victory slip from his grasp. He still had over ten thousand foot soldiers poised on the opposite bank, waiting for the signal to advance. Had these now been thrown into battle, before the struggling Egyptian divisions could have regrouped and come up to the camp, the Egyptians surely would have been overwhelmed and Pharaoh captured or killed. Yet Muwatallis hesitated. Was it indecision? Failure of intelligence? Loss of nerve? Or did Muwatallis think his twenty-five hundred chariots could finish the Egyptians off unaided? Whatever the reason, he held his men back. By dusk the beleaguered Egyptians, now reinforced by their missing divisions, were holding their own; and as darkness fell the Hittite chariots withdrew, leaving the field to the Egyptians.

Whether hostilities were resumed the following day and a truce agreed upon remains a moot point; but to all intents and purposes the battle was over and its effects irreversible. In the short term Ramesses was forced to retire and concede the loss of Kadesh and Amurru whose king, Bente-shina, was led captive to Khatte. Headmen of Canaanite towns, vassals of Egypt, were impressed by what they divined as inherent weaknesses in Pharaoh's forces: poor intelligence and a tendency to panic. Rebellion *was* possible; Egypt *could* be beaten. In the long term, however, the battle made a greater impact on the contending nations themselves. Egypt gained a healthy respect for the fighting qualities and the wiliness of their adversaries; while Khatte could not help but be impressed by the bravery, resolve, and energy of Ramesses himself. Slowly dawning on the consciousness of both must have been the realization, notwithstanding a further fifteen years of fighting, of the futility of trying to move the border north or south of its present line.

In the wake of the retreating Egyptians, all Canaan flared into open revolt. For the first time in over two hundred years Egypt could scarcely lay claim to any territory beyond Sinai. Even the frontier seemed threatened. The building of a "great and awesome new residence," Pi-Ramesses ("the House-of-Ramesses") in the northeastern Delta, was now hurried forward with all dispatch, "to strengthen the borders of Egypt."[285] It was Ramesses's darkest hour. The glorious achievements promised by the auspicious beginning of the reign had failed to materialize. The Egyptians had been worsted by the Hittites, the king had narrowly escaped capture or death, and most of the Asiatic possessions had been lost.

[285] KRI II, 269; on Pi-Ramesses, see J. Van Seters, *The Hyksos, A New Investigation* (New Haven, Conn., 1966); M. Bietak, *Avaris and Pi-Ramesse* (London, 1979).

But if we must blame Ramesses himself for the present state of affairs, we must not neglect to credit him also with the recovery of what had been lost. Doggedly he returned to the fray three years later and showed great energy and determination in his efforts to win back Palestine. In Ramesses's eighth year a massive offensive was launched against insurgents in Palestine, and town after town bearing well-known "Biblical" names (mainly from Galilee) fell to the Egyptian onslaught: Migdol, 'Ayn-no'am, Beth-Anath, Qana, Merom, Shalem.[286] About the same time—the stereotyped format of the "post-Kadesh" war reliefs do not permit an analysis into individual campaigns[287]—the Palestinian coast came in for its share of the carnage. Accho and Aphek were reduced, and the former apparently destroyed.[288] By year 10 Ramesses was pushing his forces once again into Phoenicia. A stela of that year at the Dog River[289] suggests that the southern Phoenician coast was secured with relative ease; but further north Arqata resisted and was subjected to a siege.[290]

The course of the war from this point until its termination by treaty eleven years later is little known to us. The reliefs on the west wall of the Luxor forecourt belong in this decade and indicate that the front had now moved into Amurru itself.[291] Satuna and Mutara, inland from Batrun, fell to the Egyptians who then moved through the Eleutheros Valley to assault Dapur, "a town of the Hittites in the territory of Tunip in the land of Naharin"[292] (Plate 18). Later still must come the attack on "the town that His Majesty captured in the land of Qode in the territory of Naharin,"

---

[286] The earliest record is probably on the north massif of the first pylon of the Ramesseum, Ramesses II's mortuary temple at Thebes: P-M² II, 432 (2); KRI II, 148–49. Some of the cities mentioned on the south wall of the Karnak hypostyle may also date to this campaign or series of campaigns: ibid., 157–58, 165–66. In general, it must be admitted that our knowledge of the sequence and direction of Ramesses II's offensive following the battle of Kadesh is extremely limited.

[287] At the Ramesseum and Karnak the "records" are reduced to a series of almost identical rectangular vignettes: city (with toponym in a standard column), king assaulting, captives led away, presentation to the god. At Karnak, moreover, the entire series on the south wall has been carved *over* an earlier sequence of reliefs depicting the battle of Kadesh and converging on the stela of the year 21 treaty (see Redford, *IEJ* 36 [1986], 193–95). While most of the vignettes at the Ramesseum are glossed by "regnal year 8" (but cf. Dapur!), those at Karnak are undated and represent a mélange.

[288] M. Dothan, *IEJ* 25 (1975), 165; cf. also the ostracon of year 10 of an unnamed king from the Lachish destruction level of about the same period: D. Ussishkin, *IEJ* 24 (1974), 272.

[289] R. Lepsius, *Denkmaeler aus Aegypten und Aethiopien* (Berlin, 1849), 3:197c; KRI II, 149.

[290] KRI II, 213 (Amara West).

[291] P-M² II, 333 (202-4); cf. 438 (18); KRI II, 173–76. Six of Ramesses's sons are pictured participating in the siege of Dapur.

[292] On the plausible identification of Satuna and Mutara, see Ahituv, *Canaanite Toponyms*, 146, 168.

Plate 18. Egyptian assault under Ramesses II on the Syrian town of Dapur. The seige telescopes the action: men are pulled into the city as they flee the advancing army, Egyptian shock troops mount ladders; the defenders resist; finally they capitulate and burn incense in supplication. Ramesseum hypostyle hall, western Thebes.

pictured on the west wall of Luxor in which nine princes are present.[293] If Kizzuwadna (Qode) was now within Ramesses's reach, can we conclude that Hittite resistance had collapsed?

THE TREATY BETWEEN EGYPT AND KHATTE

In fact, in the moment of their triumph, the Hittites had suffered a sudden reverse on the domestic front. Within two years of his victory at Kadesh, Muwatallis died unexpectedly, and a veiled struggle for the throne ensued between his son and his brother. Uri-teshup, the young son of Muwatallis, was duly ensconced upon his father's throne, but disaffection was evident. Hattusilis's appointment as general in the "Upper Lands" of Anatolia,[294] had gone surprisingly well. He had quelled rebellious tribes in the region and had been charged with a resettlement program for all these northern lands. On Muwatallis's death, Hattusilis grudgingly accepted his nephew's appointment, but refused to step down from his post; and Urhi-teshup on his part was forced to tolerate his uncle as a sort of coregent.

After seven years of Urhi-teshup's rule, during which a bitter hatred grew up between him and his uncle, Hattusilis staged a coup (the details of which are unknown) and incarcerated his nephew. He did not, however, kill him, but exiled him to Nukhashshe in Syria.[295] At some point Urhi-teshup escaped from his place of exile and, with a handful of followers, fled—of all places—to Pi-Ramesses in Egypt. Ramesses accepted him,[296] and was urged on by the young man to continue the war against his uncle, much perhaps as Hannibal one thousand years later was to urge Antiochus to bring war against Rome from the ends of the earth. Urhi-teshup never relented in his vendetta against his uncle: even fifteen years later we find him still trying to stir up trouble by inciting Shalmaneser I of Assyria against Khatte.[297]

But Hattusilis III faced threats more serious than those posed by an enraged nephew. Although a good administrator and excellent propagandist,[298] Hattusilis was not the soldier his father and brother had been. He

[293] P-M² II, 333 (202); Helck, *Beziehungen²*, 213.

[294] Otten, *Apologie* 1:22–23, 66–67 (north and northwest of Hattusas: A. Goetze, *JCS* 14 [1960], 46).

[295] Otten, *Apologie* 4:32; A. Goetze, *MVAG* 29 (1925), 34; on Urhi-teshup, see especially P.H.J. Houwinck ten Cate, in *Anatolian Studies Presented to Hans Gustav Güterbock* (Istanbul, 1974), 123–50.

[296] E. Cavaignac, *RHA* 18 (1935), 25ff.; W. Helck, *JCS* 17 (1963), 87–88; R. Stefanini, *Academia Toscana . . . La Columbaria* 29 (1964), 1ff.

[297] *KUB* XXVI, 70; H. Otten, *AfO Beiheft* 12 (1958), 67–68: "Urhi-teshup [wrote] to the king of Assyria, your father, [but you], Tukulti-ninurta, have sent (back) [to me] the tablet of Urhi-teshup."

[298] A. Archi, *SMEA* 14 (1971), 185–215.

took over a kingdom beset by a militant Egypt whose forces were yearly campaigning ever closer to the motherland. This time Hittite fortunes were not promising, thanks to a new configuration of international powers. With the flight and assassination of Tushratta, the empire of Mitanni had collapsed. The vacuum thus created in central Mesopotamia had been hastily filled by two successor states, one a "rump" Mitanni occupying the land between the Balikh and Euphrates under the protection of the Hittites; the other a much larger Khaniglbat ruled by a branch of Saussatar's family.[299]

Khanigalbat, however, proved too strong and soon expanded to engulf Mitanni, which disappeared as a state; early in Mursilis II's reign Khanigalbat and the Assyrians were threatening the banks of the Euphrates.[300] Things became worse when, at the turn of the century, Khanigalbat suffered two defeats in battle at the hands of an expanding Assyria, and the latter was able to confront Khatte directly in North Syria.[301] With the Eygptian war raging unabated, Hattusilis III was running the risk of isolating himself. In an effort, therefore, to neutralize the threat of Assyria, Hattusilis sought and concluded an alliance with the king of Babylon. "With an enemy who is our common foe," Hattusilis recalls saying, "[verily we will be hostile, and] with our common friends verily we are at peace. And after the king of Egypt and I became angry with each other, I wrote to (the king of Babylon) [saying 'the king of Egypt] is at war with me' and so (he) thereupon wrote [saying 'If the troops of the king] of Egypt come, then I will go with thee . . . and I will come in the midst of soldiers and chariots.' " Whether this mutual-assistance pact was ever invoked is difficult to say. The offensive Ramesses II was undertaking probably made any Babylonian aid ineffectual. We hear of no Babylonian troops and perhaps none were sent.

Hattusilis, an intelligent ruler and a "realist" by all accounts, must have appreciated the fact that negotiation was all that was left to him. Assyria had taken over the former role of the Hurrian states as eastern antagonist to Khatte and showed no signs of willingness to come to terms. Ramesses II, on the other hand, was farther removed from the scene of hostilities and, moreover, was burdened by no baggage of racial enmity toward the Hittites. Early in December 1284 B.C., in Ramesses II's twenty-first year as sole ruler, a Hittite messenger, one Tili-teshup, arrived at Pi-Ramesses bearing letters from the Hittite king,[302] proposing a treaty of peace. Ra-

---

[299] Harrack, *Assyria and Hanigalbat*, 15–24.

[300] Mursilis's annals, years 2, 9: Goetze, *MVAG* 38 (1933), 26, 117, 247–48; Harrack, *Assyria and Hanigalbat*, 48–59.

[301] Harrack, *Assyria and Hanigalbat*, 62ff.; P. Machinist, in H. J. Nissen and J. Renger, eds., *Mesopotamien und seinen Nachbaren* (Berlin, 1982), 265–67.

[302] *Palais royal d'Ugarit*, 4:106 (RS 17.137, 10–11).

messes was agreeably surprised and proved a willing negotiator. The threat from the Tigris-Euphrates Valley lent a certain urgency to the negotiations from the Hittite viewpoint; but the Egyptians apparently did not object, and the pact was concluded in haste.

The resultant treaty established a traditional "brotherhood" between the two kings, and specified the kinds of mutual assistance the two parties agreed to. The original was probably drafted in Hittite, then rendered into Akkadian; this version became the legal document to which the parties affixed their seals. One copy with Ramesses's seal was deposited in Khatte before the sun-goddess; another, with Hattusilis's seal, was sent to Egypt and laid before Re in Heliopolis. These copies, both on silver tablets, have not survived; but numerous cuneiform copies on clay have been found at Khattusas; and a paraphrase into hieroglyphic writing (of which the Karnak exemplar has survived) was posted throughout Egypt.[303]

The overriding concern of the treaty is to establish peace. The historical preamble is reduced to a minimum, and no mention is made of boundaries. Repeatedly the signatories aver that they are renouncing hostility and will never again go to war. If either is attacked by a third party—this clearly is for Khatte's benefit—the other will send troops to his assistance, though neither king is obligated to be present in person. If Hattusilis dies and a problem with the accession arises, Ramesses is honor-bound to see to it that his son succeeds him. (No similar provision is made for the benefit of the Egyptians: Ramesses was not going to allow foreigners to tamper with the "Throne of Horus.") A fairly lengthy paragraph deals with the mutual extradition of fugitives and guarantees their humane treatment. Since Urhi-teshup was still present in the court of Ramesses, these clauses may have been framed with him in mind; but apparently Hattusilis was content not to press Ramesses in this case, and to allow his nephew to remain. He only requested Ramesses to pay Urhi-teshup's troops and cover his other expenses.[304]

The war was over. Two centuries of fighting for a northern empire had come to an end. But was Ramesses aware of the cost? For when the border was drawn again, all the gains of the Ramesside kings went for nought. Ugarit and its southern coastal neighbor Siyannu[305] remained Hittite; Amurru returned to the Hittite fold, its king Benteshina reinstated, and was granted control over Arvad.[306] Kadesh too became Hittite

---

[303] *ANET*², 199–203; see especially A. J. Spalinger, *SAK* 9 (1981), 299–300; Kitchen, *Pharaoh Triumphant*, 73–74.

[304] Cavaignac, *RHA* 18 (1935), 25–26; Houwinck ten Cate, in *Anatolian Studies*, 144–46.

[305] M. Astour, *UF* 11 (1979), 13–14.

[306] Weidner, *Politische Dokumente*, 126 obv. 16–17.

once again, with close ties to Ugarit.[307] As in Amarna times Amki remained Egyptian as well as Upe to the south, and the Egyptian headquarters at Kumidi was rechristened "Ramessesburg, the city that is in the midst of Upe."[308] Nothing had changed.

But at least there was now peace to revel in, and both sides were relieved at the prospect of friendly relations and open borders. The statement of the Egyptian queen Nefertiry, in a letter to her counterpart, the queen of Khatte Putuhepa, conveys nicely the hope and exhiliration felt by both sides: "Re and the Weather-god (of the Hittites) shall uphold the treaty and Re will make it a prosperous peace, and he shall make excellent the brotherhood between the great king, the king of Egypt, and the great king, the king of Khatte, his brother, for ever and ever!" The gods were as good as Her Majesty predicted: for the remaining lifetime of the Hittite empire the treaty was never broken, and eighty years of unparalleled prosperity lay in store for the two greatest kingdoms of the ancient world.

[307] Klengel, *Geschichte*, 2:176.
[308] E. Edel, *Geschichte und altes Testament* (Geneva, 1953), 44–45; W. Helck, *MDOG* 92 (1960), 12 (equals Kumidi, which seems more likely).

CHAPTER 7

The Empire of the New Kingdom

THE WARS of the early 18th Dynasty, for the first time in Egypt's history, left it in possession of something quite new to the nation beside the Nile—an empire. Of course, from the founding of the pharaonic state Egypt had always enjoyed a sphere of influence on the upper Nile and in western Asia; but rarely had territory been annexed or permanent occupation by Egyptian settlers been practiced. Now, however, as the jingoist phrase "extending the frontiers" makes abundantly clear, the "manifest destiny" of Egypt was to expand and annex territory, which thenceforth was to be considered an Egyptian possession, and the people inside it Egyptian subjects of whom loyalty was to be expected.[1]

The two tracts that make up the New Kingdom empire, Nubia[2] and Canaan, present us with contrasts in Egypt's desires and expectations, and also how it went about achieving its goals. Nubia attracted the Pharaohs for its products and resources (especially its gold) as well as its manpower; Canaan was valued for the goods that passed along its trade routes and for its strategic location. Nubia in time came to be considered as a territory suitable for colonization, but Canaan was never so viewed. In Nubia it was determined at the outset of the wars of conquest to annihilate any power structure the Nubians themselves had erected, and by the reign of Thutmose II the erstwhile Nubian kingdom of the Hyksos age had ceased to exist. Thereafter local rule by native chiefs was replaced by an elaborate administration, modeled on that of Egypt, in which a royal plenipotentiary or "viceroy" administered a vast tract of the valley from Karoy to El Kab. In Canaan, however, it was at once realized by the Egyptians that native political institutions could not easily be replaced, as they

---

[1] For imperial concepts and mechanisms among the ancient Egyptians, see in particular D. Lorton, *The Juridical Terminology of International Relations in Egyptian Texts through Dynasty XVIII* (Baltimore, 1974); B. Kemp, in P.D.G. Garnsey and C. R. Whittaker, *Imperialism in the Ancient World* (Cambridge, 1978), 7–8; J. P. Frandsen, in M. T. Larsen, *Power and Propaganda: A Symposium on Ancient Empires* (Copenhagen, 1979), 167–68; J. Leclant, in M. Duvoyer, *Le concept d'empire* (Paris, 1980), 49–50; cf. also the excellent marshaling of the Late Bronze evidence with respect to the New Kingdom empire in Asia by J. M. Weinstein, *BASOR* 241 (1981), 1–2. A detailed treatment of the subject appears in D. B. Redford, *Egypt and Canaan* (Beer Sheva, 1990).

[2] On the Nubian empire, see in particular W. B. Emery, *Egypt in Nubia* (London, 1965); B. G. Trigger, *Nubia under the Pharaohs* (London, 1976); W. Adams, *Nubia: Corridor to Africa* (London, 1977).

partook of a degree of sophistication (thanks to their origin among the Amorites of North Syria and Mesopotamia) comparable with that of Egypt itself. In Nubia a transit corridor along the Nile had to be created and maintained, first by the creation of fortresses and later by the planting of colonial settlements. In Canaan two transit corridors already existed, the *Via Maris*, the "Way of the Sea," along the coast, and the (later dubbed) "King's Highway" through Transjordan; and all the Pharaohs had to do was to seize and maintain control over them (Plates 19, 20). In Nubia the sources of production were completely in Egyptian hands from the first, so undeveloped were native means; in the north, except for Sinai and adjacent mineral-rich regions, sources of wealth lay beyond the rim of Egypt's control.

Since the two new "provinces" Egypt had acquired differed so markedly in their resources, population, and requirements, it should come as no surprise that Egypt developed two distinct administrations for south and north. The south, deprived progressively of its autochthonous tribal base, required a wholly new and elaborate bureaucracy imposed by and from Egypt; but the north had never suffered the termination of its political structure, and thus needed no such complex framework transplanted from the Nile.

CANAANITE STATE AND SOCIETY

The lands of the Levantine littoral into which the Thutmosids had affected their belligerent entry had long since displayed a sophistication of culture and politics that defeat in battle could not efface. Canaanite society[3] of the Late Bronze Age had taken shape around a number of medium-sized but amorphous metropolitan states centered on cities that claimed, or certainly aspired to, the status of a "Great Kingship": Hazor in the upper Jordan Valley, Kadesh on the upper Orontes, Tunip in central Syria, the Nukhashshe lands south of Aleppo, Ugarit on the coast— to name but the major contenders.[4] Each of these controlled a territory comprising farmland, towns, and occasionally subjugated cities, but was constantly in a state of expansion or contraction because of the vagaries of border feuds, diplomatic marriages, purchases, sales, or rapine. None

[3] On Canaanite society, see in particular W. F. Albright, in G. E. Wright, ed., *The Bible and the Ancient Near East* (New York, 1965), 438–39; idem, *Yahweh and the Gods of Canaan* (New York, 1969); D. N. Freedman and D. F. Graf, eds., *Palestine in Transition* (Sheffield, 1983); M. Heltzer, *The Rural Community in Ancient Ugarit* (Wiesbaden, 1976); M. Liverani, ed., *La Siria nel tardo bronzo* (Rome, 1969); idem, *Three Amarna Essays* (Malibu, Calif., 1971); G. D. Young, ed., *Ugarit in Retrospect* (Winona Lake, Ind., 1981).

[4] Y. Yadin, *Hazor* (London, 1972); J.-R. Kupper, *CAH²*, II, pt. 1 (1973), 21–22; C. Epstein, *JNES* 22 (1963), 242–43; D. B. Redford, *JAOS* 99 (1979), 287, n. 151.

Plate 19. The Moabite Plateau, rising from the eastern shore of the Dead Sea, along which ran the "King's Highway."

Plate 20. Wady el-Kerak, looking east from Kerak toward the Dead Sea. Through this wady ran a transit corridor connecting the Transjordanian uplands to the Arabah and Negeb.

could claim the security of the neighboring river valley or highland states, whose longevity had bequeathed traditions of solemn sanction by the gods of a self-serving nature; and their strength and permanence seemed to bear out the gods' choice.

The head of such a metropolitan state was styled "king," but was more of a merchant prince, a *primus unter pares* among the nobility. The latter comprised a group of chariot-driving aristocracy called *maryannu* (cf. Aryan *márya*, "chariot-nobility"), who owned estates in the countryside and dominated the society of the rural towns. Membership in this nobility could be secured through inheritance, although the king could also promote favored lackeys to *maryannu* rank. Of middle rank in the social scale were the artisans who were largely a work force controlled by the palace. Renowned especially for the metalworkers in their midst, Syrian craftsmen and their products were coveted by the Pharaohs who usually turned a contemptuous eye upon manufactures from foreign parts. At the bottom of the class structure in Canaanite society was the caste of farmers, the *ḫupšu*, or "rural host" (*ṣabe nâme*), who worked the farms and other units of agricultural production (cf. the *gat* or "olive press" as a term for such a unit). Effectually tied to the land in perpetuity, the *ḫupšu* provided the local militia that fought wars or engaged in construction projects for the state. A separate group called the ʿApiru lay slightly beyond the fringe of "polite" Canaanite society of the Late Bronze Age. These were a collection of antisocial renegades, castoffs from society, who maintained a semi-independent community in the rural districts of the Canaanite states. Though often in the service of these states, the ʿApiru generally guarded their independence and freedom of movement. Much has been written in speculation on the adverse social conditions within Canaanite society that must have given rise to such a group; and it is not unlikely that a combination of mismanagement, economic straits, and natural phenomena may have combined, as in the Roman Empire in the third century A.D., to produce a "flight from the land" on the part of a disenfranchised element of the population. Whatever the reason, the ʿApiru, as their name suggests ("dust makers," i.e. people who vacate the premises with speed) display a gypsylike quality, and proved difficult for the state authorities to bring under effective control. Their heterogeneous nature is vividly illustrated by census lists from Alalakh, wherein one ʿApiru band includes an armed thief, two charioteers, two beggars, and even a priest of Ishtar.[5]

[5] The "problem" of the ʿApiru, and their alleged connection with the ancestoral Hebrews, has spawned an enormous literature. Cf. *inter alia* J. Bottero, *La problème des Habiru* (Paris, 1954); G. Buccellati, *JNES* 36 (1977), 435–36; M. Greenberg, *The Hab/piru* (New Haven, Conn., 1955); O. Loretz, *Habiru-Hebräer: Eine sozial-ling. Studie* (Berlin, 1984); R. de Vauz, *JNES* 27 (1968), 221–22; M. Heltzer, in Liverani, *La Siria nel tardo*

Canaanite society appears before us in graphic form in Egyptian reliefs, depicted either as captives from the foreign wars or as commercial agents bent on trade.[6] A less important source for their appearance is to be found in native seals and the like. From this evidence it becomes apparent that Canaanite society had evolved its own costume and coiffure, only partly dependent on adjacent cultures. At the close of the period of the Hyksos domination, during the mid-sixteenth century B.C., the wealthy nobleman would have sported a plain kilt of leather or linen as a basic garment, supplemented in winter by a sheepskin thrown about the shoulders. Occasionally, especially during the early Late Bronze Age, he might have experimented with a broad strip of decorated fabric with fringe wound around his body from waist to ankle. In northern and central Syria kings might ape the fashion of Mesopotamia by donning archaic woolen robes, supplemented by a mantle or sheepskin thrown over one shoulder, and topped by a tall rounded cap (Figure 7, no. 1).

With the coming of the Late Bronze Age, a new stage in costume development had set in. Well-to-do Asiatics from North Syria and Mitanni now appear, from the reign of Thutmose III onward, in a tight-fitting white gown with blue or red hems, reaching from neck to midcalf, with tight, wrist-length sleeves. The head is shaved and a skullcap sometimes worn (see Figure 7, no. 2), a possible reflection of Hurrian influence. It is likely that the tight-fitting, long-sleeved "sheath" served as a basic summer garment over which some kind of heavier, outer garment could be thrown in winter. This might be the heavier cloak of earlier times (cf. Figure 7, no. 1), but preference seems to have been given to a fringed mantel. The latter by the close of the fifteenth century B.C. had developed into a long piece of colorfully embroidered cloth, wound around the body from the ankles upward, and often thrown around the shoulders (cf. Figure 7, no. 3). Used in combination with the "sheath" as an undergarment, and the filet and clubbed hair as coiffure, the wraparound shawl rapidly became the customary costume of the Canaanite upper classes within the bounds of the Asiatic empire (Figure 7, no. 4).

One important repercussion of the Egyptian conquests in western Asia was the termination, within the area conquered, of the sovereignty of the large metropolitan states aforementioned. Hazor, Kadesh, and Tunip, erstwhile claimants to such leadership, were now reduced in status. *All* headmen of villages and towns, together with their former overlords, descended to a common level through the obligation of taking the oath in

---

bronzo, 34. A. F. Rainey's succinct statement in *Biblica* 70 (1989), 571, mirrors my feelings exactly.

[6] On Canaanite costume, see D. B. Redford, in *The Akhenaten Temple Project*, vol. 2: *Rwd-mnw, Asiatics and the Inscriptions* (Toronto, 1988), chap. 2; S. Schroer, *Orbis Biblicus et Orientalis* (Göttingen, 1985), 51–52.

Figure 7. Typical costume in the eastern Mediterranean during the Late Bronze Age:

1. Canaanite "wrap-around" with winter cloak and skull cap (Hazor)
2. North Syrian galabiyeh and skull cap (Theban tombs)
3. Canaanite galabiyeh and wrap and fillet (Theban tombs)
4. Typical Canaanite costume, twelfth century B.C. (tomb of Ramesses III)
5. Canaanite woman in flounced robe (Theban tombs)
6. Philistine warrior in horse-hair(?) helmet, kilt, and armor (Medinet Habu)
7. Shasu warriors in turbans and kilt (Beit el-Wali).

Pharaoh's name. Thus the towns of Canaan, now transformed into "Pharaoh's towns," constituted only the residual infrastructure of the defunct metropolitan states of the southern Levant.[7]

MUNICIPAL ADMINISTRATION

If Pharaoh now merely assumed the role of the suzerain vis-à-vis the Canaanite headmen, he carefully refrained from involving himself further in their affairs. The social structure of *maryannu* and *ḫupšu* peasantry remained intact; the headmen adopted the role of liaison. While identifying themselves in their own letters to Pharaoh, the headmen almost invariably title themselves "the man of town so-and-so"; and in the few surviving letters of Pharaoh himself the same designation is used.[8] Collectively, in the Akkadian *lingua franca* of the age, the headmen were termed *ḫazanuti*, "mayors," which is simply the equivalent of the Egyptian *ḫ³ty-'*, the "mayor" or governor of an Egyptian town. That the pharaonic administration considered the Canaanite headmen to be "mayors" in the Egyptian sense explains a good deal in respect to status, function, and obligation that these Canaanite worthies shouldered vis-à-vis the Egyptian crown.

Like their counterparts along the Nile, the Canaanite mayors were required to take the oath in Pharaoh's name,[9] and to send to Egypt whatever sons or relatives the Egyptians might require: "I have sent my son to the king, my lord, my god, my sun!" says the writer of EA 180; "behold, I have sent my daughter to the palace, to the king, my lord, my god, my sun!" parrots Shatiya of Enishazi (EA 187). "I have sent my son into the presence of the king, my lord, in order that the king, my lord, may grant me life," avers Arkhattu of Kumidi (EA 198). This seems to have been the initial act of any mayor lately arrived in office, the sign of the requisite willingness to cooperate. Thutmose III had begun the practice, as he tells us himself: "Now the children of the chiefs and their brothers were brought to be hostages in Egypt; and as for any of these chiefs that died, His Majesty used to have his son assume his post" (*Urk* IV, 690). In Egypt these "sons of chiefs" were naturally exposed to Egyptian mores and language; and the administration may even have had them educated in Egyptian fashion. Many were placed in the paramilitary units that guarded Pharaoh and ran before the royal chariot; and in later life they were to refer to themselves as "the treadway of thy (the king's) horses" (cf. EA 331). Some, dispatched to Egypt as small children, returned to their patrimonies thoroughly Egyptianized, speaking their ancestral tongue as a

[7] Heltzer, in Liverani, *La Siria nel tardo bronzo*, 31–32.

[8] G. Buccellati, *Cities and Nations of Ancient Syria* (Rome, 1967), 64–66.

[9] Lorton, *Juridical Terminology of International Relations in Egyptian Texts through Dynasty XVIII*, 31–32.

second language, and feeling more at home in Egypt than among their own people. Yakhtiri of Gaza tells us (EA 296) "when I was small (the Egyptian commissioner) brought me to Egypt, and I served the king my lord, and was stationed in the gate of the king my lord."

The Canaanite mayors suffered the same burden of obligations as the Egyptian mayors. They had to hand over taxes promptly and were required to entertain or accompany Egyptian officers passing through: "Behold! I am a trustworthy servant of the king," protests Lab'ayu of Shechem, "I have not done wrong nor have I sinned: I have not withheld my tribute, and have not refused the request of my commissioner" (EA 254). When Pharaoh went on military campaign, "chevauché" as it were, the mayor was required to house and feed the expeditionary force and to provide his own contingent of troops: "The king my lord has written," Arzawiya of Rukhizzi informs us "concerning preparations for the arrival of troops of the king my lord, and for the arrival of his many commissioners" (EA 191). Another declares: "I have prepared oxen and cattle as you have commanded me in the letter" (EA 193). Biryawaza of Damascus promises: "I am ready with my troops and my chariots, my brothers and my ʿApiru and my Sutu for the arrival of the troops (and for duty), wherever the king my lord commands" (EA 195). At regular intervals the mayor was obliged to make written report to the sovereign, employing a stereotyped, obsequious style: "To the king my lord, my god, my sun, the sun in heaven, thus (speaks) Widiya, the man of Ashkelon, thy servant, the dust of thy feet . . . at the feet of the king my lord seven times and seven times over may I prostrate myself on belly and back! Behold, I protect the place of the king which is assigned me, and whatever the king my lord has written me I have obeyed it very carefully. Who is the dog that does not obey the word of the king his lord, the son of the sun?" (EA 230).

The Canaanite mayors suffered the equivocal status of middlemen, poised midway between a demanding and unsympathetic Pharaoh, and their own people who tended toward recalcitrance. If they appeared to be "Egypt's man" to an excessive degree, they ran the risk of being assassinated; but if they failed to cooperate with the imperial administration, they ran the risk of being dragged off to Pharaoh's court to answer charges. In any case, a trip to Egypt at some point in their careers could scarcely be avoided, as the king required Canaanite nobility to grace his court at festivals (Plate 21).

THE IMPERIAL STATE DEPARTMENT

One gets the distinct impression in studying the historical records of the 18th and 19th Dynasties that the administration of the new empire was created on an ad hoc basis, with little imagination beyond a simple re-

Plate 21. Canaanite headmen adore the king at the jubilee of Akhenaten; jubilee temple of Akhenaten at Thebes (early fourteenth century B.C.).

sponse to a practical need.[10] On the morrow of the conquest, Pharaoh's government was in desparate need of able officials to keep the Asiatics in order; and we find appointed at sundry times a fortress commandant, a simple retainer, and even a construction engineer. A feeling of self-importance wells up in the biography of one Itju, who calls himself "the policeman of the Fenkhu-lands (the Lebanese coast) who punishes any who rebel against the king in the land of Retenu (the Levant in general)" (*Urk IV*, 1641). In keeping with the generally tentative efforts in the direction of the creation of a genuine "foreign service," 18th Dynasty officers sometimes reactivate an ancient title "overseer of foreign lands," taken in the Old Kingdom and later by emissaries charged with missions in foreign parts. In the New Kingdom, however, it is mainly an epithet of general application and has nothing to do with a formal "governorship" of conquered territory.[11]

[10] See W. Helck, *MDOG* 92 (1960), 1–2; idem, *Die Beziehungen Ägyptens zur Vorderasiens*[2], (Wiesbaden, 1971), 246–47; K. A. Kitchen, in Liverani *La Siria nel tardo bronzo*, 77–78; R. Hachemann, *ZDPV* 98 (1982), 1–2.

[11] On "overseer of foreign lands," see S. Groll, in M. Görg, ed., *Fontes atque Pontes* (Wiesbaden, 1983), 234–35.

Four generations after the death of the conquerer Thutmose III, a department of foreign affairs had begun to take shape; but the evidence does not always agree as to its shape and nomenclature. The Akkadian correspondence that has been preserved in the precious tablets from Amarna reflects in the main the communications passing between the Egyptian court and the Canaanite mayors of the northern empire, and as such references by title to Egyptian officials are ubiquitous. But the titles are in Akkadian. *Rabiṣu*, "supervisor," is especially common, but occasionally *šākin mâti*, "governor," *mālik* (Canaanite), "counsellor," and *sōkēn* (Canaanite), "superintendent," are also used. Are these translations of Egyptian titles? Or are they the closest Canaanite or Akkadian terms the mayors could come up with to designate an Egyptian commissioner whose real rank was wholly unknown to them? In fact, the latter is precisely the case.

When one examines the officials whose names are transcribed into Akkadian in the Amarna Letters,[12] and tries to link them with known Egyptian officials from the period of Amenophis III and Akhenaten, it becomes clear that the majority of probable identifications belong in the ranks of the *military*, with the lower echelons predominating.[13] Thus we can point to "standard-bearers," the equivalent in the ancient Egyptian army of our "captain," company adjutants, army scribes, "stable masters," the equivalent of our quartermasters, all operating in the northern territories of the empire as commissioners of Pharaoh. None is of high rank (though that does not preclude a magnate such as a vizier or king's messenger showing up on occasion), and none bears any higher status *pro tem* than a royal plenipotentiary.

The spheres of operation of these officers were constantly shifting on an ad hoc basis, and we cannot speak of "provinces" in the sense that we have become familiar with through the study of the Roman Empire. Because of his familiarity with one part of the country an officer's activity might be restricted to one region only, but the reason was a private one and had nothing to do with any prior division of the territory. When Egyptians alluded to the northern empire, they still spoke of "the land of Canaan (or Kharu, Djahy, etc.)" and the cities therein each with its own "territory," never of the "province of so-and-so." The officer is dispatched by the king on assignment and is allotted a certain number of towns in Canaan on a circuit. These he visits on his rounds, and while there exercises wide authority. He bears letters from Pharaoh, can arrest locals and convey them to Egypt, and can requisition dues and taxes; he

[12] See the standard work of W. F. Albright, *JNES* 5 (1946), 7–8; also Redford, *Egypt and Canaan.*

[13] On military titles in ancient Egypt, see the standard treatment by A. R. Schulman, *Military Rank, Title and Organization in the Egyptian New Kingdom* (Berlin, 1964).

decides cases at law and can even settle border disputes between one town and another. Sooner or later he always returns to Egypt for debriefing and consultation with the king or his officials.

If the age of the great Amenophis III had witnessed the inception of a regularized state department, the age of the Ramessides (the 19th Dynasty) carried it to the logical stage of refinement. From the voluminous records of the 19th and 20th Dynasties, it is quite clear that the provincial administrator of the time was primarily a *courier* ("king's messenger to foreign lands") who carried the king's messages and reported back to him.[14] He was recruited most often from the ranks of the military, and mainly from the chariotry corps. The curriculum vitae of one Amenemone under Ramesses II is perhaps typical: "I was a retainer of His Majesty when he was a boy; and then, when he became 'Lord' (i.e., king) he made me charioteer and overseer of the stable. My lord praised me on account of my proficiency, and appointed me battalion commander of his army . . . and he sent me as king's messenger to every foreign land, and I reported back to him about the foreign lands in every detail."[15]

The "king's messenger to every foreign land" became a romantic type in the society and literature of Ramesside Egypt, perhaps comparable with the knight-errant in medieval Europe, or the frontiersman in nineteenth-century America. From a satirical composition of the thirteenth-century B.C., Papyrus Anastasi I, which describes this profession in terms of a wholly incompetent member, we are treated to a detailed glimpse of such a courier's qualifications.[16] The king's messenger must be a "choice scribe," and "able serviceman," "leader of troops, head of the host" (P. Anast. I, 27:1), "listed in every office" (ibid., 28:2), a good charioteer and archer. In particular, he must have a good knowledge of the geography and topography of Canaan, its roads and overnight stopping points. The satirist examines his imagined messenger with a rapid stream of questions: "O serviceman, where is Raphia? What is its rampart like? How many *itr* is it to get to Gaza? (27:7–8). . . . Where is the stream of *Ntn* (the Litani?)? What is Uzu like? (21:1). . . . O serviceman, please put me on the road to the region of Accho; where does the route to Achsaph go? (21:4–5)."

Civil officers occur less frequently than the military. The occasional presence in Canaan of king's scribes and stewards may reflect the administration of pharaonic holdings in the area, and the concern for income.

Slightly more common in post–Amarna times in the roster of the ad-

[14] E. Edel, in *Geschichte und Altes Testament* (Tübingen, 1953), 55ff.; M. Vallogia, *Recherche sur les "messagers" (wpwtyw) dans les sources égyptiennes profanes* (Paris, 1976).

[15] KRI III, 274–75.

[16] A. H. Gardiner, *Egyptian Hieratic Texts*, vol. 1 (Hildesheim, 1964); A. F. Rainey, *JNES* 26 (1967), 58–59; H.-W. Fisher-Elert, *Die satirische Streitschrift des Pap. Anastasi*, vol. 1 (Wiesbaden, 1983).

ministrative personnel is the title "overseer of foreign lands," which seems by the 19th Dynasty to have graduated to the status of "governor." The cuneiform correspondence of Ramesses II and Hattusilis III, the Hittite king, refers to the king's "governor who is in the land of Upe (Damascus)," undoubtedly with headquarters in the town of Kumidi.[17] In LB II levels of several Canaanite cities, including Tel Fara (south), Beth Shean, Tel Sera', Tel Masos, Tel Hesi, Tel Jemmeh, Aphek, and others, a house type has been detected that in its layout differs markedly from the contemporary Canaanite house plan. It does, however, recall in specific detail house plans of contemporary, upper-middle-class residences in Egypt.[18] Current scholarship is probably correct in interpreting such buildings as domiciles and offices erected by and for the pharaonic administration, though needless to say one need not conjure up a "governor" wherever an Egyptian house plan is laid bare. Transport of taxes, supervision of temple holdings, and garrison duty must account for the presence of numerous petty officials and soldiers whose names have not come down to us.

Garrisons and Administrative Centers

Certain cities, enjoying strategic locations from the Egyptian point of view had, by Ramesside times, been singled out and elevated to the status of strongpoints. An armory had been added to the fortress of Sile on the lower Bubastite branch of the Nile, that frontier bastion the Egyptians considered a sort of "Ultima Thule,"[19] and a "lieutenant general of chariotry, battalion commander and king's messenger to foreign lands" appointed as commandant. Further south, in the middle of the Wady Tumilat, which had long since provided an access corridor for Asiatics from central Sinai, the fortress of Tjekku (Hebrew *Succoth*) was turned into a major police headquarters and checkpoint to monitor bedu tribes bent on entry into the Delta for pasturage.[20] A famous letter from the resident scribe, dated to the eighth year of Merenptah, yields a precious insight into this purpose: "We have finished passing the tribes of the Shasu of Edom through the fortress of Merenptah-content-with-peace, L.p.h. which is (in) Tjekku to the pools of the House-of-Atum of Merenptah-content-with-peace which is (in) Tjekku, for their sustenance and the sustenance of their flocks" (P. Anast. IV, 18, 6–7).

Although the sea route to the Lebanese coast was now familiar and well

[17] Edel, in *Geschichte*, 55ff.

[18] E. Oren, *JSSEA* 14 (1985), 37–38.

[19] Tel el-Akhmar? Cf. Helck, *Beziehungen*[2], 310–11.

[20] W. Helck, *Die altägyptische Gaue* (Wiesbaden, 1974), 173; the debate over the site of Tjekku has, through the recent excavations of J. S. Holladay, Jr., been settled in favor of Tel er-Retabeh: D. B. Redford, *LdÄ* 4 (1982), 1054ff.

traveled, the Egyptians still considered the land route from the Delta border to Gaza, 160 kilometers distant, the most important transit corridor to Asia (Plates 22–24). By the beginning of the 19th Dynasty this highway was dotted with about a dozen "way stations."[21] These are depicted in contemporary art as small, fortified "keeps," centered upon wells or pools of fresh water, and were generically called "basins" (ḥnmt). Texts describe them as being administered by bailiffs or occasionally, if they were strategically important, by battalion commanders. Two of these stations have, in fact, been excavated, one Deir el-Balah near Gaza,[22] the other Bir el-Abd in Sinai.[23] The findings largely confirm the texts and artistic depictions. Deir el-Balah comprised an elaborate Egyptian-style residence building, built during the Amarna period and replaced under Sety I by a fourteen-room tower-fort, 20 by 20 meters in extent. Adjacent to these structures was a man-made crater 5 meters deep and occupying 400 square meters, clearly intended as a reservoir.[24]

The occupation by Egyptian troops of Canaanite towns is well attested

Plate 22. Coast of the Mediterranean between Gaza and Raphia, along which ran the military route used by the New Kingdom Pharaohs.

[21] See A. H. Gardiner's classic study in *JEA* 6 (1920), 99–100.

[22] T. Dothan, *IEJ* 31 (1981), 126–27; idem, *National Geographic Magazine* 162 (1982), 738–39.

[23] E. Oren, *IEJ* 23 (1973), 112–13.

[24] T. Dothan, in E. Lipinski, ed., *The Land of Israel: Crossroads of Civilization* (Louvain, 1985), 55–56.

Plate 23. Coastal plain south of Gaza, showing sand dunes covering arable land.

Plate 24. Site of ancient Ashkelon.

in the Amarna Letters and in Egyptian inscriptions. The principal consideration governing the policy of distribution of garrisons (Egyptian *iw'yt*, "body of standing troops")[25] seems to have been strategic: the coastal towns loom large in importance. Early in the 18th Dynasty Sharuhen was garrisoned, but after the reign of Thutmose III Gaza assumed Sharuhen's role as a garrison point. Further north a "garrison commander" is mentioned in association with Tyre, and to judge by passages in the Amarna Letters, Byblos housed a similar body of troops. Several texts allude to an Egyptian-built fort, manned by a garrison "on the seashore" in Lebanon, but its exact location and nature remain to be determined. Ullaza and Ugarit both received garrisons in the early years of the empire; but the latter town was soon lost to Egypt, while by the end of the 18th Dynasty Sumur had replaced Ullaza as a garrison point.

Inland garrison cities were fewer, but reflect concern with routes and sparsely inhabited tracts that might fall into hostile hands. Jerusalem had a garrison by the close of the 18th Dynasty for the protection of what would later be called the Judaean highlands; and Beth Shean, just south of the Sea of Galilee, was assigned a similar force to keep the crossing of the Jordan under surveillance.

Garrison duty was popularly conceived as long and rigorous and utterly abhorrent to the Egyptians. Didactic texts dwell heavily on its hardships and brand it a kind of punishment or exile. If the unfortunate soldier "is sent to the garrison of Kharu . . . having left his wife and his children, his clothing is skins and his food the grass of the field, like any head of cattle" (P. Chester Beatty V, recto 5:12–15). A single tour of duty could extend up to six years. An officer, apparently sent to some coastal garrison with orders to perform construction work, complains of the conditions under which he has to work:

> I am dwelling in Damnationville with no supplies. There have been no people to knead bricks and no straw in the district. Those supplies I brought are gone, and there are no asses, (since they) have been stolen. I spend the day watching the birds and doing some fishing (all the while), eyeing the road which goes up to Djahy with (homesick) longing. Under trees with no edible foliage do I take my siesta (for) their fruit has perished. . . . The gnat attacks in sunlight and the mosquito in the (heat of) noon, and the sand-fly stings—they suck at every blood vessel—. . . if ever a jar filled with Kode wine is opened and people come out to get a cup, there are 200 large dogs and 300 jackals—500 in all—and they stand waiting constantly at the door of the house whenever I go out, since they smell the liquor when the container is opened. . . . the heat here never lets up. (P. Anast. IV, 12/5–13/7)

[25] R. O. Faulkner, *JEA* 39 (1953), 44; Schulman *Military Rank*, 17–18; Weinstein, *BASOR* 241 (1981), 17–18.

Apart from garrison posts, a few cities were taken over as permanent headquarters. Gaza, dubbed by the Egyptians "the (town) belonging to Canaan," became the principal seat of a resident who had vague jurisdiction over the coast and hill country as far as the plain of Esdraelon.[26] There was a house there for this commissioner, and a temple dedicated to Amun and the pharaonic "Genius."[27] Apart from the garrison mentioned previously, the resident was assisted by a registrar responsible for reporting on the "towns of Pharaoh"—that is, the Canaanite cities within the bailiwick just defined.[28] Arrangements for the Phoenician coast arose out of the nature of Thutmost III's conquest of the region. The great conqueror, because of his desire to use the sea route in transporting his forces to Asia, determined to secure the best Phoenician harbors at all costs; and to this end he established storage depots in certain selected coastal cities. Ullaza first became a garrison city and headquarters; later, as noted, this status was ceded to Sumur.[29] Inland, Kumidi in the Beka' Valley, north of Damascus, was made over into an Egyptian headquarters.[30]

Other cities within the empire were sometimes set aside for special purposes. Throughout the 18th and 19th Dynasties Joppa remained an important center for grain storage and the organization of the corvée; and by the 19th Dynasty a chariot depot seems also to have been established there. Yarimuta (location?) became a depot for grain storage, and Megiddo the town in charge of harvesting the plain of Esdraelon.

POLICING AND DEPORTATION

As in Egypt so in Asia, Egypt employed in addition to garrison troops and commissioners a sizable police force comprised largely of Nubians originally of the Medjay tribe. Sudanese elements had assisted the Egyptians in their struggle against the Hyksos, and by the mid-18th Dynasty had carved out for themselves such a niche that "Medjay" became virtually synonymous with "policeman." The size of the Nubian forces sent to Asia varied greatly from as few as ten to as many as a thousand. They had a reputation, it seems, for unruly behavior, but this probably worked to Egypt's advantage in cowing the local population.[31]

In the realm of what might euphemistically be termed "population con-

[26] M. Avi-Yonah, ed., *Encyclopedia of Archaeological Excavations in the Holy Land* (Jerusalem, 1976), 2:408–9; H. J. Katzenstein, *JAOS* 102 (1982), 111–12; Helck, *Beziehungen*[2], 304.

[27] R. Giveon, *The Impact of Egypt on Canaan* (Göttingen, 1978), 23.

[28] H. Goedicke and E. F. Wente, *Ostraka Michaelides* (Wiesbaden, 1962), pl. 93.

[29] Helck, *Beziehungen*[2], 304; Hachemann, *ZDPV* 98 (1982), 26.

[30] D. O. Edzard et al., *Kamid el-Loz-Kumidi* (Bonn, 1970); J. Leclant, *Orientalia* 41 (1972), 280–81; 44 (1975), 239–40.

[31] H. Klengel, in E. Endesfelder, ed., *Ägypten und Kusch* (Berlin, 1977), 227–28.

trol," the Egyptians fell back on tried and true methods. The Old Kingdom experience (as previously discussed) had proved the worth of uprooting and transporting to Egypt whole communities. At one and the same time this practice served to punish rebellious populations and increase the labor force. The policy is succinctly put by the terse instructions given by Pharaoh to his officers responsible for the empire:

> [The foreign lands beg]inning at the southern frontier of Kush [as far as Naharin . . .], Pharaoh I.p.h. has given them into your keeping for the security of her borders [in accordance with what] Pharaoh I.p.h. has [said(?)], just as was the practice of your ancestors from remote antiquity. Now [if it is] reported that some foreign peoples who know not how they should live are come [having abandoned(?)] their lands, hungry and living like wild game, [their] children [likewise], then the All-powerful shall send his victorious sword before [his host in order to] slay them and destroy their towns, and set fire [to tho]se foreign lands, and put other people in their places.[32]

Transplanting the rebellious to Nubia was a popular expedient. Akhenaten commands Zulaya of Damascus: "Send me the ʿApiru of the pasture land (?) concerning whom I sent you as follows: 'I will settle them in the cities of the land of Kush to dwell in, inasmuch as I have plundered them.' "[33]

From Palestine during the latter half of the 18th Dynasty comes convincing evidence of a certain degree of population disruption. Numerous populous sites of Middle Bronze Age date are found to have been destroyed, and a major shift of population is indicated into valleys and coastal plains, leaving the highlands sparsely occupied.[34] The immediate aftermath of the Egyptian conquest involved the intentional demolition of Canaanite towns and the deportation of a sizable segment of the population.[35] Thutmose III carried off in excess of 7,300, while his son Amenophis II uprooted by his own account 89,600. Thutmose IV implies that he carried off the inhabitants of Canaanite Gezer to Thebes, while his son Amenophis III speaks of his Theban mortuary temple as "filled with male and female slaves, children of the chiefs of all the foreign lands of the captivity of His Majesty—their number is unknown—surrounded by the

---

[32] From the Memphite tomb of Horemheb: A. H. Gardiner, *JEA* 39 (1953), 7–8; W. Helck, *VT* 18 (1968), 475–76.

[33] Edzard, *Kamid el-Loz-Kumidi*, 55–56.

[34] T. L. Thompson, *The Settlement of Palestine in the Late Bronze Age* (Wiesbaden, 1979), 59 and passim; B. Mazar, *BASOR* 241 (1981), 75; R. Gonen, *BASOR* 253 (1984), 61ff.

[35] R. Giveon, *Les bedouins Shosou* (Leiden, 1972), 219–20; D. B. Redford, in A. Hadidi, ed., *Studies in the History and Archaeology of Jordan* (Amman, 1982), 117; idem, in *Biblical Archaeology Today* (Jerusalem, 1985), 193.

settlements of Syria." Canaanite mayors were obliged, on Pharoah's demand, to round up and dispatch to Egypt specified numbers of men, women, and children: 56 from Gezer, 20 slaves to accompany the daughter of the mayor of Ammia, 10 slaves, 21 maidservants, and 80 prisoners of war from the same city. In Ramesside times sale into slavery is attested, and boatloads of Canaanite slaves were regular arrivals in Egyptian ports. Cliché-ridden allusions to "stocking (the temple's) workhouse with male and female slaves of His Majesty's captivity" continue in texts of the 19th Dynasty as frequently as before.[36]

THE TAXATION OF THE ASIATIC EMPIRE

The tax system imposed on the Canaanite population was, in essentials, that of Egypt itself transplanted abroad.[37] Like native Egyptians, the Asiatics were assessed at regular intervals and assigned tax quotas for the salaries of dependents of the Egyptian administration and for the upkeep of temples, garrisons, and so forth.[38] The Canaanite mayors, like their Egyptian counterparts, were obliged to hand in their "benevolences" (*inw*, literally "that which is brought") every New Year's day, as well as to give a portion of the "products of their labor."[39] From the period of the earliest conquests selected tracts of land as well as whole cities were confiscated and made the property of Egyptian temples: by the 20th Dynasty, the temple of Amun owned 56 and the temple of Re 103 Canaanite towns. The corvée was imposed upon the natives as an obligation to the state; and mayors were forced to cultivate unworked fields, exactly as was the practice in Egypt.[40]

Although we lack a complete file of papyri laying bare the total structure of imperial taxation, references to income from the north in annals, triumphal stelae, letters, and account ledgers have survived in some numbers. From an examination of these it may be stated that, in general, Egypt requisitioned from its northern dependencies those resources and products it could not obtain locally or from Africa. Nevertheless, Canaan and North Syria were too rich not to entice the Egyptians into milking them as much as they could. Not only was the region well endowed with native resources, but it also constituted a crossroads for trade routes orig-

[36] In general, on Asiatics in Egypt, see Helck, *Beziehungen*[2], 342–43.

[37] See in particular S. Ahituv, *IEJ* 28 (1978), 93–94; N. Na'aman, *IEJ* 31 (1981), 172–73; also Redford, *Egypt and Canaan.*

[38] D. B. Redford, in J. W. Wevers and D. B. Redford, eds., *Studies on the Ancient Palestinian World* (Toronto, 1972), 145–46.

[39] C. Aldred, *JEA* 56 (1970), 105–6; E. J. Bleiberg, *JARCE* 21 (1984), 155–56.

[40] A. H. Gardiner, *JEA* 27 (1941), 23–24; B. Menu, *La régime juridique des terres et du personnel attaché à la terre dans le papyrus Wilbour* (Lille, 1970), 92–93.

inating as far away as the Aegean and the Punjab. Taxes could be brought to the king himself when he passed through Canaan on campaign or tour of inspection; but more frequently the locals were obliged to transport the goods themselves. From southern Canaan the goods might go by land in caravan; but north of Carmel the sea route was preferred.

With respect to gems and precious metals, silver occupies the most prominent position.[41] Egypt lacks silver deposits within its own territory, while gold from the eastern desert in both Egypt and Nubia is quite plentiful. We find recorded quite large amounts of silver exacted: 200 shekels from Gezer, 1,400 from a neighboring town, 5,000 from Jerusalem.[42] Lapis lazuli, not found in Egypt, was demanded from North Syria whither it was imported from Assyria and Babylon.[43] Curiously, sources from the Amarna period lay stress on glass, which was part of the tax burden of cities in the southern coastal plain.[44]

The list of nonprecious metals, both in the form of ore and worked metals, is equally important. Dominating this category is what the Egyptians termed "Asiatic copper," possibly a copper alloy akin to bronze.[45] This was exacted mainly from Byblos and North Syria, but soon became the principal component of a lively trade and gift exchange with Cyprus. The widespread commerce involving copper is now vividly illustrated by the Ulun Buru shipwreck of late Amarna date, in which the excavator uncovered a sunken merchantman with a capacity of 5,000 tons of copper in ingot form.[46] In Egypt Asiatic copper was used for weapons, door fixtures, hinges, sockets for masts, and for cult objects such as offering tables. Trade in tin is well known from the Middle and Late Bronze Ages, and tin was exacted by Egypt as a benevolence, though in smaller amounts than copper. Iron was still quite rare and used only for luxury items; and both production and market had long since been cornered by the Hittites.

Timber of all kinds looms large in the tribute of Asia.[47] First and foremost was the cedar of Lebanon used for sacred barks, especially the bark of Amun called "Powerful-of-Prow-is-Amun." But the same wood was also employed for temple doors, flag staves, portable shrines, and cult implements. The transport of cedar to Egypt assumed top priority. Thut-

---

[41] J. R. Harris and A. Lucas, *Ancient Egyptian Materials and Industries*[4] (London, 1962), 280; J. R. Harris, *Lexicographical Studies in Ancient Egyptian Minerals* (Berlin, 1961), 41ff.

[42] Cf. EA 99:14, 287:54, 270:15, 313:7–11.

[43] Helck, *Beziehungen*[2], 388–89.

[44] Na'aman, *IEJ* 31 (1981), 175.

[45] Harris, *Lexicographical Studies*, 50ff.; R. Gundlach, *LdÄ* 3 (1980), 881–82.

[46] G. Bass: oral communication.

[47] H. Klengel, in Liverani *La Siria nel tardo bronzo*, 17.

mose III tells us: "There was felled [for me in Dja]hy each and every year fresh cedar of Lebanon, which was brought to the Palace, l.p.h. Lumber came to me in Egypt, brought south [by sea(?) in the form of] fresh [cedar] of Negaw, the choicest of (the products of) God's land, without missing a season, each and every year. My troops who made up the garrison in Ullaza came to me [by sea(?) in ships] which are of cedar of My Majesty's victories through the counsels of my father [Amun-re] who handed all foreign peoples over to me. I gave none of it to the Asiatics (for), it is the wood he loves."[48] Costly woods, boxwood in particular,[49] were also exacted from the Canaanites, especially from Amurru and the north coast. These were destined for fine furniture and cult implements.

Cattle had long been imported from Asia as milch cows and for hauling stone, less often for their beef.[50] A good number of flocks and herds rounded up on campaign must have gone immediately for the sustenance of the expeditionary force. But livestock was not a priority in the tax assessments. Exotic animals, such as chickens and elephants, occasionally appear in the lists, but these were little more than curiosities.

The grain-growing lands of western Asia did not of themselves attract the attention of the Egyptian administration, since Egypt produced cereals in superabundance; but the needs of residents, garrisons, and expeditionary forces could better be met by requisitioning local produce on the spot (Plate 25).[51] Campaigns were often timed so that the army would reach the enemy territory just when the harvest had been gathered in. Certain Canaanite mayors suffered the imposition of a sort of liturgy whereby they were obliged to harvest barley and wheat in their territory for the upkeep of local Egyptian garrisons. In particular the grain and vegetable harvests of Galilee and the Lebanon went to stock the military stores in the coastal cities in anticipation of future campaigns: "Now all the harbors His Majesty touched at were stocked with every good thing according to their yearly custom for both northward and southward journeys (with), the labor of Lebanon likewise and the harvest of Djahy, consisting of grain, incense, fresh oil, sweet oil, wine etc."[52]

Selected organic materials, not found in Egypt or perhaps coveted for their superior quality, appear regularly in tax lists. Canaanite incense was shipped home for use in Egyptian temples,[53] and moringa oil, unknown

[48] Urk IV, 1237.

[49] Helck, Beziehungen², 397–98; E. Lagrace, CRAIBL (1983), 272, n. 27; Liverani, Three Amarna Essays, 8 and n. 42.

[50] Helck, Beziehungen², 371–72.

[51] On the grain imposts of the empire, see ibid., 360–61; Na'aman, IEJ 31 (1981), 178.

[52] Urk IV, 719.

[53] On incense, see V. Loret, La resine de terebinthe (Sonter) chez les anciens égyptiens (Cairo, 1949).

Plate 25. The Plain of Esdraelon looking northeast from the mound of Megiddo, where the grain crop was harvested for the Pharaoh's court. The siege camp of the Egyptians on Thutmose III's first campaign was located in the foreground.

in Egypt, was requisitioned from the north.[54] Naharin and Cyprus are indicated as the sources of this precious commodity, and Ugaritic texts show a lively trade extending around the eastern Mediterranean.[55] Opium was exported from Cyprus in an unmistakable type of jar widely dispersed throughout the empire;[56] honey was exacted in small quantities only. Wine is a commonplace item in the lists. New Kingdom texts display an awareness of different "brands": Asiatic wines are variously qualified as "of the Ways of Horus," "of Kharu," "of Amurru."[57]

Weaponry does not figure as prominently among the taxes as might have been expected.[58] Even in the battlefield lists of booty, entered in the daybook of the King's house, personal weaponry is not given special place. This may be because weapons were construed as the private property of the soldiers who had effected the kill or capture. Ceremonial weapons, adorned with gold, silver, and gems are attested, however, with some regularity. Chariots are frequently depicted being brought by Asiatics to the king, and these too were frequently wrought in precious

[54] Helck, *Beziehungen*[2], 398–99, 415.

[55] Cf. *Palais royal d'Ugarit* (Paris, 1965), 5: no. 95.

[56] R. S. Merrillees, *Antiquity* 36 (1962), 287–88; idem, *Levant* 11 (1979), 167–68; but cf. B. M. Gittlin, *BASOR* 241 (1981), 55.

[57] A. H. Gardiner, *Ancient Egyptian Onomastica* (Oxford, 1947), 1:180*f., 187*f.

[58] On the weapons and armaments of the ancient Egyptians, see W. Wolf, *Die Bewaffnung des altägyptischen Heeres* (Leipzig, 1926); Y. Yadin, *The Art of Warfare in Bible Lands* (Jerusalem, 1961).

woods and metals. Only occasionally did Egyptians of the empire period take to Canaanite armaments. A notable exception was the body armor and helmet of the Canaanite charioteer which, under the Ramessides, was taken over by the Egyptian army.

Finally, one class of manufactured goods native to the Levant was highly prized by the Egyptians. That was ornamental metalwork. The Canaanite smith and the products of his atelier were well known in Egypt: we hear of the silverwork of Ashkelon, vases "of Hurrian type," "vessels of Djahy workmanship," and "every shining vessel" of Retenu. In fact, in schematized scenes of tribute-bringing, Syrian ornamental vases often stand symbolically, *pars pro toto*, for the totality of the taxes brought.

The assessment of all these taxes seems to have proceeded on the same ad hoc basis as the rest of the mechanisms pressed into service to run the empire. At one moment we find the king's herald responsible for "reckoning the tribute of the chiefs who are in every foreign land" (*Urk* IV, 975); at another it is the vizier or the chief treasurer that "estimates the labor of every foreign land" (KRI III, 21, 136). Whether any of these worthies ever set foot in Canaan in the process of drawing up their "budgetary estimates" is a moot point. But the king's scribe Minmose, charged with this task, actually did repair to the north in order to carry it out: "[I trod] upper [Retenu] in the train of my lord, and I taxed [upper] Retenu . . . I informed the chiefs of Retenu of [their] annual labor (tax)" (*Urk* IV, 1442).

CHAPTER 8

Asia in Egypt: Mosaic, Not Melting Pot

ANCIENT EGYPTIAN civilization was *sui generis.* The Egyptians knew they and their culture differed markedly from peoples of neighboring lands. The Egyptian way of life could not easily be transplanted and tended to wither away if uprooted from the banks of the Nile. The Egyptians knew this also and reveled in the fact. Not for them the dubious joy of "converting aliens." But now, the aftermath of empire had thrown the races together willy-nilly, and the snobbish Egyptian would have to rub shoulders with the sallow Canaanite and Nubian black. Alien cultures, belonging all to communities that had been defeated in battle by the Egyptian conqueror, were now making their presence felt within the conqueror's country itself. It was infinitely more difficult to defeat ideas, and in any case the pragmatic Egyptians felt no need to annihilate race and beliefs. As time went on they found themselves having to cast judgment about and come to terms with Canaanite mores, obliged to borrow many ideas and to reject others, and above all to treat with foreign lands as members of a world community, not as god's isolated favorite race.

THE ARMY

The most obvious sphere in which foreign examples had provided models worth copying was the military.[1] The Asiatic inventions of the chariot and the composite bow were borrowed by the Egyptians before the expulsion of the Hyksos and were developed to the point where the chariotry and archers of Egypt became the dread of the world.[2] The Egyptian terms for "chariot officer" and "charioteer" were both derived from for-

---

[1] The organization of the Egyptian army is much better known than the tactics they employed on the battlefield. In general see R. O. Faulkner, *JEA* 39 (1953), 32–47; A. R. Schulman, *Military Rank, Title and Organization in the Egyptian New Kingdom* (Berlin, 1964); J. Yoyotte and J. Lopez, Bib.Or. 26 (1969), 3–19; W. Wolf, *Die Bewaffnung des altägyptischen Heeres* (Leipzig, 1926); Y. Yadin, *The Art of Warfare in Bible Lands* (Jerusalem, 1961).

[2] On the composite bow, see H. E. Winlock, *The Rise and Fall of the Middle Kingdom in Thebes* (New York, 1947); W. E. McLeod, "The Bow in Ancient Greece" (Ph.D. diss., Harvard University, 1966); on the introduction of the chariot, see W. Helck, *JNES* 37 (1978), 337–80.

eign languages;[3] the former became a paramilitary rank comparable with our "colonel" or "group captain," whereas the latter often denoted something like our "major." Some Asiatic inventions the Egyptians were slow to master: the battering ram, for example, was adopted only after New Kingdom times. Metal armor, too, never appealed to the Egyptians partly through reasons of supply and expense, although officers occasionally used it and charioteers borrowed the Asiatic helmet (Plate 26).[4]

Although confronted by admirable models of military organization in Asia, the Egyptian army of the early 18th Dynasty remained a ragtag bunch. Task forces thrown against the Hyksos or the remnants of Middle Bronze states in Palestine were drawn from the periodic call-ups in the townships, the local militia which from the Old Kingdom had provided the fiber of the Egyptian army. It was a national force, almost a "citizens' army." In its ranks one meets such familiars from "civy street" as a butler, a steward, a barber, a secretary of bread, a treasurer, a contractor—all fighting side by side in what for a time texts are pleased to call "our army."[5]

But the prospect of prolonged conflict and the efflorescence of the ardor bred by conquest made plain to the authorities the need for a permanent force schooled in the *art* of war. Already under the 17th Dynasty the Theban kings had felt obliged to create a corps of "braves" to spearhead attacks, perhaps spurred on by the example of the warlike Medjay who had allied themselves with the Upper Egyptians as auxiliaries.[6] The same period throws up our earliest examples of the *we'u*, the "full-time" soldier, in contradistinction to the old-fashioned draftees of the militia. When grouped into squads these full-time soldiers constituted the *ᵉw'eye(t)* or "standing army," in peacetime usually divided into two brigades, one stationed in Upper Egypt and the other in Lower Egypt; when used of troops stationed abroad, the term signifies "garrison."[7] Recruitment and training centered on the barracks, literally "stable" (for chariot

---

[3] *Snny* and *ktn* respectively; cf. A. H. Gardiner, *Ancient Egyptian Onomastica* (Oxford, 1947), 1:28*; A. R. Schulman, *JARCE* 2 (1964), 87–88; D. Meeks, *Année lexicographique* (Paris, 1981), 2:332–33, 400; (Paris, 1982), 3:258.

[4] See D. B. Redford, in *The Akhenaten Temple Project* (Toronto, 1988), 2:13–22; Schulman, *JARCE* 2 (1964), 53–79; for an "armorer," see H. S. Smith, *The Fortress of Buhen: The Inscriptions* (London, 1976), 1:81.

[5] J. Wilson, *The Burden of Egypt* (Chicago, 1951), 167; for the civilians mentioned, see *Urk* IV, 1019ff., 1–24; 1026; 1442; W. Helck, *Die Verwaltung des mittleren und neuen Reiches* (Leiden, 1958), 469.

[6] Faulkner, *JEA* 39 (1953), 44; D. Meeks, *Année lexicographique* (Paris, 1980), 1:388.

[7] On these two items, see C. Vandersleyen, *Les guerres d'Amosis* (Brussells, 1971), 26–30; D. B. Redford, *Egypt and Canaan* (Beer Sheva, 1990), 29–30, 71. The term *we'u* in civilian usage denoted an "ordinary" workman: J. Černý, *A Community of Workmen at Thebes in the Ramesside Period* (Cairo, 1973), 47.

Plate 26. Egyptian infantry and chariotry at the battle of Kadesh (c. 1300 B.C.); Abydos temple of Ramesses II.

horses), a term that indicates the importance the new mobile arm had attained. Here the young recruit might be served by batmen but might have to buy his own chariot. The training was rigorous, if not brutal: "Come! I'll tell you about the condition of the soldier, the much-lacerated one! He is taken while a child and shut up in the "slammer"(?). There's a fierce blow to his body, a stunning blow to his eye and a splitting blow on his eyebrow—his head splits open with a wound, and he is laid out and beaten like a papyrus."[8]

By the 19th Dynasty a well-trained professional army had evolved, and its proud officers appear everywhere. A taxation papyrus of Sety I's third year lists the householders of a district in Memphis, and this includes, living cheek-by-jowl with priestly and civil officials, marines, an army scribe, a lieutenant general, marine standard-bearers, a group captain, charioteers, and battalion commanders.[9] The professional soldiery were often given farms in the countryside: Papyrus Wilbour of late Ramesside times apprises us of farms in the eighteenth nome of Upper Egypt assigned to officers, quarter masters, charioteers, mercenaries, and simple soldiers.[10]

Of paramount importance in the recruitment and organization of this force was the army secretariat. At the top of this department stood the "overseer of army scribes" who was usually also "scribe of recruits (or young elite)." He was charged with "registering the army in the presence of His Majesty, in mustering the new generation of recruits, letting each man know his duties in the entire army."[11] The most famous incumbent, Amenophis son of Hapu (tempore Amenophis III), elaborates on these duties:[12] "I raised up my lord's levies, my pen reckoned numbers in the myriads. . . . I taxed departments by the numbers thereof, and separated off the contingents of their departments. . . . I raised up recruits, and I set the contingents on the march to punish the foreigners in their places . . . while keeping watch on the movements of the bedu." The draft lists and related documents implied by these statements were kept by the "chief archivist of military records" in the capital,[13] and there also resided the "scribe of infantry," in rank almost equal to a general.[14] In the countryside military scribes were attached to each barracks, fort, and temple es-

[8] A. H. Gardiner, *Late Egyptian Miscellanies* (Brussels, 1937), 27; R. A. Caminos, *Late Egyptian Miscellanies* (Oxford, 1954), 98.

[9] KRI 1, 273–80.

[10] B. Menu, *Le régime juridique des terres et du personnel attaché à la terre dans le Papyrus wilbour* (Lille, 1970), 107ff.

[11] *Urk* IV, 1006; see A. Brack, *Das Grab des Tjanuni* (Mainz, 1977).

[12] *Urk* IV, 1820–21.

[13] Gardiner, *Miscellanies*, 11:4.

[14] Gardiner, *Onomastica*, 1:25* (On. Am. 88).

tate to keep local lists up to quota and to assist in the mustering. When the call-up came, every company was assigned its own scribe.[15]

For the large expeditionary forces sent abroad during the empire, personnel were mustered from all estates, villages, and units of production all over Egypt. "I am mustering," an official sent to Elephantine reports by letter, "the army and chariotry of the temple (their), staffs and the tenant farmers of the seats of His Majesty's officials."[16] Customarily one in ten of temple personnel was taken, a practice unpopular among the people;[17] for the call-up often took the form of impressment: "The vizier brought three boys and said: 'make them priests in the temple . . .' but they were seized and taken north with the intent that they should be soldiers."[18] A captain writes to garrison officers in the Delta: "Do your job diligently and do not be lax with respect to the list that I put in your hands; as for anyone in the list, do not keep him with you, but bring us men from those released(?).[19] You are to expedite the [army soldiers] who are in the towns that are in your district . . . [do not] hold back the soldiers who come from your northern district!"[20]

The army marched and fought in local contingents.[21] The expeditionary force was usually divided up into divisions, each of which we assume on the basis of a passage in a Ramesside papyrus numbered approximately five thousand men.[22] The core of a division comprised men from a particular temple estate or region and marched under the banner of the local god. Thus Ramesses at Kadesh led four divisions, one from the northeast Delta (Seth), one from the apex of the Delta and Heliopolis (Re), one from the Memphite region (Ptah), and one from the Thebaid (Amun). In a broken passage from Thutmosis III's annals a rhetorical statement might suggest that four divinely protected divisions took part also in the Megiddo campaign.[23] Divisions were further divided into companies numbering about two hundred (although the strength varied) under the command of a "standard-bearer" (i.e., a captain), and subdivided into platoons of fifty.[24] Companies were called by names appropriate to their occupation ("strong-of-weapon," "prowling Lion," "Defeating the

[15] A. Moret, Le musée Guimet (Paris, 1909), 59; KRI I, 325:14; 345:1.

[16] P. Anast. IV, 4, 8–9.

[17] P. Harris I, 57:8–9.

[18] P. Bologna 1094, 5:2–4.

[19] KRI I, 322.

[20] Ibid., 323–24.

[21] Cf. Urk IV, 1659: "Then the army of Pharaoh was mustered . . . organized in squads and assigned officers, each man being with his village."

[22] P. Anast. I, 17, 4–5.

[23] Urk IV, 652:15–653:3. We hear also of an "army of the Western River," i.e., from the western side of the Delta: Urk IV, 981:11.

[24] Schulman, Military Rank, 26–30.

Foreign Lands") or after the reigning king (". . . of Menkheperre," "Re-of-the-Rulers"), or a god ("the sun disk glitters," "Amun-protects-his-army"). The chariotry was organized into squadrons of fifty vehicles comprising five tactical units of ten.[25]

It should be born in mind that few of the encounters we have passed in review in the preceding chapter, and which our sources blow up into major victories, were pitched battles. A campaign was an armed excursion planned in advance to coincide with an optimum period for traveling in Asia, and with the receipt of "tribute" and captives as its goal. Only occasionally do the cities along the route of march offer resistance, and when this happens the Egyptian record often makes plain Pharaoh's surprise and annoyance. A skirmish might then ensue, which usually issued in favor of the Egyptians. If it did not, the Asiatics might be emboldened to shut their gates and "wait it out." The army of the Thutmosids was notorious for its ignorance of siege warfare and fortress assault, and if a town shut its gates Thutmose III or Amenhotep II would usually devastate the surrounding territory and move on. By the reign of Ramesses II, however, the Egyptian forces had gained experience and a certain degree of expertise. The use of siege mounds, protective "blinds," assault ladders, and sapping techniques are all in evidence in the elaborate reliefs recording the victories of the Ramesside kings.

Since it was accepted that at a certain season of the year "kings went forth to war," it was relatively easy to muster a large force in anticipation of one's enemy and attempt to force the issue at one stroke. That such confrontations were rare is to be explained not only by considerations of expense but also by the degree of involvement of the manpower of Late Bronze Age states in activities other than war: irrigation, cultivation, and, increasingly, monumental construction projects.

Battlefield tactics are little known to us, as texts but rarely describe or picture them. We see the infantry marching in ranks with their elliptical, raw-hide bucklers and padded caps; but their weapons (short javelins, axes, and daggers) and lack of body armor do not lend themselves to phalanx charges. Chariots, each with driver and soldier, move in ranks also, and massed charges are hinted at. Their light wicker construction meant that speed rather than armament was to be their main asset. Perhaps the most effect corps of the Egyptian army was the archers, divided into battalions of varying strength. The composite bow with which they were armed had long since proved itself to be a most devastating weapon. Modern experiments have shown that it had an accurate range of 50 to 60 meters, an effective range of 175 meters, with an exceptional shot

[25] A. R. Schulman, *JARCE* 2 (1963), 75–98.

sometimes attaining 500 meters.[26] Night attacks were sometimes tried by all armies, and these were sometimes effective since even in daylight army intelligence was woeful. A general dispatched from Ugarit to guard the passes in Amurru against a rumored Egyptian expedition bewails in a letter found at Ras Shamra (Ras Shamra 20. 33) his own tenuous position:[27]

Rs.1   To the king my lord, speak.
        Thus say Shumiy[an] thy servant. At the
        feet of my lord I prostrate myself. . . .
   4   since this Simanu (month of June)
        I have been sending to my lord, "Save me!"
        ....

  15   [for] 5 [mon]ths now I have dwelt in Amurru
        and I guard them day and night,
          and this is how I guard them: their departures and arrivals
        I guard. Half of my chariots are stationed on the seashore
        and half my [chariots] are stationed against the Lebanons
  20   and I myself dwell in the valley.
        The Rain falls and the . . . comes
        but we do not desert. . . .
  Vs. [. . .]
   4   [. . .] and they have brought in
        [. . .] in the environs of Ardata
        [. . .] my men in the middle of the night
        [and th]ey made an attack in their midst;
        but my men mopped them up and repulsed them
        and their equipment and . . .
  10   they seized by force, but only one man did they capture from them
          and I questioned him about the king of Egypt and he said
        "The king of Egypt has come forth. . . .
        and on the first day that he comes, its equipment will be issued."
        ....
  15   so let the king dispatch the troops and chariots which will come up,
        . . . truly.
        the king of Egypt will arrive quickly
        and we will not be able to prevail; (but if) truly the king of Egypt
        has gone forth without going forth, it being only the archers

[26] W. McLeod, *Phoenix* 19 (1965), 1–14.

[27] *Ugaritica* 5 (1969), 69–79; H. Cazelles, *Mélanges de l'Université de Saint-Joseph* 46 (1970), 33ff.; A. F. Rainey, *UF* 3 (1971), 131–49; M. C. Astour, in G. D. Young, ed., *Ugarit in Retrospect* (Winona Lake, Ind., 1981), 22–23.

20   that have gone forth, then we shall prevail.
      So let the king send more troops and chariots
      so that we may engage him
   and prevail. Now if
      it is the archers that have gone forth,
25   let me not perish by them, and let my lord know
   that year by year they go forth
   and that daily they come against us!"

ASIATIC PRISONERS IN EGYPT

We have already heard the Egyptian scribes and their royal master gloating over the numbers of Asiatics who were brought back to Egypt as the result of foreign conquest. They came with increasing regularity throughout the New Kingdom, first as prisoners of war, then as uprooted peasants, dissidents, or victims of internal Canaanite strife (Plate 27). They came by land in the van of the army, bound with cords or laden with booty, and the scene was common enough to be parodied: "When the victory is won His Majesty l.p.h. distributes the plunder for the return march to Egypt; (but) the Asiatic woman is exhausted by the march and is put on the shoulders of the soldiers."[28] They also came by boat, dutifully shipped off as slaves by the Canaanite mayors at Pharaoh's command.[29] Some were sold into slavery to Egypt by their own people.[30]

Once in Egypt the foreign captive would find himself in an advanced, bureaucratic society markedly different from the rustic Canaanite town where he had originated. There was no chance to escape. Not that he would wish to: at least there was food in Egypt. His name, filiation, and place of origin were registered in a special department, and he was branded with the name of the king or god he was to serve. Then he was placed within the purview of one of the state institutions (temple, government department, king's house, or the like) and directly under the authority of one of the officers of that institution.[31] A letter from the 19th Dynasty to a priest of a temple of Thoth from his scribal agent illustrates how the system worked.[32] "I have made inquiry about the Syrian of the

[28] Gardiner, *Miscellanies*, 108:15–109:1.

[29] P. Bologna 1086.

[30] Cf. A. F. Rainey, *Israel Oriental Studies* 5 (1975), 27: "His porters sold him to the Egyptians and they seized him and took his goods." On slave merchants in Egypt, selling Syrian slaves, see KRI II, 800–802.

[31] Gardiner, *Miscellanies*, 9:1; KRI II, 280:13–16; for lists of newly arrived Canaanites, see G. Steindorf, *ZÄS* 38 (1900), 15–18; G. Posener, *Syria* 18 (1956), 183ff.

[32] P. Bologna 1086; W. Wolf, *ZÄS* 65 (1930), 89–97.

Plate 27. Two Canaanite prisoners flank a Philistine captive; mortuary temple of
Ramesses III, Medinet Habu.

House of Thoth concerning whom you wrote me. I found that, as one of the slaves of the shipment brought by the fortress commander, he was assigned to be a cultivator of the House of Thoth under your charge, in regnal year three, second month of *shomu*, day ten. For your information his name is the Syrian N³q³dy, son of S³rw-r-č, his mother being Qdy of the land of Arvad, a slave of the shipment of/to this house of the ship of captain K-nr." Sometimes, however, the system permitted internal squabbling:

His keeper said, "It was the chief herald of the army, Kha-em-ope, of pharaoh's garrison who received him in order to keep him (?)." I then went to the chief herald of the army, Kha-em-ope, of the pharoah's garrison, and he denied it, saying to me expressly (?), "It was the vizier Mery-Sekhmet, who received him in order to keep him (for his own) (?)." So I went to the vizier Mery-Sekhmet, and he and his scribes denied it, saying "We have not seen him!" Today I have sought out the chief of the . . . , saying, "Hand over the Syrian cultivator of the House of Thoth whom you received, in order to return him to his priest," and I am contending with him before the great court.

The work assigned the captive population varied depending on the intelligence, skill, and prior training of the individual. Most were destined for only menial tasks, as Thutmose III had long ago determined: "To fill (Amun's) workhouse, to be weavers and make for him byssos, fine white linen . . . and thick cloth, to trap and work the fields, to produce grain to fill the granary of the god's offering."[33] Variations on this set of locutions become a standard statement in triumph stelae or a gloss on war reliefs! In addition to those who became weavers and cultivators, others were assigned to tread grapes for wine.[34] Rarely have numbers survived, but from nineteen-years' campaigning Thutmose III donated 1,588 "Kharians" to the Temple of Amun.[35] Ramesses III (twelfth century B.C.) records 2,607 foreign captives given by himself to the Theban temples, and 205 to the Temple of Ptah at Memphis;[36] while Amenophis III can speak of his mortuary temple as "filled with male and female slaves, children of the chiefs of all the foreign lands of the captivity of His Majesty . . . of

[33] *Urk* IV, 742; cf. *Urk* IV, 781, 1102–3; KRI I, 2:15, 19:14–15; 23:5–6; 38:8–9; 41:4; 48:16–49:1; II, 206, etc.; A. M. Blackman, *The Temple of Derr* (Cairo, 1913), 7–8, pl. V:1; for Canaanites in Nubian temples, see L. Habachi, *Kush* 8 (1960), 49, fig. 4; 51, fig. 5.

[34] T. Säve-Söderbergh, *Orientalia Suecana* 1 (1952), pl. 12; in wine-jar dockets that specify the vintners, many appear to be Asiatic: W. C. Hayes, *JNES* 10 (1951), 46, fig. 6:54; 56, fig. 16:251; idem, *MDAIK* 15 (1957), 81, fig. 1(D); T. E. Peet, *City of Akhenaten* (London, 1923), 1: pls. 90:152; 86:35, 55–57; J.D.S. Pendelbury, *City of Akhenaten* (London, 1951), 3: pl. 87:60, 62; KRI II, 675; 678:13–16; 694:14–695:2; VII, 50:10; 68:15; 73:8, 15; W. Helck, *Die Beziehungen Ägyptens zur Vorderasiens*² (Wiesbaden, 1972), 360.

[35] *Urk* IV, 743.

[36] P. Harris I, 10:15; 51a:9.

unknown numbers (indeed), surrounded by the settlements of Syria."[37]
The letter quoted previously[38] gives us added details on the annual quota
expected to be produced by the unfortunate field hand:

> Further: do not be concerned about the grain assessment. I have made inquiries,
> and I found three men and a boy, total four, supplying 700 sacks. I (then) spoke
> with the chief record keepers of the granary, and I said to them, "Take the god's
> three cultivators for corvée for this year," and they said to me, "Alright, yes,
> we'll do it, we understand what you say," that is what they said to me. (So now)
> I am waiting for them to dispatch the circuit scribes to the countryside, and
> (then) you shall know everything that I am going to do for you. For (one) man
> makes 200 *khar*—that's (the rate) they set for me—and so you may conclude
> that the two men and a boy make 500. But as for the Syrian cultivator who was
> given you, he will produce for you in the summer months, and his tax shall be
> requisitioned for you for the rest of his life.

Tax documents occasionally throw up the West Semitic names of these
tenants, tied to the land, and forced to produce in perpetuity.[39]

But the drudgery of farm labor was not the lot of all. A special training
was reserved for the children of Canaanite chiefs sent as hostages to
Egypt, and this program was supervised directly from the palace. The
chiefs' sons were often taken into an army company for their training,
and we find them as palace guards (Plate 28) or outrunners before Pharaoh's chariot.[40] The royal household also recruited "Canaanite slaves of
Kharu, fine youths, and fine Nehsyu of Kush, suitable for wielding sun
shades, they being shod in white sandals and wearing *sfry* garments."[41]
Some were trained in the lowest grade of the priesthood; a few might
achieve a high priesthood.[42] By Amarna times Asiatics are beginning to
appear as domestic servants or even chamberlains in the immediate entourage of the king;[43] and by late Ramesside times the Canaanite "butler"
was a ubiquitous personage in the roster of palace officials.[44] Some, perhaps by virtue of their proximity to Pharaoh, managed to expand their
influence: one, Ben-ozen of Canaanite stock from Bashan, became chief
of the department of alimentation and beverage and chief royal herald,

[37] *Urk* IV, 1649.

[38] See previous n. 32.

[39] Cf. A. H. Gardiner, *Ramesside Administrative Documents* (Oxford, 1948), 37:13,
44:5; cf. Helck, *Beziehungen*², 357.

[40] See N. de G. Davies, *The Rock Tombs of El-Amarna* (London, 1903), 1: pl. 15; (London, 1904), 2: pl. 17; (London, 1905), 3: pl. 31.

[41] P. Anast. IV, 16:4–6.

[42] KRI I, 48–49; cf. Helck, *Beziehungen*², 357.

[43] Berlin 1284 (*Aegyptische Inschriften*, 2:306).

[44] Helck, *Beziehungen*², 353–54.

under Ramesses II.[45] A high point was reached when, at the close of the 19th Dynasty, one such worthy, Bay by name, succeeded in elevating himself to a position of chancellor and virtual kingmaker. While his enemies later were to denegrate his memory, he nonetheless while alive was the real power behind the throne and could even correspond with foreign states.[46]

Specialized or "professional" occupations also beckoned to the intelligent young Canaanite, so favorably did Egyptians look upon any kind of skill in a craft (Plate 29). Asiatics are found as goldsmiths, coppersmiths, and shipwrights, and one even rose to superintendent of all construction work of the king.[47] One young Canaanite, Pas-Baʿal, possibly taken prisoner under Thutmose III, became chief draftsman in the Temple of Amun, and six generations later his descendants are still occupying this office.[48] Scribes of Syrian extraction turn up commonly, especially in the treasury.[49] A chief physician Ben-ʾanath is known, belonging to the prestigious "Mansion-of-Life."[50]

Groups of captive foreigners who had impressed the Egyptians by some inherent ability as a group were usually kept intact and settled in special foundations. Military units fall into this category. Thutmose IV established such a foundation out of the captives from Gezer, in the environs of his mortuary temple.[51] We hear of the "Fields of the Hittites" in the Memphite region under Ay,[52] and one wonders whether this settlement has anything to do with the Kurushtama people. The Ramessides continued the practice, planting enclaves of foreigners both in Middle Egypt and the Delta.[53] Ramesses II was one of the first kings to experience a confrontation with the "Sea Peoples," a group of Viking-like sea raiders who were plundering the Delta coast. He was so impressed by the fighting qualities and the armaments of one of their clans, the Shardana, that he pressed them into service as his own personal, elite guards and settled

---

[45] See J. Berlandini-Grenier, *BIFAO* 74 (1974), 1–19.

[46] On Bay, see Helck, *Verwaltung*, 355; A. H. Gardiner, *JEA* 44 (1958), 12ff.; an unpublished letter from Ugarit is from one *Beya*, from Egypt, who can only be the present worthy: P. Bordreuil, *CRAIBL* (1987), 297.

[47] Helck, *Beziehungen*², 356–57; on Benya, son of the Hurrian Aritenni, see T. Säve-Söderbergh, *Orientalia Suecana* 8 (1960), 54ff.; S. Ratié, *La reine Hatchepsout: Sources et problèmes* (Leiden, 1979), 285.

[48] D. A. Lowle, *Oriens Antiquus* 15 (1976), 91ff.

[49] Helck, *Beziehungen*², 354–55.

[50] G. A. Gabella, *JEA* 59 (1973), pl. 37:1.

[51] *Urk* IV, 1556:10–11.

[52] See p. 179.

[53] See S. Sauneron and J. Yoyotte, *RdE* 7 (1951), 67ff.; P. Harris I, 31, 8 (foundation stocked by children of the maryannu and ʿApiru at Natho, amounting to 2,093 persons); KRI VII, 84 (settlement of Asiatics in the 'Bird pool'[?] providing wine).

Plate 28. Canaanite spearman, a member of the bodyguard attending Akhenaten at his Theban jubilee; jubilee temple of Akhenaten at Thebes (early fourteenth century B.C.).

Plate 29. Musicians at Akhenaten's court. Egyptian girls perform on the left, while Asiatic musicians (from Mitanni, or Khàtte?) play a large, upright harp and lyre on the right. Their clean-shaven chins and women's garments may mark them as eunuchs or transvestites, while the blindfolds may betoken blindness.

some of them in their own camps, a practice Ramesses III was to follow. Asiatics are sometimes found on construction sites or at the granaries as unskilled labour, but this is often in conjunction with the army that traditionally fulfilled such a role; and it may be as part of their paramilitary function that the Asiatics in question are present.[54]

MERCHANT AND BEDU

As Egypt's possessions in Asia expanded, so did its trade. Egyptian temples could trade abroad, and possessed both fleets and merchants.[55] High officials also had the right to engage privately in trade with Asia,[56] and a sign of one's favor with the god was health, wealth, a house and servants, and a ship coming home from Asia. In times of peace, and especially after the Egypto-Hittite treaty, business boomed up and down the coast, and commerce resulted in an exchange of workers and merchants from Gaza to Ugarit. Egypt became familiar with distant places heretofore found only among lists of enemies, and valued them for their best products: Kizzuwatna for its beer,[57] Amurru for its wine,[58] Takhsy and Naharin for their oil,[59] Palestine for its grapes and figs,[60] Ashkelon for its silverware.[61]

To Egypt in the wake of the prisoners of war came the Canaanite merchant and by the reign of Amenhotep III this gawdy individual was already a familiar sight on the banks of the Nile. Phoenician kings of Ugarit and Tyre organized trading ventures to Egypt in which oil, wine, and copper figured prominently;[62] and what is passed off in scenes as Syrian "tribute" to Egypt is probably often nothing more than "up-front" considerations, *baksheesh* to Pharaoh and his ministers, to allow the trade to take place.[63] We hear of the trading ships of Arvad, and commercial agents from Cyprus.[64]

[54] W. C. Hayes, *JEA* 46 (1960), pl. XII, 17; P. Berlin 10621 recto 9 (tomb excavation); P. Leiden 348 verso 6, 6; 349 recto 15 ('Apiru and soldiers building a pylon); L. Christophe, *BIFAO* 48 (1949), 20 (900 'Apiru at the quarries).

[55] Cf. the dedicatory inscription of Ramesses II at Abydos, lines 87–88: "I gave thee a ship laden with cargo upon the sea, and great [marvels] of God's-land are brought in to thee; and the merchants ply their trade under orders, their labor being gold, silver and copper."

[56] D. I. Owen, *Tel Aviv* 8 (1981), 1ff.; I. Singer, *Tel Aviv* 10 (1983), 3ff.; Caminos, *Late Egyptian Miscellanies*, 138.

[57] Gardiner, *Onomastica* 1:136*.

[58] Ibid., 2:236*.

[59] P. Anast. IV, 15:3–4.

[60] P. Anast. IV, 17:5.

[61] J. J. Jannsen, *JEA* 49 (1963), 64–70.

[62] J. Nougayrol, *Palais royal d'Ugarit* (Paris, 1965), 116, no. 95:1–5.

[63] M. Liverani, *Three Amarna Essays* (Malibu, Calif., 1979), 21–33.

[64] EA 101:15–18; 39:14.

The northern suburb of Memphis became a favorite haunt of Canaan-ite merchants, who early established a community there centered upon their own temple of Baʿal, "the House of Baʿal of Memphis,"[65] and which one thousand years later when Herodotus visited Egypt still survived as "the Camp of the Tyrians."[66] Memphis in fact loomed large in the life of a foreign merchant doing business with Egypt. He knew it by the term Ḥikuptaḥ ("ku-chapel of Ptah"), a term specifically denoting the enceinte of Ptah, the chief god of the place;[67] and, while Canaanite already pos-sessed a word for "Egypt," namely Miṣrayim, Ḥikuptaḥ gradually came to connote the country as a whole. Canaanite dialects must have been commonly heard in Egyptian markets, and soon the expression "To do business in the Syrian tongue" came to mean simply "To haggle."[68]

Beside the Canaanite entrepreneur looking for trade, Egypt also played host during the empire to a class of Asiatics with which it had grown familiar for a much longer period than the merchant. These were the bedu who trekked into the eastern Delta from across the Sinai. As in those far-off days of Merikare, six hundred years before, small bands of transhu-mants with their flocks and herds still made the seasonal migration to the west, when their own wells and water holes ran dry, seeking entry to the Nile Delta. The standard illustration of this recurring migration is a model letter supposed to have been written by the scribe of a border for-tress in the Wadi Tumilat in the eighth year of Merneptah (probably):[69]

The scribe Einna greets his master, the Treasury-scribe Ka-ga[b . . .]. This is a dispatch for [my master's] information . . . to wit: we have finished admitting the Shasu-tribes of Edom (through) the fortress of Merneptah-hotpe-hi-ma'at which is ⟨in⟩ Tjekku to the water holes of the House of Atum-of-Merneptah-hotpe-hi-ma'at which ⟨are in⟩ Tjekku, for their own subsistence and that of their flocks, by the great Ku of Pharaoh L.P.H., the good sun of every land! in the year 8, epagomenal days, [birth of] Seth.[70] I have had sent a columned doc-ument to the [place where] my master is with the other specified days on which the fortress may be passed.

The bedu in the Delta roused mixed feelings among the Egyptians. Elders, traditional in their outlook, despised these wanderers and their

[65] W. Helck, Oriens Antiquus 5 (1966), 2–3 (Berlin 8169); P. Sallier IV, verso 2,8.

[66] Herodotus, 2:111; Sauneron and Yoyotte, RdE 7 (1951), 69 n. 1; A. B. Lloyd, Herod-otus Book II. A Commentary (Leiden, 1988), 3:44–45.

[67] Cf. EA 139:8 (Hi-ku-ta-aḫ); II Aqhat Vc, 20f (ḤKPT); apparently already in linear B it appears as Ai-ku-pi-ti-jo: R. R. Stieglitz, Kadmos 15 (1976), 85; R. D. Woodard, Kadmos 25 (1986), 63.

[68] J. J. Janssen, Two Ancient Egyptian Ships' Logs (Leiden, 1961), 59:14, and p. 73.

[69] P. Anast. VI, 4:11–5:5; see now H. Goedicke, SAK 14 (1987), 83–98.

[70] In the last quarter of the thirteenth century B.C. this calendric would have fallen at the end of June.

goats; the bedu were viewed as dirty and unkempt in their carriage and indifferent to the civilized ways of living. But to the young they embodied the ideal of a life of freedom from authority, as appealing then as ever the prospect of running off to the Gypsies was in the heart of a nineteenth-century child. A father scolds his wayward son in a Ramesside text:[71] "I provided your needs in all things, which others (only) hope for; I did not let you say 'O would that I had . . .' in the night, when you were lying down tossing and turning. (Yet) you are (now) on the journey of a swallow with her young,[72] you have reached the Delta on a long circuit, and have consorted with the Asiatics, having eaten bread (mixed) with your own blood![73] You have lost your wits!" Bedu society harbored criminal elements and the down and out; nice people simply did not fraternize with them: "The (band of thieves) was come into the camp and the horses were loosed . . . in the night, and your clothes were stolen. Your groom was awakened (and when) he realized what he had done, he took the rest. (Now) he has wholly gone over to a life of evil: he mixes with the tribes of the Shasu, having adopted the guise of an Asiatic."[74]

RACE RELATIONS IN IMPERIAL EGYPT

Initially, and even after the passage of time, most Asiatics remained distinct from Egyptians within Egypt. Whether brought as a prisoner or slave, or allowed to enter as a merchant or laborer, all Asiatics came in with their own names, which were rendered laboriously into Egyptian script, and now provide a fascinating source of onomastic and linguistic information primarily of interest to specialists in Hebrew and West Semitic languages.[75] Sometimes, but by no means always, an Asiatic newcomer might feel it expedient to adopt an Egyptian name, to which his foreign name would be appended employing the phrase "who is (also) called . . ." This was especially common in upper classes of immigrants who had been assigned high office as palace domestics or in the army. These often assumed Egyptian names compounded with the name of the king who had elevated them, thus: Ramesses-em-per-Re ("Ramesses-is-in-the-House-of-Re"), Ranesses-em-On ("Ramesses-is-in-Heliopolis"), Usermare-nakht ("Usermare [i.e., Ramesses II]-is-mighty), Ramesses-men ("Ramesses-endures"), and the like.[76]

[71] A. H. Gardiner and J. Černý, *Hieratic Ostraca* (Oxford, 1957), 1: pl. 78; J. Černý, *JNES* 14 (1955), 161–63.

[72] I.e., roaming aimlessly?

[73] I.e., have joined the tribe in a ceremony of blood brotherhood?

[74] P. Anast. I, 20:2–4.

[75] A partial list of Asiatic personal names will be found in Helck, *Beziehungen*², 353–67.

[76] L. Habachi, *ASAE* 52 (1954), 508, 539; Berlandini-Grenier, *BIFAO* 74 (1974), 10, n. 4; A. R. Schulman, *CdE* 61 (1986), 187ff.

At an "official" level the propaganda of the inscriptions inveighs against and derides the Asiatics and their culture in a predictable manner. The Asiatic enemies are "weak" (or "wimps" in our parlance) "doomed ones, abominated by Re"; their only destiny to become "serfs of His Majesty." A common cliché, playing on Egypt's isolation, describes the foreign chiefs as formerly "unfamiliar with Egypt," but now obliged to beg "for the breath of life." That these stereotyped notions arose out of a real racist jingoism is proved by a letter of Amenophis II to his viceroy in Nubia, which shows a lively spontaneity.[77] The letter was dictated and sent (and later proudly inscribed by the viceroy on a stela) on the occasion of the twenty-third anniversary of the king's accession, when, as the text states, the king was in his harem in Thebes drinking wine. The king prides himself on living "without opponent in any land" and goes on to characterize himself as "[the destroyer of] Naharin, the one that laid waste Khatte, viol[ator of the] Babylonian [woman], the Byblian maid, the little girl of Alalakh and the old crone of Arrapkha! And the Takhsians are nothing at all!—really what are they good for?"

While Egyptians never suppressed their traditional disdain for all things Asiatic, they approached the matter of intermarriage with a degree of tolerance. It is not unusual to find a Canaanite or Hurrian name in a family tree during the New Kingdom, and "the Syrian" (Egyptian *Paḥuru*) was by no means shunned as a nickname even for Egyptians. One charming legal document from the 18th Dynasty describes the acceptance of a foreigner into an Egyptian household; Thutmose III's barber, Si-Bastet speaks:[78] "I have a slave who was assigned to me whose name is Iuwy-Amun. I captured him myself when I was following the Ruler [on campaign]. . . . He is not to be beaten, nor is he to be turned away from any door of the palace. I have given the daughter of my sister Nebetto, whose name is Takament, to him as wife. She shall have a share in (my) inheritance just like my wife and my sister."

In contrast, however, to the traditional jingoism the new experience of empire had produced a universalism that was subtly being inculcated in the religious thought of the imperial cults. Amun-re of Thebes, the "King of the Gods" and chief of the Egyptian pantheon, had championed the wars that had created the empire and had now gravitated to the position of transcendent, universal god. As an essentially cosmic, solar deity he had created *all* mankind and differentiated the races. The hymnodist sang, at the outset of the 18th Dynasty: "Hail to thee Amun-re . . . Lord of Truth, father of the gods, who made man and created animals, lord of everything, creator of the Tree of Life, who made herbage to sustain cat-

---

[77] *Urk* IV, 1343–44; W. Helck, *JNES* 14 (1955), 22–31.
[78] *Urk* IV, 1369.

tle. . . . Atum who made the people and made their natures different, who made their colors distinct."[79]

As sun-god he was "sovereign lord of what he has created,"[80] "who created everyone and made them sustenance . . . who created them without number."[81] It was this universalist sentiment that Akhenaten fell heir to and developed within the context of his monotheism: "Thou didst create the earth according to thy desire when thou wert afar off: all men, cattle and wild game, everything upon earth which moves on legs, and what is above flying with wings; the foreign lands of Kharu and Kush and the land of Egypt, thou hast put every man in his place, thou hast provided their needs, each one with his food and a reckoned lifetime and tongues different in speech; likewise their nature and skin colors are distinguished."[82]

ÉMIGRÉ GODS

Egypt had for the moment shed its isolation and perforce had become cosmopolitan; and now through the Two Lands blew the four winds of the Egyptian empire. Nowhere is this more evident than in the pantheon where, beginning on the morrow of Thutmose I's conquests, Asiatic deities begin to make their appearance.

Foreign gods first appear in Egypt under royal patronage. Hatshepsut boasts of wearing the talismans of non-Egyptian deities (probably those of Libya or Pwenet),[83] and Amenophis II proudly displayed Astarte and Reshef as protectors of his chariot team.[84] In a celebrated case, Amenophis III besought his brother-in-law, Tushratta of Mitanni, to send him the cult statue of Ishtar of Nineveh in the hope that she might assuage some unspecified sickness from which he was suffering.[85] In none of these cases is the monarch conceding anything to a foreign community that Egypt had conquered; the "vaincueur du monde" is by no means vanquished by the gods of his subjects. Rather, the rationale is that the gods of the conquered peoples now recognize who has proved successful and "right" by his victims, and now voluntarily extend to him their favor and protection.

As soon, however, as Egypt opened its doors and accepted the presence on the Nile of an immigrant community of aliens, it also accepted their

[79] ANET², 365–66.
[80] H. M. Stewart, JEA 46 (1960), 86.
[81] ANET², 368.
[82] M. Sandman, Texts from the Time of Akhenaten (Brussels, 1938), 94–95, col. 8.
[83] See p. 152.
[84] W. K. Simpson, Orientalia 29 (1960), 63ff.; Helck, Oriens Antiquus 5 (1966), 5.
[85] EA 23.

gods.[86] The Canaanite hero-deity Ba'al, "the Lord," found a residence along with his consort Astarte among the Canaanite merchants in north Memphis.[87] Ba'al had earlier made a pilgrimage to the Nile as part of the cultic baggage of the Hyksos; but his second coming during the 18th Dynasty owes nothing to his former visit. Now he was as much a god of the conqueror as of the conquered. Both he and Astarte display openly their warlike traits, which appealed to the Egyptian military and account for their rapid assimilation into the pantheon. Anat too, and the warrior-god Reshef, appealed to the Egyptians, and the latter possessed a temple somewhere in the Delta.[88] A god of similar power, Horon (whose name is preserved in the Biblical Beth-Horon), appears in the Giza region, and Canaanites gawking at the great sphinx, believed it to be an image of this god.[89] Elsewhere the voluptuous Qadesha, "the holy one,"[90] appears as a beautiful nude woman, with a purview similar to that enjoyed by Hathor, the Egyptians' own goddess of love.

Only occasionally did the Egyptians employ *Interpretatio Aegyptiaca* to translate a Canaanite deity into an Egyptian equivalent (Seth occasionally still "stands in" for the Canaanite hero-god). For the most part the Asiatic deities were such strong personalities and now had such a large resident constituency that they entered the Egyptian pantheon with their own names and traits. Ba'al's name appears transliterated into hieroglyphics and gave rise as late as Ptolemaic times to a denominative verb in Egyptian meaning "to make war."[91] Both Anath and Astarte survive in formal lists of Egyptian gods well into Roman times;[92] and were popular enough to be used as theophoric elements in purely Egyptian names.[93] Some enjoyed "familial" adoption into the households of native gods:

[86] In general, see R. Stadelmann, *Syrisch-Palästinensische Gottheiten in Ägypten* (Leiden, 1967).

[87] Ibid., 32–33; Helck, *Oriens Antiquus* 5 (1966), 2–3; W.M.F. Petrie, *Memphis* (London, 1909), 1: pl. 15; Ba'al Saphon (Mount Casios) and Astarte are attested as early as Amenophis II's reign at Memphis: P. Leningrad 1116A verso 42.

[88] On Anat, see J. Leclant, *LdÄ* 1 (1972), 255; on Reshef, see E. Bresciani, *Oriens Antiquus* 1 (1962), 215–17; D. Conrad, *ZAW* 83 (1971), 157ff.; W. K. Simpson, *LdÄ* 5 (1984), 244–46; A. R. Schulman, in F. Junge, ed., *Studien zu Sprache und Religion Ägyptens* (Göttingen, 1984), 855ff.

[89] S. Hassan, *The Sphinx, Its History in the Light of Recent Excavations* (Cairo, 1949); C. M. Zivie, *Giza au deuxième millenaire* (Cairo, 1976), 311–18; on the god, see now especially J. van Dijk, *Fourth International Congress of Egyptology. Abstracts* (Munich, 1985), 247–48.

[90] On Qadesha, see R. Stadelmann, *LdÄ* 5 (1984), 26–27.

[91] S. Sauneron, *BIFAO* 62 (1964), 22–24.

[92] See E. Chassinat and F. Daumas, *Le temple de Dendara* (Cairo, 1934–1978), 1:152 (25); 3:192; 5:25.

[93] Cf. Padi-Astarte, Tadi-Astarte, etc.

Anath and Astarte were made the daughters of the sun-god,[94] and Reshef and Qadesha were accepted into a triad with Min.[95]

LITERATURE

The classical literature of Egypt, still being admired and copied by scribes and their pupils in New Kingdom times, dated from the halcyon days of the Middle Kingdom. It is largely of native inspiration, owing little or nothing to any influence of any sort from abroad. In it we see a self-confident if naive Egyptian, wholly in love with his country, homesick when abroad and contemptuous of foreigners.

The literature and folklore produced during the empire are quite different. Understandably themes include the exploits of those that built the empire, and turn out to be what we might call "shaggy dog" stories. They tell of the Hyksos Apophis and how he picked a quarrel with Seqenenre in Thebes by complaining that the bellowing of the hippos in Thebes was keeping him awake in Avaris, hundreds of miles way.[96] They tell of Thutmose III and his conquests in Asia,[97] and of his general Djhuty who used the Ali Baba ruse of hiding his men in donkey paniers in order by stealth to capture Joppa.[98] Other accounts, preserved for us only in later versions, apparently sought to explain the Amarna fiasco by resort to etiology,[99] or described how the great Ramesses married the daughter of the king of Khatte.[100]

Besides these legends derived from history, Egypt of the New Kingdom produced its share of pure fairy tales in which foreign influence is clear. No longer does the hero eschew travel abroad, or exhibit homesickness; but chooses to stay in Asia and marry locally. Some tales show strong Canaanite or Hurrian influence to the extent that one might almost postulate a foreign, non-Egyptian original. A prince, doomed at birth by a prediction of the "Seven Hathors"[101] that he will die either by a dog,

[94] P. Chester Beatty I, 3:4 (A. H. Gardiner, *Late Egyptian Stories* [Brussels, 1932], 40).

[95] Helck, *Oriens Antiquus* 5 (1966), 7–8.

[96] P. Sallier I, 1:1–3:3; Gardiner, *Stories*, 85–89; D. B. Redford, *Orientalia* 39 (1970), 35–38; H. Goedicke, *The Quarrel of Apophis and Seqenenre* (San Antonio, Tex., 1986).

[97] G. Botti, *JEA* 41 (1955), 64–71; it seems likely that Manetho frag. 42.86–88 (W. G. Waddell, *Manetho* [London, 1940], 86–88) conceals a popular tale based on the siege of Megiddo.

[98] Gardiner, *Stories*, 82–85.

[99] See p. 414.

[100] Cf. the Bentresh stela: A. J. Spalinger, *JSSEA* 8 (1977), 11–18; M. Lichtheim, *Ancient Egyptian Literature* (Berkeley, Calif., 1980), 3:90–94; D. B. Redford, in *Biblical Archaeology Today* (Jerusalem, 1985), 205, n. 101.

[101] The Seven Hathors, like the "Weird Sisters" of European folklore, appear at every new birth to set the fate of the newborn: see J. Vandier, *RdE* 16 (1964), 119–20; L. Kakosy, *Studia Aegyptiaca* (Budapest, 1981), 7:63; cf. Odyssey, 7:196–98.

snake, or crocodile, pursues his fortune by wandering in Asia.[102] At the palace of the king of Naharin (Mitanni) he participates and wins a contest among other princes for the hand of the daughter of the king of Naharin, who has been confined in a tower with but a single window.[103] Later, through the agency of his new wife, the prince escapes from a snake, but is seized while walking near a water hole by a crocodile. At this point the papyrus unfortunately breaks off, and we cannot discover whether the point to be made was the inevitability of one's fate or the triumph of the individual. Not only is the locale of most of the story situated in Mesopotamia, but also such motifs as the girl in the tower looking out of the window and the hero pursued by his dog(s) to the water hole recall known Canaanite themes. In the fantastic story of the "Two Brothers" the chief protagonist finds himself at one point in the "valley of the Cedar" in Lebanon living with a beautiful child of the gods with scented hair whom the monster Yam (the sea) lusts after. It is not difficult here to discern the motif of the lascivious sea monster and the goddess.[104]

A number of Asiatic myths appear rendered with very little modification into Egyptian. The aforementiond story of Yam and the Goddess, so well known from Ugarit and the Phoenician cities of the Levantine coast, has turned up in a beautiful, though fragmentary papyrus now in the J. P. Morgan library.[105] Yam exacts tribute from the gods, who reluctantly acknowledge him as overlord. When tribute is finally withheld in defiance, Astarte is sent to placate the expected wrath of the monster; but Yam still

[102] M. Lichtheim, *Ancient Egyptian Literature* (Berkeley, Calif., 1976), 2:200–203; E. Brunner-Traut, *LdÄ* 4 (1982), 1108–13; E. Cruz-Uribe, *ZÄS* 113 (1986), 18–20; on the theme of fate, see F. T. Miosi, in G. E. Freeman, ed., *Studies in Philology in Honour of Ronald James Williams* (Toronto, 1982), 69–111; cf. also W. Helck, in J. Osing and G. Dreyer, eds., *Form und Mass* (Wiesbaden, 1987), 218–25.

[103] For the "tower" motif, see S. Thompson, *Motif-Index of Folk Literature* (Copenhagen, 1955–1958), 6: M 372; the girl-in-the-tower is essentially the "Astarte-at-the-window" theme adapted in a folkloric setting: N. Robertson, *HTR* 75 (1982), 315–21; the prince beset at a water hole by dog, crocodile, and monster is similarly an adaptation of Ba'al/Adonis slain by his dogs in a fen: see p. 44, and D. B. Redford, in S. Groll, ed., *Studies in Egyptology Presented To Miriam Lichtheim* (Jerusalem, 1990), 824ff.

[104] See above, p. 43ff. On the story, see Lichtheim, *Literature*, 2:203–13; O. Spies, in M. Görg, ed., *Festschrift Elmar Edel* (Bamberg, 1979), 397ff.; E. Blumenthal, *ZÄS* 99 (1972), 1ff.; J. Assmann, *ZÄS* 104 (1977), 1ff.; L. H. Lesko, in L. H. Lesko, ed., *Egyptological Studies in Honor of Richard A. Parker* (Providence, R. I., 1986), 98–104. My skepticism regarding Asiatic elements in the story (*A Study of the Biblical Joseph Story* [Leiden, 1970], 93, n. 3) now seems ill-advised: not only are Asiatic motifs involved but, at the point where the initial episode reaches resolution and gives into the Valley-of-the-Cedar episode (6,4 to 8,6) even the syntax of the Egyptian seems influenced by some Canaanite dialect.

[105] G. Posener, *AIPHOS* 13 (1955), 461ff.; O. Kaiser, *Die mythische Bedeutung des Meeres in Ägypten, Ugarit und Israel* (Berlin, 1959), 81ff.; Stadelmann, *Syrisch-Palästinensische Gottheiten*, 125ff.; W. Helck, in M. Görg, ed., *Fontes atque Pontes* (Wiesbaden, 1983), 215ff. (where Hurrian influence is posited).

wants his tribute, and now Astarte also. The tattered fragments at the end of the papyrus do not permit connected translation, but it would appear that Seth (Ba'al) eventually championed the gods' cause and defeated Yam. Other papyri deal with the sex life of Anath and her lusty paramour of the Ba'al-type of deity. Here again Seth adopts the role of Ba'al.[106] Elsewhere both Astarte and Anath are "assigned" to Seth-Ba'al as his consorts in faithful imitation of the relationship signalized in the Canaanite pantheon.[107]

Another Egyptian "borrowing" involves a form not native to Egyptian belles lettres, namely the allegory. The Tale of Truth and Falsehood preserved in a British Museum papyrus describes how Falsehood falsely charged his brother Truth with having stolen his knife, which, to make his charge stick, he described as very valuable and of gargantuan proportions. Blinded by the Court as punishment, Truth is eventually vindicated by his son who accuses his uncle Falsehood of having eaten his bull, similarly described (and for the same purpose) as having been of fabulous proportions and value. The tale is derived from a Hurrian original, reflected in the story of Appu, and the still-living plot gravitated into Russia where it turned up as "Pravda and Krivda."[108]

Egyptian exposure to Asiatic ideas can be detected in other pieces in which the foreign influence has worked subtly on a theme while leaving the form essentially native. One such topos is the "Saturnian" age, as it were, which preceded the first sin of mankind, and in which, in contrast to the modern age, no disease or malevolence existed. "Truth descended to earth in the days (of the ancestors) and joined with those who were on earth. The land was watered, stomachs were full, there was no want in the Two Lands; walls did not collapse, the thorn did not prick. . . . food overflowed (in) the stomachs of the plebs, there was no sin throughout the land: the crocodile did not snatch, the snake did not bite—in the Time of the primeval gods."[109] The concept of the afterlife also undergoes a certain amount of coloration from an Asiatic palette, although the essentials of Egyptian belief remain. One minority view, represented in Egyptian literature as concomitant of a hedonistic life-style, had long since

[106] A. Roccati, *RdE* 24 (1972), 152–59.

[107] See n. 94; J. Vandier, *MDAIK* 25 (1969), 188–97, pl. 7a; H. Te Velde, *LdÄ* 5 (1984), 910.

[108] Lichtheim, *Literature*, 2:211–14; H. G. Gütterbock, in S. N. Kramer, ed., *Mythologies of the Ancient World* (New York, 1961), 154; J. Friedrich, *ZA* 49 (1950), 213ff.; Lesko, in *Egyptological Studies*, 98–104.

[109] O. Firchow, *Thebanischen Tempelinschriften* (Berlin, 1957), 76, 81; cf. E. Otto, in *Religions en Égypte hellénistique et romain* (Paris, 1969), 93ff.; Kakosy, *Studia Aegyptiaca*, 7:81–92.

decried the efficacy of the mortuary cult in an agnostic view.[110] Now to this approach is occasionally added a description of the beyond that owes much more to Mesopotamia and the Levant than Egypt: in the afterlife "there is no eating, no drinking, no o[ld, no you]ng, no seeing the rays of the sun disk, no breathing the north wind; darkness engulfs the face constantly; no one rises early to go forth."[111] This point-by-point rebuttal of the great Egyptian hope derives from the darkness and despair of the Canaanite *she'ol*, not the bright promise of the traditional Elysian Fields of the Egyptian sun cult.[112]

LANGUAGE

The impact Levantine and Mesopotamian culture made on Egypt of the New Kingdom is nowhere more vividly reflected than in the lexicon of the Egyptian language. Hundreds of Canaanite words turn up in New Kingdom documents, laboriously transcribed by Egyptian scribes into hieroglyphics in the fashion known as syllabic orthography. Although the Egyptian dialects resist syntactic change—most of the loanwords are nouns—their clear need for terms for new techniques, manufactures, and material results in a foreign vocabulary that constituted a gauge for the relative influence of Canaan over the whole spectrum of culture.[113]

As one might expect, fully one-quarter of those terms that can be identified have to do with the military. Technical expressions describing the chariot, its parts and accoutrements, account for half of these; while others refer to types of weapons, military ranks, architecture, and methods or activities of warfare. A limited number of nautical terms, as well, (roughly 3 percent of the whole) are attested.

Egyptian familiarity with Asia and its resources accounts for about 27 percent of the words. Terms for wood, lumber, and types of furniture amount to 12 percent, while 6 percent cover Asiatic minerals. Geographical terms amount to approximately 10 percent of the whole, of which over half designate bodies of water (wells, streams, cisterns, etc.). The

[110] On the hedonistic literature of the Harpers' Songs, see J. Assmann, in J. Assmann, ed., *Fragen an die altägyptischen Literatur* (Wiesbaden, 1977), 55–84; M. V. Fox, *Orientalia* 46 (1977), 93ff.; see also L. Kakosy, in *Religions en Égypte hellénistique*, 60–61.

[111] Gardiner, *Stories*, 91; Posener, *Drevnii Vostok* 1 (Moscow, 1975), 105ff.

[112] Cf. J. G. Griffiths, in Görg, *Fontes atque Pontes*, 193–95.

[113] The main compilation of such words remains Burchardt's massive *Die altkanaanäischen Fremdworte und Eigennamen in Aegyptischen* (Leipzig, 1909). Helck also includes over three hundred words in his *Beziehungen²*, 505ff. New treatments are to be expected from Manfred Görg and James Hoch. The percentages herein referred to are based on the author's selection of only those words that are beyond doubt Canaanite, and they may in future prove subject to slight modification.

rest comprises terms for land formations (types of fields, mountains, caves) and land travel.

The remainder of the terms illustrates what archaeological and historical evidence has already apprised us of with respect to the pervasive influence of Asiatics in Egypt. Food and its preparation account for 8 percent of the foreign vocabulary, while construction techniques, architectural features, and materials yield 7 percent. Since many of the Asiatic commodities requisitioned as tax, or coveted as trade items, came in Canaanite containers, it is not surprising that 7 percent of the terms refer to containers (ceramic or basketry). From the scales of law and international diplomacy come 4 percent of the total, the cult provides 3 percent, and international commerce 2 percent.

For four hundred years the Asiatic flood continued to inundate the Nile Delta and Valley; but today of its rise and fall scarcely a trace remains. The Canaanite communities whence the slaves, merchants, and ideas had emanated were shortly to be swept away in the catastrophe of the end of an age, and committed to complete oblivion. Nought remained of their erstwhile presence in the collective memory of the Egyptians, and in the mind-set of the brave new world that was about to dawn they could safely be assigned the scapegoat role. In the historical pastiche that ancient Israel fabricated to justify its ingress, all the iniquity of the ages is heaped upon the Canaanites, who thereby became the most maligned race in history.

The Great Migrations

The Great Migrations

CHAPTER 9

The Coming of the Sea Peoples

THE FIFTY YEARS following the Egypto-Hittite peace treaty were halcyon days for the entire Near East. In the Levant, borders were now open from Egypt to the Black Sea, and from the Euphrates to the Aegean; and international trade flourished as never before. Not only did the great treaty guarantee the peace, but a widely celebrated marriage between Hattusilis III's daughter and the mighty Ramesses II cemented relations on a family level; and although the unfortunate girl may have disappeared into the harem at Mi-wer, rarely to be seen again, nonetheless the cordial relations between Egypt and Khatte remained intact until the end of the Hittite empire.[1] While we know that relations between Khatte and Assyria had reached the stage of a cold war, the correspondence between Tudkhaliyas IV and Ramesses is concerned with nothing of greater import than perceived insults and the exchange of technicians.[2]

EGYPT AND THE AEGEAN

During the New Kingdom, Greece and the islands had enjoyed consistently good relations with Egypt, even though for popular consumption the Egyptians had passed off trading overtures from the Aegean as the proffer of tribute. By about 1520 B.C. the language of "Keftiu" (Canaanite *Kaphtor*) was sufficiently familiar to the Egyptians that spells could be transcribed into hieroglyphs.[3] Under Thutmose III, the procession of Aegean benevolence bearers in their colorful costumes (recalling Aegean frescoes) became familiar in Memphis and Thebes;[4] and under Amenophis III the sea routes around the Aegean were so familiar to Egyptian sailors that the "periplus" could be rendered into Egyptian, so that towns like Knossos, Amnissos, Pylos, and others appear in hieroglyphic script.[5]

[1] On the marriage, see now K. A. Kitchen, *Pharaoh Triumphant* (Warminster, 1982), 83–89.

[2] For example, NBC 3934 (A. Goetze, *JCS* 1 [1947], 241–42), which must be to Tudkhaliyas on the basis of the statement in line 20 "[I am] your [fa]ther's [brother]." This would refer to the treaty relationship between Ramesses and Hattusilis.

[3] J. Strange, *Caphtor/Keftiu: A New Investigation* (Leiden, 1980), 99–101 (for texts and references). The vocalization of the Egyptian syllabic orthography yields, as one might expect, an incantation in Greek.

[4] Ibid., 56–70.

[5] For sources and references, see W. Helck, *MDAIK* 39 (1983), 81–92; E. Cline, *Orientalia* 56 (1987), 1–36.

The period between 1400 and 1200 B.C. (i.e., from the reign of Amenophis III to the close of the 19th Dynasty) is dubbed the Mycenaean age, so extensively did trade centered upon the Achaean monarchy and the civilization of mainland Mycenae spread all over the Middle East.[6] It was an age when exports from the Greek world were coveted everywhere in the Levant. And so ubiquitous is the astoundingly beautiful Mycenaean pottery that it becomes a chronological yardstick for Levantine archaeologists. Not only did Egyptian and Greek bottoms ply the sea lanes of the eastern Mediterranean: it was common for merchant ships from Syria to make voyages to "Kapturi," touching at Cyprus en route.[7] Such vessels, one of which has been excavated off the south coast of Turkey, having foundered in foul weather,[8] carried copper ingots, pottery, utensils, and perhaps foodstuffs to the Aegean, along with sesame and cumin, gold, and purple dye. From Egypt came grain in return for olive oil and aromatics; to the Levant went resins, fats, and oil.[9] Over this commerce, and undoubtedly benefiting mightily from it, sat the "great king of Akhkhiyawa" as the Hittites called him, one of the five great kings of the earth at that time.[10] In contemporary Linear B documents, he is the *wanax*, the great overlord of all other lords temporal in the area.[11]

There is no reason to doubt that the Egyptian court was at all times

[6] Among the numerous works on the Mycenaean age, one might consult with profit the following: E. Vermeule, *Greece in the Bronze Age* (Chicago, 1972), 232–80; F. Stubbings, *Mycenaean Pottery from the Levant* (London, 1952); A. E. Samuel, *The Mycenaeans in History* (Englewood Cliffs, N.J., 1966); J. Chadwick, *The Mycenaean World* (Cambridge, 1976); W. Taylor, *The Mycenaeans* (London, 1983); also the pertinent chapters of *CAH*[3] II. On the Hittite sources bearing on the period, see G. L. Huxley, *Achaeans and Hittites* (Oxford, 1960); F. Schachermeyer, *Mykene und das Hethiterreich* (Vienna, 1986); on Mycenaean connections with Egypt and northern Africa, see J. Vercoutter, *L'Égypte et le monde égéen prehellénique* (Cairo, 1956); W. Helck, *Die Beziehungen Ägyptens und Vorderasiens zur Ägäis* (Darmstadt, 1979); P. W. Haider, *Griechenland-Nordafrika* (Darmstadt, 1988), 1–33. On the prior need for international security as a concomitant of trade, see N. K. Sandars, *The Sea Peoples* (London, 1985), 48–49.

[7] C.F.A. Schaeffer, *Le palais royal d'Ugarit* (Paris, 1954), 107 (RS 16.238); M. Astour, in H. Hoffman, ed., *Orient and Occident: Essays Presented to Cyrus Gordon* (Neukirchen, 1973), 17–27; Sandars, *Sea Peoples*, 48, 77; cf. the putative homeland of the Ugaritic-god Kothar in KPTR: M. Astour *Hellenosemitica* (Leiden, 1965), 110, n. 3.

[8] G. F. Bass, *Cape Gelidonya: A Bronze Age Shipwreck*, Transactions of the American Philosophical Society 57, no. 8, (Philadelphia, 1967); C. Pulak, *AJA* 92 (1988), 1–37.

[9] V. Hankey, *Melanges de l'Université Saint-Joseph* 46 (1970), 24–26; R. S. Merrillees and J. Winter, *Bronze Age Trade between the Aegean and Egypt* (Brooklyn, 1972); A. Leonard, Jr., *BASOR* 241 (1981), 87–100; Sandars, *Sea Peoples*, 57, 75.

[10] *KUB* XXIII, 1: Huxley, *Achaeans and Hittites*, 8; on Akhkhiyawa, see H. G. Güterbock, in M. J. Mellink, ed., *Troy and the Trojans* (Bryn Mawr, Penn., 1986), 33; T. R. Bryce, *Oxford Journal of Archaeology* 8 (1989), 297–310; and idem. *Historia* 38 (1989), 1–21.

[11] On this term, see D. Page, *History and the Homeric Iliad* (Berkeley, Calif., 1963), 183–88; Schachermeyer, *Mykene und das Hethiterreich*, 56 and n. 3.

during the Mycenaean age in correspondence with the court at Mycenae, although the letters have not as yet been recovered. Pharaoh corresponded with the king of Alashiya (Cyprus), as the Amarna Letters show, and Cyprus was an entrepôt in the trade with Greece.

But Egypt also had experience of Aegeans less welcome than emissaries and tribute bearers. The small communities in the islands and on the Ionian coast, hemmed in by the rugged terrain, had long subsisted on limited agriculture, fishing, and sea raiding; and this latter activity had long since been directed toward the rich cities of the Levant and the Egyptian coast. The Lukka, in whom we should see the Lycians, and the Shardana from the Ionian coast near Cyme had a name for piracy and exceptional fighting skills.[12] The latter at the beginning of the reign of Ramesses II had attacked the Delta coast, thus bringing themselves within Pharaoh's purview; and the young Ramesses was not tardy in appreciating their military prowess. Having frustrated their attack, the king lost no time in recruiting a contingent of Shardana into the Egyptian armed forces; and they were to distinguish themselves shortly at the battle of Kadesh.[13]

"THE NORTHERNERS ARE RESTLESS . . ."

While for the Middle East the closing decades of the thirteenth century were a period of peace, trade, and prosperity, there were on the horizon harbingers of evil times. The Aegean was the first region to feel the brunt of the troubles to come.

A series of largely unrelated events, which at this distance in time we can only dimly appreciate, combined to propel across the eastern Mediterranean one of the largest and most important migrations in history. It is no exaggeration to claim that the movement of the Sea Peoples, to anticipate a term to be coined for them in Egypt,[14] changed the face of the

[12] In general on the Lukka (Lycians), see Page, *History*, 24; J. Garstang and O. R. Gurney, *The Geography of the Hittite Empire* (London, 1959), chap. 6; T. R. Bryce, *JNES* 33 (1974), 395–404.

[13] The Shardana are to be linked to the "Sardonians" in the legend of Talos, and with Mount Sardena and the Sardanion plain between Sardis and Kyme on the lower reaches of the River Hermos: Strabo, 13.626; A. R. Burn, *Minoans, Philistines and Greeks* (New York, 1930), 113–14. Their distinctive helmet with ball and crescent is pictured on Ramesside monuments: A. H. Gardiner, *Ancient Egyptian Onomastica* (Oxford, 1947), 1: 199–200; Kitchen, *Pharaoh Triumphant*, 40.

[14] The epithet "of the sea" is applied only to the Sherden and Washosh (P. Harris 76.7; A. H. Gardiner, *Late Egyptian Miscellanies* [Brussells, 1933], 20:1), and "of the countries of the sea" to the Eqwesh (KRI IV, 8:9); but in most modern treatments it is extended to the entire group of northern countries who attacked Egypt under Merenptah and Ramesses III. As yet, because of the superabundance of evidence both archaeological and textual, no adequate treatment of the Sea Peoples has appeared. In addition to the words cited in n. 6, one might add F. Schachermayer, *Die ägäische Frühzeit*, vol. 5 (Vienna, 1982); A. Strobel,

ancient world more than any other single event before the time of Alexander the Great. In the history of the Near East the movement marks the end of—indeed brought to an end—one era and began another, with no continuum between the two. In Egypt, the obvious goal of the movement, the effect proved negligible when compared with what the movement of these migrants wrought in Palestine and Syria.

The ultimate causes of the movement are difficult to assess, but certain suspicious occurrences and conditions seem to have prevailed in concert. On the economic side it has been maintained that the Mycenaean states suffered an inherent weakness in being dependent on a single, high-yield crop, and having to import many raw materials.[15] The age-old practice of piracy and the recent success of the Shardana may have tempted peoples within the penumbra of the Mycenaean world to strike at the sources of the raw material. Others opt for natural disaster as the primary factor in setting the Sea Peoples in motion. Although it cannot be proved that widespread famine and crop failure in the last third of the thirteenth century disrupted life on the north shore of the eastern Mediterranean,[16] three or four sources of evidence, eight centuries removed from each other, seem to corroborate such a hypothesis. Diodorus and Herodotus preserve the memory of a famine that forced peoples from Syme, Naxos, and Sardis to emigrate,[17] and indeed contemporary documents from Egypt and Ugarit speak of famine in Anatolia.[18] It is easy to understand how the superabundance of food stocks in the Nile Valley would have proved an irresistible attraction to the hungry enclaves in the Aegean. That bubonic plague or a similar epidemic played a role is possible, but impossible to verify at this distance in time.[19]

Der spätbronzezeitliche Seevölkersturm (New York, 1976); S. Deger-Jalkotzy, ed., *Griechenland, die Ägäis und die Levant während der "Dark Ages"* (Vienna, 1983).

[15] S. Iakovides, in G. A. Christopoulos, ed., *A History of the Hellenic World, vol. 1: Prehistory and Prohistory* (London, 1974), 293.

[16] The evidence from Mycenae and the mainland is not completely conclusive: G. Shrimpton, *Echos du monde classique* 31 (1987), 137–78; cf. Sandars, *Sea Peoples*, 20 and n. 4, 24.

[17] Herodotus, 1.94; Diodorus, 5.53.

[18] G. A. Wainwright, *JEA* 46 (1960), 24–25; M. Astour, *AJA* 69 (1965), 255.

[19] It is interesting and significant to note the prevalence of ad hoc coalitions of small states, formerly vassals of larger states, in the Aegean from c. 1250 to 1175 B.C. While Amenophis III and Ramesses II encountered individual groups, the breakup of the Mycenaean age forced communities to come together on a temporary basis. For the period in question we can cite the following temporary "confederacies": the twenty-two-nation "*Bund*" under the leadership(?) of Troy, which faced Tudkhaliyas IV (see following note); the federation under the direction of Kos, which joined the Libyans against Merenptah; the Greek confederacy against Troy; the alliance of the Qayqisha and the Saii with the Libyans against Ramesses III; and the grand alliance under the leadership of the Peleset against Egypt (see Table 1). It is surprising how many of these seem to have been initiated by communities in the region of Caria and Lycia.

Did political trends assist in the collapse? Are we clear-sighted in discerning an incipient breakdown in the system of Late Bronze Age superpowers, the "great kingships"? If this was indeed taking place, it might have led to the fragmentation of the former empires, and the consequent intestine strife among the erstwhile vassals (Table 1). In this connection it should be noted that the Hittite king Tudkhaliyas IV, sometime between 1250 and 1240 B.C., was faced by a confederacy of twenty-two rebellious states along the Ionian coast from Caria (Lycia) to Wilusa (Ilion, i.e., Troy). The Hittites defeated this coalition, but the western periphery of their empire had begun to break up.[20] It was apparently this same Tudkhaliyas who conquered the island of Cyprus, thus terminating another of the prominent and prosperous exponents of the Late Bronze Age political system.[21]

The Greek mainland yields the first archaeological evidence of what was to come. About 1300 B.C. there are signs of a movement from Thessaly into Epirus of a pastoral people, later to be associated with the Dorian Greeks.[22] Half a century later they were again on the move southward, at just the time that mainland Greece seems to have been experiencing a considerable degree of internal feuding. Legend too remembers a southward flow of peoples, this time from Thrace, which swept over Naxos, Samothrace, and Euboea, and made life difficult for Thebes and Attica.[23] The sudden and thorough refortification of such places as Mycenae, Tiryns, Corinth, Athens, and Miletos about 1250 to 1240 B.C. seems to bear out the evidence just cited.[24] If this action betrays fear on the part of the Achaean inhabitants of Greece, it was well justified; for within a generation the first blow fell. About 1220 violent destruction overtook Mycenae, Tiryns, Pylos, Crisa, and Gla, to name a few, effectually terminating the culture phase called Late Helladic IIIB.[25] The once great empire of Akhkhiyawa had suffered a crippling blow.

THE FIRST MOVE ON EGYPT

The net effect of the weakening of Akhkhiyawa and the turmoil of Tudkhaliyas's reign was to liberate those lesser states in the islands and along the western coast of Asia Minor that lay between the former empires. The

[20] *KUB* XXIII, 11–13, 27–28; Huxley, *Achaeans*, 321–33; the famous Madduwattas incident is now generally dated before Tudkhaliyas IV: I. Hoffman, *Orientalia* 53 (1984), 35ff.; Schachermayer, *Mykene und das Hethiterreich*, 141–43.

[21] H. G. Güterbock, *JNES* 26 (1967), 77.

[22] N.G.L. Hammond, *CAH³* II, pt. 2 (1975), 684.

[23] Burn, *Minoans, Philistines and Greeks*, 148–50.

[24] Vermeule, *Greece in the Bronze Age*, 264–65; Sandars, *Sea Peoples*, 60–62.

[25] Hammond, *CAH³* II, pt. 2 (1975), 694; Vermeule, *Greece in the Bronze Age*, 269–70; T.B.L. Webster, *From Mycenae to Homer* (London, 1958), 136–37.

TABLE 1.
Libyans and Sea Peoples in Contemporary and Classical Sources

Amenophis III	Ramesses II	Merenptah	Ramesses III (year 5)	Ramesses III (year 8)	Hittite Sources	Classical Sources
Lukka	Lukka	Lukka	—	—	Lu-uk-ka	Lycia
Sharden	Sharden	Sharden	—	—	—	Sardonians (Lydia)
—	—	Eqwesh	—	—	—	Köos
—	—	Teresh	—	—	Ta-ru-i-ša	Tursenoi (Lydia)
—	—	Shekelesh	—	Shekelesh	Ši-ka-la-yu	Sagalassos (Pisidia)
—	Qarqisha	—	Qayqisha	—	Kar-ki-ša	Caria
—	—	—	—	Wesheš	—	Wassos (Caria)
Danuna(?)	—	—	—	Danyen	*Daniya-wana	Danaoi (Argos)
—	—	—	—	Tjakker	—	Teucrians (Troad)
—	—	—	—	Peleset	—	Pelasgiotis (Illyria?)
—	Labu	Labu	Labu	—	—	Libya
Meshwesh	—	(Meshwesh)	Meshwesh	—	—	Maxyes (Cyrene)
—	—	—	Asbata	—	—	Asbytae (Cyrene)
—	—	—	Shayu	—	—	—
—	—	—	Hasa	—	—	—
—	—	—	Baqan	—	—	Auses (Libya)

international treaties between the great powers did not bind them, and the rich states of the east were "fair game." Their fighting qualities and in particular their superior weaponry gave them a confidence the Levantine states lacked. For the Aegean and the Ionian coast had fallen heir to the great metallurgical advances attested in the Balkans during the fourteenth and thirteenth centuries, advances that manifested themselves in the long swords, shields, helmets, and body armor of sundry members of the "Sea Peoples."[26]

If, as we know it did, Egypt acted on the northerners like a great magnet, two possible routes lay open to those who wished to attack Egypt from across the Mediterranean. The most obvious lay along the coast of the eastern Mediterranean, with Cyprus as an Intermediate halting point. A less obvious, but well-traveled route, would take the voyager via Crete due south to the north African coast, with a landfall in the neighborhood of modern Mersa Matrukh. Here recent excavations have revealed an entrepôt serving trade between Crete, Cyprus, and the Delta in the fourteenth century B.C.,[27] and perhaps giving access to the inland route into Africa by way of the western oases. In any event, by the last quarter of the thirteenth century B.C., the coast west of the Egyptian Delta was familiar to seamen and caravaneer alike, and provided a direct access to Cyrenaica, which had to be carefully guarded; for in those days this vast region supported a sizable and bellicose population.[28]

The aged Ramesses II had passed away in about 1237 B.C. after a reign of sixty-seven years, and had been succeeded by his thirteenth son (in order of birth), Ramesses II having outlived the first dozen of his many sons. Merenptah was already an aged and decrepit man when he came to the throne, and although he had earlier been trained as a soldier, his active career in the army was long past. In his second year he traveled down to Thebes from his capital in the Delta "to see his father Amun, King of the Gods" and to authorize an inventory of temple treasures; but while this peaceful activity was in progress an enemy force was on the move.

From the dawn of Egyptian history, Libyan tribesmen had always been a thorn in the side of the pharaonic government, but their small numbers had prevented them from posing any serious threat to Egypt. During the New Kingdom, however, these older tribal groups had been replaced or absorbed by newcomers from the west: the Labu (who eventually gave

[26] Sandars, *Sea Peoples*, 84–97.

[27] J. Leclant, *Orientalia* 56 (1987), 293–94.

[28] For the Libyans in general, see the discussion with bibliography by J. Osing, *LdÄ* III (1980), 1015–33; for the appointment of a "Libyarch" in Ramesside times, see W. Spiegelberg, *ZÄS* 64 (1929), 95; for Ramesside fortifications in the western Delta and along the coast, see C. C. Edgar, *ASAE* 11 (1911), 277–79; J. Leclant, *Orientalia* 23 (1954), 75; L. Habachi, *BIFAO* 80 (1980), 13–30.

their name to "Libya"), the Meshwesh, the Asbuta, the Hasa, and others.[29] With long, cutaway gowns, bearded, and wearing their hair in a long curl on one side, the Labu and Meshwesh had long sinced graced Ramesside triumph scenes as the enemy whose defeat is to be celebrated. But if under the great Ramesses they had been easy prey for Pharaoh's forces, under Merenptah they proved much more formidable. For now they were joined by piratical elements from the Aegean: the sea route to Libya was now a supply route.

In his fourth book, Herodotus gives a fairly detailed account of the Libyan tribes of his day, and in chapter 191 describes one called the Maxyes (Meshwesh): "West of Triton . . . Libya is inhabited by tribes who live in ordinary houses and practice agriculture. First come the Maxyes, a people who grow their hair on the right sides of their head and shave it off on the left. They stain their bodies red and claim to be descended from men of Troy." In a similar vein Pindar (*Pythian* 5.81–83) preserves a tradition that sons of Antenor migrated to Cyrenaica from Troy. Another legend had it that, in the generation preceding the Trojan War, a certain Mopsus (or Moxos), serving as seer with the Argonauts, died of a snake bite on the north African coast and was buried at Cyrene.[30] All these traditions attest to the survival in folk memory of a historic fact: at the time of the breakup of the Akhkhiyawan kingdom, and the expedition against Troy, the route to the Libyan coast was well traveled by Aegean freebooters. The inscriptions of Merenptah record the facts of which the traditions are a dim memory.

To judge from Merenptah's account, the capital was apprised of the Libyan invasion only at the beginning of April in Merenptah's fifth year.[31] By that time the horde, with the Labu taking the lead numerically and politically, had swept over the northernmost of the string of western oases, and had entered the Delta.[32] Encouraged by Ptah in a dream, the king mustered his forces and decided to attack the invaders in early May.[33] The enemy he faced represented a coalition consciously conceived and put together by the chief of the Labu, Mereye. Besides the Meshwesh who tagged along with their cogeners, Mereye had enlisted the help of the people of the island Kos[34] and the Lycians. These in turn had persuaded

---

[29] The Meshwesh are known from the reign of Amenophis III (year 34: W. C. Hayes, *JNES* 10 [1951], fig. 10, no. 130); the Labu from the time of Ramesses II (KRI II, 475). The Asbuta are the Asbutae of Herodotus (4.168), the Hasa are the Auses of the same author (4.182).

[30] *OCD*², 700; Appolonius Rhodius, 4.1518.

[31] KRI IV, 23:6.

[32] D. B. Redford, *Pharaonic King-lists, Annals and Day-books* (Toronto, 1986), 83, no. 105.

[33] KRI IV, 20:8.

[34] The Eqwosh: D. B. Redford, *JAOS* 103 (1983), 482–83 (not the Achaeans). The island

smaller groups of Shardana, Tyrsenoi, and Shekelesh to accompany them.[35] For six hours the opposing armies hammered each other at Par-Yeru near Buto in the northwest Delta[36] until the invaders cracked and fled. Unlike the patently smaller engagements of the time of Thutmose III or Amenophis II, the rout turned into a slaughter: while the Egyptian sources conceal their own losses, over nine thousand of the enemy were killed.

But the Libyans were not to be denied. In the twenty-five years of weak government by the regimes of four short-lived kings who followed Merenptah, the Labu and the Meshwesh entered the western Delta unhindered, and settled as far east as the bank of the central Nile, destroying the towns of the Xoite township.[37] The unfortunate Siptah, who suffered not only from the effects of polio but also from the machinations of his sister(?) Tawosret and his Canaanite chancellor Bay,[38] was powerless to stop them. It was left to the family of the victor in a palace revolution, one Sethnakht, to deal with the problem; and in Ramesses III, the latter's son, Egypt had at last found a competent avenger.

The initial outbreak of hostilities centered upon the dynastic succession among the Labu. Ramesses III apparently refused to release one of the chief's children, whom he had taken captive, to succeed his father; and pursuant thereto the Libyans crossed the frontier and attacked.[39] As before the Labu were accompanied by auxiliaries: from Libya itself the Meshwesh, Asbutae, and Hasa;[40] from the Aegean, again a contingent from the southwest corner of Asia Minor, this time the Karkisa,[41] as well as another contingent from Samos and Abdera. This time the victory was more complete than under Merenptah: "See! I (Ramesses III) destroyed them and slew them at one stroke. I overthrew them, felled them in their own blood, and turned them into heaps of corpses. I turned them back from treading the frontier of Egypt. . . . I brought the rest . . . as numer-

---

boasts extensive Mycenaean remains: Huxley, *Achaeans*, 27; Stubbings, *Mycenaean Pottery*, 21–22; J. Boardman, *The Greeks Overseas* (London, 1980), 27; on decorated pottery from Kos showing plumed headdresses, see Sandars, *Sea Peoples*, 92–93; S. Wachsmann, *International Journal of Nautical Archaeology* 10 (1981), 200–201, 213.

[35] From the lists of the slain, the Eqwosh were the largest contingent by far.

[36] H. DeMeulenaere, *BIFAO* 62 (1964), 170.

[37] P. Harris I, 76, 11–77, 2.

[38] On Siptah's ailment, see J. R. Harris and K. Weeks, *Natural History* (August–September 1972), 61; on Tawosret, see R. Drenkahn, *GM* 43 (1981), 19–22; on Bay (Beya), see p. 225.

[39] KRI V, 22:15–23:4.

[40] See n. 29.

[41] Or Kayqisha (H. Gauthier, *Dictionnaire des noms géographiques contenus dans les textes hiéroglyphiques* [Cairo, 1930], 5:154, 158); both are renderings of *Karkisa*, i.e., Caria (A. Goetz, *Kleinasien*[2] [Munich, 1957], map; Huxley, *Achaeans*, 20–21; W. Helck, *Die Beziehungen Ägyptens zur Vorderasien*[2] [Wiesbaden, 1971], 195).

ous prisoners, pinioned like fowl before my horses, and their wives and children by tens of thousands."[42]

The Libyan menace was thus at an end. Although on another occasion, six years hence, the Meshwesh would mount an invasion on their own, their effort would prove feeble. But a minor detail in the records of Ramesses III in his great mortuary temple at Thebes is a harbinger of things to come: two of the captive chiefs bear quite un-Libyan types of names, Melie and Moschion, each determined by a kneeling captive with a floppy, plumed headdress.[43] Egypt was soon to see a veritable ocean of such plumes.

THE INVASION OF YEAR EIGHT

Previous encounters with the Aegean pirates had accustomed Egypt to look for hardy warriors in a few "long ships," bent on a speedy raid to be followed by as speedy a retirement. (Such raids are commemorated in the *Odyssey* 14.246ff., which may well be a faint memory of the expeditions under Ramesses II or Merenptah.) Even the Levant from time to time had been visited by individuals from the Ionian coast or the Cyclades.[44] What neither Egypt nor Palestine had experienced heretofore, however, was an outright invasion of *peoples* from the Aegean, intent on settling down. While trade with Greece and the islands had flourished as we have seen during the Late Bronze Age, there is not a particle of evidence to support the contention that prior to year 8 of Ramesses III, early waves of Sea Peoples had already settled on the coastal plain of Palestine.[45] The invasion of year 8 was sudden and unique; and all references to "Philistines" in the Bible must postdate it.

One is accustomed to think of the coalition of the seven groups that constituted the horde as taking shape suddenly, and the invasion as following quickly. In fact, year 8 simply marks the record of their defeat at the hands of the Egyptians; the founding of the confederacy may well date

---

[42] P. Harris I, 77, 3–7.

[43] KRI V, 24:14–15. These "Philistine" headdresses occasionally turn up among Egyptian auxiliary troops in early Nubian campaigns and even this first Libyan campaign (F. Schachermeyer, *Ugaritica* 6 [1969], 454–55), but whether this indicates that some Peleset already had entered Egyptian service or should simply be put down as anachronistic decoration is difficult to say.

[44] For possible Lycians at Byblos in the seventeenth century B.C., see W. F. Albright, *BASOR* 155 (1959), 71–72; for a *Šikalayu* (Shekelesh) at Ugarit, see G. A. Lehmann, *UF* 11 (1979), 481–82; E. Edel, *BN* 23 (1984), 7–8.

[45] W. F. Albright, *CAH*[3] II pt. 2 (1975), 522.

several years earlier.[46] Until recently, the only record still preserved of this incursion of peoples into the Near East was that of Ramesses III himself, preserved on the walls of his mortuary temple, Medinet Habu, at Thebes; and in spite of the exciting finds at Ugarit, this remains the sole contemporary account.[47]

> The foreign lands made a convocation(?) in their islands, bursting forth and scattering in the strife of the lands at one time; no land could stand before their arms, beginning with Khatte, (then) Qode, Carchemish, Arzawa(?) and Alashiya (Cyprus)—all cut off [at one stroke(?)]. A camp [was established] at one spot within Amurru, and they ruined his people and his land like something that had never existed. On they came, with fire prepared at their front, faces toward Egypt. Their main protection(?) was the Peleset, the Tjekru, the Shekelesh, the Da'anu, the Washosh, and the lands all united. They laid their hands on countries as far as the circuit of the earth, their hearts trusting and confident: "Our plans will succeed!"

Unlike our sources for the onslaught under Merenptah, the records of Ramesses III's year 8 give us graphic depictions as well as text; thus it becomes possible to use the accoutrements of the peoples named as evidence of their origin.[48] Most prominent in both reliefs and texts are the Peleset, with Tjekru running a close second. These wear, characteristically, a fillet from which protrudes a floppy "hoplite's" plume (unless long, natural hair has been misconstrued), and a protective piece down the nape of the neck (Figure 7, no. 6). Their armament includes long swords, spears, circular shields, and sometimes body armor. Now it has

---

[46] It is difficult to know what span of time must be allowed to accommodate the marchings and sailings implied by the Ugaritic texts, and the fight over Cyprus involving the Hittites, as well as the classical traditions of migrations (see subsequent discussion). One wonders whether Rhodes was a staging ground: the island was largely unaffected by the movement, and continued a vigorous trade with various Mediterranean ports: Taylor, *The Mycenaeans*, 160. If the completion of the siege of Troy was in fact the mainspring of the movement, then its date should establish a *terminus a quo*, but unfortunately there is no unanimity on this, dates ranging from the fourteenth century to Eratosthenes' 1194–1183 B.C.: Burn, *Minoans, Philistines and Greeks*, 52; Stubbings, *CAH*³ I, pt. 2 (1975), 350; R. B. Edwards, *Kadmos the Phoenician* (Amsterdam, 1979), 164; A. B. Lloyd, *Herodotus Book II. A Commentary* (Leiden, 1976), 1:177–80. The coalition under discussion could have taken shape in my view as early as Ramesses III's accesssion.

[47] KRI V, 39–40; W. F. Edgerton and J. A. Wilson, *Historical Records of Ramesses III* (Chicago, 1936), 53–56.

[48] Cf. works cited in n. 6 and 14, to which one might add Astour, *Hellenosemitica*, 6; Gardiner *Onomastica*, vol. 1; the numerous works of G. A. Wainwright in *JEA* and *JHS*; R. Stadelmann, *LdÄ* 5 (1984), 814–22. Regardless of what specific identifications are opted for, it is generally agreed that it is wrong to look north of the Aegean for some mysterious group of invaders who broke in upon the Mediterranean.

long been realized that the plumed headdress of the Egyptian reliefs finds a parallel in a sign (possibly a determinative) in the script of the curious "Phaistos Disk," discovered in the early part of this century at Phaistos, Crete. Several classical authors, moreover, state that crests were first used on helmets in Caria, in southwest Asia Minor, north of Lycia;[49] and interestingly, both "Carians" and "Cretans" appear as ethnic indicators in the lists of bodyguards of Judaean kings recruited from Philistia.[50] As for the terms "Peleset" and "Tjekru," the former has been compared with the "Pelasgians," a vague and rather enigmatic designation of the pre-Greek inhabitants of the Aegean.[51] The "Tjekru" recall the eponymous hero Teuker of the Troad, as well as "Zakro" in Crete.[52] Of the others, the Shekelesh (and the Teresh) wear cloth headdresses and a medallion on their breasts, and carry two spears and a round shield; their place of origin has long been considered to be Sagalassos in Pisidia.[53] The Washosh seem linked to the island of Iassos off the coast of Caria,[54] and the Da'anu have long been considered identical with the "Dana'ans" of Homer, the appellative given to Greeks in general, but originally to an Argive community.[55]

[49] On the disk, see *inter alia* Helck, *Die Beziehungen Ägäis*, 129–30; Strange, *Caphtor/Keftiu*, 135–36; on the crests, see Strabo, 14.2.27. The circular shields used by most Sea Peoples point to the Aegean world (A. M. Snodgrass, *Early Greek Armour and Weapons* [Edinburgh, 1964], 189), where they replaced the body shield in the thirteenth century (T. Dothan, *The Philistines and Their Material Culture* [Jerusalem, 1982], 12); on other armaments, see Sandars, *Sea Peoples*, 88–95. On whether we are dealing with a crest or natural hair, see K. Galling, *Ugaritica* 6 (1969), 247–48; Schachermeyer, *Mykene*, 457; Dothan. *The Philistines*, 13 and n. 49.

[50] 2 Sam. 20:23; 2 Kings 11:4, 19.

[51] On the Pelasgians, originally a Thracian tribe (*Iliad*, 2.841), possibly driven south to occupy the Troad (ibid.), Ionia and the islands (Strabo, 13.621) and Crete (*Odyssey*, 19.177), see Burn *Minoans, Philistines and Greeks*, 58–59; idem., in OCD², 794; Lloyd, *Herodotus Book II. A Commentary*, 2:232–37; if, as the later sources claim, the Pelasgians were non-Greek, a difficulty might arise if one wishes to maintain that the few "Philistine" names and words preserved for us are in fact of Greek origin. It should be noted that Xanthus (fifth century B.C.) claimed the Philistines to have been colonists from Lydia (E. Meyer, *Geschichte des Alterums* [Stuttgart, 1928], 2:1, 81, n. 1).

[52] E. Gjerstadt, *Opuscula Archaaeologica* 3 (1944), 108; G. A. Wainwright, *JEA* 47 (1961), 76; E. Forrer, *Ugaritica* 6 (1969), 214; OCD², 1048; J.D.S. Pendelbury, *The Archaeology of Crete* (Oxford, 1939), 260, n. 4.

[53] T. Smolenski, *ASAE* 15 (1915), 86 and n. 5.

[54] P. Kretschmer, *Glotta* 21 (1932), 230, n. 3; Strabo, 14.2.21. The Shekelesh, Washosh, and Qarqisha all display in their names the significant -ass(os) afformative, linking them to the Luwian/Lycian linguistic group in Asia Minor: O. R. Gurney *The Hittites²* (Harmondsworth, 1964), 122–23; J. L. Caskey, *CAH³* II, pt. 1 (1973), 139.

[55] Astour *Hellenosemitica*, 8–10; the problem is complicated, as there appears to be a doubled *n* in the original, which has often prompted comparison with the place name *Danuna* of the Amarna Letters: EA 151:50–55 (where it appears to be linked with Canaan). For a possible solution, see R. D. Barnett, *JHS* 73 (1953), 142, n. 2.

In the great invasion of year 8, then, we appear to be dealing with a coalition of peoples that encompassed the Ionian and Pisidian coasts, centering especially on Caria, and which may have involved mainland Greeks. The nautical record bears this out: the ships of the Sea Peoples, as depicted at Medinet Habu, are very much in the Aegean (rather than Cretan) tradition.[56] Can anything else be said?

The period of the onslaught of the Sea Peoples, the close of the thirteenth century B.C., is the inception of the Iron Age. It is the earliest period that lies within the compass of the dim historical memory of the later Greeks, in the historical legends of the sixth to fourth centuries B.C. Despite the passage of time, the tendency to personalize impersonal events, and the inevitable distortion or anachronism, the legends are most illuminating. Mopsus of Colophon, for example, said to have been the offspring of fugitives from Boeotia, in the years immediately following the Trojan War led "the peoples" from the Ionian coast across the Taurus mountains and into Pamphylia and Cilicia, whence some migrated further afield into Syria and Palestine.[57] Likewise, Amphilochus is also connected with a movement from the Aegean to Pamphylia after the Trojan War, and became the reputed founder of Poseidion in Syria.[58] Similarly, Teuker, brother of Ajax, who had fought in the Trojan War, led migrations that ended up in Cyprus and Cilicia;[59] and Agapenor too, king of the Arcadians, is supposed to have come to Cyprus after the Trojan War.[60] If these legends, the salient exemplars of a numerous array of similar tales, take the migration as far as Syria, founding legends linked to the later Philistine cities carry the account one step further by linking Ashkelon with migrations from Lydia and Gaza with refugees from Crete.[61]

The contemporary, as well as the classical, evidence permits us to draw the following sketchy picture. At the end of the thirteenth century B.C. a desperate effort to reunite the disintegrating Mycenaean community directed a loose coalition of former member states against Troy, the former leader of the erstwhile Ionian confederacy against the Hittites. In the

---

[56] Wachsmann, *International Journal of Nautical Archaeology* 10 (1981), 195–96, 209–10; Vermeule, *Greece in the Bronze Age*, 258–60, fig. 43; see also A. Raban, *International Journal of Nautical Archaeology* 18, no. 2 (1989), 163–71.

[57] Barnett, *JHS* 73 (1953), 140–42; *OCD²*, 239; Hammond, *CAH³* II, pt. 2 (1975), 679–80; Forrer, *Ugaritica* 6 (1969), 211–16.

[58] Herodotus, 7.91; Strabo, 14.5.17.

[59] See n. 52.

[60] M. Fortin, in *Mélanges d'études anciennes offerts à Maurice Lebel* (Quebec, 1980), 25–44.

[61] R. Drews, *The Greek Accounts of Eastern History* (Cambridge, Mass., 1973), 102; Strobel, *Seevölkersturm*, 211; M. A. Meyer, *History of the City of Gaza* (New York, 1907), 6; R.A.S. Macalister, *The Philistines, Their History and Civilization* (London, 1912), 15, 113.

years immediately following the reduction of Troy some of the members of the Mycenaean expedition, under the leadership of enclaves in Caria, banded together in a loose federation and moved east along the southern coast of Asia Minor, along with their families, to settle in the plains of Cilicia and North Syria. Branch movements spread far and wide. Sardis was occupied by Greeks around 1200 B.C.,[62] and ships of the movement made for Cyprus. In vain, Suppiluliumas II, last of the Hittite kings, attempted to salvage the situation: "Against me the ships from Cyprus drew up in line three times for battle in the midst of the sea. I destroyed them, I seized the ships and in the midst of the sea I set them on fire." Yet a few lines later we hear once more that "the enemy in multitudes came against me from Cyprus."[63] Indeed, the ships of the raiders were appearing all over the coast of Cyprus and Syria. In the latter region the autochthonous states were in no way weak or decadent, as a century of free trade had made them extremely prosperous. Ugarit alone could muster a fleet of 150 ships, a larger force than any of the fleets of the individual Greek states as reflected in the Iliad.[64] Yet the last archives of Ugarit, in the oven for hardening as the city fell, reflect the unthinkable scenario of Ugaritian forces fighting the unnamed enemy in the Taurus mountains as allies of the Hittites, while at the same time ships of the enemy raided the coast. Cyprus is hard pressed, but the king and vizier of the island can offer advice: "Beware! Twenty enemy ships were here, but now are gone, where we do not know! Enemy ships are sighted off the Syrian coast? Enclose your cities with fortifications, and take your troops and chariots inside! Watch out for the enemy and be strong!"[65] But the town cannot hold out. The last king of Ugarit sends a desperate message to Cyprus: "Now the ships of the enemy have come, and they have burned my cities in fire and have committed atrocities in my land. My father! Do you not know that all my troops are in Khatte and all my ships are in Lycia."[66]

---

[62] G. Hanfmann, BASOR 186 (1967), 37.

[63] H. Otten, MDOG 94 (1963), 21; Güterbock, JNES 26 (1967), 77.

[64] RS 18.148; Astour, AJA 69 (1965), 256.

[65] Ugaritica 5 (1968), 85–86; Enkomi on Cyprus was destroyed twice at the end of the LH IIIC (A.H.S. Megaw JHS 73 [1953], 134), after which there is evidence of abandonment (V. Karageorghis Cyprus [London, 1982], 84). There is evidence of Mycenaean warriors buried after the first destruction (ibid., 85), and "Philistine" seals and headdresses are also attested (E. Porada, in P. Dikaios, Enkomi [Mainz, 1969–1971], 801–2; C.F.A. Schaeffer, Enkomi-Alasia [1952] 1:148; 363, n. 1; Wainwright, JEA 47 [1961], 75, fig. 8). Ceramic evidence has been taken to indicate origins in the Argive plain (V. R. d'A. Desborough, CAH³ II, pt. 2 (1975), 659–62, although gray "Trojan ware" also appears among the newcomers (H. G. Bucholtz, in Bronze Age Migrations in the Aegean [Cambridge, 1974], 179–80).

[66] RS 20.238: Ugaritica 5 (1968), 87–89. None of the ships of the Sea Peoples carried many oarsmen and fighters; the raiders relied rather on speed, surprise, and superior armaments: Wachsmann, International Journal of Nautical Archaeology 10 (1981), 214.

The end was near. In truth, no one could stand before these raiders. Hattusas was destroyed, and the Hittite empire swept away in one stroke. Tarsus was laid waste, as was Enkomi on Cyprus. Alalakh and Ugarit were razed to the ground, never to be rebuilt. The Late Bronze Age of the Levant vanished in an instant: archaeology gives a graphic dimension to the terror conveyed by the written record.[67]

From their camp in Amurru—that is, in the Eleutheros Valley—the confederacy trundled south, women and children in oxcarts, while the ships kept pace off the coast. It is one of the ironic gaps in our records that nowhere has the precise location of the final battle (or battles) been conveyed to us. But in the reliefs Ramesses does (perhaps unwittingly) indicate that it was *not* in, or even on the border of, the Egyptian Delta. Pharaoh knew they were coming, and to that end he established a fortified line in Asia: "I prepared my frontier in Djahy and fortified it against them with chiefs, garrison commanders and *maryannu*. I had the Nile mouths fortified like a strong wall with a fleet of warships, cargo vessels and boats . . . manned completely from stem to stern with brave soldiers with their weapons, and infantry—all the choicest warriors of Egypt."[68] To take command of the counterattack "His Majesty departed for Djahy."[69] Djahy is too vague and archaic a term to help us in this regard; but a tradition that apparently derives from Xanthos (fifth century B.C.) places a "Lydian" army in the vicinity of Ashkelon in the period this chapter treats of.[70] And it may well be that the movement was only stopped on the southern coastal plain.

While the victory Ramesses lays claim to may not have been as complete as he would wish to have us think, nonetheless his firm stand was enough to break up the coalition and send its component members to flight. Ships that managed to break through to the Delta were quickly

[67] For Hattusas, see K. Bittel, in Deger-Jalkotzy, ed., *Griechenland, die Ägäis und die Levante während der "Dark Ages,"* 25–26; I. Singer, *Hethitica* 8 (1987), 413–21; for Enkomi, see n. 65; for Alalakh and Ugarit, see Astour, *AJA* 69 (1965), 255 (Albright, *CAH³* II, pt. 2 [1975], 507ff., is now worthless: Ugarit still stood at the very end of the 19th Dynasty [see p. 225, n. 46]): L. Woolley, *A Forgotten Kingdom* (Baltimore, 1953), 163–64; J. Frev, *Syria* 65 (1988), 395–98.

[68] KRI V, 40.

[69] Ibid., 30:5.

[70] See n. 61. Although the Sea Peoples clearly possessed *oared* galleys, the fact that the scene of the sea fight at Medinet Habu does not show oars (*Medinet Habu, vol. 1: Earlier Historical Records of Ramses III* [Chicago, 1930], pls. 37–41) has been taken to mean that the Egyptian fleet caught the enemy off guard, anchored off shore: L. Casson *The Ancient Mariners* (New York, 1959), 41–42; idem, *Ships and Seamanship in the Ancient World* (Princeton, N.J., 1971), 38. Similarly, the presence of oxcarts with women and children has been construed as indicating that the Sea Peoples were caught on the march: *Medinet Habu* 1: pl. 32. Needless to say, this is pressing the Ramesside artists (whose accuracy in *this* particular mortuary temple is sometimes suspect) much too far.

dealt with: "Those who came upon the sea, the consuming flame faced them at the Nile mouths . . . they were dragged up, surrounded and cast down upon the shore, slaughtered in heaps from head to tail."[71] Some of the Shekelesh sailed westward to Sicily (to which they gave their name),[72] the Da'anu may have found a haven on Cyprus, the Washosh disappeared. What became of the Peleset and Tjekru will be discussed in the next chapter.

[71] KRI V, 40–41.

[72] *Not* the Tjakru (W. F. Albright, *The Vocalization of Egyptian Syllabic Orthography* [New Haven, Conn., 1934], 65; Edel *BN* 23 [1984], 7), the initial sound being a voiced fricative, not a sibilant.

CHAPTER 10

"These are the Bene Yisra'el . . .": The Advent of Israel

THE PATIENT and observant reader will have noted that, up to this point in our study, no mention has been made of Israel or its ancestral patriarchs. The reason for this is an empirical one: in our sources, both Egyptian and west Asian, there are virtually no references to Israel, its congeners, or Biblical associates prior to the twelfth century B.C.; and beyond that point for four centuries a mere half dozen allusions can be elicited.

THE BIBLICAL EVIDENCE AND ITS TRADITIONAL INTERPRETATION

This dearth of citations is also paralleled on the Biblical side by a similar absence of any specific references betraying a knowledge of Egypt or the Levant during the second millennium B.C. There is no mention of an Egyptian empire encompassing the eastern Mediterranean, no marching Egyptian armies bent on punitive campaigns, no countermarching Hittite forces, no resident governors, no Egyptianized kinglets ruling Canaanite cities, no burdensome tribute or cultural exchange. Of the latest and most disastrous migration of the second millennium, that of the Sea Peoples, the Hexateuch knows next to nothing: Genesis and Exodus find the Philistines already settled in the land at the time of Abraham (cf. Gen. 26, passim; Exod. 13:17, 23:31). The great Egyptian kings of the empire, the Amenophids, the Thutmosids, the Ramessides, are absent from the hundreds of pages of holy writ; and it is only in occasional toponyms unrecognized by the Hebrew writer that a faint echo of their names may be heard.[1] Elsewhere historical figures have been transmogrified into historical heroes: the Hyksos Sheshy into a legendary Canaanite giant (Num. 13:22); Ssy-rʿ, the sobriquet of Ramesses II, into the name of a Canaanite general (Jud. 5, passim).[2] Errors persist even in periods closer in time to

---

[1] E.g., the "Land of Ramesses" in Gen. 47:11 and "Ra'amses" (the city) in Exod. 1:11 and 12:37 (see D. B. Redford, *VT* 13 [1963], 401–2; idem, in A. F. Rainey, ed., *Egypt, Israel, Sinai* [Tel Aviv, 1987], 138–39; "the Spring of Menephtoah (Merenptah)," in Jos. 15:9 (J. Simons, *The Geographical and Topographical Texts of the Old Testament* [Leiden, 1959], 140).

[2] See H. Gauthier, *Le livre des rois d'Égypte* (Cairo, 1914), 3:73–74. The common occurrence of "ra" in initial position in numerous Egyptian praenomina occasioned its wrong

the period of the Biblical writers. The Egyptian king who was expected to help Hoshea in his rebellion (2 Kings 17:4) has suffered the confusion of his *city* as his *name*. And if we remind ourselves that even Pharaoh Shabtaka (c. 697–690 B.C.) turns up in the Table of Nations (Gen. 10:7) as a Nubian tribe,[3] and that of his successor Taharqa (690–664 B.C.) is wrongly identified in the Biblical narrative (2 Kings 19:9), we cannot help but conclude that Biblical writers of the seventh to sixth centuries B.C. lacked precise knowledge of Egypt as recent as a few generations before their own time.

Such ignorance is puzzling if one has felt inclined to be impressed by the traditional claims of inerrancy made by conservative Christianity on behalf of the Bible.[4] And indeed the Pentateuch and the historical books boldly present a precise chronology that would carry the Biblical narrative through the very period when the ignorance and discrepancy prove most embarassing.[5] A totaling of the lengths of reign of the kings of Judah from Solomon's fourth year (when allegedly the temple in Jerusalem was dedicated: 1 Kings 6:1) to the destruction of Jerusalem in 586 B.C. yields 430 years and therefore would bring us back to 1016 B.C. for this point in Solomon's reign. Again, according to 1 Kings 6:1, 480 years is supposed to have elapsed between the Exodus and the dedication of the temple, thus producing a date of 1496 B.C. for the former event. Since the Sojourn in Egypt is stated to have lasted for 430 years (Exod. 12:40), the descent of Jacob and his family to the land of Goshen must have taken place in 1926 B.C. If now we add the lengths of life of Abraham, Isaac, and Jacob (290)[6] we arrive at 2216 B.C. for the birth of Abraham. This would mean that Abraham's arrival in Canaan would have to fall in 2141 B.C. (cf. Gen. 12:4), and his descent to Egypt (Gen. 12:10–19) between

---

placement in the present name, which was originally "Sesy"; and this gave rise to the Greek "Sesoosis, Sesostris," as G. Maspero long ago convincingly demonstrated: *JdS* (1901), 593ff., 665ff.; idem, *Histoire ancienne des peuples de l'Orient* (Paris, 1898), 2:267, n. 2. Unfortunately Sethe's weak but forcefully stated objections and his preference for "Senwosret" as the *Vorlage* of "Sesostris" (*ZÄS* 41 [1901], 54–55; idem, *Sesostris* [Leipzig, 1900]) swept all other views before it, and now has become virtually an article of faith: cf. A. B. Lloyd, *Herodotus, Book II. A Commentary* (Leiden, 1988), 3:16–37. Attempts to find "Sisera" in Philistine or Luwian onomastica (R.A.S. MacAlister, *The Philistines: Their History and Civilization* [Chicago, 1965], 43; W. F. Albright, *Yahweh and the Gods of Canaan* [New York, 1968], 251, n. 127) are not very convincing. The use of the *alif* in the Hebrew form, where Egyptian originally showed *ayin* is no problem; Egyptian *ayin* was notoriously weak.

[3] M. C. Astour, *JBL* 84 (1965), 422–25.

[4] See the apposite remarks of R. E. Brown, *The Critical Meaning of the Bible* (New York, 1981).

[5] Cf. H. H. Rowley, *From Joseph to Joshua* (London, 1950), 57ff.

[6] Abraham, 100 years old at the birth of Issac (Gen. 21:5); Issac, 60 years old at the birth of Jacob (Gen. 25:26); Jacob, 130 years old at the time of the descent into Egypt (Gen. 47:9).

that date and 2116 B.C., or under the 10th Dynasty of Herakleopolis. Jacob's descent would have occurred in Senwosret I's reign, and the entire Sojourn would have occupied the outgoing 12th Dynasty, the entire 13th Dynasty, the Hyksos occupation, and the early Dynasty to Hatshepsut's ninth year! In the light of Numbers 32:13, which assigns 40 years to the Wandering, the conquest of the land under Joshua must have begun in 1456 B.C., or on the morrow of Thutmose III's victorious campaigns when all Canaan belonged to Egypt, and on the eve of Amenophis II's deportation of the local population. Even more astounding are the implications of the resultant placement of the Period of the Judges, namely 1456 to 1080 B.C.[7] This is almost exactly coeval with the Egyptian empire in Asia! Yet our Egyptian sources mention neither the patriarchs, Israel in Egypt, Joshua, nor his successors, while the Bible says absolutely nothing about the Egyptian empire in the land. In fact, the Biblical writers are wholly and blissfully unaware of the colossal discrepancy to which their "history" and "chronology" have given rise.

The strength, however, of a confessional commitment to bolster a pre-judgment will not allow most conservative Jewish or Christian exegetes to discard the whole chronological arrangement, and recent work has proven Muslim scholars similarly in thrall.[8] The basic pattern of Patriarchal Age, Descent and Sojourn, Exodus and Conquest, and Judges *must* be essentially correct—Is it not inherently reasonable? Do you have a better one?—and consequently numerous ingenious solutions are devised. The most common trick has been to reduce time spans to generations: thus the 480 figure must really represent twelve generations: but 40 years per generation is too long, 20 being much closer to the average. Hence we can cut the figure in half and put the Exodus around 1255 B.C. instead of 1486, and lo! it falls squarely in the reign of Ramesses II, and thus allusion to "Ra'amses" in Exodus 1:11 can be nicely accommodated! Similarly the 430 years of the Sojourn must simply be a curious equivalent of roughly four generations—does not Genesis 15:16 virtually prove it?—and so the Descent will come to rest about the middle of the fourteenth century B.C., or at the close of the Amarna age. Although the Gargantuan ages of the patriarchs are not extraneous to the Genesis material as we now have it, but actually inform it,[9] nevertheless these too are swept away or transmogrified into normal generation estimates; and thus the "Patriarchal age" can occupy the fifteenth and early fourteenth centuries and

[7] That is, leaving 20 years for Saul, 40 for David (cf. 1 Kings 2:11), and 4 for Solomon.

[8] Cf. A. Osman, *Stranger in the Valley* (London, 1987), and D. B. Redford, *BAR* 15, no. 2 (1989), 8.

[9] Cf. Gen. 17, 21:1–2 (the birth of Isaac); 24:1 (the marriage of Isaac); 27 (the blessing of Jacob); 48:8–20 (the blessing of Ephraim). None of these stories would survive without the fantastic ages involved, integral as they are to the plot.

accommodate the alleged "Nuzi" parallels.[10] And if one is still impressed by the "appropriateness" of having Joseph rise to power under the Hyksos who, as his Semitic congeners, would have taken kindly to him (although the Joseph story clearly distinguishes Joseph from Pharaoh and his court as Egyptians), then what matter if we drop our objections to the 430 years and take them literally? Joseph would then come to Egypt around 1680, just as the Hyksos were taking power![11]

Such manhandling of the evidence smacks of prestidigitation and numerology; yet it has produced the shaky foundations on which a lamentable number of "histories" of Israel have been written. Most are characterized by a somewhat naive acceptance of sources at face value coupled with failure to assess the evidence as to its origin and reliability. The result was the reduction of all data to a common level, any or all being grist for a wide variety of mills. Scholars expended substantial effort on questions that they had failed to prove were valid questions at all. Under what dynasty did Joseph rise to power? Who was the Pharaoh of the Oppression? Of the Exodus? Can we identify the princess who drew Moses out of the river? Where did the Israelites make their exit from Egypt: via the Wady Tumilat or by a more northerly point? One can ap-

---

[10] The traditional faith in the Nuzi texts as providing fifteenth-century corroboration of the customs of the Patriarchs is well expressed in J. Bright, A History of Israel (Philadelphia, 1959), 71–79 (although long since made fashionable by Albright and his students). Unfortunately, most of the parallels have proved to be illusory: cf. J. Van Seters, JBL 87 (1968), 401–8; idem, HTR 62 (1969), 377–95; idem, Orientalia 44 (1975), 585–86; idem, In Search of History (New Haven, Conn., 1983), 226 and n. 61.

[11] Crypto-orthodox tendencies drive some scholars to ludicrous ends. For example, Albright had so convinced himself of the historicity of Moses, as well as the late date for the Exodus, that he could claim his hero was born in the late fourteenth century B.C. and died about the middle of the thirteenth, refraining only from providing the regnal year and calendrics (W. F. Albright, in F. M. Cross, ed., Magnalia Dei: The Mighty Acts of God [Garden City, N.Y., 1976], 122). The thirteenth-century date for the Exodus depends so vitally on Exod. 1:11 with its reference to the city "Ra'amses"—references in Gen. 47:11 (a land of) Ra'amses and in Ps. 78:12, 43 to Tanis actually complicate the issue—that conservatives have realized it must be held at all costs; and the difficulty of accounting for the loss of Pi in Pi-ramesses, the residence of Ramesses II, is glossed over as though quite unimportant (M. Bietak, in A. F. Rainey, ed., Egypt, Sinai and Israel [Tel Aviv, 1983], 26–28). As confidence grows, a simple denial that Exod. 1:11 is late will suffice (cf. M. Görg, Kairos 20 [1978], 278; W. H. Schmidt, Exodus, Sinai und Mose [Darmstadt, 1983], 26; yet on the slimmest grounds of the Sethnakht stela, Moses can become Amenmesse and Sethnakht the Pharaoh of the Exodus (Görg, Kairos 20 [1978], 279–80; O. Keel, Monotheismus im Alten Ägypten und seiner Umwelt [Fribourg, 1980], 281–29 and n. 57). If some allusions in the Exodus account seem more in keeping with a flight of the Israelites, while others point to an expulsion, let's have two Exoduses or even more (cf. J. J. Rowley, From Joseph to Joshua [London, 1950], 6–7, 146; R. de Vaux, Histoire ancienne d'Israel [Paris, 1971], 1:439–40; G. W. Ahlström, Who Were the Israelites? [Winona Lake, Ind., 1986], 46). It all boggles the mind.

preciate the pointlessness of these questions if one poses similar questions of the Arthurian stories, without first submitting the text to a critical evaluation. Who were consuls of Rome when Arthur drew the sword from the stone? Where was Merlin born? Where is Avalon to be located? Can one seriously envisage a classical historian pondering whether it was Iarbas or Aeneas that was responsible for Dido's suicide, where exactly did Remus leap over the wall, what really happened to Romulus in the thunderstorm, and so forth? In all these imagined cases none of the material initially prompting the questions has in any way undergone a prior evaluation as to how historical it is. And any scholar who exempts any part of his sources from critical evaluation runs the risk of invalidating some or all of his conclusions. It matters not in this case what his motivation might be—a prior confessional stance, scholarly "wishful thinking," or a misplaced pride in one's chosen discipline—the resultant vitiation of one's attempt at history will be the same. And if the Biblical material in the Pentateuch, Joshua, and Judges becomes a kind of smorgasbord of equally valid morsels of evidence, to be chosen or rejected at whim, we shall have about as many reconstructions of the premonarchic "history" of Israel as there are scholars willing to make the attempt.

Biblical historical scholarship has of late been bedeviled by the acceptance, tacitly or explicitly, of a number of arbitrary preconceptions that fail to be honestly acknowledged, and by a tedious tendency to rationalize the conservative views learned at the feet of priest, preacher, or rabbi as a philosophy of history. Under the first one might cite the commonly accepted view that ancient Israel perceived history as god's judgment on mankind leading inexorably to universal salvation through god's guidance of Israel. Such a view obviously goes hand in hand with a feeling that ancient Israel was unique, in particular, in its awareness of history and history writing: none of the great river-valley civilizations of Egypt or Mesopotamia really produced works of "history"; only Israel did, and of course Greece (with a hasty nod in the direction of a *most* prestigious discipline). Moreover, Egypt and Mesopotamia really *killed* the élan that produced an awareness of history and led eventually to history writing: "It is a well-known fact that Israel is the only people in the whole Near East where annalistic writing developed into real historiography."[12] Under the second one might cite the curious problem (or in the context a perceived problem) as to when we should begin our history of ancient

[12] S. Mowinckel, *ASTI* 2 (1963), 8; for thoughts in a similar vein, see H. Gunkel, *Die Religion in Geschichte und Gegenwart* (Tübingen, 1957–), 2:1353; H. Gese, *ZThK* 55 (1958), 41–42; G. von Rad, *The Problem of the Hexateuch and Other Essays* (Edinburgh, 1966), 170.

Israel? With patriarchs, thus in conformity with the Biblical sequence;[13] or with some later point of focus? Should we begin our history "where writing begins," or where the term "Israelites" first appears; or should we target the Davidic empire, when a nation-state seems first to appear?[14] Possibly the introduction of such terms as "pre-" and "protohistory" will help to clarify our understanding of what we are doing.[15]

Sadly, these tendencies reflect neither scientific thought nor basic intellectual honesty. The farsightedness of a *few* eighth- through fifth-century B.C. prophets who groped toward a universalism and a teleological explanation of god's activity should not be misconstrued as a national mindset, and was certainly alien to Israel as a whole.[16] One would be as little justified in ascribing the Memphite theologian's sophisticated deism to all Egyptian religion.[17] If one persists in this erroneous belief, it must be because of the dead weight of a confessional pledge that has no place in a historian's consciousness. With regard to Israel's scoring a "first" in developing a sense of history and history writing, our acceptance of this will depend on how we define history and history writing, and also on the date we give to certain specific pieces. A surprising number of scholars begin with an essentially classical definition of history and history writing,[18] and when they fail to find them in the literature of ancient Egypt or Mesopotamia, cavalierly dismiss those civilization as places where a true appreciation of "history" may not be expected. Israel is excepted on the basis of the Deuteronomistic history and the Davidic "court history," both facilely categorized as "history" (even though they have little in common with Greek examples of "history" and approximate other known genres of Near Eastern writings) and, at least in the case of the latter, assigned a tenth century B.C. date. Neither the category nor the date, as we shall see, is justified in any way.[19] Moreover, to apply classical criteria derived from the narrow study of Greek historiography is simply out of order. Gone are the days when Afro-Asiatic languages (or those of any family) are analyzed by using a linguistic jargon framed originally to describe Greek and Latin: languages are now met with on their *own* grounds, and analyzed on the basis of their own internal structures. And the approach of an individual nation to its past should similarly be hon-

---

[13] So S. Hermann, *Geschichte Israels*[2] (Munich, 1980), 63, 78, and passim; see also J. M. Miller and J. H. Hayes, *A History of Ancient Israel and Judah* (Philadelphia, 1986), 74–79.

[14] W. W. Hallo, *Biblical History in its Near Eastern Setting* (Pittsburgh, 1980), 10; J. A. Soggin, *Eretz Israel* 14 (1978), 44*ff.; A. Malamat, *ThZ* 39 (1983), 1–3.

[15] Malamat, *ThZ* 39 (1983), 1–3; cf. the incisive comments of N. P. Lemche, *Biblische Notizen* 24 (1984), 94ff.

[16] Cf. Van Seters, *In Search of History*, 241; Ahlström, *Who Were the Israelites?*, 24.

[17] On Memphite Theology, see p. 399.

[18] Cf. that of Van Seters, *In Search of History*, 2–4.

[19] See p. 299ff.

estly described on its own terms, and not automatically disqualified because it differs from the Greek approach.

As to the question where we should begin the history of ancient Israel, the problem is largely chimerical. Of much more significant reference are such questions as: Under what conditions and to what purpose did the ancestor traditions of Israel take shape? Where and when did the Exodus theme originate? Of what nature and how reliable is our evidence for the premonarchical history of the component elements of the Iron Age "Israel"? And in all our efforts to formulate the *right* questions, we should be wise to reject the application of the adjective "Biblical" to "history" and "archaeology."[20] (The only meaning I can understand in such a use is allomorphic for an adjectival genitive: "Biblical archaeology" signifies the recovery and analysis of papyri and manuscripts of the Biblical books; and "Biblical history" the history of the work itself from its initial appearance in post-Exilic times). Too often "Biblical" in this context has had the limiting effect on scholarship by implying the validity of studying Hebrew culture and history in isolation. What is needed rather is a view of ancient Israel within its true Near Eastern context, and one that will neither exaggerate nor denigrate Israel's actual place within that setting.

THE FIRST APPEARANCE OF THE HEBREWS IN PALESTINE: MODELS AND THEORIES

If we examine what evidence we have for the Israelite appearance and settlement in Canaan, we shall find that it falls into three disparate and unequal bodies of material. In the first place we have the historical traditions preserved in parts of Numbers, Joshua, and Judges, which far outweighs in sheer volume the other two; second, the extra-Biblical textual evidence; and finally, the archaeological data of excavation.

The tradition of Israel itself is perhaps most familiar through its being hallowed in the Judeo-Christian culture, and presents us with the picture of a thoroughgoing military conquest. This is supposed to have taken place in the relatively short space of time of seven years (cf. Jos. 14:7–10). Two major thrusts are discernible. The first (reported no less than three times) involves an attack from Kadesh northward into the Negev at Hormah (Num. 14:45) and Arad (Num. 12:1–3), a move declared to have been abortive in Numbers but successful in Joshua and Judges.[21] The second brings the Israelites through Edom and Moab into the plain east

---

[20] See R. B. Coote and K. W. Whitelam, *The Emergence of Early Israel in Historical Perspective* (Sheffield, 1987); G.R.H. Wright, *ZA* 78 (1988), 157.

[21] Cf. Josh. 15:13 (Caleb takes Hebron and Debir—from which direction is not specifically stated); Jud. 1:16 (Judah and the Kenites go up from the "City of Palms" [Kadesh] to take the Negev).

of the Jordan just north of the Dead Sea (Num. 21:10–21), where the attack bifurcates. One column proceeds north into Gilead (Num. 32:39) and Bashan (Num. 21:33–35) and also repulses Midian (Num. 31); the other crosses the Jordan and penetrates to the highlands north of Jerusalem at Gibeon (Josh. 2–9). From Gibeon a southward campaign secures the Judaean highlands and the foothills (Josh. 10:28–39), while a northern one reduces the coast, Galilee, and the north Jordan valley (Josh. 11:1–11). Numerous cities and regions are reported to have been peopled: Hormah (Num. 14:45), Arad (Num. 21:1–3), Midian (Num. 31), Gibeon (Josh. 9), and Jarmuth (Josh. 10:3, 23); or to have been taken and destroyed: Heshbon (Num. 21:21–30), Edre'i (Num. 21:33–35), Jericho (Josh. 2–6), 'Ai (Josh. 7:2–8:29), and Hazor (Josh. 11–11).

But even a cursory reading of this account is bound to excite suspicion.[22] Cities with massive fortifications fall easily to rustic nomads fresh off the desert (mighty Lachish in only two days according to Josh. 10:31), a feat Pharaoh's armies had great difficulty in accomplishing. Some cities are taken twice in the record (cf. Bethel: Josh. 12:16; Jud. 1:23), others three times (cf. Hebron: Josh. 10:36ff.; 15:13; Jud. 1:10; Debir: Josh. 10:38ff.; 15:15–17; Jud. 1:11; Hormah: Num. 21:3; Josh. 12:14; Jud. 1:17), suggesting conflicting traditions poorly integrated. Etiologies inform the stories to a remarkable degree;[23] and while etologies need not completely undermine the history of tradition,[24] they distance its origins within the mists of historical uncertainty and render the recorder's sources suspect. In addition to this, Egyptian personal names are wrongly understood,[25] and situations and events of the United Monarchy are anticipated.[26]

A detailed comparison of this version of the Hebrew takeover of Palestine with the extra-Biblical evidence totally discredits the former. Not only is there a complete absence, as we have seen, in the records of the Egyptian empire of any mention or allusion to such a whirlwind of annihilation, but also Egyptian control over Canaan and the very cities Joshua is supposed to have taken scarcely wavered during the entire period of the Late Bronze Age. Far more damaging, however, than this argument from

[22] Miller and Hayes, A History, 58–63.

[23] Cf. the twelve stones in the Jordan (Josh. 4:1–10), the explanation of the toponymn Gilgal (Josh. 5:2–9), the preservation of Rahab (Josh. 6:22–25), the explanation of the toponym Achor (Josh. 7), the explanation of the toponym 'Ai (Josh. 8:28), the ruin-heap in the gate (Josh. 8:29), the explanation of the servile status of the Gibeonites (Josh. 9), the stones in the cave at Mekkedah (Josh. 10:27), the altar by the Jordan (Josh. 22:10–34).

[24] Cf. B. S. Childs, JBL 82 (1963), 279–92.

[25] Sheshay in Josh. 15:14 as a son of 'Anak: Merneptah in 18:15 as the "waters of Nephtoah."

[26] The rebuilding of Jericho (Josh. 6:26; cf. 1 Kings 16:34); "sojourners" among the Israelites (Josh. 8:33–35).

silence is the archaeological record. Sites such as Hormah, Arad, Jericho, 'Ai, and Jarmuth had indeed suffered violent destruction, but this had been during the Early Bronze Age or at the end of Middle Bronze and during the Late Bronze Age they had lain unoccupied (save for squatters); others such as Kadesh Barnea, Heshbon, and Gibeon were not to be settled until the Iron Age.[27] Those sites that do show massive destruction at the transition from the Bronze to the Iron Age, about 1200 B.C., can as easily be explained as victims of the movement of the Sea Peoples.[28] The regions of Edom and Moab, represented in Numbers as sedentary states, supported only a few cities in the Late Bronze Age maintaining the north-south trade route to Damascus;[29] the Edomite and Moabite kingdoms, which Numbers wrongly understands to be already in existence, did not put in an appearance before the ninth century B.C.[30] Finally, the overall archaeological survey of settlement patterns in the final two centuries of the second millennium B.C. does not show destruction at a single point in time, but rather a gradual settlement of pastoralists (not completed until the tenth century) first in the hill country and then in regions densely populated by sedentary inhabitants.[31]

The unanimity of the archaeological record, coupled with a revulsion against the neoorthodox approach to the Bible as exemplified by groups like the Albright school, gradually resulted in a turning away from archaeological explanations to socioeconomic models. Beginning in the early 1960s G. E. Mendenhall began to preach the necessity of applying the model of the "peasants' revolt" to the Biblical record of the Conquest; and in the 1970s N. K. Gottwald refined this ingenious notion into a detailed and far-reaching theory. Basic to the discussion are three theses: that "Israel" did not originate in an ethnically distinct element, at the beginning outside Canaan spatially and culturally, but was from the outset essentially of the same stock as the Canaanites; that the Israelites were

[27] Cf. J. Gallaway, *BASOR* 196 (1969), 2ff.; J. M. Miller, in *Israelite and Judaean History* (Philadelphia, 1977), 272; R. Cohen, *Kadesh-barnea* (Jerusalem, 1983); S. Hermann, in *Biblical Archaeology Today* (Jerusalem, 1985), 48; M. Kochavi, ibid., 55. The recent attempt of Bimson to redate the Exodus and Conquest to the fifteenth century B.C. (J. J. Bimson, *Redating the Exodus* [Sheffield, 1978]; J. J. Bimson and D. Livingston, *BAR* 13, no. 5 [1987], 40ff.), while honestly trying to maintain faith with a Biblical chronology, fails in my view to face up to hard facts and glosses over difficulties.

[28] Cf. Ahlström, *Who Were the Israelites?*, 3; see also my discussion on p. 290f.

[29] D. B. Redford, *JSSEA* 12 (1982), 55–74.

[30] J. R. Bartlett, *PEQ* 104 (1972), 26–37; C. M. Bennett, in *IDB* Suppl. (Nashville, Tenn., 1976), 251–52; *pace* J. Sauer, *BASOR* 263 (1986), 10 (Iron IA sherds do not a kingdom make!).

[31] See most recently I. Finkelstein, *The Archaeology of the Israelite Settlement* (Jerusalem, 1988); F. S. Frick, *The Foundation of the State in Ancient Israel: A Survey of Models and Theories* (Sheffield, 1985); cf. also Ahlström, *Who Were the Israelites?*, 67.

not infiltrating pastoralists, but a sedentary, agricultural part of Canaanite society; and that the creation of the political entity "Israel" resulted from a violent rejection of the Canaanite city-state system, with its mechanisms of taxation, impressment, and the corvée. A corollary explains the presence of traditions implying an origin for Israel outside Canaan as applicable only to "subgroups" later taken into the tribal federation. A second corollary would see the worship of Yahweh as the cultic "cement" that unified the federation and gave it a traditional focus.[32]

The work of Gottwald, the most articulate and farsighted exponent of the theory, is like a breath of fresh air. It has had a most salutary effect in pointing up how forced some of our most cherished interpretations of archaeological remains have been in the past. Nevertheless, the "peasant revolt" theory is incapable of proof on one count, meets with opposition from circumstantial evidence on a second, and comes close to foundering on a third.[33]

No one can prove (or disprove, for that matter) that the tribal federation "Israel" originated on Palestinian soil. No one can prove that the major components of that federation had always existed on Palestinian soil. All that is known for certain is that, some time during the fourth-quarter of the thirteenth century B.C., Egypt knew of a group, or political entity, called "Israel" and occupying part of the land of Canaan;[34] but whether the group had recently arrived or taken shape is not stated in our sources. That the Hebrew language is closely related to the West Semitic dialect(s) that we subsume under the catchall "Canaanite" is a fact; but then, it is equally closely related to the dialects of Transjordan as well. To maintain that early Israel was agrarian in its economy rather than pastoralist is, I believe, to draw a false line of demarcation. As we have seen,[35] the EB IV–MB I communities in Palestine practiced some dry farming and were accomplished tinkers; yet they were essentially transhumant pastoralists nonetheless. From the Ramesside age literary descriptions of the population of upland Palestine similarly reveal to us a group of pastoralists but at this time in the process of settling down.[36]

Finally, the belief in a peasants' revolt enjoys no evidential support and

[32] Among the many books and articles written on the subject one might cite the following: G. E. Mendenhall, *BA* 25 (1962), 66–86; idem, *The Tenth Generation* (Baltimore, 1973); N. K. Gottwald, *VT Suppl.* 28 (1975), 89–100; idem, *The Tribes of Yahweh* (New York, 1979); idem, in *Biblical Archaeology Today*, 34–46; D. N. Freedman and D. F. Graf, eds., *Palestine in Transition: The Emergence of Ancient Israel* (Sheffield, 1983); Miller, in *Israelite and Judaean History*, 277–79.

[33] For rebuttals of the "peasant revolt" theory, see A. H. Hauser, *JSOT* 7 (1978), 2–19; Ahlström, *Who Were the Israelites?*, 6–9, 19–21; D. Pardee, *JNES* 48 (1989), 147.

[34] KRI IV, 19.

[35] See p. 82f.

[36] See p. 278f.

can, in fact, be shown to be most unlikely. Too much has been made of the agency of the ʿApiru, attested in the Amarna Letters, in enticing the peasantry (ḫupšu) away from the control of the local town headmen. This sometimes did happen, but it was primarily in that region that had long posed problems for the Egyptian administration, namely the great arc of no-man's land extending from north Lebanon and the Eleutheros Valley through the upper Orontes to the Golan, essentially the territory dividing the Egyptian sphere of authority from that of the Hittites. This swath of territory experienced more serious ʿApiru activity in the fourteenth century B.C. simply because this was the period that witnessed the birth of new march states in the border land between the two empires, Amurru and other lesser states to the east. The authors of this new polity, Abdi-ashirta and his son Aziru, were willing to use any group in their struggle; and if they appealed to Rib-Addi of Byblos's peasants, it was only a tactic in their insurgency, and must not be taken as an index of a common disaffection about to result in a widespread peasant revolt.[37]

A serious flaw in the peasants' revolt lies in the postulated nature and function of the "city-state." Protagonists of the theory have conjured up something that they call the "Canaanite city-state" for which they have in their mind's eye a clear picture with respect to society, economics, and relative importance, largely inspired by such well-known states as Ugarit, Alalakh, and perhaps also by the concept of the Greek *polis*. Whether or not the Syrian cities in question qualify as "city-states" on the Greek model, they share little in common with communities in Palestine. The Egyptian conquests within the Eleutheros-Qatna line had swept away the "Great Kingships" of Middle Bronze times, and drastically reduced the populations of areas with such pretensions; so that by the fourteenth and thirteenth centuries B.C. nought was left here but a handful of settlements—we can scarcely call them cities—governed by headmen wholly subservient to Egypt. These surviving villages were nothing but local patrimonies (cf. EA 179:28–29),[38] tolerated by the Egyptians but a prey to internecine blood feuds, pillaging, and extortion (cf. EA 248:14–17; 250:16–18; 263; 292:41–52; 270:14–21; 298, etc.). They were small—fifty men were enough to guard most of them (EA 238:11; 289:42; 295 rev. 6, etc.)—and flocks of sheep could be kept inside at night (EA 186:67).[39] Headmen of such settlements, far from being the "kings" or "aristocracy" that the theory requires, were often destitute as private in-

[37] M. Liverani, *The Politics of Abdi-Ashirta of Amurru* (Malibu, Calif., 1979); Ahlström, *Who Were the Israelites?*, 15–16.

[38] They were, in fact, what appears in Hebrew as the *bet 'ab*, "houses of the father": see J. Scharbart, in W. C. Delsman et al., eds., *Von Kanaan bis Kerala* (Neukirchen-Vluyn, 1982), 213–37; Miller and Hayes, *A History*, 91.

[39] Even Megiddo required only 100! EA 244:35.

dividuals (EA 316:18–22), lacking in such essentials as transport (EA 180:21–23; 198:21–23; 271:18–21), and in constant danger of having their property confiscated by the Egyptians (EA 292:29–35). When danger threatened the headmen of such illustrious towns as Jerusalem, Accho, and Achsaph, they could muster among themselves no more than fifty chariots (EA 290:20–25). It is a wild exaggeration to term these impoverished Canaanite mayors or headmen (ḫazanūti) "an agrarian elite";[40] and quite preposterous to picture the poor peasants rebelling against a powerful landed aristocracy. The ʿApiru and nomadic dissidents *always* had the upper hand: to the Canaanite headmen they were "mighty enemies" (EA 318:9), and as few as forty were sufficient to capture and destroy "cities" (EA 185:47; 186:50).

If the peasants' revolt theory is unacceptable *en tant que telle*, it has spawned another that has recently attained some respectability. This would have it that during the bad times at the close of the Late Bronze Age Palestine witnessed a demographic shift, a withdrawal of survivors from the valleys and plains into the highlands. Out of this essentially "Canaanite" phenomenon crystallized a polity that came to be known as "Israel." Those who back this theory have, it seems, been impressed by what is now an unassailable fact, namely that the culture of the Iron I period (c. 1200–1000 B.C.), when from all accounts Israel should have been passing through its formative stage, is nothing but a late development of an essentially Canaanite culture—nothing specifically "Israelite" can be discerned. But in addition to admitting the obvious, proponents of this "withdrawal" theory deny a priori that the Iron I culture represents an erstwhile pastoral community, fresh off the steppe.[41]

Unfortunately this theory has as little to recommend it as the peasants' revolt idea. While the cultural continuum between the Canaanite LB II and Iron I is a fact, the origin and identity of the Iron I peoples of the highlands cannot be sought among the fugitive Canaanite peasantry of the lowlands. Egyptian texts describe the highlanders clearly as transhumant pastoralists, and the fact that they borrowed Canaanite house types cannot be used to disprove this. (I myself have sat in houses on the Medeba plains that, by the same kind of reasoning, might be used to prove the presence there of people from Jaffa or Haifa, so closely do they conform to a Palestinian style; yet their occupants, my hosts, were recently settled bedu.) If Egyptian texts do describe any movement of people, it is always hills-to-plains, not the other way around. One need only peruse

---

[40] M. L. Chaney, in Freedman and Graf, *Palestine in Transition*, 75.

[41] A Alt, *Kleine Schriften zur Geschichte des Volkes Israel* (Munich, 1953), 97ff.; A. F. Rainey, *IEJ* 30 (1980), 250–51; Ahlström, *Who Were the Israelites?*, 27; N. P. Lemche, *Early Israel: Anthropological and Historical Studies on the Israelite Society before the Monarchy* (Leiden, 1985).

the didactic piece known as P. Anastasi I, the "Satyrical Letter," to appreciate how unsafe the Egyptian officer felt on a mission, having to traverse the Palestinian highlands, a prey not to fugitive lowlanders but to nomads; and with what relief he reached the haven of the coastal towns.[42] The mountains contained the haunts of brigands whither the unwary could be spirited away and held for ransom,[43] and whence cattle thieves could descend upon herds in the lowlands (cf. 1 Chron. 7:21).

In sum, the evidence does not support the idea of a revolt by agricultural peons from within a powerful system controlled by an urban elite, or a flight into the hills of survivors at the close of LB II. If such a system in which classes were in the throes of polarization had ever existed, it was long since a thing of the past in the outgoing thirteenth century B.C. The real threat at that time to both peasantry and their impoverished masters alike (both now subservient to Egypt) lay outside their own decrepit and moribund system, both in time and space. To find it, isolate it, and describe it, we must look south and east of Canaan.

EGYPT AND THE SHASU

The sparsely populated hill country of central Palestine, already partly stripped of its inhabitants under the 18th Dynasty,[44] held little attraction for the Egyptians who felt basically disinclined to police it. It was necessary, however, to deny it to others who might pose a threat to Egyptian interests in the region. In the fourteenth century during the Amarna period, Egypt conceived of these highlands as encompassing two spheres of responsibility, the *mâtat Urusalim*, "the lands of Jerusalem,"[45] centered upon Jerusalem and synonymous with the Judaean highlands; and the northern hill country controlled from Shechem. Since these thinly settled uplands constituted ideal staging areas and terrain for settlement for renegades, *some* kind of imperial presence was necessary to save the valleys and coastlands from marauders. Both areas, however, the Egyptians were content, if not obliged, to leave in the hands of local dynasties.[46] Shechem's sphere of influence and interference was extensive, stretching from Megiddo[47] and the caravan crossing of the Jordan[48] in the north to Gezer[49] in the southwest; but Lab'ayu, the local sheikh under Amenophis III and Akhenaten, unfortunately failed to operate in Egyptian interests

[42] P. Anastasi I, 23:3ff.

[43] Cf. EA 292:26ff.; 49ff.; on 'Apiru pressure into the Shephelah, threatening Gezer, see EA 273:18–24.

[44] See p. 208, and L. E. Stager, *BASOR* 260 (1985), 5.

[45] T. Ishida, *The Royal Dynasties in Ancient Israel* (Berlin, 1977), 129.

[46] Cf. EA 253:11–15.

[47] EA 244.

[48] EA 255.

[49] EA 253:21–22.

and had to be removed.[50] The damage was done, however, and the ʿApiru could operate freely around Shechem.[51] In the south the Egyptian authorities suspended the right of primogeniture, perhaps an indication of Egypt's greater concern for this region, and installed a younger scion of the Jerusalem house, one Abdi-khepa.[52] Several times, in contexts in which he is defending himself against misrepresentation at court, Abdi-khepa denies strenuously that he is a *ḫazānu*, a position obviously beneath him in his own view.[53] No, he is a *weʾu* (Egyptian *wʿw*), a "soldier."[54] As I have demonstrated elsewhere,[55] this is to be taken to mean that Abdi-khepa had been one of those "children of the chiefs" dispatched to Egypt and given military training there. He was now an "Egyptian soldier," and proud of it. Thus Abdi-khepa in his letters unconsciously stresses the importance the Egyptian administration placed on Jerusalem in its strategic planning: the city was *not* to be abandoned by a *military* authority.[56] The most persuasive argument he can hope to use is that "the lands (of Jerusalem) are lost," and that either a garrison is to be sent or he is to be taken back to Egypt. Jerusalem is a city "in which the king has set his name," a sure indication of the presence of an Egyptian stela in the city.[57] In fact an Egyptian building (temple?) may once have stood either within the circuit of the original walls or to the north of the present Damascus gate.[58]

[50] E. F. Campbell, *BA* 23 (1960), 19–20; idem, in G. E. Wright, *Shechem* (New York, 1965), 191–92; A. F. Rainey, in *IDB* Suppl., 869.

[51] EA 287:30–31; 289:23–24.

[52] That it was not his right of inheritance but rather pharaonic choice that determined his posting in Jerusalem is clearly indicated in EA 286:12; see Moran, in H. Goedicke and J. J. Roberts, eds., *Unity and Diversity* (Baltimore, 1975), 156; cf. Ishida, *Royal Dynasties*, 155.

[53] On *ḫazānu*, see p. 198. The term is nothing more than the equivalent of the modern *ʿomdah* or *mukhtar*.

[54] EA 285:5–6; 288:9–11; W. E. Albright, *JEA* 23 (1937), 196. *Wʿw*, meaning "(full-time) infantry-soldier" (*Wb* I, 280; A. R. Schulman, *Military Rank Title and Organization in the Egyptian New Kingdom* [Berlin, 1964], 36–37), is used generically in contrast to a "civil" posting (cf. Moran, in *Unity and Diversity*). The term can also be used of a marine-soldier (*Urk* IV, 895:9, 996:1; J. E. Quibell, *The Ramesseum* (London, 1898), pl. 27:4; C. Vandersleyen, *Les guerres d'Amosis* [Brussels, 1971], 26ff.), or of a member of a gang of workmen: J. Černý, *A Community of Workmen at Thebes in the Ramesside Period* (Cairo, 1973), 47.

[55] *Akhenaten Temple Project*, 2:17, esp. n. 52.

[56] EA 287:49–50.

[57] EA 287:60–61: *šakan šumšu . . . ana dāriš* (Moran, in *Unity and Diversity*, 155). The Egyptian idiom would be the very common *smn rn (r-nḥḥ)*: D. Meeks, *Année lexicographique* (Paris, 1982), 3:170. For similar thought, see W.M.F. Petrie, *Hyksos and Israelite Cities* (London, 1906), pls. 22, 28; R. Giveon, *Les bédouins Shosou* (Leiden, 1972), 114–15 and (5).

[58] V. Scheil, *RB* 1 (1892), 116–17; L. H. Vincent and F. M. Abel, *Jerusalem* (Paris, 1922), 774–75, pl. 79:12; L. H. Vincent, *RB* 17 (1920), 311–12; W. Ward in F. James, *The Iron*

It thus seems clear that a real fear on the part of the pharaonic administration was that the central highlands could be used as a base by elements inimical to Egyptian interests. From here they could with impunity raid the lowlands and threaten the coastal route. (It is in this context that Abdi-khepa is outraged that Ashkelon, Gezer, and Lachish—the very cities whose integrity he was trying to guarantee—had given supplies to the ʿApiru.)[59] The sheikhdom at Shechem in which the Egyptians had put their faith, had proved too obstreperous; but in all probability Jerusalem stood fast and the ruling family rewarded the confidence the Egyptians had placed in it. Nonetheless, it was into this inhospitable upland, where it was still possible to enjoy an existence largely free of imperial authority, that the great folk movement of the end of the Late Bronze Age made its dramatic ingress.[60]

Egyptian Nilotic society had, since the dawn of time, given practical and moral priority to sedentary life and poured contempt on the uncontrolled movement of people. The verb *š³s* (pronounced perhaps **shasᵉ*) meant basically to move on foot, and it is often used of journeys or of the daily motion of the sun, which is all innocent enough.[61] But very early it took on a nuance of speed and furtiveness: messengers speed on foot to far-off places, and malcontents flee punishment.[62] A participial form was applied from at least as early as the 5th Dynasty to those "wanderers" the Egyptians habitually came into contact with in the north, and rapidly became a term with societal implications. The resultant *Š³sw* (**shaswᵉ*), the "Shasu," came to be used of wandering groups whom we would call bedu, with the significant distinction that unlike their modern counterparts they lacked the camel.[63] Their lawlessness and their proclivity to

---

Age at Beth Shan (Philadelphia, 1966), 174, figs. 98:3, 99:2; G. Barkay, *7th Archaeological Congress in Israel* (Jerusalem, 1980), 19; on the possibility of an ongoing Canaanite scribal tradition in Jerusalem, see R. Hess, *ZAW* 101 (1989), 249–65.

[59] EA 287:14–16. The fact that it is the *territory* of Ashkelon and Gezer that has aided the outlaws, rather than the cities themselves, may make these places less culpable than Lachish.

[60] See Giveon, *Shosou*; D. B. Redford, *JSSEA* 12 (1982), 74, n. 155; cf. also Z. A. Kafafi, *Biblische Notizen* 29 (1985), 17ff. For the suitability of such terrain to the 'Apiru, see Liverani, *Three Amarna Essays* (Malibu, Calif., 1979), 15.

[61] *Wb* IV, 412:5; CT I 212; P. E. Newberry, *Beni Hasan* (London, 1891), 1: pl. 41(A); PT 854; A. el-M. Bakir, *The Cairo Calendar (no. 86637)* (Cairo, 1966), pl. I, 4.

[62] Book of the Heavenly Cow 66 (E. Hornung, *Der Ägyptische Mythos von der Himmelskuh* [Göttingen, 1982], 6); G. Posener, *La première domination perse en Ègypte* (Cairo, 1937), 43; P. Posener-Kriéger, *Les archives du temple funeraire de Néferirkare-Kakai* (Cairo, 1976), 1:203–4.

[63] E. Edel, *Altägyptische Grammatik* (Rome, 1964), sec. 227; Giveon, *Shosou*; on the late domestication of the camel, see *CAD*, 5:35–36; W. G. Lambert, *BASOR* 160 (1960), 43 (no earlier than mid-ninth century B.C.); I. Finkelstein, *JNES* 47 (1988), 246–47 (with references); S. Redford, *JARCE* 26 (1989), 6, n. 28.

make raids gave rise in Canaanite (and Hebrew) to the denominative verb *šasā(h)*, "to plunder."[64]

Shasu are found in Egyptian texts from the 18th Dynasty through the Third Intermediate Period. They most frequently occur in generalizing toponym lists where the context helps little in pinpointing their location. But lists from Soleb and Amarah, ultimately of fifteenth century origin[65] suggest that an original concentration of Shasu settlements lay in southern Transjordan in the plains of Moab and northern Edom.[66] Here a group of six names is identified as in "the land of the Shasu" and these include Se'ir (i.e., Edom),[67] Laban (probably Libona, south of Amman),[68] Sam'ath (cf. the Shim'ethites, a clan of the Kenites: 1 Chron. 2:55), and *Wrbr* (probably the Wady Hasa).[69] Elsewhere in texts of the 19th and 20th Dynasties, the consistent linking of Shasu with Edom and the Arabah (Timna) places the identifications on the earlier lists beyond doubt.[70]

The localization of the "Land of the Shasu" in the mountainous districts of Se'ir east of the Arabah has an interesting consequence for one name in the mentioned lists from Soleb and Amarah—"*Yhw* (in) the land of the Shasu." For half a century it has been generally admitted that we have here the tetragrammaton, the name of the Israelite god, "Yah-

---

[64] T. O. Lambdin, *JAOS* 73 (1953), 155.

[65] Giveon, *Shosou*, 26ff. (doc. 6a); 74ff. (doc 16a).

[66] The presence of toponyms compounded with "Shasu" (cf. "the Spring of the Shasu": E. Edel, *Ortsnamenlisten aus dem Toten Tempel Amenophis III* [Bonn, 1966], 25; M. Görg, *JNES* 38 [1979], 199ff.; idem, *Biblische Notizen 9* [1979], 51–52; idem, *ZDPV* 98 [1982], 14; N. Na'aman, *GM* 57 [1982], 28–29; S. Ahituv, *Canaanite Toponyms in Ancient Egyptian Documents* [Leiden, 1984], 57–58) in Lebanon and Syria no more proves the Shasu to have been indigenous to that area than Iroquois toponyms around the Great Lakes prove the "Six Nations" to have originated there. Cf. C. Wissler, *Indians of the United States* (New York, 1940), 127–28; J. B. Griffin, *The Iroquois in American Prehistory* (Ann Arbor, Mich., 1944).

[67] There is absolutely no reason whatsoever to separate the *S'rr* of the Amareh list from the normal *S'r* (M. Astour, in M. Görg, [ed.], *Festschrift Elmar Edel* [Bamberg, 1979], 17ff.). The writing with the doubled *r* is thoroughly in keeping with Late Egyptian orthography, which often sought to distinguish a consonantal "trilled" *r* from a uvularized *r* by writing it twice: A. Erman, *Neuägyptische Grammatik* (Leipzig, 1933), 209, 304, etc. *S'rr* is thus nothing but a variant of the more common *S'r*.

[68] Giveon, *Shosou*, 76; cf. also Laban's role as the progenitor of the Ammonites and the Moabites: Gen. 19.

[69] *Wrbr* I take to be a variant of *Ybr* of the Thutmose III toponym list, the transliteration of the Canaanite *'ubal* (Arabic *wabil*) "dry wady bed," and used in this section of the list to designate the major east-west wadis leading off the upland into the Jordan rift: D. B. Redford, *JSSEA* 12 (1982), 64.

[70] Anast. vi.54–56 ("clans of the Shasu of Edom"); P. Harris I, 76:9 ("Se'ir with the Shasu clans"); P. Montet, *Kêmi 5* (1937), pl. III ("despoiler of the land of the Shasu, plunderer of the mountain of Se'ir"); for the Shasu in *Kḥkḥ* (Timna), see R. Giveon, *JARCE* 8 (1969–1970), 51ff.

weh";[71] and if this be the case, as it undoubtedly is, the passage constitutes a most precious indication of the whereabouts during the late fifteenth century B.C. of an enclave revering this god. And while it would be wrong to jump to the conclusion that "Israel" as known from the period of the Judges or the early monarchy was already in existence in Edom at this time, one cannot help but recall the numerous passages in later Biblical tradition that depict Yahweh "coming forth from Se'ir" and originating in Edom.[72] The only reasonable conclusion is that one major component in the later amalgam that constituted Israel, and the one with whom the worship of Yahweh originated, must be looked for among the Shasu of Edom already at the end of the fifteenth century B.C.

While the homeland of the Shasu must be located in Moab and Edom, several corridors took these nomads on a seasonal basis for pasturage, service, and brigandage[73] into other parts of the eastern Mediterranean. Northward a natural route, in existence at least as early as the Middle Bronze Age, led via Damascus to northern Syria;[74] and through the Jordan Valley and Jezreel the wanderer could gain access to the coast and Coele-Syria. Again, via the Jordan and such Wadys as Far'a or Qilt the central highland of Palestine could be reached with ease. Westward the Arabah and Negeb offered passable routes by means of which the Shasu could approach the Nile Delta.

Although the Shasu, ever hovering just beyond the periphery of Egyptian control, had always been a thorn in Pharaoh's side,[75] they burst with especially grievous force just before the beginning of the 19th Dynasty across the Arabah and into the Negeb and northern Sinai, cutting off Egypt's coastal route. Though Sety I had little trouble in beating them back,[76] the Shasu had thus begun to frequent a new transit corridor west-

[71] B. Grdseloff, *RHJE* 1 (1947), 69ff.; S. H. Horn, *JNES* 12 (1953), 201; R. Giveon, *VT* 14 (1964), 239ff.; in context *Yhw* would probably indicate a place-name, but parallels can be adduced of deity and bailiwick sharing a common name: R. de Vaux, *The Early History of Israel* (London, 1978), 334; M. Görg, *Biblische Notizen* 1 (1976), 7ff.

[72] R. de Vaux, *Eretz Israel* 9 (1968), 28*–32*; E. Lepinski, in *The Land of Israel: Crossroads of Civilization* (Louvain, 1985), 105 and n. 37; E. Axelsson, *The Lord Rose Up from Seir: Studies in the History and Traditions of the Negev and Southern Judah* (Stockholm, 1987); Ahlström, *Who Were the Israelites?*, 57–60. Ahlström's skepticism regarding *Yhw* and the location of the "Land of the Shasu" (p. 60) is wholly unwarranted.

[73] W. A. Ward *JESHO* 15 (1972), 52–53f.

[74] Redford, *JSSEA* 12 (1982), 55–56.

[75] *Urk* IV, 36, 721 (location of campaign unknown); see Giveon, *Shosou*, 9ff.; under Amenophis II the Transjordanian enclaves spring to prominence: ibid., 26ff.; Ward, *ADAJ* 18 (1973), 45–46.

[76] Cf. *KRI* I, 9; on Sety's campaigns, see my discussions on pp. 179–81. The keynote of Sety's policy toward the north was preemptive, which may cast doubt on whether the Shasu "threat" was anything more than an excuse: cf. the phrases in R. A. Caminos, *Kasr Ibrim* (London, 1968), pls. 39–40.

ward to the Egyptian border; and during the thirteenth and the twelfth centuries they are more than once reported along the "Suez" frontier.[77] Hither they trekked with their cattle on a seasonable pattern to gain access to the watering holes in the Wady Tumilat. A second route, easily negotiated, attracted them south of the eastern Delta; and reference to the "Shasu of the Inverted Water"[78] and later settlements in Middle Egypt at Atfih[79] and Spermeru[80] prove this route to have passed through the Wady el-Shuna and the Wady 'Arabah, debouching opposite the Fayum.

In the northern hill country the presence of similar elements around Shechem posed a threat to Beth Shean, and the route between the coastal road and the Jordan was already in jeopardy at the outset of Sety I's reign. While he was again able to quell the disturbances, his records betray the presence of a strong dissident group (whom he terms ʿApiru) in the hill country where, three generations earlier, Lab'ayu had run amok.[81] One wonders to what extent these elements encouraged the Canaanite towns of the Esdraelon and Galilee to join in the revolt against Egypt on the morrow of Ramesses II's defeat at Kadesh.[82]

Egyptian reaction to the Shasu can be explained largely in the light of Egypt's prime concern with keeping the routes to the north open. By the end of his first decade on the throne Ramesses II had reconquered the coast, and the Egyptians had reappeared in the environs of Byblos.[83] Later in the reign, though undated, must fall Ramesses's wars in Transjordan, clearly occasioned by the hostility of elements there that sought to deny

[77] G. Goyon, *Kêmi* 7 (1938), 115, pls. 19, 22; P. Anast. vi.54ff.; W. Helck *JARCE* 6 (1967), 135ff.; Giveon *JARCE* 8 (1969–1970), 51ff.; Redford, *JSSEA* 12 (1982), 74, n. 155. Cf. R. A. Caminos, *A Tale of Woe* (Oxford, 1977), 72 (where "them of Se'ir" occurs in an obscure context). Their presence there is scarcely to be compared with Israel's descent: S. Herrmann, *A History of Israel in Old Testament Times* (Philadelphia, 1975), 61. While in the Delta, some may have been pressed into service in vineyards: KRI VII, 68 (wine of the Asiatics of "Bird-pool").

[78] Helck, *JARCE* 6 (1967), 135ff.; *mw-ḳd* is the Red Sea: see, among others, H. Goedicke, *GM* 10 (1974), 13ff.; G. Posener, *GM* 11 (1974), 33ff.; E. Edel, *Biblische Notizen* 11 (1980), 72.

[79] R. A. Caminos, *The Chronicle of Prince Osorkon* (Rome, 1958), 144.

[80] P. Wilbour 44:31, 36; 48:2; 61:4; 63:9. Here also was implanted the cult of a "Baʿalat" under the guise of Hathor: Giveon, *Shosou*, 147ff. On the location of Sper-meru, see Gardiner, *The Wilbour Papyrus* (Oxford, 1948), 2: chap. 1, sec. 5; idem, *Ancient Egyptian Onomastica* (Oxford, 1947), 2:110*ff.

[81] See p. 269.

[82] That a general revolt followed the defeat at Kadesh is the only plausible explanation of the stereotyped representation of the capture of cities often glossed (as at the Ramesseum) by a reference to "year 8": P-M II², 432 (2); KRI II, 148ff. Despite the availability of a fair amount of evidence, however, the course of the Egypto-Hittite war between Ramesses's fifth and twenty-first years is in need of much further study; cf. K. A. Kitchen, *Pharaoh Triumphant* (Warminster, 1982), 67ff.

[83] See p. 186.

Egypt access to the north-south route.[84] In the same context must be viewed Ramesses's attack on Ashkelon from which, in the relief, Shasu captives are shown being led away.[85] For numerous reasons[86] the reduction of Ashkelon ought to be dated late in the reign, certainly after the treaty of year 21, and construed broadly as part of the grand strategy that involved Ramesses in southern Transjordan. Thus in the sixty-year period, from about 1320 to 1260 B.C., the Shasu are chronicled as continuing to foment trouble in their native habitat of the steppe, and as pressing westward through the Negeb toward major towns along the *Via Maris*. It is not, in my opinion, an unrelated phenomenon that a generation later under Merneptah an entity called "Israel" with all the character of a Shasu enclave makes its appearance probably in the Ephraimitic highlands;[87] and the strengthened presence of the Egyptians in such towns as Beth Shean and Deir 'Allah must be seen in the light of their recent settlement in the uplands.[88]

THE SOCIETY OF THE SHASU/ISRAEL GROUP

As there is no reason to believe the Shasu were literate—Judges 8:14 curiously provides a correct reflection of this—there is no reason to expect any contemporary documents from them describing their way of life. We must instead view the Shasu/Israel of the thirteenth century B.C. through two disparate fields of vision, one contemporary but unsympathetic, the other centuries removed from the period in question.

The Pentateuch, Joshua, and Judges are not silent on nascent Israel, and from these sources a perception can be gained of what social conditions were later conceived to have been before, during, and immediately after the occupation of the land. Dominating the primitive concepts of the community was the notion of a contract between Yahweh the god of the group and the human community (although not the individual: apart from the community the individual had no rights). Sovereignty resided

---

[84] Kitchen, *JEA* 50 (1964), 47ff.; these campaigns are difficult to date before year 5 (as does W. Helck, *VT* (1969) 18, 478), in the light of the known sequence of events of the first half of the decade of the reign: cf. D. B. Redford, *JEA* 57 (1971), 110–11.

[85] P-M II², 133 (493). That the relief dates from Ramesses II's reign and not Merneptah's (as F. Yurco, *JSSEA* 8 [1978], 70; idem, *JARCE* 23 [1986], 89–90) is now virtually certain: D. B. Redford, *IEJ* 36 (1986), 188–200. Whether Merneptah *also* reduced Ashkelon (cf. the famous passage in the Merneptah stela: H. Engel, *Biblica* 60 [1979], 373ff.; G. Fecht, in M. Görg, ed., *Fontes atque Pontes* [Wiesbaden, 1983], 106ff.; E. Hornung, in ibid., 224ff.; G. W. Ahlström and D. Edelman, *JNES* 44 [1985], 59ff.; L. E. Stager, *Eretz Israel* 18 [1985], 56*ff.) remains a moot point; but the Karnak relief cannot be invoked as evidence.

[86] *IEJ* 36 (1986), 188–200.

[87] See n. 85.

[88] On Beth Shean, see p. 292; on Deir 'Allah, see J. Yoyotte, *VT* 11 (1961), pl. 4; 12 (1962), 464ff.; in general, J. M. Weinstein, *BASOR* 241 (1981), 18ff.

with Yahweh, not the community (Jud. 8:23); and while the latter repeatedly reneged on the contract, Yahweh never did. The rules he laid
down, unilaterally in fact—the human party to the contract had no say in
the matter—were Draconian in the extreme, and the deity's will utterly
barbaric. Alien groups whose actions or even presence were deemed in
opposition to Israel are consigned to genocidal slaughter at the behest of
Yahweh (Exod. 17:14; Num. 31; 1 Sam. 15:3); even fraternization with
foreigners brings the plague (Num. 25:9, 18). Anyone who dissents Yahweh burns up (Num. 11:1–3; 16:35); anyone who complains he strikes
with plague (Num. 11:33; 14:37; 16:49), or sends poisonous snakes after
(Num. 21:6). Aberrant cultic practices, even though indulged in innocently, bring death (Exod. 32:35; Num. 15:37–40).

The will of the deity was interpreted and implemented by a leader chosen on an ad hoc basis, often because it is sensed that the charisma of
Yahweh is upon him.[89] Although the fiction is maintained that the deity
has chosen him, the offer is made formally by the "elders of the assembly"
(Jud. 21:16; cf. 11:5; 1 Sam. 8:4), and sanctioned by the "people" (Jud.
11:11), both terms conjuring up the image of that common phenomenon
in primitive societies in the ancient Near East—the tribal assembly of
weapon-bearing men and the presiding tribal fathers, as the expression of
the power to legislate and sanction. Often the leader is chosen in the face
of a crisis of military proportions, and so, imbued with the spirit of god,
leads the tribal levies in battle (cf. Jud. 2:16 and passim; 10:18). His
power often seems to be the equivalent of a dictator in the early Roman
republic, and when he "blows the trumpet" (Jud. 3:27), all the host must
assemble (1 Sam. 10:17). Nevertheless the chosen leader is designated by
the civil term "judge," and at times is found really judging (cf. Jud. 4:4–
5; 1 Sam. 7:15–16). The occasional qualification of the judge as a "seer"
(1 Sam. 9:11–13) or a long-haired "Nazarite" (Jud. 13:5; cf. 4:2) introduces a charismatic or ecstatic element derived from the cult.

In contrast to the "judge" and his dictatorial approach, the day-to-day
running of tribal affairs sounds a little more sophisticated. Towns number
landowners and moneyed citizens among their populaces (Jud. 9:2) and
are governed by "magistrates" (sarim: Jud. 4:15; 8:6; 9:30); villages are
unwalled (cf. Deut. 3:5; Ezek. 38:11). The host is ordered by "lawgivers"
and "they that march with the scribal rod" (Jud. 4:14), and "deputies"
(paqid) are attested (Jud. 9:28).

It is difficult to say whether this picture displays an inherent integrity
of time and place, or whether it is a composite of several different times
and places.[90] In some details it sounds like what one might expect of the

---

[89] A. Alt, *Essays on Old Testament History and Religion* (New York, 1968), 231–32;
A. Malamat, in Cross, *Magnalia Dei*, 152–68.

[90] Studies on the period of the Judges, while genuflecting in the direction of the admission

society of Early Iron Age Palestine, but this may attest to nothing more than the longevity and universality of certain traits held in common by many primitive societies in the region over time. (The brutal nature of Yahweh may be an artifice to stress the recalcitrance of early Israel and to underpin reform legislation of a later period.) Titles such as "judge" (*šō-fēt*) or "seer" find no corroboration (as yet) in contemporary nomenclature,[91] though "head" (*ro'š*), once applied to Jephtha (Jud. 10:18, 11:8, cf. *qasin* "leader," Jud. 11:6), sounds vaguely like the "chief" (*ʾ*) Egyptian sources speak of in Shasu society. On the other hand, the society of the town as described in Judges sounds like that of the monarchic period, or even later. And anachronisms do indeed abound, robbing the book of the credence one might have placed in it. Iron is common for chariots and implements (cf. Jud. 1:19; 4:3 13; cf. 1 Sam. 13:19–21), although historically it did not replace bronze until well into the monarchy.[92] Camels are ubiquitous—in fact, the plot of the Gideon story depends on them—(cf. Jud. 6:5; 7:12; 8:21, 26); yet camels do not appear in the Near East as domesticated beasts of burden until the ninth century B.C.[93] The author knows of kings in Moab (Jud. 2:12–30; 11:25) and Ammon (Jud. 11:13, 28), although these monarchies did not take shape until well into the first millennium B.C. as noted previously. He also frequently mentions Sidon—to the exclusion of Tyre—as a strong city that is able to offer protection, a clear reflection not of the Iron Age when Tyre dominated, but to the period of Sidon's hegemony during the Persian period.[94] The roster of pagan gods, too, with whom Israel has to contend sounds like the di-

---

that the Deuteronomic framework of the present form of the book is genuinely late, have too often proceeded on the unstated premise that the material within the framework is genuinely ancient: cf. *inter alia* A. Malamat, in B. Mazar, ed., *The World History of the Jewish People*, 1 (Tel Aviv, 1971), 3:134 ("despite all the shortcomings of the Book of Judges as a historical source, the narratives therein are . . . a true portrayal of the mode of life and the historical phenomena distinguishing the period"); idem, in Cross, *Magnalia Dei*, 152–68; Bright, *History*, 130–32; E. L. Ehrlich, *A Concise History of Israel* (New York, 1962), 25ff.; D. N. Freedman, in H. Goedicke and J.J.M. Roberts, eds., *Unity and Diversity* (Baltimore, 1975), 3–35; Lipinski, in *The Land of Israel: Crossroads of Civilization*, 95 and n. 6. It is refreshing to note some remarks of dissent: H. Engel, *Die Vorfahren Israels in Ägypten* (Frankfurt, 1979), 77–78; J. M. Sasson, *Ruth, A New Translation* (Baltimore, 1979), 250; Van Seters, *In Search of History*, 342–46.

[91] Ishida, *Royal Dynasties*, 33–37; H. Rosel, *Biblica* 61 (1980), 251ff.; idem, *BZ* 25 (1981), 180ff.; N. P. Lemche, *Biblische Notizen* 20 (1983), 44ff.; Miller and Hayes, *A History*, 93; on the term, see references in Ahlström, *Who Were the Israelites?*, 78, n. 74.

[92] See J. C. Waldbaum, in T. A. Wertime and J. D. Muhly, eds., *The Coming of the Age of Iron* (New Haven, Conn., 1980), 86.

[93] See n. 63.

[94] Cf. Josh. 11:8, 13:4; Jud. 1:31, 10:6, 19:28. H. Donner and W. Rollig, *Kanaanäische und aramäische Inschriften* (Wiesbaden, 1962–1964) 2:19–23; L. I. Levine, *Caesarea under Roman Rule* (Leiden, 1975), 144, n. 6.

vine enemies of Elijah's day (cf. Jud. 10:6); and the legendary heroes are so far in the past that their names and identities can be misconstrued.[95]

The contemporary, Egyptian, description of the Shasu enclaves in the highlands differs somewhat from that given in Judges of the early Israelites. The number of pastoral transhumants within the bounds of Cis- and Transjordan from the fourteenth through the twelfth centuries B.C. accounted for a substantial proportion of the population. Already in the second half of the fifteenth century B.C. they comprised some 36 percent of the Palestinian captives brought back by Amenophis II, and although the latter's tally is not to be construed as a census list, it nonetheless represents a cross-section of the population of the land.[96] They are consistently described as being divided into "clans,"[97] each governed by a "chief" (ʿ₃) in contradistinction to towns and states for whose leaders the Egyptians reserved the title "grandee" (wr).[98] Membership in the clans was not exclusive: outcasts and ne'er-do-wells could gain admittance, and a ceremony of blood-brotherhood seems to be attested.[99] Their proclivity for internecine strife drew expressions of contempt from Egypt.[100] Their conflict with Pharaoh and, to a lesser extent, the latter's surrogates within the Canaanite principalities arose not out of objections to taxation or the draft[101]—Egypt was little able and less interested in so dominating them—but in their well-deserved reputation as robbers and brigands whose code of conduct admitted little mercy on their victims.[102] They lived in tents,[103] in mountainous districts[104] remote from towns, where woods and predators made travel risky.[105] Their principal source of wealth was their cattle[106] and they were also renowned for an aromatic

[95] Cf. the figure of the demigod Shamgar, son of ʿAnat, misunderstood as an early hero, and the folk etymology of the personal name Yerubbaʿal (Jud. 6:32).

[96] Urk IV, 1309; excluding the Nukhashsheans and the total for the families.

[97] Mhwt: Wb II, 114:8; Giveon, Shosou, 47–48, 66; P. Anast. i.20.4; vi.54–56; P. Harris I, 76:9–10.

[98] Wb II, 114:10; see the instructive list in Medinet Habu: P-M II², 173 (6).

[99] Cf. P. Anast. I, 20:2–4; A. H. Gardiner and Cerný, Hieratic Ostraca (London, 1958), pl. 78:4–6; J. Cerný, JNES 14 (1955), 161ff.; J. L. Foster, JSSEA 14 (1984), 88ff. On the phenomenon of tribal disintegration and reintegration, see M. B. Rowton, JNES 36 (1977), 183–90.

[100] KRI I, 9:3–5, 16:9ff.

[101] Pace N. K. Gottwald, IDB Suppl., 629.

[102] Cf. especially P. Anast. I, 17, 7; 23, 7–8.

[103] P. Harris I, 76, 10 (ihrw = [אֹהֶל]); on the camp tradition in Israel, see M. Weinfeld, VT 38 (1988), 324–32.

[104] Cf. P. Montet, Kêmi 6 (1937), pl. 3 (dw n Sʿr, "the mountain of Seʿir"); Petrie, Hyksos and Israelite Cities, pl. 32 (nₐy.sn tswt, "their hills").

[105] Cf. P. Anast. I, 19, 1–4 (lions, leopards, and bears); cf. similarly W. Helck, Die Lehre des Dwₐ- Htji (Wiesbaden, 1970), 2:xvi.a.

[106] Cf. P. Anast. VI, 54–56; P. Harris I, 76:11; W. Westendorf, Koptisches Handwörterbuch (Heidelberg, 1977), 327, for Coptic šōs, "herdsman, shepherd."

gum, which perhaps they found in the wild.[107] But their life must have seemed to the Egyptians so Spartan that they contemptously referred to them as "living like wild game."[108]

The Shasu settlement in the Palestinian highlands, or nascent Israel as we should undoubtedly call it, and whatever related group had begun to coalesce in the Judaean hills to the south, led a life of such rustic simplicity at the outset that it has scarcely left an imprint on the archaeological record.[109] When after the close of the thirteenth century B.C. they began to develop village life,[110] it is significant that in large part they mimicked settlement patterns and domestic architecture that were borrowed from the Canaanite towns of the lowland.[111] Artifacts from cultural assemblages show a continuum throughout the thirteenth and twelfth centuries, similarly indicating a borrowing of styles and standards already present in the land.[112] Economic patterns discernible in the transition to sedentary life were also copied from Canaanite prototypes,[113] and it is probable that

[107] P. Turin B verso 1,8 = R. A. Caminos, *Late Egyptian Miscellaneous* (Oxford, 1954), 467.

[108] Vienna block from Horemheb's tomb: Bergmann, *ZÄS* 27 (1889), 125ff.; J. H. Breasted, *Ancient Records of Egypt* (Chicago, 1906), 3: sec 11; A. H. Gardiner, *JEA* 39 (1953), 7; Helck *VT* 18 (1968), 472ff. In my view the inscription on this block is a *general* statement of pharaonic policy (not a reference to a specific incident), placed in the mouth of Horemheb as spokesman for the king to the officers in charge of Asia and Kush.

[109] For the original settlement in the highlands, see J. M. Miller, in J. H. Hayes and J. M. Miller, eds., *Israelite and Judaean History* (Philadelphia, 1977), 279ff.; Miller and Hayes, *A History*, 83–85; also G. W. Ahlström, *JNES* 39 (1980), 65, and the literature there cited. On the settlement of the Israelite tribes in general, see in particular Alt, *Kleine Schriften*, 1:126ff.; M. Weippert, *The Settlement of the Israelite Tribes in Palestine* (London, 1971); S. Mittmann, *Beiträge zur Siedlungs- und Territorialgeschichte des nordliche Ostjordanlandes* (Wiesbaden, 1970), 208ff.; B. Mazar, *BASOR* 241 (1981), 75ff.; also the excellent survey of B.S.J. Isserlin, *PEQ* 115 (1983), 85ff., and review of the evidence by Gottwald, Herrmann, and Kochavi in *Biblical Archaeology Today*. Though many of the tribal ingredients clearly have a long history, there seems little justification in interpreting the Israelite confederacy as an 'Apiru defensive reaction datable to the Hyksos period: so W. R. Wall, *ZAW* 95 (1983), 197ff. The settlement of Israel will be further discussed in the next chapter.

[110] On the dramatic increase in population density in the central highlands during the course of Iron I, see M. L. Chaney, in Freedman and Graf, *Palestine in Transition* 49–50; L. E. Stager, *BASOR* 260 (1985), 3, 25; Kochavi in *Biblical Archaeology Today*, 55–56.

[111] H. K. Beebe, *BA* 31 (1968), 49; G. W. Ahlström, *JNES* 41 (1982), 133 and n. 2; A. Mazar, in *Biblical Archaeology Today*, 61ff. For the settlements at Arad, Dhiban, Gibeon, and Ai on virgin sites, see J. Callaway, *BASOR* 196 (1969), 9; nevertheless, in the course of time characteristic house types and town planning do appear: Y. Shiloh *IEJ* 28 (1978), 36ff., and the literature in n. 1 and 2; Stager, *BASOR* 260 (1985), 11ff.; A. Mazar, as cited. For a much needed note of caution in the interpretation of such archaeological sites as Tel Massos, see N. K. Gottwald, in *Biblical Archaeology Today*, 40–42.

[112] Cf. O. Negbi, *Tel Aviv* 1 (1974), 159ff.; R. Amiran, *Ancient Pottery of the Holy Land* (Jerusalem, 1970), 192.

[113] Cf. the judicious remarks of Isserlin, *PEQ* 115 (1983), 90, and V. Fritz, *BASOR* 241 (1981), 70ff.; also Y. Aharoni, *BA* 39 (1976), 74ff., and G. Mendenhall, ibid., 152ff.

in some cases tribal borders reflect the preexistent territories of older Canaanite states.[114] Nevertheless, distinctive traits do appear among the newcomers, such as their proclivity to locate their shrines away from settlements, thus emphasizing the discontinuity with the antecedent cultic tradition of the Canaanites.[115] Another aspect of the religious life of the Shasu/Israelites is reflected in the phenomenon of a single, outdoor cult site serving the needs of a number of surrounding villages as a central place of worship. Moreover, it seems undeniable, although still based on an argument from silence, that from the beginning Israel tended to shy away from artistic representations of the deity such as the Canaanites favored. This aniconic tradition is to be compared not so much with the "empty shrine" motif of solar theology, but rather with the aversion to images found among certain tribal groups in Arabia.[116]

But it is important to note that, while the Canaanites may have unwittingly provided models to copy or shun, their towns in the lowland or on the coast were as incapable as Egypt of exerting effective *political* control over the Palestinian highlands, nor is there any evidence that they wished to do so. In the Amarna age such towns as Ashkelon, Gezer, and Lachish experienced pressure *from* the highlands to do *their* will;[117] and in Sety I's reign it is groups from these same highlands that descend to compromise the integrity of coast and valley. In Ramesses II's first decade the Canaanite towns along the coast and in Galilee made a modest attempt to effect an act of will, but it is directed against Egypt itself, not the people of the highlands. With their defeat at the hands of Ramesses's forces, the Canaanites were weaker than ever. After 1200 B.C. when the Sea Peoples overwhelmed the coast, and "Israel" is firmly attested, the Canaanites as a political force were dead.[118] And so, effectually, was the Egyptian empire of the New Kingdom.

[114] C. Meyers, BASOR 252 (1983), 55; perhaps also Z. Gal, Tel Aviv 9 (1982), 79ff.

[115] N. Na'aman, ZDPV 103 (1987), 13–21.

[116] E. F. Campbell, *Interpretation* 29 (1975), 145; cf. the Nabatean predilection for the "god-block." For the possible social origins of the aniconic tradition, see R. S. Hendel, CBQ 50 (1988), 365–82.

[117] See n. 59.

[118] It is a curious rejection of hard evidence to claim that the Israelite movement, a "broad alliance of extended families, protective associations and tribes that managed to throw off the central authority . . . had to defend itself against the counter-revolutionary thrusts of the ousted authorities," and that "in Canaan, with Egyptian imperial influence weakened, the Israelites faced a multiplicity of these small states" (N. K. Gottwald, in *Palestine in Transition*, 30). How easily can preoccupation with a model make one oblivious of the need for an empirical approach.

Egypt and the Hebrew Kingdoms

PART FOUR

Egypt and the Hebrew Kingdoms

CHAPTER 11

Horses and Pharaoh's Daughter: Egypt and the United Monarcy

In 1075 B.C. the Egypt of the Ramesside empire still existed, albeit weakened, impoverished, and disillusioned; one short generation later the country had crossed a "great divide" and entered the deepening twilight of the postimperial, "Tanite" era. What had happened?

Tanis and Thebes: The Transition to the 21st Dynasty

One can, of course, appeal persuasively to a concatenation of economic and climatic factors that wrought havoc with Egyptian society in the twelfth century B.C. The destruction of the Hittite empire and the overrunning of the Levant by the Sea Peoples had effectively deprived the Pharaohs of access to the silver- and iron-bearing regions of Anatolia, just when these metals were about to become all important in international coffers and arsenals. By the third-quarter of the century the Sinai turquoise mines had shut down, the Timna copper mines were less frequented (if not abandoned), and the Nubian gold mines had begun to show signs of exhaustion. Consequently, by 1115 B.C. both gold and copper grew suddenly much more expensive. An extended period of drought in northeast Africa resulted in successive low Niles and poor harvests,[1] and the country was plagued by inflation and labor strikes. A quantity of emmer wheat (2.25 bushels) that was valued at 1 copper deben at the close of Ramesses III's reign cost 5 scarcely twenty years later; and the official reports of investigating commissioners frequently contained such notes as "regnal year 29, 2nd month of *proyet*, day 10—on this day the workers crossed the 5 checkpoints of the necropolis and said 'We are hungry! Sixteen days have gone by in the month!' and they sat down (i.e., refused to work)."[2]

With prices high and wages low or in arrears, it was difficult to resist

---

[1] C. Brooks, *Climate through the Ages* (New York, 1970), 336.

[2] On the shutting down of the mines, see W. B. Emery, *Egypt in Nubia* (London, 1965), 206–7; R. Giveon, *The Impact of Egypt on Canaan* (Göttingen, 1978), 51ff.; B. Rothenberg, *Timna* (Aylebury, U.K., 1972), 163; on the economics of the period, see J. Černý, *JWH* 1 (1954), 903–21; J. J. Janssen, *SAK* 3 (1975), 127–86; idem, *Commodity Prices from the Ramessid Period* (Leiden, 1975).

the temptation posed by the enormous treasure lying buried in the royal and private tombs on the west bank at Thebes. During the reign of Ramesses IX (last quarter of the twelfth century) come the first reports of grave robbing both in the royal and private necropolises. Starting with accessible graves of the Second Intermediate Period at the north end of the cemetery, the robbers had graduated by the end of the century to the main interments of the empire period, and were even rifling the eternal resting places of Sety I and Ramesses II. The authorities tried to post guards and apprehend the culprits, and in many cases were successful, as the surviving transcripts of the tomb-robbery trials eloquently attest.[3] But, as in the case of the drug problem in our present society, the need for a recirculation of this wealth was too great and government officials too corrupt to do much more than attack the tip of the iceberg. By the eleventh century B.C. the pious priests were driven to the resort of secreting the mummies of the royal ancestors in a succession of tombs, one step, as it were, ahead of the indefatigable robbers. At last, in the tenth century B.C., they transferred in desperation the remaining royal mummies of the 17th through the 20th Dynasties to a secret shaft at Deir el-Bahari where they rested in peace until discovered in the nineteenth century of our own era.[4]

In making the obligatory search for "causes" in history, one sooner or later turns to the human factor. The details elude us, but the testimony is unanimous: after Ramesses III died, "kings succeeded to the throne for seven generations who were confirmed sluggards and devoted only to indulgence and luxury. Consequently in the priestly record no costly building of theirs nor any deed worthy of historical record is handed down in connection with them."[5] Although this is in part an etiology on the very lack of record Diodorus seeks to explain, the impression is a correct one: the family of Ramesses III had fallen into a prolonged internecine feud, perhaps because of the circumstances of the assassination, and the latter end was completely discredited.

The long-lived but ineffectual Ramesses XI (c. 1105–1075 B.C.), whom one cannot help but regard with a degree of pity (although why is difficult to say in want of evidence), proved to be the last of the Ramessides and the last imperial Pharaoh. His equivocal reputation was won while he yet lived: "As for Pharaoh, how can he ever reach this land (i.e., Thebes in the south)? Of whom, indeed, is Pharaoh the master? . . . do not be con-

---

[3] See T. E. Peet, *The Great Tomb-Robberies of the Twentieth Egyptian Dynasty* (London, 1930).

[4] G. Maspero, *La trouvaille de Deir el-Bahari* (Cairo, 1883); idem, *Les momies royales de Deir el-Bahari* (Cairo, 1887); J. E. Harris and K. R. Weeks, *X-Raying the Pharaohs* (New York, 1973), chap. 3.

[5] Diodorus, 1.63.1

cerned about what he might do!" Thus a magnate of Thebes to his timorous secretary during the last years of Ramesses XI.[6] An outbreak of civil war during the first decade of his reign had contributed to the impression of Ramesses XI's weakness. Although the troubles had not unseated him, it had nonetheless wrought havoc in Thebes and Middle Egypt, and temporarily removed the king's protégé, the high priest of Amun, one Amenophis. The viceroy of Kush, Paynehsi, the principal opponent of the king, was with difficulty driven back into Nubia where the rebellion had started; but it was at the cost of appointing another power-seeking army officer, Herihor, to the high priesthood of Amun. Beginning with the grandiose titles of "he-who-is-over-the-Two-Lands, ... high priest of Amonrasonther, Field Marshal of Upper and Lower Egypt, and duke," Herihor, in year 19 of Ramesses XI and after receiving a favorable oracle from Amun, without further ado proclaimed himself king.[7] Ramesses XI is scarcely heard of again.

Egypt entered the second quarter of the eleventh century B.C. in a state of military and economic decline, and there could be no question of maintaining traditional forms of empire. The Ramesside house had wholly discredited itself. Amun had set them aside and declared in favor of Herihor. In the north, in the oracular parlance of the times, Amun had "appointed" as an "officer" for "the north of his (Amun's) land"[8] a certain Nesubanebdjed, who had in all probability been nought but a trusted official of the last Ramesses. This worthy, catapulted (by marriage?)[9] to the kingship, and the four generations that followed him, ruled from Tanis, the new city that had arisen "Phoenix-like" from the ruins of Pi-Ramesses in the northeast Delta. Founded on flats called "the Field of the Storm" close to the mouth of the easternmost, Bubastite, branch of the Nile, Tanis was intended to replace Pi-Ramesses, about thirty kilometers to the south (Plates 30, 31). For some reason the great Ramesside residence was abandoned at the close of the 20th Dynasty (although a settlement lin-

[6] A. H. Gardiner, *JMEOS* 2 (1912), 61; E. F. Wente, *Late Ramesside Letters* (Chicago, 1966), 79.

[7] D. B. Redford, *LdÄ* 2 (1977), 1129–33.

[8] Cf. Wenamun 2:35 (A. H. Gardiner, *Late Egyptian Stories*, [Brussels, 1931] 70). The term "officer" (*snn{ty}*) was originally the military "chariot-warrior" (A. H. Gardiner, *Ancient Egyptian Onomastica* [Oxford, 1947], 1:28*; A. R. Schulman, *JARCE* 2 [1963], 87–88; D. Meeks, *Année lexicographique* [Paris, 1981], 2:332–33; [Paris, 1982], 3:258); but here it means something like "the official in charge." Wenamun's locution seems to betoken an oracular appointment.

[9] Tant-amun was daughter of a simple "esquire (*s³b*)" Nebseny: See H. Gauthier, *Livre des rois* (Cairo, 1914), 3:258 (L); P. Montet, *Le drame d'Avaris* (Paris, 1941), 189, n. 4. But attempts have been made to see in her the former queen of Ramesses XI; See A. Niwinski, *JARCE* 16 (1979), 50–51. Nesubanebdjed's mother *may* have been Nodgme, wife of Herihor, but even this is far from certain; see E. Wente, *JNES* 26 (1967), 174.

Plate 30. Statuary and pylon at Tanis, all Ramesside in origin and taken from the abandoned capital of Pi-Ramesses.

Plate 31. Trunk and legs of a colossus of Ramesses II, originally from Pi-Ramesses, now at Tanis.

gered on, contemporary with the earliest years of Tanis), and the builders of the new city felt free to use the derelict buildings of the former capital as a quarry.[10] So many Ramesside blocks in fact were hauled from the old site to Tanis that early archaeologists mistook Tanis for Pi-Ramesses itself.[11]

In spite of two new men in the south and the north, the prospect of national revival was never fulfilled. For a century and a half Egypt continued to decline. Although Herihor had boldly usurped the royal prerogative, his successors (with a few notable exceptions) eschewed the cartouche and retained only the high priesthood of Amun, command of the army, and the (now moribund) viceroyalty of Kush. The bond between the royal house and Thebes was severed. No longer did kings make the journey from the Delta to Thebes for the festivals of the king of the gods; no longer were their embalmed corpses taken up river to be buried in the Valley of the Kings.[12] No more booty from foreign wars or taxes from Asia were deposited in the coffers of the temple of Amun. All Thebes had left was the cult and priesthood of the once imperial god, and the memories of past glories.

The 21st Dynasty thus witnessed the sure decline of Thebes. Once its principal relationship with the royal house had become a thing of the past, the prestige that had buoyed it up over six centuries and had made it the second metropolis of Egypt, "the southern city," was irreparably broken. As excavations have shown, the population suddenly declined at the beginning of the 21st Dynasty, and large sectors of the city were abandoned. By year 48 of the Tanite king Psusennes I (c. 1002 B.C.), in the pontificate of the Theban Menkheperre, the temple of Amun was delapidated, its enclosure wall was in ruins, and the houses of the people were

[10] It is difficult to assign a precise date to the founding of Tanis. The name (apart from its possible appearance in the compound Sḫt-Dʿ: R. A. Caminos, *Literary Fragments in the Hieratic Script* [Oxford, 1956], 19–20) appears first in Wenamun (1:3 = Gardiner, *Stories*, 61) of 20th Dynasty date, and in the Onomasticon Amenemope (A. H. Gardiner, *Ancient Egyptian Onomastica* [Oxford, 1947], 2:199ʿff.) of the early 21st Dynasty. Pi-Ramesses was still the residence under Ramesses III (cf. A. H. Gardiner, *JEA* 5 [1920], 192, no. 23, and 192–93, no. 25; V, 230), and is still in existence at the close of the dynasty (On. Am. 410 = Gardiner, *Onomastica* 2:171ʿff.), thus overlapping with Tanis for a short time. As is now abundantly clear, the latter was a foundation of the outgoing 20th Dynasty.

[11] J. Van Seters, *The Hyksos, A New Investigation* (New Haven, Conn., 1966), 128ff.; M. Bietak, *Tell el-Dabʿa* (Vienna, 1975), 2:179ff.; idem, *Proceedings of the British Academy* 55 (1979), 278–79.

[12] The last royal tomb at Thebes is the unfinished hypogaeum of Ramesses XI Valley of the Kings (4: P-M I², 501). The term "royal tomb" disappears from the Theban administrative texts by the mid-21st Dynasty and the administration of the royal necropolis a generation later: J. Černý, *A Community of Workmen at Thebes in the Ramesside Period* (Cairo, 1973), 26, 52.

encroaching on the sacred courts.[13] Pathetic are the lightly engraved rec-
ord-texts announcing that high priest so-and-so has repaired this gate or
renewed this wall: the fact is there was no money and no manpower to
build anything new.

And yet the god Amun had bequeathed such a hallowed tradition and
such a strong base of power that the family of Herihor could for six generations wield enormous control over all Upper Egypt. The extent and
wealth of the temple of Amun in the twilight of the New Kingdom is
staggering. On the death of Ramesses III it owned 600,000 acres of land,
421,362 head of cattle, 433 gardens, 65 towns (9 in Canaan), 46 carpenters' shops, and a fleet of 83 cargo boats. Over 85,000 chattels and farmers labored on the god's estate, exclusive of the priests. The bequests of a
single Pharaoh (Ramesses III) to Amun included nearly 1.5 tons of gold
and silver, 2.5 tons of copper, over 1,000 jars of incense, over 25,000 jars
of wine, 310,000 measures of grain, besides substantial amounts of flax,
vegetables, and fowl.[14] In the 21st Dynasty Amun's "estate" is coextensive with Upper Egypt.[15] Here the high priests were virtually sovereign,
and their wives, the "Divine Adoratresses" of Amun, were given the double cartouches as though they were queens.[16]

In the absence of royal authority and the de facto power of the priests,
it is not surprising to find a reorientation of state theory toward the eccle-
siastics. Priests now take over civil authority and the high priests become
governors with headquarters not in Thebes but in a new fortress called
Teudjoy on the east bank of the Nile, not far south of the Fayum.[17] In
place of the king the gods are invoked to an increasing extent as sources
of political authority. The priestly families get rich and the fragmentary
picture we can reconstruct shows them buying up large tracts of land in
field and town throughout the south, such purchases being sanctioned
and guaranteed by oracles of Amun.[18]

Only the descendants of Nesubanebjed at Tanis are credited in the king
list with the kingship, and their names only appear as members of the
21st Dynasty; but even this regime, though separated from Thebes, was
wholly informed by the cult and worship of Amun. A high priesthood of
"Amunre king-of-the-gods" is known at Tanis, and the title is even taken

[13] P. Barquet, *Le temple d'Amon-rê à Karnak* (Cairo, 1962), pl. 32b, and p. 36–37.

[14] See the lists in the Great Harris Papyrus: W. Erichsen, *Papyrus Harris I* (Brussels,
1933); J. H. Breasted, *Ancient Records of Egypt* (Chicago, 1906), 4:124ff.

[15] Cf. how "Thebes," "the House of Amun," and "Upper Egypt" alternate in titles during
the Late Period.

[16] See E. Graefe, *Untersuchungen zur Verwaltung and Geschichte der Institution der Got-
tesgemahlin des Amun* (Wiesbaden, 1981).

[17] Today the mound of El-Hibeh: see R. J. Wenke, *Archaeological Investigations at El-
Hibeh, 1980* (Malibu, Calif. 1984).

[18] A. H. Gardiner, *JEA* 48 (1962), 57ff.

by the king himself, sometimes within his cartouche.[19] Other epithets reminiscent of the halcyon days of the empire include "Theban Ruler," "Beloved of Amun," and "Rising in Thebes."[20] Amun grants the king victory and might in battles,[21] and the king in gratitude claims to have constructed great "monuments in Karnak"(sic).

Hollow though these claims may appear to us, endowed as we are with hindsight, they betray an honest but pathetic attempt to live up to the standards of a lost past. Part of that standard included the obligatory exploits of a hero-king in Asia. But what of Asia now?

TANIS AND PALESTINE

If the early Hebrews by the circumstances of their entry and distribution in the land were not brought into extended contact with Egypt in the thirteenth century B.C., the invasion of the Sea Peoples in the twelfth century wholly excluded any significant cultural influence from the Nile. The Shasu had threatened Egypt's use of the Transjordanian route in the 19th Dynasty, and had harrassed the coastal route as well; the Philistines and Teukrians now cut the Via Maris permanently.

Ramesses III had maintained, perhaps with some justification, that he had himself settled the enclaves of the Sea Peoples within his territory and bound them in his own service: "I settled them in fortresses (nḫtw) confined through my name. Their draftees were numerous approaching hundreds of thousands, and I supplied them all by tax with clothing and provisions (reckoned) against the treasury, the granaries each year."[22] Although it cannot be denied that some of these settlements were in Egypt,[23] the king is also referring to enclaves of the Philistines and Teukrians whose settlement in the coastal plain he acquiesced in and (post eventum) authorized. Towns in the region, rebuilt by the king, provided with gates emblazoned with his cartouche—to "confine" the occupants—and garrisoned with people, qualify precisely as nḫtw, "fortresses"; and there is little doubt that the later Philistine towns of Gaza, Ashkelon, and the rest would have been covered by the term.[24]

[19] Cf. P. Montet, Les constructions et le tombeau de Psousennès I à Tanis (Paris, 1951).

[20] Ibid., 108, fig. 44, pl. 72 (no. 413); 136, fig. 51, pl. 107 (no. 482).

[21] Ibid., 149, fig. 54; 150, fig. 55.

[22] P. Harris 76:8–9.

[23] For later references to remnants of the Sea Peoples in Egypt, see A. H. Gardiner, Rameeside Administrative Documents (Oxford, 1948), 7:12–13 (mid-20th Dynasty); J. Černý, Late Ramesside Letters (Brussels, 1939), 19:21 (21st Dynasty); G. Daressy, ASAE 15 (1915), 141 (mid-22nd Dynasty).

[24] On the word "fortress" (nḫtw: Wb II, 317:11–12) two revealing passages from Ramesses II's reign convey the nature of the institution: "Retenu, the settlements, the fortresses of the king, the towns settled and provided with men" (KRI II, 330:15); and "filling the

Although as we have seen Ramesses III had been able, by dint of military activity, to reassert his authority over much of Palestine and perhaps parts of Syria as well, his successors proved incapable of maintaining control of the area. Ramesses IV and V, with difficulty we may imagine, continued the maritime trade with Phoenicia, continued to work the copper and turquoise mines in the Sinai and Arabah, and did not blanch at using the grandiose epithets of imperial victory.[25] Scattered objects from Palestinian excavations continue to mention the Pharaohs down to Ramesses VI,[26] under whom Canaanites are still found in the work force west of Thebes.[27] Thereafter Palestinian mounds fall silent, although Ramesses VII can still be spoken of as "shooting arrows against the land of Kharu . . . entering into the land of Khatte having leveled (literally, overturned) its mountains."[28]

Within fifteen years of the passing of Ramesses III, Egyptian control of its former northern dependencies had been lost; and it was then, less than a century after their arrival in the Levant, that the resident Sea Peoples moved to establish themselves independent of the aegis of Egypt. Their advent under Ramesses III and the latter's war to reestablish his empire had already leveled many a town along the coast; and now a second aggrandizement of the Philistine sphere brought additional woe to the region.[29] Gaza, Ashkelon, and Ashdod suffered the complete destruction of

---

fortresses he (i.e., the king) had built with those whom his sword had plundered" (KRI II, 206:16).

[25] KRI VI, 27:4 (Ramesses IV's trade with the Lebanon); 228:15–16 (Ramesses V's boast of "crying out to the Lebanon"); Rothenburg, *Timna*, 163; KRI VI, 10:9–10; 228:1–2, 15–16 ("Retenu is his by capture, burdened with their tribute"; "slayer of Kharu . . .").

[26] Cartouche of Ramesses IV from Tel Delhamia in the Jordan Valley (J. Leclant, *Orientalia 51* [1982], 485, fig. 83); scarab of Ramesses IV from Tel Fara South (A. Rowe, *A Catalogue of Egyptian Scarabs, Scaraboids, Seals and Amulets in the Palestine Archaeological Museum* [Cairo, 1936], no. 8); a bronze of Ramesses VI from Megiddo (KRI VI, 278); scarabs of Ramesses VI from Gezer (P-M VII, 375), Gaza (R. Giveon, *Tel Aviv* 4 [1977], 66–67, fig. 1, no. 2), and Beth Shemesh (Rowe, no. 834). I doubt very much whether there are scarabs of Ramesses VIII from Tel Fara South (as T. L. McLellan, *Journal of Field Archaeology* 6 [1979], 67; cf. now A. Mazar, *IEJ* 35 [1985], 98, n. 9).

[27] KRI VI, 269:1–4.

[28] KRI VI, 394; cf. also the banal phrases appropriated by Ramesses IX (KRI VI, 461): "His battle cry is in the foreign lands, crusher of mountains . . . awe of him pervades the hearts of the northerners"; (ibid., 466) "who wins in the fray, expert in crushing the foreigners, leading officer in any rout, who crushes the foreign land with overwhelming victories." We should beware, however, of allowing the banality of the phraseology to cloud our historical sense: the decision to use phrases of this sort may well have been occasioned by some real event. In point of fact, it is probably Ramesses IX who is alluded to by the king of Byblos contemporary with Herihor (Wenamun 2, 51–53) as having sent envoys to his fathers. Cf. also the inlay of Ramesses IX from Gezer: P-M VII, 374.

[29] For a judicious interpretation of most destruction levels in Levantine sites separating LH IIIB and IIIC, see V. Fritz, *UF* 5 (1973), 123ff.; also see J. D. Muhly, *AJA* 86 (1982),

their last Late Bronze Age cities,[30] while further to the north coastal towns such as Aphek, Tel Abu Huwam, and Tel Keisan had already gone up in spectacular conflagrations.[31] The Philistines began to broaden their horizons, bursting out of their fortresses and occasionally founding new towns.[32] In the south they took over way stations formerly belonging to the Egyptian administration,[33] while to the southeast they spread their settlements along the Nahal Besor.[34] The fertile, grain-growing countryside of the Shephelah beckoned also, and here Lachish was taken and committed to the flames,[35] Tel Mikne (Ekron?) occupied and rebuilt,[36] and Tel Sera seized.[37] At Tel Fara South a large residence was built, and a "princely" family can be traced through the great tombs spanning five generations in the adjacent cemetery.[38]

In the north the achievement of an autonomous stage of expansion, free at last from Egyptian tutelage, is in evidence likewise from the end of the reign of Ramesses VI (or thereabouts), although here the ancient Hebrews

---

135. The contention that two destruction levels at some sites reflects two waves of invaders is to be wholly rejected: W. F. Albright, *CAH*³ II, pt. 2 (1975), 507ff.; A. Malamat, *World History of the Jewish People*, 1 series (Tel Aviv, 1971), 3:29; R. W. Hutchinson, *Prehistoric Crete* (Harmondsworth, 1962), 314. At these sites there is either a double destruction within a short space of time, or a hiatus between the destruction of the Late Bronze town and the appearance of "Philistine" pottery, in which LH IIIC 1b ware is found (cf. Ashdod [T. Dothan, in *Biblical Archaeology Today* (Jerusalem, 1985), 167], Tel Sera [E. Oren, *IEJ* 24 (1974), 270], Tel Ma'arabim [ibid.], Tel Mikne [S. Gittin and T. Dothan, *IEJ* 33 (1983), 128; 36 (1986), 106; 37 (1987), 64, 67], Tel Batash [*IEJ* 27 (1977), 168; 32 (1982), 153]). We are dealing clearly with two distinct phases in the initial establishment of the Sea Peoples: the destruction that was concomitant to their invasion of year 8 of Ramesses III, and a second violent expansion sometime shortly after in the generation following the death of that king. Cf. A. Mazar, *IEJ* 35 (1985), 95ff. (esp. 97, where a terminus of Ramesses VI's reign is strongly suggested for the breakout).

30 W. J. Pythian-Adams, *PEFQS* (1923), 13, 27ff.; 62, 77–78; T. Dothan, *The Philistines and Their Material Culture* (Jerusalem, 1982), 36–37.

31 M. Kochavi, *IEJ* 24 (1974), 261; 26 (1976), 51; 27 (1977), 54; B. Mazar, *BASOR* 124 (1951), 25; *IEJ* 32 (1982), 63; but cf. Mazar, *IEJ* 35 (1985), 99 (where an earlier date is suggested).

32 E.g. Tel Qasile: A. Mazar, *IEJ* 25 (1975), 77ff.

33 Cf. Deir el-Balah: T. Dothan, in E. Lipinski, ed., *The Land of Israel: Crossroads of Civilization* (Louvain, 1985), 63–67; Tel Jemmeh (G. van Beek, *IEJ* 24, [1974] 139), where there are two strata (Philistine) separated by a burnt level: Dothan, *The Philistines*, 34.

34 *IEJ* 28 (1978), 194–95.

35 D. Ussishkin, *IEJ* 25 (1975), 166; after Ramesses III: J. Leclant, *Orientalia* 51 (1982), 486.

36 See n. 29; also Dothan, in *The Land of Israel*, 70–72.

37 E. Oren, *IEJ* 24, 139, 270.

38 W.M.F. Petrie, *Beth-Pelet* (London, 1929), 1:17ff.; Dothan, *The Philistines*, 29–30; Mazar, *IEJ* 35 (1985), 98. The alleged influence from the Aegean (J. C. Waldbaum, *AJA* 70 [1966], 331–40; see Dothan, in *Biblical Archaeology Today*, 171) has, however, been called into question: W. H. Stiebing, Jr., *AJA* 74 (1970), 139–44.

(and moderns in their wake) may have misapplied the ethnic "Philistine" to an original Teukrian component.[39] Beth-Shean had always been viewed by the Egyptians as a key fortress on the route via the Jezreel Valley to the Jordan and north to Damascus; and it may have been under Ramesses III himself that a garrison of Sea Peoples was ensconced in this fortified city side by side with an Egyptian contingent.[40] The early 20th Dynasty city was, however, brutally fired,[41] and at the same time settlements of Sea Peoples began to appear in the Esdraelon plain and down the Jordan Valley as far as Tell es-Saʿidiyeh and Tell Deir ʿAlla.[42] The Philistines and their congeners were, by 1100 B.C., ringing the central highlands.

Out textual evidence by and large confirms the archaeological. The Onomasticon of Amenemope, which may be dated to around 1100 B.C., follows a list of the toponyms of the Phoenician coast and Coele-Syria with six place-names of which four are certainly in the Philistine plain:[43] Ashkelon (262), Ashdod (263), Gaza (264), Yasur (265),[44] Subaray (266), and one lost in a lacuna (267). These are then followed by three names of Sea Peoples: [Sh]ardana (268), Teukrians (269), and Philistines (270). In all probability the six town-names designate the principal *municipia* that the three groups in question occupied in the period after Egypt withdrew from Asia; but while the first two may have initially been present, they were soon swallowed up in the (we may assume) much larger Philistine matrix.[45] Subsequently the six were reduced to a "tripolis," to be expanded around the time of the founding of the Hebrew monarchy to the traditional "Pentapolis" known from the Bible.[46] Of the northern group

[39] Teukrians inhabited Dor under Ramesses XI: cf. Wenamun 1, 8–9. It seems reasonable to infer that the slight cultural differences between the north and the Jordan Valley, and the Philistine plain are to be put down to this ethnic bifurcation.

[40] E. Oren, *The Northern Cemetary at Beth Shean* (Leiden, 1973); Philistine pottery is, however, rare: F. W. James, *The Iron Age at Beth Shean* (Philadelphia, 1966), 150.

[41] J. Garfinkel, *IEJ* 37 (1987), 224.

[42] A. Ben-Tor, *IEJ* 25 (1975), 169; J. B. Pritchard, in W. A. Ward, ed., *The Role of the Phoenicians in the Interaction of Mediterranean Civilizations* (Beirut, 1968), 99–112; H. J. Franken, *Excavations at Tell Deir ʿAlla*, vol. 1 (Leiden, 1969); R. H. Dornemann, A. Hadidi, ed., in *Studies in the History and Archaeology of Jordan* (Amman, 1982), 1:135–40.

[43] Gardiner, *Onomastica*, 1:190ʿff. (nos. 257–60).

[44] On the identity of this place, see A. Alt, *Schweizerische Theologische Umschau* 20 (1950), 65.

[45] Dor certainly was a Teukrian settlement around 1075 B.C. (see n. 39). It has been suggested that *Dhikerin* (Dikera) between Bit Jibrin and Ashdod (R.A.S. MacAlister, *The Philistines: Their History and Civilization* [London, 1911], 75) and *Ziklag* (G. A. Wainwright, *JEA* 47 [1961], 77) derive from *Tjekker* (Teuk[rians]), and thus betray erstwhile Teukrian enclaves.

[46] S. Yeivin, *The Israelite Conquest of Canaan* (Istanbul, 1971), 113, n. 213; B. Mazar, *The Philistines and the Rise of Israel and Tyre* (Jerusalem, 1971), 10. The tripolis in question has nothing to do with that of Jos. 15:46–47 (Ekron, Ashdod, Gaza) which, like 2

and those in the Jordan Valley our sources are silent; although to judge by the ease of access enjoyed by the Philistines to Beth Shean (2 Sam. 31:10), their control in the north must have lasted until the early tenth century. Whether the Philistines maintained control of the sea is a moot point; but scattered references suggest they did at least for a short time. Teukrian ships have no difficulty in pursuing a miserable Egyptian envoy to Byblos, and demanding that he be arrested;[47] and the much later Greek tradition preserves a memory of the "Lydians" (Sea Peoples) maintaining the rule of the sea from Ramesses III's eighth year for ninety-two years.[48]

Philistine culture, although its root was cut by the end of the twelfth century B.C. with the destruction of the Aegean civilization, lived on until the end of the millennium, and displays itself especially in the beautiful polychrome pottery of the age (see Figure 8).[49] Even in the tenth century

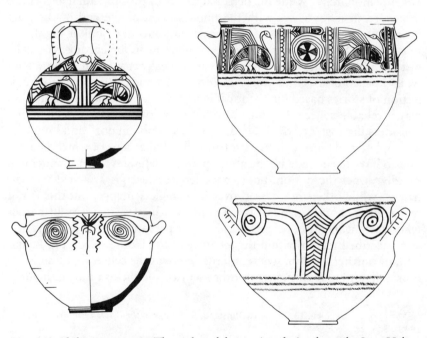

Figure 8. Philistine pottery. The styles of decoration derive from the Late Helladic IIIC ceramic tradition of the Aegean, with Cypriote influence.

Chron. 26:6, omits Ashkelon simply because it postdates 605 B.C. when Ashkelon was destroyed by Nebuchadrezzar II and temporarily abandoned.

[47] Wenamun 2, 64–66.

[48] On the thalassocracy lists, see R. Helm, *Hermes* 60 (1926), 241ff.

[49] R. Amiran, *Ancient Pottery of the Holy Land* (New York, 1970), 266–69; Dothan, *The Philistines*.

Philistine names like Goliath and Achish continue to recall the Aegean origin of the group;[50] and while by the eighth century the native onomasticon had been replaced by a Semitic one, nonetheless a distinctive "patois" was preserved in the Philistine cities down to the first century B.C.[51]

This is the background against which the curious melodrama entitled by us moderns "the Period of the Judges" is played out. In the collective memory of the Israelites of these their formative years in the land, no recollection of Egypt was retained. This is not surprising, since the evolution of "Israel" as a political entity postdated the Ramesside age and took place, as we have seen, in an upland remote from Egyptian imperial control.

This plausible silence notwithstanding, the Book of Judges is an equivocal source for the history of the two centuries prior to the rise of the Israelite monarchy. While the personal names of the individual heroes are in accord in many cases with the onomasticon of the end of the Late Bronze and Early Iron Ages,[52] the organization of the book is highly artificial and the tales, as we have seen, abound in anachronisms.[53] The historian must, if he uses it at all, treat Judges pretty much as he would treat the medieval "Grail" legends, or the Alexander Romance: as a collection of stories based on historical figures dimly remembered, but in no way a reliable source. He must also be aware of one salient fact. If one considers the roster of the individual judges, both "major" and "minor," a complete and representative list from all tribal groups of which Israel is said to have been made up, a careful perusal of Judges and 1 Samuel will rapidly dispel the notion. Some have lengthy legends attached to their names, while others are passed over in a single sentence; but this is not the striking characteristic of the list. In fact the vast majority of heroes who warrant mention originated, lived, or performed their exploits in a circumscribed region within the territory of the House of Joseph, Benjamin, or northern Judah, wherein Jerusalem was the center of administration, religion, and culture.[54] In other words, the inclusion of individual

---

[50] See p. 252.

[51] Strabo, 16.2.2; Neh. 13:24; A. T. Olmstead, *A History of the Persian Empire* (Chicago, 1948), 351; cf. Zech. 9:5.

[52] Cf. among others 'Eglon (cf. 'gly: P. Montet, *Kêmi* 17 [1964], 63, fig. 1); Yabin (cf. Yabin-ilu, EA 328:4); Abimelech (cf. EA 146–55); Ben Anath (W. Helck, *Die Beziehungen Ägyptens zur Vorderasien*[2] [Wiesbaden, 1971], 356); Eli (ibid., 364).

[53] See p. 277; on the organization and theological framework of the material, see now J. Van Seters, *In Search of History* (New Haven, Conn., 1983), 337–46.

[54] Joshua lives in Ephraim (Jos. 19:50); the tribes assemble in Shiloh (Jos. 22:12) and Shechem (Jos. 24:1); Ehud comes from Benjamin (Jud. 3:12–30); Deborah hails from Ephraim (Jud. 4:5); Gideon and Abimelech are both from Manasseh and rule from Schechem (Jud. 6–9; Ahlström, *Who Were the Israelites?*, 69); the Jephthah saga features Ephraim prominently (Jud. 10:6–12:7); Tola, although born in Issachar, judges from Ephraim (Jud. 10:1–2); Ibzan comes from Bethlehem (Jud. 12:8–10); Abdon is of Pirathon

traditions in Judges reflects nought but the dominance of Jerusalem in the *selection* process and has nothing to do with historical reality in the period in question. If we but had a compendium of like traditions that achieved inscripturation at Samaria in the northern part of the land, we might be struck by the number of names and tales that did not survive, and which found no place in the canonical Book of Judges.

The division of Israel into twelve tribes is, even on the basis of the Biblical record, a somewhat artificial arrangement, and may owe more to a calendrical criterion employed by the later monarchy than to historical origins.[55] Firm ground is reached only when it is rejected. Reasonably certain would appear the postulate that in the "Israel" of Merneptah's stela we should construe what the Bible calls the "House of Joseph," ensconced on Mount Ephraim around Shechem (where in fact it may have enjoyed an embryonic existence since Amarna times).[56] The House of Joseph exhibits a lateral connection eastward across the Jordan—Did this axis reflect an original path of entry?—with the clans of Machir and Gilead in Transjordan; while on the Josephites' southern flank their uterine congeners, the tribe of Benjamin (i.e., "southerners"), in tribal lore offspring of the same mother Rachel, occupied the highland just north of Jerusalem.[57]

Thus far the original Israel. Other regions harboring clans traditionally considered part of the twelve-tribe framework were added to the Israelite "federation" relatively late. A judicious reading of both the archaeological and the textual record militates in favor of the eleventh to the tenth centuries for the settlement and the early monarchic period for the addition of the four Galilean tribes.[58] In the Judaean highlands to the south the date may be even later and the overall picture more complicated. Kenites, Yerahmeelites, Calebites, Othnielites, and others constituted the population of the rugged country called *Har Yehudah*, "the mountain (district) of the gorge(s)."[59] Extensive occupation of the region is not attested before the close of the second millennium or the early monarchic

---

in Ephraim (Jud. 12:13–15); Samson, a Danite, is buried in Ephraim (Jud. 16:31), Eli and Samuel are both resident in Ephraim, and the story of the Levite and his concubine takes place in Bethlehem and Ephraim (Jud. 19:1); and the subsequent intertribal war takes place in Benjamin (Jud. 20:14ff.).

[55] For a criticism of the amphictyony, see Van Seters, *In Search of History*, 231–32 and n. 81; idem, *Abraham in History and Tradition* (New Haven, Conn., 1975), 143–48; N. P. Lemche, *Studia Theologica* 38 (1984).

[56] Ahlström, *Who Were the Israelites?*, 66–67.

[57] K. D. Schunk, *Benjamin* (Berlin, 1963); W. C. Hayes and J. M. Miller, eds., *Israelite and Judaean History* (Philadelphia, 1977), 92–98.

[58] Ahlström, *Who Were the Israelites?*, 63–64, 92, 95; I. Finkelstein, *The Archaeology of the Israelite Settlement* (Jerusalem, 1988), 94–110; Z. Gal, *TA* 9 (1982), 79–86.

[59] M. Noth, *The History of Israel* (London, 1959), 56–58; E. Lipinski, *VT* 23 (1973), 380–81; R. de Vaux, *The Early History of Israel* (Philadelphia, 1978), 547.

period.[60] Other southern communities are more elusive: Amalek occurs in no contemporary extra-Biblical text (although possibly attested now archaeologically),[61] and Simeon is conspicuous by his absence from all bodies of evidence.

Dan presents a special case. The name has invited the ingenious comparison with the name of that component of the Sea Peoples known as *Danune*;[62] but there is no extra-Biblical evidence for the settlement of a large remnant of this community in southern Palestine. Until the time that such evidence is forthcoming, it is better to reserve judgment.

If the Egyptians were intimately knowledgeable about what was going on in hither Asia in the later eleventh and early tenth centuries B.C., no detailed record of theirs has come down to us. Whatever relationship the last Ramessides had attempted to perpetuate with the Asiatics, there could be no question of the 21st Dynasty's inability to claim suzerainty over any territory east of the Delta. Even Byblos, the oldest state in the Levant to have been subverted by Egypt, demanded payment for its goods; and the present ruler averred strenuously that his ancestors had been paid for their services:[63] in response to the statement that his fathers had willingly sent timber, Zakar-Baʿal replied:

> Of course they did, and if you pay me something I will do it! But my (fathers) performed this service only after Pharaoh l.p.h. had despatched six cargo boats laden with Egyptian products and they were unloaded into their storehouses (i.e., in payment). And you? What have you brought for me? . . . Now if the ruler of Egypt were my lord, and if I were his vassal, he would not have to cause gold and silver to be brought with the request "Perform the business of Amun!" . . . But I am not your vassal, nor the vassal of him that sent you!

Unable to command compliance with their demands, the Tanite kings consciously fostered a commercial policy that involved them in cartels with the now-independent states of the coast.[64] Through the latter diplomatic contact was still maintained with the great states of inner Asia, including Assyria, whose thrusts toward the Syrian coast were now being felt in the Levant.[65] Military commands that echo exploits of old credited

[60] I. Finkelstein, *JNES* 47 (1988), 250–51.

[61] M. Kochavi, *BAR* 6 (1980), 27; Finkelstein, *JNES* 47 (1988), 243.

[62] See p. 252; Y. Yadin, *Australian Journal of Archaeology* 1 (1968), 9ff.; on the Danite migration, see A. Malamat, *Biblica* 51 (1970), 1–16.

[63] Wenamun 2:5–13 (Gardiner, *Stories*, 67–68). His statement is, in fact, a tissue of lies.

[64] W. F. Albright, *JAOS* 71 (1951), 260–61; idem, in *Studies Presented to David Moore Robinson* (St. Louis, 1951), 1:223ff.; idem, *CAH*² II, pt. 2 (1975), 507ff. J. Leclant, in W. Ward, ed., *The Role of the Phoenicians in the Interaction of Mediterranean Civilization* (Beirut, 1968), 9ff.; for Egyptian imports at Philistine sites, see A. Mazar, *BA* 40 (1977), 85; T. Dothan, in *Biblical Archaeology Today*, 174; deim, *IEJ* 36 (1986), 107.

[65] For the incursion of Tiglath-Pileser I into the Phoenician coast, probably during Ramesses IX's reign, see *ANET*², 275a; on the diplomatic presents sent by a king of Egypt

to the mighty Ramesside princes are indeed found at the Tanite court; and Psusennes I's titulary is insistent on triumph over Asiatics.[66] But whether they are evidence of military activity in Palestine is wholly unknown. Our sparse sources for the period occasionally throw up servants of Asiatic origin, but whether they arrived in Egypt as prisoners of war or through the slave trade remains uncertain.[67] Egypt did, indeed, remember vividly the territory in the north over which it had once exercised sovereignty, as the detail in the geographical section of the Onomastica of Amenemope clearly shows; but it was a region that no longer delivered taxes or received Egyptian commissioners.[68]

THE RISE OF THE IRON AGE STATES IN THE LEVANT

The beginning of the first millenium B.C. witnessed the assimilation (from an Egyptian point of view) of the "indigestible" elements of the outgoing Late Bronze Age in western Asia into a framework at once familiar and manageable. This was not a "district of northern foreign lands," as a New Kingdom scribe might have termed it, reduced to subservient status, but rather the ingredients of a "sphere of influence" encompassing a group of disunited states that Egypt gradually came to realize could be used as a buffer against threats more remote.

Everywhere in the Levant except the Phoenician coast, new states largely unrelated to the defunct principalities of the Bronze Age began to rise in the eleventh and tenth centuries B.C. In contrast to the Bronze Age states, which were essentially patrimonies identified with and centered upon individual cities, the new political sovereignties took their rise within the ethnic communities that often gave their tribal name to the new state. From the outset they constituted a political expression of the *Volk*, and were designed to provide a framework within which the *Volk* could function. While the ruling families of such states might select a city

---

(Nesubanebdjed, or Psusennes I), see E. F. Weidner, *AfO* 6 (1930–1931), 88; M. Elat, *IEJ* 25 (1975), 32; idem, *JAOS* 98 (1978), 22; for the votive bead of the lady Napalte, possibly evidence for a diplomatic marriage with the Pharaoh, see E. Dhorme, in Montet, *Psousennès*, 139ff.; R. Borger, *Einleitung in die assyrischen Königsinschriften* (Leiden, 1964), 20–21.

[66] Cf. the "chief generalissimo of His Majesty, chief steward of Amunrasonther, chief charioteer of His Majesty . . . Onkhefenmut," Montet, *Psousennès*, 59, fig. 21, pl. 39; "general and commander (*ḥ³wty*) of Pharaoh's battalions . . . Wenbanebdjed," ibid., 84, fig. 31; see further D. B. Redford, *JAOS* 93 (1973), 4–5.

[67] Cf. Akh-amun-nekhy and Akh-ptah-nekhy, specifically referred to as "Syrian servants" in the endowment stela of Sheshonq son of Namlot from Abydos: A. Mariette, *Catalogue générale d'Abydos* no. 1225, 10–11; A. M. Blackman, *JEA* 27 (1941), 92; cf. also Shepet, commander of shield bearers, in the El-Hibeh letters (mid-eleventh century B.C.): W. Spiegelberg, *ZÄS* 53 (1921), no. 33, verso 2.

[68] Cf. R. A. Caminos, *A Tale of Woe* (Oxford, 1977), 67 (if indeed *Nhrn* is to be read).

as a residence and capital, it was the tribe or region that identified the polity.

Because of the nomadic past of the peoples who constituted these "national" states, kinship tended to dominate as the underlying criterion of communal and political identity; and the erstwhile god of the tribe gravitated to supreme national deity, sometimes to the exclusion of others. Since their formative stage had witnessed an economy of pastoralism and transhumance, boundaries meant less to the Iron Age states than to the city patrimonies of the Bronze Age; and the former exhibited a disquieting proclivity for expansion by uprooting autochthonous populations and dispossessing them of their former lands.[69]

The ethnic makeup of the Levant at this time likewise attests the new winds blowing in the post-Sea Peoples era. The composition of North Syria reflected, however dimly, the heyday of that region's incorporation into the Late Bronze Age empire of the Hittites. The states of Samal, Cilicia, Gurgum, Carchemish, and Hamath (which had supplanted Ugarit, Aleppo, and Nukhashshe) bore the appellative "Hittite" and, whether Hittite in racial composition or not, certainly made use of the late Hittite hieroglyphic script. In inland Syria further south, the dissolution of Amurru, Tunip, Kadesh, and Upe had opened the door to a group, already present during the Bronze Age, but now unchallenged by any superior power. These were the Aramaeans, a people speaking a West Semitic tongue related to but quite distinct from the Pheonician dialects of the coast or the Canaano-Hebrew dialects of the south. Aramaean enclaves gained the ascendancy on the Orontes and in Coele-Syria, and in the tenth century were in the process of founding powerful states at Hamath, Geshur (in north Palestine), and especially at Damascus.[70] Along the southern coast, from Gaza to Mount Carmel, enclaves of the Philistines and Teukrians (now partly Semitized) maintained a firm hold of the broad coastal plains and, as the Egyptians had done before them, exercised a tentative but preemptive influence over the inland mountains. In response to the Philistine presence, Israel and Judah in the uplands were moving toward the creation of a state.[71]

Only along the coast north of modern Haifa, and extending as far as

[69] G. Buccellati, *Cities and Nations of Ancient Syria* (Rome, 1967), 92 ff.

[70] On the Neo-Hittite kingdoms, see J. D. Hawkins, *CAH²*, III, pt. 1 (1982), 372–441; O. R. Gurney, *The Hittites²* (Harmondsworth, 1962), 39–46; J. G. Macqueen, *The Hittites* (London, 1986), 154–56; on the later use of the term "Hittite," see J. Van Seters, *VT* 22 (1972), 64–81; on the Aramaeans, see B. Mazar, *BA* 25 (1962), 98–120; A. Malamat, in D. J. Wiseman, ed., *Peoples of Old Testament Times* (Oxford, 1973), 134–55; W. T. Pittard, *Ancient Damascus* (Winona Lake, Ind., 1987).

[71] On the role of the Philistines as a menace that helped to unite the Hebrew tribes, see A.D.H. Mayes, *VT* 23 (1973), 151ff.; cf. also K. Koch, *VT* 19 (1969), 78ff.

Arvad, did the original Canaanite population maintain itself inviolate in the age-old city-states of Tyre, Sidon, Beirut, Byblos, and Arvad. These coastal Canaanites, now appearing under the rubic "Pheonician,"[72] were more than ever oriented toward the sea, and shortly we shall trace the route and impact of their maritime activity.

Strangely Egypt too during the tenth century in a certain sense falls into the category of "new state." Ever since their crushing defeat in battle by Ramesses III, the Libyan tribes had reverted to the less obvious tack of infiltrating the Nile Valley and Delta in small groups and making themselves useful to the state as a mercenary fighting force. The Meshwesh came in the largest numbers and one of their chiefs, Buyuwawa, settled during the 20th Dynasty in the environs of Herakleopolis where there had been an army barracks and military governorate since the time of Ramesses II. Further north, the western districts of the Delta around Sais became the stamping ground of a community of Labu. (In Upper Egypt the Mahaswen appear occasionally during the outgoing New Kingdom but never gained a permanent foothold.) By the close of the 21st Dynasty the Meshwesh chieftaincy at Herakleopolis had made itself indispensible to the Tanite royal house, and the incumbent, one Sheshonq, had achieved the rank of generalissimo of all armed forces. An older man with grown sons during the reign of Psusennes II, Sheshonq had acquired a number of notable family connections. The high priest of Memphis was his uncle through marriage, his eldest son Osorkon had been married to the king's daughter, a second son had married into the family of the fourth prophet of Amun, and a third son was commander at Herakleopolis. It is small wonder that, when Psusennes II died around 930 B.C., apparently without heir, Sheshonq acceded to the throne without incident and founded a new house, which Manetho later numbered the 22nd.[73]

THE PROBLEM OF THE SOURCES

Apart from the tenth century herein under discussion, there are few periods in the history of the Levant for which one can gain totally opposed impressions depending on one's secondary sources. The problem is threefold: the almost total silence of our written sources,[74] our inability to evaluate critically much later sources on the period, and the equivocal

---

[72] On the Phoenician cities in the Iron Age, see M. Noth, WO 1, no. 1 (1947), 21ff.; D. Baramki, *Phoenicia and the Phoenicians* (Beirut, 1961); D. Harden, *The Phoenicians* (Hardmondsworth, 1971); J. D. Muhly, in *Biblical Archaeology Today*, 177–91; E. Gubel et al., eds., *Studia Phoenicia*, I vol. 1 (Louvain, 1983).

[73] In general on the Libyans, see the works cited in chapter 12, n. 19.

[74] Cf. A. Malamat, in T. Ishida, ed., *Studies in the Period of David and Solomon* (Tokyo, 1982), 189–90.

nature of the archaeological record. Thebes, which for five centuries has supplied us with royal inscriptions, grist for the historians' mill, ceases to be a center where triumphal inscriptions are set up once the connection with the royal family is severed at the close of the 20th Dynasty. Whether the kings of the 21st Dynasty similarly broadcast their exploits in stelae and reliefs at Tanis is difficult to say, but the practice seems to have become passé, and very few "historical" texts have been recovered from the site.[75] Needless to say, the tenth century B.C. has bequeathed us no contemporary inscriptions from the states of Palestine and Syria.

Thrust back to later sources purporting to give a historical picture of the age, we can only bewail the absence of any gauge by which their accuracy can be measured. Two sources are here in question: the snippets of a classical history of Tyre vouchsafed in epitome by Josephus,[76] and the text of the two books of Samuel and the first two chapters of 1 Kings. The former amounts to little more than a king list, but by and large it seems in accord with the Biblical tradition of 1 Kings in placing an Eiromos (Hiram) in the second quarter of the tenth century, roughly contemporary with Solomon. The Biblical sources are much more extensive and infinitely more seductive. Although the Biblical historian is forced to admit that he has no means of checking the historical veracity of the Biblical texts, "nevertheless materials relevant for the historian can be gathered from the narratives . . . (and) the work appears to be rich in materials of high value to the historian."[77] If we are still inclined to doubt, we are reassured by such statements as "there seems no reason to question (the) general reliability and the substantial accuracy of (the account's) chronological sequence,"[78] or "there seems to be no good reason to doubt the existence of a historical kernel."[79] The case is argued no further, and one is left to wonder what clues the writer has which the reader lacks. Bewilderment increases when one reads "our sources are the products of later working and editing, so that the original elements, more often than not, cannot be isolated with any exactitude."[80] Yet the writer obviously feels he *has* isolated them, and can stamp one passage "a rather realistic report of what actually happened," another episode "legendary," yet other details "non-controversial matters of fact," and still others "impossible to

[75] Tanis was, comparatively speaking, a new city with no tradition reaching back into imperial times. In addition to this, the 22nd Dynasty was Libyan in origin, and may not have shared or fully appreciated the New Kingdom penchant for publishing records of triumph.

[76] Cf. H. J. Katzenstein, *The History of Tyre* (Jerusalem, 1973), 78ff.; Van Seters, *In Search of History*, 195ff.

[77] J. A. Soggin, in Hayes and Miller, *Israelite and Judaean History*, 335–37.

[78] Ibid., 346.

[79] Ibid., 361.

[80] Ibid., 362.

consider . . . a historical record."[81] One feels impelled to cry out: what criteria of evaluation are you using? What unpublished evidence do you possess? Sadly, in most cases of this kind, there is no answer to either question.

For the standard scholarly approach to the history of Israel during the United Monarchy amounts to nothing more than a bad attack of academic "wishful thinking." We have these glorious narratives in the books of Samuel and 1 Kings, so well written and ostensibly factual. What a pity if rigorous historical criticism forces us to discard them and not use them. Let us, then, press them into service—what else have we?—and let the burden of proof fall on others.[82] And so, as in the case of Josephus's use of the same material, the modern historical treatment of the Age of Saul, David, and Solomon degenerates into little more than a paraphrase of the Biblical text, interlarded with arcane interpretations of a political or sociological nature.

In fact over the years Biblical scholarship has established a woeful record in soberly and dispassionately analyzing the sources in 1 and 2 Samuel on the United Monarchy.[83] While one might be unwise to impute cryptofundamentalist motives, the current fashion of treating the sources at face value as documents written up in large part in the court of Solomon arises from an equally misplaced desire to rehabilitate the faith and undergird it with any arguments, however fallacious. Two observations in particular seem to have fostered the growth of this new apologetic. One is essentially an aesthetic judgment: "The so-called 'Story of David's Succession' in 2 Sam. ix–xx and 1 Kings i–ii is a prose composition superior to anything we know in biblical narrative . . . . The original work [was] written by a highly skillful scribe who either had personally witnessed many an event or had been guided by an eye-witness."[84] So we are to conclude that literary excellence is evidence of contemporary authorship? One (perversely perhaps) longs to see the result of the application of such a criterion to Geoffrey of Monmouth's treatment of Arthur, to the anonymous *Joseph and Asenath*, to the Alexander Romances, or a host of other Pseudepigrapha. Mesmerized by the literary quality of much of the writing in 1 and 2 Samuel—it is in truth a damned good story!—many

[81] Ibid., 351–53, 338, 364.

[82] Cf. the apt comments of M. Liverani, *Oriens Antiquus* 16 (1977), 105.

[83] The picture is changing: among others, one may read with refreshment and profit such insightful works as Van Seters, *In Search of History*; W. C. Hayes and J. M. Miller, *A History of Ancient Israel and Judah* (Philadelphia, 1986); B. Halpern, *The First Historians* (San Francisco, 1988).

[84] E. Lipinski, in J. A. Emerton ed., *Congress Volume. Jerusalem 1986* (Leiden, 1988), 160–61; cf. A. Alt, *Kleine Schriften zur Geschichte des Volkes Israel* (Munich, 1959), 2:15; T.N.D. Mettinger, *King and Messiah* (Lund, 1976), 31.

scholars take a further step: "The Succession story must be regarded as the oldest specimen of ancient Israelite history writing."[85]

The second observation, innocent enough in itself, is that monarchic states in antiquity, exercising hegemony over a broad region, depend upon a large cadre of scribes to make them run. This is true. The argument continues that such scribes would need training, which, in systems of long standing, would have been provided by the bureaucratic tradition itself. But in Solomon's case the empire had come into being but yesterday, and no scribes or training mechanism existed. Models were needed to set up the whole framework in a hurry; and where better to find such models than in the highly sophisticated scribal tradition of Egypt, just next door? We know the range of written works to which Egyptian scribes were exposed for their education during the New Kingdom: besides such forms for practical use as letters, accounts, memoranda, and reports, there were also poetry, hymns, aphoristic literature, stories, onomastica, hemerologies, and magical and medical texts. If Solomon imported the Egyptian system, it would have come with all this "belle-lettristic" baggage in tow. And does not, in fact, the bruited wisdom of Solomon sketched in 1 Kings 4:29–34 sound remarkably like the content of some of these Egyptian genres?[86] Having convinced oneself of the likelihood of an interest in "literature" at the court of Solomon—how like an institution of the European eighteenth century this sounds!—it is but a step to conjure up a scribal class with an interest in committing the past to writing (the contemporary Egyptian scribe on whom the imagined Solomonic scriveners are supposed to be modeled exhibited no such interest in history, but that seems to have escaped our apologists). And so the Succession Document, the great J-epic and even the Joseph story can be credited to the literary activity of Solomon's court, and we can be comforted that our faith in their essential historicity was not misplaced.[87] The "Census Lists of David" and the "Annals of Solomon" become a fact.[88]

[85] G. von Rad, *The Problem of the Hexateuch and Other Essays* (Edinburgh, 1966), 176; cf. H. Gunkel, in *Religion in Geschichte und Gegenwart*³ (Tübingen, 1957–), 2:1112ff.; M. Burrows, in R. C. Denton, ed., *The Idea of History in the Ancient Near East* (New Haven, Conn., 1955), 110; the view is extremely widespread and would not repay extending this note into a headcount. For a cogent argument that the "Succession Document" begins at 2 Sam. 2 (if not earlier), see Van Seters, *In Search of History*, 281–82.

[86] Alt, *Kleine Schriften*, 2:94–96; but cf. M. V. Fox, *VT* 36 (1986), 302–10.

[87] Gunkel, in *Religion in Geschichte and Gegenwart*³, 2:1112ff.; G. Von Rad, *Gesammelte Studien zum alten Testament* (Munich, 1961), 225–37; idem, *The Problem*, 203; M. Noth, in *Religion in Geschicte und Gegenwart*³, 2:1498–1504; R.B.Y. Scott, *VT* Suppl. 3 (1955), 262–79; O. Eissfeldt, *Introduction to the Old Testament* (New York, 1965), 247; Lipinski, in Emerton, *Congress Volume*, 157–64; Burrows, in Denton, *Idea of History*, 112; J. Blenkinsopp, *VT* Suppl. 15 (1966), 44–57; T. Ishida, *Royal Dynasties of Ancient Israel*

It is difficult to decide whether it is worthwhile to attempt a rebuttal of such irrelevant arguments, the one wholly subjective, the other a priori. But as they reinforce a perception of a key period in Israelite history when Egyptian influence is invoked, the attempt must be made.

In the first place it should be apparent that the literary quality of a retrospective piece has nothing to do with how close in time the author was to the events. The Succession Document of 2 Samuel 13 to 1 Kings 2 exhibits the same traits as the stories in 1 Samuel about David's early career under Saul: skillful concentration on dramatic turns of the plot, imagined conversations (which the author could not possibly have been privy to), sensitivity to psychological nuances, subtle development of character, irony and the like. None of these characteristics marks the work as *historical* of necessity, or militates in favor of contemporary composition. They are rather the hallmarks of hero tales and well-crafted *Mächen* the world over.[89]

Second, the claim that Solomon's reign constituted an "enlightenment" rests on no solid basis, and can be shown to be unlikely. Premonarchic communities, at the moment of their transformation into more sophisticated nation-states headed by kings, make solely practical demands of that novel mechanism for expediting state affairs, namely the script.[90] In Egypt and Mesopotamia, for example, at the moment of the creation of the nation state or the urban community, the script served three basic needs: the need to keep accounts, the need to identify, and the (perceived) need to commemorate. The first two arise from the day-to-day exigencies experienced by the civil service; the third reflects the self-consciousness of the head of state in his new role as the embodiment of the community's ideals. The first two produce tax lists (identifying individual, commodity,

---

(Berlin, 1977), 136, 148; G. Rendsburg, *The Redaction of Genesis* (Winona Lake, Ind., 1986).

[88] N. Na'aman, *Borders and Districts in Biblical Historiography* (Jerusalem, 1986); E. W. Heaton, *Solomon's New Men* (London, 1974); Z. Kallai, *Historical Geography of the Bible: The Tribal Territories of Israel* (Jerusalem 1986); A. F. Rainey, *Abr-Nahrain* 27 (1989), 178; D. Edelman, *JNES* 50 (1991), 69–73.

[89] Hayes and Miller, *A History*, 152–60; folkloristic motifs abound: the childless wife (1 Sam. 1:11); the ribald tale of discomfiting the conqueror (1 Sam. 5); selection of the youngest son (David: 1 Sam. 16:1–13; Solomon himself!); the "David-Goliath" motif (1 Sam. 17); the eye-gouging motif (F. M. Cross, in E. Tov, ed., *The Hebrew and Greek Texts of Samuel* [Jerusalem, 1980], 105–19); the hundred foreskins as bride-price (1 Sam. 18:25; 2 Sam. 3:14). Figures belong in the realm of fantasy, yet are often integral to the plot: e.g., 1 Sam. 4:2, 10 (4,000 and 30,000 killed); 1 Sam. 11; cf. 15:4 (Judah musters 10,000, Israel 300,000); 1 Sam. 13:2 (30,000 chariots, 6,000 cavalry); 2 Sam. 6:1 (select troops 30,000 in number); 2 Sam. 8 and 10, 18:7 (22,000, 18,000, and 20,000 slain in David's battles); 2 Sam. 12:13 (the fantastic weight of the Ammonite king's crown).

[90] For what follows, see D. B. Redford, *Pharaonic King-lists, Annals and Day-books* (Toronto, 1986), 133–34.

and amount), bills, dockets, memoranda, lists, and even letters; the third produces the triumphal relief, with or without glossing text, the biographical statement, and the compendium (of useful information formerly transmitted orally, such as the pharmacopoeia and the like). Belles lettres are *not* represented at this moment in the incipient evolution of the state, and are in fact far in the future. Material with the specific intent of an apology, or propaganda in favor of a royal house, an individual king, a divine covenant, or the like will take the form not of a hero tale, subtly composed and committed to a scroll in the archives—Who is going to read it?—but a simple, direct biographical statement, inscribed on stone and posted for all to see and hear a scribe read. Evidence from other Levantine states of the Iron Age (Samal, Carchemish, Cilicia, and Damascus to name a few) proves that the published building text or biographical or statue inscription was the norm. We should expect the same and nothing more from the monarchy of David and Solomon.[91]

But we need not confine the rebuttal to a demonstration of the unlikelihood of a Solomonic date for the materials in 1 and 2 Samuel (or its immediate *Vorlage*); an argument of empirical reference can be set forth. The presence of numerous etiological passages detracts, as it did in the case of Judges, from the degree of confidence one can place in the stories to which the etiologies are attached, and makes a Solomonic date for in-

[91] Those who are inclined to think that, because we "now" know Israel was "more literate" than formerly supposed, it was quite possible for the ancient Israelites to commit their historical and prophetic works and their ruminations on imponderables to writing from the outset, should be reminded of some sobering facts. First, "literate" is a relative adjective, and we must be told the gauge by which in a given instance literacy is being measured. If it is against scholars' earlier expectations, we may as well dismiss the whole subject. Many scholars have long suspected that during the monarchy there were far more scribes jotting down administrative dockets than the evidence suggested; and the recovery of written texts to date from excavations wholly bears out this suspicion (cf. I. T. Kaufman, *BA* 45 [1982], 29–39; F. Vattioni, *AION* 28 [1978], 227–28; A. R. Millard, in *Biblical Archaeology Today*, 301–12). Nonetheless, the paltry few hundred ostraca and handful of seals and bullae that have come to light have, under no circumstances, given grounds to believe in a "literate" society in ancient Israel. Far more written material has come to light from Ptolemaic Egypt; but to call Egyptian society of the second century B.C. "literate" would give a quite misleading impression. Second, the mere fact that some of the Hebrews *could* have written down belle-lettristic compositions does not mean that they did in fact do so. The Egyptians *could* have written down stories about Khufu, Pepy II, Apophis, and Khamwese during or shortly after the lifetimes of these individuals: they had the means, the script! Yet they did not do so, and the extant stories of these famed characters were composed centuries later. Third, we must always bear in mind that in antiquity, until Hellenistic times, writing in *all* cultures (not excepting Hebrew and Greek, save the mark!) was but an *aide-memoire*, and no stigma attached itself to being illiterate. When great imaginations set about to compose, their owners, whether able to read and write or not, put together their pieces for oral delivery; and if we possess written copies of what they extemporized, we owe this to the entirely secondary and irrelevant process of transcribing.

scripturation, just one generation after the event, rather improbable.[92] In fact, the etiologies associated with David's taking of Jerusalem and his early battles with the Philistines are linked to material so slight that the etiology in question seems the sole and adequate explanation of the tradition itself.[93] Numerous passages presuppose the existence of a monarchy of considerable antiquity,[94] while Moab, Ammon, and Edom are already monarchic states in the author's view.[95] Here and there one encounters allusions to motifs and traditions that either originated or were developed to the point presupposed by the Samuel passages at a much later date.[96] Blatant anachronisms are more numerous than a record with reliable sources should contain: coined money (1 Sam. 13:21), late armor (1 Sam. 17:4–7, 38–39; 25:13), the use of camels (1 Sam. 30:17) and cavalry (distinct from chariotry: 1 Sam. 13:5; 2 Sam. 1:6), iron picks and axes (as though they were common: 2 Sam. 12:31), and sophisticated siege techniques (2 Sam. 20:15).[97] Nor is the core of the "Succession Document" (2 Sam. 13 to 1 Kings 2) free from clear indications of a date long after the events described. The author has his characters wear archaic clothing (2 Sam. 13:18),[98] talk of coined money (2 Sam. 18:11–12), call up a troop of Gargantuan size for an immediate pursuit (2 Sam. 17:1), engage in a battle with twenty thousand casualties (2 Sam. 18:7), and use cavalry (1 Kings 1:5). Moreover, one of the army runners is described by the generic "the Kushite," a term that points to a period after the last quarter of the eighth century B.C. and recalls the prowess of the Nubian army under Taharqa in running. The passage could only have been written when the presence of Kushites as servants and paramilitary in Palestine was sufficiently common to make the inclusion of one in the story believable.[99]

[92] Cf. the etiology of topographic phenomena: stones (1 Sam. 6:18, 7:12, 23:28), a well (2 Sam. 2:16), a monument apparently anepigraphic (2 Sam. 18:18); of political facts (1 Sam. 13:14, 31:7; 2 Sam. 4:3, 6:23), of precedents (1 Sam. 30:25).

[93] 2 Sam. 5:8 (based surely on the presence of a temple notice restricting access to the shrine: cf. S. Sauneron, *BIFAO* 60 [1960], 111–12.

[94] 1 Sam. 2:1–10 (a royal psalm); chap. 8; 10:17–19; 12:6–25.

[95] 1 Sam. 14:47, 22:3.

[96] The plague narrative (1 Sam. 4:8); the hardening of Pharaoh's heart (1 Sam. 6:6); the annihilation of Amalek (1 Sam. 15:2); the death of Abimelek (2 Sam. 11:21); the anti-Baʿal polemic of the later monarchy (1 Sam. 7:3–4); the law of Moses (1 Kings 2:3).

[97] The use of mounds and rams in the southwest, especially by a lesser state, sounds premature.

[98] See E. A. Speiser, *The Anchor Bible: Genesis* (New York, 1964), 289–90.

[99] Kushites (Medjay) are known in Palestine in Amarna times (H. Klengel, in *Ägypten und Kusch* [Berlin, 1977], 227–33), and the transfer of Kushite communities for resettlement in the north is known from the 19th Dynasty (KRI II, 206); but these were imperial measures discontinued when the empire collapsed. For three centuries from about 1050 B.C. Nubia was virtually cut off from Egypt, lower Nubia depopulated, and Kushites almost wholly

A favorite recourse adopted to lessen the embarrassment is to ascribe the anachronisms, etiologies, and folkloristic elements to glosses or editorial framework; but this is nought but subterfuge. The vast majority of the examples I have marshaled belong to the very fabric of the stories recounted. They date the storyteller himself and (from a modern historian's point of view) impugn his sources. The more extensive and fully worked his sources, and the more he esteemed them, the less would be his own input and the more easily identified his additions. But the historian in 1 and 2 Samuel—and one need not deny a variety of "hands" and multitiered sources—has no documents or informants who *themselves* do not view the United Monarchy as a remote heroic age.

If the extended "Succession" Document (not to mention the earlier Saulide narratives) is a late composition, and not very useful at face value for eliciting the facts of David's reign,[100] it remains legitimate to ask why it was written.[101] One will receive a number of bewildering answers. Is it intended as a counterblast to the pious tradition of the "good king David," which runs through much of the rest of the Old Testament? (Yet certainly from 2 Samuel 13 to 1 Kings 1, David is not presented as an evil or Macchiavellian figure, but rather as an inept, malleable nonentity with essentially good intentions.)[102] Is it an "antimonarchic" statement?[103] (But where is this ever spelled out?) Is it political propaganda contemporary with the early monarchy and intended to exculpate David from dynastic bloodguilt?[104] (Poorly argued and unconvincing, one might con-

---

absent from Egypt: B. G. Trigger, *History and Settlement of Lower Nubia* (New Haven, Conn., 1959), 112–14; T. Säve-Söderbergh, *Temples and Tombs of Ancient Nubia* (New York, 1987), 38–39. With the rise of the kingdom of Kush, however, in the second half of the eighth century B.C., Kushites once more insinuated themselves into the northern Nile Valley. Isaiah 20 is probably the earliest reference to Kush in the Old Testament, all other passages being demonstrably later (Redford, *King-lists,* 323 and n. 165; similarly in Phoenician, Z. Harris, *A Grammar of the Phoenician Language* [New Haven, Conn., 1936], 113). It is at the same period that the personal name "The Kushite" in Egyptian onomastica suddenly springs to popularity with the reemergence of Nubia in Egypt during the 25th Dynasty (711–663 B.C.): J. Leclant, *Enquête sur les sacerdoces et les sanctuaires égyptiens à l'époque dite "éthiopienne"* (Cairo, 1954), 70–71. Under Taharqa the Kushites were noted for their running (690–664 B.C.): A. M. Moussa, *MDAIK* 37 (1981), 331–38, pl. 47.

[100] Use of the Succession Document as historical source at face value renders any investigation, no matter how erudite, a mere exercise, devoid of substance: cf. A. Malamat, *JNES* 22 (1963), 1ff.; idem, in Ishida, *Studies in the Period of David and Solomon,* 189ff.; Ishida, *Royal Dynasties,* 175ff.; F. Langlamet, *RB* 89 (1982), 5ff., and a host of others.

[101] Cf. J. Van Seters, *JSOT* 1 (1976), 22–29; F. Langlamet, *RB* 83 (1976), 321ff.

[102] Cf. Van Seters, *In Search of History,* 283, who contrasts the David of the Saulide narratives, always leading his men into battle, with the David of the Succession Document, *never* leading his men into battle!

[103] L. Delekat, *BZAW* 105 (1967), 26–36.

[104] R. N. Whybray, *The Succession Narrative* (London, 1968), 50ff.; cf. N. P. Lemche, *JSOT* 10 (1978), 9–25; idem, *Biblische Notizen* 24 (1984), 106–7.

tend, and avoiding the difficulties of the manifold signs of late authorship.) Does it convey an "antimessianic" message from post-Exilic times?[105] (The writer may well have harbored a sentiment that might have expressed itself in such a narrative; but by the very subtlety of his delivery would the message not have been in danger of being missed?)

That the Succession Document does depict David in an unfavorable light and that this was appreciated anciently are adequately proved by the omission of the piece from the Book of Chronicles, which idolizes the House of David without stint. But the succession Document also explains other twists of history perceived at a distance. How did a brigand from Bethlehem supplant the house of Saul, even though he had married into it? How do the quirks of later history find a rationalization in David's sin? How came it that David was followed by a lesser son, Solomon, in view of his other illustrious and older offspring, well known in folklore? The story does, in fact, provide an explanation of the Judaean dynasty in the form it was known to later generations: descended through the line of the wise Solomon (not the lustful Amnon, the power-hungry Absolom, or the presumptuous Adonijah), thoroughly Jerusalemite—Solomon of all David's sons in the running is the only one born of a woman of Jerusalem—a prey to cabals and would-be kingmakers, a state to be saved by the hard, implacable Solomon, not the emotional, lenient David.

In short, in addition to rationalizing history, the Succession Document also provides a model to be shunned for those who would reform or reestablish the Davidic state. Caveat Josiah and Zerubbabel!

The dual function of explanation and warning, and the sensitive literary treatment of the theme, bring the Succession Document close to that type of text represented by Pediese's history of his family's relations with the city of Teudjoy in Middle Egypt.[106] Written in 513 B.C., this lengthy narrative exhibits characteristics of style and thematic treatment that, *mutatis mutandis*, show through in the Succession Document also: interest in the checkered history of a family through time, sensitivity to the emotional reaction of individual characters, imagined conversations, skillful use of dramatic turns of the plot.[107] As the *stated* purpose of the Succession Document appears to be how the "Kingdom was established in the hand of Solomon" (1 Kings 2:46), so Pediese's work purports to explain "how Teudjoy went to ruin."

[105] Van Seters, *In Search of History*, 290–91.

[106] P. Rylands IX: F. L. Griffith, *Catalogue of the Demotic Papyri in the John Rylands Library, Manchester* (Manchester, 1909).

[107] These characteristics are shared by another genre, viz. the expanded historical biography of private individuals, which is found during the Kushite-Saite period. Here also, in contrast to earlier biographical statements, there is a genuine interest in the participation of individuals in momentous historical events.

No one doubts that Pediese himself and his *dramatis personnae* were historical, although considerable uncertainty hangs over many details of his story. Similarly, it would be ill-advised to deny historicity to the characters of the Succession Document, but their heroic size and the events they participated in are most certainly suspect. In fact, the Succession Document may tell us as little of the tenth century B.C. as the *Morte d'Arthur* does of the sixth century A.D.

When we proceed beyond the Succession Document and come to the block of material describing the reign of Solomon (1 Kings 3–11), we are surrounded by a completely different atmosphere. The style of the writer and his treatment of details degenerate immediately. Sensitivity to plot, detail, and characterization is replaced by the banality of folktale, parable, and list.[108] There can be no doubt that we are confronted by an author different from him of the Succession Document.

The thematic material of this section may be summarized as follows:

1. Solomon's marriage to Pharaoh's daughter (3:1, 7:8, 9:16, 24)
2. Solomon's dream at Gibeon, asking for wisdom (3:4–14)
3. The parable of the two harlots (3:16–28, in illustration of 2)
4. List of Solomon's officers and alimentation (4:1–19, 22–27)
5. General remarks on Solomon's wisdom (4:29–34, illustrating 2)
6. Narrative of the pact with Hiram and the quarry work (chap. 5)
7. Building and description of the temple (chap. 6)
8. Building of palace and administrative offices (7:1–12)
9. Furnishings by the Tyrian smith Hiram (7:13–47)
10. Inauguration of the temple (8:1–21)
11. Solomon's prayer (8:22–53)
12. Solomon's blessing and sacrifice (8:54–66)
13. Solomon's second vision and Yahweh's promise (9:1–9)
14. Cession of part of Galilee to Tyre (9:10–14)
15. Forced labor to build cities (9:15–22)
16. Merchant fleet on the Red Sea (9:26–28; 10:11–12, 22)
17. Visit of the Queen of Sheba (10:1–10, 13)
18. Solomon's income and wealth (10:14–21)
19. Solomon's trade in horses (10:26–28)
20. Solomon's acts of apostasy (11:1–13)
21. Solomon's adversaries (11:14–44, as punishment for 20)

Far too much of this is so general that it fails to yield a clear insight into what historical facts, if any, underlie the disjointed verbiage.[109] The com-

---

[108] How anyone could characterize 1 Kings 3–11 as "carefully structured" is difficult to imagine (so B. Porten, *HUCA* 38 [1967], 124), except by eisegesis.

[109] On the "Book of the Deeds of Solomon" and his reputation for wisdom, see M. Noth,

piler, or author, is at pains much of the time to impress us with how wise and famous Solomon was, and how this redounded to his financial benefit. The description of the temple could have been penned by anyone who saw the structure prior to 586 B.C., while the pious prayers and promises of 10 through 13 envisage the Exile. Distilled to basics, the account of Solomon's reign reduces itself to the following "facts":

1. He was a very wise man and author of "Wisdom" writings
2. He built the temple with Phoenician help
3. He married a Pharaoh's daughter
4. He had a fleet on the Red Sea and engaged in trade
5. He was visited by a South Arabian queen
6. He built many cities
7. He had a number of (named) officials

Only "facts" 6 and 7 yield specifics; the rest is vague and cast as legend. The fashioning of Solomon's figure from such ingredients as imperial hegemony, prowess in building, foreign trade (especially up the Red Sea), wealth, wisdom, and marriage to a great king's daughter suggests the obvious parallel of the semilegendary emperor of the remote past who took shape from the sixth century B.C. on in the person of "Sesostris." Sesostris, an amalgam of the historical Thutmose III and Ramesses II, is certainly no figment of the imagination; but the tales told of him in Herodotus, Diodorus, and others are quite unreliable. For his part, Solomon, as he appears in 1 Kings, has assumed the guise of the "Sesostris of Israel."[110]

EGYPT AND THE ISRAEL OF DAVID AND SOLOMON

As historians we crave a way out of the impasse of inferior textual sources, but willy-nilly are thrown back onto the less than satisfying record of the spade. Here no new texts have come to light. Not even the names "David" and "Solomon" appear, either in West Semitic or Egyptian inscriptions.

The archaeological record is not, however, as unhelpful as its failure to unearth epigraphic evidence might lead us to believe. For once there is a consistency in the general thrust of the data. The cities that Solomon is

---

VT Suppl. 3 (1960), 226; R.B.Y. Scott, VT Suppl. 3 (1960), 262, 279; J. Liver, *Biblica* 48 (1967), 75–101; Porten, *HUCA* 38 (1967), 93–128.

[110] D. B. Redford, in *Biblical Archaeology Today*, 199–200. It is easy to be led astray in Sesostris studies into the mistaken conclusion that the historical figure behind the legend is Senwosret III of the 12th Dynasty (see most recently C. Obsomer, *Les campagnes de Sesostris* [Brussels, 1988]); in actual fact the problem goes back to a mistaken identification in the Manethonian epitome.

supposed to have built, in particular Hazor, Megiddo, and Gezer, show certain distinctive features of architecture such as casemate walls, triple-access gateways, and governors' residences that have the stamp of a single intent or master builder.[111] Moreover the tenth century *does* give evidence of expanded settlements and the kind of town planning one might associate with a strong central monarchy;[112] and the contemporary presence of a strong authority in Judah and the Negeb, able to control the trade routes and to build fortresses, cannot be denied.[113]

If we wish to adopt an a priori position, as Egyptologists we cannot quibble with much of what the Bible says about Egypt during the reigns of David and Solomon. By and large the record is plausible. It is not impossible that wandering Egyptians came within the ambit of Judaean groups in the first quarter of the tenth century (cf. 1 Sam. 30:11; 2 Sam. 23:21). It is conceivable that Egypt was delighted at the genesis of the kingdom of Israel, opposed as it was from the outset to the Philistine occupation of the coastal plain. It is even acceptable to postulate Egyptian attacks, early in the tenth century B.C., on Philistine and Canaanite enclaves in the Shephelah, one of which, Gezer, was destroyed in a spectacular conflagration:[114] some of the Pharaohs of the 21st Dynasty display evidence of bellicose intent toward Asia in their titulary and iconography.[115] But it is also conceivable that Pharaoh's court could have given aid and comfort to dissidents and rebels against Solomon.[116] The present

---

[111] Cf. Y. Yadin, *IEJ* 8 (1958), 80–86; idem, *Hazor* (London, 1972), 135–64; K. Kenyon, *Royal Cities of the Old Testament* (New York, 1971), 53–70; D. Ussishkin, *IEJ* 16 (1966), 174–86; idem, *BA* 36 (1973), 78–105; Y. Aharoni, *IEJ* 24 (1974), 13ff.; W. G. Dever, *IEJ* 35 (1985), 217–30.

[112] Cf. Y. Shiloh, *IEJ* 28 (1978), 36–51.

[113] Finkelstein, *JNES* 47 (1988), 241–52. This does not, however, exonerate those who seem to treat any or all of the material in Judges and Samuel as a body of "proof texts" to be drawn on at will to elucidate their archaeological finds: cf. *IEJ* 28 (1978), 268 (where the authors cavalierly suggest that an abandonment of Izbet Sarta was occasioned by the battle of Ebenezer!); or *IEJ* 35 (1985), 187 (where the authors yield to the temptation to see the "Camp of Dan" [Jud. 18:12] in a level of pits!). At least we can thank such writers for providing us with comic relief.

[114] The evidence, such as it is, is conveyed by 1 Kings 9:16; an excellent survey of the state of the question is given in A. R. Green, *JBL* 97 (1978), 353ff.; cf. also Malamat, in Ishida, *Studies in the Period of David and Solomon*, 198–99. Unfortunately a good deal of unnecessary and idle speculation has been indulged in over the underlying motivation of the unnamed Pharaoh (cf. A. R. Schulman, *JNES* 38 [1979], 188). One disquieting impression the cited verse leaves with the reader is that it was inserted into the account of Solomon's building program simply to explain how it came about that Gezer was (now) a Hebrew possession.

[115] Psusennes I (c. 1050–1000 B.C.) is the best example (Montet, *Psousennès*, 74, 136, and passim).

[116] K. A. Kitchen, *The Third Intermediate Period in Egypt* (Warminster, 1973), 274–75; B. Halpern, *JBL* 93 (1974), 523; J. R. Bartlett, *ZAW* 88 (1976), 205ff.; H. Donner, in Hayes

writer personally has a little more difficulty in construing Solomon's marriage to Pharaoh's daughter as historical.[117] But it must be admitted that the tenth century, significantly enough, witnessed the prominence of several members of the distaff side of the great noble and royal families of Egypt, whose marital unions were understood to be important for economic and political purposes.[118]

But where do we go from here? Branding a proposition as "plausible" represents a minimal gain from the standpoint of the historian. One wishes to investigate probability, not whether an alleged event *could* have happened (the answer in the latter case will almost always be "yes"). In the present equivocal state of our knowledge, it seems foolhardy in the extreme (and at the very least pretentious) to go on writing learned tomes about such topics as "the foreign policy of David and Solomon," economics of defense, constitution of the state, royal legitimation, or organs of statecraft. At the very most one will gain a limited insight into what the Deuteronomist writer considered to be the nature of the United Monarchy.[119]

Let us learn to live with ambiguity. Some day evidence may be produced on Solomon's trade in horses or on his marriage to Pharaoh's daughter. Until then these must remain themes for midrash or fictional treatment.

---

and Miller, *Israelite and Judaean History*, 386; R. North, in *Homanaje a Juan Prado* (Madrid, 1975), 200ff.

[117] Redford, in *Biblical Archaeology Today*, 203, n. 42.

[118] For the intermarriage of the Sheshonq family, see p. 299; for Hent-towy, granddaughter of the high priest Menkheperre, and Makare, daughter of Psusennes II, see A. H. Gardiner, *JEA* 48 (1962), 57ff.; for the marriage of princesses to commoners, see Kitchen, *Third Intermediate Period*, 276, 282.

[119] Cf. such works as those of Z. Kallai, *EIJ* 27 (1977), 103–9; S. Talmon, in G. Rendsburg et al., eds., *The Bible World* (New York, 1980), 239–48.

CHAPTER 12

Egypt and Israel in the World of Assyria

FOR A BRIEF PERIOD, datable to the two generations spanning the last quarter of the tenth century and the first quarter of the ninth, there is evidence of an attempt, on Egypt's part, to revive the empire by force. Enough evidence has already been amassed in this book to demonstrate the recurring pattern of growth of political power in Palestine exciting Egyptian concern, and followed by military action (or the threat of it) to reduce or subvert this power. The pharaonic government never failed to be greatly exercised by any political structure in Palestine beyond a segmentary society. Any threat to the freedom of passage along coastal or inland route, or the potential for any part of Palestine being used as a base for hostility, provoked the same reaction along the Nile: execration by the gods and mustering of the troops. The chiefdom of Saul and the monarchy of David could be viewed as beneficial to Egypt's interests as both leaders directed their belligerence toward the Philistines, Egypt's old enemies. But, the battle won in Israel's favor, the peace and rising prosperity of Solomon's kingdom could only rouse Egypt's anxiety.

SHESHONQ'S ATTACK

At an as yet unknown date, but probably early in his reign (i.e., in the 930s),[1] Sheshonq I founder of the 22nd Dynasty, led a major military campaign across the Sinai frontier into Palestine. He lists 154 towns as having been destroyed by the Egyptian forces, and while neither Judah nor Israel is mentioned by name, the geographical range of place-names indicates that both sectors of the country were targeted by Pharaoh's planners. At some point Sheshonq marched toward Jerusalem and "took away the treasures of the House of Yahweh and the treasures of the king's

---

[1] The argument that Sheshonq's campaign took place late in the reign (W. F. Albright, *BASOR* 130 [1953], 4ff.; D. B. Redford, *JAOS* 93 [1973], 10, n. 62) is not compelling. The Gebel es-Silsileh text of year 21 (R. A. Caminos, *JEA* 38 [1950], pl. 13) refers to the building of a "broad court," which (wherever it was) must have been left unfinished on Sheshonq's death (cf. Spencer, *The Egyptian Temple, A Lexicographical Study* [London, 1984], 69–70). It is a good guess that certain cornice blocks (unpublished) now lying in the Karnak Outdoor Museum, with the cartouche of Osorkon I carved on them, came originally from this structure. The triumphal relief, on the other hand, is on the external face of the Bubasite Gate, and there is no certainty that this was construed as part of the "broad court."

house; he took away everything. He also took away all the shields of gold which Solomon had made" (1 Kings 14:26). At last the Bible has given us a definite link between the histories of Egypt and Israel, the earliest, in fact, of the precious few links that have come down to us.

Students of Sheshonq I's great campaign against Judah and Israel have concentrated largely on the toponym list as a reflection of the route taken by the Egyptians,[2] and the evidence that can be adduced bearing on Biblical chronology.[3] The question arises whether the toponym list, which is indeed an itinerary, can still be used in conjunction with destruction levels detected archaeologically as has sometimes been done. The present author has argued against such a use for the 18th Dynasty list of Thutmose III, in the light of the inability of Thutmosid armies to mount successful siege operations.[4] By Ramesside times, however, Egyptian forces were conversant with assault techniques and while siege mounds and rams were still to come in the Iron II period, sappers, scaling ladders, testudines, and covering barrages are already attested.[5] Psusennes I of the 21st Dynasty, moreover, is dubbed in one of the minor objects from his tomb a "seizer of cities," a curious anticipation of πολιορκητης.[6] The very sophisticated techniques of siege warfare that emerge suddenly into the full light of history with the Piankhy stela of the eighth century must have a considerable antecedent period of development; and it is not at all unlikely that the Libyan kings two centuries earlier were already masters of the art.[7] Thus it is highly likely that Sheshonq's itinerary can also be construed as a swath of destruction and captured cities, reduced either through siege or voluntary surrender.

It would be most gratifying to have on hand a version of the Egyptian account of Sheshonq's invasion. At present we have only a fragmentary stela from Karnak and the triumphal scene on the south wall of the hypostyle.[8] The stela yields only a few scattered phrases, suggesting an Asi-

[2] See K. A. Kitchen, *The Third Intermediate Period* (Warminster, 1973), 295ff.; M. Noth, *ZDPV* 61 (1938), 277ff.; S. Herrmann, *ZDPV* 80 (1964), 55ff.; B. Mazar, *VT Suppl.* 4 (1956), 57ff.; N. Na'aman, *Tel Aviv* 12 (1985), 91–93.

[3] Albright, *BASOR* 130 (1953), 4ff.; idem, *BASOR* 141 (1956), 23ff.; D. N. Freedman, *The Bible and the Ancient Near East* (New York, 1961), 275; A. R. Green, *JBL* 97 (1978), 359, n. 30; J. M. Miller, *JBL* 86 (1967), 276ff.; additional bibliography in J. H. Hayes and J. M. Miller, *Israelite and Judaean History* (Philadelphia, 1977), 678–79.

[4] D. B. Redford, in A. Hadidi, ed., *Studies in the History and Archaeology of Jordan* (Amman, 1982), 1:115ff.; idem, *JSSEA* 12 (1982), 55ff.

[5] A. R. Schulman, *Natural History* 73 (1964), 13ff.; on Assyrian siege-craft, which was dominant in the Iron Age, see I. Eph'al, *Tel Aviv* 11 (1984), 60–70.

[6] P. Montet, *Les constructions et le tombeau de Psousennès* (Paris, 1951), 74, fig. 27 (714).

[7] See in particular A. J. Spalinger, *JSSEA* 11 (1981), 37ff. and the literature there cited.

[8] Stela: G. Legrain, *ASAE* 5 (1904), 38ff.; Grdseloff, *RHJE* 1 (1947), 95ff.; Kitchen,

atic initiative for the battle; but it is still questionable whether it refers to the campaign in Rehoboam's fifth year at all. The triumphal scene likewise refers to the Asiatics "who had taken to attacking thy (the king's) frontiers,"[9] but these are referred to by the stereotyped, ancient phrases "the Montiu of Asia," and once as "the battalions of the army of Mitanni."[10] Since one can scarcely credit Sheshonq with having fought his way as far north as the plains of Mesopotamia, the term must have been drawn, somewhat carelessly, from the military reliefs of Thutmose III on the same temple.

The outward manifestations of his Asiatic campaigning clearly show a conscious attempt to revive Ramesside forms: the stela announcing the *casus belli*, the stela set up in conquered territory,[11] the head-smiting scene, and toponym list.[12] In addition to this there is good evidence that Sheshonq set up his residence in the same stretch of territory on the eastern branch of the Nile in the Delta where Pi-Ramesses had once been located, and that he even preserved part of the ancient name in his new toponym.[13] One of the battalions of his army was named after the praenomen of Ramesses II, Usermare,[14] and at Karnak his triumphal relief is

---

Third Intermediate Period, 294; triumphal scene: G. R. Hughes, ed., *Reliefs and Inscriptions at Karnak, vol. 3: The Bubastite Portal* (Chicago, 1954).

[9] Hughes, *Bubastite Portal*, pl. 3, col. 7. It is an intriguing possibility that Sheshonq's military activity, localized by the stela as beginning from the *Km-wr* on the eastern side of the Delta, was sparked by earlier Solomonic expansion into the Negeb. For Solomon's trade with the south, see A. Malamat, in *Studies in the Period of David and Solomon*, 201ff.; S. Yeivin, *JQR* 50 (1960), 1933ff.; idem, *JEA* 48 (1962), 75ff. On the destruction of sites in the Negeb, which could plausibly be ascribed to Sheshonq, see C. Meyers, *BA* 39 (1976), 148ff. and 151, n. 4; R. Cohen, *IEJ* 36 (1986), 114–15.

[10] Hughes, *Bubastite Portal*, cols. 18–19, 23; on Mitanni, see D. B. Redford, *LdÄ* 4 (1982), 149ff.

[11] Kitchen, *Third Intermediate Period*, 299, n. 303.

[12] On the head-smiting scene as a genre, see H. Schafer, *Junker Festscrift* (Vienna, 1957), 168ff.; on toponym lists, see now H. Beinlich, *LdÄ* 3 (1980), 1061–62. There is another head-smiting and topographical scene of Sheshonq I at El-Hibeh (cf. P-M IV, 124; also E. Feucht, *SAK* 6 [1978], 69ff.), but unfortunately it is in a very fragmentary condition.

[13] Cf. Caminos, *JEA* 38 (1950), pl. 13, cols. 39–40 ("the residence [called] 'The House of Isis of the Great *Ka* of Re-harakhty' "); cf. also D. B. Redford, *Pharaonic King-lists, Annals and Day-books* (Toronto, 1984), chap. 9.

[14] Cf. P. Tresson, *Mélanges Maspero* (Cairo, 1934), 1:817ff. (line 13): *ꜣ n thrw n Wsr-mꜣꜥt-rꜥ*. On the *thrw* see W. F. Albright, *The Vocalization of Egyptian Syllabic Orthography* (New Haven, Conn., 1934), 52, who rightly derives the name as a loanword from, (דהר,) "to dash" (of a horse). Other derivations which have been put forward seem impossible philologically (cf. W. Helck, *Die Beziehungen Ägyptens zur Vorderasiens*² [Wiesbaden, 1972], *Die Beziehungen Ägyptens und Vorderasiens zur Ägäis* [Darmstadt, 1979], 135ff. [cf. D. B. Redford, *JAOS* 103 (1983), 482]). That the word is Hittite (*ANET*², 239, n. 3) I very much doubt: they are already present on the Phoenician coast under Thutmose III: *Urk* IV, 686:5. A. R. Schulman renders "foreign troops" (*JARCE* 5 [1965], 35, n. g with references), but it is surely not their alien origin that distinguishes them: a commander of

side by side with the record of Ramesses II's northern wars. Under his two successors banal phrases redolent of great victories sometimes turn up in texts, but one gets the impression only of "role playing."[15]

On the question of how Sheshonq's raid dovetails with the political events of Rehoboam's reign as described in 1 Kings 12, we have no information. The sacking of Jerusalem is dated to Rehoboam's fifth year, and in the internal sequence of chapter 12 this would fall *after* the split in the kingdom. Verses 1–16 of this chapter, however, are put together to capitalize on the dramatic effect of a popular motif of storytelling: the wise, old king is followed by the foolish, young king, the statesman gives place to the tyrant.[16] The latter's outrageous demands are then used as historical explanation as to why disaster followed. In the light of the woeful state of the sources of Kings bearing on the early Divided Monarchy, one would seriously err to accept this at face value.[17] Sheshonq's invasion could have easily fallen on the yet undivided state of the late Solomon, and Jereboam (an erstwhile exile in Egypt) could have started his career as an Egyptian protégé.[18]

The Libyan Dynasts and Their Troubles

In retrospect the reign of Sheshonq appears as a "flash in the pan." Resourceful and energetic he may well have been, but the state over which he exercised rule had no unity of purpose. The Meshwesh tribesmen who now resided in separate communities throughout Lower and the northern parts of Middle Egypt were an independent lot, not eager to assimilate, and given to uproar and feuding. They stubbornly preserved titles in the Libyan tongue and personal names native to the Libyan onomasticon, and to the end of their tenure of power in Egypt preserved the barbaric feather insignia as headgear.[19]

---

the *thrw* in Herakleopolis under the Ramessides has a perfectly good Egyptian name (see D. Kessler, *SAK* 2 [1975], 103ff., pl. 2). The clear link with the root DHR makes one think of "assault troops."

[15] Redford, *JAOS* 93 (1973), 13.

[16] Cf. the following contrasted pairs: Snefru–Khufu (M. Lichteim, *Ancient Egyptian Literature* [Berkeley, Calif., 1976], 1:216–22), Rhampsinitus–Cheops (Herodotus, 2.124.1), Psammetichos II–Apries (Herodotus, 2.161.2), Cyrus–Cambyses (Herodotus, 3.16, 29, etc.).

[17] Cf. in this regard the wide divergence between the Masoretic text and the Septuagint: W. Gooding, *VT* 17 (1967), 173–89; Hayes and Miller, *Israelite and Judaean History*, 232–33; on the form of criticism of 12:1–19, see I. Plein, *ZAW* 78 (1966), 8–24.

[18] On Jereboam's career, see H. Seebass, *VT* 17 (1967), 325–33; R. W. Klein, *JBL* 89 (1970), 217–18. There is no inherent necessity to treat the reference to Sheshonq in 1 Kings 11:40 seriously. "Sheshonq" was the only pharaonic name the Deuteronomist histories knew of at this period and they naturally assumed him to be the king in question.

[19] On the Libyans, see G. Möller, *ZDMG* 3 (1924), 36ff.; W. Hölscher, *Libyer und Ägyp-*

The refractory nature of the Libyan temperament caused two grievous rebellions by the native Egyptians of the Theban region in the third-quarter of the ninth century B.C.; and although neither proved successful, the Herculean effort required to restore order effectually wrecked the unity of Egypt.[20] Thereafter in the Delta the local chiefs of the Meshwesh and the Labu began to construe their role as that of virtual sovereigns and their bailiwicks as autonomous "fiefs." While they continued to offer lip service to the 22nd Dynasty Pharaoh, the progeny of Sheshonq now resident in Tanis, they sometimes slighted him by writing his names with cartouches left blank. These chiefs erected buildings in their own name, portrayed themselves in guises usually reserved for kings, and even adopted royal kingship myths and spoke "Horus-fashion" of their pre-destinations by the gods. While they exercised both civil and military authority within their principalities, they took obvious pride in their military function. They adopted the title "First (one), or leader," the equivalent in reference of the late Roman imperial *dux*, "(military) leader," and their sons were given the rank of general. It is probable that within each principality the Libyan soldiery was bound to the chief by a quasi-feudal bond and was given plots of land, which the soldiers held in return for military service.[21]

For its part, the native Egyptian stock, now ousted from the position of "*maîtres chez eux*," retired increasingly into a parochial, priest-ridden society in which social mobility was more difficult than it had formerly been. The priesthood of this period comprised a small number of aristo-

---

ter (Glückstadt, 1937); J. Yoyette, *Mélanges Maspero* (Cairo, 1961) 4, no. 1:121ff.; F. Gomàa, *Die libyschen Fürstentümer des Deltas* (Tübingen, 1974); J. Osing, *LdÄ* 3 (1980), 1015ff.; R. A. Fazzini, *Egypt, Dynasties XXII–XXV*, Iconography of Religions, XVI, 10 (Leiden 1988). The Meshwesh, like the modern Awlad 'Ali (see M. Awad, *Bull Soc Geog Egypt* 32 [1959], 11), were divided into two groups, one of which settled in Egypt, the other remaining on the Libyan coast to the west, where they were still living in Herodotus's day (4.191.1; W. W. How and J. Wells, *A Commentary on Herodotus* [Oxford, 1928], 1:358). Throughout the period of their dominance in Egypt, the Libyans were as much concerned with the west where lay their homeland as they were with the unfamiliar Asian sphere. In Egypt the Libyans soon gained an unsavory reputation for obstreperous behavior: J. Černý, *CAH³* II, pt. 2 (1975), 616ff.; G. Maspero, *Memories sur quelques papyrus du Louvre* (Paris, 1875), 110ff.

[20] The account of the rebellions is given in the biographical statement of the king's son Osorkon: see R. A. Caminos, *The Chronicle of Prince Osorkon* (Rome, 1958). Contemporary texts sometimes use the term "rage," which can also refer to civil strife; but this may allude only to the temperament of individual Libyan kings: cf. "I served kings and was unscathed by their rage" (*CGC* 42208 f, 15); "I it was that soothed his (the king's) heart when he fell into rages" (*CGC* 42210); "(I am) one that calms down the sovereign in his rages" (*CGC* 42211).

[21] For a detailed treatment of the Libyan dynasties of Egyptian history, see the works cited in nn. 2 and 19 (especially those of Yoyotte, Kitchen, and Gomàa).

cratic families at the top, presiding over a larger body of middle-ranking priests. All jealously guarded their functions and prebends, and made sure that they were passed on to the younger members of the family. When the monarchy had been central in Egyptian society, people had been proud of their associations with the royal family and had boasted of it in their private inscriptions. It gives a certain status and security in a rank-conscious community. With the withdrawal, however, of the kingship to the Delta and its gradual weakening, members of the priesthood found the social framework in which they had enjoyed a special identity no longer in existence. Now they fell back on the glories of an illustrious pedigree as a source of support for their position in society and would include in their statue inscriptions long family trees.[22]

Inevitably the tone of this "Brave New World" is a parochial one, and movement both physical and social becomes more and more confined to one's ancestral environs, that is, the hometown.[23] What might have been a necessity to begin with, however, soon turned into a virtue: to remain at home is right and good, to rove abroad dangerous and wanton. As the political uncertainties of the period caused provincial society to turn in upon itself for protection and stability, the community and family began to loom large: the Wisdom texts of the post–New Kingdom era reflect the atmosphere of a small town, rural, agrarian, and suspicious of outsiders. "Do not stay in a district in which you have no people (of your own kin) . . . do not let your son marry a wife from another village";[24] be on your guard against a woman from abroad . . . do not express your whole heart to a stranger";[25] "the god who is in the city is the one on whom the death and life of people depend. The person without god who goes abroad gives himself into the hand of the [enemy(?)]."[26] The dominance of the local town in Egyptian life had important socioeconomic ramifications. Lack of obligation beyond the immediate community produced a new feeling for the importance of personal property and the owner's right to dispose of it. With respect to the propriety of making a bequest to his daughter, one priest of the period has occasion to allude to "the statement of the great god (i.e., Amun in a regulatory pronouncement): 'Let each man exercise control over his (own) property.' "[27] In a rare burst of enlightened self-interest, the upper and middle class of this Tanite age had adopted the custom of devoting a portion of their land to the local temple. By contract

[22] D. B. Redford, *A Study of the Biblical Joseph Story* (Leiden, 1970), 6.
[23] E. Otto, *Die Biographischen Inschriften der ägyptischen Spätzeit* (Leiden, 1954), 87–88.
[24] Onkhsheshonqy 21/24–25; cf. 15/15.
[25] *ANET²*, 420.
[26] P. Insinger 28/11–29/1.
[27] CGC 42208, c, 14.

the temple had the use of the land, paid part of the produce to the erstwhile owner, and agreed to look after the owner's mortuary arrangements in perpetuity. Since this meant real income for the owner's descendants, the practice had the effect of ensuring economic security for both the ecclesiastical and private sectors.[28]

This then was the Egypt that, though weak and pusilanimous, nonetheless bore an awesome reputation for power into uncharted politics of a new age. Some reaches of the former empire seemed to have remained unchanged—Nubia remained a backwater and the Phoenician coast an admiring dependent—but in reality a cold new wind was blowing.

Whatever power the southern Levantine hinterland had recently exhibited in the form of the Solomonic state was a thing of the past. Linguistic and cultural sectionalism had now replaced whatever "empire" David had erected with a welter of new West Semitic–speaking communities, based in part on tribal origins. The Hebrew Kingdom had split into a greater and a lesser successor state: the prosperous Israel in the central highland, Galilee, and Transjordan (the true descendant of the tribal amalgam that had taken shape in the thirteenth century B.C.), and the weak southern kingdom of Judah centered upon Jerusalem.[29] Beyond the Dead Sea and the Arabah three desert kingdoms were in the process of crystallization around the southern reaches of the important trade route known as the "King's Highway": Ammon, a hill community just south of the Beka'a Valley; Moab, encompassing the rich farmlands between the Wady Wala and the northern end of the Dead Sea; and Edom (ancient Seʿir), a "Shasu" enclave in the mountainous region between the Zered and Aqaba.[30]

None of these posed Egypt any problem; in fact, they were to a certain extent cut off from direct contact with the Nile. When a major power threatened the region from the north, these communities to a greater or lesser degree regarded Egypt as their champion. And so Pharaoh tried to be (with what success we shall shortly learn); for to preserve these principalities meant to ensure a buffer against invasion from Asia.

Philistia too was no longer the threat to Egyptian security, but a poten-

---

[28] For "donation" stelae, see D. Meeks, in E. Lipinski, ed., *State and Temple Economy in the Ancient Near East* (Leiden, 1979), 605–88; and the additions in D. Berg, "The Genre of Non-Juridical Oracles in Ancient Egypt" (Ph.D. diss., University of Toronto, 1988), 154ff.

[29] The most recent and in some ways the most up-to-date treatment of this period is to be found in J. M. Miller and J. H. Hayes, *A History of Ancient Israel and Judah* (Philadelphia, 1986), 218–376.

[30] On the Transjordanian kingdoms, see among others K.-H. Bernhardt and J. M. Miller, in Hadidi, *Studies in the History and Archaeology of Jordan* 1:163–74; J. R. Bartlett, *PEQ* 104 (1972), 26ff.; J.F.A. Sawyer and D.J.A. Clines, eds., *Midian, Moab and Edom* (Sheffield, 1983); J. A. Sauer, *BASOR* 263 (1986), 1–26.

tial "early warning" zone against invasion from the north. Though ruled now by descendants of transmarine immigrants, the coastal district continued to be informed by the role assigned to it in the days of the Egyptian empire. Gaza, one of the headquarters cities during the New Kingdom, retained a prime role as "border kingdom," at once the nerve center for the north Sinai and western Negeb, and a principality acting on more than one occasion as a surrogate for Egypt.

ONCE AGAIN . . . THE SOURCES

The absence of sources during the 21st Dynasty, which we bemoaned for both western Asia and Egypt, continues to bedevil attempts to write a history of relations between the two regions in the first third of the first millennium. Egyptian history perhaps suffers most from this gap in sources.[31] Monumental, triumphal inscriptions such as provided the backbone of our sources during the New Kingdom, have not come to light; and it is doubtful whether the Libyan Pharaohs published any. Epigraphic material emanating from the royal cities of Tanis and Bubastis belongs in the main to the sphere of standard cultic depictions. Private biographical statements, often carved on votive statues placed in temples, are long on genealogical information and pious snippets of "Wisdom," and extremely short on historical references. One genre whose exemplars abound in this period is the donation stela, a sort of legal conveyance devoid of historical notices. Minor texts shed only a tiny ray of light. Letters, dockets, records of Nile levels, phylacteries, contracts—these are the spotty and often irrelevant categories one is forced to sift, often with no results at all.

As a last recourse the historian must go outside Egypt for his sources. The Assyrian records, rich and detailed for most of the period covered in this chapter, offer not a little information, especially those that date to the eighth and seventh centuries B.C.[32] Greece, Anatolia, and North Syria offer nothing, the former two concealed in the shadows of a Dark Age. The Phoenician cities yield a very few texts, and much more circumstantial evidence in the realm of art and architecture. But it is from Judah and Israel, with their comparative wealth of historical writing, that one expects the most.

The author of 1–2 Kings has produced his work from the vantage point

[31] Egyptian sources of the period are nowhere dealt with comprehensively, but most histories of the period adequately introduce the reader to the historiographical problems. See Redford, *King-lists*, 305–31.

[32] Apart from those sources cited in the following notes, one might consult the relevant translations in *ANET²*; A. K. Grayson, *Assyrian and Babylonian Chronicles* (Locust Valley, N.Y., 1975); idem, *Assyrian Royal Inscriptions* (Wiesbaden, 1972–76).

of a much later age. He knows of the reign of Josiah[33] (1 Kings 13:2) and of the Exile (both that of the northern kingdom, Israel, as well as the Babylonian: 1 Kings 14:15; 2 Kings 21:10–15). His point of view is clear: he measures every king against the rigorous iconoclastic monotheism and cultic puritanism that, for him, the reign of Josiah exemplifies to best advantage (2 Kings 23:25); and does not stint in expressing his admiration or disapprobation. The slightest trace in his sources of an act that can be judged on the basis of his ethic, or construed as fulfillment of prophecy is bound to excite his penchant for editorializing. That he does not have any more events on which to comment than are now present in his work does not mean that he has been selective in his choice of materials, but rather that his material contained nothing more. He has given us all his sources gave him.

Yet this "Deuteronomist" historian, as he is called from the similarity of his views to those of the Book of Deuteronomy, published in the seventh century B.C.,[34] did not manufacture all of his tiresome message out of whole cloth. Two sources show through his heavy-handed editing, one a collection of stories about prophets, and the other a sort of chronicle with historical notices. The Tales of the Prophets (Table 2)[35] treat mainly, though not exclusively, of dealings with kings and give prominence to predictions and their fulfillment. The largest group, and those most fully worked as narratives, center upon the doings of Elijah and Elisha, and make them protagonists in the Baʿal-Yahwist polemic, predictors of doom, and *agents provocateurs* in Israelite and Damascene politics. How much history is to be assumed in all this is difficult to say: the figures are undoubtedly genuine, but the stories may reflect the view from the sixth century B.C. or even later. Of the rest, the prophecies of Ahiyah, Shemaiah, and the unnamed prophets of 1 Kings 12:25–13:32 and 2 Kings 21:10–15 look artificially prescient, and the notices regarding Isaiah take us into the full light of the book that bears his message.

[33] Hezekiah and Josiah corresponded to the Deuteronomist historian's ideal king: G. E. Gebrandt, *Kingship according to the Deuteronomic History* (Atlanta, 1986), 1–43; cf. I. W. Provan, *Hezekiah and the Book of Kings* (Berlin, N.Y., 1988).

[34] On the Deuteronomist historian, see among others E. W. Nicholson, *Deuteronomy and Tradition* (Oxford, 1967); M. Weinfeld, *Deuteronomy and the Deuteronomic School* (Oxford, 1972); M. Noth, *The Deuteronomistic History* (Sheffield, 1981); J. Van Seters, *In Search of History* (New Haven, Conn., 1983), 322–53; F. H. Cryer, *BN* 29 (1985), 58ff. For the date shortly after 587, see W. Wurthwein, *Die Bücher der Könige* (Göttingen, 1984), 485ff.

[35] M. Noth, *Überlieferungsgeschichtliche Studien* (Tübingen, 1957), 78–87; A. Rofé, *JBL* 89 (1970), 427–40; idem, *VT* Suppl. 26 (1974), 143–64; idem, *The Prophetical Stories: Narratives about the Prophets in the Hebrew Bible, Their Literary Types and History* (Jerusalem, 1988); Van Seters, *In Search of History*, 303–6.

TABLE 2.
Tales of the Prophets

Prophet	Passage(s)	Content
1. Shemaiah	1 Kings 12:1–24	Explanation of why Rehoboam was deterred from attacking Israel
2. Ahiyah	1 Kings 11:1–40; 14:1–18	Prophecies against Jereboam
3. —	1 Kings 12:25–13:32	Prophecy against Rehoboam because of his introduction of pagan rites
4. Jehu	1 Kings 16:1–4, 7	Prophecy against Ba'asha
5. Elijah	1 Kings 17–21	Condemnation of Ahab
6. Micaiah	1 Kings 22:1–38	Prophecy against "king of Israel" concerning his proposed attack on Jabesh (cf. no. 9)
7. Elijah	2 Kings 1:1–17	Prophecy of Ahaziah's death because he inquired of Ba'al
8. Elijah	2 Kings 2	Elijah's death; Elisha demonstrates God's charisma
9. Elisha	2 Kings 3:4–27	Prophecy of ruin of expedition against Mo'ab
10. Elisha	2 Kings 4:1–8:15	Miracle stories of Elisha (chap. 6 against "king of Israel"; 8:7–15 regarding Haza'el)
11. Elisha	2 Kings 9:1–27; 30:10–31	Encitement of Jehu to rebellion and the resultant massacre
12. Elisha	2 Kings 13:4–21	Elisha's death
13. Jonah	2 Kings 14:25–27	Prophecy that Jereboam II would restore empire of Israel
14. Isaiah	2 Kings 18:13–19:37; 20:1–19	Isaiah and the Assyrian invasion
15. —	2 Kings 21:10–15	Prophecy against Manasseh and prediction of Jerusalem's destruction

The chronicle passages[36] stand out clearly as a framework that appears at intervals from 1 Kings 14:21 to the end of 2 Kings. In isolation the stereotyped formulas of which this framework consists apply primarily to the Davidic dynasty in Jerusalem and set on record the name of the king's father, his age at accession, length of reign, mother's name, parentage and birthplace, circumstances of the king's death, and place of burial (Table 3). Not all this information is given for each king: only from the end of Manasseh's reign is this the case. For earlier centuries there are obvious gaps and patently unreliable information. Only with Jehoshaphat, for example, does the scribe begin to provide the age at accession,[37] and only with Joash is the queen mother's town of origin added. Abiya and Asa (father and son) have the same mother, and only four of the eleven kings before Hezekiah are provided with maternal grandfathers. Until Manasseh (with the exception of Ahaziah) the vague "city of David" suffices as a reference to place of burial.

By contrast, the "chronicle" of the kings of Israel is so woefully deficient in information that one is led to doubt that it ever existed. Usually only length of reign and paternity is present, there being no dockets at all on queen mothers;[38] and place of burial is referred to as "in Samaria" or "Tirzah." One does not need to postulate any independent "chronicle" for Israel to account for this meager fare!

The Judaean chronicle does, however, faithfully record the year of one king's accession in terms of the equivalent regnal year in the neighboring kingdom. There is no reason to suppose that this is the result of "scholastic" research undertaken by the Deuteronomist historian himself; rather, it must reflect on the ongoing practice of Judaean "archivists" from an early period. In this regard it should be remembered that during the ninth and eighth centuries in Egypt the frequency of coregency and the breakup of the kingdom into a number of virtually independent principalities made it necessary from time to time to render specific dates in terms of two regnal year systems.[39] Pragmatic considerations alone underlie this practice. The business life of the community, in all its varied aspects, transcended the petty political divisions that had temporarily appeared; and business transactions crossed erstwhile borders with ease. Commercial

---

[36] See S. R. Bin-Nun, *VT* 18 (1968), 414–32; Van Seters, *In Search of History*, 292–302; T. Ishida, *The Royal Dynasties of Ancient Israel* (Berlin, 1977), 156–57 (on the list of queen mothers); R. D. Nelson, *The Double Redaction of the Deuteronomist History* (Sheffield, 1981), 29–42.

[37] Rehoboam's age at accession (1 Kings 14:21) is clearly fallacious.

[38] Ishida, *Royal Dynasties*, 157.

[39] See in general Kitchen, *Third Intermediate Period*; W. J. Murnane, *Ancient Egyptian Coregencies* (Chicago, 1977). Coregencies are not directly involved in all this, having a purpose that did not necessarily involve two dating systems: A. Schaefer, *ZAW* 113 (1986), 44–55.

documents, therefore, of necessity had to bear dates according to the political jurisdictions of both contracting parties. Undoubtedly a similar interconnection of the business and commercial life of Israel and Judah lies at the root of the phenomenon in the Judaean chronicle.

One important point to note is that, with the presence of cross-dates of Israelite kings in the Judaean chronicle, all the information on the basis of which filiation and length of reign could be computed is already accounted for. There is thus no need to postulate the existence of a separate "chronicle of the kings of Israel."

Apart from the chronicle framework, the Tales of the Prophets and the extensive editorial sections provided by the Deuteronomist historian, a number of historical notices are strewn throughout 1 and 2 Kings relating to the Davidic dynasty (Table 4). These are not very varied, but group themselves basically into three categories: notices regarding building operations or dedications in the Jerusalem temple; construction activities outside Jerusalem; and notices of military activity. The record of building operations begins with the plans laid by Joash and the collection of a subvention, both dated to his twenty-third year, and continues with Jotham's gate-building, the renovations of Ahaz, the aqueduct of Hezekiah, the altars of Manesseh, and the extensive renovations of Josiah. Each of these notices relates to a concrete addition to a building (or in Josiah's case a series of removals) that undoubtedly would have found its initial record in the form of a *dedicatory building inscription*, possibly dated (cf. the year 23 of Joash). We have no means of knowing whether the Deuteronomist historian had access to a complete list: he may not have had, for Ezekiel 43:7–8 conveys the impression of the clutter resulting from royal building operations within the precincts of the temple. Besides building inscriptions, a number of passages clearly point to *votive dedications* in the temple: the replacement of gold with bronze shields under Rehoboam (which occasions the reference to Sheshonq), and the votives of Asa, Joash, Amaziah, Ahaz, Hezekiah, and Manasseh. These references one and all conjure up in the mind's eye one of the most common types of docket in early epigraphy, the dedication text written or incised on a vessel. Such vessels (or related paraphernalia of precious substance) were usually carefully kept from generation to generation, and could easily have been viewed decades or centuries after their manufacture. Even if the objects themselves were not on view, the "checklist" of cultic objects dedicated by a particular king (and even a checklist of objects removed!) is attested archaeologically in comparable contexts.[40] Thus it is safe to

[40] Such lists are common. Apart from the Qatna inventories (see p. 145), cf. *inter alia* Thutmose III's list of dedications to the Theban triad, "from year 1 to year 46 and for millions of years" (P-M II², 95 [275]); the benefactions that Ramesses III performed for the gods during this thirty-one years of reign are the burden of the enormous checklist that

TABLE 3.
Chronicle Passages with Historical Notices

Name	Father Given	Age	Reign	Mother	Father-in-law	Place	Death	Burial
1. Rehoboam	Yes	41	17	Na'amah	—	(Ammon)	Natural	City of David
2. Abiya	Yes	—	3	Ma'acah	Abishalom	—	Natural	City of David
3. Asa	Yes	—	41	Ma'acah	Abishalom	—	Foot disease	City of David
4. Jehoshaphat	Yes	35	25	Azubah	Shilkhi	—	Natural	City of David
5. Jehoram	Yes	32	8	—	—	—	—	City of David
6. Ahaziah	Yes	22	1	Athaliah	—	—	Killed	City of David
7. Joash	Yes	7	40	Zibiah	—	Beersheba	Assassinated	City of David
8. Amaziah	Yes	25	29	Jehoaddin	—	Jerusalem	Assassinated in Lachish	City of David
9. Azariah	Yes	16	52	Jecoliah	—	Jerusalem	Leprosy	City of David
10. Jotham	Yes	25	16	Jerusha	Zadok	—	Natural	City of David
11. Ahaz	Yes	20	16	—	—	—	Natural	City of David
12. Hezekiah	Yes	25	29	Abi	Zechariah	—	Unknown	—
13. Manasseh	Yes	12	55	Hephzibah	—	—	Natural	Tomb in the garden of Uzza

TABLE 3. (continued)
Chronicle Passages with Historical Notices

							Assassinated	Tomb in the garden of Uzza
14. Amon	Yes	22	2	Meshullemeth	Haruz	Yotbah	Killed	Own tomb
15. Josiah	Yes	8	31	Jedidah	Adaiah	Bozkath	Natural	—
16. Jehoahaz	Yes	23	3 mos.	Hamutal	Jeremiah	Libnah	Natural	—
17. Eliakim	Yes	25	11	Zebida	Pedaiah	Rumah	—	—
18. Jehoiakin	Yes	18	3 mos.	Nehushta	Elnathan	Jerusalem	—	
19. Jedekiah	Yes	21	11	Hamutal	Jeremiah	Libnah		

TABLE 4.
Historical Notices Relating to the Davidic Dynasty

King	Passage	Content	Source[a]
1. Rehoboam	1 Kings 14:25–28	Shishak invasion, paying of tribute	T
2. Abiya	1 Kings 15:6–7	(General statement about wars)	Dtr
3. Asa	1 Kings 15:12	Removed male cult prostitutes	Dtr
	1 Kings 15:13	Demotion of mother because she made an idol	Dtr (etiology?)
	1 Kings 15:15	Dedication of votives	T
	1 Kings 15:16–22	War and the building of Rama; hiring of Ben Hadad	B(?)
4. Jehoshaphat	1 Kings 22:45	(Wars and peace with Israel)	Pr. (chap. 20, 22
	1 Kings 22:46	Exterminates male prostitutes	(Doublet of 1 Kings 15:12)
	1 Kings 22:47–49	Wreck of Tarshish fleet	Stela (of Amaziah?)
5. Joram	2 Kings 18:20–22	Revolt of Edom (and Lebonah[!])	Stela (of Amaziah?)
6. Joash	2 Kings 11	Coronation and murder of Athaliah	T or B (but heavily embellished); note how topography of temple and palace is basic to plot
	2 Kings 12:14–16	Collection to repair temple	T
	2 Kings 12:17–18	Strips temple votives to pay Haza'el	T
7. Amaziah	2 Kings 14:5–7	Revenge on father's assassins and defeat of Edom, etc.	Stela (triumphal)
	2 Kings 14:8–14	War with Israel, destruction of wall, pillaging temple	T
8. Amaziah	2 Kings 14:21	Installation by people	(Chronicle frame)
	2 Kings 14:22	Built Elath	B or triumphal stela
9. Jotham	2 Kings 15:5	Regent for father	(Chronicle frame)
	2 Kings 15:35	Built upper gate of temple	B & T
10. Ahaz	2 Kings 16:5	Siege of Jerusalem	Pr. and Isa. 7
	2 Kings 16:6	Edom retakes Elath	(Folk memory?)
(10. Ahaz)	2 Kings 16:7–9	Sends votives and temple treasures to Assyria to "buy" Tiglath-pileser	T

TABLE 4. (*continued*)
Historical Notices Relating to the Davidic Dynasty

King	Passage	Content	Source[a]
	2 Kings 16:10–18; 32:12	Construction, renovations, and new cult paraphernalia in temple	T and B
11. Hezekiah	2 Kings 18:7–8	Rebellion against Assyria and defeat of Philistines	Dtr (from Pr. and oral tradition)
	2 Kings 18:4	Removes Moses' bronze snake	T
	2 Kings 18:15–16	Removes temple treasure to give to Assyrians	T
	2 Kings 20:20	Construction of conduit	B
12. Manasseh	2 Kings 21:3–7	Altars, images, and cult paraphernalia set up in temple	T and B (with Dtr overtones)
13. Josiah	2 Kings 22:1–23:23	Finding of Book of Law, cultic purification and renovation, account of passover	T (or stela), reworked by Dtr
	2 Kings 23:29–30	Killed in battle	(Chronicle frame)
14. Eliakim[b]	2 Kings 23:34	Necho makes Eliakim king	(Chronicle frame)
	2 Kings 23:35	Raising of tax to pay Necho	Dtr

[a] B = building inscription; Dtr = Deuteronomist redactor; Pr. = Tales of the Prophets; T = temple notice (votive inscription, inventory or other priestly record, originally kept in the temple).

[b] After no. 14, Dtr's record becomes an original text based on memory, eyewitness accounts and brief notices salvaged from the Neo-Babylonian destruction.

conclude that building inscriptions and votive dedications, both on view on the temple mount, could have provided the ultimate source for all the Jerusalem temple notices.[41]

The second group of notices—of construction activity outside Jerusalem—is much more limited and brief in the extreme. Only one Judaean king is connected with building towns, Azariah and the building of the Elath.[42] All the rest are Israelite kings: Jeroboam who built Shechem, Pen-

constitutes Papyrus Harris I (J. H. Breasted, *Ancient Records of Egypt* [Chicago, 1906], 4:87–206); cf. the list of votives Osorkon I made to the gods during a period of three and a quarter years: E. Naville, *Bubastis* (London, 1891), pl. 51; this list could easily be extended ad nauseam.

[41] Of course both sources of material may well have been separated from the present text of kings by an intermediary sort of "midrashic" document. I doubt whether "invasion notices" from royal annals figured in the sources: T. Vuk, *Wiederaufkaufte Freiheit. Der Feldzug Sanheribs gegen Juda nach dem Invasionsbericht 2. Kon 18:13–16* (Jerusalem, 1984).

[42] The passage in Chronicles relating his building activity (2 Chron. 26:9–10, 14–15) seems, like most of the Chronicler's non-Kings sources, to be highly suspect: catapults were

uel and Bethel (in a passage influenced by the Deuteronomist historian), Baasha who built Rama, and Omri and Ahab who built Samaria. None of this information is at all *recherché* and, as we shall see, could have been derived by the Deuteronomist historian from common knowledge or the Tales of the Prophets. The laconic references themselves indicate that no additional sources need be invoked.

The notices of military activity constitute a mixed bag. Some are so vague that they depend on nothing more than a *general* assumption by the Deuteronomist historian on what the probable situation might have been (cf. for example 1 Kings 15:6, "now there was war between Rehoboam and Jereboam all the days of his life"; 1 Kings 22:44–45,[43] etc.) The account of Amaziah's war with Jehoash (2 Kings 14:8–14), which also reminds us of the votive inscription and the votive checklist, depends also upon Jerusalem's topographic history embellished by a folktale; and thus we are again thrust back into local Jerusalem tradition and folk memory.

A significant number of references, on the other hand, to Elath, Ezion-geber, and Edom take us into the realm of another source entirely. These references may be listed as follows:

1. Solomon's Red Sea fleet out of Ezion-geber (1 Kings 9:26–28)—success
2. Jehoshaphat's fleet wrecked at Ezion-geber (1 Kings 22:47–49)—failure
3. Revolt of Edom and Lebonah[44] under Joram (2 Kings 8:20–22)—failure
4. Amaziah's defeat of Edom (as no. 5)
5. Azariah's rebuilding of Elath (2 Kings 14:7, 22)—success

These notices, in their stress on city building and political hegemony, as well as their terse wording, indicate one kind of source only (and, one might add, without embellishment or interpretation by the exerptor), and that is the triumphal, biographical stela. These are common in the Iron Age and always tend to contrast the activity of the speaker's forebears (or the situation that prevailed before his time) with the halcyon days and signal accomplishments of his own reign.[45] One might almost reconstruct the very words of an Azariah stela: "I am Azariah, the son of Amaziah, the son of Joash, king of Judah. Formerly the Edomites were subservient to David, the father of my fathers, and in the days of Solomon, his son, the ships used to go south from Ezion-geber . . . But from the days of

---

not to be invented for nearly four centuries! Cf. A. Ferril, *The Origins of War* (London, 1988), 170–74.

[43] Presumably derived from the Prophetic Tales: cf. chap. 20.

[44] Emended from Libneh. Undoubtedly the Edomite town is intended (Num. 33:20–21; Deut. 1:1); cf. R. Giveon, *Les Bedouins Shosou* (Leiden, 1971), 76.

[45] Cf. e.g. the Kilamuwa text (ninth century B.C.): H. Donner and W. Röllig, *Kanaanäische und aramäische Inschriften* (Wiesbaden, 1962–1964), 1: no. 24; M. Miller, *PEQ* 104 (1974), 9–18; F. M. Falles, *WO* 10 (1979), 6–22; Van Seters, *In Search of History*, 194.

Jehoshaphat the ships ceased to go forth; and in the time of Joram, his son, Edom and Lebonah rebelled against Judah. But Amaziah, my father, defeated Edom and restored it to Judah, and took Sela' and renamed it . . . and I restored Elath to Judah and rebuilt it; and I built in it."

If the search for the ultimate source of notices of military and building activity in 1 Kings and 2 Kings takes us back to *standing stelae* in the environs of the Yahweh temple and royal palace at Jerusalem, another monumental, epigraphic source at once springs to mind as having been part of that renowned complex; and that is the relief decoration on dado or stylobate. The practice (found in the Bronze Age in both Egypt and Khatte)[46] involves carving figures, sometimes glossed by identifying texts, marching in procession along the facade of a temple or palace toward the entrance. In the Levant, the composition of the processional may vary to include commoners: scribes, officials, and soldiers appear along with the king himself and his heir.[47] Even on a stela, a ruler may deign to include his secretary in the vignette as well as himself.[48] All the indications are that a visitor entering the precincts of the Jerusalem temple and the adjacent royal apartments would have been confronted by a considerable amount of commemorative epigraphy and relief decoration. Wall reliefs, inscribed gates, and statuary (with texts?) are all alluded to in Biblical passages reflecting eyewitness accounts of the temple mount;[49] and stelae are now attested archaeologically.[50] It is quite likely that this epigraphic adornment also included a decorated dado of inscribed orthostats, as at Carchemish, dating from the origin of the temple, and commemorating Solomon, his son, and his officials; and it is in the form of this kind of concrete, graphic record, visible to all, that we must imagine the ultimate source of the prosopographic details in 1 Kings 4:2–6 and similar passages rather than a document of dubious historicity from Solomon's time.

From the beginning of the reign of Jotham we are within the penumbra of a body of texts that themselves can be dated to the eighth century B.C. Isaiah's career, for which contemporary documents are extant, dates from the year of Azariah's death (Isa. 1:6). The major event of 735–34 B.C., the coalition of Israel and Damascus against Judah with the intent of turning it into a puppet under the "Son of Taba'el,"[51] left a virtually con-

---

[46] Examples from Ramesside Egypt show the sons and daughters of the king, proceeding in order of birth, each identified by formulas giving filiation, title, and name: K. A. Kitchen, *Pharaoh Triumphant* (Warminster, 1983), 101–13.

[47] M. Vieyra, *Hittite Art* (London, 1955), pls. 35–38; H. G. Güterbock, *JNES* 13 (1954), 102–14.

[48] H. Frankfort, *The Art and Architecture of the Ancient Orient* (Harmondsworth, 1954), pl. 162.

[49] Cf. 2 Kings 21:7, 23:11; Ezek. 8:10, 43:7–8.

[50] J. Naveh, *IEJ* 32 (1982), 195–98.

[51] W. F. Albright, *BASOR* 140 (1955), 34.

temporary record in Isaiah 7 and 8; and this is all that need be called up as a source for the notices under Jotham and Ahaz (2 Kings 15:37, 16:5), which are simply editorial packing by the Deuteronomist historian. In the same vein, 18:7–8 is nought but the same historian's introduction to the rebellion narrative (18:13ff.) and derives from it.

It might be objected at this point that a source named in the Bible is being ignored. Some fifteen times in 1 and 2 Kings the author has occasion to refer his reader for further details on a king's reign to the "Book of the Diurnal Deeds of the Kings of Judah."[52] Now compositions called "daybooks" are well known in Egypt (where the form originated) and were kept by such institutions as temples, corporations, courts of law, and even the king's house itself.[53] Not a few have survived, but if one expects them to comprise a diary of historical events, disappointment awaits. For the first, and perhaps the only reason for writing such a log was purely practical: to keep a running account of doings and dealings of importance to the institution, especially with respect to its *finances*. In the case of the king's house, the daybook notes the arrival and dismissal of emissaries and visiting dignitaries, the movements of the king, the progress of the army (when the king is on campaign), but first and foremost the receipt of commodities of all varieties, and the disbursement of salaries and rations. The story of Wenamun[54] shows that the daybook form was transplanted as a means of recording to the municipal administrations of Levantine cities by the close of the New Kingdom—again the passage in question proves the contents to have been accounting entries—and there is little doubt that inland cities like Jerusalem borrowed the genre from the coast. But the daybook is *not* a diary or journal in our understanding of the term, *still less* a set of annals;[55] and even if abridged, it would be virtually useless as a historical source. A far closer parallel would be a modern butler's housekeeping ledger.

Even the most cursory examination of the passages citing the "Book of the Diurnal Deeds of the Kings of Judah" will show beyond a shadow of a doubt that, whatever the book was, we can under no circumstances categorize it as a "journal." It seems to refer more to events, but then in such a stereotyped and formulaic manner that we are led to wonder whether the Deuteronomist historian really conceived of his source as an-

---

[52] Noth, *Überlieferungsgeschictliche Studien*, 72–78; J. Liver, *Biblica* 48 (1967), 77–78.

[53] Redford, *King-lists*, 97–126; idem, *LdÄ* 6 (1986), 151–53.

[54] Wenamun 2, 8.

[55] Cf. H. Gressmann, *Die älteste Geschictsschreibung und Prophetie Israels*² (Göttingen, 1910), xi, who postulates daybooks or summaries made from them. J. A. Montgomery, *JBL* 53 (1934), 46–52; idem, *The Book of Kings* (Edinburgh, 1951), 31–37, and G. Fohrer, *Introduction to the Old Testament* (Nashville, Tenn., 1968), 97, suggest the existence of dated annals as a source.

nalistic, or indeed whether he even saw his "source" at all. Eleven of the fifteen passages (with only minor variants) yield the banal formulas "(A) Now the rest of the acts of N, and (B) all that he did, are they not written in . . ."; and in three of the remaining four a third element, (C) "his might," is added. Thus in none of these cases is any specific, additional material alluded to, but *only the impression* is given that such exists. In the passage attached to Jehoshaphat's reign "how he fought" is added as another element; but this, if genuine—it is missing in the Septuagint—is simply an allusion to the battle of Jabesh already covered in 22:29–33 from the Tales of the Prophets. The passage attached to the name of Asa refers us to the "Diurnal Deeds" for the cities that he built (again missing in the Hexapla), and in the preceding section the building of a city is indeed the subject: Geba of Benjamin! An added element to the formula in Hezekiah's case cites the "Diurnal Deeds" for the construction of the aqueduct from Gihon to Siloam, a feat commemorated for all to see in the famous Siloam inscription.

The most revealing occurrence of the formula is that in 2 Kings 21:17 (Manasseh), which adds to the simple pattern A plus B "and the sin which he committed." No daybook ever contained such condemnatory statements of a moralizing kind. In fact, this phrase clearly refers to the excoriation of verses 10–15, which again comes from the Tales of the Prophets.

A glance at the references to the "Book of the Diurnal Deeds of the Kings of Israel" confirms our suspicion. The basic formula A plus B is found several times (faultily in 2 Kings 15:11), and with formula C added in four other cases. Twice, with Zimri and Shallum, one is referred to the "Diurnal Deeds" for the conspiracy each was guilty of, and which has just been put on the record in the preceding verses! Of the remaining four citations, that attached to the reign of Jereboam—"how he reigned and how he fought"—refers to what has just gone before, the Tales of the Prophets Ahiyah and Shemaiah. The reference for Ahab—"the ivory house that he built, and all cities that he built,"—need have no other source than what we already have in another prophetic work to which the Deuteronomist historian had access, the Book of Amos (cf. 3:15). The addition to the formula under Jehoash leads us back to the same alleged source for "how he fought with Amaziah king of Judah"; but this has just been treated in verses 8–14 in the folktale that had grown up around an incident in Jerusalem's topographic history. Finally "how (Jereboam II) fought and recovered Damascus and Hamath" is nothing but a statement of the fulfillment of the Jonah prophecy in 14:25, again an allusion to a (now lost) prophetic tale.

It is remarkable how few, if any, of the references to the "Diurnal Deeds" of either kingdom have any substance at all; while those few that contain more than the basic formulas connect with information cited or quoted *in extenso* in the Tales of the Prophets. One can only conclude that a formal source that went under the rubric the "Diurnal Deeds" never existed, and that the term applies pseudonymously to the prophetic tales that the Deuteronomist historian had already used.

AN EMBELLISHED KING LIST

While on the face of it there is no empirical connection between the chronicle framework and historical notices, analogy militates strongly in favor of the inclusion of both in a single document to which the Deuteronomist historian had access.

The Levant and northeast Africa during the second and third quarters of the first millennium B.C. witnessed the rise in popularity of a genre of chronicle history writing different in origin from those chronicle forms derived from annals. This Levantine form was basically a king list interlarded with brief notices or characterizations and (in a later stage) embellished with narrative derived from folklore. The best example is to be found in Manetho's *Aegyptica*, but the work of this third century B.C. priest represents only one (surviving) stage in a long process.[56] The Ramesside form of the king list, reflected in the Turin Canon,[57] shows us the prior shape of the genre, intent on recording the exact length of reign of each Pharaoh and occasionally (though rarely) giving length of life and (very rarely) including a historical statement. But it must have been the Kushite-Saite period (711–525 B.C.) with its heightened interest in the past and its archaizing that stimulated the rapid growth of the chronicle and established the parameters followed by Manetho two centuries later. It seems certain that Egypt exerted a certain influence over the Phoenician chronicle form, as represented in the "Annals of Tyre," Philo's "history," and the lost works of Mochus, Dius, and others, even though the Phoenician writers did not set out slavishly to copy the alien genre.[58] Here too we are dealing with a king list into which length of life and notices of occasional historical facts have been inserted, a synthesis of which the writers were conscious. Eusebius, reporting on Philo, or rather on the earlier Phoenician history that Philo renders into Greek, speaks of three strands woven into the final form of the work:[59] "succession lists of the kings of Phoe-

[56] Redford, *King-lists*, 206–30.

[57] Ibid., 1–18.

[58] For explicit evidence of the dependence of Phoenician literati on Egypt, cf. the statement of Zakarbaʿal (eleventh century) acknowledging that Byblos was indebted to Egypt for its scholarship and craftsmanship; also the prominence enjoyed by Thoth in the mythological histories of Phoenician writers: see nn. 60–61.

[59] Eusebius, *Praepartatio Evangelica* 1.9.21.

nicia"; "city records"; and "temple archives." The parallel to Kings is close: a chronicle interwoven with historical notices and prophetic and cultic stories. Moreover, the time period within which a self-conscious archaism in Phoenicia prompted the collection of material and the production of the earliest chronicle is the same as that in Egypt, seventh to sixth centuries B.C. Sanchuniaton, the writer whom Philo claims to have used and translated into Greek, can best be fitted into the sixth century B.C.;[60] and his reputed source Hierombalos to the ninth through seventh centuries B.C.[61]

Remarkably the nature and date of our putative "Judaean Chronicle" (if we may be permitted to coin such a label)[62] that informs 1 and 2 Kings parallel those of the "Phoenician History" and the "Manethonian" king list tradition closely. (Perhaps it is not so remarkable, as Judah lay within the culture sphere of Egypt and the eastern Mediterranean, and could not help but share form, theme, and treatment of the general literary tradition of the whole.) From the internal Biblical evidence adduced previously, it seems clear that the chronicle, like those in Phoenicia, was begun in the seventh century B.C., probably some time between the beginning of the reign of Manasseh and the beginning of the reign of Josiah, and may reflect the continuation of the literary activity the Bible attests under Hezekiah.[63] At the center is a skeletal king list in which matrilineal descent and cross-dating with Israel assume a prominent place; and flesh was added to this in the form of historical notices and didactic stories. The former derive exclusively from what was on view and well known *in Jerusalem*, and have absolutely nothing to do with court annals or daybooks.[64] If

[60] Cf. W. F. Albright, *The Bible and the Ancient Near East* (New York, 1965), 470; idem, *Yahweh and the Gods of Canaan* (New York, 1968), 225; cf. also R. du Mesnil de Buisson, *Nouvelles études sur les dieux et les mythes de Canaan* (Leiden, 1973), 70; admittedly the evidence is circumstantial, but some statements are much too negative: H. W. Attridge and R. A. Oden, *Philo of Byblos. The Phoenician History* (Washington, D. C., 1981), 3–9.

[61] Hierombalos—whether the personal name is genuine or not is immaterial: Attridge and Oden, *Philo*, 24, n. 22—is contemporary with an Abi-ba'al, king of Beirut, and although this person cannot yet be identified, the personal name is attested from Phoenicia and Israel from the early ninth to the mid-seventh centuries B.C.: P-M² VII, 388; ANET², 291, 296, 321.

[62] What the state of historiography was in Israel is unknown to us, as the references to the kings of Israel and their *res gestae* in the Book of Kings do not constitute an independent source; and it is only the tiresome wishful thinking of scholars that would make it into one.

[63] Cf. Prov. 25:1.

[64] Daybooks probably were kept at the courts of Israel and Judah, but we have no idea whether the practice of keeping formal annals was followed. While Assyria might have provided a model, in Egypt the annals form seems to have been so transmogrified that it no longer conformed to the regular record of yearly events we know existed in the Old Kingdom: D. B. Redford, in F. Junge, ed., *Studien zu Sprache und Religion Ägyptens* (Göttingen, 1984), 327–41.

such had been available to the chronicle writer, we should have had an infinitely richer but substantially different account than in fact we now have. Moreover, if *any* annalistic type of source had survived from the time of Solomon, we should not have been left with the block of puerile nonsense in 1 Kings 3–12. Our experience of Manetho is the same: we expect solid history from monuments we no longer have but which Manetho saw—could he not read the hieroglyphs?—yet we are constantly thrown back on outlandish folklore that he extracted from his temple library. In both cases we moderns overestimate both the *availability* of court records to an early "historian" and the *interest* of the latter in this type of record. Scholarly collection of evidence was wholly foreign to him. The past for him served only to stress a clear and simple moral, and pious legends proved far more useful than court records that were both unavailable and irrelevant.

TANITE EGYPT: TENTATIVE TRADING PARTNER

If the chronicles of Phoenicia and Israel have disappointed us in our search for a specific record of contact with Egypt, the results of archaeology help to a limited extent to fill in the cultural picture.

The tradition of a glorious isolation, which the Libyan kings did not deviate from, did not prevent the passage of merchantmen to and fro between the Nile Delta and the Phoenician coast. With Byblos the Libyan kings maintained the traditional cordiality, although the initiative may have been a Phoenician one. Votive statues, or fragments thereof, of Sheshonq I, Osorkon I, and Osorkon II have been unearthed there, the former two with applied Phoenician texts telling of their Egyptian provenience and their dedication by the Byblian king to Baʿalat on his own behalf.[65] With Sidon too the 22nd Dynasty enjoyed good relations, as attested by Osorkon II's gift of alabastra;[66] and votives of the same material with the names of Osorkon II, Sheshonq II, and Takelot II may point to Tyre's efforts to cultivate the Egyptian link.[67] Certainly the Egyptians continued throughout the Iron Age to purchase timber in Tyre.[68] The Phoenicians for their part had for centuries absorbed the broad spectrum of Egyptian cultural and religious expression without themselves

[65] P. Montet, *Byblos et l'Égypte* (Paris, 1929), 49–57, figs. 17–18, pls. 36–38; idem, *Fouilles de Byblos* (Paris, 1937), 1:116, no. 1741, pl. 43; Donner and Röllig, *Kanaanäische und aramäische Inschriften*, 2: nos. 5–6.

[66] W. von Bissing, *ZA* n.s. 12 (1940), 155ff.; W. Cilican, *Levant* 2 (1970), 28ff. (found at Ashur whither they had been carried as booty).

[67] Later taken to Spain, where they were excavated: I. Gamer-Wallert, *Ägyptische und ägyptisierende Funde von der iberischen Halbinsel* (Wiesbaden, 1978).

[68] H. F. Saggs, *Iraq* 17 (1955), 127–28.

relinquishing their own creative spirit; and when a new and eclectic efflorescence of Phoenician art burst in the eighth century B.C., it is small wonder that exponents of the new forms should have borrowed heavily from
Egypt both in motifs and architectural forms.[69] Simultaneously with the
appearance of the new art—Greek tradition was later to date it as contemporary with the reign of Takelot III about 760 B.C.—the period of
Phoenician trade and colonization began in the western Mediterranean;
and it was in Phoenician bottoms that Egyptian and Egyptianizing art
objects found their way to remote islands and the Italian and Iberian Pen-
insulas.[70]

The impact of Egypt on the Hebrew kingdoms of the Iron Age is more
difficult to document and perhaps more elusive (see further discussion in
chapter 13). Contact was certainly less direct since the hinterland found
the sea route inaccessible; and the land route was difficult to negotiate,
not only because of desert conditions, but also because it was in the control of others. Nevertheless, there is good evidence that both Judah and
Israel communicated regularly with Egypt (cf. Hosea 7:11, 12:1, etc).
And while Egypt remained the only major power in the region on whom
the Levantine cities could rely, its inherent weakness and divisions were
not lost on the astute observer. It is not imprecise observation nor a hyperbolic cast of writing that makes Isaiah describe Egypt in chapter 19 of
his book as anarchic and disunited. Anyone proceeding in the mid-eighth
century B.C. from Judah to the Delta and up the Nile would have encountered no less than seven "fiefs" of the "Great Chiefs of the Meshwesh"
and two "kings" in Lower Egypt, two additional "kings" in Middle
Egypt, and the vast temple estate of Amun in the Thebaid. The "legitimate" king of the 22nd Dynasty directly controlled only Tanis and its
environs, Athribis and Memphis: all other lords temporal, while they offered him lip service, ran their own bailiwicks independently.

It is interesting to examine Hebrew familiarity with the Egyptian landscape as reflected in the toponyms evidenced in Biblical documents of the
eighth through sixth centuries B.C. (excluding the toponyms in the Exodus account, on which see my subsequent discussion). Most frequently
mentioned are Zo'an (Tanis), Memphis, and Daphnae, with seven occurrences each,[71] followed by Thebes (No "the city") with five and Migdol

---

[69] See I. J. Winter, *Iraq* 38 (1976), 16; J. D. Muhly, in *Biblical Archaeology Today* (Jerusalem, 1985), 184; P. Wagner, *Der ägyptische Einfluss auf die phönizische Architektur*
(Bonn, 1980); G. E. Marfoe, *BASOR* 279 (1990), 13–26.

[70] Muhly, in *Biblical Archaeology Today*, 178–80; Gamer-Wallert, *Ägyptische Funde*.

[71] Zoan: Num. 13:22; Isa. 19:11, 13, 30:4; Ezek. 30:14; Psalm 78:12, 43, Memphis:
Hos. 9:6; Isa. 19:13; Jer. 2:16, 44:1, 46:14, 19; Ezek. 30:13. Daphnae: Jer. 2:16, 43:7, 8,
9; 44:1, 46:14; Ezek. 30:18.

with four.[72] Then follow Sais, Bubastis, Pelusium, Herakleopolis, and Aswan with one each.[73] Significantly absent from the list are Pi-sapdu (modern Saft el-Henneh), Pi-gerer, Sambehdet, Per-kheby, Busiris, or Athribis. In other words, an Israelite or Judaean contemplating a real or imagined trip to Egypt would have conceived of an entry via the Bubastite branch of the Nile only, and not via the Wady Tumilat or the central branch (the "Great River").[74] Israel and Judah were thus more familiar with the seat of 22nd Dynasty Pharaohs and, with their decline, with the "rump" state of Ra'-noufe (i.e., the lower reach of the Bubastite branch between Bubastis and Sile) over which the 23rd Dynasty ruled.[75] It is in connection with Israel's prior familiarity with the Ra'-noufe region of the northeast Delta that the overriding popularity of the winged scarab in Israelite glyptic art must be viewed.[76] For it was to this northeastern quarter of Lower Egypt that the cult and myth of the winged Khopry were native.[77] According to a late tradition, Khopry the beetle had come forth from the brow of Osiris and flown from Heliopolis to Sile, in which site he resided as an avatar of Horus, "Lord of Mesen," under the appellation "the august, winged scarab, protector of the Two Lands, the great god, residing in Sile."[78]

Despite its political weakness, however, Egypt remained a repository

[72] Thebes: Nah. 3:8; Jer. 46:25; Ezek. 30:14, 15, 16. Migdol: Jer. 44:1, 46:14, Ezek. 29:10, 30:6.

[73] Sais: 2 Kings 19:9 (see subsequent discussion); Bubastis: Ezek. 30:17; Pelusium: Ezek. 30:15; Herakleopolis: Isa. 30:4; Aswan: Ezek. 30:16.

[74] A. H. Gardiner, *Ancient Egyptian Onomastica* (Oxford, 1947), 2:153*ff.

[75] Piankhy Stela, lines 19, 114 (see N.-C Grimal, *La stèle triomphale de Pi(ankh)y* [Cairo, 1981]; possibly the environs of Tanis (Yoyotte, in *Mélanges Maspero*, 4, no. 1:129, n. 2; J. Vandier, *RdE* 17 [1965], 170ff.), applied as a designation of Osorkon IV's kingdom between Sile and Bubastis (W. Helck, *Die altägyptische Gaue* [Wiesbaden, 1974], 190; H. Gauthier, *Dictionnaire des noms géographiques contenus dans les textes hiéroglyphiques* [Cairo, 1926], 1:190; 3:130; P. Montet, *Géographie de l'Égypte ancienne* [Paris, 1959], 1:201), and closely associated with the cults of the eastern frontier (E. Chassinat, *Le temple d'Edfu* [Cairo, 1892–1934], 1:130; Montet, *Kêmi* 8 [1946], 64, pl. 15; G. Daressy, *BIFAO* 11 [1914], 35–36). Later the term seems to have been reinterpreted as *hrw-nfr*: P. Dem. 31169 recto ii, 4. It has become fashionable of late to deny that the Osorkon and Takelot found on several monuments at Karnak are in fact members of the Manethonian 23rd Dynasty. This notion, which is based on false premises and misreading of evidence, will be answered by the present author in due course.

[76] On the winged scarab on Israelite seals, see the discussions and literature cited in A. D. Tushingham, *BASOR* 200 (1970), 71ff.; A. F. Rainey, *BASOR* 245 (1982), 57ff.

[77] See J. Vandier, *RdE* 17 (1965), 172ff.; on Khopry's solar identification, see K. Mysliwiec, *Studien zum Gott Atum* (Hildesheim, 1978), 1:75ff.; E. Brunner-Traut, *Gelebte Mythen* (Darmstadt, 1981), 7ff.

[78] A. Kamal, *Stèles ptolémaiques* (Cairo, 1905), 187; G. Daressy, *BIFAO* 11 (1914), 29ff.; the legend is contained in the texts accompanying an Edfu offering scene: Chassinat, *Edfu*, 6:316 (pl. 151).

and a source of wealth, as well as a transit corridor to points in central Africa. One need only peruse Osorkon I's list of bequests to the gods[79] or the readjustment Prince Osorkon effected in the revenues of Amun[80] to appreciate the fact that the absence of architecture on an imperial scale has nothing to do with the wealth of the country. Although northern Nubia remained largely uninhabited[81] and the African empire terminated, goods from the south continued to trickle in, albeit on a reduced scale, along the Nile and through the oases.[82] In the north, the Libyan kings probably viewed the *Via Maris* with as much concern as their New Kingdom forebears had done. To preserve the trade that passed along this ancient route, diplomatic gifts of exotic African products might be sent to the king of Assyria,[83] and Egyptian ambassadors and scribes dispatched to Assyria, Samaria, and the Philistine cities.[84] For their part the inhabitants of western Asia welcomed trade in the exotic products Egypt had to offer—gold, horses, linen, apes, elephants, and crocodiles[85]—and in return sent south the commodities that we have learned from its imperial experience Egypt hankered after: oil (Hosea 12:1), unguent (Gen. 37:25), wine, alum, and spices.[86] An index of the importance of this commercial relationship is the rapid adoption by the Hebrew states during the Iron Age of the system of weights, measures, and numerals used by Egypt.[87]

[79] E. Naville, *Bubastis* (London, 1891), pl. 51. This wealth is now ingeniously ascribed to Sheshonq's pillaging of Jerusalem a generation earlier: A. R. Millard and K. A. Kitchen, *BAR*, 15, no. 3 (1989), 20–34. One might encourage these authors to explore further, whether, for example, the economic decline of the 20th Dynasty was occasioned by Israel's "despoiling" the Egyptians (Exod. 12:35–36); or whether the lines of worry on Amenemhet III's statuary reflect the sickness inflicted on Pharaoh because of Sarah (Gen. 12:17).

[80] Caminos, *The Chronicle of Prince Osorkon*.

[81] G. A. Reisner, *Archaeological Survey of Nubia* (1908–1909) (Cairo, 1911), 29; B. G. Trigger, *History and Settlement of Lower Nubia* (New Haven, Conn., 1959), 112ff.; T. Säve-Söderbergh, *Kush* 12 (1964), 37; cf. W. B. Emery, *Egypt in Nubia* (London, 1965), 206ff.

[82] Caminos, *Chronicle of Prince Osorkon*, 125–26; D. B. Redford, *JSSEA* 7 (1977), 7–8.

[83] M. Elat, *IEJ* 25 (1975), 32; idem, *JAOS* 98 (1978), 22ff.; H. Tadmor, *IEJ* 11 (1961), 143ff.

[84] See H. Tadmor, in H. Goedicke and J.J.M. Roberts, eds., *Unity and Diversity* (Baltimore, 1975), 42 (on the Egyptians at the court of Adad-nirari III); cf. also A. Reifenburg, *Ancient Israelite Seals* (London, 1950), 31, no. 9 ("belonging to Pediese," a seal from Samaria); cf. also the alabaster of Osorkon II from Samaria: G. A. Reisner et al., *Harvard Excavations at Samaria* (Harvard, 1924), 1:247, fig. 205; 2: pl. 56g.

[85] Elat, *JAOS* 98 (1978), 120ff.

[86] E. Chassinat, *Le temple de Dendera* (Cairo, 1936–), 4:66, 5:71; S. Sauneron, *Le rituel d'embaumement* (Cairo, 1952), 3:1–2; D. J. Wiseman, *Iraq* 28 (1966), 155.

[87] The royal cubit: Y. Aharoni, *BA* 31 (1968), 24; the *deben* (c. ninety-one grams, to which the shekel was adjusted): idem, *BASOR* 184 (1966), 18; R.B.Y. Scott, *BASOR* 200

THE THREAT OF ASSYRIA

We have described earlier the long-standing national animosity that existed between the principality of Assyria, whose center lay in the city of Ashur on the upper Tigris, and the Hittite empire whose perceived sphere of expansion was eastward into the plains of Mesopotamia (see chapter 6). With the passage of the Sea Peoples and the sudden demise of Hittite hegemony in Asia Minor, this Bronze Age contretemps became a thing of the past; but the weakened condition of Assyria at the time did not permit them to capitalize on the power vacuum that had resulted. It was not until the reign of Tiglath-pileser I (c. 1115–1077 B.C.), a contemporary of Ramesses XI in Egypt, that a sufficiently strong government emerged at Ashur to consider once again a major westward thrust.[88]

But now another ethnic group, by geopolitical posture also opposed to Assyria, had adopted the former Hittite goal, and was moving eastward into Mesopotamia, and this was the Aramaeans. Here was a force to be reckoned with, young and vibrant, and with all the vigor associated with a tribal state. Twenty-eight times, so Tiglath-pileser tells us, he was obliged to lead punitive campaigns against the encroaching Aramaeans, until finally he burst through into Syria. The startled Phoenician cities of Sidon, Byblos, and Arvad followed time-honored practice and "bought off" the newcomer with presents, facilitated his cutting of timber in the mountains, and even took him fishing for game fish on the Mediterranean.[89] But Tiglath-pileser's exploits proved ephemeral. His successors for over 150 years were wholly incapable of resisting Aramaean pressure; and by the third-quarter of the tenth century B.C., just as Sheshonq I was seating himself on the throne in Egypt, the invaders had reached the Tigris.[90]

The Aramaeans themselves, however, found it difficult to sustain their own momentum, and once the disciplined military might of Assyria had been marshaled by an effective head of state, they gradually gave ground. For exactly three centuries from the accession of Adad-nirari II the story of Assyria is one of almost uninterrupted expansion as Assyria transformed itself into the scourge of the ancient world (911–612 B.C.). At its greatest extent its empire stretched from northeast Africa to the Caucasus, and from the Mediterranean to the mountains of Iran.

(1970), 64. On the influence of hieratic notation on the Hebrew script of the eighth to seventh centuries, see Aharoni, *BASOR* 184 (1966), 13ff.; idem, *BA* 31 (1968), 15; idem, *BASOR* 201 (1971), 35–36; A. F. Rainey, *BASOR* 202 (1971), 23ff.; S. Yeivin, *IEJ* 16 (1966), 152ff.; idem, *JEA* 55 (1969), 98ff.; I. T Kaufman, *BASOR* 188 (1967), 39ff.

[88] G. Roux, *Ancient Iraq* (Harmondsworth, 1966), 252–53.

[89] On "tribute," see Tadmor, Goedicke and Roberts, in *Unity and Diversity*, 37.

[90] Roux, *Ancient Iraq*, 254.

For Egypt and its clients and neighbors in the Levant, the moment of truth came during the reign of Shalmaneser III (858–824 B.C.). Following up the advantage gained by his predecessor over the Aramaeans of Mesopotamia, Shalmaneser crossed into North Syria and established himself in the captured principality of Bit-Adini; but when he turned south to advance up the Orontes, he was met by formidable opposition. At last all Syria had been galvanized into action, and twelve independent states united under the leadership of Hada-ezer of Damascus, including Hamath, Cilicia, Arvad, Israel (Ahab is here mentioned), Musri, Ammon, and even an Arabian tribe. With nearly seventy thousand troops, the coalition met the Assyrians at Qarqar on the Orontes in 853 B.C. and fought them to a standstill. Repeated attacks by Shalmaneser in the years that followed failed to crack the unity of the Aramaean front ranged against him; and it was only when an internal conspiracy swept Hadad-ezer off the throne of Damascus and replaced him with a usurper, Haza'el, that the Assyrians were able to make some headway in Syria. Still the major cities of Hamath, Damascus, and Samaria resisted attack with considerable success; and Shalmaneser had to content himself with the usual diplomatic gifts from the circumspect cities of the Phoenician coast.[91]

The interesting entry in the breakdown of the coalition is Musri, which is almost certainly Egypt.[92] The Egyptian king of the 22nd Dynasty who was an (earlier) contemporary of Shalmaneser III was Osorkon II (c. 873–844 B.C.), and numerous texts from his reign or lifetime show a preoccupation with affairs of Asia. One wonders whether the epithet "smiting the Asiatics" taken by Osorkon at his accession betrays preconceived plans;[93] and, if he is the "Osorkon Maiamun" of a British Museum oracular decree in favor of a newborn prince, Amun's prediction takes on a new meaning: "I (Amun) will cause that Pharaoh Osorkon Maiamun, my good child, send him at the head of a great army and he (the prince) will bring back report . . . 'Great of Magic' (the uraeus) the Mistress of Buto, will be fixed on his head, and every chief of every foreign land and country will say to him 'I will, I will!' "[94] Osorkon II's gifts of alabaster have been recovered in the excavations at Samaria (presumably sent to Ahab),

[91] On the battle of Qarqar, see *ANET²*, 278–79; Elat, *IEJ* 25 (1975), 25–35; Tadmor, in Goedicke and Roberts, *Unity and Diversity*, 38–40; J. A. Brinkman, *JCS* 30 (1978), 173–75; W. T. Pitard, *Ancient Damascus* (Winona Lake, Ind., 1987), 126–28.

[92] On the identification of Musri with Egypt, see A. T. Olmstead, *History of Assyria* (New York, 1923), 134; idem, *History of Palestine and Syria* (New York, 1931), 384; E. Meyer, *Geschichte des Alterums* (Stuttgart and Berlin, 1928), 2:2, 333; Tadmor, in Goedicke and Roberts, *Unity and Diversity*, 39.

[93] H. Gauthier, *Le livre des rois d'Égypt* (Cairo, 1914), 3:337–38; H. K. Jacquet-Gordon, *JEA* 46 (1960), 14, n. 1.

[94] I.E.S. Edwards, *Hieratic Papyri in the British Museum*, 4th ser. (London, 1960), 2: pls. 16:34–17:37.

and one of his ambassadors there may have deigned to have his name carved on a seal in Hebrew script.[95] Osorkon may well have flattered himself on his contribution to the coalition that fought at Qarqar, but his paltry one thousand troops indicates only tokenism and perhaps a secret hedging of the bet. When, in the years subsequent to that great battle, it appeared that Assyria had been neither worsted nor discouraged, Osorkon or his successor considered it politic to join the Phoenicians and dispatch diplomatic presents to the Assyrian capital; and two generations later Egyptian envoys are to be found residing in Assyria.[96]

The same pattern of indecisive confrontation between the Tigris-based power of Assyria and the Mediterranean coastlands was to prolong itself for over one hundred years after the battle of Qarqar. Haza'el, who in the last quarter of the ninth century B.C. and in spite of the Assyrians, had subverted most of the states between Damascus and Gaza to his rule,[97] died around 800 B.C., bequeathing to his son Bar-Hadad III(?) a state preeminent in the Levant. Although Bar-Hadad, before his death about 775 B.C., was to suffer the attenuation of his domains through the revolt of Jehoash of Israel,[98] he nonetheless maintained the core of his principality intact. A renewed attempt to organize a coalition on the part of Bar-Hadad led to the siege of the reluctant king of Hamath in his capital city, an investment from which he was (apparently) saved only by the timely intervention of Adad-nirari III of Assyria in 796 B.C. Adad-nirari even assaulted Damascus itself but failed to take the city, and had to content himself with the receipt of the usual gifts from Tyre, Sidon, Israel, Edom, and the Philistine cities.[99] Nonetheless Assyrian attacks did not slacken. On no less than four occasions in the eighteen-year span ending in 755 B.C. Assyrian sources list forays against Damascus.[100] Egypt, suffering from the weakness attendant upon its intestine feuding, is absent from all these records.

The year 745 B.C. marks one of those major turning points in history the significance of which is often lost on layman and scholar alike. Jereoboam II died about that time, and Takelot III had just been made coregent at Bubastis; but neither of these inconsequential events makes the year special in any way. What was happening in Assyria in 745 infuses

[95] See n. 84.

[96] ANET² 281; J. V. Kinnier-Wilson, The Nimrud Wine Lists (London, 1972), 102, 127, 139, and passim; Tadmor, in Goedicke and Roberts, Unity and Diversity, 42.

[97] Pitard, Ancient Damascus, 151–58.

[98] J. M. Miller, ZAW 80 (1968), 337–42.

[99] On Adad-nirari's records, see ANET², 281–82; H. Tadmor, Iraq 35 (1973), 141–50; W. H. Shea, JCS 30 (1978), 101ff.; on the date, see Pitard, Ancient Damascus, 163–66; on the Zakkir stela, see Donner and Röllig, Kanaanäische und aramäische Inschriften, 2: no. 202; ANET², 501–2; E. Lipinski, AION 31 (1971), 393–99.

[100] Pitard, Ancient Damascus, 175–77.

that twelve-month span with an importance comparable to that of 586 B.C. (the fall of Jerusalem), or 333 B.C. (Alexander's crossing of the Hellespont) or 31 B.C. (Octavian's victory at Actium). For it was in 745 that a civil war in Assyria unseated the royal family and catapulted a general named "Pul" known to history as Tiglath-pileser III, to the throne of the empire. This usurper proved to be an organizational genius and a master strategist, worthy of comparison with Hannibal or Scipio. By relentless campaigning and indiscriminate use of mass deportation, he encompassed the destruction of Damascus and Israel and by 732 B.C. even threatened Egypt.[101]

At the outset he faced formidable opponents. The upstart state of Urartu (Biblical Ararat) had expanded into North Syria and the northern Zagros, thus encircling the Assyrian heartland. Arpad in North Syria was Urartu's ally, and elsewhere in Syria no state felt obliged to offer presents. Tiglath-pileser's action was swift. By skillful campaigning he completely defeated Urartu in two years and repaired to Syria in 743 to receive tribute.[102] The next year he expanded by force his conquests in North Syria, deported the enemy ruler and laid seige to Arpad, which fell after a three-year investment.[103] The years 740 and 738 witnessed the sacking of Ullubu and Kullanu in the north, and it became evident that Tiglath-pileser III aimed at nothing less than the liquidation of all states in the Levant to the border of Egypt.

One can imagine the panic that must have seized Damascus and Samaria as they saw the irresistible advance southward of the Assyrians. Both states were now considerably weakened in the hands of usurpers, Rezin in Damascus and Menahem, the butcher of the house of Jereoboam (2 Kings 15:14–16) in Samaria, and their first impulse was to proffer a propitiatory tribute to Tiglath-pileser, which they did, probably in 738 B.C.[104] Was it pursuant thereto that an anti-Assyrian(?) rebellion carried off Menahem's short-lived son and replaced him with Pekah, that "smouldering stump of a firebrand" as Isaiah calls him (Isa. 7:4)?[105] In any case, probably in 736 B.C., Rezin and Pekah attempted to revive the old anti-Assyrian coalition. At the same time Hanno of Gaza, Mitinti of

---

[101] In general see H.W.F. Saggs, *The Greatness That Was Babylon* (New York, 1962), 116–19; for the lamentable state of Tiglath-pileser III's annals and a masterful analysis and reconstruction, see H. Tadmor, *Proceedings of the Israel Academy of Science and Humanities* 2 (1968), 168–87; on his use of mass deportation, see B. Oded, *Mass Deportations and Deportees in the Neo-Assyrian Empire* (Wiesbaden, 1979), 19.

[102] H.W.F. Saggs, *Iraq* 17 (1955), 146.

[103] *ANET²*, 282; Saggs, *Iraq* 17 (1955), 133 (letter 15).

[104] H. Tadmor, *Scripta Hierosolymitana* 8 (1961), 252–58; B. Oded, in Hayes and Miller, *Israelite and Judaean History*, 424; W. H. Shea would date the tribute to 740: *JNES* 37 (1978) 49; see 2 Kings 15:19–20 (1,000 talents).

[105] So W. H. Hallo, *BA* 23 (1960), 48.

Ashkelon, and Hiram of Tyre agreed to create a front against Tiglath-pileser. Only Ahaz of Judah remained outside the group, and when he showed reluctance to cooperate, the Damascene and Israelite forces invested Jerusalem with the goal of replacing Ahaz with a puppet.[106] Again Tiglath-pileser responded with a speed and determination that bewildered his enemies. Adopting a strategy of attacking the weaker, coastal allies and of driving a wedge between Israel and Damascus, he descended upon Phoenicia in the spring of 734 B.C., capturing Sumur, Arka, and Byblos, and forcing Tyre to pay tribute and suffer partial deportation.[107] Accho was assaulted and reduced to ashes, the territory of Naphtali annexed, and the Assyrians were able to march clean through Philistia.[108] Mitinti subsequently suffered a fatal attack and Hanno fled to Egypt allowing Tiglath-pileser to enter Gaza unopposed. The Assyrian king took booty, including the (relatively modest) sum of eight hundred talents of silver, imposed an annual tribute, and set up a victory stela in the temple of Gaza.[109] Two years later, after a desperate struggle of which no record has as yet come to light, Damascus fell, its population was deported, Rezin killed, and his territory annexed as a province. Israel temporarily escaped, thanks to the timely assassination of Pekah and the immediate submission of the usurper Hoshea who had, however, to witness passively the annexation of Israel's territory in Galilee and Transjordan, and the reduction of his state to little more than the environs of Samaria.[110]

None of the implications of this spectacular spread of Assyrian power could have been lost on the Egyptians. In 732 B.C., as a follow-up to the final smashing of Damascus and the reduction of Israel, Tiglath-pileser III had appointed the chieftain of an Arab tribe south of Gaza to the ad hoc post of "gatekeeper over Egypt," a sort of warden of the marches,[111] per-

---

[106] Pitard, *Ancient Damascus*, 184–86; Oded, in Hayes and Miller, *Israelite and Judaean History*, 425–26 (cf. 2 Kings 16:5); D. J. Wiseman, *Iraq* 18 (1956), 125 reverse 5–8 (cf. 2 Chron. 28:16–18). On the identity of "Ben-Taba'el" of Isa. 7–6, see W. F. Albright, *BASOR* 140 (1955), 34ff.; B. Mazar, *IEJ* 7 (1957), 236–37; Pitard, *Ancient Damascus*, 184, n. 104.

[107] Wiseman, *Iraq* 18 (1956), 117–29; *ANET²*, 283b; on the overall strategy, see Hallo, *BA* 23 (1960), 48; H. Tadmor, *BA* 29 (1966), 88 (who posits a secondary interest of securing coastal trade); on Tyre's relations with Assyria, see G. Kestemont, in E. Gubel et al., eds., *Studia Phoenicia* (Louvain, 1983), 1:53–78.

[108] M. Dothan, *IEJ* 25 (1975), 164; D. J. Wiseman, *Iraq* 13 (1951), 21ff.; A. Alt, *Kleine Schriften zur Geschichte des Volkes Israel* (Munich, 1953), 2:150ff.

[109] *ANET²*, 283; Wiseman, *Iraq* 13 (1951), 21ff.; Tadmor, *BA* 29 (1966), 88ff.; Oded, in Hayes and Miller, *Israelite and Judaean History*, 425; N. Na'aman, *TA* 6 (1979), 68–69.

[110] Cf. 2 Kings 17:1; Hallo, *BA* 23 (1960), 50; Pitard, *Ancient Damascus*, 186–87; Oded, *Mass Deportations*, 64; on the creation of the provinces of Magiddu and Gal'azu out of Israelite territory, see Oded, in Hayes and Miller, *Israelite and Judaean History*, 427; on Assyrian rule in Transjordan, see B. Oded, *JNES* 29 (1970), 177ff.

[111] *ANET²*, 282; Tadmor, *BA* 29 (1966), 89; Na'aman, *TA* 6 (1979), 69.

haps in the expectation of an imminent Egyptian collapse. While from 732 to 725 B.C. the Assyrians were occupied elsewhere, it was but the calm before the storm. It may well have looked to observers on the Nile that Assyria considered expansion into Africa its "manifest destiny."

KUSH AND ASSYRIA: THE CONTEST FOR EGYPT

Egypt by 735 B.C. had become a political vacuum. Sheshonq IV at Tanis in that year celebrated a traditional jubilee,[112] apparently unaware or unconcerned about the momentous events about to transpire 450 kilometers to the northeast. Of his neighbor Takelot III at Bubastis we know nothing, except that he continued to while away his uneventful reign. Takelot's young, virgin sister Shepenwepet was in that year occupying the post of "Divine Adoratress" and "God's wife of Amun" at Thebes, thus titular head of the Southland; and elsewhere the patchwork of chiefdoms and "kingships" of which the Delta and Middle Egypt were made up existed as I have described it previously (p. 335f.). It was to be sure a most disunited front that Egypt's rulers presented to the outside world, weak, grudging of loyalty to a central government, and lacking willpower.[113]

Another power in the Nile Valley was already, by 735 B.C., displaying the strength, unity, and élan that in Egypt was wanting. The Dark Age into which Kush had been plunged at the end of the New Kingdom, lasted about two centuries and, as we have already noted, virtually cut off the region south of the second Cataract from Egypt proper.[114] Around 860 B.C. interest focuses on the Dongola reach with its ancient district capital of Napata, where the worship of Amun had thrived from the early 18th Dynasty; for here a power center was in process of forming around a family of influential Kushite chieftains. While their origins are shrouded in mystery, they were certainly of Sudanese stock and may have enjoyed a Negro strain in their ancestry.[115] The simple tumulus burials in the earlier part of the tribal cemetary at Kurru near Napata point to a parochial culture, little different from that which had held sway in the area from

---

[112] P. Montet, *Le lac sacré de Tanis* (Paris, 1966).

[113] It is significant that during the decade of the Syro-Ephraimitic war and the machinations of the coastal states in their efforts to prepare a defense against Assyria, no reference is made to the expedient of looking to Egypt for support. True, Hanno flees from Gaza to Egypt for refuge; but this is more a commentary on the natural horizon as a border city (Na'aman, *Tel Aviv* 6 [1979] 74ff.). In short Egypt was *not*, until after 730 B.C., a political power from whom help might realistically be sought.

[114] See p. 337. A very little trade is attested: Caminos, *Chronicle of Prince Osorkon*, 125–26f.; but this is negligible when compared with the amounts recorded during the New Kingdom.

[115] G. A. Reisner, *HTR* 13 (1920), 30; J. Leclant, *Recherches sur les monuments thébains de la XXVᵉ Dynastie* (Cairo, 1965), 331–32.

the third millennium. But after 800 B.C. the rich archaeological evidence shows that these chieftains were beginning to aggrandize their territory, and to fall increasingly under the influence of Egyptian civilization. Square, stone-built mastabas begin to appear at Kurru, an Egyptian form of monarchy was mimicked and the title "king" adopted by chief Alara, as well as the full-fledged hieroglyphic script.[116] It was the influence of the old, Ramesside ruins in Nubia, and in particular the temple and cult of Amun in Nubia, that informed Alara's and his successor's adopted culture;[117] but it was a species of Egyptian culture that was somewhat old-fashioned and fraught with a solemn, conservative piety. Adherence to such a "straight-laced" fundamentalism, always stronger in a convert, was to enhance the Kushites' loathing of their contemporaries, the Libyan rulers of Egypt who—horror of horrors!—had loose morals, showed no reverence for ancient dietary laws, and always acted perfidiously.

The zeal for Amun displayed by the new Kushite kings created a bond of mutual self-interest with Thebes and the Egyptian south in general. Alara dedicated his sisters to Amun with the hope that the great god would favor his house, and his brother Kashta who succeeded him around 750 B.C. was accepted by the inhabitants of the Thebaid and allowed to erect stelae. His son Piankhy, who followed Kashta in turn, in 735 B.C., dispatched his younger sister Amunirdis to Thebes, but not to serve in the manner of other dedicated princesses as a mere songstress or priestess. For Amunirdis was appointed by her brother as a *coregent* of the functioning "Divine Adoratress" Shepenwepet.[118] The latter was not ousted from her queenly office, nor as far as we know did she suffer a diminution of her power; but she was obliged to adopt the little Kushite girl as her "daughter" with the full panoply of titles and regalia.[119] The move not only set a precedent to be followed by other potentates desirous of controlling Thebes for the next two hundred years, but it also secured the Thebaid for Piankhy; and when later he moved a garrison into the city,[120] Piankhy's border must have extended as far north as Asyut.

Thus the remarkable advance of the Assyrians toward the Delta from

---

[116] A. J. Arkell, *A History of the Sudan to 1821* (London, 1959), 116; D. O'Connor, in *Ancient Egypt, A Social History* (Cambridge, 1983), 269–70; J. Leclant and J. Yoyotte, *BIFAO* 51 (1951), 7; S. Wenig, *Africa in Art: The Arts of Ancient Nubia and the Sudan* (Brooklyn, 1978), 2:56, 63.

[117] E. Russmann, *The Representation of the King in the 25th Dynasty* (Brooklyn, 1974), 25–26.

[118] L. F. MacAdam, *The Temple of Kawa* (Oxford, 1949), 1:16; Leclant and Yoyotte, *BIFAO* 51 (1951), 15; P-M² V, 227; Gauthier, *Livre des rois*, 4:5 (2, 1), n. 2; J. Leclant, *ZÄS* 90 (1963), 74ff.

[119] H. Kees, *Das Priestertum im ägyptischen Staat* (Leiden, 1953), 266; Kitchen, *Third Intermediate Period in Egypt*, 151; Redford, *King-lists*, 314.

[120] Breasted, *Ancient Records of Egypt*, 4: sec. 821.

745 to 732 B.C. finds a curious parallel in the sweep of an equally irresistible force in the opposite direction down the Nile during the same years. While it must remain a moot point as to whether Tiglath-pileser III harbored any farsighted design on Lower and Middle Egypt, it cannot be denied that the Kushites certainly did. As devout worshipers of the gods and protégés of Amun, the Sudanese rulers felt it their mission to move on to the shores of the Mediterranean and to reform Egypt. The question now was which of these new, major powers would win the race for the lower Nile, and would the Delta remain a power vacuum?

Lower Egypt was not prepared to continue in its accustomed guise of an inactive pawn in the political game between the great powers. This passive roll, politically and commercially, was exchanged by the Egyptians in the last third of the eighth century for the part of an aggressive if not belligerent protagonist. Assyrian sources indicate that Egyptian and Philistine trade with Lebanon for timber was of sufficient concern under Tiglath-pileser III to call forth an explicit interdiction from the Assyrian authorities.[121] Interestingly, the thalassocracy lists record for the eighth year of a Psammous of the 23rd Dynasty a reflection of Egypt's resurgence in the field of maritime commerce;[122] and while these lists are uneven in historical worth, they often preserve a curious kernel of truth.[123] It was probably the prosperous trade that was converging on the south Philistine coast from the Nile and south Arabia that prompted Tiglath-pileser III to turn Gaza into a *bît kâri*, and later Sargon II to promote actively direct trade between Egypt and Assyria on the Egyptian border.[124]

One would be mistaken not to discern behind this revival of Egypt's interest in the north the vitality that attended the expansion of the Kingdom of the Western Delta under the leadership of the city of Sais.[125] To-

---

[121] ND 2715: Saggs, *Iraq* 17 (1955), 127ff.; N. Postgate, *Taxation and Conscription in the Assyrian Empire* (Rome, 1974), 390ff.; cf. Tadmor, *BA* 29 (1966), 88. On Assyrian use of Lebanese timber, see J. Elayi, *JESHO* 31 (1988), 14–40.

[122] Eusebius, *Hieronymus Chronikon* (ed. Helm), 85: *Aegypti post Foenices mare optinuerunt.* Shalmaneser V may, on his Israelite campaign, have undertaken operations against Tyre to prevent Egyptian maritime activity on the Phoenician coast: A. Malamat, *IEJ* 1 (1950), 152.

[123] On the thalassocracy lists, see R. Helm, *Hermes* 60 (1926), 241ff.; A. R. Burn, *Minoans, Philistines and Greeks* (Oxford, 1931), 63.

[124] C. J. Gadd, *Iraq* 16 (1954), 179; H. Tadmor, *JCS* 12 (1958), 77ff.; idem, *BA* 29 (1966), 92; Elat, *JAOS* 98 (1978), 27ff.

[125] The "Archaismus," which is often qualified as of "Kushite" origin, would better be termed the "Saite Risorgimento," and construed as a phenomenon having to do with the resuscitation of ancient models in art, script, religion and society. The Kushites had nothing to do with it: the 25th Dynasty merely aped a fad they found already in vogue in Egypt. See H. Brunner *LdÄ* 1 (1975), 386ff.; idem, *Saeculum* 21 (1970), 151ff.; R. A. Fazzini, *Miscellanea Wilbouriana* (Brooklyn, 1972), 64–65f; H. Kees, *Das Priestertum im ägyptischen Staat* (Leiden, 1953), 198; J. Yoyotte, *Histoire de l'art* (Paris, 1961), 1:238.

ward the close of the reign of Sheshonq III, in the second quarter of the eighth century, Sais had fallen into the expanding bailiwick of the chief-taincy of the Labu, one of the foreign enclaves that could trace its presence in Egypt back to the outgoing second millennium. Just before Sheshonq IV died after four decades of rule, a chief of the Labu named Tefnakhte is attested at Sais with suzerainty over the Saite, Xoite, and West nomes of the Delta.[126] By the beginning of the period covered by the Piankhy stela[127] he had succeeded in subverting the whole Delta, and securing the submission of the valley as far as Hermopolis but not, however, without determined opposition from some quarters. Although Piankhy claims to have trounced Tefnakhte, it is significant that he did not proceed with his army beyond Memphis, and was satisfied with the token submission of the Delta. Sais was obviously much stronger than Piankhy would have us believe, and Tefnakhte remained sufficiently independent to pass on his mantle to his son Bocchoris. Both of them now stand at the head of the "Manethonian" version of the 26th Dynasty.[128]

The dominance of Sais in the history of Egypt from the close of the 22nd Dynasty to the beginnings of the 25th in 711 B.C., when Bocchoris was captured and executed,[129] puts a different slant on the international politics of the Levant. In place of the nonentity who had occupied the Tanite throne, there now ruled an energetic monarch willing to take on superior forces and fight them to a standstill. If Hoshea, eager for backing in his bid for independence, had not sought it from Tefnakhte of Sais, it is a puzzle where he *would* have gone.[130] In my opinion this consideration lends strong prima facie probability to Goedicke's twenty-year-old suggestion that in 2 Kings 17:4 we construe סוא as a rendering of "Sais,"[131] or perhaps a *nisbe* derived from the toponym.[132] Similarly in 720 B.C.

---

[126] Yoyotte, *Mélanges Maspero*, 1, no. 4:152ff.; idem, *BSFE* 24 (1957), 53, fig. 1: D. B. Redford, *BES* 5 (1983), 85–86.

[127] See Grimal, *La stèle triomphale de Pi(ankh)y*.

[128] See the complete discussion in Redford, *King-lists*, chap. 9.

[129] From a combination of the contemporary Assyrian chronology with the data from the Serapeum texts, it transpires that the arrival of Sabaco in Egypt can be dated no earlier than January 711 B.C. The execution of Bocchoris will probably have followed fairly shortly. See my discussion on the chronology of the period in *JARCE* 22 (1985), 5–15.

[130] Hoshea's appeal to Egypt would have been made in 726 or 725 B.C.; on the chronology, see J. Reade, *Syro-Mesopotamian Studies* 4 (1981), 1–9; that Hoshea's insurrection was part of a wider revolt against Assyria seems certain: Miller and Hayes, *A History of Ancient Israel and Judah*, 334–36.

[131] H. Goedicke, *BASOR* 171 (1963), 64ff.

[132] D. B. Redford, *JSSEA* 11 (1981), 75ff. All other suggestions are decidedly less likely. There is no proof whatever that the name "Osorkon" could be shortened to resemble the word in question (Kitchen, *Third Intermediate Period*, 373–74), nor can it be a rendering of *nsw* "king" (Oded, in Hayes and Miller, *Israelite and Judaean History*, 433), which in transcription always shows an unassimilated *n*: *s³-nsw* > Σιονσις; *Imn-m-nsw* > Αμενεμνῆς; *nsw-bity* > in-si-bi-ya; see further Redford, *King-lists*, 327 and n. 187.

when the rebellious Hanno of Gaza elicited Egyptian support to take on Sargon II,[133] it is inconceivable that anyone other than the Saite king should have offered a realistic hope of effective support. Osorkon IV of Bubastis and Ra'noufe was situated geographically closer to the Palestinian frontier, but the Piankhy stela portrays him as a pliant weakling, siding with whichever of the warring forces was in the ascendant. It is not without significance that his only appearance in Assyrian sources is as a docile bringer of tribute;[134] and in this act his envoys may well have rubbed shoulders with the emissaries from Judah, Philistia, and Transjordan.[135]

That it was indeed Tefnakhte who, in response to these pleas from Israel and Gaza, busied himself with armed intervention in Asiatic affairs, may be supported by two pieces of circumstantial evidence. The first is a late tradition preserved in Diodorus and Plutarch:[136] "Tnephachton the father of Bocchoris the wise, while on campaign in Arabia, ran short of supplies because the country was desert and rough . . . he was obliged to go without food for one day and then to live on quite simple fare at the home of some ordinary folk." The account goes on, in a rather "Hellenic" tone, to describe Tnephachton's new-found delight in this rustic existence, as opposed to the sophisticated urban life he was used to, and concludes with a moralizing counterblast against a life of luxury. Stripped of its Hecataean moralizing, this story may derive from a genuine memory of Tefnakhte's expedition across the Sinai—"desert and rough"—to the aid of Hanno of Gaza.

The second piece of circumstantial evidence is an inference based upon the reliefs of the fifth room at Khorsabad.[137] The costumes, weaponry, and physiognomy of some of the combatants depicted here in the battles and sieges associated with Ekron and Gibbethon seem to point to the Nile Valley. If Reade is correct in dating the content of these reliefs to the Phil-

---

[133] On the Gaza campaign, see ANET², 285; H. Tadmor, BA 29 (1966), 91; N. Na'aman, Tel Aviv 6 (1979), 68ff.

[134] Tadmor, JCS 12 (1958), 78; Albright, BASOR 141 (1956), 24. That this "Osorkon" (Silkanni) is the last scion of the 23rd Dynasty has been argued elsewhere: Redford, Kinglists, chap. 9. It is quite likely that he appears as Pir'u, the giver of an unspecified quantity of tribute, again including horses, in the aftermath of Sargon's victory at Gaza: A. G. Lie, The Inscriptions of Sargon II King of Assyria vol. 1: The Annals (Paris, 1927), 22:123–25.

[135] Osorkon's tribute may be reflected in a letter from Nimrud telling the king that legates from Egypt, Gaza, Judah, Moab, and Ammon have arrived with tribute: Saggs, Iraq 17 (1955), 134; Tadmor BA 29 (1966), 92ff.; for a fragmentary letter referring to five Egyptian horses as part of the tribute, see R. F. Harper, Assyrian and Babylonian Letters (Chicago, 1892–1914), no. 1427.

[136] Diodorus, 1.45.1–2: A. Burton, Diodorus Siculus, Book I. A Commentary (Leiden, 1972), 144–45; Plutarch, De Iside et Osiride 8. The inscription is said to be at Thebes; but this attests simply the attraction of this great city of ruins in folklore of the Late Period.

[137] M. El-Amin, Sumer 9 (1953), 35ff., figs. 2–6.

istine campaign of 720,[138] then we must conclude that already *before* the battle of Raphia the Egyptians had acted upon the calls for assistance from Palestine and had dispatched auxiliary forces to the cities of the Philistine plain. The Negroid appearance, however, of some of the faces in the reliefs[139] poses a problem, as Sudanese elements in Nilotic forces should not be expected prior to 711 B.C. If the racial type has been correctly identified, then we must either redate the reliefs of the fifth room to later in the reign, or assume that the sculptor introduced anachronistic details into his depiction of an event that had taken place much earlier.[140]

To Kush went the initial triumph. In the years following 720, as the Delta and the valley of the Nile began to line up behind Tefnakhte, Piankhy must have grown increasingly concerned (although official propaganda endows him with a charming insouciance during this period). At last, with the siege of Herakleopolis by Tefnakhte's minions, Piankhy dispatched an expeditionary force. While Tefnakhte escaped to the comparative safety of his bailiwick in Sais, his coalition was broken up and his attempt to reunite Egypt frustrated (c. 717–716 B.C.).[141] Piankhy, however, made no serious effort to subvert the Delta and replace the local administrations with his own governors; and the dynasts at Bubastis and Sais (Osorkon IV and Bocchoris, Tefnakhte's son, respectively) were left free to dabble in Asian intrigue or to send their tribute to Assyria. When, in the spring of 712 B.C., Assyrian punitive forces descended on Ashdod in the Philistine plain, it may have looked that Egypt too (with whom Ashdod had conspired) was destined for invasion. Piankhy's decease about this time and the accession of his younger brother Shabaka to the throne brought fresh enthusiasm to the regime; and late in 712 (or possibly January 711) Kush invaded Egypt. Memphis was easily seized, Bocchoris captured and executed, and Sudanese rule imposed throughout Upper and Lower Egypt.[142]

Egypt and the Arabs

From the activity of Tiglath-pileser III and Sargon II in the southwest it was becoming clear that Philistia and the Sinai were destined to become

[138] J. Reade, *JNES* 35 (1976), 100ff.

[139] Ibid., 100 and n. 2.

[140] Cf. Tadmor, *BA* 29 (1966), 94. It should be noted, however, that the prognathous, "southern" mode of representing the human profile that we associate with the Sudanese art of the 25th Dynasty is already present in Egypt before 720 B.C.: see *Neferut net Kemit: Egyptian Art from the Brooklyn Museum* (Tokyo, 1984), no. 57, and notes thereto by R. A. Fazzini.

[141] See Spalinger, *JSSEA* 11 (1981), 37–58; Grimal, *La stèle triomphale de Pi(nakh)y*; J. Leclant, *LdÄ* 4 (1982), 145–48.

[142] D. B. Redford, *JARCE* 22 (1985), 5–15.

the scene of confrontation between Egypt and Assyria. One ethnic element that was to play an important role as an intermediary here was the enclave of the Arabs.[143] Egypt until the end of the second millennium had maintained a working relationship with the early tribes of the 'Arabah in an effort not only to mine the material resources of the region but also to control the incense trade.[144] Following the decline and withdrawal of the Egyptian empire, there is some evidence during the Iron I period of growing prosperity among the nomadic tribes of the Negeb, as they sought to capitalize on local trade routes. A progressive sedentarization centering on the large and rich site of Tel Masos is also in evidence and may reflect the chiefdom that has come down in history under the rubric "Amalek."[145]

Thereafter, however, the entire area fell under the control of Asiatic principalities with the result that the Egypto-Arab link was ruptured.[146] Precisely when a significant number of Arab tribesmen began to filter westward across the Negeb and into Sinai is a moot question; and it ill behooves us to take statements in such late and unreliable sources as the Chronicler at face value.[147] In the first half of the eighth century, however, it would appear that the Judean *risorgimento* under Uzziah resulted in the reassertion of Judean control over the 'Arabah, Edom, and Ezion-geber;[148] while at the same time extensive tracts of the western Negeb fell into Philistine hands.[149] On the eve of Tiglath-pileser III's accession, it

---

[143] E. A. Knauf, BN 20 (1983), 34–33; 21 (1983), 37–38; 22 (1983), 25ff.; idem, *Ismael. Untersuchungen zur Geschichte Palästinas und Nordarabiens im 1. Jahrhundert* (forthcoming); see also M.A-K. Muhammed, *ASAE* 64 (1981), 95ff.; A.-A. Saleh, "Arabia and the Arabs in Ancient Egyptian Records" (in press).

[144] A.-A. Saleh, *Orientalia* 42 (1973), 370ff.; P. Parr, in Hadidi, *Studies in the History and Archaeology of Jordan* 1:129–30. On the "Midianite" pottery from northwest Arabia found at Tel Fara and Tel el-Yehudiya, see T. Dothan, *The Philistines and Their Material Culture* (Jerusalem, 1982), 28, and the literature there cited.

[145] M. Kochavi, *BAR* 6 (1980), 27; I. Finkelstein, *JNES* 47 (1988), 241–52.

[146] On the Solomonic expansion into the central Negeb, see C. Meyers, *BA* 39 (1976), 149.

[147] Cf. for example Elat, *JAOS* 98 (1978), 28, n. 49.

[148] See p. 328; J. Bright, *A History of Israel* (Philadelphia, 1959), 239–40; on the trade with Arabia, see N. Gleuck, *BA* 28 (1965), 86.

[149] Evidence is so far lacking for the history of Philistia during the first two centuries of the first millennium. The only city of the Philistines mentioned in the passages recounting David's career is the inland Gath (1 Sam. 17:5ff.; 27ff.; 2 Sam. 21:15–22; 8:1, 5:17–25); but the list in 1 Sam. 6:17 suggests the following sequence of political priority (at least for the ancient writer): Ashdod, Gaza, Ashkelon. 2 Sam. 1:20 mentions the "market streets" of Ashkelon, presaging the commercial importance of the city. With Amos in the early eighth century we are on firmer ground: while Gath has disappeared in Uzziah's destruction (H. J. Katzenstein, *The History of Tyre* [Jerusalem, 1973], 197 and n. 24), Gaza boasts palaces, and Ashkelon knows a sceptor-wielding potentate (Amon 1:8). Ashkelon, in some unrecorded turn of its fortunes, had probably extended its control over the region to the south-

was Philistine and Me'unites, an Arab tribe of the north Sinai, that largely controlled the vast southern wilderness.[150] And it is significant that, when in 734 Tiglath-pileser struck south, it was not against any inland state that he marched, but against Phoenicia, the coastal plain, Gaza, and the Sinai route to Egypt.[151] The setting up of a stela in Gaza and at the Brook of Egypt, and the defeat of the Me'unites with 9,400 casualties,[152] signaled the importance the Assyrian king placed on the coastal plain and the routes that led through it.

Both Tiglath-pileser III and Sargon II appointed local sheikhs as "march lords" with general oversight over the Sinai approaches to the Delta.[153] In the light of the traditional treatment of the nomads of this area by the Egyptians as "lesser breeds without the law," such a policy was enlightened to say the least; and probably from this period dates the Arab predilection for supporting the states of western Asia in their confrontation with Egypt. Under Hezekiah the Me'unites were partially displaced from the environs of greater Gaza by the Simeonites;[154] but at the time of Esarhaddon's invasion the Arab tribes of the northern Sinai were so firmly ensconced and so numerous that their support for the Assyrians was crucial to their victory.

Evidence from Egypt is scant as to relations between these early Arabs and the pharaonic administration. It is debatable whether the "sandy ones," the ḥryw-š' on the Shabaka scarab, can be construed as a reference to the Sinai nomads, although this would be plausible.[155] The "Mntiu of Asia" in Taharqa's texts from Kawa is an equally archaic term that could as well apply to Philistines, Judeans, or even Assyrians![156] On the whole during the period presently under discussion Egypt seems to have exhibited little ability to control the Sinai, but also little inclination to tolerate the ingress of transhumant groups into the Delta. During the first half of the first millennium there are far fewer Asiatic groups resident in Egypt

east of the city (cf. A. Alt, *Kleine Schriften zur Geschichte des Volkes Israel*, 3:420, n 1; N. Na'aman, *Tel Aviv* 6 [1979], 70), and I suspect that Gaza (though evidence is lacking) had taken over territory in north Sinai. One can sense the feeling of strength enjoyed by Hanno of Gaza and Mitinti I of Ashkelon, which prompted them in 735–734 to present an ephemeral united front to Tiglath-pileser III and boldly to expand into the Shephelah: A. F. Rainey, *BASOR* 251 (1983), 14–15.

[150] Tadmor, *BA* 29 (1966), 89; idem, in B. Uffenheimer, ed., *Bible and Jewish History* (Tel Aviv, 1972), 223–24.

[151] See p. 342.

[152] Oded, in Miller and Hayes, *Israelite and Judaean History*, 425; Na'aman, *Tel Aviv* 6 (1979), 68–69.

[153] Tadmor, *JCS* 12 (1958), 77–78; idem, *BA* 29 (1966), 89; Na'aman, *Tel Aviv* 6 (1979), 69.

[154] 1 Chron. 4:41.

[155] Toronto ostracon: bibliography in J. Leclant, *LdÄ* 5 (1983), 512, nn. 93–94.

[156] M. F. Laming MacAdam, *The Temples of Kawa* (Oxford, 1949), 1: nos. 6, 20–21.

than during the New Kingdom.[157] This disinclination to dominate the approaches to the eastern Delta as of old, combined with the relentless pressure of the Arabs westward, resulted ultimately in the permanent presence of Dedanite groups in the Wady Tumilat from about 500 B.C. onward.[158]

During the century and a quarter that elapsed between Shabaka's conquest of Egypt in January 711 (Plate 32) and the fall of Jerusalem in 586, one can sense a renewal of the age-old concern with controlling the *Via Maris* and ensuring that the governments of the Levantine coast were friendly to Egypt, while largely ignoring the needs of inland states. We cannot be sure that trade was uppermost in the Sudanese Pharaoh's minds. Certainly Gaza and Ashkelon must now have become the beneficiaries of an incipient commerce passing from south Arabia via the Negeb and the 'Arabah.[159] But many of the aromatics and tropical products traversing this route were available to the 25th Dynasty in their homeland far to the south on the Nile.

ASSYRIA ON THE NILE

Continuing the policy of Sais with greater effectiveness, the 25th Dynasty burst on the Palestinian scene with an aggressiveness that must have surprised contemporaries, the more so as the initial stance of the Kushites on the morrow of their conquest of Egypt suggested a rapprochement with Assyria was in the offing.[160] As "King of Egypt and Kush," adorned with the double uraeus to symbolize that fact, Shabaka instituted a large-scale program of rebuilding the enclosure walls of all temples in Upper and Lower Egypt.[161] When, probably in 704–03 B.C. Hezekiah of Judah took the lead (at Babylonian instigation?) in organizing the Phoenician and Philistine cities against Assyria, we may be confident that he found ready support in Egypt.[162] When Sennacherib appeared on the march, making for Philistine Ekron, the call went out for "the kings of Egypt and the archers, chariotry and cavalry of the king of Kush—an army beyond

[157] D. B. Redford, *JAOS* 93 (1973), 17.

[158] F. V. Winnett, *Ancient Records from North Arabia* (Toronto, 1970), 115–17; W. J. Dumbrell, *BASOR* 203 (1971), 33ff.; A. Lemaire, *RB* 81 (1974), 63ff.

[159] Note how, pursuant to the victory at Gaza, Sargon enumerates together the tribute of Pir'u of Musri (Egypt), Samsu, queen of Arabia, and Ita'mar the Sabaean: A. G. Lie, *The Inscriptions of Sargon II, King of Assyria*, vol. 1: *The Annals*, 22:123–25.

[160] On evidence of diplomatic correspondence between Shabaka and his Assyrian contemporaries, cf. his seal impressions found in Sennacherib's palace at Nineveh: A. H. Layard, *Discoveries in Nineveh and Babylon* (London, 1853), 156–59; on his return of political fugitives, see Redford, *JARCE* 22 (1985), 6–7.

[161] Cf. Cairo JdE 44665: J. Leclant, *Enquêtes sur les sacerdoces et les sanctuaires égyptiens à l'époque dite "éthiopienne"* (Cairo, 1954), 35.

[162] Cf. Isa. 18:1ff. where the prophet strongly denounces Hezekiah's action.

Plate 32. Schist head of a 25th Dynasty king, possibly Sabaco. (Photo: Courtesy, Brooklyn Museum)

counting."[163] The ease and swiftness with which Shabaka led a substantial expeditionary force to the plains of Eltekeh to engage the Assyrians in 701 militates in favor of a large standing army poised in the Delta for precisely this purpose, and certain bases of operation in the northern Sinai and the Philistine plain. Even though our sources for Eltekeh are confined to the Assyria records—Egyptian relief and textual material employ stereotyped images of uncertain application[164]—there can be no doubt that it was an unexpected and serious reverse for Assyria arms, and contributed significantly to Sennacherib's permanent withdrawal from the Levant.[165]

[163] ANET[2], 287. The "kings of Egypt" are undoubtedly the Delta chieftains, the Libyan dynasts whom the Assyrians persist in mistaking for "kings," (pace N. Na'aman, VT 29 [1979], 65). The single reference in 2 Kings 19:9 to Taharqa as the Egyptian king involved has caused an incredible amount of "revisionist" history writing. Since Shabaka came to the throne in 712 and enjoyed over fifteen years on the throne, it follows that he was king in 701 (Redford, JARCE 22 [1985], 13), not his second successor; even if his nephew Shebitku, who succeeded him directly, had been a coregent for three years, the conferal of this dignity would still be in the future in 701! (See Murnane, Ancient Egyptian Coregencies, 189–90, where the case for a coregency is based solely on an inference from 2 Kings 19:9 itself.) Taharqa's arrival in Egypt from his native Nubia is described in plain and unequivocal terms in the famous Kawa text (MacAdam, Kawa, 1:28): "Now I came from Nubia among the king's (Shebitku's) brothers whom he had called up thence, and I was with him, for he loved me more than all his brothers and all his children . . . (my mother) was still in the land of Nubia; for I had left her as a youth of 20 years when I came with His Majesty to Lower Egypt." The summoning of the princes is never stated to have been in connection with any preparation for war (so K. A. Kitchen, RdE 34 [1982–1983], 65): Shebitku is simply forming his court at Memphis after the death of his predecessor, Shabaka. Thus in 701 Taharqa was still a lad in Nubia, and his first trip to Egypt proper lay years in the future. To take the reference to Taharqa in 2 Kings 19:9 seriously (cf. Na'aman VT 29 [1979], 65; Kitchen, RdE 34 [1982–1983], 65) is unwarranted and produces misleading results. (Of course Egyptian expeditionary forces were sometimes split into different divisions, but campaigns are not identified by the subordinate commander's name, in this case "the prince . . . with the second division.") Quite simply, Taharqa's was the only Pharaonic name known to the author of 2 Kings 19 for the period about which he was writing; and he mistakenly assumed he was already on the throne. On the tradition of Taharqa the conqueror, see Strabo, 1.3.21; 15.1.6; G. Goosens, CdE 22 (1947), 239ff.

[164] Cf. standard head-smiting scene (J. Leclant, Recherches sur les monuments thébains de la XXVᵉ dynastie dite éthiopienne [Cairo, 1965], 2: pl. 82B; 1:339, n. 4); contemporary business documents of 710, 702, and 700 sometimes include the phrase "may he (Pharaoh) be healthy and may Amun grant him the victory!" (M. Malinine, Choix de textes juridiques [Paris, 1953], P. Louvre 322b, d, and e); the Toronto scarab (see n. 154) reads: "He has slain his enemies in Upper and Lower Egypt and in every foreign land. The sand-dwellers who rebelled against him fall to his slaughter; they come of their own accord as living prisoners, each one seizing his fellow." On the reliefs from Gebel Barkal, see n. 185.

[165] The ink spilled, splashed, and poured over Sennacherib's campaign against Philistia and Judah in 701 has become nothing less than an inundation. Among the more reliable and significant contributions, one may cite the following: Tadmor, BA 29 (1966), 86–102; B. S Childs, Isaiah and the Assyrian Crisis (London, 1967); Oded, in Hayes and Miller,

On Shabaka's death very early in 697 B.C. he was succeeded by his erstwhile coregent, Shebitku, his nephew, the son of Piankhy. In the fall of 697 he underwent a coronation in Thebes, the first Kushite monarch we know of to do so;[166] and modeled part of his titulary in pious fashion after the epithets of the great conqueror Thutmose III.[167] Shebitku was to undergo a curious transmogrification in later tradition; largely forgotten in the Nilotic king list, he was to survive in Hebrew memory, misunderstood as the name of a Kushite tribe.[168] His adopted titulary sketches his proposed policy toward the north: "With great respect in all lands, mighty-armed who smites the Nine Bows, content with victory."[169] On the facade of the little temple of Osiris Lord of Eternity that he refurbished and enlarged at Karnak, Shebitku is shown receiving the sword from Amun, and the scene is glossed by the expected promises and boasts of victory in foreign parts.[170]

The reign of the succeeding king, Taharqa, began auspiciously some time in 690. A coronation in Memphis, in the first year, was followed by a formal "appearance" in the temple of Amun at Thebes in the third year (688), and an especially high Nile in the sixth year (685).[171] Thereafter Taharqa began to take the initiative in his dealings with the states of Palestine.[172] In the inventory lists from the temple of Kawa in Nubia, records were kept of Taharqa's donations to the local cult from his second year to his tenth inclusive.[173] Up to his eighth year the donations include ves-

---

Israelite and Judean History, 446–51; D. Ussishkin, *IEJ* 29 (1979), 137–42; idem, *The Conquest of Lakish by Sennacherib* (Tel Aviv, 1982); M. Hutter, *BN* 19 (1982), 24ff.; F. Goncalves, *L'expédition de Sennacherib en Palestine dans la litterature hébraïque ancienne* (Paris, 1986), 352–63; P. Dion, *Bulletin of the Canadian Society of Biblical Studies* 48 (1988), 3–25. On the Egyptian perspective on Sennacherib's campaign, see F. J. Yurco, *Serapis* 6 (1980), 221–39; K. A. Kitchen, in M. Görg, ed., *Fontes atque Pontes* (Wiesbaden, 1983), 243–53. An uncritical preoccupation with the reference of "Tararqa," together with an evaluation of 2 Kings 18:17–19:35 as encompassing the record of two separate events, has prompted some scholars to postulate two campaigns by Sennacherib, one in 701 and the other in 688 (cf. Bright, *History*, 285–88; W. H. Shea, *JBL* 104 [1985], 401–18; cf. H. Horn, *Andrews University Seminary Studies* 4 [1966], 1–28). This, however, has become such an exercise in ingenuity and a travesty of methodology that it ceases to amuse.

[166] Cf. J. von Beckerath, *JARCE* 5 (1966), 53, n. 33. The verb "to appear," used in this graffito, most likely refers to a "coronation."

[167] Leclant, *Recherches*, 237, n. 1.

[168] M. Astour, *JBL* 84 (1965), 422–25.

[169] Leclant, *Recherches*, 340, n. 3.

[170] Redford, *JARCE* 22 (1985), 14, fig. 3.

[171] Redford, *King-lists*, 300, n. 19; Leclant, *Recherches*, 347; idem, *LdÄ* 6 (1986), 156–67; Yoyotte, *BIFAO* 51 (1952), 16; J. Leclant and J. Yoyotte, *RdE* 10 (1949), 37ff.; W. Helck, *ZÄS* 93 (1966), 74–79.

[172] On Taharqa's northern policy, see A. J. Spalinger, *Orientalia* 43 (1974), 295–326; idem, *CdE* 53 (1978), 22–47.

[173] MacAdam, *Kawa*, 1:5ff., 33ff.

sels of gold, silver and bronze, cloth, aromatic substances, and cult utensils, but nothing that could be construed either as tribute or as pieces commemorative of foreign wars. Then in his eighth year the list includes "one bronze statue of the king smiting foreign countries (III, 15)," "every kind of timber including acacia, cedar and persea (III, 21)," and "the children of the chiefs of the Tjehenu (III, 22)." In the narrative section appended to the tenth year he mentions "cedar, juniper, acacia (VI, 14) . . . true cedar . . . Asiatic bronze (VI, 18) . . . good gardeners of the *Mntiu* of Asia (VI, 20–21)." In stela VII, 3–4, it is recorded that "His Majesty ordered that true cedar of Lebanon be brought southward." Taharqa's governor of Thebes, Montuemhat, likewise speaks of "true cedar from the best of the terraces (scil., of the Lebanese mountains)," which he used to construct a sacred bark, and of "Asiatic copper" used for the manufacture of cult paraphernalia.[174] In the light of these passages it is probable that a flurry of military activity occupied Taharqa in the years immediately following 684. We might postulate a campaign of a punitive nature against some Libyan clan that had been disturbing the western border of the Delta in that year, followed shortly by a more ambitious expedition into Asia in 683–682. It may have been this latter incursion into the Levantine theater that occasioned the erection of a statue of the king on which was carved a list of conquered, foreign principalities.[175] The genre of text had been a common one during the New Kingdom; but even the most detailed exemplars often sacrificed accuracy to the need to glorify Pharaoh. Taharqa's lists are simply an unimaginative reproduction of the best-known places that might have been in any New Kingdom list. Nevertheless, the fact that he makes use of this genre—he is the first to do so since Sheshonq I 250 years earlier—shows that for precedents Taharqa was looking back to the period of the empire.

To sum up: there is circumstantial evidence of moderate weight only to suggest an increased presence of Egyptian forces in the Levant during the two decades from 710 to 690. Thereafter in 684–683 and 682–681 all indications are that formal campaigns were mounted that reached as far north as the Phoenician coast. In the light of this Egyptian evidence the cordial relations between Taharqa and Ba'lu of Tyre and Abdimilkutte of Sidon take on new meaning.[176] It has plausibly been suggested that Taharqa diverted some of the southern trade he controlled to Tyre;[177] and one wonders whether the "22 kings of Khatte" whom Esarhaddon later counted as wholly subservient to himself had originally constituted a

---

[174] J. Leclant, *Montouemhât, quatrième prophète d'Amon et prince de la ville* (Cairo, 1961), 197, line 2; 213, line 11.
[175] Cairo 770. Taharqa's involvement in Libya is reflected in an unpublished Karnak stela.
[176] *ANET²*, 290.
[177] S. Yeivin, *JQR* 50 (1959–1960), 226.

loose coalition, organized under Tyre at the instigation of Taharqa.[178] It is quite likely that Ashkelon at least, of the Philistine cities, had sided openly with Egypt, to judge by the allusions in Assyrian sources on the conquest of 671.[179]

While Egypt's interest, as of old, led it to concentrate most of its efforts in the coastal plain, there is nonetheless good evidence that the late eighth and seventh centuries were marked by an increase in relations, commercial and political, between Judah and Egypt.[180] Although there is no direct evidence that Hezekiah had approached Egypt in the preparations for the anti-Assyrian stand, the goals of both countries did indeed coincide; and the sudden appearance of Sabaco at Eltekeh was partly responsible for removing the immediate threat to Jerusalem.[181] Isaiah implies that Judah was beginning to profit from Egyptian trade across the Negeb,[182] and some of the items in Hezekiah's tribute to Sennacherib suggest an African provenience.[183] The prospect of political alliances with Egypt gladdened the heart of Judah as it pleased the Philistine states, and the generally favorable attitude toward such alliances shows through clearly in Isaiah's invectives.[184] Knowing the sequel, we are apt to forget the impression Taharqa's Egypt at first made on the Near East. A new stela from Dahshur expresses the glowing pride with which Taharqa contemplated the precision and physical prowess of his well-trained troops, and underscores the high morale that imbued these forces.[185] An Asiatic surveying

---

[178] Katzenstein, *History of Tyre*, 263.

[179] R. Borger, *Die Inschriften Asarhaddons Königs von Assyrien* (Graz, 1956), 102. In connection with Taharqa's hegemony over the Philistine plain, one must mention the systrum fragment recently unearthed at Miqne (S. Gitin, *BAR* 16, no. 2 [March–April 1990], 41). The dedication to "Amunre, Lord of the Thrones of the Two Lands, preeminent in the Holy Mountain (i.e., Gebel Barkal) at the Horns of the Earth [. . .]" points to the Napatan form of the god, and a fortiori a deposit during the time of the 25th Dynasty, not the 26th (as the excavator apparently maintains).

[180] With the "buffer" of Damascus and Israel gone, the south Levantine states were obliged more than ever to turn to Egypt for assistance. One might opine that whatever lexical, institutional, and cultural impact Egypt made on Judah (see pp. 350–394) was effected at this time; cf. for example, the striking Egyptian influence evident in the cult objects from Beer-sheba: Y. Aharoni, *BA* 35 (1972), 124, fig. 17.

[181] See p. 353.

[182] Isa. 30:6–7.

[183] *ANET²*, 288a.

[184] Isa. 30:1–5, 31:1–3.

[185] A. M. Moussa, *MDAIK* 37 (1981), 331–37. The massive building program in evidence in Egypt during this reign (J. Leclant, *LdÄ* 6 [1986], 56–67) indicated efficient organization of manpower. Taharqa's triumph scenes are stereotyped and draw on Old Kingdom phraseology: Leclant, *Recherches*, 297–98; R. A. Parker et al., *The Edifice of Taharqa by the Sacred Lake at Karnak* (Providence, R.I., 1982), 57, pl. 27. On the tradition of Taharqa as a conqueror, see Strabo, 1.3.21, 15.1.6; Goosens, *CdE* 22 (1947), 239–44; J. Janssen, *Biblica* 34 (1953), 34. In this regard one might consider the enigmatic reliefs once in the temple

this "new Egypt" from afar may be forgiven if he misconstrued it as a sort of "wave of the future." And if in fact Manasseh of Judah was coerced into contributing auxiliaries to Ashurbanipal's campaign against Egypt, this need not in itself be interpreted as a volte-face in Judaean policy.

But the clock could not be put back. A Thutmose III could—and would—have seized all the principalities in western Asia by force. Taharqa found it expedient, and probably less expensive, to use most of them as allies, for the posture events were forcing on Egypt was one of defense. Taharqa's befriending of the Phoenician cities can only be interpreted as the strengthening of a flank in the expectation of an Assyrian thrust toward Egypt. Further south, the Philistine cities were in an uncomfortable position, as they were more vulnerable to attack than Tyre and Sidon. While eager for ties with Egypt, they could not afford to discontinue their tribute to Assyria.[186] Inland states like Judah were in the same compromised position. Judah at the time was ruled by the irresolute Manasseh who had been cowed by Assyrian power and was probably incapable of the effective anti-Assyrian activity his father had engaged in.[187]

During the 680s Sennacherib's weakness invited Taharqa's involvement in the Levant in a manner ever more anti-Assyrian; while the civil war that raged in Assyria for three months following his murder[188] may well have looked like the end of that state. If Taharqa had so interpreted

---

of Gebel Barkal, which Spalinger has drawn to our attention: *JSSEA* 11 (1981), 46–49 and fig. 4. These show soldiers with Assyrian helmets being defeated by an Egypto-Nubian force in chariots. Spalinger attempts to set a *terminus ante quem* of Sennacherib's reign on the basis of the conical helmet and the presence of the scene in a section of the temple built by Piankhy (ibid., 49; cf. D. Dunham, *The Barkal Temples* [Boston, 1970], plan B502). This type of helmet, however, continued through the reign of Sennacherib and into the seventh century (D. Ussishkun, *The Conquest of Lakish by Sennacherib* [Tel Aviv, 1982], pls. 66, 69–72 and passim; H. Hall, *Babylonian and Assyrian Sculpture in the British Museum* [Paris, 1928]; cf. the fine example found near the Ramesseum: Leclant, *Recherches*, 181 [E,1]); and the hall in question was most certainly in process of decoration in later reigns: P-M VII, 219–20. It is tempting to see in this scene a 25th Dynasty record of either Elketeh or one of Taharqa's early campaigns.

[186] See R. Zadok, *WO* 9 (1977), 35ff.; *ANET*², 291, 294.

[187] On the reign of Manasseh, see Oded, in Miller and Hayes, *Israelite and Judean History*, 452–58; it is quite likely that Manasseh, in concert with other vassals of Esarhaddon, had had to sign a vassal treaty obligating him to support Assyrian aims and to refrain from rebelling: Miller and Hayes, *A History of Ancient Israel and Judah*, 370–72; subsequent Assyrian demands were for garrison posts (Oded, in Miller and Hayes, *Israelite and Judaean History*, 455), and their influence may have extended to the cult (M. Weinfeld, *JNES* 23 [1964], 202–12). His erstwhile close relations with Tyre (cf. Katzenstein, *History of Tyre*, 263–64) need not mean that he was actively involved in rebellion; and the tribute of Judah at the time seems rather light: R. F. Harper, *Assyrian and Babylonian Letters Belonging to the Kouyunjik Collection(s) of the British Museum* (Chicago, 1892–1914), no. 632.

[188] Roux, *Ancient Iraq*, 293–94.

events, he was sadly mistaken; for by March 681 the civil war had ended abruptly and Sennacherib's youngest son Esarhaddon sat firmly upon the Assyrian throne. Shortly he was to become Taharqa's nemesis and the scourge of Egypt.

Esarhaddon, who cannot help but have viewed the alliances of Taharqa with Tyre and Sidon as a *casus belli*, from the outset adopted a strategy of outright war with Egypt. The trading post that over forty years before Sargon had established south of Gaza was but a preliminary move in establishing bases in the south against Egypt. By Esarhaddon's time the western Negeb had been taken over by the Assyrian military, a governor ensconced in Tel Jemmeh, and garrisons posted in sites between Raphia and Beer-Sheva.[189] Within twelve months of Esarhaddon's accession, Assyrian troops were operating in the north Sinai, where they removed in chains the sheikh of a local tribe—had he been openly intriguing with Taharqa?—and sent him to Assyria.[190] Two years later Esarhaddon turned against Taharqa's Phoenician allies. The typically sudden and well-planned Assyrian attack resulted in the destruction of Sidon, and the execution, after a futile attempt at flight, of its king. Ba'lu of Tyre surrendered and was forced to sign a treaty with Esarhaddon, which bound him completely, economically and politically, to Assyria.[191] Taharqa had, to his chagrin and probably to the damage of his image in the Levant, been unable to save his allies.

As though to broadcast his unquestioned hold over Palestine and the coast, Esarhaddon summoned "all the kings from the Hatti-country (Palestine and Syria) and from the seacoast and made them build a town for me on a new location, calling its name Kar-Esarhaddon."[192] Here was proof of sovereignty: it was Esarhaddon that all Palestine obeyed.

Now that Taharqa had been discredited (as it seemed), Phoenicia reduced, and the Negeb firmly held, the time seemed right for the final confrontation with Egypt. The events of the next decade show clearly that annexation simply, and not punitive or preventive action, was the chief aim of Assyria. It was undoubtedly expected that the forthright persual of this policy would result in the fall of the next state in the "domino chain" that had begun to collapse sixty-five years before with the triumphs of Tiglath-pileser III; and this may very well have inspired the Assyrians with a confidence not warranted. For Egypt was something

---

[189] For the residence of the Assyrian governor at Tel Jemmeh and the presence there of Assyrian palace ware, see G. Van Beek, *IEJ* 24 (1974), 139, 274; 27 (1977), 172; Na'aman, *Tel Aviv* 6 (1979), 72–73, 81.

[190] *ANET*², 290, 302; R. Campbell Thompson, *The Prisms of Esarhaddon and Ashurbanipal* (London, 1931), 18, lines 39ff.; Borger, *Inschriften*, 50.

[191] Borger, *Inschriften*, 107–9; *ANET*² (Suppl.), 533–34; Katzenstein, *Tyre*, 267ff.

[192] *ANET*², 291; Borger, *Inschriften*, 48.

more than a Damascus or a Sidon. The events of 701 might have suggested to Esarhaddon that the Kushites were no mean adversaries, and that they too could acquit themselves well, at least when not blinded by the dazzle of their own propaganda.

Whatever the reason, the first attempt to invade Egypt went badly. In the early spring of 674 B.C. the Assyrian army marched across the north Sinai but suffered a repulse, probably on the eastern frontier of the Delta.[193] Naturally the Assyrian sources say nothing, and it is only in the terse entry of a later chronicle that we read "In the month of Addaru, on the fifth day, the army of Assyria was defeated in a bloody battle in Egypt."

Part of the cause of the Assyrian defeat may well have been the route chosen to break into Lower Egypt. For, like most of his predecessors, Esarhaddon's probable path lay along the coast past Raphia, el-Arish, and Lake Sirbonis and ended at Sile, the well-fortified frontier station. This is essentially the medieval caravan route from Syria to Salhieh in the Delta; in the Bible it is called "the Way of the Land of the Philistines."[194] But there is a more southerly route that, striking in a southerly direction from el-Arish, could be used to enter Egypt by way of the Wady Tumilat and the Bitter Lakes. Bedu from the Negeb and Sinai had frequented this route from time immemorial, but it had rarely if ever been followed by a large, well-equipped army.

Esarhaddon's defeat in 674 must have buoyed Taharqa's hopes. Now was the time to take the initiative and strike again into Asia. In the months following the Assyrian defeat, Taharqa's forces moved into the Philistine plain, turned Ashkelon into a base of sorts, and may have attempted to organize a coalition of the local rulers.[195] The outcome of the great chess game between the two superpowers still defied prediction, and for his part Esarhaddon felt uneasy. Prayers were offered to the sun-god Shamash: "Should Esarhaddon, king of Assyria, plan and strive to set out with his troops, his chariots and his armor to march to the Trans-Euphra-

---

[193] On URU Ša.LU of the Esarhaddon chronicle, see S. Smith, *Babylonian Historical Texts* (London, 1924), 10–11; *ANET²*, 303; H. von Zeissl, *Äthiopen und Assyrer in Ägypten* (Glückstadt, 1944), 36. It is difficult to separate this town from the one in Babylonia, and it seems more than likely that,as Landsberger and Bauer contend (*ZA* 37 [1937], 78), a minor, local Assyrian campaign has been inserted in the chronicle to avoid the embarrassment of having to mention a defeat. Fecht's attempt (*MDAIK* 16 [1958], 116ff.) to see in the name a reference to the frontier fort of Sile is highly ingenious, but founders on the problem of the unlikely transliteration: See Spalinger, *Orientalia* 43 (1974), 300–301.

[194] On these routes, see J. Clédat, *ASAE* 15 (1915), 16; C. S. Jarvis, *Three Deserts* (London, 1936), 116ff.; J. Baines and J. Malek, *Atlas of Ancient Egypt* (New York, 1980), 19–20, 188; Y. Aharoni, *The Land of the Bible: A Historical Geography* (London, 1979), 197–200.

[195] *ANET²*, 293; Borger, *Inschriften*, 102; M. Etan, *JAOS* 98 (1978), 33.

tes to Ashkelon? . . . will (the Egyptians) plan and strive to wage war against Esarhaddon, king of Assyria, in the region of Ashkelon?"[196] Omens were required. On the march in early summer of 671 Esarhaddon visited a temple at Harran in central Mesopotamia, and while there two crowns were placed on his head, a sure sign that this double uraeus diadem of Egypt would soon grace his brow.[197] If this was a good omen, an eclipse that happened in July of that year was considered inimical, and the troops had to be reassured.[198]

Still Esarhaddon pressed on. His exact route is somewhat in doubt: we can trace it as far as Raphia, but thereafter the king waxes eloquent in describing the horrible terrain he and his men traversed and the two-headed snakes and flying green things he had to overcome (Figure 9). We emerge again into the light of reality when he tells us he was assisted with food and water by the camels of the local Arab tribes, and mentions the point of his "landfall" in Egypt, namely Migdol on the eastern edge of the Delta, northeast of modern Qantara.[199] It would seem that, whichever route across the Sinai Esarhaddon had opted for, he appeared in the Delta unexpectedly and at a point Taharqa least expected. It was not until the Assyrians had gained "(The Mansion) of *Was-khupri" near modern Faqus[200] that the Kushites could muster their forces and offer resistance.

The element of surprise worked wonders. Though Taharqa fought a desperate rearguard action, and was wounded five times (so Esarhaddon tells us), he was forced to fall back on Memphis, which he had no time to fortify. In early July the city fell in half a day, and Taharqa fled precipi-

---

[196] J. A. Knustzon, *Assyrische Gebete an den Sonnengott* (Berlin, 1893), 2: nos. 69, 70; Tadmor, *BA* 29 (1966), 100.

[197] S. Parpola, *Letters from Assyrian Scholars to the Kings Esarhaddon and Ashurbanipal* (Neukirchen-Vluyn, 1970), no. 117.

[198] L. Waterman, *Royal Correspondence of the Assyrian Empire* (Ann Arbor, Mich., 1930–1936), no. 276.

[199] For Esarhaddon's fantastic account, see *ANET²*, 292. The problem as to which route Esarhaddon took to enter Egypt turns on the identification of Migdol in part. This is usually taken as the Biblical Migdol (J. Simons, *Geographical and Topographical Texts of the Old Testament* [Leiden, 1959], sec. 424), and identified most recently with Site T 21, twenty kilometers northeast of modern Qantara (E. Oren, *BASOR* 256 [1984], 7–44). If this is correct, then undoubtedly Esarhaddon entered Egypt via the coastal route from Gaza. But the problem is that P. Dem. 31169, a most important geographical papyrus, much in need of a reedition, mentions at least four "Migdols" on the eastern frontier (D. B. Redford, in A. F. Rainey, ed., *Egypt, Israel, Sinai* [Tel Aviv, 1987], 143, 154 and n. 14). It is conceivable that one or more of them stood south of Qantara, guarding the entry into Wady Tumilat.

[200] Assyrian *Ishkupri*, undoubtedly a foundation encorporating the praenomen of Sety II (c. 1225–1220 B.C.): Gauthier, *Le livre des rois d'Égypte* 3:130–39; it is to be identified with the like name in P. Dem. 31169, which G. Daressy (*ASAE* 17 [1917], 128) places in the environs of Salhieh; see also Fecht, *MDAIK* 16 (1958), 118–19.

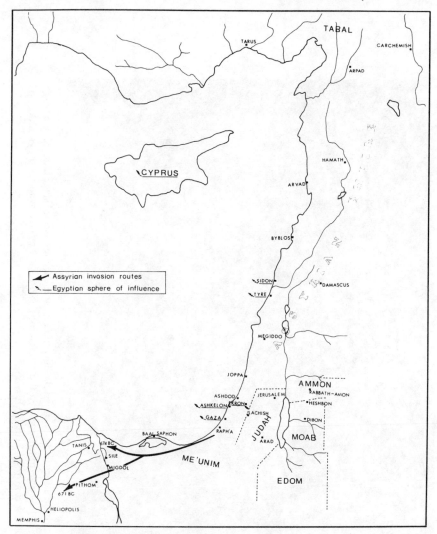

Figure 9. The Levant in the seventh century B.C.

tously southward, leaving his queen and family to fall into enemy hands.[201]

The next eight years in Egypt's history, from 671 to 663 B.C., were characterized by contemporaries as that period of "The raging of the foreign lands," or "that evil time (Plate 33, 34)."[202] It was a period of confusion

[201] ANET², 293.
[202] Leclant, Montouemhât, 83, line 6; P. Rylands IX, vi.16–18.

Plate 33. Assyrian assault on a fortified city, possibly Egyptian. As some troops ascend siege ladders to engage the defenders, sappers below attempt to weaken the foundations. Note the battered walls and pylonlike aperture on the right. (Photo: Courtesy, British Museum)

Plate 34. Assyrian soldiers lead away captives from the city under siege. The "Sudanese" appearance of the prisoners on the right and the kilts and feathered filets of the high-ranking prisoners in the center suggest a 25th Dynasty milieu. (Photo: courtesy, British Museum)

in which, though Assyrian arms had been proved unbeatable, the Assyrian administration proved incapable of holding the country, and the Delta dynasts, caught between Kush and Ashur, played the Vicar of Bray to the best of their ability. Esarhaddon attempted to enfeoff the local rulers, and the Assyrians appointed one Necho, the son of the wretched Bocchoris of Sais,[203] as their local governor. But even he proved not to have Assyria's best interests at heart: when Taharqa emerged out of the south the year following Esarhaddon's attack and recaptured Memphis, the whole Delta came over to him. When Assyrian troops reappeared in Egypt under Ashurbanipal, Esarhaddon's son, in 666 B.C., and Taharqa again fled south, Necho cleverly convinced the enemy that he had been powerless in the face of the Kushite power, and managed to have himself reinstated as Assyrian regent. This "fence sitting," however, between two powers much stronger than tiny Sais, could deceive the opposing camps for only so long; and when in 664 Taharqa died and was succeeded by Tanwetaman, Necho was a marked man. Tanwetaman's uncontested advance to Memphis left Necho isolated, and he was probably put to death.[204]

The last act in this story drama was, from Egypt's point of view, the worst; but from history's the dawn of a new day. The murder of his regent and the advance of the Kushites could not be ignored by Ashurbanipal. In 663 he dispatched a punitive expedition that chased Tanwetaman all the way to Nubia, and this time pursued him as far as Thebes. For the first time in a thousand years Thebes, still loyal to the Kushite 25th Dynasty, was brutally sacked and its treasures carted off to Assyria, including silver, gold, gems, costumes, chattels, and even obelisks.[205] Everywhere in Africa Assyrian arms were triumphant—but Necho's son yet lived!

[203] On Necho (I), see D. B. Redford, *LdÄ* 4 (1982), 368–69; idem, *King-lists*, 326–27.

[204] On Tanwetaman and the recapture of Egypt, see Spalinger, *JAOS* 94 (1974), 316–28; A. Leahy, *GM* 83 (1984), 43–46; S. M. Burstein, *JSSEA* 14 (1984), 31–34.

[205] *ANET²*, 295; some of the booty has turned up in excavation in Assyria: W. K. Simpson, *Sumer* 10 (1954), 193–94; V. Vikentiev, *Sumer* 11 (1955), 111–16; idem, *Sumer* 12 (1956), 76ff.; B. Parker, *Iraq* 17 (1955), 119; Leclant, *Orientalia* 27 (1958), 96; 30 (1961), 394; P. Barguet, *Le temple d'Amon-rê à Karnak* (Cairo, 1961), 135.

Specter or Reality? The Question of Egyptian Influence on Israel of the Monarchy

IT WOULD BE passing strange if Israel and Judah during the Iron Age lived out their relatively brief lives as independent states wholly isolated from influences emanating from the closest major nation-state in the region, Egypt. (The two capitals, Jerusalem and Samaria, are only 440 and 470 kilometers distant from Memphis respectively). And yet if one is perfectly frank, one will have to admit that signs of Egyptian influence in the Bible, or specific borrowings by Israelite culture, are remarkably few and certainly do not pop out instantly, at least upon a cursory reading of the Bible. Where then are they; or are we mistaken in our prior assumption? Certainly the culture of the ancient Hebrews, with roots in their nomadic, Shasu past, borrowed most heavily from Canaan and their congeners who lived in Syria and on the coast. Israel was a community of speakers of the Canaanite language of the West Semitic subfamily, and their way of life and material culture were endemic to the Levant. With Egypt they had never in the formative period of their history come into direct contact; and Pharaoh had always appeared to them, in the borrowed vision of the Canaanite townspeople, as a severe master and almost a tyrant.

Yet for five centuries the impact of the Egyptian empire had been felt all along the western horn of the fertile crescent; and although it diminished with the disintegration of the empire it by no means ceased altogether. We are perfectly justified, therefore, in searching for traces of Egyptian influence in the Bible, if the search is undertaken in a balanced and reasoned manner and if certain caveats are kept in mind.

First, it serves no scholarly purpose to let enthusiasm loose, cast caution to the wind, and conjure up an Egyptian word or phrase behind every Hebrew *hapax*, or an Egyptian custom behind every otherwise unexplained Hebrew practice. Not so long ago a welcome reaction set in against a like tendency to imagine Old Testament scripture shot through with an all pervasive, "Pan-Babylonian" influence. God forbid that a "Pan-Egyptianism" should now take its place! As an undergraduate the present writer received a salutary reproof from his Greek history professor when he opted as an essay topic for "Foreign Influence in Art of the Archaic Period." Eyeing me with that suspicion that only a threatened classicist can have for one involved in a Near East training, the old man muttered: "Very well, you may do it. But I'll not have you concluding it all came from Egypt!" Regardless of his motives, the professor's ire sounded a note of caution: scholarly commitment to a particular area or discipline should not be turned into a sort of biased apologetic.

Second, even if a word, motif, practice, or artifact that probably has an Egyptian origin can be isolated, one cannot automatically assume that the Hebrews of the monarchy borrowed it directly from contemporary Egypt. The legacy of the Bronze Age empire of Egypt had been considerable, and it is unthinkable that it should not have survived for the Hebrews to draw on. Because of the drastic reduction in the number of written sources for the 21st through 24th Dynasties, it becomes substantially more difficult than it was in the New Kingdom to describe in specific detail the culture of Egypt during the Tanite or Libyan hegemony.

Third, it is a fact that during the Iron II period Judah and (especially) Israel enjoyed much closer contact with the Phoenician coast than with the Nile. Styles in art and architecture show clearly that Israel borrowed Egyptian motifs via the Phoenicians; and if that is the case, why not lexical items and ideas as well? In short, whatever stray Egyptian influences we find may simply reinforce our belief in the "Phoenician connection."

THE IDEOLOGY OF KINGSHIP

We begin in the realm of kingship. Here a vast gulf seems to be fixed between the divine kingship of the Pharaohs, dogmatically expressed in mythological instruments and fundamental to the concept of the Egyptian state, and the much paler, ephemeral image of the Israelite monarchy. The mythological identity and role of Pharaoh had been established during the first half of the third millennium B.C., and the royal cult fixed it immutable for all time.[1] The king of Egypt was the avatar of the dynastic patron Horus on earth, son of the sun-god, enjoying at death an apotheosis as the chthonic Osiris. Guarantor of the fertility of the land, defeator of the forces of chaos, divine celebrant of the cult, upholder of the order of the universe, Pharaoh towered over creation like some elemental deity descended to earth. Changing times, of course, brought modifications. In the second millennium the king's earthly function comes to the fore.[2] He has been selected by the gods; he appears as the likeness of his father the

---

[1] On Egyptian kingship studies are legion. See in particular H. Frankfort, *Kingship and the Gods* (Chicago, 1949); H. W. Fairman, in S. H. Hooke, ed., *Myth, Ritual and Kingship* (Oxford, 1958), 74–104; G. Posener, *De la divinité du pharaon* (Paris, 1960); W. Barta, *Untersuchungen zur Göttlichkeit des regierenden Königs* (Munich, 1975); D. Lorton, *JAOS* 99 (1979), 460ff.

[2] See D. B. Redford, "Kingship in the 18th Dynasty," in *Symposium on Egyptian Kingship* (Denver, forthcoming).

sun. Great stress is laid on his physical strength, his military acumen, his inventiveness, and his human intelligence. By the beginning of the first millennium foreigners sat on the throne(s) of Egypt, and there is a further weakening in the bond between mythical role and terrestrial reality. The once prestigious title "king" becomes little more than a synonym for "head of state." City rulers who call themselves "king" proliferate at a single moment in time, and we are not sure that the resultant travesty done to the Horus myth was born in upon the Egyptian mind.[3] The link between ruler as protégé and a particular deity who selects or extends the aegis becomes firmer during the first half of the first millennium.[4]

The Hebrew monarchy, on the other hand, belongs to a Levantine kind of kingship markedly different from that of Egypt.[5] Here the king is a "latecomer," beneficiary of a charisma bestowed on him, but bound by a contractual agreement with his people, and with the national god. As a "soter" figure he leads in battle and administers justice, but is beholden to the national god, whose surrogate and agent he is. As leader of a nation but lately freed from a nomadic state, he boasts kinship and long lineage; yet he is selected by the deity and maintains his approval. In many ways the Hebrew king is thus something of a "middleman" between god and people, in much the same manner as the ḫazānu of Late Bronze Age Canaan was the intermediary between his people and Pharaoh. He was under the loyalty oath, as the king was under the covenant: both stood in the position of vassals.

In neither origin, formulation, nor ideology, therefore, are the Egyptian and Hebrew monarchies comparable; but self-conscious sociopolitical structures that have achieved a degree of sophistication may well mimic admired parallels. Is this the case with the monarchy in Israel?

Even here it is difficult to discern an "Egyptian veneer" in the practices and concepts of the Israelite kingship. In rites of inauguration, for example, it is often claimed that the "statute" (Psalm 2:7) and "testament" (2 Kings 11:12) that were part of the coronation ritual in Judah designate a "fivefold titulary" of Egyptian type;[6] but the Hebrew words in question

---

[3] For the condition of Egypt in the eighth century, see p. 335–6.

[4] M. A. Bonhême, Les noms royaux dans l'Égypte de la 3ème période intermediare (Cairo, 1987), 266ff.; Tanis, Bubastis, Herakleopolis, and Hermopolis, where "kingships" are attested for the eighth century B.C., all were dominated by gods with "royal" connections.

[5] The Hebrew concept of kingship has spawned a wide variety of literature: see, among others, G. Buccellati, Cities and Nations of Ancient Syria (Rome, 1967); I. Engnell, Studies in the Divine Kingship in the Ancient Near East (Oxford, 1967); B. Halpern, The Constitution of the Monarchy in Israel (Chicago, 1981); T. Ishida, The Royal Dynasties in Ancient Israel (Berlin, 1977); A. R. Johnson, Sacred Kingship in Ancient Israel (Cardiff, 1967); T.N.D. Mettinger, King and Messiah (Lund, 1987); K. W. Whitlaw, The Just King (Sheffield, 1979).

[6] G. von Rad, Gesammelte Studien zum Alten Testament (Munich, 1961), 205ff.

have absolutely nothing to do with setting the royal name.[7] The naming of the messianic king in Isaiah 9:6 has been likened to the five-part pharaonic title or "great name," but the Hebrew has four names, none of which sounds remotely Egyptian.[8] And that the poignant story of the unfortunate offspring of the union of David and Bathsheba recalls the concept of the royal *ka* in ancient Egypt is forced, tendentious, and insensitive to the loftiness of the plane on which the Hebrew story is written.[9]

The anointing of the king in Israel and Judah was a rite integral to the royal investiture.[10] By contrast, although in Egypt anointing as a symbol seems to have been excluded from the coronation rites,[11] it is attested in the appointment of officials and vassals.[12] Whether this provides the Hebrew ritual with a meaningful parallel, the king being now Yahweh's officer and vassal is an intriguing though ingenious notion. On the other hand, there is good evidence for the common practice of anointing at coronation throughout the monarchic communities in western Asia, at least in the Late Bronze Age;[13] thus the phenomenon in Israel may be an indigenous development rather than a borrowing from Egypt. As for accoutrements, it has been claimed that the Hebrew word for "crown," *nezer*, derives from an Egyptian word *nsr*, "flame," which is used of the uraeus serpent on the king's headdress and by metonymy of the crown itself.[14] While it is true that the Egyptian double crown and the *atef*-crown passed into Levantine iconography in the Iron Age,[15] if not before, it is not at all certain that they were actually used as headgear by the rulers of the Palestinian states. Linguistically the equation of *nezer* and *nsr* looks suspect: the Egyptian word would undoubtedly have been carried over into the first millennium Hebrew as *nes(er)*, not *nezer*.[16] Solomon's

---

[7] K. A. Kitchen, *Ancient Orient and Old Testament* (London, 1966), 106ff.

[8] For the use of a fivefold designation in Egyptian literature apart from king's name, see H. Ranke, *ZÄS* 79 (1954), 72; for the Isaiah passage, see A. Alt, in *Festschrift Alfred Bertholet* (Tübingen, 1950); cf. also S. Morenz, *ZÄS* 79 (1954), 73–74.

[9] N. Wyatt, *UF* 19 (1987), 399–404.

[10] Cf. Mettinger, *King and Messiah*, 185ff. and n. 1 (references).

[11] Barta, *Untersuchungen zur Göttlichkeit des Regierenden Königs*, 45–50.

[12] E. Kutsch, *Salbung als Rechtsakt im Alte Testament und im alten Orient* (Berlin, 1963), 34ff.; E. Martin-Pardey, *LdÄ* 5 (1984), 367–69.

[13] Cf. KBo I, 14 rev. 6–10: see now A. Harrack, *Assyria and Hanigalbat* (Hildesheim, 1987), 74.

[14] M. Görg *BN* 3 (1977), 26; 4 (1977), 7–8, in the wake of Sethe, Ember, and Calice; R. Gundlach, in M. Görg, ed., *Feschrift Elmar Edel* (Bamberg, 1979), 210.

[15] W. F. Albright, *Archaeology of Palestine* (Harmondsworth, 1949), pl. 12 (Balu'ah stela); H. Frankfort, *Art and Architecture of the Ancient Orient* (Harmondsworth, 1954), pl. 168 (Phoenician ivories); for other iconographic influences, see A. J. 'Amr, *PEQ* 120 (1980), 55–63.

[16] Cf. Coptic NHC from Egyptian *nsr*, "flame": J. Osing, *Die Nominalbildung des Ägyptischen* (Mainz, 1976), 178.

throne with its lion armrests (1 Kings 10:18–20) certainly recalls Egyptian prototypes common from Amarna times to the 20th Dynasty; but it would seem to have entered the Israelite sphere through the medium of Phoenician craftsmanship.[17] The royal psalms sometimes confront us with the concept of the king as the son, or image, of god (cf. especially Psalms 2, 8, 72, and 110), although it must be admitted that the notion is but lightly stressed in the surviving literature. This may derive in some vague way from Egypt,[18] although in the historical depictions of the kings of Judah and Israel in the Books of Kings it plays almost no role at all. In conclusion it may be said that, whatever Mesopotamian influence may be evident in the nature of Hebrew kingship, the Egyptian contribution was minimal. The Levantine form of monarchy developed largely autochthonously.

GOVERNMENT FUNCTIONARIES AND MECHANISMS

For half a century it has been commonplace to look for parallels to the officials of the Hebrew kingdoms (especially those named in 2 Samuel 8:16–18, 20:23–26 and 1 Kings 4:2–6) in the government offices of neighboring Egypt.[19] David and Solomon, it is argued, in setting up a bureaucracy where none had before existed, would have stood in need of a model, and what better model than that provided by the centuries old and highly efficient civil service of Egypt? The Canaanite "city-states" that the Hebrew kingdom had supplanted were deemed to have been too small and parochial in their outlook for Israel to have copied them: the "empire" in any case was a quantum leap above the "city-state." Moreover, awareness of the Egyptian administration could not have been acquired by slow, cultural osmosis, for the matter was immediate and pressing. No, Egyptian scribes themselves must have been present at the Jerusalem court in an advisory capacity.

Now several caveats ought to be expressed before we swallow this ar-

---

[17] See F. Canciane and G. Pettinato, *ZDMG* 81 (1965), 103–8.

[18] Cf. J. de Savignac, *VT* 7 (1957), 82–90; Mettinger, *King and Messiah*, 265–74; cf. Görg *BN* 3 (1977), 7–13; V. A. Toben, in S. Groll, ed., *Pharaonic Egypt, the Bible and Christianity* (Jerusalem, 1985), 237–48. The charming image of Psalm 110:1 of the king sitting beside the deity with his enemies beneath his feet recalls the common statue type from Egypt depicting king and god seated side by side, with the "nine bows" beneath their feet or depicted on the sides of the dais: O. Keel, *Die Welt des Altorient in Bildsymbolik* (Zurich, 1972), 233, 240, 246.

[19] The principal advocates are R. de Vaux, *RB* 48 (1939), 394–405; idem, *Les institutions de l'ancien Testament* (Paris, 1961), 183–203; J. Begrich, *ZAW* 58 (1940), 1–29; E. W. Heaton, *Solomon's New Men* (London, 1974); T.N.D. Mettinger, *Solomonic State Officials* (Lund, 1974); Ishida, *Royal Dynasties*, 68; cf. also U. Rutersworden, *Die Beamten des israelitischen Königszeit* (Stuttgart, 1985).

gument whole. In the first place, the case is entirely a priori. I know of no Biblical passage that names an Egyptian scribe at the court of either David or Solomon; nor is there a single title in the Hebrew civil service that is a straight transcription or even translation of an Egyptian original.[20] Second, while the vast majority of Late Bronze Age towns in Canaan were small affairs—"city-state" is a much too grandiose title for most of them—the coastal towns were much more sophisticated and fully as large as the Judaean community for which Jerusalem functioned as a capital. The natural routes of contact from hillcountry to coast would have put the Hebrews in touch with those models first. Finally, the day-to-day functioning of a state in its relative degree of complexity and its specific nature arises out of local conditions of society, economy, and demography; and it poses mainly practical problems. State mechanisms developed elsewhere may be transplanted, but only if similar conditions prevail and if they have proved themselves practicable. Titles likewise will spontaneously take form with the local purview and function of the officer in question in mind, and will be borrowed without modification only for purposes of enhancing prestige.

The Levantine state the administration of which we know most from contemporary sources is Byblos. In the second quarter of the eleventh century B.C. the report of Wenamun gives us a vivid picture of the Byblian court, albeit through the eyes of an Egyptian who could not control the local dialect and therefore might be prone to postulate an Egyptian institution or use an Egyptian term when at a loss for the appreciation of the Canaanite form. The headman Zakar-Ba'al, undoubtedly a "king" in his own eyes, is accorded the title "chief" pursuant to Egyptian practice; and his personal scribe, *sōpēr* in Phoenician, becomes a "letter-scribe" to Wenamun (2, 64). In fact he does write a letter once, but then doubles as the messenger (2, 34, 37), and also functions as a food purveyor (2, 68). In keeping with its location, Byblos has a "harbor master" (1, 43) and a labor force with supervisors for the cutting of timber (2, 42–43). For consultation, advice, and physical support the king can call on "his council" (2, 71),[21] and his court is made up of, among other groups we may presume, a cadre of adolescent "pages" (1, 38–39).[22] Zakar-Ba'al does indeed have Egyptians in his employ, but they seem more a showy luxury for a town proud of its long association with the Nile: a butler Penamun (2, 46), and a singer Tanno (2, 69).[23] Yet Zakar-Ba'al apparently under-

---

[20] That the "Shisha" who in 1 Chron. 18:16 is listed as a scribe of David bears a name-form influenced by the Egyptian term for letter-scribe (*sš š't*: cf. A. Cody, *RB* 72 [1965], 381–93) is very doubtful: cf. Rutersworden, *Beamten*, 88, n. 126.

[21] *mw'd* = Hebrew *mō'ed*; J. Wilson, *JNES* 4 (1945), 245.

[22] So long ago, and rightly, Golénischef: see G. Posener, *RdE* 21 (1969), 147.

[23] For other Egyptian singers at Canaanite courts, see H. Hickman, *Le métier de musicien au temps des pharaons* (Paris, 1954), 286–87.

stands Egyptian and can conceivably write a stela inscription in hieroglyphics (2, 59–60).

Byblos is probably typical of that kind of coastal city to which Ashkelon, Gaza, and even Tel Fara belonged, in which a basically Canaanite
administration is veneered with a number of "luxury" functions inspired
by Egyptian originals. It is a moot point as to whether such pretensions
were suggested only by the presence of expatriot Egyptians to fill the
roles.

Whether Jerusalem belongs in the "Byblian" category may be the subject of debate; but the evidence is far more difficult to use to prove this
association than the data of Wenamun. Leaving aside the suspect nature
of the three lists,[24] the nature of the officials' spheres of responsibility
under David and Solomon arise for the most part out of the substance of
the Davidic and Solomonic traditions. There is a commander of the host
and a commander of the royal bodyguard—these owe nothing to Egypt—
and a bevy of priests, kōhenīm, an autochthonous function with no Egyptian overtones whatsoever. The officer charged with the "corvée" perpet-
uates the supervision of a mechanism of major work projects known from
Amarna times;[25] but the Egyptian official responsible for the same kind
of labor in Egypt bore an entirely different title—"royal scribe and superintendent of recruits"—and his field of activity was broader.[26] "He-who-
is-over-the-house" (i.e., the palace), if derived from a literal rendering of
an Egyptian original, poses a conundrum, for the ḥry-pr was a much less
important officer, and "vizier" with whom the title is often compared
enjoyed an infinitely broader purview as head of the entire civil service.
And if the Hebrew king possessed one or two "scribes" (sōferīm), so did
Penamum of Samal or Zakir of Lu'ash or Azitawadda of the house of
mpš. There is absolutely no reason to drum up a supposed Egyptian function as inspiration. Writing up accounts was far too basic a need, and
there is no evidence that Elihoreph or Akhiya wrote in hieratic.

The one title that, more than others, has led scholars to imagine an
Egyptian Vorlage is mazkir, "remembrancer" (in Septuagint), which has

[24] The ordering of the lists seems in part to be a pale reflection of the status and order of
entry of the dramatis personae. Thus in lists 1 and 2 (Temp. David), Joab occupies first
position; while in the third the son of the priest instrumental in putting Solomon on the
throne takes precedence. Elsewhere the genealogical sequence poses problems. While it is
conceivable that a long-lived Jehoshaphat should have served both David and Solomon as
mazkir, is it possible that Zadok and Abiathar, of the generation of Saul, should still have
been in office under Solomon? Further: list 1 hops from the military to the civil to the sacerdotal, back to the civil, then the military and finally to the sacerdotal again in a much less
satisfying manner than list 2 or even 3.

[25] I. Mendelsohn, BASOR 167 (1962), 31–35; A. F. Rainey, IEJ 20 (1970), 191–202;
Rutersworden, Beamten, 72–73.

[26] D. B. Redford, Akhenaten, the Heretic King (Princeton, N.J., 1984), 47.

been equated with *wḥmw* from a root WḤM, meaning "to repeat, do again, act a second time." But not only is the meaning of the root fundamentally different, the derived function diverges as well. For the *wḥmw* is one "who stands in for . . . ," "a representative," a "front man," and in his function comes close to what, in terms of the modern U.S. presidency, would be the "White House chief of staff."[27] He has nothing whatsoever to do with "calling to remembrance."

In the mechanics of government we may well expect to find some parallels to Egyptian practice, and are not in fact embarrassed in this hope. As hinted already, the imposition of the corvée (or forced labor) in the era of Solomon probably owes much to its common practice formerly during the Late Bronze Age within the bounds of the Egyptian empire in Canaan. The writer has elsewhere pointed out the parallel between Solomon's twelve districts, designated one per month to supply the court with food, and the Egyptian practice of dividing the tax base into twelve parts to meet an ongoing budgetary requirement on a calendrical basis.[28] Others have compared the occasional use in Egypt of the "coregency" as a means of smoothly bridging two reigns with a similar dyarchy in Israel from David on, even though in tenth-century Egypt it is not attested.[29]

One postulated ingredient in the political makeup of ancient Israel, which is often contrasted with the absolutism of Egypt, is the tendency toward democracy that issued, it is alleged, in a sort of bicameral assembly under the monarchy.[30] Now "democracy" is one of the most misused terms of our era, being treated at one and the same time as a synonym for representative elective government, social justice, equality before the law, freedom of speech and assembly, and even a humanistic approach to life in general. This semantic spread in the range of the word's application does not, moreover, result from fuzzy thinking, but seems to be a subtle and unwarranted attempt to derive all the basic "goods" from a specific system of government, an evolutionary scheme at variance with historic

[27] The writer is preparing a brief treatise on the *wḥmw*.

[28] D. B. Redford, in J. W. Wevers and D. B. Redford, *Studies in the Palestinian World* (Toronto, 1972), 141–56; the mechanism is too old and widespread in Egypt to admit of a reversed direction of influence: A. R. Green, *BASOR* 233 (1979), 59ff.; on Solomon's tax districts, see Y. Aharoni, *TA* 3 (1976), 5–16.

[29] E. Ball, *VT* 27 (1977), 268–79; W. H. Shea, *ZDPV* 101 (1985), 15. Yet coregency as a mechanism too obviously stems from practical necessity to have been borrowed. Note how often in the past fifty years vice-presidents in the United States have become president (Truman, Johnson, Nixon, Bush); this admittedly was not "programmed" in the system, still less copied from some other, but its practical value has begun to dawn on the electorate.

[30] Cf. A. Malamat, *JNES* 22 (1963), 247–53 (where such "loaded" terms as "consultative bodies," "political assembly," "citizens," and "representative institutions" are freely bandied about); D. G. Evans, *JNES* 25 (1966), 273–79; Mettinger, *King and Messiah*, 111–30.

fact.[31] For order, freedom, fair dealing, and humanitarianism characterize a society because of its specific ethnicity, history, and social custom, and do not arise out of that society's predilection for any particular form of government, democratic or otherwise. It is better, therefore, in the present case to return to a literal understanding of the term as "rule by the *demos*, or enfranchised body of citizens."

On this definition one cannot find the institution anywhere in the ancient Near East during historic times. The very concept of a "citizen"—a free man owing loyalty to his *polis* or city-community, with the entailment of rights and duties—is wholly alien to thinking in the ancient Near East, including that of the rustic Levantine enclaves of which the Hebrews formed a part. In the Levant the individual was, from the perspective of the state, nought but "a live one" (our "warm body"), a "head" or "counted one,"[32] a "servant (subject)" without even so basic a right as freedom of movement.[33] And there is no use in pointing to the occasional phenomenon of the "assembly" or "council" in an effort to establish the case for "primitive democracy," for such convocations of selected members of the community were ubiquitous throughout the area, including such states as the undemocratic regime of the Pharaohs. Already in Ugaritic we hear of the ʿd, "the conclave," and the phr (or mphr), "the assembly,"[34] and Iron Age Phoenicia has given us the mʿd, "the scheduled council," and the mphrt, "the assembly."[35] Egypt too throws up during most periods of its history the "council" or "board of magistrates."[36] But none of these bodies is elective in our modern sense, though undoubtedly deemed representative of the population at large in an ill-defined way.[37]

[31] My basic freedom derives from *habeas corpus*, and certain fundamental principles of Germanic society and Roman law. The former is a royal writ, and in my day has been suspended by democratically elected governments, always of course in the interests of the public safety. The extension of the franchise may prevent one from attaining unconstitutional power, but it cannot guarantee that a blackguard, sadist, or simpleton will not represent us. With a majority of red-necks in the electorate, a modern democratic state cannot avoid barbarism.

[32] Hebrew *nephesh*, "breathing (human) thing"; Egyptian *tp* "head", or *ḥsb* "counted one."

[33] Buccelati, *Cities and Nations*, 58–61.

[34] C. H. Gordon, *Ugaritic Textbook Glossary* (Rome, 1965), nos. 1816, 2037.

[35] See p. 370; R. S. Tomback, *A Comparative Semitic Lexicon of the Phoenician and Punic Languages* (Ann Arbor, Mich., 1978), 191. With the disappearance of monarchy in the Phoenician cities, these councils were, as institutionalized oligarchies, to form the backbone of the administration: D. Harden, *The Phoenicians* (Harmondsworth, 1971), 71–72.

[36] S. Gabra, *Les conseils de fonctionnaires dans l'Égypte pharaonique* (Cairo, 1929); A. Theodorides, *RIDA* 16 (1969), 109ff.; idem, *AIPHOS* 22 (1978), 83ff.; D. Meeks, *Année lexicographie* (Paris, 1980), 1:388–89.

[37] It is quite unwarranted, e.g., to read into references in the EA to "the people of town X" something like a "popular assembly" (Ishida, *Royal Dynasties*, 20), or to employ such

Mode of selection to these councils and assemblies at present escapes us, although age and family probably weighed heavily. All were administrative and consultative, with additional juridicial obligations; none was a legislative organ. Israel was a member of the cultural world that produced this governmental organ, and differs in no way from its neighbors. The story of 1 Kings 12 is not history writing but folklore, in which the "old men" represent the prudence of age, and the "young men" the rashness of youth. To read into the story a bicameral legislature is not only poor judgment—could anyone be so insensitive to literary motifs?—but it smacks of the perverseness of wishful thinking. In Israel in early times we are justified in postulating the existence of little more than a tribal or communal "moot," scarcely different in nature or purpose from the early Germanic institution.[38]

KÖNIGSNOVELLE

Over fifty years ago the German Egyptologist Alfred Hermann was so impressed by the *Tendenz* and literary forms of a group of Egyptian texts that center upon certain acts of the king that he coined the term *Königsnovella*, or "royal romance" to define them. Although each is clearly based on a historic incident, the facts have undergone a "poetical" embellishment consonant with Egyptian political concepts and Pharaoh the individual has disappeared behind the mask of Pharaoh the archetype. Stress is laid on such themes as the king's superior intelligence, his piety toward the gods, their favor for him (often vouchsafed in dreams), the spontaneous adulation of mankind (represented by the court), and the success of his mighty deeds.

It is important to remember that the *Königsnovella* is not a formal genre—Biblical scholars sometimes appear to be treating it as such—nor does the word itself correspond to any ancient Egyptian technical term. In Egyptian there is no word or phrase that can be translated "royal romance." Hermann's examples comprise a heterogeneous lot that displays in common nought but a focus on a deed of the king and a heavy literary treatment. If we range in review a representative sample of the type of text Hermann is addressing (Table 5), we can better appreciate the disparate nature of the material.

---

pretentious terms as "voice of the people" (P. Artzi, *RA* 58 [1964], 159–66), "urban representative institutions," or the like (H. Reviv, *JESHO* 12 [1969], 283–97). These leave the impression of "democratic" tendencies, when all we in fact have evidence of is a gerontocracy of elders or an oligarchy of landowners. In some cases, monarchic states can be referred to in legal documents by reference to their people alone without mention of their king: Buccelati, *Cities and Nations*, 58; 64, n. 173.

[38] Tacitus, *Germania* 11–12; *OCD*², 464.

TABLE 5.
Examples of *Königsnovelle*

	Type	*Topos*
Montuhotep I?	—	—
Senwosret I, Berlin leather role	Royal audience record	Court's adulation
Senwosret I, Tod, Elephantine and Theban stelae	Embellished, daybook and royal audience record	—
Neferrenpet stela	Embellished, royal audience record?	Courtier's advice, king-in-library
Kamose stela	Triumph stela, royal authorship?	King-rejects-counsel
Thutmose III annals Thutmose III Gebel Barkal	Embellished, daybook and royal audience record	King-rejects-counsel. Court's adulation
Thutmose III 7th pylon	Royal audience record	Court's adulation
Amenophis II Sphinx stela	"Collection of mighty deeds"	—
Thutmose IV Dream stela	Derived from the "Collection of mighty deeds"	Dream
Akhenaten's "inaugural"	Royal audience record	[Court's adulation]
Redesiyeh stela	Royal audience record	[Court's adulation]
Kubban stela	Royal audience record	Court's adulation
Inscription dedicatoire	Royal audience record	Court's adulation
Luxor building text	Embellished, royal audience record?	[Courtier's advice? King-in-library]
Manshiet el-Sadr	Daybook and royal audience record	—
Piankhy Tanwetaman	Thorough literary treatment on basis of eyewitnesses	King-rejects-counsel Dream
Thutmose II (Aswan stela) Sety I (Karnak stela) Sety I (Beth Shean stela)	"One came to tell His Majesty . . ."— daybook with heavy embellishment	Exasperation of the king

TABLE 5. (*continued*)
Examples of *Königsnovelle*

	Type	Topos
Merenptah (Karnak stela)	—	Dream
Ramesses IV (Abydos stela)	Royal authorship?	King-in-library
Smendes (Silsileh text)	—	—
Sheshonk I (Ehnasya stela)	Day-book with embellishment	Brilliance of king's son

In all cases the particular historical incident that is chosen for publication in stela form, suitably embellished, comes from the roster of what might well be called the "mighty acts of the king." The building or restoration of temples, the fashioning of statues, selection by gods—all illustrate the divinity of the king and his physical prowess and intellectual genius. But none of the resultant creations can be subscribed under a single heading insofar as source and form are concerned, and "royal romance" is a singularly inappropriate term from the standpoint both of the ancients' approach to the subject and of the moderns' attempt to make sense of it.

The sources (in order of frequency) that underly the pieces in Table 5 are four: the record of a "royal audience" (*ḥmst-nsw*); the daybook of the king's house; a special commissioned treatment; and a "collection of the mighty deeds." The royal audience (literally, "sitting of the king," "royal seance") was a formal convening of the court, common during the Middle and New Kingdom, at which the king delivered a speech usually of intent, occasionally of report. A modern parallel might be the speech from the throne, or the U. S. president's periodic address to Congress, in both of which future policy and report of past success are often considered. The daybook of the king's house is the journal kept by a royal secretary in which is recorded the day-by-day accounting of income and disbursement and the record of events of significance in the life of the government. A few of the stelae cited previously are accounts either commissioned or authored by the king, involving much royal diction, but which derive from neither a formal speech nor a journal entry. Finally, the "collection of mighty deeds" (of the king) is a designation given (anciently) to a genre of chatty court prose or poetry, intended for dissemination, in which the accomplishments of the king in sport and war are celebrated.

In almost all cases a brief, laconic record in the source has provided the basis for the text as we have it. The record has been embellished by the use of images and terms that are part of the stock-in-trade of one who composes in the oral tradition; and a number of stock topoi have become standard. These include the court's spontaneous "applause" at the conclusion of the king's speech, the council's advice to the monarch (usually conservative and usually rejected), the king's recourse to the library to consult a reference book, the god's will communicated in a dream, and the arrival of a messenger with bad news.

In none of these widely differing genres can we detect anything remotely comparable with any extant piece in Hebrew literature. As we have seen, the status of Pharaoh and the adulation this called forth finds no real parallel in Israel; and the dream topos is so common in folklore that it serves no purpose in eliciting "Biblical visions" as parallels to the *Königsnovella*. Needless to say, the other topoi characteristic of the Egyptian pieces are conspicuous by their absence from Hebrew literature.

AKHENATEN AND MOSES: THE CLASSIC "RED HERRING"

One "discovery" that never ceases to fill the hearts of students and laymen with modest pride and their eyes with the light of recognition is the alleged similarity between the religion Akhenaten preached and "Mosaic monotheism." Even Freud was carried away by what he perceived to be more than a superficial resemblance,[39] and later writers, not so familiar with the primary sources, have made of Akhenaten a teacher of Moses and a forerunner of Christ.[40] Were not the Israelites in Egypt for a 430-year period spanning the Amarna age, and, if the Exodus be dated to the reign of Ramesses II, might not the (then) 80-year old Moses have lived part of his life under Akhenaten?[41] Do not, in fact, a number of later independent historians, including Manetho, date Moses and the bondage to the Amarna period?[42] Surely it is self-evident that the monotheism preached at Mount Sinai is to be traced back ultimately to the teachings of Akhenaten, the heretic king. Even those who would deny direct contact nonetheless allow themselves to compare the two systems and to marvel at the points of similarity.

A note of caution, however, ought to have been struck if and when the enthusiastic investigator delved a little deeper into the matter. For if he

[39] S. Freud, *Moses and Monotheism* (New York, 1959).

[40] Redford, *Akhenaten*, 226, 232.

[41] On the flights of fancy that can result from the attempt to intermesh the literal Biblical text with Egyptian history, see especially H. H. Rowley, *From Joseph to Joshua* (London, 1950), 70–71 and passim.

[42] See p. 260.

did, he would have learned that the Exodus is most unlikely to have occurred when and under the conditions and involving the people the Pentateuch says it did.[43] In fact probably no part of the Israelites was even in Egypt during the New Kingdom in a capacity that later gave rise to the Sojourn and Bondage narratives. With the prima facie probability thus removed, the conscientious student would be hard put to persevere with the comparison.

Nonetheless the label "monotheism" often provides the incentive to continue in disregard of the historical facts; and in any case no one ought a priori to discourage a comparison (although in retrospect it may be deemed a waste of time). But in the comparison one must avoid the pitfall of assuming greater significance for an alleged point of contact than is actually the case. It is easy to point to aspects of activity, universality, divine sonship, justice, and messianism in both Israelite and Amarna belief, but these are so widespread in all ancient religions (including the normative religion of Egypt) that to posit specific contact is quite misleading.

One question that arises at the outset has to do with what we are comparing. On the one side Amarna "religion" seems clear, in terms of textual sources, chronological limits, and content. "Mosaic monotheism," on the other hand, is a will-o'-the-wisp. Most scholars would deny that, in the thirteenth century B.C., the traditional time slot for Moses, the Hebrews had in their religious thought approached anywhere near the exalted plane of "monotheism," preferring to see the prophetic movement of the Iron Age culminating in Jeremiah and Deutero–Isaiah as the point when there crystallized a sophisticated concept of the supernatural to which the appellative "monotheism" might be applied. Shall we then isolate the religion of Israel in the thirteenth century and compare that with Akhenaten's beliefs? Or shall we allow ourselves to squeeze in Israel's monarchic concepts of the ninth century to provide us with comparable material? And can we by stretching a point include the advanced concepts of a Deutero-Isaiah of the sixth to fifth centuries in our conception? What results unfortunately from this fudging is a grand mélange of points amassed from over nine hundred years of evolution, which are then compared with a specific, heretical movement pinpointed to a single generation in time.[44] Such a comparison is obviously meaningless.

A second question that might be posed has to do with nomenclature: is "religion" the appropriate term for both phenomena? Adoration of the supernatural by the community in a prescribed manner, involving a ritual,

---

[43] See p. 408ff.

[44] This, it seems to me, mars what is otherwise a very useful comparison by V. A. Tobin: see *Pharaonic Egypt, The Bible and Christianity* (Jerusalem, 1983), 231ff.

a code of conduct, and a divine-human relationship constitutes a fair description of ancient Hebrew religion, but not Akhenaten's program. Hebrew religion, at least in the formative stage in which we see it in the later Iron Age, is credal, involving a confession of faith in Yahweh.[45] What Akhenaten put forward in no way involves a creed; it is more a royal statement regarding the king's relationship with his father than a religion of the people. As such it thrusts a teaching role upon the monarch in which he, as the sole individual privy to god's will, is obliged to make plain to the people the nature of god and the king's place in creation. There is nothing comparable in early Hebrew religion with the "teaching" of Akhenaten:[46] no one fills an essential didactic role, and, when later the prophets emerge, they prove to be outside the system. For Hebrew religion is essentially indigenous to a particular ethnic group, and underwent a natural evolution over centuries of prehistory. Akhenaten's program is a self-conscious modification of an existing system, undertaken at a known point in time, based in the highest circles of the realm and involving a contretemps with a coterie of high officials.[47]

If now we begin our comparison by attempting to isolate the natures of the deities Akhenaten's program and the early Hebrew religion put to the fore, we encounter a marked, nay a jarring, contrast. For Akhenaten's god is celestial and solar, identified as "light" and the "sun disk"; he creates brightness and therefore his own essence.[48] The name by which he is known is not new, but in its formulation sums up the nature of the god exactly: "Re-harakhty is he who rejoices in the Horizon in his name 'Light which is in/from the sun disk.' " By contrast the Hebrew god Yahweh displays atmospheric and chthonic traits, being intimately associated with the wind, earthquake, fire, and thunder. Light by no means constitutes the essence of this god. In late metaphorical jargon it may be associated with him in the same way as in most ancient cultures it is conjured as a symbol of purity and truth. In the accepted folk tradition he is a new deity, unknown to the fathers, by the name "Yahweh." As a personality, the sun disk is a pale cipher, arousing little response in the worshiper. On the other hand, Yahweh is a wrathful, vengeful god prone to violent outbreaks of temper, but also capable of compassion and forgiveness, very much in keeping with the class of Canaanite deities.

For Yahweh is in very truth a power of the environment who reveals himself directly through the cosmos and has little need of an intermediary. When the community of Israel enters the light of history and becomes

[45] On the creed, see G. von Rad, *The Problem of the Hexateuch and Other Essays* (New York, 1966), 1–78.

[46] Tobin, in *Pharaonic Egypt*, 249–50.

[47] Redford, *Akhenaten*.

[48] D. B. Redford, *JARCE* 13 (1976), 53.

self-conscious, Yahweh becomes a "god of history" and his "mighty acts" are bruited abroad, almost as though he were a great king.[49]

The sun disk, on the other hand, is a "timeless" royal deity without any *res gestae*. Where Yahweh is a hero-god whose triumphs are to be trumpeted ad nauseum, the sun disk is a sophisticated symbol, a projection of kingship into the heavens on a universal scale. His name is written in cartouches, and his sway is universal. As he is king in heaven, so his son Akhenaten mirrors his father's kingship on earth.[50] Derived from tendencies already present in religious thought of the earlier 18th Dynasty, universal kingship shared in a sort of diarchy between heaven and earth and is peculiar—and central—to Akhenaten's program.[51] Thus is explained the concentration throughout the reign on such celebrations of royalty as the jubilee, never before celebrated on so grand a scale as in the heretic's third year,[52] the grand "durbar" for the reception of foreign tribute,[53] and the constant bestowal of largesse and rewards on "worthies."

All of this is quite foreign to Yahweh. When Israel graduated to the level of monarchy, the ethnic god naturally partook to a limited extent in the jargon and panoply of this more sophisticated form of government. But the monarchic aspects of Yahwism are wholly peripheral, appearing as part of the hyperbolic metaphor of enthronement Psalms;[54] while universalism is encountered only in the late, fully developed theology of a Deutero-Isaiah (which owes more to the universalist theologies of the sixth to fifth centuries B.C. than to remote Akhenaten).

The modes of representation of the godhead likewise defy comparison. Although Akhenaten throughout his reign shows a progressive aversion to any anthropomorphic or theriomorphic depictions in art or literature of the deity or anything else, he allows himself a symbolized representation of a disk with many arms—an abstraction but nonetheless an icon.[55] Moreover, the new divine symbol forms but a part of a new canon of art designed, apparently, to convey something of the "meaning" of Akhenaten's teaching.[56] In Israel, despite a general aniconic tendency in "state" religion during the Iron Age[57]—what do we know of the earlier formative stage?—there seems to be no reluctance to describe god in literature using

[49] Tobin, in *Pharaonic Egypt*, 261, 265.

[50] Redford, *JARCE* 13 (1976), 49ff.

[51] On the 18th Dynasty concept of kingship, see Redford, "Kingship."

[52] D. B. Redford, *JARCE* 17 (1980), 21–23.

[53] C. Aldred, *Akhenaten, King of Egypt* (London, 1988), 178–81.

[54] Tobin, in *Pharaonic Egypt*, 261, 265.

[55] Redford, *JARCE* 13 (1976), 55–56; idem, *Akhenaten*, 172–75.

[56] On the Amarna style of art, see principally C. Aldred, *Akhenaten and Nefertity* (New York, 1973).

[57] J. S. Holladay, in P. D. Miller et al., eds., *Ancient Israelite Religion* (Philadelphia, 1987), 249ff.

a bold, anthropomorphic vocabulary. Needless to say, Israelite religion is linked at no stage in its history with a distinctive art form.

The central and fundamental position occupied by Akhenaten in the new order knows no parallel among the early Hebrews. He occupies "center stage" in every scene of art, he alone knows his "father" the sun disk,[58] he receives obeisance and worship equally with the disk. Great stress, perhaps to the point of being the single most important feature of Akhenaten's system, is laid on the filial link with his father the sun disk; and the widest variety of imagery is employed in the texts to describe the relationship.[59] With the Egyptian people the sun disk enjoys no special or direct relationship other than within creation or through the intermediary of his son. As is becoming increasingly clear, the sun disk crystallized in Akhenaten's thinking from an apotheosis of his own father Amenophis III, whose sobriquet significantly was the "Dazzling Sun Disk." This deity could never be a *personal* god, except to his son, and therefore was not imbued with the plebeian quality of compassion.[60] Nor did he demand any particular code of ethical behavior different from what had dominated Egyptian society from time immemorial.

By contrast, Yahweh was very much a god of his people and contained from the outset all the ingredients of a personal deity. A rigid code of ethics is strongly stressed, and becomes an integral part of Hebrew religion, as in all Near East religions. What is more, there existed between him and Israel a bond quite unknown between an Egyptian god and his people, and that was the covenant. Yahweh had chosen Israel and entered into a contractual agreement with it.

We now come to the one aspect of the two gods that more than any other has suggested a point of direct affiliation: the attitude toward plurality of deity. Enough has been written and enough evidence produced to prove beyond a shadow of a doubt that Akhenaten's was an uncompromising monotheism that denied other gods. Not only does the ubiquitous occurrence of such terms as w', "sole, unique," $nn wn ky hr hw.f$, "there is no other of his kind," and the like point in this direction, but the erasure of the plural "gods" and the unequivocal reference to the gods having "ceased" clinch the matter beyond the reach of debate.[61] Along with this uncompromising denial went a rejection of myth, the vehicle through which the gods worked effectively. No myth is told of the sun disk, and his creation is never described in detail.

For the earliest stages in the development of the Hebrew religion, Yahweh is perceived as but one among the gods.

[58] J. Assmann, *SAK* 8 (1980), 15.
[59] Redford, *JARCE* 17 (1980), 25–26.
[60] Ibid., 26.
[61] D. B. Redford, *BES* 3 (1981), 87–102.

As for mythology, although the scriptures as they descended through the filter of the Deuteronomists and the post-Exilic priests have suffered the expurgation of most mythical allusions, enough remains to place Yahweh squarely in the class of Canaanite hero-creator gods. His inaugural battle with the monster "Sea" is recalled by snippets that refer to his dompting of Rahab, Leviathan, or the "Waters."[62] His creation of man from clay and woman from a rib (Gen. 2) is as crass as most foreign contemporary accounts, and the Flood story, though edited by the P-writers, remains within the ambit of a well-known type of myth.

The differences listed here cease to be surprising when one reflects upon the wholly different sociological milieus in which Akhenaten and the early Hebrews fashioned their respective communities. Yahwism was strongly patriarchal, favoring the males and denigrating the females,[63] and accentuating cultic purity and defilement. His cult arrangement had originally been rustic in the extreme, and was preserved fetishlike in later times when a once necessity was now translated into a virtue. Altars were to be constructed of earth or unhewn stone;[64] the god dwelt within the curtains of a portable shrine. When later a private chapel for the king at Jerusalem became the state shrine, there was no doubt that Yahweh dwelt *within* this house, his presence manifest in the mystic Shekinah.

Akhenaten's circle was that of the most sophisticated court in the world, and it stamped his program indelibly. For generations this court had been strongly influenced if not dominated by the royal females, and its customs, life-style, and art are influenced by a sort of feminine energy. Cleanliness and purity were taken for granted. The cult arrangements were reduced to a minimum, but were anything but rustic. Elaborate altars of cut stone and cult paraphernalia of gold and electrum abounded in the centers where worship was carried on. While the simplistic perception of a people from the steppe dictated that Yahweh actually dwelt in his tent, the more sophisticated Egyptian concept promoted the notion that god did not have a terrestrial house: "Heaven is thy temple" sang the hymnist.[65] Earthly shrines comprising open-air courts with offering tables were really viewing places and worshiping centers for the people, not the abode of the sun disk.

THE CULT

When we pass to the cult, it is similarly difficult to find more than a scattering of superficial features that recall Egyptian practices. The Israelite

---

[62] C. Kloos, *Yahweh's Combat with the Sea* (Leiden, 1986).

[63] Cf. Lev. 12:5; Num. 5:11–30, 12:14; Deut. 22:18–21, 25:11–12.

[64] Exod. 20:24–26.

[65] M. Sandman, *Texts from the Time of Akhenaten* (Brussels, 1938), 71:8.

offering cult has long since appeared in its rightful context within the Late Bronze Canaanite tradition, thanks to the evidence from Ugarit. Its festivals are tied to the Levantine agricultural calendar and the Egyptian prototypes suggested seem farfetched.[66] On the other hand major festival cycles of the Egyptian calendar are not represented at all among the Hebrews.[67]

The points of lexical contact or similar procedure one must pass in review are meager in the extreme. The washing off of a magical text written in ink on a papyrus and the drinking of the resultant "water of bitterness" (Num. 5: 23–24) are identical to the very common Egyptian practice of consuming for magical or therapeutic purposes the solution of the ink of a written text with water. The implied apotropaic magic in Psalms 68:2 in which enemies are cursed "as wax melts before the fire" recalls the Egyptian practice of making images of Seth, Apophis, and Pharaoh's enemies of wax and consigning them to the flames.[68] The musical accompaniment of a ritual by a harpist[69] finds a curious parallel in late Libyan Egypt.[70] Certain cult implements have names clearly derived from Egyptian, although this points to loanwords through secular, cultural contact, rather than specifically through the cult.[71] The cult emblem incorporating a bronze serpent (Num. 21:8, 9) called *nes* in Hebrew may well conceal the Egyptian word *nsrt*, "flaming (serpent)," vocalized NHC in the late period.[72] The formal offering of libations to the covenant deity by the heads of the twelve tribal groups (Num. 7:12–88) recalls the periodic libations to the god guaranteeing the peace made by the heads of the twelve principalities in Egypt on the eve of the founding of the 26th Dynasty.[73]

[66] E.g., *Pesaḥ*, "passover," from Egyptian *p³ sḥ* "the sacrifice" (not common in this meaning).

[67] One may cite the royal jubilee rites (the *sed*–festival), the Osirian festivals, those associated with the mortuary cult, the feasts associated with the New Year and the seasons, the fertility rites celebrated in connection with the inundation, the ithyphallic Min and other deities of the same ilk. In origin, form, and ethos, Israel owes nothing to the Egyptian cults.

[68] *Wb* II, 83:7; S. Schosske, *LdÄ* 5 (1984), 1014; R. Fuchs, *LdÄ* 5 (1984), 1090.

[69] 2 Kings 3:15; S. M. Olyan, *Asherah and the Cult of Yahweh in Israel* (Atlanta, 1988), 30–31.

[70] J. Yoyotte, *Les principautés du Delta* (Cairo, 1961), pl. 1; P. Bucher, *Kêmi* 5 (1935), pls. I, II.

[71] Cf. *Kalahat*, "cauldron," (1 Sam. 2:14, Mic. 3:3) from Egyptian *Krht*: M. Ellenbogen, *Foreign Words in the Old Testament* (London, 1962), 149; *'aḥ*, "brazier" (Jer. 36:22–23), from an Egyptian word of the same meaning: Ellenbogen, 21; *paḥ*, "plate" (Exod. 39:3, Num. 17:3) from Egyptian *pḥ³*: ibid., 130.

[72] See n. 16. M. Görg (*BN* 14 [1981], 11ff.) suggests a derivation from the Egyptian *nsw*, "king," and recalls standards consisting of the king's cartouche. There are, however, linguistic and iconographic difficulties to this view.

[73] Herodotus, 2.151. Cf. A. B. Lloyd, *Herodotus Book II. A Commentary* (Leiden, 1988), 3:130.

Some derivatives stretch credulity. Does Hebrew *Še'ol*, "underworld," really come from the Egyptian "Lake of Reeds"?[74] Or do *tōhu* and *bōhu* of Genesis 1:2 derive from the Egyptian roots "to go astray" and "to flee" respectively?[75] That Absalom's pillar (2 Sam. 18:18) should be compared with the Egyptian practice of raising a memorial stela[76] is not convincing.

Certain it is, however, that some of the technical terms designating priestly costume are Egyptian in origin. The "sash" or "girdle" (Hebrew *'abnet*: Exod. 28:4, 29:9, 39:29; Lev. 8:7, 13, etc.) is a loanword from an Egyptian root meaning "to wrap"; while the "ephod" (Exod. 28: 4, 6; 1 Sam. 2:18, 6:14, 22:18, etc.), often of linen, comes from a common Egyptian word for a type of linen perhaps distinguished by the weave.[77]

There is not enough evidence to establish when, or under what circumstances, Israelite culture incorporated these heterogeneous traits. Some, like the items of priestly apparel, clearly go back to Canaanite borrowings during the New Kingdom when Egyptian imperial influence was strong;[78] others, like the folk motif of the twelve tribal heads, may be quite late. Nor is there certainty regarding the route whereby the bequest was effected. Canaanites or Phoenicians could easily have acted as intermediaries, as they did in other matters of culture.[79]

VOCABULARY AND IDIOM

A certain Egyptian influence is discernible in Hebrew vocabulary and imagery, although not perhaps as much as from other West Semitic languages.[80] Again the old problem rears its head: can we always be sure

[74] M. Görg, *BN* 17 (1982), 26–34; Cf. W. Wifall, *ZAW* 92 (1980), 325–32.

[75] Wifall, *ZAW* 92 (1980), 431–34; *BN* (1981), 18–19. *Bohu*, for one, seems an indigenous West Semitic designation of watery chaos: cf. M. Astour, *Hellenosemitica* (Leiden, 1965), 115, n. 6, and 116, n.1; H. W. Atridge and R. A. Oden, Jr., eds., *Philo of Byblos. The Phoenician History* (Washington, D.C., 1981), 80, n. 43.

[76] B. Ockinga, *BN* 31 (1986), 31ff.

[77] I. Friedrich, *Wiener Beiträge zur Theologie* 20 (1968), 32, 47, 52; Ellenbogen, *Foreign Words,* 2; M. Görg, *Biblische Zeitschrift* 20, no. 2 (1976), 242ff. Other terms for items of sacerdotal costume, however, have little to do with Egypt. The word for "bloom," or perhaps "rosette" (*sis*) is West Semitic, and itself descended to Egypt as a loanword in the New Kingdom (*Wb* V, 636), where it is used of the rosette appliqués attached to chariot covers: P. Anastasi IV, 16, 9; R. A. Caminos, *Late Egyptian Miscellanies* (Oxford, 1954), 213. Görg wishes to link Hebrew *me'il*, an overgarment (Koehler-Baumgartner, 2:579), with Egyptian *m'r* known especially (but not exclusively) from the Ptolemaic period: *Wb* II, 49:2; Görg, *Biblische Zeitschrift,* 20 no. 2 (1976), 242ff. The word was probably, however, pronounced with an *r*, thus *ma'ar*; and would thus have nothing to do with the Hebrew.

[78] Cf. "Ephod" already well known in Ugaritic and in the Akkadian texts from Ras Shamra: Koehler-Baumgartner, 1:75 (references).

[79] See p. 366.

[80] See in particular, T. O. Lambdin, *JAOS* 73 (1953), 145ff.; Ellenbogen, *Foreign Words*; R. J. Williams, in J. R. Harris, ed., *The Legacy of Israel* (London, 1971), 262–69.

that in the case of a particular word or idiom it was monarchic Israel that effected the borrowing; or are we again faced with transfers that belong to a much earlier stratum in the history of Canaanites in the area?

Of the forty-odd words that can reasonably be assigned an Egyptian derivation, some thirteen designate manufactures (including furniture and weights and measures), while five are terms for clothing and cloth. As we have seen, the cult accounts for much of this list, while certain scribal implements (seal, ink, writing palette) show a dependence on the Nilotic scribal art. Israel well knew such political terms as "Pharaoh," "king's wife" (Tahpenes), and "magician"(ḥartōm), and was familiar with Egyptian ships.[81] Trade goods from the south that must have found their way into Israel and Judah retained their Egyptian names: reeds, lotus, acacia wood, ebony, apes, natron, gold, alabaster, and other building stones. Architectural forms, usually those having to do with Solomon's temple, are a little more suspect.[82] Of terms for natural phenomena only ye'or, "river" (i.e., the Nile), seems to have stuck, Hebrew having a wealth of words for such things. A few technical terms derived from Egyptian society and bureaucracy found their way into Hebrew: 'ebyon, "poor" (from Egyptian bin, "evil, bad"), 'uggat, "bread" (from Egyptian 'ḳw, "rations"),[83] ger, "visitor, alien" (from Egyptian K³ry, "neighbor").[84] Finally, the Egyptian word for "power," often used of Pharaoh, was familiar enough to be transcribed into Hebrew in Isaiah 30:30.[85]

Egyptian idiom too seems to have occasionally made an impact on Hebrew. Such expressions as "eternal house," "wall of bronze," "broken-armed" (i.e., weak, ineffectual) recall common Egyptian locutions;[86] while the concepts of "the way of the living" and the "tree of life"[87] seem indigenous to Egyptian wisdom and mythology. The image of god in his

---

[81] Ellenbogen, Foreign Words, 145, 154.

[82] 'ulam, "fore-hall" or the like (1 Kings 6:3) does in fact seem to derive from Egyptian (M. Görg, BN 13 [1980], 22ff.); and rimon of 1 Kings 7:18 has been ingeniously compared with an Egyptian root meaning "to support" (Görg, 20–21). But the other terms explained as Egyptian derivatives seem farfetched (Cf. M. Görg, BN 1 [1976], 29–30; 5 [1978], 12; 13 [1980], 19; ZAW 98 [1977], 115–18; GM 20 [1976], 22–23; Y. M. Grintz, Leshonenu 89 [1974–1975], 163–68).

[83] M. Görg, BN 19 (1982), 22–23.

[84] M. Görg, BN 25 (1984), 10–13. This, however seems doubtful, as the Coptic shows that, in the case of krr, "foreigners," the r conceals an l; and that in the case of k³ry the r had been uvularized by the New Kingdom.

[85] Ellenbogen, Foreign Words, 112.

[86] Williams, Legacy, 264–66; cf. J. K. Hoffmeir, Biblica 67 (1986), 378–87; cf. also A. Jirku, ZDMG 103 (1953), 372.

[87] Williams, Legacy, 267; Wb III, 342:2–4; C. Kayatz, Studien zu Proverbien 1–9 (Neukirchen-Vluyn, 1966), 105ff.

creative aspect as a potter[88] and in his custodial capacity as a shepherd[89] also have excellent Egyptian credentials, and may well have influenced Israelite thought. Occasionally Hebrew psalmody indulges in that pessimistic appraisal of present conditions exemplified in Psalm 12:1–2:[90] "There is no longer any that is godly, for the faithful have vanished from among the sons of men. Everyone utters lies to his neighbors." With this one might compare the misanthropic clichés of Middle Kingdom literature: "Hearts are rapacious and there is no man in whom one can trust. . . . there are no just persons and the land is abandoned to wrongdoers."[91] Again: that figure in which a reversal of fortunes in society becomes a source of wonderment (cf. 1 Sam. 2:4–5)[92] harks back to a very common motif in the Pessimistic literature in Egypt during the second millennium: "Really, the rich are in mourning while the poor rejoice . . . princes hunger grievously while the servants are served."[93]

The indications of Egyptian influence on language and idiom we have just passed in review betray the subtle influence of the Nile rather than conscious borrowings by Israel in the areas of trade, the cult, and that amorphous sphere known in Egyptian as "Teaching" and in Hebrew as "Wisdom." Israel, lying so close to the Mediterranean coast and the land crossing to North Africa, belonged within the Egyptian cultural penumbra, and could not help receiving unconsciously such linguistic and lexical influence.

HYMNS AND POETRY

It would be curious if the long association of Egypt and Canaan during the empire had not resulted in the transfer of certain Egyptian images and forms within the sphere of hymnology and poetry.[94] Belle-lettristic creations in metric form constituted an oral tradition disseminated all over the Near East, but only in certain centers (like Egypt) was there an indigenous source powerful enough to foster mimesis in adjacent regions. A quick perusal of polite forms of address contained within the Amarna corpus will prove this to have been the case. The Canaanite mayors,

[88] S. Morenz, ZÄS 84 (1959), 79–80.

[89] D. Muller, ZÄS 86 (1961), 143.

[90] Cf. Psalm 53:3, 142:4, etc.

[91] R. O. Faulkner, JEA 42 (1956), 29.

[92] "The bones of the mighty men are broken, but the weak put on strength; those (formerly) well fed have hired themselves out for bread, but those who were hungry have ceased to hunger."

[93] Ipuwer: M. Lichtheim, *Ancient Egyptian Literature* (Berkeley, Calif., 1976), 1:149–63.

[94] Cf. A. Barucq, *L'expression de la louange divine et de la prière dans la Bible et dans l'Égypte* (Cairo, 1962).

through their enforced sojourn in Egypt in their youth, were more familiar than the rest of their countrymen with polite forms of discourse current at Pharaoh's court; and these abound in their private letters to the
king. It was solar "theology," to the exclusion of other more recondite
aspects of Egyptian imagery, that cast a spell over the Canaanite. Pharaoh
to them was "my god, my sun, the Sun in heaven," "the son of the Sun,"
"hale like the Sun in heaven," "the Sun of (all) lands"—all direct translations of native Egyptian phrases. In fact one extended salutation in a
letter of the king of Tyre, Abi-milki (EA 147: 5–13), really constitutes an
Egyptian sun hymn done directly and literally into Akkadian! "My lord
is the Sun god who rises over the foreign lands every day as his gracious
father the sun has ordained; one who gives life by his sweet breath and
languor when he is hidden, who pacifies the entire land with the power of
his mighty arm, who emits his roar in heaven like Ba'al, and the whole
earth shakes with his roar."[95]

The solar imagery remained firmly fixed in the poetic repertoire of Canaan, especially the coastal cities, long after the disappearance of the
empire. The marvelous panegyric on the nature and activity of god in
Psalm 104, written during the second-quarter of the first millennium B.C.,
draws on both ancient Canaanite epic and Egyptian solar hymns. Verses
3 to 18 describe Yahweh in terms of Ba'al, triumphant over Prince Yam,
ensconced on the mountains and sustaining the earth, whereas verses 2
and 19 to 30 draw specifically on the phraseology and imagery of Akhenaten's hymn to the sun disk.[96] (Table 6).

PENITENTIAL PSALMS

Nearly one-third of all the material contained in the Book of Psalms falls
into a category of the individual complaint or penitential psalm.[97] These
are personal appeals to god by a victim of sickness, depression, or villifi-
cation who ascribes his suffering either to the malefic affects of outside
sorcery, or to his own sinful conduct. He states his confidence in the deity,

[95] See W. F. Albright, *JEA* 23 (1937), 191ff.; also D. B. Redford, "The Nature of Kingship
during the 18th Dynasty" (forthcoming).

[96] Text in Sandman, *Akhenaten*, 93ff., and V. A. Tobin, "The Intellectual Organization
of the Amarna Period" (Ph.D. diss., Hebrew University, 1986), 29ff. A translation appears
in Tobin, 29ff.; see also P. Auffret, *Hymnes d'Égypte et d'Israel* (Göttingen, 1981). I am
also indebted to an insightful study of Psalm 104 incorporated in a paper delivered to the
Oriental Club of Toronto by Professor Paul Dion in 1988, at the moment of writing unpublished.

[97] S. Mowinckel, *The Psalms in Israel's Worship* (Nashville, Tenn., 1962), 1:225–46;
2:1–25; J. W. Wevers, *VT* 6 (1956), 80–96; G. W. Anderson, *BJRL* 48 (1965), 16–29;
E. Gerstenberger, in J. H. Hayes, *Old Testament Form Criticism* (San Antonio, Tex., 1974),
198–205.

TABLE 6.

Comparison of Akhenaten's Hymn to the Sun Disk and Psalm 104

Hymn to Sun Disk	Psalm 104
O thou great living sun disk . . . lord of heaven and earth . . . thou risest beautiful on the horizon of heaven, . . . shining on the eastern horizon, having filled every land with thy beauty!	O Yahweh my god! Thou art very great . . . (who) coverest thyself with light as with a garment (1–2)
Thou hast made the heavens afar off in order to shine in it	. . . who hast stretched out the heavens like a tent (2)
Thou hast made the seasons in order to nurture all that thou hast made	Thou hast made the moon to mark the seasons (19)
Thou settest on the western horizon and the land is in darkness in the manner of death	The sun knows its time of setting (19) Thou makest darkness and it is night (20)
Every lion comes forth from his den, and all the serpents bite	. . . when all the beasts of the field creep forth; the young lions roar for their prey (20)
Dawn comes (only) when thou risest on the horizon	When the sun rises . . . (22)
The whole world, they do their jobs	. . . man goes forth to his work (23)
The fish in the river leap before thee; thy rays are within the Sea	Yonder is the sea, great and wide which teems with things innumerable, living things both small and great (25)
Ships sail both north and south	There go the ships (26)
Thou puttest each one in his place, thou providest their needs each one with his food	These all look to thee to give them food in due season (27)
How manifold is what thou hast done	O Yahweh! How manifold are thy works! (24)

excoriates his enemies or confesses his sin, and vows to reform and testify should god heal or save him. A related genre concentrates on the erstwhile sufferer's plight from the later vantage point of one saved and now under obligation to give thanks. Numerous examples of the same type from the cuneiform world prove that this genre in Hebrew is but part of the much larger phenomenon of the "Lament" of the sufferer throughout the ancient world.[98]

The penitential psalm is also attested in Egypt.[99] Well over 90 percent of the thirty-five-odd examples come from the workmen's village of Deir el-Medina on the west bank of Thebes and date from the 19th and 20th Dynasties; but the earliest date from Tutankamun's reign, and sporadic examples from the Third Intermediate Period prove that the haphazard of preservation has skewed our view. The Egyptian penitential psalms are preserved on stelae, often with a depiction of the speaker in the pious attitude of adoration, and were destined for public display in a temple or shrine. The text betrays all the earmarks of oral-formulaic composition[100] and usually incorporates an appeal to the god, a description of the sickness (blindness or a respiratory ailment), a confession of sin, and a vow to testify to the god's saving power. An extension of the situation has the victim, now healed and once again in the god's good grace, fulfilling his vow by delivery of a "testimony" and enjoying the praising of the deity by all and sundry.

Despite a number of parallels, there can be no question of Israel's dependence on Egypt for the penitential psalm. The "life situation" from which the psalm arises is too common to posit dependence; and it may not be fortuitous that it appears in Egypt only with the increased contact with Asia occasioned by the empire.

In poetry a certain similarity in genre and treatment can be established between extant New Kingdom love poetry and the Song of Songs. Although the latter is Exilic or post-Exilic in date, the form harks back to Egyptian love poetry one thousand years earlier;[101] and while the Bible piece has been "spiritualized" by purblind and unfeeling exegetes, the origin remains an erotic though discreet creation probably within the purview of a sophisticated court.

WISDOM

In Egypt, beginning certainly as early as the last century of the third millennium B.C., our sources throw up an amorphous category of composi-

[98] G. Widengren, *The Accadian and Hebrew Psalms of Lamentation* (Stockholm, 1936); W. H. Hallo, *JAOS* 88 (1968), 71–89.

[99] Cf. A. Erman, *Denksteine aus der thebanischen Gräberstadt* (Berlin, 1911); see also S. Allam, **MDAIK** 24 (1969), 10ff.; J. J. Clère, *RdE* 27 (1975), 70ff.; M. Görg, in *Fontes atque Pontes*, ed., M. Görg (Wiesbaden, 1983), 162ff.

[100] Cf. R. C. Culley, *VT* 13 (1963), 113–25; idem, *Oral Formulaic Language in the Biblical Psalms* (Toronto, 1968).

[101] For the most impressively erudite treatment of the subject and its related problems, see M. V. Fox, *The Song of Songs and the Ancient Egyptian Love Songs* (Madison, Wis., 1985).

tions intimately associated with the training of scribes.[102] Throughout Egyptian history the filling of posts that demanded an ability to read, write, and impart skills or exercise technical expertise always created a tension between two unrelated urges: the natural desire of a father that his son should follow him in office, and the equally pressing need for choosing the best man for the job. At all periods (though especially in the early Old Kingdom), the sons of a great scribe may well turn out to follow the scribal profession also, but as time went on the increasing complexity of bureaucracy demanded that formal schools be set up, associated with the court. A charming word-vignette of the 19th Dynasty[103] describes for us the deportment of the ideal pupil and the desired approach to learning: he is to be prompt, neat of dress, equipped with his book; arithmetic and reading are important, and he is to do his calculation silently, not aloud; he must be diligent and emulate his instructors.

In order to facilitate instruction the scribes amassed a body of texts, compiled if not composed, with pedagogic intent. Much or perhaps most of this was prosaic in the extreme and had to do with the kind of routine administration the scribe would be faced with in pursuance of his calling: accounts, memoranda, letters, dispatches, reports. But a certain amount of it comprised poetical or prose compositions that at one and the same time aimed to entertain and to teach. By copying these texts under the supervision of his teacher the student would develop a good hand, learn the accepted style of composition, and absorb the wisdom precepts of the ancestors. The libraries, which have either survived or been reconstructed from book lists and inventories, show the range of materials with which the fully trained scribe was supposed to be familiar:[104] stories, king lists, annals, diaries, mythological treatises, sign lists, geographies, ritual books, magical texts, manuals, inventories, letters, accounts. Even a private collection of a trained scribe might include stories, love poetry, hymns, magic, medicine, and oneiromancy.[105]

A certain amount of this material can be separated out—the ancients themselves so separated it—and grouped under the broad heading of "Teaching" (*sbo³yet*). Whether this term should be construed as a "genre" designation becomes an argument for schoolmen; and the word, admittedly, bears more on intent or purpose than form. "Teaching" may consist of practical instruction from a master craftsman to an apprentice;

[102] On scribal training in ancient Egypt, see R. J. Williams, *JAOS* 92 (1972), 214–21; H. Brunner, *Altägyptische Erziehung* (Wiesbaden, 1972).

[103] P. Anastasi V, 22/6–23/7; Caminos, *Late Egyptian Miscellanies*, 262–63.

[104] D. B. Redford, *Pharaonic King-lists, Annals and Day-books* (Toronto, 1986), 215–223.

[105] A. H. Gardiner, *The Library of A. Chester Beatty* (London, 1931).

from a scribe on how to write; instruction on behavior from a king to his untutored pages (or courtiers), or even from a god to a devotee. It can be applied to the kind of "learning" that comes from perusal or a "satirical letter," or from a lexicon. But by and large "Teaching" in Egyptian means a form of composition in which a wiseman (father, king, or superior) addresses a discourse comprising a range of worldly wisdom[106] to a subordinate (son, subject, trainee, or the like). Consequently the *sboyet* will turn out to be a monologue, didactic, and preceptive. Any deviation from this basic format can arguably be maintained to be an extension or even a misuse of the term.[107]

The content and thrust of the "Teaching" may well vary: propaganda is attested side by side with advice on "lifemanship"; reference material is found with satire and biography. But all, broadly speaking, are intended to instruct in some fashion or other.[108]

Scholars have long recognized a marked similarity between Egyptian "Teaching" and Biblical "Wisdom" texts such as those contained primarily in Proverbs, in both idiom and content.[109] The common Egyptian for-

[106] The contention that Egyptian Wisdom gravitated from a secular to a more sacred or religious perspective over the centuries has been used of late as a "strawman" (H. H. Schmid, *Wesen und Geschichte der Weisheit* [Berlin, 1966], 8ff.; Williams, *VT* Suppl. 28, [1975], 245), and Breasted's contention, it is true, may have been simplistic. But no one can deny a striking contrast between the pragmatic, yea *opportunistic* advice of a Ptahhotpe of the third millennium, who mentions god comparatively rarely, and the sickeningly maudlin piety and sentimentality of the self-righteous Amenemope of the late second millennium. The linking of piety with ethic was not complete until Hellenistic times: cf. M. Lichtheim, *Late Egyptian Wisdom Literature in the International Context* (Göttingen, 1983), 186–87.

[107] This is not the place to enter into a disquisition on the thorny question of "genre" in ancient Egyptian belles lettres (H. Brunner, *ZÄS* 93 [1966], 29; J. Assmann et al., *Fragen an die altägyptische Literatur* [Wiesbaden, 1977]; K. A. Kitchen, in E. Hornung and O. Keel, eds., *Studien zu altägyptischen Lebenslehren* [Göttingen, 1979], 235–83; S. Purdy, *ZÄS* 104 [1977], 112ff.; M. V. Fox, *ZÄS* 107 [1980], 128; R. J. Williams, *JAOS* 101 [1981], 7). Suffice it to say, in anticipation of a position adopted by the present writer in a forthcoming treatment of oral tradition in ancient Egypt, that the ancients must be allowed to communicate to us their own categories. Too often we impose our own classifications (which incidentally often arise inconsistently from preoccupation with such disparates as purpose, form, and style), and draw them unconsciously from the translation language.

[108] On teaching in general, see W. McKane, *Proverbs: A New Approach* (London, 1970), 51–150, and for specific examples thereof, see R.B.Y. Scott, *Proverbs, Ecclesiastes* (New York, 1965), xlii–xlvii; R. N. Whybray, *Wisdom in Proverbs* (London, 1965), 53–54; H. Brunner, *Handbuch der Orientalistik²*, vol. 1, pt. 2 (Leiden, 1970), 113–39; idem, *LdÄ* 3 (1980), 964–68; M. V. Fox, *ZÄS* 107 (1980), 128.

[109] "Wisdom" (*hokma*) does not, however, render Egyptian *sb³yt*, which is rather the equivalent of *musar*: Whybray, *Wisdom* 62; while there is a resemblance between the hypostasis of Wisdom in Proverbs and the personification of *ma'at* in Egypt (Kayatz, *Studien zu Proverbien*, 93–98 and passim), I do not find a true equivalent of the concept of *ma'at* in Hebrew thought as some apparently have done: H. Gese, *Lehre und Wirklichkeit in des*

mula "if (you are a . . .)," "better is . . . than . . ." and the use of the vetetive appear in Hebrew in strikingly similar contexts,[110] while the recollection that the present father-son chat simply mirrors a current situation—my father taught me also!—is shared by both traditions.[111] Again: such motifs as the typical fool, the ideal man (silent, patient, obedient), flogging as pedagogic tool, and the ear as the receptacle of instruction are found both in Egypt and Israel.[112]

Although it might be agreed that these similarities arise from a common background of "Wisdom" shared by Egypt and Canaan from remote times, it would be difficult to deny that a more direct dependency seems to underlie some specific passages, and that it is Israel's dependence on Egypt that is the question. The most famous example, and indeed the primary one, is the Wisdom of Amenemope written probably during the 20th Dynasty (c. twelfth century B.C.) but continuing popular until the 26th Dynasty (seventh century B.C.).[113] Proverbs 22:23 to 23:11, with its "Thirty Sayings," strikingly mirrors the "Thirty Chapters" of Amenemope in content to the extent that one can scarcely escape the conclusion that the former is a "version" of the latter.[114] But elsewhere Proverbs is dotted with individual parallels,[115] and several occur in the Psalter. Of the latter, one of the more charming is the likening of the "Ideal Man" (the "godly") and the "Heated Man" (the "ungodly") in Psalm 1 to different trees: the origin of the motif is clearly chapter 4 of Amenemope.[116] Psalm 34:11–14, which begins "Come O sons! Listen to me and I will teach you the fear of Yahweh," bears more than a passing resemblance (*mutatis mutandis*) to similar calls from as early as the Amarna age.[117]

---

alten Weisheit (Tübingen, 1958), 33–38; U. Skladny, *Die altesten Spruchsammlungen in Israel* (Göttingen, 1962), 89–92.

[110] P. Humbert, *Recherches sur les sources égyptiennes de la litterature sapientiale d'Israel* (Neuchâtel, 1927), 57; Kayatz, *Studien zu Proverbien*, 26ff.; J. M. Thompson, *The Form and Function of Proverbs in Ancient Israel* (The Hague, 1974), 40, 62.

[111] Whybray, *Wisdom*, 35–36, 45.

[112] Ibid., 59–61, 65–67; N. Shupak, *RB* 94 (1987), 98–119.

[113] Translation: Lichtheim, *Literature*, 2:146–63; A. Alt, in M. Noth and D. W. Thomas, eds., *Wisdom in Israel and the Ancient Near East* (Leiden, 1955), 16–25; see also S. Morenz, *ZÄS* 84 (1959), 79–80; R. J. Williams, *JEA* 47 (1961), 100–106; W. Helck, *AFO* 22 (1968–1969), 21–27; G. E. Bryce, *A Legacy of Wisdom: The Egyptian Contribution to the Wisdom of Israel* (London, 1979); on the date see R. J. Williams, *JAOS* 101 (1981), 10. That a common Egyptian source lies behind both Proverbs 22 and 23 and Amenemope seems to be a needless and farfetched assumption: I. Grumach, *Untersuchungen zur Lebenslehre des Amenope* (Munich, 1972).

[114] Scott, *Proverbs, Ecclesiastes*, 135ff.; McKane, *Proverbs*, 369–74; M. V. Fox, *ZÄS* 107 (1980), 130–31.

[115] Cf. the list in R. J. Williams, *VT Suppl.* 28 (1975), 245 and n. 85.

[116] Lichtheim, *Literature*, 2:150–51.

[117] Cf. Davies, *The Rock Tombs of Amarna* (London, 1909), 6: pl. 32; *Urk* IV, 1998 "Ho,

What has been examined to this point in the form of evidence of "literary" impact of Egypt on Israel suggests a circuitous route via an intermediary. Egypt, during the empire and later, cultivated direct ties with the cities of the Levantine coast; the mountains inland interested the Egyptians little, as we have seen. If genres, styles, and specific compositions lived on in some form in the cultural baggage of the Asiatics living close to the Egyptian frontier in the first millennium B.C., it is highly likely that this took place in the maritime cities from Gaza in the south to Byblos in the north; and if the invasion and settlement of the Philistines and Teukrians effected a real hiatus in the life of the cities of the south coastal plain, then we can narrow our search to that stretch of coast between Accho and Arvad. Here we must postulate—the figures of Hierombalos and Sanchuniaton bolster the case—the existence of a scribal "elite," still in touch with or mindful of Egypt from the 21st through the 26th Dynasties, that perpetuated the celebrated creations of the Egyptian New Kingdom and kept alive style and form in however bastardized a manner. Just as Israel was placed in the debt of Phoenicia for most of the Egyptian influences in art, architecture, and historiography,[118] so also in the realm of belles lettres Egyptian literature and style passed through the sieve of the Levantine coast before arriving at Jerusalem.[119]

"Sieve" may not be an inappropriate term, for one major characteristic of Hebrew passages derived from Egyptian calls for comment: none of these pericopes is a verbatim translation. Observation of this fact has given rise to a variety of explanations: Hebrew writers quoted from memory; the transmission process was "lengthy"; Israel owed only a "general debt" to Egypt in the sphere of Wisdom. All of these propositions offer a valid, if limited, insight into the problem; but none fastens upon the two factors at work here—rendering of idiom and theme into a foreign tongue, and oral composition and transmission.[120] No Hebrew in Jerusalem could possibly have packed Biblical Wisdom with so many Egyptian inspired phrases and images had not they come to him in his own language. And the wide gap between the wording and adaptation of the Hebrew and that of the Egyptian originals would not exist had the Hebrew wise man possessed a translation and been content therewith. Once again, for that necessary intermediate stage in the transmission one is drawn to the Phoenician cities of the coast, where long-standing familiar-

---

all living upon the earth and ye who shall be young men some day! I shall tell you the way of life." Cf. also B. Couroyer, *RB* 57 (1950), 174–79.

[118] See pp. 366.

[119] C.I.K. Story, *JBL* 64 (1945), 319–37; Scott, *VT* Suppl. 3 (1955), 262–79; Williams, *VT* Suppl. 28 (1975), 250–51.

[120] Again the reader is referred to the writer's forthcoming treatment of oral tradition in ancient Egypt.

ity with Egyptian culture and (in some quarters) fluency in Egyptian were characteristic of the intelligentsia. Here is the society in which the Egyptian originals passed into a Semitic tongue, not necessarily by means of written translations, but through an oral, targumic rendering, admired and imitated but noncanonical.

CHAPTER 14

Four Great Origin Traditions

A MOMENT'S REFLECTION will confirm the contention that comparatively rarely in human history does a movement of people occur that completely annihilates or supplants an earlier or autochthonous population. Most of the checkered nature of the old world's history has far more to do with the ebb and flow of political and cultural hegemony than with wholesale demographic shifts or even colonization. The spread in sequence of Assyrian, Neo-Babylonian, Persian, Hellenistic, and Roman rule did not result in violent changes in basic populations; even the deportations of recalcitrants or the immigration of elite groups may have taken place for broad reasons of security. When shifts resulting in annihilation *do* occur, it is not surprising that in the sequel there is the devil to pay. The victims are not likely to accept with equanimity the claims by the ingressing group that they are doing so with divine approval, or that the victims' land has been handed over by the god to the newcomers: that a man has an absolute right to live on his ancestral plot is an unquestioned privilege buried deep in the human soul, which even a god finds well-nigh impossible to rescind.

One of the few destructive movements of peoples covered by the chronological range of this book is the invasion of the Sea Peoples. Here at least we stand on safe ground if we postulate widespread upheaval of states and shifts of ethnic groups. In the aftermath it is perhaps not surprising to find in the native lore of incoming tribes a preoccupation with these origins, and a desire to explain the taking of land once not theirs. The cities of the southern coastal plain long remembered that the ancestors of at least some of their inhabitants had emigrated from the Aegean and western Asia Minor, and Amos 9:7 reflects a similar origin tradition among the Aramaeans of the Iron Age.

Israel of the monarchy too took a conscious interest in its origins, and these eventually assumed the shape of the present Pentateuch.[1] Assembled, edited, and partly written by the P-writers[2] (priests in all probability

---

[1] T. L. Thompson, *The Origin Tradition of Ancient Israel* (Sheffield, 1987).

[2] On the P-source, see A. Hurvitz, *RB* 81 (1974), 24–36; S. E. McEvenue, *The Narrative Style of the Priestly Writer* (Rome, 1971); G. Vink, *The Date and Origin of the Priestly Code in the Old Testament* (Leiden, 1969); P. Weimar, *BN* 24 (1984), 12ff., 138ff.; Z. Zevit, *ZAW* 94 (1982), 481–511.

spiritually descended from the intellectual elite of Jerusalem in the late monarchy), the Pentateuch includes four major traditions in which Egypt figures prominently, either as a subtle influence or as an explicit component. These are the accounts of creation, the Table of Nations, the Sojourn in Egypt, and the Exodus. Of these the first two are largely, though not entirely the product of P; the latter two, on the other hand, enjoyed an earlier existence and transmission.

THE CREATION ACCOUNTS

On the two creation accounts in the Book of Genesis, 1:1–2:4, and 2:4–24, reams of scholarly comment have been written; and the present writer is not prepared either to provide a critique of it, or even to summarize it. Both have long been claimed to display clear dependence on Mesopotamian creation stories;[3] while the appended accounts of the origin of certain aspects of civilized living (Gen. 4:17–22) show marked similarities to Phoenician tales.[4]

This would appear to end the search for sources of influence on the Hebrew writer(s), were it not for the principal tool of creation in Genesis 1, namely the "divine *fiat*": "God said: 'let there be . . .' " Here we are reminded not of Asiatic myth but of Egyptian.

The most common myth pattern in ancient Egypt regarding the origin and nature of the world[5] derives its varied detail from the landscape of the Nile Valley: the annual inundation turning the valley into a sort of primeval "sea," the dry land emerging as the water recedes, the black alluvium teeming with life. In almost all primitive creation stories in Egypt, the eternal substance that existed in the beginning and whose origin is not explained is water, the primeval ocean, Nun.[6] From the waters emerges a mound[7] on which the creator god, in reptilian, insect, or avian form, is sitting; and from this vantage point he engages in the creative activity that takes its most crass form as an act of expectoration, self-fertilization, masturbation,[8] or the like. Since this motif achieved its classic form in the sun cult of Heliopolis, the creation god is often conceived of as a falcon, and the primeval mound as an egg from which it hatches

---

[3] E. A. Speiser, *Genesis* (New York 1956), 8ff.; W. G. Lambert, *JTS* 16 (1965), 287–300.

[4] Eusebius, *Praeparatio Evangelica* 1.10.8–13; H. W. Attridge and R. A. Oden, Jr., *Philo of Byblos. The Phoenician History* (Washington, 1981).

[5] On Egyptian creation stories, see S. Sauneron and J. Yoyotte, *La naissance du monde* (Paris, 1959); J. Assmann, *LdÄ* 5 (1984), 677–90.

[6] Cognate with West Semitic word *nun*, "fish": F. Cornelius, *Geistegeschichte der Frühzeit* (Leiden, 1960) 2:1, 75–78.

[7] A.-A. Saleh, *MDAIK* 25 (1969), 110ff.

[8] P. Derchain, in *Religion en Égypte hellénistique et romaine* (Paris, 1969), 31ff.

and the halves of which subsequently become heaven and earth.[9] Creative mythological thought transmogrified the mound into other images that made possible a wider range of associations: a lotus flower, a floating reed,[10] even a human head.[11] In all cases the subsequent creation of mankind is not of moment to the narrator, and has to be pieced together from disparate sources. A popular and widespread motif credited the sun-god's lament on seeing the earth barren and lifeless on the morning of creation with the emergence of man: the tears (Egyptian *rimi*) of the sun-god fell to earth and became men (Egyptian *rome*).[12] Another version had it that Khnum, the potter god of Elephantine, fashioned men and animals on his wheel out of alluvial clay, and breathed his breath into them.[13] This notion was equally popular and of relative antiquity. Amenemope (twelfth century B.C.) says: "Man is clay and straw, God is his fashioner." Some texts dwell on the fabrication of the body as though it were a task for a basketmaker, and speak of "the tying on of heads, the affixing of necks, the knotting of backbones."[14]

Another creation motif, less common perhaps than the "Primeval-Ocean-and-Mound" type, centers upon sexual union as the prime element in the act of creation. Heaven (female) and earth (male) were one, locked in an embrace in the Nun, and the act of creation consisted of the separation of the pair by the insinuation of Atmosphere (or, Light, i.e., the god Shu) between them. The resultant elevation of the (now impregnated) heaven, called in Egyptian "The Uplifting of Shu," meant that the subsequent birth of her offspring would be celestial; and the heavenly luminaries and all the starry host duly appeared and found their natural passage along the belly of the heaven, to be swallowed by her at night.[15]

That category of creation story in which a hero-god is pitted against a dragon or monster of chaos is indeed attested in Egypt, but usually the plot has been divorced from creation and serves as a tale of inauguration or an etiology (e.g., of solar eclipse).[16] As a creation account it is adumbrated in the Instruction for King Merikare of the twenty-first century B.C., and may well be much older.[17] "Mankind," says Merikare's father,

[9] S. Morenz, *Aegyptische Religion* (Stuttgart, 1960), 187ff.

[10] E.A.E. Reymond, *CdE* 40 (1965), 61ff.; idem, *JEA* 48 (1962), 81ff.

[11] Lucian, *De dea Syria* 7.454–55.

[12] Assmann, *LdÄ* 5 (1984), 681.

[13] S. Sauneron, *BIFAO* 62 (1964), 33–37; idem *Le temple d' Esna* (Cairo, 1963), 2:35ff.

[14] CT II, 37–38f (Spell 80): Middle Kingdom.

[15] Cf. H. Te Velde, *Studia Aegyptica* 3 (Budapest, 1977), 163ff.; E. Hornung, *Das Amduat* (Wiesbaden, 1963), 2:188; on the swallowing of the children, see H. Frankfort, *The Cenotaph of Sety I at Abydos* (London, 1933), 82ff.

[16] See D. B. Redford, S. Groll, ed., *Studies in Egyptology Presented to Miriam Lichtheim* (Jerusalem, 1990), 834.

[17] W. Helck, *Die Lehre für König Merikare* (Wiesbaden, 1977), 83.

"is god's flock. He made heaven and earth for their benefit (when) he had defeated the water monster, and he had made breath that their noses might live. They are his images,[18] who came forth from his body." At Hermopolis, apparently, the fight between god and dragon played a part in the myth. Imperfectly known to modern scholarship but involving a certain degree of syncretism of borrowed elements, the Hermopolitan cosmogony centered upon the primeval ocean characterized by four negative qualities: bottomlessness (Nunu), darkness (Keku), boundlessness (Hehu), and imperceptibility.[19] All four concepts, which in their inability to be qualified by degree approach Anaximander's principle "the Unlimited," were personified for purposes of the cult by four pairs of deities; and these were termed the "Eight" (Greek "Ogdoad"), "the very great primordial ones, the august ones who came forth from him . . . after whom all being came into being."[20] While the mound emerging from the waters and the uplifting of the sky also figure in the Hermopolitan account, a battle with the monster (in this case the Neheb-kau snake) may also have been included: compare PT 229, "O adze of Atum which is in the vertebrae of Nehebkau, which terminates the strife in Hermopolis . . . !"[21]

The coarse and unsophisticated nature of these basic concepts needs no stressing. As in most cultures the most fundamental spiritual tenets took their rise in remote antiquity, if not prehistory, and the intelligentsia of a later, more polished society found themselves saddled with an embarrassingly primitive baggage. Without discarding anything, however, the Egyptian wiseman reinterpreted and shaped his crass traditions into something at once both sophisticated and imponderable.

Several elements in these creation tales already show sensitivity and insight. The concern with "being" and "coming into being" and the concept of autogenesis strike us as unusually advanced. The time before creation is described in terms suggesting a striving after the idea of "nonbeing,"[22] and creation itself is often called "the first deed (occasion)." In the

---

[18] *Snn*; the same word can mean "statue": J. J. Clère, in *Hommages Sauneron* (Cairo, 1979), 357, n. 1. Interestingly, the reverence accorded whole species of animals in the Late Period (which resulted in the huge animal necropolis that so offended Greeks and Romans) stems from the belief that all members of a particular species were "images" of the theriomorphic god they were associated with: A. Hunt and C. C. Edgar, *Select Papyri* (London, 1927), 2: no. 329.

[19] K. Sethe, *Amun und die acht Urgötter von Hermopolis* (Berlin, 1929); J. Wilson, in H. Frankfort, *Before Philosophy* (Baltimore, 1946), 61; Assmann, *LdÄ* 5 (1984), 679–80.

[20] E. Chassinat, *Le Temple d'Edfu* (Cairo, 1892–1934), 1:288.

[21] A. W. Shorter, *JEA* 21 (1935), 43; B. Altenmüller, *Synkretismus in den Sargtexten* (Wiesbaden, 1975), 96–98.

[22] H. Grapow, *ZÄS* 67 (1931), 34ff.; "when nothing at all had come into being, when the earth was in total darkness": H. Junker, *Das Götterdekret über das Abaton* (Vienna, 1913),

creation of man there seems also to be an overriding fascination with breath insinuated into the throat as the key element that quickens the inert flesh.[23]

The pinnacle of the quest after the First Principle in ancient Egypt was reached with the composition of the so-called Memphite Theology.[24] In form a dramatic-cultic text glossed by a commentary at the end, the Memphite Theology is found on a block now in the British Museum that dates to the reign of Shabaka (712–697 B.C.), who claims to have found the original on a papyrus "which the ancestors had made, worm-eaten and unknown from beginning to end." While the veracity of this statement has been challenged and an early date for the *Vorlage* called into question,[25] no one can deny that the contents became known (again?) only at the beginning of the Kushite period around 710 B.C. and were disseminated during the following two centuries. The commentary, among other novel ideas, advances the proposition that the essence of the creator god, Ptah, resides in "heart" and "tongue," that is to say mind and creative utterance. Mind conceived of being, and the creative word made it concrete. So the creation itself becomes in a sense an emanation of the creator, or at least that part of it which has life-force: "Thus it happened that the heart and the tongue gained control over every other member of the body through the teaching that he (Ptah) is in every body and every mouth, of all gods, all men, all cattle, all creeping things and everything that lives, by thinking and commanding everything that he wishes." Ptah's ubiquity can also be extended as the fundament of the entire creation: "No entity exists without him. Being is his being continually as he has decreed."[26]

Over the past half century there have been scholars who have plumped for several of these patterns and details passed in review as comprising a background that exerted an influence on the writers of Genesis 1–2; and of late their numbers have begun to proliferate.[27] While one cannot as yet

---

9. Creation is, however, never quite conceived of as from nothing: W. Altenmüller, *WO* 10 (1979), 116.

[23] R. J. Williams, in G. E. Kadish, ed., *Studies in Honor of John A. Wilson* (Chicago, 1969), 93–94.

[24] J. H. Breasted, *ZÄS* 39 (1901), 39–54; C. Desroches-Noblecourt, *MDAIK* 16 (1958), 83ff.; W. Erichsen and S. Schott, *Fragmente memphitischer Theologie in demotische Schrift* (Wiesbaden, 1954); J. G. Griffiths, *The Origins of Osiris and His Cult* (Leiden, 1980); H. Junker, *Die Götterlehre von Memphis* (Berlin, 1940); K. Sethe, *Dramatische Texte zu altägyptischen Mysterienspielen* (Berlin, 1928).

[25] F. Junge, *MDAIK* 29 (1973), 195–204.

[26] O. Koefoed-Petersen, *Les stèles égyptiennes* (Copenhagen, 1948), no. 37.

[27] Cf. among others, A. H. Sayce in S.R.K. Glanville, ed., *Griffiths Studies* (Oxford, 1932), 419ff. (Hermopolitan cosmogony); R. Kilian, *VT* 16 (1965), 420–38 (the Ogdoad); S. Herrmann, *TLZ* 86 (1961), 413–24 (Onomastica); J. K. Hoffmeier, *JANES* 15 (1983),

speak of a "Pan-Egyptianizing" movement, it would be well to view these tendencies in perspective. Although within Egypt the mythologies of creation have a long history, it is not until the period of cultural renewal of the 24th to 26th Dynasties, the period of so-called archaizing, that such sophisticated treatises as the Memphite Theology have any impact on the outside world. It is at that period, the two centuries say between 725 and 525 B.C., that Egypt and the entire eastern Mediterranean including the Aegean found themselves thrown together in a cultural, an economic, and, more importantly, a spiritual community of interests. This period has never been adequately explored by scholars. Until such time as the complexities of cross-cultural fertilization during the Kushite-Saite period are fully examined from Ionia to Iran and from the Sudan to Urartu, it seems premature to commit oneself to a judgment on the possibilities of Egyptian influence on the Genesis creation account. It may in fact prove to be a simple case of linear borrowing, albeit accompanied by a purposeful intent to "demythologize"; or it may turn out to be a mere sideshow in a far more widespread and complex pattern of cultural exchange.

THE TABLE OF NATIONS

If Genesis 1–2 proffers the tantalizing possibilities of Egyptian influence on Hebrew thought during the seventh and sixth centuries B.C., Genesis 10 clinches the matter.[28] For this chapter gives us a primitive attempt to chart the genealogy of mankind using the meager data available from the close of that period, distorted by the myopic view from Jerusalem.

The Table of Nations comprises a genealogy of a primary tabular form, expanded at points into a narrative genealogy. The table is found in verses 2–4, 6, 7, 22, and 23. After the enumeration of the progeny of each son two formulas are added, one giving a geographical reference for the aforementioned people, and the second a summation. From these verses the family tree presented in Table 7 emerges:

The descendants of Japheth and Shem are carried to the third generation from Noah, those of Ham to the fourth. Whether this has anything to do with Ham's late arrival in the triad, its original members being Japheth, Shem, and Canaan, is a moot point. Of those descendants whose

---

39–49 (Hermopolitan cosmogony); K. Koch, *ZThK* 62 (1965), 251–93 (Memphite theology); H. Goedicke, in *Biblical and Related Studies Presented to Samuel Iwry* (Winona Lake, Ind., 1982), 73–76 (creation of Eve); J. Duchesne-Guilleman, *CRAIBL* (1982), 512–23 (spirit of god).

[28] On Genesis 10, see G. Hölscher, *Drei Erdkarten* (Heidelberg, 1948); J. Simons, *OTS* 10 (1954), 155–84; W. Brandenstein, in *Sprachgeschichte und Wortbedeutung* (Bern, 1954), 57–83; R. North, *A History of Biblical Map Making* (Wiesbaden, 1979), 31–34; J. Van Seters, *In Search of History* (New Haven, Conn., 1983), 27–28; Thompson, *The Origin Tradition*, 77–80.

TABLE 7.
Family Tree According to the Table of Nations

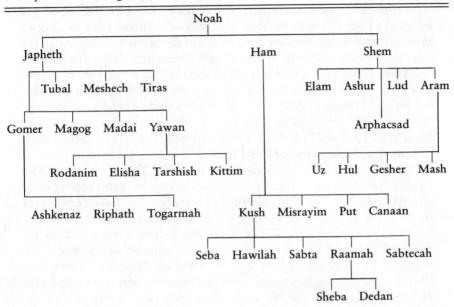

progeny is specified in detail, only the Scythians (the offspring of Gomer, i.e. the Cimmerians), the eastern Greeks, the north Arabian tribes,[29] and the Araemaeans figure in the genealogy. Thus the list has serious gaps, only partly filled by the narrative genealogy that has been inserted.

The narrative genealogy makes use most frequently of the *qal* of √YLD. In verses 21 and 25 alone is the passive of the *qal* found. The former verse is unnecessarily redundant, and, as it is not paralleled by any similar formula in the case of Japheth or Ham, it may safely be classed as a gloss.[30] Verse 25 informs us of the two branches that descended from Eber, who is also mentioned in verse 21.

The narrative sections carry on the families of two (Misrayim and Canaan) of the Hamite races, and one (Arphacsad) of the five Shemites. Japheth is ignored. If, as many would have us believe, we are here faced with the "J" Table of Nations, we must admit that it is incomprehensibly incomplete. Has the P-writer, who is supposed to have provided the framework for the chapter,[31] omitted a good deal of his "J" source, or

[29] With the exception of Sabtecah and possibly also of Sabtah, the sons of Kush are all to be placed in Arabia: M. Astour, *JBL* 84 (1965), 422–23.

[30] Cf. Simons, *OTS* 10 (1954), 170.

[31] S. R. Driver, *An Introduction to the Literature of the Old Testament* (New York, 1956), 14–15; cf. Thompson, *The Origin Tradition*, 77–80, 191–94.

was the latter simply of markedly inferior standard? Clearly the narrative genealogy must be more closely examined.

As Simons has well demonstrated,[32] verses 8–12 which tell of Nimrod are alien to their present context. Not only was Nimrod not mentioned in verse 7 where one would expect him, but the section makes use of the *wayyehi* formula and deals in history rather than genealogy. The point of departure in verses 8 and 9 was the elucidation of a proverb, in that of verses 10–12 the need to amplify the bare mention of Ashur in verse 22. But since the origin of Ashur was Nimrod's kingdom, and since through an erroneous identification Nimrod's father was Kush, verses 10–12 clung to verses 8 and 9, and could not migrate to verse 22 or thereabouts.

In their consistent use of third masculine plural gentilics in place of eponyms, verses 13 and 14 are unique in the table. The writer cannot pass off these eight names as those of *heroes eponymi*; he seems merely to be saying that Egypt is the place of origin of these peoples. But by employing plural forms he has ruptured both the smoothness and the credibility of the genealogy. Verses 16–18a have the same detrimental effect on the tone of the chapter, for they list nine singular gentilics as additional off-spring of Canaan, whose two sons have already been cited (verse 15). That the section is a hasty and unfortunate interpolation by a redactor who thought that the Canaanites should receive fuller treatment is a virtual certainty.[33]

Verses 24 and 25, which deal with the descent of Arphacsad, are derived from the same traditions as are reflected in Genesis 11:12–17. But whereas the latter chapter continues with the progeny of Peleg, 10:26ff. concentrates exclusively on the sons of Joktan, Peleg's brother.

It is clear that the narrative genealogy in the Table of Nations is not a unity but a heterogeneous collection of material. Some is ill-suited to the tabular genealogy and harmonizes poorly with it (e.g., verses 13 and 14, and 16ff.); some is interpolated etiology (e.g., the Nimrod digression) and is out of place in a formal genealogy; and some clearly anticipates what is to come in the next chapter. No matter, then, what judgment one passes on the genuineness of the content of the narrative genealogy, one is forced to admit that it is secondary and supplementary to the table proper. The writer of Genesis began with a table of the sons of Shem, Ham, and Japheth, into which either he or a later redactor inserted a variety of glosses and additions. As might be expected, material for such additions was more readily accessible when it bore upon Hamites or Shemites, who were more familiar to Israel than the distant Japhethites.

The Table of Nations strangely omits to mention the descent of Israel.

---

[32] Simons, *OTS* 10 (1954), 163ff.
[33] Ibid., 167–68.

Even when the writer deals with the progeny of Shem he assiduously avoids the Peleg line, being content perhaps with a scarcely perceptible nod in the direction of the Hebrews by twice referring to Eber, their eponymous ancestor (verses 21, 25). Joktan, Peleg's brother, on the other hand is credited with no fewer than thirteen sons, the enumeration of whom serves only to emphasize the bypassing of Peleg. In the light of Peleg's key position in the descent of Abraham, the lopsidedness of Genesis 10 cannot be set down to chance. The whole chapter it would seem is proleptically supplementary to the descent of Abraham in Genesis 11. The latter is the work of the post-Exilic writer of Genesis whose intent was to trace the ancestry of the Hebrews and thus to define the pedigree of his own race.[34] In the process he felt obliged to place Israel within the broader context of the foreign peoples he was familiar with, and the Table of Nations was the product of his labors.

The discussion thus far has led us to suspect a post-Exilic date for the composition of Genesis 10. Does an examination of the eponyms themselves support this suspicion? Let us examine the tabular genealogy first.

The Japhethites are strung out in a great arc extending on the east to Iran (the Medes) and on the west to the Ionian Greeks on the west coast of Anatolia.[35] This takes in the northern Zagros, Armenia, and all of Asia Minor—that is, the mountainous region that threatens and encloses the Fertile Crescent on the north and northeast. It is coextensive with the incipient empire of the Medes and Persians in the mid-sixth century B.C. Bringing us within the same or a slightly later time range is the list of Yawan's sons, which includes Cyprus and Rhodes.[36] The racial distribu-

---

[34] D. B. Redford, *A Study of the Biblical Joseph Story* (Leiden, 1970), 34–35. Concerning a post-Exilic Yahwistic edition of Genesis, see N. E. Wagner, *CJT* 13 (1967); also, F. V. Winnett, *JBL* 84 (1965), 1–19; Van Seters, *In Search of History*; idem, *Abraham in History and Tradition* (New Haven, Conn., 1975), 125–30 and passim.

[35] E. Dhorme, *Syria* 13 (1932), 35–36.

[36] Kittim and Ridanim; the former is *KTY* in contemporary Semitic inscriptions (see G. A. Cook, *A Textbook of North-Semitic Inscriptions* [Oxford, 1903], 56, 66, 78, 352; Y. Aharoni, *Arad Inscriptions* [Jerusalem, 1981], 12–13; Koehler-Baumgartner, 2:480); the latter is usually taken to be Rhodes (so H. Gunkel, *Genesis* [Göttingen, 1901], 153; Dhorme, *Syria* 13 [1932], 48; J. Simons, *Geographical and Topographical Texts of the Old Testament* [Leiden, 1959], 80), although Schmidtke with much less likelihood has suggested Egyptian *Rtnw*, a vague term for Syria in the second millennium: see his *Die Japhethiten der biblischen Völkertafel* (Breslau, 1926), 84. Of the other two names in this verse, Tarshish has been identified with Tartessos in the western Mediterranean (Dhorme, *Syria* 13 [1932], 45–46; W. F. Albright, *BASOR* 83 [1941], 21–22; U. Täckholm, *Opuscula Romana* 10 [1974–1975], 41–57; M. Elat, *OLP* 13 [1982], 55–69), but this has not commanded universal respect (cf. J. D. Muhly, in *Biblical Archaeologist Today* [Jerusalem, 1985], 185). Elisha is something of a problem. Often in the past it has been equated with Alashiya (Cyprus), a name common in the second millennium (Dhorme, *Syria* 13 [1932], 44; Speiser, *Genesis*, 66; Koehler-Baumgartner, 1:55); but was it still used in the middle of

tion envisaged here was brought about by the Greek colonization of the eastern Mediterranean, which began at the end of the eighth century B.C.[37] The Hebrews first became familiar with Greeks during the Exile (Ezek. 27:13, 19); but it was not until after the Exile that they began to encounter them frequently (Isa. 66:19, Joel 4:6, Zech. 9:13, Dan. 8:21, 10:20, 11:2). Heading the sons of Japheth is Gomer, the eponymous ancestor of the Cimmerians.[38] The latter appear, according to Assyrian sources, in Urartu in the late eighth century and are grouped with the Medes and the Manai in texts of Esarhaddon's time.[39] In 644 B.C. the Cimmerians swept over Lydia, capturing Sardis and slaying Gyges the Lydian king. Thereafter their decline was fairly rapid, and from about 630 B.C. on their place was taken by the Scythians.[40] Now in verse 3 Gomer is made the father of Ashkenaz (the Scythians); in other words the succession of the Scythians to the seat of their Cimmerian predecessors is known to the writer, and the *terminus a quo* must in consequence be the last quarter of the seventh century.

The sons of Ham number four: Kush, Misrayim, Libya (Put),[41] and Canaan. The order here is not geographical but political.[42] The precedence of Kush over Egypt is a clear reflection of the political preeminence the kingdom of Kush (Napata) enjoyed from its conquest of Egypt about 711 B.C. down to its defeat by Psammetichos II (c. 593 B.C.).[43] Even after

---

the first millennium? Simons, *OTS* 10 (1954), 178, has suggested Strabo's Elaioussa, an island off the coast of Asia Minor, and Skinner long ago compared Elissa, the legendary foundress of Carthage (*Genesis* [Edinburgh, 1910], 198), but neither suggestion commands respect.

[37] M. I. Finley, *Early Greece: The Bronze and Archaic Ages* (London, 1981), 90ff.; J. Boardman, *The Greeks Overseas* (London, 1980); R. H. Pfeiffer, *JBL* 56 (1937), 92–93; idem, *Introduction to the Old Testament* (New York, 1948), 206. To say that the verse reflects the situation which obtained around 710–610 B.C. is too vague; it reflects rather the situation *first brought about* during that period, but since the Greeks remained on Cyprus for centuries this is only to establish a *terminus a quo*.

[38] Skinner, 196; Simons, *Geographical and Topographical Texts*, 38–39.

[39] Dhorme, *Syria* 13 (1932), 29ff.; L. F. Hartman, *JNES* 21 (1962), 25–37; A. J. Spalinger, *JAOS* 98 (1978), 400–409.

[40] Helck, *LdÄ* 5 (1984), 990–91.

[41] Egyptian *Pywd*, Coptic *Phaiat*, Persian *Putaua*; R. G. Kent, *JNES* 2 (1943), 306; the name of a tribe that came to prominence in the ninth century (H. K. Jacquet-Gordon, *JEA* 46 [1960] 20), and later became eponymous for Libya: see G. Posener, *La première domination perse en Égypte* (Cairo, 1936), 186–87; Simons, *Geographical and Topographial Texts*, secs. 149, 198, 1313; Koehler-Baumgartner, 3:866–67.

[42] *Pace* Hölscher (*Dreid Erdkarten*, 52–53), whose preconceived idea that the list proceeds from east to west leads to the fantastic conclusion that Canaan stands for Punic Carthage.

[43] E. Drioton and J. Vandier, *L'Égypte*[4] (Paris, 1962), 594–95; see also W. Spiegelberg, *Ägyptologische Randglossen zum alten Testament* (Strasbourg, 1904), 9–10; D. B. Redford, *JARCE* 22 (1985), 5–15.

that date Kush continued to hold the first rank in tradition, as Herodotus and Diodorus attest.[44] Libya is in third place; the Libyan supremacy of the 22nd and 23rd Dynasties (c. 950–720 B.C.) is in the distant past. Last comes Canaan, a faint reminder of the erstwhile extent of Nilotic influence.[45] But Canaan is a mere name; its heyday is in the remote past, and neither Genesis 10 nor the Patriarchal Tales know much about it or its legendary inhabitants. One of the sons of Kush is a certain Sabtecah, who has been plausibly identified with the Kushite king Shabtaka (697–690 B.C.)[46] But here he masquerades as an eponymous ancestor. In sum the evidence would seem to point to late seventh or early sixth century as the *terminus a quo* for the situation envisaged by the Hamitic list.

The presence of Elam at the head of the Shemites might transport us back to the mid-seventh century, before the annihilation of that state at the hands of Ashurbanipal. The second name, Ashur, suggests a *terminus ad quem* of 612 B.C. when Assyria was overthrown. But if we take these *termini* seriously, we are probably unwisely disregarding the survival of great names even after the place to which they refer no longer exists. Tradition is tenacious and toponyms often have a long life. Arphacsad is usually taken as a designation of Babylonia, whose absence from the table (except in verse 10) would be otherwise inexplicable.[47] Lud may be Lydia, though by what rationalization it was brought into the family of Shem remains a mystery.[48]

In the tabular genealogy the evidence is almost unanimous: the last half of the seventh century B.C. is the *terminus a quo* for the political and ethnic distribution that lies behind the Table of Nations. The picture revealed is, as it were, the last glimpse the Judaeans as an independent nation had of the world before the Exile claimed them; and with some modifications it was also the picture they conjured up when they emerged from their enforced sojourn abroad.

The evidence to be gleaned from the narrative genealogy does nothing to weaken this hypothesis. The seven sons of Egypt comprise the first branch of the Hamites we encounter in the narrative genealogy. The only certain member of the group is Pathrusim, which is a masculine plural back formation from Egyptian p^3t^3rsi, "the south land," a designation of

[44] According to Herodotus (3.19ff.) Cambyses was unable to conquer Kush, and showed himself to be inferior to its king. On the tradition that civilization had entered Egypt from Kush, see Diodorus 3.3; A. B. Lloyd, *Herodotus Book II. A Commentary* (Leiden, 1988), 3:94, 168.

[45] Simons, *Geographical and Topographical Texts*, 19.

[46] E. G. Kraeling, *Rand McNally Bible Atlas*, 49; Astour, *JBL* 84 (1965), 421ff.

[47] Hölscher, *Drei Erdkarten*, 46–47; Simons, OTS 10 (1954), 174; idem, *Geographical and Topographical Texts*, 9.

[48] Hölscher's strange localization of Lud on the Palestinian coast (*Drei Erdkarten*, 51–52) is out of the question.

Upper Egypt originating in the New Kingdom, but common in the form cited (i.e., with the article) only in demotic.[49] Scholarly consensus identifies Kaphtor with Keftiu, a name for some region of the Aegean (probably Crete), and Lehabim with the Labu, a Libyan tribe.[50] In my opinion, there is no reason to reject the identification of the Ludim with the Lydians of Asia Minor.[51] Elsewhere in the Old Testament the Ludim are referred to as fierce fighters (cf. Isa. 66:19, Jer. 46:9, Ezek. 27:10); and it was the bellicosity of the Lydians that led Herodotus to call them the best fighters in all Asia.[52] About 655 B.C. Psammetichos I of Egypt entered into an alliance with Gyges of Lydia,[53] and it was probably pursuant to this treaty that Lydians began to enter Egypt as mercenaries. The sequence of consonants '-N in Anamim suggests the name '(y)n, a frequent designation of bodies of water in the Egyptian Delta,[54] but Albright's identification with the Anami, a people occupying the north African coast in the time of Sargon of Assyria (721–705 B.C.), is probably the best suggestion to date.[55] By its position in the list Naphtuhim might appear to be a term for the Delta, as the next entry Pathrusim is of the valley, and so Erman[56] and Spiegelberg[57] both understood it. Erman's *Patmuhim*, however, involves an arbitrary emendation, and Spiegelberg's Natho not only an emendation but a misunderstanding as well.[58] The consonant sequence P-T-Ḥ suggests the presence of the god's name "Ptah," and Hirsch long ago reconstructed a *Niwt-ptḥ* "the City of Ptah" (i.e., Memphis) as the Egyptian *Vorlage*.[59] In spite of Spiegelberg's objection that no such place was forth-

---

[49] I.e., from about 600 B.C. on: cf. H. Gauthier, *Dictionnaire des noms géographiques contenus dans les textes hieroglyphiques* (Cairo, 1931), 6:27. D. B. Redford, in *Anchor Bible Dictionary*, s.v. "Pathros" (forthcoming). Other Biblical occurrences of Pathros (cf. Isa. 11:11, Jer. 44:1, 15) presuppose the Diaspora.

[50] Gauthier, *Dictionnaire*, 3:117; Simons, on insuffcent grounds it seems to me, is opposed: cf. *Geographical and Topographical Texts*, 56.

[51] Skinner, *Geographical and Topographical Texts*, 57; idem, *Genesis*, 212; Speiser, *Genesis*, 68.

[52] Herodotus, 1.80–81.

[53] F. K. Keinitz, *Die politische Geschichte Aegyptens vom 7. bis zum 4. Jahrhundert vor der Zeitwende* (Berlin, 1953), 12; Spalinger, *JAOS* 98 (1978), 400ff.

[54] Gauthier, *Dictionnaire* 1:145–46; P. Montet, *Géographie de l'Égypte ancienne* (Paris, 1957), 1:66.

[55] *JPOS* 1 (1921), 191–92.

[56] *ZAW* 10 (1890), 118–19.

[57] *OLZ* 9 (1906), 276ff.; Spiegelberg, *Ägyptologische Randglossen*, 6.

[58] The place name *Natho* is not *N³-idhw*, "the Delta Marshes", but *N³y-t³ḥwt*, literally "those belonging to the Mansion [of Ramesses III]"; see A. F. Gardiner, *Ancient Egyptian Onomastica* (Oxford, 1947), 2:146˙ff.; W. Helck, *Die altägyptische Gaue* (Wiesbaden, 1974), 178.

[59] Hirsch, *Vierteljahrsschrift für Bibelkunde*, 2:413ff. W. Vycichl (*ZÄS* 76 [1940], 88–89) derives it from פַּתְמֹחִים.

coming from ancient Egyptian texts,[60] the idea is an attractive one and finds some support in *Niwt-Imn* (Hebrew *No-Amon*), "the City of Amun," a late appellative of Thebes.[61] Finally Kasluhim is utterly obscure. Müller's emendation to Nasmonim and subsequent identification with a north African tribe mentioned by Herodotus involve too risky a modification of the Hebrew.[62] One would like to see in Kasluhim a garbled form of Kalasiries, the warrior class mentioned in demotic and in classical authors;[63] but this too necessitates a shaky prior assumption.

One thing seems certain: the writer of verses 13–14 knew these terms as appellatives of whole peoples and felt no need or justification for conjuring up eponymous ancestors for them. In some cases (Ludim, Lehabim, probably Anamim) he was correct; in others (Pathrusim, Caphtorim, probably Naphtuhim) he was creating gentilics from toponyms. To say that Egypt fathered peoples, rather than specific sons whose names are then listed, is a clear weakening of the metaphor on which the form of the genealogy is shaped. The content of verses 13–14 represents Egypt's position vis-à-vis certain peoples and states for which no expression in the traditional metaphor of genealogy had heretofore been deemed necessary. When we plot on a map the geographical extent of Egypt's "family," we find it reaching into Libya and along the north African coast, to the Aegean and Asia Minor; absent is Kush and the coast of Palestine and Syria. This is precisely the limits of Egypt's sphere of influence and interest during much of the Saite Period (26th Dynasty).

The brief notice of Canaan's progeny in verse 15 transports us within the same period. "Heth" is an allusion, not to the Hittites of the second millennium and their homeland, but to the states of Syria collectively called Khatte by the Assyrians and Babylonians from the ninth[64] to the sixth centuries B.C.[65] That Sidon should be classed as the firstborn of Canaan instead of Tyre, which is not even mentioned, points to a period when Tyre's fortunes were at a low ebb, and Sidon was the leading city of Phoenicia. Such a situation obtained between Nebuchadrezzar's destruction of Tyre in the early sixth century B.C.[66] and the Tennes rebellion of the fourth.[67]

We cannot escape the conclusion that the narrative genealogy, like the

[60] *OLZ* 9 (1906), 278.
[61] Gardiner, *Onomastica*, 2:24*f.
[62] *OLZ* 5 (1902), 474.
[63] Spiegelberg, *ZÄS* 43 (1906), 87ff.
[64] Simons, *OTS* 10 (1954), 167.
[65] D. J. Wiseman, *Chronicles of Chaldaean Kings* (London, 1956) 25, 68ff.
[66] D. Baramki, *Phoenicia and the Phoenicians* (Beirut, 1961), 30–31.
[67] D. Barag, *BASOR* 183 (1966), 6ff.

tabular, reflects a sixth to fifth century placement of peoples and states.[68] It is essentially the view of the world that the Jews carried with them into Exile, slightly modified by their descendants who returned to their native land three or four generations later. If there be any elements of genuine antiquity in this picture, it is due to the political and ethnic condition of Israel's world in the Saite period, not to any independent Hebrew traditions of long standing. The Egypt that shows through in the Table of Nations is the Egypt of Psammetichos I and his descendants, the 26th Dynasty. To contend that the Hebrews must have been familiar with Egypt from high antiquity is to belabor a truism. But the post-Exilic editor was publishing for his contemporaries; and the Egypt he felt obliged to explain for them was the Nilotic power of his own time.

THE SOJOURN AND EXODUS

There is perhaps no other scriptural tradition so central to the reconstruction of Israel's history that Deuteronomy presents us with than the Exodus of the Hebrews from Egypt. It has become a prototype of salvation, a symbol of freedom and the very core of a great world religion. Yet to the historian it remains the most elusive of all the salient events of Israelite history. The event is supposed to have taken place in Egypt, yet Egyptian sources know it not. On the morrow of the Exodus Israel numbered approximately 2.5 million (extrapolated from Num. 1:46); yet the entire population of Egypt at the time was only 3 to 4.5 million![69] The effect on Egypt must have been cataclysmic—loss of a servile population, pillaging of gold and silver (Exod. 3:21–22, 12:31–36), destruction of an army—yet at no point in the history of the country during the New Kingdom is there the slightest hint of the traumatic impact such an event would have had on economics or society. As we have already seen, the Asiatic population in Egypt had lingered during the New Kingdom and a part of it had been assigned construction tasks (p. 221ff.); but the "store-cities" of the Exodus story (1:11) are a purely Israelite phenomenon, and the progressive assimilation of the Asiatic population during the New Kingdom is not reflected in the Exodus at all.

Clearly something is wrong. Are we approaching the subject from the proper direction? Have we been reading the primary source in Exodus too naively? Is there evidence we have missed?

The almost insurmountable difficulties in interpreting the Exodus narrative as history have led some to dub it "mythology rather than . . . a detailed reporting of the historical facts" and therefore impossible to lo-

[68] Certainly not the end of the second millennium, as S. Herrmann, *A History of Israel in Old Testament Times* (London, 1975), 42.

[69] Cf. K. Baer, *JARCE* 1 (1962), 44.

cate geographically.[70] This is a curious resort, for the text does not look like mythology (at least on the definition of the latter as a timeless event set in the world of the gods). The Biblical writer certainly thinks he is writing datable history, and provides genealogical material by means of which the date may be computed. He also thinks it is possible to locate this event on the ground, and packs his narrative with topographical detail. That the resemblance in plot pattern and motif (especially in the "Song of the Sea") to the "Hero-god versus the Monster Sea" suggests a mythic basis to the story, which only later underwent historicization, is more ingenious than illuminating. After all, the feats of Ramesses II on the battlefield occasion the abundant use of imagery drawn from the motif Hero-god versus Chaos; but Kadesh was a real battle nonetheless!

Of prior concern here should be the date of the sources in Exodus 1–14 judged empirically on the basis of datable details. The latter, it must be admitted, are few and most are of a toponymic nature.[71] Research on these place-names, however, has proceeded far beyond the stage of Cazelle's classic article of thirty-five years ago;[72] and we can now genuinely speak of a unanimity of the evidence.[73] Whoever supplied the geographical information that now adorns the story had no information earlier than the Saite period (seventh to sixth centuries B.C.). The eastern Delta and Sinai he describes are those of the 26th Dynasty kings and the early Persian overlords: his toponyms reflect the renewed interest in the eastern frontier evidenced for this period by fort building and canalization. He knows of "Goshen" of the Qedarite Arabs, and a legendary "Land of Ramesses." He cannot locate the Egyptian court to anything but the largest and most famous city in his own day in the northeastern Delta, namely Tanis, the royal residence from about 1070 to 725 B.C. (cf. Psalm 78:12, 43), which survives as a metropolis into Roman times;[74] and he mistak-

---

[70] G. W. Ahlström, *Who Were the Israelites?* (Winona Lake, Ind., 1986), 46–49; Cf. S. Mowinckel, in *Die Religion in Geschichte und Gegenwart*[4] (Tübingen, 1960), 1274–78; C. Kloos, *Yhwh's Combat with the Sea* (Leiden, 1986), 139ff.

[71] The toponymic detail is usually assigned to the P-redaction of the Exodus account, the earliest focus of the tale locating the major incident only at "the Sea" (P. Weimar, *Die Meerwundererzählung* [Wiesbaden, 1985], 68ff.). The traditional source division of Exodus 1–14, however, perhaps makes the problem seem a little more complicated than it in fact is: ibid., passim; M. North, *Exodus* (London, 1962).

[72] H. Cazelle, *RB* 62 (1955), 321–64.

[73] For the details, see D. B. Redford, in A. F. Rainey, ed., *Egypt, Israel, Sinai* (Tel Aviv, 1987), 137–61.

[74] On Tanis, see most recently M. Romer, *LdÄ* 6 (1986), 194–209. Incidentally, efforts to put forward passages in the Joseph and Moses narratives about the proximity of the royal residence to Goshen as proof of the veracity of the Biblical account (see e.g. N. Sarna, *Exploring Exodus* [New York, 1986], 10) are quite wrongheaded. Even if the sources were not folkloristic in origin, throughout the 18th Dynasty the principal royal residence was at Memphis, or in its environs, with the brief interval of some twenty-five years when the court

enly presses into service the adjacent marshy tract "the reed-(lake)" as the "Reed-sea,"[75] the scene of Israel's miraculous passage to safety. The route he is familiar with is that which traverses the same tract as the canal of Necho II (610–594 B.C.) from Bubastis to the Bitter Lakes; then he moves north in his mind's eye past the famous fort at Migdol to Lake Sirbonis (Ba'al Saphon) where Horus had already in the mythical past thrown Seth out of Egypt. In short, with respect to the geography of the Exodus, the post-Exilic compiler of the present Biblical version had no genuinely ancient details. He felt constrained to supply them from the Egypt of his own day and, significantly perhaps, cited several places where Asiatic elements and especially Judaean mercenaries resided in the sixth and fifth centuries.[76]

When we move beyond toponymy, the Egyptian origin of specific details and even the Egyptian locale of the tale become very hazy indeed. The Nile and its plant life are mentioned, as well as mud brick as a building material (especially common in the Delta); and certain plagues (e.g., frogs, gnats, flies) seem appropriate to a Nilotic setting. A knowledge of the agricultural year in the Nile Valley may also be attested by 9:31–32. But apart from these few features of the plot, the story could have taken place anywhere.

A perusal of the Bondage and Exodus narratives strains the imagination to elicit Egyptian background; but the following details may be passed in review. The term "Pharaoh" is ubiquitous and is used, as it was in the first millennium B.C., as a synonym for the word "king," or even misunderstood as a personal name (cf. Exod. 6:29).[77] The birth of Moses and his being secreted in the rushes has been likened to the fate of Horus in late mythology;[78] but in fact the motif of the "Birth of the Hero" has much wider currency in antiquity and is not Egyptian in origin.[79] The rod that turns into a serpent (Exod. 4:2–4, 7:10–12) recalls the wax model

---

resided at Thebes and Amarna. It is dangerous to confuse origin—the 18th Dynasty came originally from Thebes—with place of domicile.

[75] Hebrew *sup*, usually derived from Egyptian *twfy*, "reed lake" in the northeast Delta. Much has been written on this body of water, sometimes in an effort to discount this identification: J. R. Towers, *JNES* 18 (1959), 150–53; N. H. Snaith, *VT* 15 (1965), 395–98; N. Lohfink, *JBL* 85 (1966), 137–58; B. S. Childs, *VT* 20 (1970), 406–18; B. F. Batto, *JBL* 102 (1983), 27ff.; see the trenchant comments of Kloos, *Yhwh's Combat* 153–57; also Weimar, *Die Meerwundererzählung* 258–61.

[76] Cf. Migdol (Jer. 44:1); cf. J. Fitzmyer, *JNES* 21 (1962), 19. The absence of the Exodus tradition from early Biblical material should also be noted: S. Norin, *Es Spaltete das Meer* (Lund, 1977), 195–96.

[77] J. Osing, *LdÄ* 4 (1982), 1021.

[78] W. Helck, *VT* 15 (1965), 48.

[79] D. B. Redford, *Numen* 14 (1967), 209–28; J. S. Ackerman, in K.R.R. Gros Louis, *Literary Interpretations of Biblical Narrative* (Nashville, Tenn., 1974).

that turns into a live crocodile when grasped;[80] and the "magicians" who can emulate this trick derive their designation from an Egyptian loan-word.[81] Apart from a vague appropriateness of some of the afflictions, the Ten Plagues are not especially "Egyptian" in background, although pestilence and cataclysm were very well known in ancient Egypt.[82] The motif of turning the river into blood (7:20–24) is known from Mesopotamia, as well perhaps as a plague of flies.[83] Darkness (10:21–23) certainly was feared by the Egyptians, and failure of the sun to shine signaled a desperate state of affairs;[84] but it could not be construed as a plague. The slaying of the firstborn does, indeed, enjoy some parallels in Egyptian mythology (none however of much prominence); and attention has been drawn with respect to blood on the doorposts (12:22)[85] to the apotropaic use of the color red among the Egyptians. The possibility of offending the Egyptians by offering items that are somehow taboo (Exod. 8:26) recalls the piety attached to wholesale animal worship in the Late Period and the revulsion caused by the inadvertent killing of individuals.[86] The "pillar of fire" curiously recalls a common figure used in high-flown jargon of the Egyptian king leading his troops into battle as a "sun disk (or other luminary) at the head of his army."[87] Finally, the rolling back of the water to get at the dry bottom, and the flood of water to drown enemies are both known in Egyptian folklore.[88]

None of this suggests a close familiarity with Egypt. But it might be explained as a "demythologizing" tendency, or even a sort of *Interpretatio Hebraica* of certain myths and cultural traits, indulged in by Israelite

[80] A. Erman, *The Ancient Egyptians: A Source Book of Their Writings* (New York, 1966), 38.

[81] See p. 385.

[82] On the widespread parallels to the individual plagues, see F. Dumermuth, *ZAW* 76 (1964), 323–25; On the literary transmission and present organization of the plague narrative in Exodus, see G. Fohrer, *Überlieferung und Geschichte des Exodus* (Berlin, 1964), 62–70; D. J. McCarthy, *CBQ* 27 (1965), 336–45; idem, *JBL* 85 (1966), 137–58; M. Greenberg, in *Fourth World Congress of Jewish Studies* (Jerusalem, 1967), 1:51–54; W. H. Schmidt, *Exodus, Sinai und Mose* (Darmstadt, 1983), 49–54.

[83] S. N. Kramer, *Ar Or* 17 (1949), 399–405; idem, *The Sumerians* (Chicago, 1963), 162–64; W. G. Lambert and A. R. Millard, *Atra-hasis: The Babylonian Story of the Flood* (London, 1969), III, 46–vi, 4.

[84] Cf. W. Helck, *Die Prophezeiung des Nfr.tj* (Wiesbaden, 1970), 43–45.

[85] M. Gilula, *Tel Aviv* 4 (1977), 94ff.; Y. Koenig, *Journal Asiatique* 273 (1985), 8–10.

[86] Herodotus, 2.65–76; A. B. Lloyd, *Herodotus Book II. A Commentary* (Leiden, 1975), 1:141ff.; 2:291ff.

[87] D. B. Redford, *JARCE* 13 (1976), 49–50.

[88] Magicians are adept at dividing the waters: cf. Westcar 6, 8–14 (Lichtheim, *Ancient Egyptian Literature* [Berkeley, Calif. 1976], 1:217): I Khamois 3, 30–31 M. (Lichtheim, *Ancient Egyptian Literature* [Berkeley, Calif., 1980], 3:130). On waters diverted to drown enemies, see Herodotus, 2.100 (Nitocris's revenge on her brother's murderers).

aliens living among Egyptians, or close enough to have limited and distorted knowledge of their customs.

Despite the lateness and unreliability of the story in Exodus, no one can deny that the tradition of Israel's coming out of Egypt was one of long standing. It is found in early poetry (e.g., Exod. 15) and is constantly alluded to by the prophets.[89] One cannot help but conclude that there was an early and persistent memory of a voluntary descent into Egypt by pastoralists in which one Jacob, who was later to achieve a reputation as an ancestral figure, played a leading role. Those who had made the descent, the tradition went on to elaborate, had not only prospered and multiplied, but had for a period of four generations grown exceedingly influential in Egypt. Subsequently a strong hostility had been evinced by the autochthonous population toward the Asiatic interlopers; and the latter had been forced to retire to the Levanthine littoral whence they had come.

There is only one chain of *historical* events that can accommodate this late tradition, and that is the Hyksos descent and occupation of Egypt (see chapter 5). The memory of this major event in the history of the Levant survived not only in Egyptian sources. It would be strange indeed if the West Semitic speaking population of Palestine, whence the invaders had come in MB IIB, had not also preserved in their folk memory this great moment of (for them) glory. And in fact it is in the Exodus account that we are confronted with the "Canaanite" version of this event, featuring the great ancestral leader Jacob, the four-generation span, the memory of political primacy, the occupation of the eastern fringe of the Delta, and so on. It became part of the origin stories of all the Semitic enclaves of the area, and from there it even spread to the north and west where it became current among the non-Semites.

Since we have next to nothing by way of textual witnesses to the folklore of the Canaanites of the Levant, traces of an "Exodus" tradition apart from the Hebrew version are difficult to find. But they do exist. Strabo preserves the memory of an army drowned in the sea, localized on the Palestinian coast north of Acre, and is aware of similar phenomena at Mount Casius "near Egypt."[90] Legend had it that certain communities in Asia and Mesopotamia had originated in Egypt;[91] and in early Roman times the population of Palestine was considered to have originated from "Egyptian, Arabian and Phoenician tribes."[92]

But the best-preserved non-Biblical memory of the sojourn and Exodus

---

[89] E.g. the eighth-century prophets: Hosea 11:1, 12:9, 13; Amos 3:1, 9:7, etc. On the date of Exodus 15, see now Ahlström, *Who Were the Israelites?*, 50–51 (with literature).

[90] Strabo 16.2.26.

[91] Diodorus 1.28.1; Herodotus, 2.104; A. Burton, *Diodorus Siculus Book I. A Commentary* (Leiden, 1972), 118.

[92] Strabo, 16.2.34.

was that preserved in "Phoenician" legend, and surviving today in classical sources.[93] From at least as early as the fifth century B.C. and perhaps earlier—the details are already a commonplace in Herodotus—Levantine communities remembered a descent to the Nile of one Io, her marriage to the reigning king and the list of her descendants through her son Epafos (Apophis). Io's line ruled over Egypt for four generations, whereupon her great grandson Agenor retired to Phoenicia, where he became a great king, and his brother Belos (Baʿal) to Mesopotamia. Belos's son Danaos, after a contretemps with his brother Aegyptos, fled to Argos.[94] Both the origin and the ultimate settlement, however, of the main elements of the movement are linked with "Phoenicia": Epaphos's brother is said to be "Phoenix" and Epaphos himself at one stage in his career was in Byblos, while Kadmos, son of Agenor, in concert with Danaos, led the foreigners expelled from Egypt.[95]

In sum, therefore, we may state that the memory of the Hyksos expulsion did indeed live on in the folklore of the Canaanite population of the southern Levant. The exact details were understandably blurred and subconsciously modified over time, for the purpose of "face-saving." It became not a conquest but a peaceful descent of a group with pastoral associations who rapidly arrived at a position of political control.[96] Their departure came not as a result of ignominious defeat, but either voluntarily or as a flight from a feud, or yet again as salvation from bondage. Nor are we justified in construing as a difficulty the discrepancy between the bondage tradition of Exodus 1:11–14 and the historical reality of the Hyksos expulsion: the Biblical writer has here incorporated another figment of legend for which, in fact, he had Egypt to thank.

During the Saite and Persian periods there took shape in Egypt two types of popular story, redolent with a patriotic jingoism. One took as its plot the invasion of Egypt from the north, the destructiveness of a foreign occupation, and the eventual expulsion of the invaders by Egyptian forces coming from the south. The other centered upon the infestation of Egypt by plague-ridden or leprous peoples (usually foreign), and the steps taken

[93] See in particular M. Astour, *Hellenosemitica* (Leiden, 1965), 83–92, and passim. I use "Phoenician" in the sense the classical writers employed it, i.e. as a designation of the east Mediterranean littoral from Orthosia to Pelusium (Strabo, 16.2.21).

[94] Apollodorus, 2.1.3–4; 3.1.1; cf. J. Berard, *Syria* 29 (1952), 1–43; idem, *RHR* 151 (1957), 221–30.

[95] Jacoby, *FGr. Hist.* IA.3, frag. 21, 86; IIIA, 264 frag. 6; R. B. Edwards, *Kadmos the Phoenician* (Amsterdam, 1979), 23–29. Epaphos' spiriting away to Byblos has Osirian overtones: J. G. Griffiths, *De Iside et Osiride* (Cardiff, 1970), 443. One wonders whether the slaughter of the sons of Aegyptos has anything to do with the slaying of the firstborn.

[96] Io marries into the royal family; Joseph is virtual ruler of the land, and in fact in later apocryphal literature and Targums is called "king": G. T. Zervos, in J. H. Charlesworth, *The Old Testament Pseudepigrapha* (New York, 1985), 2:469.

to rid Egypt of their blight. It takes little discernment to recognize in the first plot pattern a repeated motif in Egyptian history—Thebes in the south had thrice attempted to spearhead wars of liberation against the north—but in its present formulation the story owes more to the national fervor awakened by the disastrous invasions (or attempted invasions) of the Assyrian, Neo-Babylonian, and Persian states from 671 to 525 B.C. The second story-type, on the other hand, has deeper roots, although it too was shaped and brought to relevance by the ubiquity of foreign enclaves in Egypt from Saite times on. As we have them for the Hellenistic age—none earlier have survived—examples show that both plot patterns could be welded into a single tale, although they also appear separately.[97] Certainly the earliest to come down to us in detail—Hecataeus of Abdera bears an earlier but imperfect witness—is the account in Manetho's *Aegyptica* (first half of the third century B.C.).[98] The "bare bones" of Manetho's account runs as follows:

A.	1.	The King (Amenophis/Hor) desires to see the gods.
	2.	Amenophis son of Paapis the seer declares he may if he cleanses the land of lepers.
	3.	The King sends all lepers to the quarries east of the Nile.
	4.	Amenophis the seer predicts an invasion of thirteen years.
	5.	Amenophis commits suicide.
	6.	The lepers ask that they be allowed to live in Avaris.
	7.	In Avaris the lepers choose as their leader Osarsiph, priest of Heliopolis.
	8.	Osarsiph makes monotheistic and racially exclusive laws.
BRIDGE	9.	Osariph invites the Shepherds "back" to Avaris.
B.	10.	The Shepherds return.
	11.	The King hides the divine images and sends his five-year-old son to safety.
	12.	The King declines to fight the Shepherds and retreats to Ethiopia.
	13.	The Shepherds lay Egypt waste.
GLOSS	14.	Reiteration of the PN Osarsiph and identification with Moses.
A + B	15.	Amenophis and his son Rapsaces drive out the Shepherds.

It is clear that numbers 10–13 with the addition of 15 is but a variant of the "Invasion-from-the-North" theme. In fact, the details of numbers

---

[97] Most will be found translated in M. Stern, *Greek and Latin Authors on Jews and Judaism*, vol. 1 (Jerusalem, 1974); see also S. K. Eddy, *The King Is Dead* (Lincoln, 1961); D. B. Redford, *Pharaonic King-lists, Annals and Day-books* (Toronto, 1986), 281–96.

[98] Redford, *King-lists*, 282–83.

12 and 13 point directly to the inspiration of the popular view of events in the seventh and sixth centuries. Both Taharqa and Tanwetaman, as noted, had beat a hasty retreat from Memphis to Nubia, not wishing to engage the Assyrians in battle. And in the slaughter of the sacred animals, the Shepherds emulate the reputed acts of the Persians.[99]

But items 1–8[100] and one form of 15 compose our version of the tale of the unclean ones, and here at least the underlying historical reality can be extracted easily. "Amenophis" the king (or Hor, a sobriquet) is Amenophis III, and his desire to see the gods a folk interpretation of passages from his inscriptions.[101] Amenophis son of Paapis is Amenhotep son of Hapu, the historical secretary of labor who served under Amenophis III, gained a reputation for wisdom while he lived, and for over fifteen centuries was revered as a healing "demigod."[102] The dispatch of the impure ones to quarries east of the Nile is an etiological explanation of the whirl-wind of quarrying and construction that went on during the reigns of Amenophis III and Akhenaten, prominent textual records of which remained on view for all to see. Memorial stelae commemorating the quarry work were inscribed at Tura opposite Memphis in Middle Egypt under Amenophis III;[103] and the stela of Akhenaten at Gebel Silsileh is the most prominent monument at the site.[104] The text of the latter suggests a magnitude for the operation not much different from that of Amenophis's roundup of lepers: "The first occasion when His Majesty issued a command . . . to pursue all work from Elephantine to Sam-behdet,[105] and to the commanders of the army to levy a numerous corvée for quarrying sandstone in order to make the great *benden* of Re-harakhty . . . the princes, courtiers, supervisors and managers were in charge of its impressment for transporting the stone." The use of the Greek terms "lepers" and "unclean" suggests a pejorative in the original Egyptian (or demotic) that in Pharaonic propaganda was customarily attached to undesirable antisocial elements, whether native or foreign. In the present case it seems clear that the devotees of Akhenaten's sun cult are the historical reality underlying the "lepers," and this is confirmed by the iconoclastic nature of the lepers' legislation and the figure of thirteen years for the occupation, which corresponds to the period of occupation of Amarna.[106] Osarsiph moreover is remembered as a priest of Heliopolis,

[99] A. T. Olmstead, *History of the Persian Empire* (Chicago, 1948), 89–90.

[100] With the exception of 4–5, which as it now stands anticipates 10–13.

[101] Redford *King-lists*, 248–51.

[102] D. Wildung, *Imhotep und Amenhotep* (Berlin, 1977).

[103] *Urk* IV, 1677, 1681.

[104] *Urk* IV, 1962, Redford, *King-lists*, 293, n. 113.

[105] I.e., from the First Cataract to the Mediterranean.

[106] I.e., eleven full years under Akhenaten and two under Tutankhamun.

where sun worship was endemic, and his name may be construed as a pejorative applied in later tradition to Akhenaten.[107]

From what has been adduced to this point it is clear that the first half of Manetho's Osarseph tradition (the "A" pattern) descends from an etiological tale bearing upon the Amarna period of Egyptian history. The story probably originally concluded with the 19th Dynasty kings Sety I (Mernepath) and his son Ramesses II finally putting an end to the Amarna interlude; thus it would conform to the revised king list of later Ramesside times, in which the four "Amarna" reigns are excised and their years added to Horemheb, so that the 19th Dynasty follows Amenhotep III immediately. The pattern A, then, would probably have originated toward the end of the New Kingdom, as one of the many legends told of illustrious kings of the 17th and 18th Dynasties;[108] but it must have come into Manetho's hands in a demotic version of the Saite or early Persian periods.

The fate of the victims in the Osarsiph legend differs from that of the Hyksos. The latter were expelled through war, whereas the lepers were enslaved. It is from Osarsiph or its prototype that the "Bondage" tradition of Exodus originated. To the conceivable argument that the direction of dependence might be reversed, a cogent rebuttal can be given. The assignment of quarry work and heavy-stone construction to captives in Egypt is better attested than brick making,[109] and is thus more appropriate in a tale with an Egyptian setting. The use of brick is, of course, ubiquitous in Egypt, and especially in the Delta; but "store-cities" are an Asiatic phenomenon and brick making as the appropriate job for a captive servile population is well known in the Neo-Assyrian empire.[110]

If one cannot resist the urge to read scripture uncritically as history, the blocks of material describing the lives and careers of Moses and Joseph teem with pitfalls. For there are no more enigmatic and elusive figures in the entire Bible.

Moses, in the final form the P-editor gave to the Pentatuch, is tied to

---

[107] See D. B. Redford, in N. Swelin, ed., *Alexandrian Studies Presented to Daoud abu Daoud* (forthcoming).

[108] Cf. the story of Apophis and Sekenenre.

[109] See p. 221ff.; also Redford in Rainey, *Egypt, Israel, Sinai*, 145–47. It is true that in the famous scene from the tomb of Rekhmere, the brickmakers are identified as "the captivity which His Majesty brought for work on the Temple of Amun" (N. de G. Davis, *The Tomb of Rekhmire at Thebes* [New York, 1943], pl. 59); but the workers look no different from the Egyptians, and where they were captured is not stated.

[110] B. Oded, *Mass Deportations and Deportees in the Neo-Assyrian Empire* (Wiesbaden, 1979), 54–58, 90, 111. Of course no one can deny that brickmakers constituted a major part of the Egyptian labor force, and we have the texts and reliefs to prove it (cf. K. A. Kitchen, *Tyndale House Bulletin* 27 [1976], 136–47); but that Asiatics were primarily assigned this form of labor is not the case.

four major traditions: the Exodus itself, the law-giving at Mt. Sinai,[111] the wandering in the wilderness, and the initial stages of the conquest.[112] The question as to which of these traditions did Moses originally belong, if not to all,[113] is one that has bedeviled scholarship for decades. It is tempting to argue that the law-giving as well as the institution of passover and related agricultural feasts had in their origin nothing to do with the Exodus, and should be removed from the previous list.[114] The blanket denial of the Prophets that Israel in the wilderness had possessed the elaborate cultic laws that are now credited to Moses' mediation in Exodus and Leviticus could only have meaning if this was a commonly accepted view at the time.[115] It was only in post-Exilic times, then, that Moses became the great "lawgiver." On the other hand, that Moses is somehow associated with formulation of the Yahweh covenant, as a "prophet," may enjoy deeper roots in Israelite tradition.[116] That is not to say that this was Moses' *historical* origin; but a quasi-priestly role is one of his functions in the tradition.

The connection with Egypt in the Mosaic tradition holds primacy of place in popular and scholarly thinking.[117] But this belief cannot look to the birth narrative for support, for the motif of the exposed child has nothing intrinsically to do with Egypt. Nor can one base this contention on Moses' confrontation with Pharaoh, since it would appear that this was secondarily imposed on an earlier tradition in which the Israelite elders directly negotiated with the Egyptian monarch.[118] Yet, it has been maintained, the PN "Moses" (Hebrew *Mōše[h]*) enjoys excellent credentials as an *Egyptian* name; and indeed it does. The verbal affix *-mose*, which turns up in such well-known names as Thutmose, Amenmose, and Ptahmose, was in the New Kingdom pronounced *-mase*, and in the first

[111] E. Nielsen, *VT* 32 (1982), 87–98; H. Gese, *ZAW* 79 (1967), 143–44; G. W. Coats, *Moses: Heroic Man, Man of God* (Sheffield, 1988), 177.

[112] M. Noth, *A History of Pentateuchal Traditions* (Englewood Cliffs, N.J., 1972), 156–75.

[113] A modern trend does, indeed, appear to be gravitating back to this position: E. F. Campbell, *Interpretation* 29 (1975), 144; W. H. Schmidt, *Exodus, Sinai und Mose* (Darmstadt, 1983), 15–19; H. Schmid, *Die Gestalt des Mose* (Darmstadt, 1986), 103.

[114] Cf. W. Johnstone, *ZAW* 99 (1987), 32–34; Norin, *Es Spaltete das Meer*, 182ff.

[115] Cf. Amos 5:21–25; Jer. 7:22; cf. Hos. 8:12–13; Mic. 6:6–8.

[116] J. Muilenberg, *VT* 9 (1959), 347–65, idem, in J. P. Hyatt, ed., *The Bible and Modern Scholarship* (Nashville, Tenn., 1965), 87; B. S. Childs, *The Book of Exodus* (Philadelphia, 1974), 353; cf. Hos. 12:13.

[117] Cf. S. Herrmann, *Israels Aufenthalt in Ägypten* (Stuttgart, 1970), 70; A.H.J. Gunneweg, *Geschichte Israels* (Stuttgart, 1984), 26–27; M. Metzger, *Grundriss der Geschichte Israels* (Neukirchen-Vluyn, 1983), 34; H. Donner, *Geschichte des Volkes Israel* (Göttingen, 1984), 109; G. Fohrer, *Geschichte Israels* (Heidelberg, 1982), 64; M. L. Chaney, in D. N. Friedman and D. F. Graf, eds., *Palestine in Transition* (Sheffield, 1983), 65.

[118] Noth, *History of Pentateuchal Traditions*, 71.

millennium -*mose*. Moreover, whereas the vocalization did not fossilize but kept pace with the times, the sibilant with which the name was transcribed into Hebrew shows that the name must have entered the language *before* the eighth century B.C., and perhaps even in the late New Kingdom itself.[119]

That Moses was originally a "priestly" figure with Midianite connections and associated with an early cult center of the proto-Israelite tribes at Kadesh has of late become popular. Does not the presence in neighboring Seʿir of a Shasu tribe that bore the tetragrammaton as a designation lend support to such a suggestion?[120]

It is hard in the present state of our knowledge to come to any decision in this matter. One cannot rid oneself of the dismay attendant upon the realization that our lengthy and detailed account of Moses, in all his roles, is late, either Exilic or post-Exilic; and that, although the figure of this charismatic leader may well have been the focus of legend much earlier, for us this prior stage in the formulation of the tradition is a dead letter. Moreover, one cannot help but sense in the entire Mosaic tradition, as we now have it, a pervasive, informing element, which produces nought but effect. From the outset Moses' rejection by his own people provides a tension that runs through the whole; his slowness of wit and inarticulateness make him virtually useless to god. He is, in addition, skeptical of his ability and at times of the almighty as well. All this constitutes a convenient backdrop against which the power of Yahweh may be seen to greater advantage. All this may be highly entertaining; but it is literary artifice, not history. The author is playing secondarily upon a primary Mosaic tradition that he does not allow us to see. The vast majority of the "facts" he now gives us about Moses are demonstratively late, and worthless in the task of uncovering the historical basis for the early "hero."

Another source of chagrin is the suspicion that even the present P-redaction of the Moses story is not a prime source, but conceals and omits certain details widely known at the time. The burial on Mount Nebo (Deut. 34:1–6) and the hint of a Mosaic origin for the Danite priesthood are passing allusions to stories now lost. To what extent would they shift the center of our search for the historical Moses to Transjordan and the Jordan Valley? It is sometimes maintained that, of all the Israelite tribes,

---

[119] See J. G. Griffiths, *JNES* 12 (1953), 225–31; cf. J. Černy, *ASAE* 41 (1941), 349–54; but see now the remarks of J. Vergote, *Bulletin de la Société d'égyptologie de Genève* 4 (1981), 89–95; also Astour, *Hellenosemitica*, 229ff.; idem, *Ugaritica* 6 (1969), 15 and n. 39 (who derives the name from *mt*, a chthonic god at Ugarit, and compares *Mus*, the serpent god).

[120] M. Weinfeld, *Tarbiz* 56 (1987), 449–60; H. Schmid, *Die Gestalt des Mose* (Darmstadt, 1986), 41–42 (lit.); Coats, *Moses*, 25–29 (lit.).

only that of Levi displays Egyptian names in its onomasticon; but this is somewhat misleading. Apart from "Moses" the only *PNN* that are indubitably of Egyptian origin are Hophni and Phinehas, and once again we find ourselves in a certain milieu at Shiloh,[121] with a priesthood explicitly stated to date from the time of the Bondage (1 Sam. 3:27–28). Again: the laconic reference to Moses' marriage in Numbers 12:1 (immediately followed by the editor's assurance that this had taken place) is an inadvertent slip apprising us of the sometime existence of an incident now lost. It is usually assumed that this is the ultimate source of much of the tangential midrash about Moses' early career that one finds in Judaica of the intertestamental period.[122] And yet, could this not be a reference to a preexistent tale relating Moses to Kush? In particular, Artapan has been thought to preserve a genuine, extra-Biblical tradition, although it is quite true that most of his work takes the form of an implicit rebuttal of Manetho.[123] In particular his story of the invasion of the Kushites and the great seige of Hermopolis in which Moses took part[124] is a clear reminiscence of the invasion of Piankhy around 717 B.C.[125] There are parallels between Moses and Tefnakhte of Sais (c. 724–717 B.C.): both organized peoples in the Delta against oppression, and both led hosts into "Arabia" where living proved rigorous.[126]

WHAT REALLY HAPPENED AT THE EXODUS?

It seems fatuous to attempt to answer this question, but perhaps it must be posed.

To this point the discussion has established the following scenario. In Egypt the Hyksos occupation and expulsion were remembered fairly accurately in the king list tradition, although the folk memory tended to confuse the events of the fall of Avaris with the siege of Megiddo.[127] In Canaan it was remembered too, but here no fixed narrative or king list held imagination in check. Memory fastened on the century of occupa-

---

[121] For Hofni, see H. Ranke, *Die altägyptische Personennamen* vol. 1 (Glückstadt, 1935), 239:12–13 (= "tadpole"); for Phinehas, see ibid, 113:13 (= "the Southerner"). Other proposed candidates, such as Aaron and Merari, have nothing to do with Egyptian at all.

[122] Cf. J. G. Cager, *Moses in Greco-Roman Paganism* (Nashville, Tenn. 1972); T. Rajak, *JJS* 29 (1978), 11–22; G. Vermes, in *Moise, l'homme et l'alliance* (Paris, 1955), 66–74. It should be noted that in the legend of the descendants of Io (see p. 413) Aegyptus who went to "Arabia" married an Ethiopian wife: Apollodorus, 2.1.5.

[123] J. J. Collins, in J. H. Charlesworth, ed., *The Old Testament Pseudepigrapha* (New York, 1985), 2:892; A.-M. Denis, *Museon* 100 (1987), 49–65.

[124] Collins, in Charlesworth, *Pseudoepigrapha*, 2:898–900.

[125] N. C. Grimal, *La stèle triomphale de Pi(ankh)y au musée de Caire* (Cairo, 1981).

[126] Cf. the Tefnakhte story in Diodorus, 1.45; Plutarch, *De Iside et Osiride* 8.

[127] See p. 128; D. B. Redford, *Orientalia* 39 (1970), 1–51; idem, *King-lists*, 245.

tion, translated into a four-generation span; the names of illustrious leaders Sheshy, Ya'akob, Io, and Apophis; the antipathy between Egyptian and Asiatic; the withdrawal of the Hyksos to Palestine; and the attendant cataclysm.

One might dwell for a moment on this final point. Sources contemporary with the expulsion of the Hyksos apprise us of curious atmospheric disturbances, strange for the Nile Valley, although not entirely unknown there. The snippet of a diary now preserved on the verso of the Rhind Mathematical Papyrus[128] records the final events leading up to the fall of Avaris: "Year 11, tenth month—one[129] entered Heliopolis; first month, day 23—the Bull of the South(?) gores his way as far as Tjaru;[130] day 20 [+ x]—it was heard tell that Tjaru was entered; year 11, first month, 'Birth of Seth'[131]—the sky rained." This rainstorm may or may not be identical with another downpour that proved very destructive and was recorded on a stela of Ahmose together with the measures the king took to alleviate the resultant misery of the people. "The sky came on with a torrent of rain, and [dark]ness covered the western heavens while the storm raged without cessation . . . [the rain thundered(?)] on the mountains, (louder) than the noise at the 'Cavern' that is in Abydos. Then every house and barn where they might have sought refuge [was swept away, . . . and they] were drenched with water like reed canoes . . . and for a period of [x] days no light shone in the Two Lands."[132]

The striking resemblance between this catastrophic storm and some of the traditional "plagues" seems more than fortuitous.[133] The subsequent interpretation of such an event by the Canaanites as divine punishment on the Egyptians in this moment of triumph would be a natural construction to place upon it. And it is but a step from interpreting the disaster as punishment on Egypt *for an expulsion*, to construing it as pressure exerted *to effect a release*.

One other legend helped to shape the tradition, and this was a native Egyptian reworking of the Amarna event. Here the "renegade leader"

---

[128] A. B. Chace, H. P. Manning, and L. Bull, *The Rhind Mathematical Papyrus: B. M. 10057 and 10058* (Oberlin, Ohio, 1927–1928), pl. 108, (par. 30, no. 87); Redford, *Kinglists*, 110.

[129] Presumably Ahmose.

[130] Border fortress on the east side of the Delta, northeast of Avaris.

[131] Epagomenal days, intercalated before the first month of the calendar year; in the middle of the sixteenth century B.C., roughly the third week in August.

[132] C. Vandersleyen, *RdE* 19 (1968), pls. 8, 9; W. Helck, *Historisch-biographische Texte der 2. Zwischenzeit* (Wiesbaden, 1975), 106–7.

[133] On the plagues as they now appear in Exodus, see Noth, *Exodus*, 62–84; Z. Zevit, *JQR* 66 (1975–76), 189–92; J.-L. Ska, *Biblica* 60 (1979), 23–35; 191–215; Schmidt, *Exodus, Sinai und Mose*, 49–54; N. H. Sarna, *Exploring Exodus* (New York, 1986), 63–80.

and the prior enslavement of an antisocial group provided themes that entered the Canaanite tradition and partly transformed it.

Since World War II a number of theories have been hatched that attempt to "explain" by a single, comprehensive stroke some or all of the supernatural concomitants of the Exodus. Thus, an unusually high inundation caused by heavy rainfall in Abyssinia is put forward as the catalyst that occasioned a sequence of natural disasters, which have come down to us in the narrative as the Ten Plagues.[134] Or, a comet passing too close to the earth caused not only the plagues but a tidal wave at the Red Sea and volanic erruptions, which account for the pillar of fire and cloud, the Mountain of God, manna in the wilderness and probably anything else you would like to throw in which this ingenious author has forgotten.[135] Or again, the eruption of the island of Thera produced a tidal wave that overwhelmed and drowned an Egyptian army in pursuit of some runaway Hebrew slaves who were saved because they were on high ground.[136]

There are several things wrong with this approach. First, as far as motivation is concerned—and I know it is unfair to *impute* motives—the prior concern with those who produced such theories is in explaining a miracle taken for granted, not in holding its historicity up to scrutiny. Thus they become part of that quaint nineteenth-century occupation of providing Christ's miracles as described in the received texts of the Gospels with rational, scientific explanations, without once questioning the received texts. Second, an overarching theory that fastens on *one* basic factor as responsible for the entire event appeals to those lazy enough to feel comfortable with ignoring evidence in disciplines they cannot control. This yields in turn a highly tendentious approach: evidence I cannot control is not important and I will easily reject it; while data not "in sinc" with my presuppositions I can skew or reinterpret.[137] In actual fact, it is very rare that a problem area in history, worked over for generations of scholars, will suddenly be wholly solved by a single event, unnoticed and unrecorded in contemporary records. This kind of "open Sesame" smacks of sheer fantasy. Third, the three explanations of the Exodus account just adumbrated, accept without any question as their starting

---

[134] G. Hart, *ZAW* 69 (1957), 84–103; 70 (1958), 48–59.

[135] E. Velikowsky, *Ages in Chaos* (New York, 1946); *Worlds in Collision* (New York, 1950).

[136] H. Goedicke, various oral communications; see H. Shanks, *BAR* 7, no. 5 (September–October 1981); idem, *BAR* 7, no. 3 (May–June 1982); E. Oren, *BAR* 7, no. 6 (November–December 1981); I. Wilson, *The Exodus Enigma* (London, 1985).

[137] This shortcoming is seen to best advantage in the works of Velikowsky (see n. 135). Although the astronomical parts of his work I cannot deal with, I know that when he must handle Egyptian evidence he commits the most egregious and laughable errors. Although it would be a waste of space to list them here, I will be happy to oblige any reader with more details.

point the latest P-form of the Exodus account. There has been no prior assessment of the sources. Yet Goedicke's reconstruction of the Exodus, for one, depends heavily on the geography of Exodus 1–15, the very data that is demonstrably untrustworthy.

It is ironic that the Sojourn and the Exodus themes, native in origin to the folklore memory of the Canaanite enclaves of the southern Levant, should have lived on not in that tradition but among two groups that had no involvement in the historic events at all—the Greeks and the Hebrews. In the case of the latter, the Exodus was part and parcel of an array of "origin" stories to which the Hebrews fell heir upon their settlement of the land, and which, lacking traditions of their own, they appropriated from the earlier culture they were copying. One batch of tales centered upon an "ancestor" called Abram whose memory lived on in Beer Sheva and in the Negeb; another took its rise at Shechem in the highlands and revolved around the figure of a Canaanite leader Jacob. The Canaanite origin of these figures is now only dimly reflected, as most of the Biblical stories told about them took shape much later and served etological needs felt by Israel in the first millennium B.C. But they themselves were undoubtedly bona fide historical figures of the Middle Bronze Age.

One final irony lies in the curious use to which the Exodus narrative is put in modern religion, as a symbolic tale of freedom from tyranny. An honest reading of the account of Exodus and Numbers cannot help but reveal that the tyranny Israel was freed from, namely that of Pharaoh, was mild indeed in comparison to the tyranny of Yahweh to which they were about to submit themselves. As a story of freedom the Exodus is distasteful in the extreme—I much prefer the account of Leonidas and his three hundred at Thermopylae—and in an age when thinking men are prepared to shape their prejudice on the basis of 3,000-year old precedent, it is highly dangerous.

JOSEPH

No piece of prose elsewhere in the Bible can equal the literary standard attained by the Joseph story of Genesis 37–50; and few extra-Biblical works in the ancient Near East can rival it for excellence of style and composition. The story is constructed around a beautifully turned and symmetrical plot that displays a unity and integrity that bespeak single authorship. The author's style is spare and unpretentious, and, because of the dramatic effect, achieves a height it might otherwise have missed. No mechanism or tool is alien to this matter: he can retard or accelerate the pace of the plot to heighten suspense; he can develop character more subtly yet deftly than anywhere else in scripture, save perhaps in the Succession Document; he uses a gentle and superb irony throughout his work to provide unity. Doublets and recapitulation can be deadly; yet in the Joseph story they provide emphasis. Embellishment can be tiresome; yet our author uses it, though sparely, to the best advantage. In short, the nine or so chapters that comprise the Joseph story show all the earmarks of a *composition*, rather than a *record*.[138]

For, as has long been realized, the Joseph story is in fact a novella or short story. It shares with other Egyptian and Near Eastern stories of the same genre a number of specific characteristics. As in folktales and wisdom there is a preference for the generic "god" as opposed to the name of the deity,[139] and proper nouns are likewise avoided. Terms of relationship ("father," "older brother," "younger brother") and titles are preferred to names; and toponyms, while a few are present, are generally suppressed. This all contributes to an atmosphere of timelessness and placelessness in the setting of the story: admittedly, as the story is now placed, it takes place in Egypt; but the basic shape of the plot does not demand a Nilotic setting.

The identification of the genre of the Joseph story as that of the novella helps to explain why the narrative makes such a "poor fit" as a component in the chain of Patriarchal Tales in Genesis. Not only is there a marked change in style when one passes from the short and disjointed sections dealing with Abraham, Isaac, and Jacob to chapter 37 of Genesis, but the author's interest and purpose change also. Unlike the earlier narrative, the Joseph story proper shows no interest at all in cult topography or origin tales; god and his angels do not descend to earth or stand on ladders, make promises, blow up cities, or engage in wrestling matches. Genesis 12–36 has focused repeatedly on the covenant of God with the patriarchs, has reiterated the promises time and again, and sought to establish precedents for the Israelite occupation and cult associations. In the Joseph story these voices fall silent, and these concerns cease to inform the narrative. The "poor fit" of the Joseph story extends to factual detail. According to Genesis 45:11 the descent of Jacob and his family was an ad hoc measure to help them survive the remaining years of famine; elsewhere it is clear their purpose was to settle in Egypt. Again, the Joseph story brings all the sons of Jacob to Egypt, where they live out their lives, even the "baby" Benjamin already blessed with ten sons! This contradicts emphatically the traditions of individual tribes in later times in which the

[138] See the Redford, *Joseph Story*; C. Westermann, *Genesis 12–50* (Darmstadt, 1975), 56–68; idem, *Genesis* (Neukirchen, 1981), 1–19; Thompson, *The Origin Tradition*, 116–31; for bibliography and discussion over the last two decades, see L. Ruppert, *BZ* 29 (1985), 31–48; J. Scharbert, *BN* 37 (1987), 104–28.

[139] M. V. Fox, *ZÄS* 107 (1980), 123–26; R. J. Williams, *JAOS* 101 (1981), 11–12, for literature and discussion.

eponymous ancestors live, marry, raise families, and die in Canaan.[140] Finally, in contrast to the ubiquitous use of "Joseph" as the eponymous ancestor of the "House of Joseph" (Ephraim, Manasseh, Machir) in the central highland, "Joseph" the hero of the novella is almost totally absent from the rest of the Bible until the intertestamental period is reached. In short the Joseph story could easily be excised from the Patriarchal Tales without doing any damage to the main course of the history of Proto-Israel.

In spite of the fact that the basic plot of the story, as pointed out, is in no special way tied to a Nilotic setting, a number of details that color the present version of this plot motif do, indeed, point to Egypt. Most obvious are the Egyptian personal names,[141] of which four are produced in passages rather tangential to the main story line (Gen. 39:1, 41:45): Ṣaphnathpane'aḫ, Asenath, Potiphar, and Potipherah. The last two being variants of one name, we are left with three Egyptian names in the story. Ṣaphnathpane'aḫ is unanimously agreed to be the transliteration of an Egyptian name-type that means "God N speaks (or spoke) and he lives." The type begins in the 21st Dynasty, becomes very common in the ninth through seventh centuries B.C., and thereafter peters out, though sporadic examples survive in Greco-Roman times. Asenath is usually derived from a name "Belonging-to-Neith," which is specifically attested from Greco-Roman times but belongs to a category that begins in the New Kingdom and becomes very common in the first millennium B.C. The interpretation of the consonant cluster N + T as the goddess Neith is, however, open to question, as it could indicate nūt⁽ᵉ⁾, the vocalization of the Egyptian word for "god"; and "Belonging-to-(the)-goddess" is an attested personal name in the Late Period.[142] Potiphar and its variant are modeled on a very common type of name, namely P³-di + God's name, meaning "He-Whom-God-N-gives." These begin at the close of the New Kingdom, increase in frequency in the 21st and 22nd Dynasties, and become very common from the Kushite 25th Dynasty to Greco-Roman times. Thus the mean period when all three name-types had achieved a maximum popularity vis-à-vis the others can be said to be the seventh and sixth centuries B.C., or the Kushite-Saite period.

Titles and epithets occur here and there that have been thought to have had an Egyptian origin, but some have reference so general that they

[140] In Genesis 38 Judah marries, settles down, and raises a family in Canaan; Simeon marries a Canaanite (Gen. 46:21); Ephraim dies in Palestine (1 Chron. 6:20–24); Manasseh married an Aramaean (1 Chron. 7:14) and his son Machir was at home in Gilead (Num. 32:40; cf. 1 Chron. 2:21–22).

[141] See A. R. Schulman, SAK 2 (1975), 235–43.

[142] Ranke, Personnenamen, vol. 1, 177:24; the feminine might, however, have occasioned the appearance of an r after the t.

could turn up in any administration. Such is "chief of the Bakers" (Gen. 40:2–3), which seems now to be attested for the Jerusalem court in the seventh century B.C.[143] "Father to Pharaoh and lord of all his house" (45:8) are not constructed on any special Egyptian model: the technical Egyptian title "god's father" has quite a different connotation, and in any event "father" to a king has good credentials in Hebrew.[144] The "guard" of whom Potiphar is captain (37:36, 39:1, etc.) likewise is a known institution in Judah at the end of the monarchy, and there is no need to conjure up an Egyptian derivation.[145]

On the other hand, some descriptions have direct application to Egypt. The term "overseers" in Genesis 41:34, the officials whom Joseph advises Pharaoh to appoint, is an Aramaic title ubiquitous in the Egyptian administration during the Persian period (525–410 B.C.).[146] The word saris of Genesis 37:36, rendered variously "officer" or "eunuch," has long been recognized to be a rendering of ša rêši, the common Akkadian title of the Assyrian administration.[147] Whether in fact it here means "eunuch" is beside the point. The title seems only to be found in the Persian administration of Egypt, where it is applied to high-ranking governors.[148]

Although the Joseph story is not interested in the cult etiology of Israel, it does show a wide-eyed interest in how the economy of cereal production and storage and pharaonic ownership of land and chattels came to the state with which the writer was familiar. In short: it was Joseph that brought about these economic and agrarian reforms.

In detail, what does the author know (or think he knows) about these matters? To him Pharaoh is the owner of all the land of Egypt, except temple land, as well as all the livestock; the inhabitants are his slaves, while the priests were his salaried employees. At planting seed is handed out to the peasants, and at harvest one-fifth of the produce goes to Pharaoh. Now this is a pretty fair though general description of the state of things in the Nile Valley during many widely scattered periods, from the Old Kingdom on (although in the third millennium we would probably not hear of "the land of the priests");[149] and no "Joseph" of the nineteenth or seventeenth or fifteenth century B.C., or whenever one wishes to

---

[143] E. Mazar, IEJ 37 (1987), 62.

[144] Redord, Joseph Story, 191, n. 7.

[145] Koehler-Baumgartner, 2:353.

[146] Redford, Joseph Story, 207–8; G. R. Driver, Aramaic Documents of the Fifth Century B.C. (Oxford, 1965), 15–16.

[147] Koehler-Baumgartner, 3:727; on eunuchs see G. E. Kadish, in Kadish, Studies in Honour of John A. Wilson, 55–62, see also M. Görg, BN 53 (1990), 14–20.

[148] Redford, Joseph Story, 200–201; also P. Rylands IX passim, where the srs is the term given to the Persian provincial governors.

[149] Cf. B. Menu, Recherches sur l'histoire juridique, économique et sociale de l'ancienne Égypte (Paris, 1982), 1–42.

place him, was responsible for it. Some details can be elucidated. The handing out of seed and the implied prognostication of the harvest is well known at all periods of Egyptian history, although details of the mechanism varied over time.[150] Priests from the New Kingdom enjoyed privileged positions, broadly speaking, although the complicated obligations in New Kingdom sources show that they were liable for dues, taxes on royal land under their authority, and service of one kind or another. To an outsider, of course, this may not have looked like taxation. But in the sixth century we have an explicit statement that, except for that "Time of Troubles" (possibly an allusion to the Assyrian occupation of 671–663 B.C.), the great temples were usually not taxed.[151] With respect to the 20 percent that went to Pharaoh, it is possible to elicit this rate elsewhere in the tax structure of Late Period Egypt;[152] but Papyrus Rylands IX yields unequivocal evidence. There it is stated that, in the Saite period the temple income (in edibles) was alloted as salaries to the four phyles of priests into which the temple staff was divided, 20 percent per phyle (P. Rylands IX, 13, 8). The remaining 20 percent was called the "Portion of Pharaoh" (P. Rylands IX, 3, 17–18; 15, 3-4) and could be disposed of at Pharaoh's discretion.[153] Finally, the text of Genesis 47:21, which in the Hebrew states that Joseph removed the people into cities, sounds suspiciously like the population movements effected by Sesostris when he built new cities on mounds to keep settlement clear of the annual flood.[154]

Various incidental details find some degree of correlation in Egyptian texts. The trade with Egypt in aromatic substances enjoyed by Transjordanian camel-bedu (Gen. 37:25) finds its best parallels from the seventh to third centuries B.C. The knowledge of the Zodiac (37:9), the cow as a symbol for "year," the importance placed on the celebration of the king's birthday—all seem to find a reflection in the Egypt of the second half of the first millennium B.C. Genesis 42:35 seems to envisage the meaning "(coined) money" for kesep, "silver,"[155] kept in a pouch small enough to be stuffed in the mouth of a sack.[156] The investiture of Joseph bears com-

---

[150] B. Menu, *CRIPEL* 3 (1975), 143–49.

[151] P. Rylands IX, 6, 16.

[152] Redford, *Joseph Story*, 237, n. 3.

[153] In fact the family of the priest Pediese had appropriated this stipend, until stripped of it under Psammetichos II: P. Rylands IX, 9, 13, 19; 11, 4.

[154] Diodorus, 1.57.1.

[155] The use of the word "silver" meaning "money" was established already in New Kingdom Egypt, although prices were usually expressed in weight units of copper, and the terms used indicate units of value rather than coins (J. J. Janssen, *Commodity Prices from the Ramessid Period* [Leiden, 1975], 101–05). Exchange remained, during this period, barter or money-barter (ibid, 545ff.).

[156] Wenamum 1,11, refers to silver in a bag, but these were nothing more than small, loose items of a size able to fit in a container and not important enough to be specified.

parison with similar procedures in pharaonic times, especially those of the seventh to sixth centuries B.C. Joseph's accusation that his brothers are "spies" come "to see the weakness of the land" (Gen. 42:9), trumped up though it may be, employs a word used of intelligence agents sent out just prior to an invasion; since the brothers have already said they came from Canaan (42:7), such an accusation would make no sense if it were not conceivable that a hostile power, in possession of Canaan, was about to pounce on Egypt, a political configuration unknown in the New Kingdom but familiar from the Saite period.

Scholarly treatments of the background of the Joseph story have often singled out details that enjoy parallels that happen to come from the New Kingdom, while arguing that data from the Third Intermediate Period and Saite age need not force us to lower our date since—Who knows?— it may be only haphazard preservation that robbed us of similar New Kingdom data. This is not really fair, as it at one moment shows a confidence born of an empirical approach, and at another claims uncertainty by pointing to the slim margin of what is possible. But you cannot be an empiricist one moment and an agnostic the next.

In fact, a compelling case can be made for a seventh or sixth century date for the story, regardless of the contentious issue of background detail. Several motifs, none of which are in any way peripheral, inform the plot of the Joseph story. These may be listed as follows: the young man who surmounts many problems, endures many trials, and eventually comes out on top (the "rags-to-riches" or "from-prison-to-throne" motif); the wiseman who emerges from an unexpected quarter (sometimes the dungeon) to save the king and the nation; the great reformer or lawgiver, ultimately responsible for the good system we now have. Common to all three is the figure of the "wiseman," a favorite among storytellers throughout Egyptian history. But there is a marked difference between the way in which the author uses his "wiseman" in this story, and the function of the wiseman in stories of the second millennium date.

The classical Egyptian "wiseman" is the ḫry-ḫb (ḫry-tp) "the (chief) lector-priest,"[157] literally "the (chief) one-who-carries-the-ritual-book"; and because he is a *lector* (i.e., one who reads the liturgy) he must be literate, and then in Egyptian thinking it would follow that he is learned. Since magic is such a major component in all ancient Egyptian religious literature, the "lector" easily translates into "magician." It is this aspect of the lector, his ability to work magic, that forms the core of his role in stories from the Middle Kingdom and New Kingdom in Egypt. The magician knows how to make a wax crocodile that will turn into the real

---

[157] Latest discussion is in J. Quaegebeur, in S. Groll, ed., *Pharaonic Egypt, the Bible and Christianity* (Jerusalem, 1985), 162–72.

thing in order to catch an adulterer; he knows how to roll back water in order to retrieve a broach accidentallly dropped in a lake; he can fix severed heads back on bodies; he can tame wild animals; and so forth.[158] The magician is also a "wise scribe" who can make predictions, and whose "teaching" survives in writing;[159] but this reflects a function at home in the realm of Wisdom literature.

In contrast to the motive of trivial entertainment that lies behind such Middle Egyptian stories, the stories of the Late Period confer on the wiseman a far more serious role. A princess is sick unto death and a wiseman is dispatched to save the situation (which he does by diagnosing her ailment and recommending a healing god).[160] Pharaoh himself has but days to live, and a young lector (intentionally prevented from contact with the king by jealous wisemen) saves the day.[161] The Nile does not flood, a famine ensues, and a wiseman is called in to investigate.[162] Pharaoh and the country are threatened by an evil Nubian magician, and a wiseman is summoned to rescue the king.[163] A temple lies in ruins and Isis appears to the king in a dream, after which a wiseman is summoned to solve the problem.[164] It is precisely the same function fulfilled by Daniel on two occasions with Nebuchadrezzar (Dan. 2) and Belshazzar (Dan. 5) in tales of Hellenistic date. Into this Daniel material there also enters the motif of wrongful incarceration and final rehabilitation of the wiseman, a plot pattern shared by such narratives as those of Mordecai, Tobit, and Ahikar in Israel, and Onkh-Sheshonqy and Hy-Hor in Egypt, all dating from the second half of the first millennium B.C.[165]

That the character and function of Joseph in the story in Genesis fits this role of savior and erstwhile persona non grata of these later tales should be clear on even a cursory perusal. Joseph too was wrongly jailed, prevented from entering Pharaoh's ken, and later rehabilitated; and he too was called forth when Pharaoh was troubled by dreams, and went on

---

[158] Cf. Papyrus Westcar where the role of the wiseman in Middle Kingdom literature can be seen to best advantage: Lichtheim, *Literature*, 1:216ff.

[159] Chester Beatty IV, verso 2:5ff.

[160] Thotemheb in the Bentresh stela: *ANET*², 29–31 (22nd to 26th Dynasty date).

[161] Meryre, in P. Vandier: G. Posener, *Le Papyrus Vandier* (Cairo, 1985) (dated between c. 650 and 350 B.C.).

[162] Imhotpe in the Siheil famine inscription: P. Barguet, *La stèle de la famine à Séhel* (Cairo, 1953); *ANET*², 31–32 (Ptolemaic date).

[163] Si-Osir in Khamois II: Lichtheim, *Literature*, 3:138–51 (Ptolemaic date).

[164] Phritiphantes in Chaeremon: (Redford, *King-lists*, 287–88 and n. 99 [Ptolemaic date]) following Codex Laurentianus, rather than the Latin which *Phritibautes*: H. St. J. Thackeray, *Josephus Against Apion* (London, 1976), 1:280, n. 1 (*Contra Apionem* 1.289). The Latin clearly is the less acceptable, as it attests the confusion of labials and the faulty copying of *upsilon* we should expect in Byzantine times.

[165] Redford, *Joseph Story*, 97; J. J. Collins, *JBL* 94 (1975), 224–27; J. M. Lindenberger, in Charlesworth, *Pseudepigrapha*, 2:479–507.

to save the nation from a dire fate. The currency of this type of story from the late Libyan period into Hellenistic times is not fortuitous.

We conclude that, on a judicious appraisal of the evidence, the Biblical Joseph story was a novella created sometime during the seventh or sixth century B.C. (the end of the Judaean monarchy or the Exile). Its present position provides a free expansion on the theme of Israel's descent to Egypt, although it is wholly unnecessary to the ongoing account of the Patriarchs: Jacob and family arrive on the banks of the Nile without the help of Joseph in the earlier tradition. As the Sojourn and Exodus narrative is an adaptation by Israel of an earlier Canaanite tradition, so the Joseph story is the Hebrew exemplar of a widespread story line much in use in Egypt and the Levant at the time the Pentatuch was being committed to writing. There is no reason to believe it has any basis in fact—the absence of the story from the earlier tradition in the prophets speaks against such a belief—and to read it as history is quite wrongheaded.

CHAPTER 15

Egypt and the Fall of Judah

As THE ARMY of Ashurbanipal disappeared over the horizon in the summer of 663 B.C. and returned to Assyria, few would have predicted anything but a servile, provincial status for the land of the Nile, now permanently reduced to a vassal of the great king in Nineveh. In the Delta the landed families of Libyan chieftains continued jealously to guard their patrimonies, always suspicious of each other, never able to unite. Upriver the great cities of Herakleopolis, Hermopolis, and Asyut constituted independent bailiwicks, and the Thebaid was now virtually cut off from the north under its priest-mayor Montuemhat. The further south one went, and especially in the long stretch of the valley governed by Thebes, the stronger one discovered the ties to the Sudanese kingdom to be; and no one could be sure that Tantwetaman, though worsted by Ashurbanipal, would not advance downriver again. Not that he would be welcome in the north: the Delta families hated him almost as much as they hated the Assyrians. Even the presence of Necho I's son, Nabushezibanni (to give him his Assyrian name), functioning as a sort of Assyrian viceroy, did not seem able to ensure any subservience or concerted stance on the part of these families.[1] And sitting in the fortress at Memphis, taking full advantage of the disunity of Egypt, sat a small but powerful Assyrian garrison.[2]

But within a decade the impossible had come true. The Delta families had been stripped of their power, the Assyrian garrison expelled, and the country reunited under the leadership of Sais. How had all this been effected?

THE SAITE RESTORATION OF EGYPT

To begin with, the accomplishment must be ascribed to the perspicacity and diplomacy of one man, Nabushezibanni, the son of Necho, whom we

---

[1] The political configuration of Egypt at the beginning of the 26th Dynasty is reflected best in Ashurbanipal's records: see in particular the discussion of A. J. Spalinger, *JAOS* 94 (1974), 316–28; K. A. Kitchen, *The Third Intermediate Period in Egypt* (Warminster, 1973), 394–403.

[2] For Assyrian rule in Egypt, see H. Lewy, *JNES* 11 (1952), 280, n. 83; B. Oded, *Mass Deportations and Deportees in the Neo-Assyrian Empire* (Wiesbaden, 1979), 45, and n. 30; M. Elat, *JAOS* 98 (1978), 26.

shall henceforth call by his birth-name, Psammetichos.[3] His seizure of power and establishment of a new, 26th Dynasty are not reflected in contemporary documents, which are extremely scarce; and we are perforce thrown back on the memory of later generations, especially those tales told to the Greek historian and traveler Herodotus when he was in Egypt. Herodotus, visiting shortly after 450 B.C., lived within the penumbra of the 26th Dynasty, the last great independent regime that survived in the longing memory of an Egypt now subverted to Persia. Recency and nationalistic fervor made this memory sharper than that of any earlier period of Egypt's history.[4] One of the stories recounted to Herodotus purported to describe Psammetichos's coming to power.[5] He had been, it was said, one of twelve warring dynasts in the Delta who had reluctantly agreed upon a truce, solemnized in the Temple of Hephaistos at Memphis. Once a year they came together in the temple to reaffirm their agreement by pouring libations. An oracle had declared that the future ruler of the land would be the one that poured his offering from a bronze vessel, and pursuant to the apprehension thus aroused the dynasts had banned bronze vessels from the temple. On one occasion when the twelve were lined up for the libation, with Psammetichos, at the end of the row, the priestly celebrant distributed only eleven cups; and Psammetichos, finding himself without a vessel, innocently removed his helmet and poured his libation from that. The other dynasts at once realized the prophecy had been fulfilled and drove him from the temple; and he was forced to flee for his life to the Delta marshes. A second oracle predicted that Psammetichos would receive help from bronze men who would come out of the sea; and one day, as he walked on the coast of the Mediterranean in his place of exile, he encountered a stranded boat bearing Ionian hoplites, blown off course. With the help of these he won the day against his rivals.

Although they telescope events, these yarns contain something more than a modicum of truth. Correctly remembered is the period of stasis and anarchy after the withdrawal of the Assyrians. Probably also correct is the recollection of Psammetichos's flight in the face of the hostility of the Delta families to the remote marshes of the north for safety. And certainly true, as we shall see, is the theme of military assistance from Greek freebooters.

Sober records of this earliest period of the reign are few indeed; but we shall probably be not far off the mark if we reconstruct Psammetichos's

---

[3] On Psammetichos I and his accomplishment, see Kitchen, *Third Intermediate Period*, 399–404; A. J. Spalinger, *JARCE* 13 (1976), 133–47; idem, *Orientalia* 47 (1978), 12–20; idem, *LdÄ* 4 (1982), 1164–69.

[4] H. D. Meulenaere, *Herodotos over de 26ste Dynastie* (Louvain, 1951).

[5] Herodotus, 2.151–52. See A. B. Lloyd, *Herodotus Book II. A Commentary* (Leiden, 1988), 3:130–32. See also my discussion, p. 383.

career roughly along the following lines. At the time of Ashurbanipal's withdrawal from the Nile, Psammetichos was ensconced as *orpayes* ("heir apparent") and Assyrian protégé in Athribis, about sixty-five kilometers north of modern Cairo; but his collaboration with the invader must have made him anathema to neighboring town rulers, and almost at once, we may imagine, he was obliged to quit Athribis and flee to his old patrimony in Sais. It is altogether likely that at first Psammetichos made full use of the support proffered by the Assyrian garrison to reenter Memphis and deter the local factions from acting against him; and it may also have been with the garrison's help that he threw back a second attempt by Tanwetaman to retake the north by defeating the invading Nubians just south of Memphis.[6]

Now the coast was clear and the momentum had turned in Psammetichos's favor. By 660 B.C. he had begun to reorganize the economy and taxation structure of the townships of Middle Egypt; and four years later he felt strong enough to make overtures to Montuemhat in Thebes. This worthy, himself a Nubian appointee and president of a local administration still loyal to Tanwetaman, was sufficiently realistic to appreciate the change in the configuration of political power that had come about in Egypt.[7] Psammetichos either had expelled, or was about to expel, the Assyrian garrison in Memphis, and the incursions of the Cimmerians in the spring of 657 B.C.[8] and the Assyro-Elamite war[9] prevented Ashurbanipal from undertaking punitive action. Montuemhat allowed himself to acquiesce in Psammetichos's proposal to appoint his little daughter Nitocris to a sacerdotal function in Thebes; and in the winter of 656 B.C. a flotilla of royal ships conveyed the girl to Thebes.[10] In a masterstroke of diplomacy Psammetichos refrained from ousting Shepwenwepet II, the Divine Worshiper of Amun and titular head of the Thebaid, who was a scion of the Kushite royal family, but obliged this "High Priestess" to adopt Nitocris as her protégé and junior partner. A large number of towns and grandees was obliged to cede property and goods to the young princess as part of her "dowry"; and the Thebaid reverted legally and permanently to the Egyptian crown. Two years later in 654 B.C. punitive action against certain Libyan enclaves on the western fringes of the lower valley estab-

---

[6] The precise historical role played by Tanwetaman is still unclear, however; see D. B. Redford *LdÄ* 4 (1982), 368–69; S. M. Burstein, *JSSEA* 14 (1984), 31–34; Lloyd, *Herodotus*, 3:130.

[7] On Montuemhat, see J. Leclant, *Montuemhat, 4ème prophète d'Amon, prince de la ville* (Cairo, 1961); M. L. Bierbrier, *LdÄ* 4 (1982), 204.

[8] A. J. Spalinger, *JAOS* 98 (1978), 400–409.

[9] G. Roux, *Ancient Iraq* (Harmondsworth, 1966), 300–301.

[10] R. A. Caminos, *JEA* 50 (1964), 71–101.

lished Psammetichos's mastery of that ethnic element.[11] At virtually the same time Gyges of Lydia, eager for any help he could get against the Cimmerian threat from the north, approached Psammetichos for an alliance; and pursuant thereto a contingent of Greek soldiers from that part of Ionia under Lydian control crossed the sea to enter Egyptian service.[12] These were the harbingers of a veritable flood of Greek mercenaries which for the next three and a half centuries was to flow southward into pharaonic employment in ever increasing numbers. With them the Egyptian military, which Psammetichos must have realized could not come up to contemporary standards, was ready to take on the world, and once again Egypt could present itself as a united and powerful state to the outside world.

Thus was inaugurated the 26th, or "Saite" Dynasty, the last period of imperial and cultural renewal of native inspiration ancient Egypt was to experience. Although the family of rulers of Sais came from Libyan stock—they had in fact held the office of "chief of the Labu-(tribe)"[13]—there was nothing alien about Psammetichos or his coterie of brilliant advisors. The revival was an Egyptian one, conceived on Egyptian lines and patterned on such ancient models that some have sought, not without justification, to speak of cultural archaism.[14] During the 140 years that Psammetichos and his able descendants ruled Egypt, the frontiers stood, as classically they had under the Old Kingdom, at the First Cataract and the Mediterranean.

Internally the country underwent a vigorous reorganization, which strengthened it immeasurably. In the capital, now removed to Sais, a large court took shape, evoking the past glories of empire; and the local temple of the goddess Neith virtually was transformed into the state treasury.[15] A strong federal system under the vizier and remodeled judiciary put an end to the centuries of weak parochialism. In the provinces Psammetichos successfully deprived the landed families of political power by setting up strong local governments responsible to Sais: each township received a governor and a secretary, responsible for agricultural production, land distribution, justice, and law enforcement.

[11] H. Goedicke, *MDAIK* 18 (1962), pl. 1.

[12] Spalinger, *JAOS* 98 (1978), 402–3; J. Boardman, *The Greeks Overseas* (London, 1980), 112–13.

[13] J. Yoyotte, *Mélanges Maspero* (Cairo, 1961), 4:142–51.

[14] Cf. Spalinger, *Orientalia* 47 (1978), 12–13; D. B. Redford, *Pharaonic King-lists, Annals and Day-books* (Toronto, 1986), 328–31.

[15] On Sais (modern Sa-el-Hagar), see L. Habachi, *ASAE* 42 (1943), 369ff.; R. el-Sayed, *Documents relatifs à Sais et ses divinités* (Cairo, 1982); idem, *La déesse Neith de Sais* (Cairo, 1982); J. Baines and J. Malek, *Atlas of Ancient Egypt* (Oxford, 1980), 170. Memphis, however, probably remained the center of administration: A. B. Lloyd, in *Ancient Egypt, A Social History* (Cambridge, 1983), 332.

Not least the potential wealth of Egypt and the revenue to be derived from foreign trade dominated the policies of Saite kings. A major part of the township governor's responsibilities had to do with the collection of taxes, which even extended to temples, and there is some evidence that, before the close of the period, a primitive income tax had been introduced.[16] In the light of the contemporary importance placed upon commercial traffic, it should come as no surprise that "harbormaster" (in charge of transit dues) and "master of shipping" were two of the most important titles of the regime.

Saite interest in foreign trade acted like a tonic on Egypt (Figure 10). In all probability the long Libyan hegemony had witnessed a falling off in native interest in sending ships and merchants far afield in search of goods for which to trade. In any case taking the initiative in matters of trade did not sit well with the Egyptians, accustomed as they were to exercising an imperial control over foreigners who themselves were obliged to bring their produce to Egypt. The first three centuries of the first millennium had witnessed the continued circulation of Egyptian goods throughout the Levant thanks solely to the agency of Phoenician traders.[17] Now, however, a new family, and one with a keen mercantile sense, was in control of Egypt, and no more fortuitous juncture in history can be conceived: for Phoenician trading activity was at its height, Greek vessels ranged the Mediterranean to colonize distant shores, and the routes to South Arabia, the Caucasus, Iran, and the Punjab lay open to the merchant.

Egypt's foreign trade can be reconstructed from such literary sources as classical authors and the Bible, from scattered allusions in Akkadian texts, and especially from temple reliefs of the Ptolemaic period, the inspiration for which is to be sought in Saite prototypes. Although a customs post had been set up at the First Cataract, Egypt enjoyed less trade than formerly with its mortal enemy, the Sudanese kingdom to the south. Egypt did, however, control the western oases route through Dakhleh, Kharga, and Dush, which provided an alternate route south to the upper Nile,[18] and by the close of the seventh century B.C. had begun to evince a renewed interest in the traditional "Puntite" coasts at the southern end of the Red Sea. In this regard one can only marvel at the enterprise and far-sightedness of Necho II who dug a canal between the Nile and the Red Sea through the Wadi Tumilat and built docks on the coast, presumably in the environs of modern Suez. That all this was in anticipation of mar-

---

[16] On the duties of the "nomarch," see Herodotus, 2.177; Aristotle, *Oeconomica* 1351a16–1352; Diodorus, 1.73.1; Strabo, 17.1.13, 54.

[17] See p. 334f.

[18] A. Fakhry, *The Oases of Egypt* (Cairo, 1973), 1:150ff.; (Cairo, 1974), 2:64–65, 79–80; D. B. Redford, *JSSEA* 7 (1977), 7–9.

itime activity, at least in part of a commercial nature, with the south can scarcely be doubted (though this particular king as we shall see was also beset by military preoccupations).[19] In the course of all these naval operations one of the Phoenician crews in Necho's employ disappeared down the Red Sea only to reemerge three years later via the straits of Gibraltar. Herodotus, our informant, pours scorn on the account: according to *his* geography such a circumnavigation would have been impossible.[20]

Despite the turmoil of contemporary politics in western Asia, Egypt continued to enjoy relatively free access to the products it craved: wine and alum from Phoenicia, medicinal herbs from Palestine, aromatic substances and bitumen from Transjordan; and from across the Sinai, to be tapped at Gaza, flowed a stream of exotic products from south Arabia.[21]

But by its geographical position Sais, a true precursor to Alexandria, looked northward and to the west, and it should come as no surprise that its rulers valued most highly the commerce they enjoyed with Greece. Following on the heels of the mercenaries Psammetichos had acquired from Gyges came Greek merchants and adventurers bent on colonization; but, while elsewhere along the Levantine coast Greek colonists had experienced little difficulty in establishing themselves, in highly populated Egypt problems developed. An early trading post established around 630 B.C. at the mouth of the Canopic branch of the Nile ran afoul of the natives and, in order to obviate any problem arising from the clash of cultures, Psammetichos toward the close of his reign founded a special town further inland and within the greater environs of the capital Sais. This settlement, Naukratis by name, was given over as an emporium to a consortium of Greek cities, and through it flowed the lucrative trade in grain, papyrus, oil, wine, and pottery between the Nile and the Greek mainland.[22]

THE 26th DYNASTY AND JUDAH

"When the 15th year of Pharaoh Psammetichos came (650 B.C.) the Southland was faring very well indeed. Pedeise son of Yerterow was taken into the Chancery, and the silver and grain he (had raised as tax) had increased 100 percent."[23] The year 650 found not only the "Southland"

---

[19] See p. 447f.

[20] Herodotus, 2.158–59; A. B. Lloyd, *JEA* 63 (1977), 142ff.; idem, *Herodotus*, 3:149–51.

[21] On Saite commerce, see E. Drioton and J. Vandier, *L'Égypte*[4] (Paris, 1962), 583–84.

[22] On Naukratis and its precursor, "The Camp of the Milesians," see Strabo 17.1.18; F. K. Kienitz, *Die politischen Geschichte Ägyptens vom 7. bis zum 4. Jahrhundert* (Berlin, 1953), 38; A. Bernard, *Le Delta égyptien d'après des textes grecs* (Cairo, 1970), 799ff.; Boardman, *Greeks Overseas*, 118–35; Herodotus, 2.178; Lloyd, *Herodotus*, 3:222–4.

[23] P. Rylands IX, viii. 14–15.

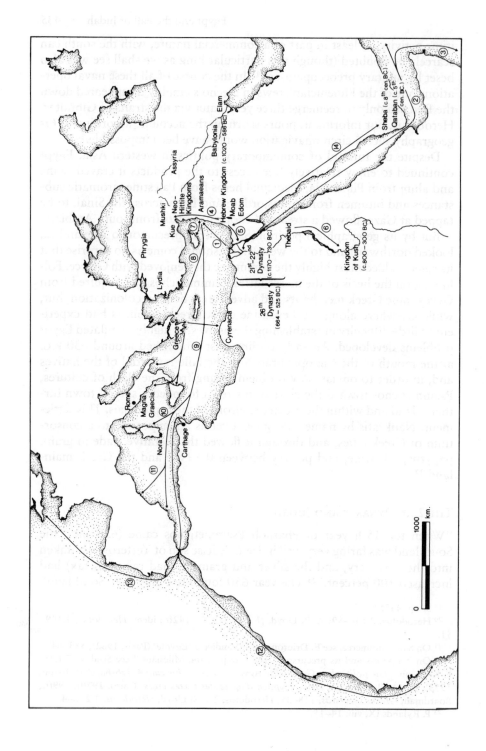

(Upper Egypt) but the entire Levant within the Egyptian penumbra basking in the glow of a revivified Egypt. The aged Manasseh, a true "Vicar of Brae" if there ever was one, was approaching the end of his fourth decade on the throne of Judah in the year 650; and his younger contemporaries, Sil-bel of Gaza, Mitinti II of Ashkelon, Ikaushi of Ekron, Amminadab of Ammon, Musuri of Moab, and Kaushgabri of Edom, were probably at the peak of their careers.[24]

To say the very least Manasseh has had bad press. Today he would be described as a political realist and, in matters of religion, one tolerant of pluralism. But the ravening iconoclasts of a later age, distorting history with hindsight, branded him an idolator of the worst sort who brought the wrath of god down upon his people.[25] Yet the worship of the "Lord" (Ba'al) and "his Lady" (Asherah) of the local city and its bailiwick, *dei civitatis* in fact, was endemic in the religion of the Levant from at least as early as the Late Bronze Age, and probably much earlier. Though more common in the cities of the Levantine coast, the Lord and Lady combination was also found in the more rustic cities of the hinterland, like Hamath, Damascus, and Jerusalem. But here they had to vie with cults of a more puritanical flavor originally at home among the more austere communities of the desert steppe whence the inland states had taken their rise. Such a deity was Yahweh who had not, in very truth, been averse to taking unto himself an "Asherah."[26] But the "crime" of Manesseh, in concert with the vast majority of kings before him, lay in treating the temple in Jerusalem as Solomon had intended—as a *royal chapel* wherein, although Yahweh held primacy of place, guest cults of other deities could be

[24] *ANET*², 294.
[25] On the reign of Manasseh, see E. Nielsen, in *Fourth World Congress of Jewish Studies* (Jerusalem, 1967), 1.103–6; B. Oded, in J. H. Hayes and J. M. Miller, eds., *Israelite and Judaean History* (Philadelphia, 1977), 452–58; J. H. Hayes and J. M. Miller, *A History of Ancient Israel and Judah* (Philadelphia, 1986), 365–76.
[26] See S. M. Olyan, *Asherah and the Cult of Yahweh in Israel* (Atlanta, 1988), for references.

Figure 10. (opposite) Trade in the first half of the first millennium B.C.:
1. Egypto-Phoenician axis of trade and cultural exchange
2. Red Sea route of trade with the east
3. Route of circumnavigation of Africa under Necho II (609–594 B.C.)
4. Israel-Cilician axis of trade through Aram
5. Egypto-Israelite trade and cultural exchange
6. Egypto-Kushite route of commerce
7–11. Phoenician trade routes with Mediterranean regions
12. Carthaginian exploration and colonization (fifth century B.C.)
13. Carthaginian trade in tin (fifth century B.C.).

housed. There was nothing at all unusual about this by contemporary standards; but it ill suited the mind-set of the puritanical innovators of two generations later.

Nonetheless, Manesseh's reign proved to be a time of peace for his land, undoubtedly because of his wholesale acquiescence in the larger revamping of the international power structure of his day. In the 660s he had been obliged to toe the Assyrian line with his Philistine and Transjordan colleagues, and Assyria continued to maintain garrisons in such Shephelah towns as Gezer and Lachish until 649 B.C..[27] And even in the years immediately following the latter date Ashurbanipal was still able to strike out successfully against the Arab tribes adjacent to Palestine.[28] But Psammetichos's star was on the rise, and any other minor ruler might well have found himself in a quandary; but Manasseh had meekly bowed to Assyria, and he was now equally prepared to bow to Egypt. The result was an absence of warfare in his kingdom for five decades. Excavations in Jerusalem both on the western hill and the east slope of the original Davidic city[29] have illustrated graphically how the prosperity of this reign was mirrored in the expansion of domestic and cultic occupation outside the line of the defensive walls of Hezekiah. On the slope of the Kedron Valley above the spring of Gihon the remains of stone-built shrines have been recovered, associated with caves and masseboth oriented toward the rising sun.[30] The physical and ceramic context would admirably fit the reign of Manasseh when solar worship may well have become inordinately popular.

THE SCYTHIAN INVASION

If no other faction had been introduced into the political equation, Egypt and Assyria might, in the years following 650 B.C., have tacitly agreed to maintain separate spheres of influence and have divided the ancient world between them. But a new element from an unexpected quarter was about to impinge on the weary old states of the river-valley civilizations: a whirlwind was arising out of the north.

In the early centuries of the first millennium B.C. there resided in the steppes of southern Russia a nation of horse-rearing seminomads known

[27] R.A.S. MacAlister, *The Excavations of Gezer* (London, 1911), 1:23ff.; in 646 B.C. there was still an Assyrian governor at Samaria: R. A. Henshaw, *JAOS* 88 (1968), 478. Assyria could still exact reprisals as late as around 644: A. Malamat, *JANES* 5 (1973), 270, n. 12.

[28] Roux, *Ancient Iraq*, 302; J. M. Myers, in H. Goedicke, ed., *Near Eastern Studies in Honor of William Foxwell* (Baltimore, 1971), 379.

[29] M. Broshi, *IEJ* 24 (1974), 21–26.

[30] K. Kenyon, *PEQ* (1967), 65ff.; (1968), 97ff.; idem, in M. Avi-Yonah, ed., *Encyclopedia of Archaeological Excavations in the Holy Land* (Jerusalem, 1975), 2:595–97.

as the Cimmerians. Warlike and mobile, the Cimmerians belonged linguistically to the Indo-Aryans and are mentioned by Homer (tenth to ninth centuries B.C.) as a remote little-known people. Around 750 B.C. some of the Cimmerians suffered displacement at the hands of a related Asiatic people known as the Scythians and were obliged to move southward through the Caucasus. The whole rapidly assumed the aspects of a folk movement, which fell upon Urartu in the closing decades of the eighth century and, a little further to the west, overwhelmed the kingdom of Phrygia. Repelled with difficulty by Esarhaddon in 679 B.C., the Cimmerians gravitated toward the Aegean through Anatolia and after several decades of periodic rape and pillage succeeded in capturing Sardis and killing Gyges king of Lydia, Psammetichos's erstwhile ally.[31]

In the wake of the rampaging Cimmerians now came the Scythians via the same route. These marauders were to exert a baleful influence over three centuries of Near Eastern history and, thanks to Darius I's abortive campaign against them, were to win a lengthy passage in Herodotus's history. In the early 670s the sudden appearance of the threatening Scythian host on his border had prompted Esarhaddon of Assyria to offer his daughter in marriage to the Scythian chieftain Partatua.[32] Thereafter the Sycthians, possibly in sympathy with Assyria, turned upon the Medes, a rising and major enemy of Assyria in western Iran.[33] At this point Herodotus's account runs as follows:[34]

A battle was fought in which the Medes were defeated and lost their power in Asia, which was taken over in its entirety by the Scythians. . . . During the twenty-eight years of Scythian supremacy in Asia, violence and neglect of law led to absolute chaos. Apart from tribute arbitrarily imposed and forcibly extracted, they behaved like mere robbers, riding up and down the country and seizing people's property. At last Cyaxares and the Medes invited a greater number of them to a banquet at which they made them drunk and murdered them. . . . They (the Medes) captured Nineveh . . . and subdued the Assyrians.

For Herodotus the onslaught of the Scythians on the Levantine coast, which had taken place twenty-eight years before the fall of Nineveh, had involved Psammetichos I in a desperate parlay to buy the invader off

[31] On the Cimmerians, Biblical "Gomer," see L. Waterman, *Royal Correspondence of the Assyrian Empire* (Ann Arbor, Mich., 1930–1936), nos. 146, 197; L. F. Hartman, *JNES* 21 (1962), 25ff.; M. Van Loon, *JNES* 29 (1970), 67; H. Cazelles, in L. G. Purdue and B. W. Kovacs, eds., *A Prophet to the Nations* (Winona Lake, Ind., 1979), 136, 141–43, and passim; *OCD²*, 240. The traditional date 652 B.C. has lately been disputed: for a conspectus of the chronological problem, see Spalinger, *JAOS* 98 (1978), 400ff.

[32] Roux, *Ancient Iraq*, 295.

[33] H. R. Hall, *The Ancient History of the Near East* (London, 1950), 495–96.

[34] Translation of A. de Selincourt, *Herodotus. The Histories* (Harmondsworth, 1954), 84–85 (1.104–6).

through negotiation.[35] Eventually he succeeded and the Scythians, who had penetrated to the very border of Egypt, retired voluntarily by way of Ashkelon, which they pillaged. The story of their being smitten ever after with a "woman's disease" smacks of etiology and the same ribald overtones that surround the tale in 1 Samuel of how the Philistines, in the very environs through which the Scythians passed, were afflicted with hemorrhoids because of their defilement of the ark.

The account in Herodotus of the Scythians' lightning raid down the coast of the Levant has met with varying acceptance on the part of scholars. By some it had been dismissed as fictional, falsely patterned on the Cimmerian depredations in Asia Minor. To others it is a distortion of a historical assignment of Scythian mercenary troops, in Assyrian employ, to posts in Palestine and their subsequent altercation with Egypt. While earlier Biblical scholars construed the earliest oracles of Jeremiah as prompted by the Scythian invasions, current trends date these chapters much later and tend to impune the historicity of the incursions.[36]

In fact, a raid far to the south by such roving horsemen as the Scythians are known to have been is well within the realm of possibility. If they, from their base in Iranian Kurdistan,[37] could have operated at will throughout the powerful mountain kingdoms of Phrygia and Lydia, there is every reason to believe that with even greater ease they could have negotiated the well-traveled routes of the Mediterranean coast. And there was much to attract them, in the coastal cities of Ashkelon and Gaza, to say nothing of the prospects of plunder along the Nile.

As to the date of the incursion, the datum of twenty-eight years for their domination stands out prominently. This clearly does not correspond to any real length of regime but is simply computed by totaling the numbers of years between their first appearance in the west (i.e., the raid) and their sudden reduction, coeval in Herodotus—by inference—with the fall of Nineveh. The ultimate source of the latter event, surviving in numerous later histories, was the Babylonian chronicle;[38] and we may surmise that the source of the raid itself was likewise the same chronicle.[39] Twenty-eight years before the fall of Nineveh in 612 would bring us to 641–640, the twenty-fourth year of Psammetichos I; and interestingly it

---

[35] Herodotus, 1.105–6; Lloyd, Herodotus Book II. A Commentary (Leiden 1975), 1:76.

[36] Cf. the papers of H. H. Rowley and H. Cazelles in Purdue and Kovaacs, Prophet; see also Hayes and Miller, A History, 382–85; A. Malamat, in The Age of the Monarchies. Political History (Jerusalem, 1979), 4:349, n. 4; A. R. Millard, in J. Ruffle, ed., Glimpses of Ancient Egypt (Westminster, 1979), 119–22.

[37] M. Van Loon, Urartian Art: Its Distinctive Traits in the Light of Recent Excavations (Istanbul, 1966), 21–22.

[38] D. J. Wiseman, Chronicles of Chaldean Kings (London, 1956).

[39] The tablets covering the years in question have not yet come to light.

is to this very year that Eusebius in his chronicle adds the terse statement "Scythii usque ad Palaestinam penettraverunt."[40] Within months Amon the young king of Judah and son of Manasseh was assassinated in a palace conspiracy and his juvenile offspring catapulted to the throne on the tide of a popular uprising.[41] One can only suspect a connection between this precipitous action on the part of a populace filled with panic and the havoc caused by a recent raid of barbarians never seen before and possibly still roving the countryside.[42]

THE SAITE EMPIRE IN THE LEVANT

Josiah the boy-king entered upon his reign in a world in which Egypt was beginning consciously to reassert its hegemony in the traditional regions of its interest along the Levantine coast. Egypt could afford to take the initiative in the Levant, not as an agent of a withdrawing Assyria (whose protégé Egypt had briefly been), but as a supplanter acting in its own behalf. Ashurbanipal in fact construed Psammetichos's independence of action as rebellion. He could, however, do little by way of retaliation. A suspended war with Elam was followed by a grievous civil war with Ashurbanipal's brother, the regent of Babylon (652–648 B.C.) A brief punitive raid followed against the Arabs in Transjordan east of the Dead Sea; but it was the Assyrian army's last appearance in the west. The disastrous war with Elam was shortly resumed and dragged on for most of the decade. Ashurbanipal's eventual victory (639 B.C.) can in reality be aptly termed "Pyrrhic," for it left Assyria exhausted and ill-equipped to withstand the storm of resentment that was shortly to arise.

Throughout the Saite period military and paramilitary commanders are found with increased frequency in posts in the eastern Delta; and fortifications and entrepôts begin to proliferate on a line from the Bitter Lakes to Lake Sirbonis. In one of these, "Daphnae" (Egyptian "The Mansion-of-the-King"), a contingent of Ionian hoplites had been stationed before the close of Psammetichos I's reign.[43] Beyond the eastern frontier, too, the Egyptians were moving north. Probably shortly after the withdrawal of the Scythians, Psammetichos followed up his diplomatic triumph by seiz-

[40] *Hieronymus Chronikon* (ed. Helms), p. 96; R. Labat, *Journal Asiatique* (1961), 1–12.

[41] 2 Kings 21:23–24; on the "people of the land," see the references in E. Lipinski, in *The Land of Israel: Crossroads of Civilization* (Louvain, 1985), 104 and n. 34; T. Ishida, *VT Suppl.* 40 (1986), 96–106. While it may be that their action reflects an anti-Egyptian stance (Malamat, *JANES* 5 [1973], 271; idem, *VT Suppl.* 218 [1975], 126), it is misguided to construe this innocuous term as synonymous with a kind of "party" with political goals.

[42] On the date of about 640 for the Scythian penetration, see H. Kees, in Pauly-Wissowa-Kroll, *RE*² II, 2 (Stuttgart, 1923), 1868ff.

[43] Boardman, *Greeks Overseas*, 132–35; cf. also E. Oren, *BASOR* 256 (1984), 7–44.

ing the Philistine city of Ashdod, if Herodotus is to be believed.[44] And there can be no doubt that by the close of his reign, Psammetichos's direct control extended along the coast as far as and including Phoenicia, where he boasts that his officers supervised timber production and export.[45] The Saite reduction of Phoenicia to vassal status once again restored the paradigm of antiquity and provided a stereotype for political propaganda: the reliefs and inscriptions on Ptolemaic temples, five centuries later, echo the Saite triumph with the recurrent refrain "the Fenkhu bear to thee (Pharaoh) their tribute."[46] We are ill-informed at present as to how the major Philistine states, apart from Ashdod, entered the pharaonic fold. Gaza and Ashkhelon may well have passed into Egyptian control voluntarily, with the coincidence in time of the weakening of Assyria, the Scythian raid, and the renewed Egyptian initiative. The "good relations" mentioned in the "Adon-letter" (see subsequent discussion) undoubtedly reflect the formal treaty relationship many a south Palestinian city now entered into with its Egyptian overlord.[47] We know little of the fate of the south Phoenician coast after the destruction wrought by Ashurbanipal's army (c. 645), but certainly well before the close of Psammitichos I's reign Egyptian control has been extended to Tyre, and probably Arvad as well.[48] There is even evidence of an incipient infrastructure of "provincial" officials assigned to the new dependencies in the Levant. A messenger, probably of Saite date, is known whose bailiwick included "Pekan-a'an of Philistia," that is Gaza; and a text from 613 B.C., commemorating the burial of Apis, tells us that the chiefs of Lebanon "were subjects of the palace with a royal courtier appointed over them, and their taxes were assessed to the (Egyptian) Residence, in the same manner as the land of Egypt."[49]

An unexpected consequence of Egypt's enlarged horizons and extended

[44] Herodotus, 2:157; Lloyd, *Herodotus*, 3:146–48. H. Tadmor (*BA* 29 [1966], 102) suggested the figure "29," which in Herodotus indicates the *length* of the siege in years, should be construed as the regnal year of Psammetichos I, viz. 635 B.C. The fact that the traditional hegemony of the Scythians is "28 years" may be understood together with this datum to indicate that it was in the years following the Egypto-Scythian encounter that Psammetichos effected the capture of the city: see A. Malamat, *JNES* (1950), 218: J. Strange, *Studia Theologica* 20 (1966), 136; H. Cazelles, *RB* 74 (1967), 25–26, 42. The seizure of the site may be reflected in the destruction of stratum VII; T. Dothan, *Atiqot* 9–10 (1971), 21–115.

[45] D. B. Redford, *JAOS* 90 (1970), 477. On Psammetichos I's control of the Philistine coast, see G. Steindorff, *JEA* 25 (1939), 30–33; Malamat, *The Age of the Monarchies*, 4:1, 205; idem, *VT* Suppl. 28 (1975), 125.

[46] Cf. E. Chassinat, *Le temple d'Edfu* (Cairo, 1892–1934), 1:30, 7:165; E. Chassinat and F. Daumas, *Le temple de Dendera* (Cairo, 1934–1978), 2:200, 4:66, etc.

[47] W. Moran, *JNES* 22 (1963), 173ff.

[48] P-M VII, 393; J. J. Katzenstein, *History of Tyre* (Jerusalem, 1973), 299, n. 24; 313, n. 100.

[49] See n. 45.

hegemony involved manpower exchanges with the nations within its sphere of influence of paramilitary purposes. The inverted snobbery of the literate and other sophisticates of the empire period had long since contributed to the stultifying of the spirit of militarism in Egypt; it became fashionable in scribal circles toward the close of the New Kingdom to pour scorn on the calling of the army officer. So prominent a role was assigned in literature to the stereotype of the luckless soldier on foreign assignment beset by all sorts of problems not of his own making that on the morrow of the fall of the House of Ramesses most Egyptians would not even consider soldiering an acceptable career but were content to leave it in the hands of resident aliens of lower status who were willing to fulfill its harsh duties. This practice, not conducive to the art of war in Egypt, conspired with the scarcity of iron and modern weaponry to produce a Nilotic army decidedly inferior to the armed forces of western Asia. Undoubtedly Psammetichos had realized this, hence his willingness to hire the best warriors available. We have seen his acceptance of Ionian hoplites, the cultural and military heirs of those well-armed Sea Peoples who had left such a favorable impression in the Egyptian memory six centuries earlier[50] but he also coveted contingents from Palestine and Syria, more familiar with the skillful tactics and superior armaments of Assyria than the Egyptians were.

In the event Saite Egypt became a highly desirable employer for Asiatics as well as Greeks. Syrians came to Egypt and are found in communities at Migdol, Athribis, Memphis, Thebes, and Aswan, and at special encampments in the Delta. Although much of our detailed evidence regarding the life and occupation of these communities derives from the private letters from their descendants two centuries later during the Persian period, we may nonetheless extrapolate in order to shed light on the period of origin. It is clear, then, that the prime function of all these enclaves was paramilitary, although nothing prevented any of them from engaging in commerce.[51] They were organized into "garrisons,"[52] and paid salaries from the royal treasury. Although their own internal organization and their command system was not dispensed with, the Egyptians nonetheless insisted on assigning their own liaison officers to each garrison.[53] Since the foreigners enjoyed a certain degree of autonomy and moreover often proved unruly, the Egyptian officer's task was very difficult. En-

[50] On the tradition of the Sea Peoples surviving in Egypt during the Late Period, see J. Yoyotte, RdE 12 (1952), 92–93; Edfu, 4:236; 9: pl. 90.

[51] E. Bresciani, La lettere aramaiche di Hermopoli, 366–67; B. Porter and J. Greenfield, ZAW 80 (1968), 225.

[52] Dgl: cf. J. A. Fitzmyer, in Albright Festschrift, 148.

[53] Kientz, Geschichte, 41ff.; J. Leclant, BIFAO 50 (1951), 171, n. 2; H. De Meulenaere, BIFAO 63 (1965), 21ff.

lightening in this regard is the plaintive reminiscence of one such Egyptian commander who had been assigned to a contingent of foreign troops on the southern frontier: couched in an address to his god are the words "as thou didst deliver me from the difficult situation caused by the troops of Asiatics, Greeks, Syrians and others" who had planned to defect to the Sudan and been dissuaded by the speaker.[54]

It would be strange if the same magnetic attraction Saite Egypt had extended to the rest of the eastern Mediterranean did not make itself felt in Judah. In fact the evidence is unequivocal. One of the fifth century B.C. papyri recovered in the excavations of the Jewish quarter at Elephantine states that the local shrine that the garrison had built was already standing when Cambyses conquered Egypt in 525 B.C.;[55] and the adoption stela of Psammetichos I's ninth year (656 B.C.) already knows of the settlements of the "Shasu of the south" in the Delta.[56] The practice of which these allusions are a reflection is specifically, if tersely, condemned in Deuteronomy 17:16 "Only he (i.e., the king) is not to multiply horses; nor shall he send the people back to Egypt in order to multiply horses." Since it is beyond doubt that the "Book of the Law" found in the Jerusalem temple in Josiah's eighteenth year (c. 623 B.C.) was an early version of Deuteronomy, the dispatch of Judaeans to Egypt must have been royal policy at the time in question—during the first two decades of Josiah's reign—and perhaps already under Manasseh and Amon. In any case, the period is coeval with the initial "Drang nach Norden" of the 26th Dynasty.

In the context of Psammetichos's reassertion of control over the Levantine coast, the mercenary troops he had acquired were also used to garrison the strongpoints. One such post has come to light through excavation at Mesad Hashavyahu on the coast not far from Ashdod. Here Greek pottery of the period 625 to 600 B.C. attests the presence of Hellenic occupants,[57] though documents from the site suggest a local society bound by custom known to us from the Bible. Southeast, similar pottery has come to light at Tel Melah in the Negeb. In the same area, at the Judaean frontier fortress of Arad, the archives that have been unearthed in the excavations of Aharoni mention contingents of *Kittiyim*, the word used in the Bible for "Greeks," to whom the Judaean authorities issue rations.[58] Rather than to assert that inland Judah independently em-

[54] H. Schaefer, *Klio* 4 (1904), 157, pl. 2; J. Vercoutter, *BIFAO* 48 (1949), 175.

[55] Cf. *ANET²*, 492.

[56] Caminos, *JEA* 50 (1964), 94–95.

[57] J. Naveh, *IEH* 12 (1962), 89ff.; Tadmor, *BA* 29 (1966), 102; Strange, *Studia Theologica* 20 (1966), 136–37.

[58] Y. Aharoni, *IEJ* 16 (1966), 4ff.; idem, *Arad Inscriptions* (Jerusalem, 1981), 12–13 and passim.

ployed Greek soldiers from across the sea, it seems wiser to construe their presence in the area as the result of Egyptian imperial encroachment. Whether Judah, already under Josiah, had signed a treaty with Psammetichos, whereby it suffered reduction to vassal status, is a moot point: the Bible does not mention such a treaty, but an understanding of some sort might well explain the exchange of Judaeans for military service in Egypt in return for horses and Greek garrison troops.

The year 627 B.C. saw the twenty-one-year-old Josiah engaged in a cultic purification of his realm, which he had set on foot some months earlier. In Egypt Psammetichos I's daughter Meret-neit, afflicted by an eye disease, in this year besought the divine healer Amenophis son of Hapu for release from her ailment. In Babylon 627 was the year of the death of Kandalanu, the regent appointed two decades earlier by the Assyrians. Further afield 627 witnessed the continued hegemony in the north of the Scythians, the increasing rise to prominence of the Medes in Zagros, the seizure of power by Periander of Corinth, and the final suppression of Cylon's coup in Athens. More important for the entire ancient world, it was the year of Ashurbanipal's death.[59]

Although with our modern benefit of hindsight there can be no mistaking the significance of this event, it was unlikely that contemporaries realized immediately what it meant to the balance of power. Increasing unrest had broken out as the ailing monarch had drawn closer to the end, and following his death serious insurrection bedeviled his son's accession. The rebellion of Babylon, of which there had been harbingers before Kankalanu's death, now broke out with unprecedented force. In November 626 a Chaldaean, Nabopolassor, seized the throne of Babylon, and for two years fought off counterattack after counterattack by the Assyrian army. By 623 it was clear that the revolt had succeeded: Babylon was free and growing strong, while Assyria had suffered a serious defeat and was experiencing a crisis in leadership.[60]

Reaction among the national elements of Assyria's sphere of influence followed rapidly, some remaining loyal, others siding with the Babylonian rebels. In the west Josiah in 623 took advantage of the situation by annexing the Assyrian province of Samerina,[61] and carrying his cultic reforms to an extreme that might in earlier times have been interdicted by the Assyrian authorities.[62] Probably Judah's response to the international situation is representative of what went on elsewhere in Palestine and

---

[59] R. Borger, *JCS* 19 (1965), 59ff.; idem, *Iraq* 27 (1965), 135ff.

[60] Roux, *Ancient Iraq*, 33ff.

[61] 2 Kings 23:15–20.

[62] Cf. *inter alia* his eradication of stellar and solar worship in the Jerusalem Temple: 2 Kings 23:5, 11–12.

Syria, as Assyrian garrisons and governors were removed and the insignia of its hegemony destroyed.

Egypt's reaction on the other hand was at once unexpected yet far-sighted. The world view was significantly different on the banks of the Nile from what it had been at the same vantage point two generations earlier when Assyria had perpetrated its excesses against the cities of Egypt. Now Assyria was on the verge of annihilation. Those about to supplant Assyria came from the ranks of the illiterate barbarians, the Chaldaeans, the Medes, the Scythians, who had long since demonstrated how atrocious their behavior could be toward the sophisticated old cultures of the urbanized Near East. The balance of power in western Asia, which had remained static for three centuries, was in danger of being upset with unknown consequences in the area of most concern to a merchant prince, trade and commerce. It was thus most probably a desire to maintain the international status quo, rather than any love for Assyria, that prompted the aging Psammetichos to undertake the surprising military moves that mark the last decade of his life. For as in the years following 623 the Babylonians continued to push back the Assyrian forces on the Tigris, positioning themselves seriously to threaten the heartland of the former empire, Psammetichos decided to take sides and actively to assist his former tormentors. In the late summer of 616 B.C. as Nabopolasser and his troops ravaged the land of the middle Euphrates, an Egyptian expeditionary force appeared and in concert with Assyrian forces pursued the retiring Babylonians partway down the Euphrates. No engagement occurred and both sides retired in good order; but Egypt had shown its hand.

The next four years proved crucial to the outcome of the hostilities.[63] In 614 Cyaxares and his Median troops suddenly overwhelmed the city of Ashur, and then signed a treaty of alliance with Nabopolasser. In May 612, the combined forces of Babylon, Media, and the Scythians finally laid siege to Sin-shar-ishkun, the Assyrian king, in his capital at Nineveh. In August of the same year the city fell, as Sin-shar-ishkun immolated himself within his palace, and was given over to merciless plunder and destruction. Although a remnant of the royal family under the crown prince Ashur-uballit II escaped to the west and set up a government in exile in Harran, Assyria as a nation-state ceased to exist, and few if any shed tears of regret. Nahum's words probably echo the sentiments of the world: "Woe to the bloody city, all full of lies and booty! . . . there is no assuaging your hurt, your wound is grievous. All who hear the news of you clap their hands over you; for upon whom has not come your unceasing evil?"[64]

[63] Wiseman, Chronicles, 57ff.
[64] Nahum 3:1, 19.

Egypt's inactivity during this period—no pharaonic forces are mentioned in the Babylonian Chronicle for the entries from 615 to 610 B.C.—is very difficult to understand. Certainly we cannot doubt that the Assyrians could have benefited from Egyptian help, even though their ultimate fate might only have been slightly delayed. Two facts probably have to be taken into consideration. First, for an Egyptian expeditionary force to operate on the upper Euphrates, as had been the case in 616, was feasible and offered a chance of success: the Egyptian-dominated coast was close at hand, and the river constituted a defensible line behind which one could retire if need be. On the other hand, to come to the aid of Ashur and Nineveh on the Tigris far to the east was nothing short of inviting disaster, especially in light of the control exercised by the Medes and Scythians over the plains of Mesopotamia. Second, in 615 B.C. Psammetichos I was most likely in the neighborhood of seventy years of age, and may well have been afflicted with disease.[65] One can only imagine how the unsuccessful expedition of 616 might have affected an aging potentate whose every decision of state in fifty years had been characterized by circumspection and caution. Psammetichos may well have foreseen the imminent collapse of his erstwhile ally and refrained from committing troops to a doomed cause.

With Psammetichos's death in 610 the policy of intervention was resumed. Even before his passing Psammetichos I may have authorized garrison troops along the coast (in Phoenicia?) to proceed to Harran to assist Ashur-uballit:[66] the old king's last days were spent at his garrison posts in the eastern Delta,[67] a fact that could be interpreted to suggest that he was still concerned with management of expeditions. In any case his son and successor, Necho II, was very much in favor of a renewal of military involvement.

Among the members of the 26th Dynasty, Necho II has received the worst press.[68] A man of action from the start, and endowed with an imagination perhaps beyond that of his contemporaries, Necho had the ill luck

[65] There is some evidence of sickness in the family (cf. H. Wild, MDIAK 16 [1958], pl. 33; Aelian, 10.21), but whether it affected the king is unknown.

[66] There is no compelling reason to think that the force mentioned in the chronicle in 610 was anything but a contingent comprising *available* forces, scraped together from garrisons already in residence in Egyptian-controlled Syria; the question as to whether the Egyptians went by sea thus becomes meaningless: Freedy and Redford, *JAOS* 90 (1970), 482; Malamat, *JANES* 5 (1973), 273, n. 23.

[67] Inferred from the fact that his embalming house was in the environs of Daphnae: W. Erichsen, *Eine neue demotische Erzahlung* (Copenhagen, 1942), 24, pl. 3:3.

[68] For a summary of Necho II's reign, see Lloyd, *Herodotus*, 3:149–64; Spalinger, *Orientalia* 47 (1978), 19–21; D. B. Redford, *LdÄ* 4 (1982), 369–71; for a rare relief depiction of this king, see B. V. Bothmer, *Egyptian Sculpture of the Late period* (Brooklyn, 1960), pl. 39.

to foster the impression of being a failure: in hindsight his bent to action was perceived as impetuosity, his imagination unrealistic dreaming. If a certain authoritarian tendency in his makeup (coupled with a temper?) is discernible in the scant records, this must be balanced by the brief glimpse of him in folk literature, which reveals a fair and generous adjudicator.[69]

The earliest months of the new reign were not auspicious. The Egyptian contingent dispatched to Harran to assist Ashur-uballit II proved perhaps too small in the event; and, in October 610 at the advance of the Babylonians and the Scythians in concert, the Assyrian king and his allies fled across the Euphrates leaving the city to fall into Nabopolasser's hands.[70] This was too much for Necho, who spent the winter mustering a much larger expeditionary force than had theretofore been sent into Asia;[71] and in the spring of 609 it was prepared to set out. The route along the coast followed the same track used 850 years before by the great conqueror Thutmose III, across the Sinai to Gaza, through the Philistine and Sharon plain to the Carmel range, and via the pass to the Jordan Valley. And like his illustrious precursor, Necho too suffered an unexpected ambush.

A good deal of ink has been spilled in trying to establish what Josiah's motivation must have been to take on the Egyptian forces at Megiddo.[72] But viewed from the vantage point of the spring of 609, his action makes eminent sense. In five years the alliance of the Babylonians, Medes, and Scythians had suffered no defeat, but had mounted an irresistible offensive. The Assyrians had done nothing but retreat: Ashur and Nineveh had been overwhelmed, and now Harran had been abandoned. The Egyptians had proved themselves powerless to stem the tide: once their intervention was ineffectual and a second time, within months of Josiah's momentous decision, they had withdrawn ignominiously in the face of the enemy. The Babylonian advance looked like the wave of the future. For a century, moreover, ever since the overtures of Marduk-baladin II to Hezekiah,[73] Judah had perceived itself as sharing a community of interest with Babylon in international politics. Josiah simply saw himself as an ally of the forces of right in the final destruction of Assyria.

Josiah's intervention at the Megiddo pass, though a courageous move, failed at the cost of the thirty-nine-year-old king's life. Judah must have been shocked and dismayed: many kings lose battles, few lose their lives in the process. When Josiah's body entered Jerusalem, revolution broke

---

[69] Cf. the king (by implication Necho II) who plays a judicial role in the fragmentary tale published by Erichsen, Erzahlung.

[70] Wiseman, Chronicles, 63; Malamat, JANES 5 (1973), 274–75.

[71] Cf. the locution used in BM 21901 obv. 66 umman KURMi-ṣir ma-at-tu.

[72] Cf. among others, Malamat, JANES 5 (1973), 267–78; idem, in W. Claassen, ed., Text and Context (Sheffield, 1988), 120–22; Hayes and Miller, A History, 402.

[73] 2 Kings 20:12–13.

out, and the common people seized power and placed Jehoahaz, one of Josiah's younger sons on the throne.[74] This was a deliberate act designed to remove from power the heir apparent Eliakim, Josiah's eldest son,[75] whose grandfather from Galilee,[76] Pediah, had borne a quasi-Egyptian name, and who, as it turned out, proved to represent a pro-Egyptian faction at the Judaean court.

Necho did not at once gain intelligence of these events. His march northward was otherwise unimpeded, and by late June he had effected a junction with Ashur-uballit's forces, crossed the Euphrates and laid siege to Harran.[77] After four months the investment terminated with a failure to take the city, but before its end Necho had set up his headquarters at Riblah in central Syria, and begun the reorganization of all the territory as far north as Carchemish into an Egyptian dependency. To Riblah in the late summer he summoned the parochial rulers of Palestine and Syria, and bound them to the Egyptian crown by oaths, treaties, and tax obligations. To judge by the example of Judah, pro-Egyptian parties were encouraged. To Jehoahaz Necho was not sympathetic. He was dethroned forthwith and sent in chains to Egypt, and his older brother Eliakim put in his place.[78] With his name changed to "Jehoiakim" by Necho, the new ruler repaired to Jerusalem and sought forthwith to raise the necessary taxes. This he could not have done without help in the face of the hostility of the people, and we may presume that he had access to Egyptian troops.

The momentous events of 609 B.C. had awakened in the Judaean state a factional strife dormant for thirty years. The 'am ha'ares, the common autochthonous population, anti-Assyrian and therefore in the event anti-Egyptian as well, and in the present configuration of Near Eastern politics pro-Babylonian, had lost its obvious leader, the young Jehoahaz; his younger brother Mattaniah who, as events were to show, turned out to be initially pro-Babylonian, was but ten years old and not yet politically committed. The upper echelons of the court, however, led by the eldest son of Josiah, King Jehoiakim, proudly asserted their pro-Egyptian inclinations now that their star was in the ascendant. But the situation was still volatile and the political posture of Judah insincere: "How lightly you gad about, changing your way! You shall be put to shame by Egypt as you were by Assyria!"[79]

The author of these words, who probably would have classed himself among the common people, must be ranked as the most gifted tragic poet

---

[74] 2 Kings 23:31.
[75] Born in approximately 634 B.C., when his father was fourteen: 2 Kings 23:36.
[76] Malamat, VT Suppl. 28 (1975), 126–27; idem, The Age of the Monarchies, 4:206–7.
[77] Wiseman, Chronicles, 63.
[78] 2 Kings 23:33–34.
[79] Jer. 2:36.

the ancient Hebrews ever produced and the formulator of a theological concept never surpassed for its sublimity in the entire history of Judaism. Jeremiah came of a rural family of priests resident in Anathoth, north of Jerusalem,[80] and did not move easily in the sophisticated population of the capital where he was ever to remain a rustic, excluded from court life. Born in about 627 B.C., the thirteenth year of Josiah,[81] Jeremiah grew up in the heady, iconoclastic atmosphere of reform; and although in the process of centralizing the cult in the Jerusalem temple his own family must have been to some extent disenfranchised, he nonetheless grew to support the reform for its ethical content. The sophisticated temple cult, however, with its ritual and sacrifice, the careful prescription of which was later to be enshrined in Leviticus, Jeremiah had no use for and went as far as to deny that it had any basis in the nation's tradition. "Keep on with your burnt offerings and sacrifice," he represents Yahweh as saying to the people, "and eat the flesh! But I did not speak with your forefathers and I issued no command to them on the day I brought them out of Egypt concerning burnt offering and sacrifice!"[82] Whether Jeremiah had begun to make such public utterances before Josiah died is a moot point;[83] but certainly the events of 609 called forth a torrent of words.

The social phenomenon of a holy man playing the role of spokesman of the deity is known from most ethnic groups in the ancient world, including the Egyptians, during most periods of their history. Whether it is the "lector-magician" in Egypt, the "seer" or the "prophet" in the states of western Asia, or the prophet-priest in Mesopotamia,[84] the divine mouthpiece functions similarly: he has unnatural powers that are easily recognized, possesses the gift of oratory, and often by his championing the cause of the oppressed runs afoul of the authorities. The prophet is the "escape valve" of the community.

The speed with which the political alignment of the nations was changing from 623 B.C. called forth a plethora of such prophets. Some like Zephaniah, spurred by the destruction of Nineveh,[85] execrated those guilty of social injustice, and reveled in the prospect of the Chaldaean

[80] H. H. Rowley, in Perdue and Kovacs, *A Prophet to the Nations* (Winona Lake, Ind., 1979), 37ff., for sources and discussion.

[81] This seems to me the obvious conclusion from an analysis of Jer. 1:1–4: the association of verse 2, namely that Jeremiah was first called in Josiah's thirteenth year, is a clear interpretation of verse 4: "Before you were born I consecrated you and appointed you." Cf. J. P. Hyatt, *Interpreter's Bible. Jeremiah* (New York, 1956), 779, 798.

[82] Jer. 7:21–22.

[83] Rowley, in Perdue and Kovacs, *Prophet*, 35ff.

[84] See, among others, R. J. Williams, *JAOS* 101 (1981), 1–19; H.-P Muller, *ThWAT* 5, nos. 1-2 (1984), 140–63; idem, *BN* 29 (1985), 22–27; G. Dossin, *Sur le prophetisme à Mari* (Paris, 1966); B. Uffenheimer, *VT* Suppl. 40 (1988), 257–69.

[85] Cf. Zeph. 2:13–15.

invasion, as though it were the instrument of god to punish Judah.[86] Some few, in the zeal that popular frustration at Jehoiakim's rise to power promoted, directed their public diatribes toward a much more sensitive topic: the very survival of Jerusalem and its temple. Uriah in Kirjath Jearim[87] and Jeremiah in Jerusalem[88] gave vent in a public forum to predictions of doom. But Jehoiakim's pro-Egyptian alliance was, from 609 to 605 B.C., riding the crest of a wave and encouraged by the vigorous action taken by the new Pharaoh; and it was not about to tolerate such opposition from the ranks of the plebeians. The king issued warrants for Uriah's arrest and, when the prophet fled to Egypt, sought Egyptian permission to extradite him. The miserable Uriah was brought back to Jerusalem and executed.[89] But for the timely intervention of the royal officer Ahikam, Jeremiah would certainly have suffered the same fate.[90]

The tide indeed seemed to have turned in Necho's favor. Although his siege of Harran had been aborted, nonetheless the size of the army he had been able to muster must have impressed Nabopolasser, for until September 607 the Babylonians refrained from pursuing their aims in western Mesopotamia. The Babylonian Chronicle does not mention the presence of Egyptian expeditionary troops until 606; so the likelihood is that Necho's campaign in 609 and the garrison he left behind must have been sufficient to galvanize Syria against the new menace of Babylon.

Necho used these two and a half years (autumn 609 to spring 606) to initiate a number of new projects. It was now that he conceived the notion of canalizing the Wady Tumilat by cutting a waterway, "the canal of the east," probably from the Kharom Lake midway along its length to the northern tip of the Gulf of Suez.[91] On its northern bank about twenty-four kilometers from the gulf he founded a frontier fort and entrepôt called "The House of Atum," a god intimately associated with this eastern tract; the Egyptian form of the name, *Pr-itm*, rapidly passed into Hebrew toponymy as "Pithom" and was later identified as one of the cities built by the Israelites in bondage.[92] The intent of this ambitious operation was to be able to operate freely on both Nile and Red Sea, and possibly

---

[86] Hab. 1:6–10; 2:6–16.

[87] Jer. 26:20.

[88] Jer. 26:1ff.

[89] Jer. 26:21–23.

[90] Jer. 26:24.

[91] Cf. Pithom stela, 10 (*Urk* II, 90); Herodotus, 2.158, 4.39; Pliny, *Natural History* 6.165ff.; Diodorus, 3.43.5; cf. J. Ball, *Egypt in the Classical Geographers* (Cairo, 1942), 130.

[92] J. Leclant, *Supplement au dictionnaire de la Bible* 42 (1967), 1–6; Redford, *LdÄ* 4 (1982), 1054–58; that Pithom's foundation dates from the early years of Necho II is now certain, thanks to the recent excavations of J. S. Holladay: *The Wady Tumilat Project. The Excavations of Tell el-Maskhuta* (Malibu, Calif., 1982).

open up alternate avenues of attack on Mesopotamia. To this end triremes manufactured by Greek shipwrights[93] were based in docks constructed on the Red Sea coast,[94] and presumably commissioned to undertake operations in the gulf of Akaba and southward toward the straits of Bab el Mandeb. Necho's strategy was sound, if not brilliant, in the face of Babylonian expansion; but it had unexpected *commercial* results. As already noted, a crew of Phoenician sailors in Necho's employ, dispatched south down the Red Sea, appeared three years later in the Mediterranean, having circumnavigated Africa.[95] The feat can only astound us moderns. But for the ancients the opening up of old Pwenet in East Africa and the resultant trade in tropical goods must have seemed much more important.

In addition to preparations for war, Necho used his earliest years, in the time-honored fashion of good Egyptian kings, to set on foot building operations. In "the year after the coronation" (i.e., probably late 609, immediately after his return from Syria) he opened a new gallery in the Tura quarries to extract building stone.[96]

In 607 Nabopolasser returned to the attack in western Mesopotamia.[97] The presence of a strong Egyptian garrison at Carchemish could not be tolerated by Babylon if Mesopotamia was to remain in its hands and free of outside interference. To dislodge the Egyptians, however, by a frontal attack on Carchemish was a move that could not have succeeded; and so Nabopolasser sought at first merely to isolate the garrison by driving a spearhead across North Syria further south. To that end in the early fall of 607 he led his troops across the Euphrates some forty-five kilometers south of Carchemish and captured the town of Kumukh. With the city firmly in Babylonian hands and a garrison in place, Nabopolasser felt free to retire to Babylon in February 606 B.C. Necho, however, was not prepared to leave the enemy thrust unanswered. The army was called out in the spring of 606, and dispatched forthwith to North Syria. Kumukh was immediately invested and reduced in the late summer, after a four-month siege. In an act of ferocity that at once indicates his determination as well a streak of cruelty, Necho put the Babylonian garrison to the sword.[98]

The war had now acquired a momentum of its own: neither side was willing to desist. Within weeks of the fall of Kumukh Nabopolasser coun-

---

[93] A. B. Lloyd, *JHS* 95 (1975), 45ff.

[94] Herodotus, 2.158, 4.39.

[95] Herodotus, 4.42.2–4; A. B. Lloyd, *JEA* 63 (1977), 148–55.

[96] G. Daressy, *ASAE* 11 (1911), 260.

[97] Wiseman, *Chronicles*, 21, 65.

[98] There is no reason to infer (Wiseman, ibid., 21) that the Egyptian besiegers did not represent the full strength of Necho's forces: the period of the siege (spring–summer) certainly implies the presence of an expeditionary force.

terattacked. By early October 606 his forces had encamped at Qurumati on the Euphrates south of Kumukh and were raiding across the river. The attacks, however, did not seriously weaken the Egyptian position. In fact, when in late January 605 Nabopolasser left his army at Qurumati and returned to Babylon, the Egyptian garrison at Carchemish quickly crossed the Euphrates and marched on Qurumati, sending the Babylonian forces scurrying southeastwards.

From this point the *élan vitale* of the Babylonians seems to have revived. It was to be the last appearance of Nabopolasser on the battlefield, and his unexpected withdrawl to Babylon in the winter of 605 might suggest that he was sick. In any case, his place was taken by his eldest son, the crown prince Nebuchadrezzar II, who for two years had been assisting his father with operations. Thanks to his equivocal appearance in the Bible Nebuchadrezzar has acquired an unsavory reputation for tyranny, but there is little in the historical record to suggest that he was any better or worse in his moral conduct than any other king at the time. Simply, he had the misfortune to be the king who—with reason according to the practice of the day—destroyed Jerusalem, terminated the existence of Judah, and authored the "Babylonian captivity." For this he has received a notoriously "bad press."

His initial action in the spring of 605 betrays the spirit of an energetic young man, a genius on the battlefield, possibly motivated at the moment by a feeling of revenge for the atrocity at Kumukh. Undoubtedly April 605 witnessed the mustering of the Egyptian army and its march north. The army was a large one and besides Egyptians included the various auxiliary forces of which Saite Egypt could boast: Nubians, Libyans, and Ionian Greeks.[99] Whether Necho II was in command and present at the subsequent battle is at present unknown; and the Babylonian Chronicle is broken at the point where he might have been mentioned.[100] Josephus states that Necho was present,[101] while Jeremiah's reference is equivocal.[102] In the light of the outcome of the hostilities in this year, it is difficult to see how Necho would have escaped the annihilation of his forces without some reference somewhere to an ignominious flight. The engagement itself is described in the Chronicle as follows:[103]

[In the 21st ye]ar the King of Akkad (i.e., Nabopolasser) stayed in his land. Nebuchadrezzer, his eldest son and [cr]own prince [mu]stered [the army of Ak-

---

[99] Jer. 46:9. For a Greek shield unearthed in the excavations of Carchemish, see L. Woolley, *Carchemish* (London, 1921), 2:123ff. On the Libyan *Put*, see p. 404.

[100] Wiseman, *Chronicles*, 84.

[101] *Antiquitates Judaical* 10.6.

[102] Jer. 46:2.

[103] BM 21946 obv. 1ff. (Wiseman, *Chronicles*, 66).

kad] and took the lead of his troops. He set out for Carchemish which is on the banks of the Euphrates, and crossed the river [against the army (?) of Eg]ypt which was ensconced in Carchemish. [. . .] they joined battle and the army of Egypt fled from before him. He effected their [defeat] and utterly annihilated them. The rest of the army of Egypt [which . . .] defeat sped quickly, not having (yet) joined battle, in the environs of Hamath the army of Akkad encountered them and defeated them (so badly) that [not] one man returned to his country.

There is no mistaking this account, but how was such a major defeat possible? Had not Egyptian forces more than held their own in previous encounters, and were they not four years hence to acquit themselves commendably once more against the same adversaries?

Three factors may be cited in the proposed explanation of this dramatic and unexpected victory by the Babylonians. First, the change of command clearly had an exhilarating effect on the Babylonian troops. From all accounts Nebuchadrezzar was a brilliant tactician; and if in fact Necho was not leading the Egyptians, the latter may simply have been "out-generaled." Second, we may assume that Nebuchadrezzer's advance was far more rapid than the Egyptians expected. Third, the *direct* attack on the headquarters at Carchemish must have come as a complete surprise, since in earlier encounters Nabopolasser had avoided such a gamble.

The course of the battle, as described in the Chronicle, permits two possible reconstructions. Either the Babylonian attack was so sudden that a sizable portion of the Egyptian army, already encamped at Carchemish, could not put itself in battle array quickly enough, but panicked and fled south. Or the main Egyptian expeditionary force, marching north from the Delta, did not arrive in time, but was intercepted after the battle of Carchemish near Hamath, and destroyed.

In either case the result was the same: Egyptian control of the Syrian hinterland was permanently terminated. An index of the appalling losses Necho suffered is Nebuchadrezzer's ability to march his troops in desultory fashion around Syria from the autumn of 605 (after his father's death) to January 604, and to do the same further south beginning in June 604. Egypt had nothing to oppose him with. Jeremiah exulted in Necho's defeat. "Go up to Gilead," he taunted Egypt, "and get balm, O virgin daughter of Egypt! In vain you have used many medicines, (but) there is no healing for you. The nations have heard of your shame, and the earth is full of your cry; for warrior has stumbled against warrior, and they have both fallen together!"[104] Swept away by the magnitude of the Babylonian victory, Jeremiah declared Nebuchadrezzer to be god's instrument and confidently predicted the destruction of all the states of the

---

[104] Jer. 46:11–12; in general cf. C. F. Whitley, *ZAW* 80 (1968), 38ff.

world.[105] It seemed a total defeat for the Egypt-sympathizers who constituted Jehoiakim's coterie.

The progress of the Babylonians through Syria beginning in June 604 must have been watched with increasing anxiety by the states of Palestine.[106] For Nebuchadrezzer and his forces were clearly heading south, bypassing Phoenicia and inland Palestine to attack Egyptian dependencies in the south coastal plain. Numerous must have been the pleas from the coastal cities to Necho imploring action on their behalf. Fortunately one such request has turned up in the form of an Aramaic letter on papyrus, sent from Adon, the king of Ekron, whose city lay in the path of the Babylonian advance.[107] Adon appeals to the treaty he has signed with Egypt, and pleas for armed forces from Egypt, for he is unable to withstand the enemy who is already in Aphek (plain of Sharon). Undoubtedly other local heads of state such as Aga of Ashkelon and Jehoiakim himself hastened to dispatch similar letters, beseeching assistance;[108] but Necho was unable to comply. As the Babylonian army entered the Philistine plain Jehoiakim proclaimed a fast in Jerusalem. Now was a pointless time for pro-Babylonian speechmaking, just when the Judaean administration was *in extremis*. Nevertheless Jeremiah chose this occasion, in November 604 B.C., to assign his emanuensis Baruch the task of reading his recently prepared book of utterances in public, in the Jerusalem temple.[109] The book was forthwith confiscated, read to the king, and destroyed; and Jeremiah and Baruch went into hiding with a price on their heads.

Meanwhile, in the same month, Nebuchadrezzer invested Ashkelon. Before the end of December it had been captured and utterly destroyed.[110] Antimenidas, a Greek mercenary and brother of the poet Alcaeus, was serving with the Babylonian army on this occasion; and a fragment of Alcaeus in honor of his brother's homecoming describes the awful fate of the city, many of whose inhabitants had been sent to the House of Hades.[111] The remaining population together with Aga the king was deported to Babylonia, where an expatriate community calling itself "Ashkelon" was to be found in the following century.[112] The uninhabited ruins

[105] Jer. 25:9, 17–26.

[106] Wiseman, *Chronicles*, 28, 68.

[107] J. Fitzmyer, *Biblica* 46 (1965), 41ff.; 42, n. 1, for bibliography; on the identity of the writer, see B. Porten, *BA* 44 91981), 36–52.

[108] A fragmentary ostraca from Arad mentioning the king of Egypt may date to this period: Y. Yadin, *IEJ* 26 (1976), 9ff.; but see A. Malamat, in Claassen, ed., *Text and Context*, 120–22.

[109] Vividly described in Jer. 36: see A. Malamat, *IEJ* 6 (1956), 252; idem, *IEJ* 18 (1968), 141; idem, *VT* Suppl. 28 (1975), 130–31.

[110] Wiseman, *Chronicles*, 68; Hayes and Miller, *A History*, 406.

[111] J. D. Quin, *BASOR* 164 (1961), 19–20.

[112] Tadmor, *BA* 29 (1966), 102, n. 62; R. Zadok, *BASOR* 230 (1978), 61; Oded, *Mass Deportations*, 25, n. 34.

were to stand a haunt for the wild beasts for over a hundred years, a mute witness to the Babylonian fury.

In January 603 Nebuchadrezzar quit Ashkelon and made his way back to Babylon, but three and a half months later he returned with siege machinery.[113] If, as seems most likely, the fragmentary lines of the Chronicle are here to be restored with a reference to "Gaza,"[114] Nebuchadrezzar's strategy is chillingly clear: he was intent upon wholly neutralizing and reducing the Philistine plain and the coastal highway to Egypt by utter destruction and depopulation. Gaza fell we may be sure, and shortly an exiled community of Gazaeans turns up in Babylonia.[115] Philistia was barren, its kings and population in exile: the road lay open to Egypt.

The affect of these overwhelming victories and the "Babylonian fury" on Judah can easily be imagined. Nebuchadrezzar had not yet turned his attention to the hinterland—his overall strategy demanded reduction of the *Via Maris* and a direct attack on Egypt—but Jehoiakim could not doubt that sooner or later the Babylonian siege engines would be dragged eastward up into the mountains toward Jerusalem. It was most likely in 601, that upon the appearance of the Babylonian army in the west, Jehoaikim capitulated and dispatched the tribute expected of him to Nebuchadrezzar's headquarters.[116] It was precisely this moment that Nebuchadrezzar had chosen for the showdown with Egypt. The chronicle does not tell us the month in which the Babylonians set out, but it was probably later than usual, perhaps toward the end of summer. The settling of affairs of Judah, which may have involved a march to Jerusalem formally to accept the obeisance of Jehoiakim, will have occupied Nebuchadrezzar until well into the fall; and it was not until late November 601 that his troops assembled at their staging point somewhere on the coastal plain and set forth against Egypt. Jeremiah was in a paroxysm of glee. The king, his sworn enemy, had lost face and the pro-Egyptian party had lost credibility; and now his prophecies were about to be completely vindicated, for Nebuchadrezzar was about to destroy Egypt. "Prepare yourselves baggage for exile!" he taunted, "O inhabitants of Egypt! For Memphis shall become a waste, a ruin without inhabitant!" Then, in a parody of the Io legend,[117] "a beautiful heiffer is Egypt, but a gadfly from the north has come upon her. Her hired soldiers in her midst are like fattened calves; yea, they have turned and fled together, they did not stand. . . . the

---

[113] Wiseman, *Chronicles*, 28–29, 70.

[114] Malamat, *JANES* 5 (1973), 277, n. 33; idem, *VT* Suppl. 28 (1975), 131, n. 18.

[115] Zadok, *BASOR*; 230 (1978), 61; I. Ephal, *Orientalia* 47 (1978), 80.

[116] Cf. Josephus, *Antiquitates Jud* 10.6.1, where Judah's subversion to Babylonian hegemony is dated to Jehoiakim's eighth year; Wiseman, *Chronicles*, 70; H. Tadmor, *JNES* 15 (1956), 229, n. 22.

[117] See p. 412f.

daughter of Egypt shall be put to shame, and shall be delivered into the hand of a people from the north!"[118]

It was over sixty years since an invading force had trodden the highway south from Gaza toward the eastern Delta; but in the interim Saite concern with the northeast frontier had produced a border far more securely fortified than the one Ashurbanipal had had to cross. Ashurbanipal and his father Esarhaddon had entered the Delta virtually unopposed and had fought their first engagements with the enemy well inside Egyptian territory. Now, however, Saite settlements and strongpoints lined the eastern frontier and the road to Gaza. Just south of the latter, at or near Raphia, was the "town of Pahsay."[119] On the land strip between Lake Bardawil and the Mediterranean now lay the shrine and settlement of "that town of Ba'al Sapon,"[120] and thirty-five kilometers to the west was the city of Pelusium at the mouth of the easternmost branch of the Nile.[121] As the road turned southwest, down the right bank of the Pelusiac branch, one encountered, scarcely eight kilometers from Pelusium, the "tower" par excellence, the fortified keep of Migdol, which now, since the coming to power of the 26th Dynasty, constituted the true border fort of the northeast frontier and the entry to Egypt proper.[122] The fort of New Kingdom date, which earlier had fulfilled this function, Sile, still stood thirty-two kilometers distant to the southwest. The title of the high priest of the town—"the fighter, Possessed of Justification"—recalled the military purposes of the settlement's location;[123] a "fort" (ḥnrt)[124] still stood there protecting a "depot" ('t),[125] and at this point the marshy tracts of the Delta began, stretching off to the west and beyond the river. Another thirty-two kilometers due west brought the traveler within sight of the strongly fortified Daphnae with its garrison of Greek troops; and forty kilometers southwest again to the town of *Weskhupri* which seventy years

---

[118] Jer. 46:13–26; J. P. Hyatt, *JBL* 75 (1956), 282–83; J. G. Snaith, *JSS* 16 (1971), 15ff.; Malamat, *JNES* 5 (1973), 267ff.

[119] P. Demot. Cairo 31169 (iii), 23; A. H. Gardiner, *JEA* 6 (1920), 110, 113; H. Gauthier, *Dictionnaire des noms géographiques contenus dans les textes hieroglyphiques* (Cairo, 1925–1931), 3:22.

[120] D. B. Redford, in A. F. Rainey, ed., *Egypt, Israel, Sinai* (Jerusalem, 1987), 143–44, nn. 15–16.

[121] P. Montet, *Géographie de l'Égypte ancienne* (Paris, 1957), 1:199.

[122] Tell el-Her and site T.21 on the north: Gauthier, *Dictionnaire*, 3:21; G. Daressey, *Sphinx* 14 (1910), 169; P. Demot. Cairo 31169.iii.20; for description of the sites, see J. Cledat, *BIFAO* 18 (1920), 193–94; Oren, *BASOR* 256 (1984), 7–44; cf. for the garrison J. A. Fitzmyer, *JNES* 21 (1962), 19.

[123] G. Daressy, *BIFAO* 11 (1914), 29ff., 36; Montet, *Géographie* 1:189ff.

[124] Gauthier, *Dictionnaire* 2:121; Cairo 29306.

[125] Gauthier, *Dictionnaire* 1:163; Nitocris stela, 25; O. Koefoed-Petersen, *Les stèles égyptiennes* (Copenhagen, 1948), pl. 54.

earlier had witnessed Esarhaddon's entry into Egypt.[126] If the traveler or expedition was intrepid enough while yet in Palestine to strike inland through Kadesh-Barnea, then west via the Nitla pass, they would have approached Egypt through the "wasteland of the Wall"—that is, the desert due east of Ismailia where the Egyptian fortification began.[127] Here they would have passed by the "Scorpion Lake"[128] (some part of the modern Bitter Lakes), skirted the hill of Gebel Maryam where already watchposts may well have been established,[129] and come face to face with the recently built fortress of Pithom. If their journey was not challenged at this point, the fortress of Pi-Sopdu forty kilometers to the west would have blocked their final entry into the Delta proper.

In the event Nebuchadrezzar eschewed the inland route and led his forces confidently down the coast. On this occasion, however, he could not achieve the surprise that had aided him at the battle of Carchemish. The advanced outposts gave Necho ample warning, and when the Babylonians came within sight of Migdol,[130] they found the Egyptian army drawn up and waiting.

The Chronicle and Herodotus constitute our sole records of the battle. Both are laconic. The former reads[131] "In the month of Kislev (November–December 601) [Nebuchadrezzar] took the lead of his army and marched to Egypt. The king of Egypt heard of it and mustered his army. In open battle they smote the breast of each other and inflicted great havoc on each other. [Nebuchadrezzar] and his troops turned back and returned to Babylon." Herodotus records that Necho "attacked the Syrians (sic) by land and defeated them at Magdolus."

The battle amounted to a signal defeat to Babylonian arms. Jeremiah and the doomsayers were confounded. For not only had the Egyptians fought Nebuchadrezzar to a standstill, but Necho seized the opportunity of the Babylonian retreat (in defiance of Jeremiah's opinion of him)[132] to

---

[126] See chapter 12, n. 194; its position in P. Demot. Cairo 31169 puts it in context: Weskhupri (ii, 22), "House of the Valley" (ii, 23), the Pelusiac branch (ii, 24), Fakus(?) (ii, 25) . . . Bubastis (iii, 6). The loss of w-, (or w + V) corresponds to the absence of w (or w + V) in contemporary Akkadian transcription; cf. Šilkanni for W₃srkn, Hophra or Uḫpara for W₃ḥ-ib-rʿ, Ἐνμωνθις for Wn-mntw etc.

[127] On Shur, see J. Cledat, BIFAO 16 (1916), 215; 18 (1920), 169; N. Na'aman, Tel Aviv 7 (1980), 95–110; A. F. Rainey, Tel Aviv 9 (1982), 132–33.

[128] Chassinat, Edfu, 4:28.

[129] J. Cledat, BIFAO 1 (1900), 110–11; idem, RT 32 (1910), 193–94.

[130] Cf. Herodotus, 2.159, which passage refers to the present engagement, not to that of 609 B.C.: see Malamat, JANES 5 (1973), 275–76 and n. 30; I. Lipinski, AION 22 (1972), 235ff.

[131] Wiseman, Chronicles, 70.

[132] Jeremiah (46:17) had punned on Necho's name, "Loud-mouth who lets slip (probably Maʿebir/Wḥm-ib-rʿ) the opportune time."

follow up his advantage and seize Gaza, now deprived of its fortifications through the recent siege.[133] One wonders to what extent this double victory was due to the presence of Greek auxiliaries; for Necho dedicated the armor he used in battle to Apollo's temple at Branchidae.[134]

For the Babylonians Migdol had meant the loss of troops and equipment, and no further hostilities could be envisaged for the immediate future. In fact from January 600 to late November 599 Nebuchadrezzar remained at home in Babylon in order "to gather together his chariots and horses in great number."[135] Pursuant thereto Jehoiakim withheld his tribute and began again to make friendly overtures to Egypt.[136] The tide definitely appeared to have turned against Babylon, and when in December 599 Nebuchadrezzar came again to the west, it was a weak show of force. On this occasion the Babylonians united at Kadesh could mount only a few punitive raids into the desert to quell Arab unrest.[137] Always ready to seize upon any event as portending ultimate disaster for anyone, Jeremiah prophesied the destruction of Kedar;[138] but Nebuchadrezzar was obliged to return to Babylon in March 598, leaving only small contingents to raid further south on the borders of Judaea.[139] Throughout the summer and fall no foreign army set foot in Palestine.

But it was only a matter of time, for Nebuchadrezzar determined to punish Judah for its desertion. In late November 598 the muster of troops took place in the plains of Akkad, and the long march began to the west. Just a few days later, and probably before news of the Babylonian advance had reached him, Jehoiakim died on December 6, at the age of thirty-six.[140] The heir apparent was his eight-year-old son,[141] Jehoiachin, who duly took the throne, unwitting of the disaster about to fall. The sudden and unexpected investment of the city by the Babylonians

[133] Herodotus (2.159) refers to the capture of "Kadytis" immediately after the battle of Migdol. The name is clearly "Gaza," derived through an Egyptian source: cf. M. A. Meyer, *History of the City of Gaza* (New York, 1907), 38; Tadmor, *BA* 29 (1966), 102; Malamat, *JANES* 5 (1973), 275–76, Lipinski, *AION* 22 (1972), 236–37; H. J. Katzenstein, *VT* 33 (1983), 249–50; Lloyd, *Herodotus*, 3:162–63.

[134] Herodotus, 2.159.

[135] Wiseman, *Chronicles*, 31, 70.

[136] 2 Kings 24:1, cf. D. N. Freedman, *BA* 19 (1956), 54; J. P. Hyatt, *JBL* 75 (1956), 281; Tadmor, *JNES* 15 (1956), 229.

[137] Wiseman, *Chronicles*, 31–32, 70.

[138] Jer. 49: 28–32; cf. Tadmor, *JNES* 15 (1956), 230; Malamat, *IEJ* 6 (1956), 254–55; Hyatt, *JBL* 75 (1956), 283; W. J. Dumbrell, *BASOR* 203 (1971), 39.

[139] 2 Kings 24:2; Freedman, *BA* 19 (1956), 55, n. 18.

[140] See 2 *Chronicles* 36:9, which gives three months and ten days as the time intervening between Jehoiakim's death and the fall of Jerusalem on March 16: cf. Hyatt, *JBL* 75 (1956), 278–79; Freedman, *BA* 19 (1956), 55, n. 22.

[141] In light of the event, Chronicles is here to be preferred over the record of 2 Kings 24:8, which makes Jehoiachin eighteen at his accession.

must have come as a rude shock to the court and the inhabitants of the city, unprepared as they must have been for a protracted siege. The Babylonian Chronicle is preserved at this point and yields a rare and precious reference to an event reflected in the Bible: "In the seventh year (i.e., 598–597) in the month of Kislev (November–December) the king of Akkad mustered his troops, marched to the Hatti-land (i.e., Palestine-Syria) and besieged the city of Judah. On the 2nd day of the month of Adar (March 16, 597) he seized the city and captured the king."[142] Undoubtedly prevailed upon by his mother and his courtiers, the young Jehoiachin, to prevent starvation in the city and to ensure good treatment for his subjects, had opened the gates of Jerusalem and given himself up after only two months.[143] The adviser's foresight proved correct: Jehoiachin and the court were reasonably well treated. But the treasury and temple were stripped and Nebuchadrezzer "received its (the city's) heavy tribute, and sent it to Babylon."[144] To judge by the more judicious records of Jeremiah 52:28–30, 3,023 of the Jerusalem upper class, including we may be sure a goodly number of families of the pro-Egyptian party, were uprooted from their homes and carried captive to Babylon.

In the event, Jehoiachin was the happy survivor of the catastrophe that was Judah's end. Kept under arrest in Babylon along with his brothers, Jehoiachin was maintained at state expense, as evidenced by cuneiform ration lists that mention "[Ya]-u-kin, king of Ya-[u-da]" as being alloted 10 *sila* of oil.[145] When the rest of the royal family had perished in the final destruction of Jerusalem in 586 B.C., Jehoiachin found himself the object of Judah's hopes, and the sole legitimate heir to the kingship.[146] At long last, when he was forty-five years old, Nebuchadrezzar's successor released him from prison, and he ended his days in comparative ease at the court in Babylon.[147]

Nebuchadrezzar's lightning strike against Jerusalem had been a gamble. After the defeat of 600 B.C. he was not strong in the west, and he must have appreciated his weakness. There was every reason to believe that Necho might follow up his advantage and move actively into Syria, and certainly that the appearance of Nebuchadrezzar so far south in the Levant would have promptly called forth the Egyptian levies.

But Nebuchadrezzar had correctly sized up his man: Necho II was occupied elsewhere, and did not march to Jerusalem's relief.[148]

[142] Wiseman, *Chronicles*, 72.

[143] Cf. 2 Kings 24:10–12; Hyatt, *JBL* 75 (1956), 279.

[144] Wiseman, *Chronicles*, 72.

[145] E. Weidner, *Mélanges Dussaud* (Paris, 1939), 2:923ff.

[146] On the continuing loyalty of Jerusalem to Jehoiachin, even before 586, see H. G. May, *JNES* 4 (1945), 221, n. 21.

[147] 2 Kings 25:27–30.

[148] See p. 462.

The events of the succeeding years seemed to confirm suspicions that Babylon had overextended itself and had been severely weakened by its defeat on the borders of Egypt. In January 596 Nebuchadrezzar could manage only a one-month tour of inspection, which did not extend south of Carchemish; and in December of the same year Elamite forces invaded Babylonia.[149] Although the Elamite thrust was parried, Nebuchadrezzar was partly discredited and disaffection spread throughout the ranks of the army. In December 595 rebellion broke out in Babylon and was suppressed two months later with great bloodshed. Notwithstanding a tour of Syria by Nebuchadrezzar at the turn of the year to collect tribute, it must have looked from the vantage point of the Levantine coast that his star had set.

In Jerusalem there was a flurry of diplomatic activity, as pro- and anti-Babylonian spokesmen vied for the ear of the people. Eyeing the international scene at all times, but motivated by more zeal than foreknowledge, Jeremiah had predicted doom for Elam in 596: "Behold! I shall break the bow of Elam, the mainstay of their might. . . . I will bring evil upon them. . . . I will send the sword after them until I have consumed them; and I will set my throne in Elam and destroy their kings and princes, says the Lord."[150] But the promised destruction failed to materialize, and the anti-Babylonian faction became vocal. The "prophets, diviners, dreamers and soothsayers" began to preach to the people "you shall not serve the king of Babylon."[151] In debate before the people Jeremiah's enemy, the prophet Hananiah of Gibeon, broke the yoke Jeremiah was wearing as a pitiable object lesson, and prophesied "thus says the Lord of Hosts, the god of Israel: 'I have broken the yoke of the king of Babylon. Within two years I will bring back to this place all the vessels of the Lord's house which Nebuchadrezzar king of Babylon took away. . . . I will also bring back Jehoiachin son of Jehoiakim king of Judah and all the exiles.' "[152] The tide was running high for the patriots: it was only a matter of time and Babylon would be crushed. Probably in the autumn of 594, with hopes uplifted by the revolt in Babylon only months before, Zedekiah convened a conference of envoys from the surrounding states: Edom, Moab, Ammon, Tyre, and Sidon.[153] Clearly the object was rebellion, and

[149] Wiseman, *Chronicles*, 72.

[150] Jer. 49:35–38. The oracle is dated "In the beginning of the reign of Zedekiah King of Judah" (verse 34) and is clearly occasioned by the events of 596. See Tadmor, *JNES* 15 (1956), 230, n. 27; Hyatt, *JBL* 75 (1956), 283.

[151] Jer. 27:9.

[152] Jer. 28:2–4.

[153] The Septuagint for Jer. 27:1 reads "in the Fourth year of Zedekiah": Hyatt, *JBL* 75 (156), 281; Freedman, *BA* 19 (1956), 58. There is no reason to reject the historicity of the event.

equally clearly Zedekiah was prepared to gamble on the new Egyptian ruler.

Necho II died in the fall of 595 B.C.,[154] leaving three daughters and one son, Psammetichos II who succeeded him.[155] Since the encouraging victory of 600, Egyptian activity had concentrated on another theater of interests, the south, perhaps since the general consensus was that the northern frontier was now safe. In the south the 25th Dynasty had continued to maintain itself as the ruling power over vast reaches of the Sudan from its traditional seat at Napata;[156] and nothing could dissuade these rulers from considering their eventual return to Egypt inevitable. As a consequence Psammetichos I had had to fortify the southern border at Elephantine[157] and station a strong garrison there, which, as we have seen, included a Judaean element.

Fortunately for the Saites, the immediate successors of Tanwetaman remained quiescent in their southern fastness. But under Anlamani (c. 623–593 B.C.), perhaps encouraged by Egyptian reverses in Asia, the Kushites began to move northward ostensibly to punish tribesmen raiding from the eastern desert.[158] We cannot be sure, but it may have been in response to this threat that Necho II, late in his reign, mounted a riverine expedition southward from Elephantine against the "Nubian bowman." A block uncovered by the Germans at Elephantine apprises us of "the horses and [chariots](?)" and of "the fleet that went south carrying them upon the river." This flotilla numbered something in excess of eighteen vessels, led by the king's flagship(?) called "Necho-is-Soul-like," and comprising great and small transports.[159]

The fragmentary nature of the inscription leaves us in doubt as to the outcome of the expedition, but the threats to Egypt remained, as Kushite troops continued to occupy forward posts against Egypt. Clearly a preventive strike of crushing force was required. An opportunity presented itself when in 593 Anlamani died, and trouble developed over the succession. An oracle of Amunre had to be invoked to decide who among the princes was to take the throne, and the divine choice was Aspelta, the

[154] Kienitz, *Geschichte*, 158 (between May 4 and November 23); on the corrected dates, see Lloyd, *Ancient Egypt, A Social History*, 281.

[155] R. el-Sayed, *BIFAO* 74 (1974), 35.

[156] A. J. Arkell, *A History of the Sudan to 1821* (London, 1961), 138ff.; W. B. Emery, *Egypt in Nubia* (London, 1965), 222ff.

[157] H. Ranke, *ZÄS* 44 (1901), 42–43; De Meulenaere, *BIFAO* 63 (1965), 21ff.; Lloyd, *Herodotus*, 2:126–30.

[158] M.F.L. MacAdam, *The Temples of Kawa* (Oxford, 1949), 1:46ff.

[159] *MDAIK* 31 (1975), pl. 28(b); K. Jansen-Winkeln, *GM* 109 (1989), 31. This campaign must fall late in the reign after 600 B.C., as prior to that time Necho's moves seem fully accounted for.

younger brother of Anlamani, who for reasons unknown ran afoul of the Amun priesthood.[160]

Within months the blow fell. In 593, the third year of the young Psammetichos, a large expeditionary force was assembled comprising native conscripts under general Amasis, the royal plenipotentiary,[161] and the mercenary contingents of Ionian and Doric Greeks and Phoenicians under general Potasimto.[162] Psammetichos himself accompanied the army as far as Elephantine where he stayed in expectation of their return. Triumphal stelae erected at Thebes and the first cataract depict the young king at the end of October "cooling his heels" at Elephantine and engaging in desultory promenades until the news reached him.[163] "Then His Majesty wandered through the nesting places in 'Neferibre-lake,' and made the circuit of its pools, hastening over its islands and banks, viewing the tree groves of 'God's land.' . . . Then one came to tell His Majesty 'the army that your majesty dispatched to Nubia has reached the highland of Pnubs! It is a land with no (suitable) battlefields, a place devoid of horses. Nubians of every land have overwhelmed it, their hearts filled with haughtiness!' " The text at this point goes on rather confusingly to describe the Egyptian victory as due to the presence of the king on the field of battle; but another fragmentary stela from Aswan ascribes the slaughter to "the army of His Majesty."[164] The Egyptians proceeded to occupy Dongola, burned Napata, and even pushed further on toward Meroë. With garrisons now permanently in place south of the First Cataract,[165] the army returned downriver at a leisurely pace, some soldiers scratching their names and an account of themselves at Abu Simbel while gawking tourist-fashion at the mighty monument of Ramesses II. The 25th Dynasty had lost 4,200 soldiers as captives and countless others among the dead. No more would Kush seriously threaten Egypt.

The news of this victory, remembered long afterward for generations, must have had an electrifying effect on the Near East, and especially on Judah. The preceding year Nebuchadrezzar must have got wind of Zedekiah's deliberations with the surrounding states of the south Levant, for he had summoned the Judaean king and some of his ministers to Babylon for a dressing down.[166] But they had not been detained and had returned to Jerusalem in time to hear of the Egyptian victory. Moreover, Psammetichos II for all his frailness, seemed intent on pursuing an active

[160] Arkell, *Sudan*, 144.

[161] See Bothmer, *Egyptian Sculpture of the Late Period*, pls. 48–49.

[162] S. Raite, *BIFAO* 61 (1962), 43–53; S. Pernigotti, *StudClassOriental* 17 (1968), 251ff.

[163] H.S.K. Bakry, *Oriens Antiquus* 6 (1967), 225ff.

[164] L. Habachi, *Oriens Antiquus* 13 (1974), pl. 20(b).

[165] Arkell, *Sudan*, 145.

[166] Jer. 51:59; M. Greenburg, *JBL* 76 (1957), 305–6.

policy toward western Asia. No sooner had he returned from Nubia than he laid plans for a similar expedition in the north.

"Now in the fourth year of Pharaoh Psammetichos (II) Neferibre dispatches were sent to the great temples of Upper and Lower Egypt as follows: 'Pharaoh, life, prosperity and health! goes to the land of Palestine (*Ḫ³rw*); let the priests come with the bouquets of the gods of Egypt to take them to the land of Palestine with Pharaoh!' "[167] What ensued was a triumphal progress by king, court, priests, and army to the cities of Philistia and Judah,[168] and in the event it was unchallenged by Babylon. Psammetichos undoubtedly pursued the route of so many of his predecessors, and continued on up the coast to the Phoenician cities of Tyre and Byblos. His aim must have been to lift the spirits of the anti-Babylonian resistance and to cement alliances, rather than to collect tribute; and in this he must have been signally successful. The loyal Phoenician cities were to supply timber for ships, as they had since time immemorial. Judah was to be the center of the opposition to Nebuchadrezzar and, with a victorious Egypt behind it, could not unrealistically hope for success. Even in Babylon the Judaean exiles were asking the prophet Ezekiel when they were to go home.[169] Optimistic predictions were rife in the exile community that Babylon's fortunes were about to decline, and that the exiles would soon be released.[170] Even though Jeremiah in his maverick fashion continued to excoriate any majority sentiment that held out hope, he too was driven by the experience of Babylonian barbarity to damn to eventual doom this equivocal instrument he had conceived the Lord God as wielding against his chosen people.[171]

But once again events took a strange turn. Necho had died at an inopportune moment, depriving the south Levant of a proven ally just when Nebuchadrezzar seemed to be weakened. Now, in 591, on the return from his Palestinian expedition Psammetichos fell ill,[172] and (he was to die within twenty-four months) he may have from this moment lingered on in a progressively worsening condition. He succumbed finally in early February 589, and his son Wahibre (Greek *Apries*, Hebrew *Hophraʿ*) took the throne.

Contemporary views and expectations are lost to us, but it is a fair guess that Apries's accession was considered a boon by Egyptians and Judaeans alike.[173] Probably a young man in his early twenties when he

---

[167] P. Rylands IX, 14:16–19; K. S. Freedy and D. B. Redford, *JAOS* 90 (1970), 479ff.

[168] J. Yoyotte, *VT* 1 (1951), 143; Freedy and Redford, *JAOS* 90 (1970), 479ff.

[169] Ezek. 20:1ff.; Freedy and Redford, *JAOS* 90 (1970), 480.

[170] Cf. Jer. 29:21–23, 26–32.

[171] Cf. Jer. 50–51.

[172] P. Rylands IX, 15:8–9.

[173] Herodotus (2.161) conveys an early (and favorable) judgment of the reign: Lloyd, *Herodotus*, 3:170.

came to the throne, Apries set about to pursue the general policies of initiative in western Asia that his father had conceived. Herodotus records that Apries made an expedition to Sidon, and it is in keeping with what we know of the impetuosity of this young man that he should have accomplished this in the first year of his reign, probably late spring and summer of 589.[174] If Zedekiah had been chastened by his interrogation in Babylon and the fatal sickness of Psammetichos II, the prospect of the victories of the latter's energetic heir must have quickened his pulse and encouraged him in his last and fateful decision. Probably before the summer of 589 had come to an end, Zedekiah had formally renounced any allegiance to Babylon he may have reaffirmed at his meeting with Nebuchadrezzar.[175] The die was cast.

In the succeeding months Nebuchadrezzar proved once again that he surpassed his contemporaries in strategic concept and daring tactics alike. Babylon may well have recouped its losses from the rebellion of 595 B.C.—we cannot say, as our chronicle covering the years from 594 is yet to be found—but Apries's dash and energy seemed more than to offset any advantage Nebuchadrezzar may have gained.

It was probably in the late autumn of 589 that Nebuchadrezzar made his move. The Babylonian forces marched to central Syria, and Nebuchadrezzar set up his headquarters at Riblah[176] from where he purposed to direct operations. The army was divided, one column dispatched to the Lebanons to counter Apries's move along the coast, and the other sent to invest Jerusalem to destroy once and for all Egypt's buffer on its northeast border.[177] Along the Lebanese coast Nebuchadrezzar's efforts were indecisive. Although he claimed to have rid the country of "the enemy" (Egyptians), and to have brought off timber for construction work in Babylon, he was forced to lay siege to Tyre, an action that tied down part of his forces in a protracted and fruitless investment.[178] Moreover, Apries's fleet could operate at will along the coast and bring aid to the beleagured city.

The expeditionary force sent to Judah at first experienced equally slow going. Zedekiah was able to send word to Egypt before the Babylonian forces closed in and surrounded the city in January 588 B.C.[179] An impor-

---

[174] Nebuchadrezzar's Wady Brisa text, which records his operations in Lebanon probably in 588–586, justifies his attack on the allegation that the Lebanese mountains were being tyrannized by a "foreign enemy who was exploiting the region and putting its inhabitants to flight" (ANET², 307). The enemy could only have been Egypt. For a dissenting voice, see Lloyd, Herodotus, 3:171–72.

[175] Freedy and Redford, JAOS 90 (1970), 480 and n. 100.

[176] Cf. Jer. 39:5.

[177] For discussion with references, see Freedy and Redford, JAOS 90 (1970), 481ff.; B. Oded, in Hyatt and Miller, Israelite and Judaean History, 472ff.

[178] Josephus, Contra Apionem 1.21; ANET², 307.

[179] May, JNES 4 (1945), 218–19.

tant discovery in the excavations of Lachish between World Wars I and II was a cache of twenty-one Hebrew ostraca, constituting hurried dispatches from an outpost to the commandant of Lachish.[180] Dated to this final siege of Jerusalem, they provide a vivid, in fact breathtaking picture of the confusion and despair that attended the event. One of the earliest, no. 3, includes the report that "the commander of the host, Coniah son of Elnathan has come down in order to go to Egypt."[181] Coniah's mission must have been successful, for shortly, probably in the fall of 588, Apries and his army departed Egypt and wended their way along the coast, making for Jerusalem. Some of Apries's officers are well known to us from statuary they have left, and one is inevitably drawn to wondering how many of them accompanied their sovereign on this fateful campaign. There was Neferibrenakht, commander of infantry, "king's messenger who fights on his lord's behalf in every foreign land . . . overseer of the door of northern foreign lands";[182] and Amun-Tefnakht, commander of the king's bodyguard and of elite troops.[183] Potasimto late of the Nubian campaign may also have been present: he too "fought on his lord's behalf in every foreign land,"[184] as did also several other generals dated about this time.[185]

But the involvement of these worthies in the relief of the besieged city was short-lived. The Babylonian forces quickly withdrew from Jerusalem and sped westward into the coastal plain.[186] Their march was apparently so swift and their front so intimidating that Apries with the limited number of troops he had brought[187] saw neither the opportunity of marching up-country to Jerusalem nor any realistic chance of overcoming the enemy in an open battle. Ignominiously the Egyptians withdrew. City after city in the Shephelah capitulated until only Lachish and Azekah remained to hold out,[188] and the Babylonians resumed their siege of the capital. Jerusalem's fate was sealed.

The prophetic outbursts became shrill. The optimists were gone. Jeremiah prophesied the expected doom even more vehemently than before, and was summarily incarcerated by the executive and the military;[189] even though the timorous and vacillating king privily continued to seek

---

[180] H. Torczyner, *The Lachish Ostraca* (London, 1938); W. F. Albright, in *ANET*², 321–22.

[181] *ANET*², 322.

[182] Cairo 895.

[183] Z. Saad, *ASAE* 41 (1941), 386.

[184] A. Rowe, *ASAE* 38 (1938), 170.

[185] Cf. Cairo 1209; H. Gauthier, *ASAE* 22 (1922), 97.

[186] Jer. 37:11.

[187] A. Malamat, *IEJ* 18 (1968), 151.

[188] Jer. 34:7; *ANET*², 322.

[189] Jer. 37:15–21.

his advice.[190] Even from Babylon the exiled Ezekiel taunted the luckless Apries: the Pharaoh who had taken as part of his titulary the epithet "strong-armed" had now had his arm broken by the Lord.[191]

Although the military was committed to carrying on the war and treated dissidents as traitors,[192] there was now no real hope unless Egypt would venture to try again. The Transjordan states were much too small to provide effective help, although they did offer sanctuary to fugitives from Judaea.[193] In the final act of the unfolding drama they stood aloof.[194] Zedekiah in desperation manumitted all the slaves, probably to raise new levies;[195] and consulted Jeremiah for political advice.[196] But to no avail. Large numbers of the population continued to defect to the Babylonians, and as time passed famine and plague gripped Jerusalem.

The end came some eighteen months into the renewed siege. The historical corpus of Mesopotamian texts has long familiarized us with the sophisticated siege equipment the Assyrians and Babylonians could bring to bear on a city; and these techniques employing towers, siege mounds, and battering rams had long since passed to the west, as the Piankhy stela indicates. We may well imagine that in the spring of 586 mounds began to rise against Jerusalem's walls, probably on the north or west (perhaps both); here the lie of the land beyond the fortifications was not precipitous, thus favoring the attack of siege engines (Plate 35). Aided by famine, which weakened the defenders, the Babylonians launched a concerted attack in the summer months, perhaps in the vicinity of the reservoirs later to become the pool of Bethesda, north of the temple and palace.[197] During the daylight hours of July 18 the wall was breached and the attackers entered the city (Plate 36), the Babylonian command immediately occupying the "Middle Gate."[198] The defenses collapsed, and the Judaean government disintegrated. That same night the king, his family, and remnants of the army fled via the gate of the south of the original City of David into the Kidron Valley and thence into the Judaean desert. They did not make for Egypt: every avenue of access to the Sinai was cut off. Instead they made for the Jordan valley and the hills of Ammon beyond,

---

[190] Je. 38:14–28.

[191] Ezek. 30:20ff.; Malamat, *IEJ* 18 (1968), 152; Freedy and Redford, *JAOS* 90 (1970), 482–83; J. K. Hoffmeier, *JSSEA* 11 (1981), 166–70; idem, *Biblica* 67 (1986), 378–87.

[192] Cf. Jer. 38:4; *ANET*², 322.

[193] Jer. 40:11; M. Noth, *A History of Israel* (London, 1959), 292.

[194] J. R. Bartlett, *PEQ* 114 (1982), 13ff.

[195] Jer. 34: 8–10; M. David, *OTS* 5 (1948), 63ff.; Malamat (*IEJ* 18 [1968] 153) dates the manumission before Apries's countermove.

[196] Jer. 38:14ff.

[197] On the hasty quarrying and defenses thrown up by the defenders of the city on the north and west, see A. D. Tushingham, *ZDPV* 95 (1979), 53–54.

[198] Jer. 39:3; cf. N. Avigad, in *Biblical Archaeology Today* (Jerusalem, 1985), 471–72.

Plate 35. Eastern wall of the City of David (c. early seventh century B.C.), above the spring of Gihon. This was probably the city wall standing when the Babylonians assaulted the city in 586 B.C.

Plate 36. Pillar, wall, and staircase from an early sixth century B.C. house in the northeastern quarter of the City of David, destroyed in the Babylonian assault of 586 B.C.

where Ba'alis, the Ammonite king, would undoubtedly have offered refuge. But it was not to be. The Babylonians pursued the royal party, captured them near Jericho and transported them to Nebuchadrezzar's headquarters in Syria. There Zedekiah was blinded and his family executed. One month later Jerusalem went up in flames and its population and wealth carried captive.

Epilogue

THE EVENTS of 586, construed at the time as but a stage in the annihilation of the independent states of the southern Levant, were to prove a major watershed in the history of the Hebrews. The rump community that returned to Jerusalem from Babylon at the close of the century was a new beginning, markedly different from what had gone before in politics, culture, and religion. To us moderns the Judaism of an Ezra or a Nehemiah is familiar and living, the religion of an Amos or a Jeremiah strange and almost "prehistoric."

Egypt's moment of truth was shortly to come, in 525 B.C., when the expanding Median empire of Cambyses overwhelmed the forces of Psammetichos III; but for the Nilotic community the cultural impact was less traumatic. True, the state lost its independence and was demoted to the status of a remote province in a vast, world-empire; but the administration, religion, and cultural expression changed only imperceptibly. Only experts can distinguish between statues and texts of the fifth century and those of the seventh or sixth; and while the fourth century was to throw up Egyptian rebels who took the crown and proclaimed themselves Pharaoh, their short-lived regimes were but extensions of the earlier Saite experience.

The political defeats of 586 and 525 B.C. were destined ultimately to exert a deleterious influence on the intellectual life of both Egypt and the Levant. The reputation of Egypt for "metaphysical" inquiry into imponderables, which brought many a Greek of the seventh and sixth centuries to the feet of an Egyptian priest, vanished in the fifth and fourth, as Greek admiration gave way to contempt. Similarly the heights achieved by the Hebrew prophets in ethics and theology before the Exile dwarf the attainments in the same spheres of the restrictive, ritual-conscious community of the Second Temple. The dominance of foreigners in the affairs of Egypt and Judah set the intelligentsia in both communities in a defensive posture. In Egypt, certainly from the Greek conquest, the temple personnel turned in upon themselves, and with the progressive loss of patronage and approbation by the authorities, began to consider themselves the last repository and bastion of the old ways of pharaonic times. In Judah, in a reactionary effort to hold the line, the sacerdotal mentors of the community linked orthodoxy with nationalism, and produced the intransigence of the Maccabees and the savagery of the zealots. The stultifying trends in both communities may be observed to advantage in the literature each produced: the Egyptian temple, the arcane lore of cryptographic inscriptions; the Judaic community, the Mishnah. Neither enjoyed an acceptable fit in the new world of Hellenism.

One might almost say that "God was dead." The erstwhile parochial deities of Thebes and Memphis, Jerusalem and Tyre had all *mutatis mutandis* hitched themselves to nationalist resistance, and in so doing had determined their own fate. Their municipal bailiwicks during the two centuries at the turn of the present era became hotbeds of jingoist sentiment; and some, like Thebes and Jerusalem, reveled in the role of beleaguered fortresses of the old order now under attack.

But Amun and Yahweh had failed. Both Egypt and western Asia proved powerless to withstand the onslaught of Greek and Roman arms on the battlefield, and retreated perforce in the realm of ideas as well. Resistance was futile: by the end of the first century the temple of Amun lay derelict, Yahweh's house destroyed. Literary "counterattacks" proved to be nothing more than pitiable attempts to curse the impure *ḫ³styw* (foreigners) or the vile *Kittim* (Greeks or Romans). The best this folk literature could offer was the promise of a brighter day ahead, a forlorn and desperate hope. Through all the railing of the faceless apocalyptic writers one can discern the frustration of disenfranchised cultures that have been outstripped by a new and imaginative way of life from across the seas.

Yet in this long and lamentable twilight of the old communities of the eastern Mediterranean, the autochthonous populations might have taken satisfaction in one signal achievement. Where national gods had failed, the *numina populi* began to exert on the European conquerors an irresistible appeal, which eventually compromised any loyalty they might have showed toward their own pantheons. Zeus could not compete with Serapis, nor Athena with Cybele. The old nation-states whose long and checkered history we have traced were now defunct, and no longer provided security or fulfillment for the communities that had once compromised them. The individual had now perforce to seek his salvation elsewhere, outside the group, outside the nation. He was on his own in a brave new world where no one cared. The personal need thus evinced elicited a response, as far as the masses of the new Hellenized world were concerned, from one source: the circle of personal, "humanized" deities who filled the spiritual void in every psyche. Like the human sufferer, they too had suffered; like the mortal soul, they too had faced death and judgment. The parallel demanded a spiritual union, and called forth piety and repentance. Only in the Mysteries could union with the divine and salvation be achieved.

The effects are still with us. The saving grace of an Isis, a Christ, or Mithra triumphed everywhere in the Mediterranean world of the universal empire of Rome, and in a transmuted state has even descended to the twentieth century. But all this is another story.

Index